I0752466

KERUX COMMENTARIES

HEBREWS

KERUX COMMENTARIES

HEBREWS

A Commentary for Biblical Preaching and Teaching

HERBERT W. BATEMAN IV
STEVEN W. SMITH

Herbert W. Bateman IV
EDITOR

KREGEL MINISTRY

Hebrews: A Commentary for Biblical Preaching and Teaching

© 2021 by Herbert W. Bateman IV and Steven W. Smith

Published by Kregel Ministry, an imprint of Kregel Publications, 2450 Oak Industrial Dr. NE, Grand Rapids, MI 49505-6020.

All rights reserved. No part of this book may be reproduced, stored in a retrieval system, or transmitted in any form or by any means—electronic, mechanical, photocopy, recording, or otherwise—without written permission of the publisher, except for brief quotations in printed reviews.

Unless otherwise indicated, the translation of the Scripture portions used throughout the commentary is the authors' own English rendering of the original biblical languages.

All Scripture quotations, unless otherwise indicated, are from the New American Standard Bible® (NASB), Copyright © 1960, 1962, 1963, 1968, 1971, 1972, 1973, 1975, 1977, 1995 by The Lockman Foundation. Used by permission. www.Lockman.org

Italics in Scripture quotations indicate emphasis added by the authors.

The Hebrew font, NewJerusalemU, and the Greek font, GraecaU, are available from www.linguistsoftware.com/lgku.htm, +1-425-775-1130.

All photos are under Creative Commons licensing, and contributors are indicated in the captions of the photos.

Maps on pages 48 and 145 are from the *Kregel Bible Atlas* by Tim Dowley, copyright © 2003 Angus Hudson Ltd./Tim Dowley & Peter Wyatt trading as Three's Company. Used by permission.

ISBN 978-0-8254-5839-2

Printed in the United States of America
21 22 23 24 25 / 5 4 3 2 1

Contents

APPLICATION (11:1—13:25)

EDITOR'S PREFACE TO THE SERIES

The Kerux Commentary series, unlike other commentaries written for preachers, joins experts in biblical exegesis with experienced communicators of biblical truth. Together they bring a heightened refinement in the handling of the Bible. Every volume emphasizes text-based truths that bridge from the context of the original hearers and readers to the twenty-first-century world. The name *kerux* (KAY-rüxs) captures the aim of the series. Just as a *kerux* was one who proclaimed the official announcement of the king, so the forty-five volumes in this series will enable the preacher or teacher to accurately and authoritatively communicate the message of our divine King.

Every volume presents preaching units that offer *exegetical, theological,* and *homiletical* material to guide preachers and teachers to accurately interpret the Bible and ultimately engage today's world.

EXEGETICAL ANALYSIS	➡	**THEOLOGICAL FOCUS**	➡	**PREACHING/ TEACHING STRATEGY**

Solid *exegetical analysis* of the biblical text reveals the literary-theological movement of every biblical passage. The exegetical authors (trained experts in interpretation) engage the biblical text by interacting with original languages that shed light on interpretation (e.g., syntax, grammar, structure), hermeneutical issues relevant to a given passage (e.g., genre analysis), and pertinent secondary literature. From the exegetical analysis is derived a theological focus. The gnomic truths of a passage—those truths that transcend time and culture—emphasize the *theological focus* of each preaching unit. Following the careful exegetical analysis and insightful theological synthesis, homiletical authors (trained experts in preaching) offer suggestions for communicating the text. Based on the popular "big idea" preaching model, every preaching unit offers *preaching strategies,* contemporary connections, suggestions for creative presentation, illustrations, and more. These tools help the preacher and teacher effectively proclaim Scripture.

Kerux commentaries are written for trained pastors and teachers who speak regularly, who have some knowledge of Greek and Hebrew, and who spend a significant time preparing to preach and teach God's Word. As a result, each volume offers:

- a detailed introduction and outline.
- a summary of all preaching sections with their primary exegetical, theological, and preaching ideas.
- preaching pointers that join the original historical context with the contemporary one.
- insights from the Hebrew and Greek text.
- a thorough exposition of the text.
- sidebars of pertinent information and historical background.
- appropriate charts and photographs.
- a theological focus to passages.

- a contemporary big idea for every preaching unit.
- present-day meaning, validity, and application of a main idea.
- creative presentations for each primary idea.
- key questions about the text for study groups.
- lists of books and articles for further reading.

Many thanks to Jim Weaver, Kregel's former acquisition editor, who conceived of this commentary series and further developed it with the team of Jeffrey D. Arthurs, Robert B. Chisholm, David M. Howard Jr., Darrell L. Bock, Roy E. Ciampa, and Michael J. Wilkins. Much appreciation is extended to Dennis and Paul Hillman, whose thirteen-year tenacious commitment to the series contributed to Kerux becoming a reality. Finally, gratitude is extended to the two authors for each Kerux volume; the outside reviewers, editors, and proofreaders; and Kregel staff who suggested numerous improvements.

—Herbert W. Bateman IV

EXEGETICAL AUTHOR'S PREFACE

To my longtime friends from our PhD days at Dallas Theological Seminary: James McGahey, Karl Pagenkemper, and William Webb

During the mid-1990s while attending a required faculty development forum, the faculty was challenged to undertake a professional goal, to embark on a project that we'd like to complete before retiring. Some set their eyes on entering a doctoral program, others wanted to publish their dissertation, and still others wanted to plant a church. For me, it was to write a commentary on the book of Hebrews. With that goal in mind throughout my teaching career, I taught the book of Hebrews, presented papers on Hebrews, wrote book reviews on Hebrews's commentaries, published journal articles on Hebrews, and wrote books on Hebrews. Furthermore, my work on Second Temple history and literature have influenced numerous aspects of this commentary. So, I'm pleased to share what I consider my *magnus opus* with you.

Naturally, I'm extremely grateful for the many commentaries on Hebrews that have helped focus my initial independent study in Hebrews. Commentaries by F. F. Bruce (1964), H. W. Attridge (1989), A. C. Mitchell (1989), P. Ellingworth (1993), G. Guthrie (1998), W. L. Lane (1991), C. R. Koester (2001), L. T. Johnson (2006), and G. Cockerill (2012) are some of the authors with whom I interacted as well as the numerous English translations. Yet with all these commentaries available today, it seems reasonable to ask, why add another to this rather impressive list?

What separates this commentary on Hebrews from all others is the preaching portions presented for each expositional unit. Steven W. Smith has not only taught preaching; he's currently the senior pastor at Immanuel Baptist Church in Little Rock, Arkansas. His contributions distinguish this commentary from all others. Another distinguishing feature of the expositional portion is the historical and cultural background identified for each unit so that Steven was able to make a legitimate link from the past to the present. In all fairness to Steven, the homiletical portions did not always agree with some of my historical conclusions such as authorship; nevertheless, that never detracted from his ability to make a link from a past context to a present.

I'm also grateful for the two consulting editors for this volume: Jon Lannsma and Dennis Hillman. Jon C. Laansma is the Gerald F. Hawthorne Professor of New Testament Greek and Exegesis at Wheaton College in Illinois. Among his many publications, he is the author of *"I Will Give You Rest": The Rest Motif in the New Testament with Special Reference to Mt 11 and Heb 3–4* (WUNT 2/98; Mohr Siebeck, 1997) and *Christology, Hermeneutics and Hebrews: Profiles from the History of Interpretation* (coedited with D. J. Treier; T&T Clark, 2012). Jon and I served as co-chairs of the Hebrews Study Group that met annually at the Evangelical Theological Society (2007–12). Dennis R. Hillman is a retired pastor (1979–93) and served as a senior editor, publisher, and academic and ministry director for Kregel Publications (1993–2018). His expertise in transforming exegetical material into sermons provided great insight into Steven's work.

—Herbert W. Bateman IV

PREACHING AUTHOR'S PREFACE

This book is dedicated to my friend Jarrett Stephens.

The book of Hebrews is an exegetical and theological challenge. It is a challenge for which no preacher, including me—especially me—feels equipped. Having recently preached through Hebrews again, I was struck by how many passages stump commentators, challenge parishioners, and worry preachers. It's just hard. Clarity in preaching comes at a cost. In this fight, I am encouraged by the exegetical skill of Herb Bateman. He is a fine exegete, a friend, and a winsome personal apologist for understanding the biblical text. What a joy to learn from him in this process. For that I am very grateful. There are a few homiletical portions where the portions are his or are influenced by his work. For that I am also grateful.

As with all Scripture, there is great joy in wrestling with the text. The wrestling is worth it as we read ourselves clear. Rich blessings on your study and proclamation!

—Steven W. Smith

OVERVIEW OF ALL PREACHING PASSAGES

Hebrews 1:1–4

Exegetical Idea
Unlike in times past when God spoke through many prophets, God had spoken in this new era through a single divinely appointed, divinely related, and divinely authoritative spokes*man*, "a son," to whom had been given a name superior to even that of the celestial sons of God.

Theological Focus
In this new era, God speaks to people through a new and superior spokes*man*, Jesus.

Preaching Idea
Tuning out the many makes it possible to hear the one and only voice that *really* matters.

Preaching Pointers
While Hebrews 1:1–4 is at once elegantly simple and brutally complicated, the message is quite simple: God spoke through his messianic Son of promise. The language of these beautiful verses, as will be seen in the exegetical section, was unveiling the NT motif of Jesus as the messianic Son of promise in both explicit and nuanced ways. Obviously, the original readers knew Jesus as Messiah, but did they know him as God's ultimate spokes*man*, his final word? Their challenge was the many prophetic voices—and, we might even add, the competing Jewish interpretations of those voices—that detracted from the one voice that really mattered.

Today, we too struggle with competing voices. There are the voices at work demanding our attention. There are the community voices like Big Brothers and Big Sisters of America entreating our participation in mentoring youth. There are voices at church appealing for our commitment, time, and money. There are also the family voices at home. Do you ever feel as though you are just drowning in a sea of voices? Prioritizing the important from the not-so-important voices is difficult to do. Yet there are times we need to tune out some of these voices. This passage appeals to our need to tune out the many, so that we can hear the voice that *really* matters.

Hebrews 1:5–14

Exegetical Idea
In explaining the distinction between "a Son" and "the sons of God" (e.g., angels), God spoke of the Son's prominent relationship with him, contrasted the Son's royal and creator status with that of the celestial sons of God, and promised the Son—whom angels served—a future absolute authority over all creation.

Theological Focus
The messianic Son of promise has been exalted to a prominent relationship with God, with a superior status to that of angels, and with a promise of absolute authority over all of creation that distinguishes him from all celestial sons of God.

Preaching Idea
Distinctions make a difference.

Preaching Pointers
Whereas Hebrews 1:1–4 underscored Jesus as God's superior spokes*man*, verses 5–14 provided the reason why he was God's preferred spokes*man* over the angels. The first-century Jewish community had a high regard for angels as powerful beings (Dan. 12:1; 1 En. 6:1–4a; 7:1–6; 1QM). Angels also delivered messages to people from God (Dan. 9:21; Luke 1:11, 26). Yet, Jesus was not an angel. So, distinguishing Jesus from the angels was important. Jesus was not to be confused with angelic beings, even though he too was sent by God.

In Hebrews 1:1–4, the emphasis for today addresses the question, what voices do we listen to that are inferior to the Son of God? However, in Hebrews 1:5–14 the emphasis is a cosmic hierarchy. Prophets spoke with God's authority, angels spoke with God's authority, but in this era Jesus speaks with God's authority. He is the new and developed thought of God. Or, to say it more precisely, the prophets were leading to Jesus who affirmed and completed their message (Matt. 5:17). Do we exhibit a hierarchy of spokesmen or spokeswomen when it comes to preachers and teachers? Who are the current or recorded voices to whom we might listen? Alistair Begg? Tony Evans? Timothy Keller? Thomas Long? Otis Moss III? John MacArthur? John Piper? Andy Stanley? Chuck Swindoll? Barbara Brown Taylor? Today's "celebrity" preachers are endless. But in Hebrews 1:5–14, the general assumption is a high view of God's voice by way of Scripture in order to establish the authority of the messianic Son of promise, Jesus. Barnabas defers to Scripture to reinforce Jesus as God's one and only exalted Son. There is no other. Distinctions make a difference.

Hebrews 2:1–4

Exegetical Idea
In his warning to concentrate on and listen to God's revelation about the messianic Son of promise, Barnabas recalled the physical punishment the exodus generation received when they defied God's revelation given through a myriad of celestial "sons of God," as a form of comparison about God's future punishment for those who would reject God's most recent revelation about the messianic Son of promise through whom God had spoken, eyewitnesses confirmed, and whose message God endorsed.

Theological Focus
God will punish any person who defies his revelation, especially those who reject his recent revelation about his messianic Son of promise through whom God has spoken, whom eyewitnesses confirmed, and whose message God endorsed.

Preaching Idea
Our focus determines our future.

Preaching Pointers
Hebrews 2:1–4 represents the conclusion to Hebrews 1. If Jesus was both superior to the prophets and to the angels, Barnabas needed to warn his readers not to lose sight of the message about Jesus. This was Barnabas's first of several stern warnings. How this passage is approached sets the tone for the other warning passages that follow. In order to drive the point home, Barnabas used a word picture of "slipping away." However, as we will see, he was not commanding them to keep from slipping; he was commanding them not to lose focus that will cause them to slip away. This was a significant difference. It was Jesus who kept them from slipping away, therefore Barnabas focused on him. The original audience would appreciate the strong historical precedent for focusing on the words of angels and of prophets. They would have understood how God kept people accountable for listening to their words. Now, God's greater spokes*man* had spoken. Therefore, the Roman followers of Jesus were expected to focus on what God said about Jesus.

Today, people may or may not listen to what a preacher is saying. In many people's minds, the preacher may or may not have authority. One reason is that we preachers have, perhaps unwittingly, presented ourselves as one voice among many that can demand attention. This, coupled with the reality that those who consider themselves "active" in the faith attend church only part-time, gives them the impression that focusing on Jesus is optional. This compounded indifference to the spoken word makes the warning of 2:1–4 more relevant today than ever. If we lose focus we will slip away. Our focus determines our future.

Hebrews 2:5–9

Exegetical Idea
God's plan for his messianic Son of promise—and *never* the angels—was that the Son's authority be expanded to an absolute ruling authority over all of creation, even though his Son, Jesus, existed ever so briefly as a man, died a gruesome death on behalf of all people, and then was exalted to his currently partial rule.

Theological Focus
God's plan for the messianic Son of promise to rule with absolute authority begins with Jesus's life as a man, his death for all people, and his exaltation as God's messianic Son of promise.

Preaching Idea
Great plans require perceptive thinking and time.

Preaching Pointers
The anticipation of a messiah was part of Jewish theological thinking ever since Jeremiah and Ezekiel prophesized the demise of Judah at the hands of Nebuchadnezzar. It was part of God's plan. As a result, most of the Jewish people of the first century made *conjectures* about a future

messiah and were at times misguided and driven by current social, religious, and political affairs (Bateman et al., 2012, 211–49). And despite their misunderstandings, the Messiah came according to God's plan. This passage hints at what would be further explained in chapter 3, namely, God's plan. Jesus was faithful to fulfill the plan of God. Yet, God's plan was expanded to fulfill far more than what was anticipated in Jesus.

Even today, when people think of God's plan, they often do not see it as active but static. They understand creation, Christmas, and Easter, but beyond that they might wonder if the plan of God has stalled out. Yet, God is active today in fulfilling his plan. This is the flow of the text: Jesus is the means by which the plan will be executed because he has an expanded but hidden role and because of his dying on behalf of all people. Thus, we should be encouraged that people today can actually be active in God's plan by making much of Jesus. And so, these verses have the feel of encouragement—we are encouraged to be aggressively waiting for Jesus to fulfill his plan. Great plans require perceptive thinking and time.

Hebrews 2:10–18

Exegetical Idea

Whereas the result of Jesus's gruesome death was God's way to equip him to be the leader of the family household with whom he worshipped and trusted God, Jesus's incarnation created a human connection that defeated Satan, eliminated the fear of death, and qualified him for service as high priest—one who was able to aid members of the household family of faith in their physical, emotional, and spiritual struggles.

Theological Focus

God equips Jesus perfectly to lead the household family of faith with whom he worships and trusts God and for whom he defeated Satan, conquered death, and currently serves as a high priest who is able to identify with the physical, emotional, and spiritual struggles of all family members.

Preaching Idea

Jesus is a better leader.

Preaching Pointers

During the Greco-Roman period, the family unit was an essential element to society: husband, wife, children, and slaves. They were the household family unit. It was a microcosmic unit of the Roman Empire over which Caesar ruled as the head of all family units. The family was crucial in the Greco-Roman world.

Even today, the family is critical to society. However, what makes the family different in today's society is the acceptability of wrong behavior among our leaders that trickle down into our families. We tend to assume that leaders will lie, steal, cheat, and even manipulate the law in their favor. We recognize that many are not respectable. Whether they be our bosses, political leaders, or church leaders, integrity is lacking, the love of money abounds, and immoral behavior is blatantly flaunted in public and on television. Yet, the leadership of Jesus is radically different. He is our "founder," or, we might say, our "captain." Jesus is our better leader. He is a trustworthy leader over the numerous household families of faith that make up God's kingdom.

Hebrews 3:1–6

Exegetical Idea

Members of the household family of faith were to give careful consideration to the confession about Jesus as God's sent spokes*man* and high priest, who deserved greater honor than even Moses as well as their persistent allegiance.

Theological Focus

Persistent allegiance to Jesus as God's sent spokes*man* and high priest that exceeds all other loyalties is both urged and expected.

Preaching Idea

Loyalty involves careful deliberation, deserved respect, and steadfast commitment.

Preaching Pointers

No matter where they lived in the world, Jewish people of all ages tended to be loyal to their Jewish homeland, their Jewish law, and their Jewish celebrations. This was certainly the case during the time of Barnabas. Jewish people throughout the Roman world believed God had called them, established them in Judaea, and would act on their behalf to execute divine justice in Judaea. This sense of *nationalism* began in the Sinai desert under the leadership of Moses, who was their national hero. He was well known, his service respected, and his name venerated. A Jewish person's national connection to Judaea was generally strong and his or her sense of loyalty profound.

We too exhibit loyalties. Loyalties are often evident in our choices of a particular sports team whether they be at the high school, college, or professional level. Where we work, worship, and window-shop may expose our loyalty to a particular place or product. Oftentimes, however, loyalty to people such as our bosses, friends, and family are unmistakable. As we shall see, Barnabas is going to emphasize that the features of loyalty to Jesus involve careful deliberation, deserved respect, and steadfast commitment.

Hebrews 3:7–19

Exegetical Idea

While God exhorted the household family of faith to resist stubborn unbelief as evidenced in the exodus community, Barnabas expected believers to take heed of any potential stubbornness as well as take steps to avoid it because of the family's allegiance with Jesus, the messianic Son of promise, and because of the stubborn unbelief of the exodus generation that infuriated God.

Theological Focus
Vigilance in heeding, avoiding, and resisting stubbornness against God is based upon the household family of faith's present relationship with Jesus and the historical willful unbelief of God's people in the past.

Preaching Idea
Stubborn unbelief leads to straying.

Preaching Pointers
The Roman household family of faith was well aware that stubborn disbelief was an obstacle to overcome. Historically, stubborn unbelief resulted in Jewish people straying from God that had devastating consequences for the exodus generation, especially at Mount Sinai (Exod. 32:1–33:6) and again at Kadesh Barnea (Num. 14; cf. Ps. 106:7–27a). Consequently, Barnabas not only exhorted the household family of faith about stubborn disbelief; he also explained why it was a problem before issuing his warning about it.

Even today, we struggle with disobedience that leads us to *straying* from God rather than *staying* with God. Many ministries fly a banner about security (= eternal security) in Jesus. However, this sort of security preached, to the neglect of a call for obedience, oftentimes leads to spiritual lethargy. We are all prone to wander and prone to leave the one we love. Therefore, we need the warnings in Hebrews to motivate us to stay close to Jesus when, in reality, we want to wander. We too need to be warned about stubborn unbelief that leads to straying.

Hebrews 4:1–13

Exegetical Idea
The household family of faith was expected to fear failure because of the historical stubborn unbelief of the exodus generation, and yet, based upon God's invitation for a future Sabbath celebration, the household family of faith was expected to strive to be successful in not repeating the historical failures of the past.

Theological Focus
God's promise of a future celebration with him is available to all those who do not take their future with God for granted and thereby do not cease striving to succeed in joining God in his future celebration.

Preaching Idea
People who fail to learn from the past are guaranteed to repeat it.

Preaching Pointers
Time and again, Jewish leaders and Jewish people throughout the Roman Empire rejected Jesus, the message about Jesus, and his messengers. The kingdom Jesus proclaimed was turned down. Yet, Judaeans living during the mid-60s assumed they could rebel against Rome, declare their independence, and exist apart from the Roman Empire as "God's Jewish kingdom." They displayed repeatedly a fearless audacity that threatened Rome's

revered *Pax Romana* (= Roman peace). Their stubbornness led to a rebellion that revealed self-assurance, feelings of fearlessness, and defiant activities, whether they be aggressive or passive-aggressive behavior. The Jewish family of faith in Rome was well aware of the Judaean revolt in much the same way as those who had been taken captive to Babylon in 605 and 597 B.C. were aware of the happenings in Jerusalem during the time of Jeremiah. From beginning to end, Barnabas addressed the original readers' current story by showing connecting points between the Jewish rebellion against Rome in Judaea with the exodus rebellion against God at Kadesh Barnea. Thus, Barnabas recalled a similar sort of rebellion against God's plan for his people.

Even today, we too wrestle with rebelling against God's plan. The plan God has for my life is impacted by Jesus's words in the Sermon on the Mount and aspects echoed in Hebrews 13. Jesus demonstrated life in the kingdom by painting a picture of people who love their enemies, divest in this world to invest in the life to come, and to not worry about what tomorrow might bring. All those kingdom virtues are very counterintuitive. I want to dispose of my enemies, hoard in this life, and fret over tomorrow. We all tend to rebel against God's plan. This passage addresses a rebellion that has eternal consequences. It's the type of rebellion that can lead to a failure to enter the rest of God. Thus, when we fail to learn from the past we are guaranteed to repeat it.

Hebrews 4:14–5:10

Exegetical Idea
Jesus, the household family of faith's high priest to whom they were to cling and through whom they had safe access to God in order to experience God's compassion, met the qualifications for the high priesthood in keeping with his divinely appointed tasks as regal high priest.

Theological Focus
Clinging to Jesus, God's appointed regal high priest, makes it possible for the household family of faith to approach God in safety in order to experience his compassion.

Preaching Idea
Everyone needs compassion, but where do we get it?

Preaching Pointers
For the Jewish household family of faith in Rome, access to God was initially by way of the Levitical priesthood. A priest's eligibility for priesthood was based upon his descent from Aaron's male line (e.g., patrilineal descendants), being chosen by God, and being officiators of temple sacrifices on behalf of God's people. Unfortunately, not all priests, particularly the high priest, were God's chosen nor were they ethical and willing to be compassionate. The truth of this passage for the original readers of Hebrews was that Jesus, God's chosen high priest, made it possible for the followers of Jesus in Rome to have access to God and experience God's compassion without going to the temple in Jerusalem.

Even today, there are many charlatans who preach, "Thus sayeth the Lord," but lack in demonstrating compassion. But like the believers in Rome, we too need to experience compassion. Whether it be at work when we make a mistake and the boss says, "It's OK. I too have made mistakes"; at school when we don't seem to be getting it and the teacher says, "It's OK, let's meet after school and see if we can improve your understanding of the course material"; or at home when we crash the car and Mom and Dad say, "It's OK, I'm just glad you're not hurt"—everybody needs to experience compassion.

Hebrews 5:11–6:12

Exegetical Idea

The household family of faith in Rome, reprimanded for their inability to advance in their understanding of Jesus as regal high priest and in discerning life situations, was exhorted to press on in their understanding about the messianic Son of promise in conjunction with a motivational word of encouragement.

Theological Focus

Everyone who claims to be a follower of Jesus must understand the details of Jesus as God's messianic Son of promise.

Preaching Idea

The mind is a terrible thing to neglect.

Preaching Pointers

During the Greco-Roman period, the literate person was in the minority. Very few could afford an education; even fewer could read and write. This was not because they were incapable of learning; they just learned differently. They learned orally. Naturally, this could lead to stagnation in advancing in knowledge and understanding of new subjects. In this unit, Barnabas expressed his disappointment in the Roman Jewish household family of faith about their inability to advance in their understanding of Jesus as regal high priest. So, he reprimanded them and exhorted them to press on in their orally taught understanding about the messianic Son of promise, to move from their ruts and stop neglecting their need to advance in their understanding.

Even today, as literate as our society is, it's very easy to stagnate and become apathetic about advancing in our understanding about issues. It's a common leadership maxim that people within an organization will do anything in the world to keep from thinking. The temptation in an organization is simply to execute our roles without thinking about how our work affects the larger picture. We find this temptation in our adolescence, where academic pursuits simply become checking boxes and a means to the end of getting a degree. We, perhaps unwittingly, are programmed to check boxes and not to think outside of them. The spiritual danger is that we treat our relationship with God like a relationship with other organizations. We simply want to check boxes. However, the mind is a terrible thing to neglect.

Hebrews 6:13–6:20

Exegetical Idea
God's pledge to Abraham about heirs, conferred to Abraham by way of his perseverance, was certified by way of God linking his vow to his pledge, which had unchangeable certainties about Jesus as God's royal-priest.

Theological Focus
Followers of Jesus can trust that God will fulfill his pledge to those who persevere because of his trustworthy word about Jesus, his royal high priest.

Preaching Idea
God's promises are not like human promises—they are guaranteed.

Preaching Pointers
For the first-century Jew, Abraham was the recognized forefather of God's theocratic nation of Israel, whose existence was traced back to early Mesopotamia and the times of the Egyptian Pharaohs. "Abraham is often mentioned," according to Evans (2001, 2), "as the ideal example of Jewish piety and orthodoxy." In fact, he was considered God's friend, because he observed God's commandments. He was recognized as faithful to God. Here in Hebrews 6:13–20, Barnabas focused attention on *God's pledge to Abraham*, namely, that he would be a "father of a multitude." Abraham believed God, and God kept his pledge.

Today, verbal pledges or commitments are part of everyday life. We make pledges to our spouses during wedding ceremonies. We make commitments to volunteer in community organizations like Big Brothers Big Sisters, the Boy Scouts, or the Girl Scouts. We make pledges to provide monthly donations to World Vision, St. Jude Children's Research Hospital, and the church. We sign contracts for services to be completed within a timely manner. Unfortunately, obligations to an agreement is an endangered expectation. We don't always believe them. We don't always fulfill them. How does the everyday reality that not everyone keeps their promises, affect us? Is it true that God's promises are not like human promises—that they are in fact guaranteed?

Hebrews 7:1–28

Exegetical Idea
Scripture's silence about Melchizedek and Abraham's encounter with Melchizedek served to underscore the imperfection of the Levitical system and exalt the status of Jesus as regal priest.

Theological Focus
Jesus's exalted status as royal high priest permanently supplants the cultic system of Judaism.

Preaching Idea
Jesus is permanently for us.

Preaching Pointers

The Jewish household family of faith in Rome was no doubt aware of interpretive stories about biblical figures that were part of Jewish tradition. According to these stories, the "sons of God" left heaven to have intercourse with women (1 En. 6:1–7:6), Sarah's beauty was embellished (1Q20), Manasseh's penitential prayer was a proposed theological supposition (Pr Man), and the Letter of Jeremiah was an embellishment of Jeremiah 10 about idols. Similarly, there were embellished stories about Melchizedek. Yet, Hebrews 7 recalled, interpreted, and applied the biblical encounter between Abraham and Melchizedek in Genesis to underscore the imperfection of the Levitical system, and its replacement by way of the exalted status of Jesus as regal priest in the order of Melchizedek.

Even today, when a novelist wants to explain something, he or she will release a "prequel." A prequel is a story released after the original story but concerns events that took place before the original. This is the sense of Hebrews 7. Hebrews 7 is the prequel to the life of Jesus. The book of Hebrews was written after Jesus went back to heaven but contains events that led up to this coming. In a similar way, when we encounter Jesus, we can hardly imagine the amount of backstory there is. Hebrews 7 explains that the backstory to Jesus is the Levites, and the backstory to the Levites is Melchizedek. A good prequel will help the reader appreciate the original. In this case the prequel—the story of the Levites and Melchizedek—is not a better or embellished story, but a story that helps us appreciate even more our engagement with Jesus. Jesus is permanently for us.

Hebrews 8:1–13

Exegetical Idea

Jesus's ministry as regal high priest in a heavenly sanctuary was of better quality than the ministries performed in earthly sanctuaries because the nature of the first covenant was incomplete and God's people were repeatedly breaking it, so God inaugurated a new internalized covenant that replaced the first one.

Theological Focus

Jesus's ministry as God's regal high priest is of better quality than those ministries performed on earth due to God's inauguration of his new set of covenantal promises.

Preaching Idea

What is perfect will not be obsolete.

Preaching Pointers

For Barnabas, Hebrews 8 was a significant turning point in his discussion. From 8:1 until 10:39, the tone changed from hard warnings, to discussions of Melchizedek. It was a long expository section on the superiority of Jesus, and the old or first covenant. For the Jewish person who was a member of the household family of faith, the Mosaic law was extremely important, even for those who were first-generation followers of Jesus. Yet, the transition to the new covenant was difficult (cf. Acts 15; Rom 7; Gal. 2; Eph. 2; etc.). The Jewish believers living in Rome wrestled with understanding God's plan expressed in Scripture (HB LXX) as it was accomplished through Jesus. Barnabas could have discussed in this section why Jesus was *supreme*, but instead he discussed why Jesus was *superior*. He did not use the superlative but the comparative.

Today, we accept and celebrate the new covenant during our communion services without much thought given to the old. There is the temptation to downplay the old covenant due to its imperfections. Yet the point of the new covenant is its superiority to the old because it is better than the first due to Jesus who inaugurated it. In a similar way, we accept new car models that are placed yearly on the market with improved shapes and often confusing new digital accessories. We give little thought to Ford's Model-T, which is the basis of the modern car. Like Ford's Model-T, the first covenant was magnificent. If we stop to appreciate the design of the old covenant (like Ford's Model-T), it makes the new covenant (or new cars) even more glorious. The problem is that its design had an internal expiration date built in leading to God's new covenant due to the perfection of Jesus who showcased the new covenant. Yet unlike new car models, the divine perfections of the new covenant will never expire due the perfection of the one who inaugurated. It will never become obsolete.

Hebrews 9:1–28

Exegetical Idea
In contrast to the cultic regulations for the earthly tabernacle and the ineffectiveness of cultic rituals, the arrival of Jesus as God's regal high priest and his entrance into God's heavenly presence guaranteed an efficacious cleansing of a person's conscience, and as God's mediator of a new covenant, Jesus intended to establish an inheritance for the Jewish household family of faith.

Theological Focus
Jesus is the mediator of God's new covenant, and royal high priest whose self-sacrifice makes it possible to purge a person's conscience of guilt as well as experience God's promised inheritance.

Preaching Idea
Previews determine the plan.

Preaching Pointers
Since the time of Moses (ca. 1446 B.C.), the Levitical cultic system of sacrifice was intended to be front and center for God's chosen people of Israel. For more than 1,500 years, the cultic practice of animal sacrifice—first practiced in the tabernacle, then Solomon's temple, then Haggai's temple, and finally in Herod's rebuilt temple—had been part of Judaea's history. In this section, Barnabas developed the idea that Jesus's sacrifice was better than the Levitical cultic system of animal sacrifice. By way of a synopsis, Barnabas developed a brief picture of the tabernacle. Since the household family of faith in Rome knew it so well, they did not need a full review, just a synopsis. Consequently, Barnabas pointed out particular aspects for the purpose of his illustration, and he even used the term "parable" (*parabole*)in verse 9. The tabernacle was an illustration, a metaphor, or a picture.

Today, the church building is an illustration, a metaphor, or picture of God, particularly as it concerns Jesus. Some churches have stained glass windows, rather than curtains where cherubim were displayed. Rather than a place where burnt offerings were to take place in the tabernacle's courtyard, today's churches feature a cross. And rather than an ark of the covenant located in the Holy of Holies, churches today display a table with an inscription: "The Lord's Table" or "Do This in Remembrance of Me." Yet as was the case during Israel's history, today's tabernacle (= church building) where worship occurs conjures various perspectives, some good and some not so good. Nevertheless, the church is meant to exemplify something better. Previews determine the plan.

Hebrews 10:1–18

Exegetical Idea
The symbolic acts of Judaism's blood sacrifices offered through its inadequate covenantal system were replaced with Jesus's efficacious sacrificial death, which completed God's will, established a new covenant, and set into motion the household family of faith to be set apart for God as well as to experience God's forgiveness.

Theological Focus
Jesus, through his efficacious sacrificial death, fulfilled God's will, replaced symbolic acts of animal sacrifices, established a new covenant, and set into motion believers being set apart for God and experiencing forgiveness.

Preaching Idea
The shadow is irrelevant when the reality is here.

Preaching Pointers
As the Jewish household family of faith in Rome heard this portion of Hebrews read for the first time, they would have been very familiar with the Jewish cultic system of ritual sacrifices. Herod's temple had not yet been destroyed. So, there remained in place an active sacrificial system despite the religious corruption of the high priests. The ritual sacrifices and imagery were accessible to all who went to Jerusalem and worshipped. Thus, when Barnabas explained that these cultic systems were "shadows" and thus inadequate due to their repetitive nature, we can imagine how this passage resonated with the first-century listener. They would also identify with the inability of the sacrifices to make someone truly clean and pure before God. The idea of inadequacy was a perfect segue into the discussion of the complete adequacy of Jesus and his sacrifice.

Today people are largely unfamiliar with first-century cultic rituals. Yet, they are familiar with "shadow" realities. From early on, we develop dependence on certain "shadow" realities in our life. We become familiar with family and church structures that are "shadows" of biblical expectations. We engage financial systems that are mere "shadows" of security. We become dependent on federal and state government social services that are "shadows" of a standard of living. Yet, God makes it clear that all things, material or immaterial, are imperfectly represented in this life. Every imperfect thing in this life is a "shadow" to point us and to lead us to Jesus. The imperfect bodies in this imperfect world systems, including the church, are filled with imperfect people, and that makes us long to see Jesus, our regal high priest, and to see the kingdom of God. So, while the "shadows" we experience today are good, they are pale and incomplete representations of reality. "Shadows" are representations, not a reality on which to depend. The shadow is irrelevant when the reality is here.

Hebrews 10:19–39

Exegetical Idea
Jesus as God's royal high priest, whose once-for-all self-sacrifice provided confidence to enter God's presence, warranted responsibilities, exhibited limitations for apostates, and expected the recollection of successes and perseverance in their faith in Jesus until he returns.

Theological Focus
Confidence in Jesus is limited to those who maintain their believing faith, because apostates will eventually face God's judgment.

Preaching Idea
Confidence demands evidence.

Preaching Pointers
The first-century world to which Barnabas was writing was hard. There were no social systems to take care of people in their time of need. It was easy to feel alone with no one to help. In their lowest moments, help was inaccessible. Faith in God might have seemed equally distant or as though God was inaccessible. The focus of the OT was not on his immanence but his transcendence. God was "wholly other." It was into this world that the word "confidence" (v. 19) comes streaking in like a meteor. What one did not have, ever, when approaching the throne of God, as represented in the Holy of Holies, was confidence. That confidence allowed them to draw near (v. 22). It motivated them to hold fast (v. 23) and stir each other up to good works (v. 24). Jesus brought them into the presence of hope.

Today people live without confidence for many reasons. Our confidence may be shaken with the crib death of our son, when our husband suffers a major heart attack and dies on Christmas day, when diagnosed with breast cancer, or when our daughter is being abused by her spouse. Where's God? Hurting people lean into their faith when they feel alone. Perhaps, not unlike in the first century, we live without confidence because we feel God is not accessible. To them God is aloof. God is real but apparently untouched by their suffering. Into this dark way of thinking bursts the Light of the World, who brings us near to the Father. For this reason, this passage may be more relevant now than ever. Confidence demands evidence.

Hebrews 11:1–40

Exegetical Idea
Many well-known Jewish ancestors, who were recognized for their righteousness, believed in the certainty of an unseen creator God's existence and trusted him for their future realities.

Theological Focus
Righteous people believe in the certainty of an unseen creator God and trust him for future realities.

Preaching Idea
Faith is real confidence in unseen realities.

Preaching Pointers
Hebrews 11 is a literary monolith, yet one that has parallels in other Jewish literature (Sir, 3 Macc, CD). Barnabas's listing of Jewish heroes, however, draws attention to those who have triumphed in faith. It is as beautiful as it is daunting. While the beauty of this passage is appropriately well noted, what must not be missed it how breathtakingly intertextual this is. We have in this passage some explanations of the life of Noah and of Abraham that give us more information than in the original books of Genesis and Exodus, respectively! Beyond this, the OT characters are spoken of in terms of Jesus. For example, Moses is described as having considered the reproach of Christ. So, this beautiful passage helps us understand how the compositional nature of Scripture speaks to its oneness.

Throughout life we understand that people are successful because they believe. Like a golfer envisioning a ball going in the hole before he ever swings his putter, we know that successful people believe. They envision their success and therefore succeed. While that is true, what is going on here in Hebrews 11 is much deeper than that. This is not holy hoping. This faith is an absolute confidence in the kingdom of God. And as a result, this confidence is rewarded by God's commendation (v. 39). Faith is real confidence in unseen realities.

Hebrews 12:1–13

Exegetical Idea
Members of the household family of faith were expected to endure life's challenges, like an athlete, and to be encouraged that as members of God's family God was providing educational opportunities for them, like a father to his children.

Theological Focus
Enduring life's challenges and engaging in divine educational opportunities are commonplace for anyone who is a member of God's family.

Preaching Idea
Nothing of eternal value can be won without endurance and discipline.

Preaching Pointers
Greco-Roman life revolved around the household family and sporting events held at Rome's massive Coliseum located in the center of the city. Elite athletes ran great distances. But the reality was that even a runner of shorter distances, in a way, had to endure the race. They were expected to complete the race. The idea was always that running implied completing, whether the distance was 40 yards or 100 kilometers. Barnabas placed the context of the

passage in the great hall of faith. So, the motivation for the running was the onlookers, the great cloud of witnesses. The cloud of witnesses was not just full of faith—they were also full of endurance. The Jewish household family of faith in Rome were running to join the cloud of witnesses.

Even today, we run to join the cloud of witnesses. And yet, this is not a pep talk to endure being given in a vacuum without context. Our motivation to endure comes from being under the discipline of the Lord. The Lord's discipline marks us believers. There is not an explicit sense that the discipline is necessarily *corrective*; it may equally be considered the *instructive* discipline of the Lord. This divine education comes with various opportunities to learn and involves a regimen of training that exercises our faith. So we are running, yes, but not just to run. We are running *into* the discipline of the Lord, toward something that is good for us. The goal is to finish the race set out for us. This is the explicit application of the faith we have as followers of Jesus, faith that endures as we embrace divine discipline. Nothing of eternal value can be won without endurance and discipline.

Hebrews 12:14–29

Exegetical Idea
Barnabas encouraged living in harmony with all people despite their difficulties unlike the exodus generation, and he expected the Roman household of faith to pay attention to and not reject the message about Jesus and thereby join those in God's heavenly kingdom.

Theological Focus
All who live morally harmonious lives, who pay attention to and do not reject the message about Jesus, will join the righteous who currently inhabit the heavenly kingdom of God.

Preaching Idea
Living demands choosing our moments.

Preaching Pointers
Living harmoniously as a Roman household was paramount to people living during the Greco-Roman world. For the Roman Empire, maintaining the "peace of Rome" was essential. Yet, during the time Barnabas wrote Hebrews, a violent movement in Judaea was about to erupt. Yet, despite what was going on in Judaea, Barnabas insisted that the Jewish household family of faith in Rome live morally harmonious lives by refraining from decisions that would make it impossible for repentance, as was the case for the exodus generation. The events in Judaea were profound, disturbing, and tempting for Jewish people.

Even today, there are moments in life that are more profound than others. A first conversation with one's future spouse, or the moment we decide to put ourselves out there for a job or for a promotion, are examples. None of these things would be possible if we did not choose our moments. We call these instances "defining moments" because they cause the trajectory of our life to pivot or change course. And these changes forever become a part of who we are. Not only the choice to move forward, but also the choice to stand still, both have life-shaping consequences. There's no middle ground when followers of Jesus consider the dangers and penalties of refusing God. Living demands choosing our moments.

Hebrews 13:1–25

Exegetical Idea

Barnabas's admonition to persist in loving one another involved expectations for ethical living regarding hospitality and concern for others, the private life relating to social nuptials and confidence in God as helper, and community life concerning its leaders and the continuity of God's message about the sacrificial death of Jesus, which served as the basis for rejecting Judaism's cultic system.

Theological Focus

Persistent love for one another manifests itself in caring for others, honoring marriage vows, revering church leaders past and present, and maintaining God's message about Jesus as exalted royal high priest.

Preaching Idea

How do we recognize the real family of God?

Preaching Pointers

For Rome's Jewish household family of faith, there was an expectation in the culture to exhibit unselfish dispositions and practices that involved mutual sharing of possessions and participating in community activities. These were forms of "brotherly love." Barnabas admonished the household family of faith to persist in loving one another, which comprised expectations for ethical living regarding hospitality and the concern for others. For private life, this included honoring marriage in society and trusting God to provide despite societal threats; and for community life, this included remembering and obeying leaders and ensuring the continuity of God's message about the sacrificial death of Jesus, whom God had not only raised but also exalted as royal high priest.

Even today families have expectations. This final chapter of Hebrews carries much of the language of family (brothers, and brotherly love) and the idea of community. There is a community identity to a group of people who alone exclusively have the right to eat around a certain table, a table that by its very existence includes some and excludes others. In fact, this idea of family as community here in this final chapter is a fitting ending to the sermon series on the book of Hebrews. The high view of Jesus allows us to see practically what Jesus won for his household family of faith by giving us, his family, access to the throne of God. As well, the warning passages are warnings to those who think they are in the family but do not have the character traits (such as endurance) of family members. The mood of the text flows forth from the expectation of a confident, enduring believer. We do not endure on our own, but in the family of faith, and as such, we live out all aspects of our life together with family expectations in view.

ABBREVIATIONS

GENERAL ABBREVIATIONS

A.D.	in the year of our Lord (*anno Domini*)
B.C.	Before Christ
B.C.E.	before the Common Era
C.E.	Common Era
DSS	Dead Sea Scrolls
ET	English translation
HB	Hebrew Bible
LXX	Septuagint (the Greek OT)
NT	New Testament
OT	Old Testament

TECHNICAL ABBREVIATIONS

agcy.	agency
ap.	apposition
b.	born
ca.	ca.
cf.	compare (*confer*)
ch(s).	chapter(s)
col(s).	column(s)
con.	*contra*, against
cond.	condition(al)
d.	died
des.	descriptive
e.g.	for example
etc.	and so forth, and the rest (*et cetera*)
et al.	and others (*et alii*)
flor.	flourished (*floruit*)
frag.	fragment
gen.	genitive
i.e.	that is (*id est*)
idem	the same
impf.	imperfect
impv.	imperative
indep.	independent
inf.	infinitive
n(n).	note(s)

neut.	neuter
p(p).	page(s)
par(r). *or* //	Gospel parallel(s)
pass.	passive
perf.	perfect
pres. tense	present tense
ptc.	participle
repr.	reprinted
rev.	revised
sbjv.	subjunctive
subj.	subject
s.v.	under the word (*sub verbo*)
temp.	temporal
trans.	translation
txt.	text
var.	variant
v(v).	verse(s)

BIBLICAL

Old Testament

Gen.	Genesis
Exod.	Exodus
Lev.	Leviticus
Num.	Numbers
Deut.	Deuteronomy
Josh.	Joshua
Judg.	Judges
Ruth	Ruth
1 Sam.	1 Samuel
2 Sam.	2 Samuel
1 Kgdms.	1 Kingdoms (LXX)
2 Kgdms.	2 Kingdoms (LXX)
1 Kings	1 Kings
2 Kings	2 Kings
3 Kgdms.	3 Kingdoms (LXX)
4 Kgdms.	4 Kingdoms (LXX)
1 Chron.	1 Chronicles
2 Chron.	2 Chronicles
1 Par.	1 Paraliponmenon (LXX)
2 Par.	2 Paraliponmenon (LXX)
Ezra	Ezra
Neh.	Nehemiah
Esther	Esther
Job	Job
Ps./Pss.	Psalm(s)
Prov.	Proverbs
Eccl.	Ecclesiastes
Song	Song of Songs
Isa.	Isaiah
Jer.	Jeremiah
Lam.	Lamentations
Ezek.	Ezekiel
Dan.	Daniel
Hos.	Hosea
Joel	Joel
Amos	Amos
Obad.	Obadiah
Jonah	Jonah
Mic.	Micah
Nah.	Nahum
Hab.	Habakkuk
Zeph.	Zephaniah
Hag.	Haggai
Zech.	Zechariah
Mal.	Malachi

New Testament

Matt.	Matthew
Mark	Mark
Luke	Luke
John	John
Acts	Acts
Rom.	Romans
1 Cor.	1 Corinthians
2 Cor.	2 Corinthians
Gal.	Galatians
Eph.	Ephesians
Phil.	Philippians
Col.	Colossians
1 Thess.	1 Thessalonians
2 Thess.	2 Thessalonians
1 Tim.	1 Timothy
2 Tim.	2 Timothy
Titus	Titus
Philem.	Philemon
Heb.	Hebrews
James	James
1 Peter	1 Peter
2 Peter	2 Peter
1 John	1 John
2 John	2 John
3 John	3 John
Jude	Jude
Rev.	Revelation

EXTRABIBLICAL SOURCES

Old Testament Apocrypha

Tob	Tobit
Jdt	Judith
Wis	Wisdom of Solomon
Sir	Wisdom of Jesus the Son of Sirach (Ecclesiasticus)
Bar	Baruch
Add Esth	Additions to Esther
Add Dan	Additions to Daniel
Bel	Bel and the Dragon
1 Macc	1 Maccabees
2 Macc	2 Maccabees
1 Esd	1 Esdras
Pr Man	Prayer of Manasseh
3 Macc	3 Maccabees
2 Esd	2 Esdras
4 Macc	4 Maccabees

Old Testament Pseudepigrapha

Apoc. Ab.	Apocalypse of Abraham
As. Mos.	Assumption of Moses
2 Bar.	2 Baruch (Syriac Apocalypse)
Ep. Arist.	Epistle of Aristeas
Jos. Asen.	Joseph and Aseneth
Jub.	Jubilees
1 En.	1 Enoch (Ethiopic Apocalypse)
2 En.	2 Enoch
4 Ezra	4 Ezra

Odes Sol.	Odes of Solomon
Pss. Sol.	Psalms of Solomon
Sib. Or.	Sibylline Oracles
T. 12 Patr.	Testaments of the Twelve Patriarchs
T. Benj.	Testament of Benjamin
T. Dan	Testament of Dan
T. Iss.	Testament of Issachar
T. Jos.	Testament of Joseph
T. Levi	Testament of Levi
T. Adam	Testament of Adam
T. Mos.	Testament of Moses
T. Sol.	Testament of Solomon

Classification of the Dead Sea Scrolls

[a], [b], [c], etc.	manuscript identifiers
Ap	Apocalypse (e.g. 4QMessAp)
ar	Aramaic (e.g., 1QapGen ar)
apocr	apocryphon (e.g., 1QapGen)
1Q	Cave 1, Qumran
4Q	Cave 4, Qumran
11Q	Cave 11, Qumran
frag	fragment
Mess	Messianic (e.g. 4QMessAp)
ord	ordinances (e.g., 4Qord[a])
p	pesher (e.g., 1QpHab)
pap	papyrus (e.g., 4QpapParaKings)
Q	Qumran
tg	targum (e.g., 11QtgJob)

Dead Sea Scrolls

Number	*Abbreviation*	*Name*
CD	Damascus Document	Cairo Genizah copy of the Damascus Document
1QM	1QWar Scroll	Milḥamah *or* War Scroll
1QpHab		Pesher Habakkuk
1Q20	1QapGen ar	Genesis Apocryphon
1Q28	1Q28	Rule of the Community
1Q28a	1QSa	Rule of the Congregation
1Q28b	1Q28a	Rule of Blessings
4Q159	4Qord[a]	Ordinances[a]
4Q161	4QpIsa[a]	Isaiah Pesher[a]
4Q174	4QFlor	Florilegium
4Q175	4QTest	Testimonia
4Q185		Sapiential Work
4Q246	4QapocDan ar	Apocryphon Daniel

4Q252	4QCommGen A	Commentary on Genesis A
4Q266	4QD[a]	Damascus Document[a]
4Q285	4QSM	Sefer ha-Milḥamah
4Q369	4QPEnosh	Prayer of Enosh
4Q376	4QapocrMoses B[b]	Apocryphon of Moses B[b]
4Q377	4QapocrMoses C	Apocryphon of Moses C
4Q382	4Qpap paraKings	Paraphrase of the Kings
4Q400	4QShirShabb[a]	Songs of the Sabbath Sacrifice[a]
4Q401	4QShirShabb[b]	Songs of the Sabbath Sacrifice[b]
4Q402	4QShirShabb[c]	Songs of the Sabbath Sacrifice[c]
4Q403	4QShirShabb[d]	Songs of the Sabbath Sacrifice[d]
4Q404	4QShirShabb[e]	Songs of the Sabbath Sacrifice[e]
4Q405	4QShirShabb[f]	Songs of the Sabbath Sacrifice[f]
4Q406	4QShirShabb[g]	Songs of the Sabbath Sacrifice[g]
4Q407	4QShirShabb[h]	Songs of the Sabbath Sacrifice[h]
4Q423	4QInstruction[g]	
4Q458	4QNarrative A	
4Q493	4QM[c]	War Scroll[c]
4Q496	4QpapM[f]	War Scroll[f]
4Q504	4QDibHam[a]	Words of the Luminaries[a]
4Q521	4QMessAp	Messianic Apocalypse
4Q544	4QAmram[b] ar	Visions of Amram[b]
4Q546	4QAmram[d] ar	Visions of Amram[d]
11Q13	11QMelch	Melchizedek
11Q17	11QShirShabb	Songs of the Sabbath Sacrifice
11Q19	11QT[a]	The Temple Scroll[a]

Midrashim, Midrash Rabbah (Rabbinic Works)

Gen. Rab.	Genesis Rabbah
Exod. Rab.	Exodus Rabbah

Apostolic Fathers

Barnabas	Hellenized Jew, early Christian missionary; d. ca. A.D. 61
Ignatius (of Antioch)	Syrian bishop, church father; ca. A.D. 50–ca. 110
Eph	*To the Ephesians*
Phld	*To the Philadelphians*
Smyrn	*To the Smyrnaeans*

Classical and Ancient Christian Writings (Greek and Latin Works)

Aristophanes	Greek Athenian playwright; 446–386 B.C.
Av.	*Birds* (*Aves*)
Aristotle	Greek philosopher, scientist; 384–322 B.C.
Ath. pol.	*Constitution of Athens* (*Athēnāin politeia*)
Pol.	*Politics* (*Politica*)
John Chrysostom	From Antioch, Bishop of Constantinople; A.D. 344–401

Hom. Heb	Homlies from the epistle of Hebrews (*Homiliae in epistulam ad Hebraes*)
Demosthenes	Athenian orator, statesman; 384–322 B.C.
Andr.	*Against Androtion* (*Adversus Androtionem*)
CApat	*Against Apaturius* (*Contra Apatourium*)
CDionys	*Against Dionysodorus* (*Contra Dionysodorum*)
CMac	*Against Macartatus (Contra Macartatum)*
Dio	Roman statesman and historian of Greek and Roman origin (A.D. 155–235)
Hist. of Rome	*History of Rome*
Dionysius (of Halicarnassus)	Greek historian, teacher of rhetoric; flor. ca. 20 B.C.
Ant. rom.	*Antiquitates romanae*
Eusebius (of Caesarea)	Bishop and church historian; ca. A.D. 264–ca. 340
Hist. eccl.	*Ecclesiastical History* (*Historia ecclesiastica*)
Heliodorus (of Emesa)	Greek writer; flor. third or fourth century A.D.
Aeth.	*Aethiopica*
Irenaeus	Bishop of Lyon, Greek theologian; ca. A.D. 130–ca. 200
Haer.	*Against Heresies* (*Adversus haereses* [*Elenchos*])
Isocrates	Athenian orator, teacher of rhetoric; 436–338 B.C.
Trapez.	*On the Banker* (*Trapeziticus* [*Or. 17*])
Josephus	Romano-Jewish historian; A.D. 37–100
A.J.	*Jewish Antiquities* (*Antiquitates judaicae*)
B.J.	*Jewish War* (*Bellum Judaicum*)
C. Ap.	*Against Apion* (*Contra Apionem*)
Vita	*The Life* (*Vita*)
Origen	Christian theologian, biblical scholar; ca. A.D. 185–ca. 254
Comm. Jo.	*Commentarii in evangelium Joannis*
Philo (of Alexandria)	Jewish philosopher; ca. 20 B.C.–A.D. 50
Abr.	*On the Life of Abraham* (*De Abrahamo*)
Aet.	*On the Eternity of the World* (*De aeternitate mundi*)
Agr.	*On Agriculture* (*De agricultura*)
Cher.	*On the Cherubim* (*De cherubim*)
Conf.	*On the Confusion of Tongues* (*De confusione linguarum*)
Congr.	*On the Preliminary Studies* (*De congressu eruditionis gratia*)
Decal.	*De decalogo*
Det.	*That the Worse Attacks the Better* (*Quod deterius potiori insidiari soleat*)
Deus.	*That God Is Unchangeable* (*Quod Deus sit immutabilis*)
Ebr.	*On Drunkenness* (*De ebrietate*)
Flacc.	*Against Flaccus* (*In Flaccum*)
Fug.	*On Flight and Finding* (*De fuga et inventione*)
Gig.	*On the Giants* (*De gigantibus*)
Her.	*Who Is the Heir?* (*Quis rerum divinarum heres sit*)
Ios.	*On the Life of Joseph* (*De Iosepho*)
Leg.	*Allegorical Interpretation* (*Legum allegoriae*)

Legat.	*On the Embassy to Gaius* (*Legatio ad Gaium*)
Migr.	*The Migration of Abraham* (*De migratione Abrahami*)
Mos.	*Life of Moses* (*De vita Mosis*)
Mut.	*On the Change of Names* (*De mutatione nominum*)
Opif.	*On the Creation of the World* (*De opificio mundi*)
Plant.	*On Planting* (*De plantatione*)
Post.	*On the Posterity of Cain* (*De posteritate Caini*)
Praem.	*On Rewards and Punishments* (*De praemiis et poenis*)
Prob.	*That Every Good Person Is Free* (*Quod omnis probus liber sit*)
Prov.	*On Providence* (*De providentia*)
QG 1, 2, 3, 4	*Questions and Answers* 1, 2, 3, 4
Sacr.	*On the Sacrifices of Cain and Abel* (*De sacrificiis Abelis et Caini*)
Sobr.	*On Sobriety* (*De sobrietate*)
Somn.	*On Dreams* (*De somniis*)
Spec. 1, 2, 3, 4	*On the Special Laws* (*De specialibus legibus*)
Virt.	*On the Virtues* (*De virtutibus*)
Philodemus (of Gadara)	Greek poet, philosopher; ca. 110–35 B.C.
Lib.	*De libertate dicendi*
Pindarus	5th century BCE
Pyth.	*Pythian Odes* (*Pythionikai*)
Plato	Greek philosopher; 427–347 B.C.
Leg.	*Laws* (*Leges*)
Phaed.	*Phaedo*
Phileb.	*Philebus*
Resp.	*Republic (Respubica)*
Tim.	*Timaeus*
Pliny (the Elder)	Roman statesman, polymath; A.D. 23–79
Nat.	*Natural History* (*Naturalis historia*)
Plutarch	Greek biographer, essayist; ca. A.D. 46–120
Cat. Min.	*Cato the Younger* (*Cato Minor*)
Def. orac.	*De defectu oraculorum*
Mor.	*Moralia*
Per.	*Pericles*
Pomp.	*Pompeius*
Polybius	Greek historian; ca. 200–ca. 118 B.C.
Hist.	*Historiae*
Strabo	Greek geographer, historian; ca. 63 B.C.–ca. 23 A.D.
Geogr.	*Geography* (*Geographica*)
Suetonius	Roman biographer, historian; A.D. 69–122
Claud.	*Divus Claudius*
Tib.	*Tiberius*
Tacitus	Roman senator, historian; A.D. 56–120
Ann.	*Annales*
Hist.	*Historiae*

Tertullian	Early Christian theologian, polemicist; ca. 160–ca. 240
Pud.	*Modesty* (*De pudicitia*)
Thucydides	Greek historian; ca. 455–ca. 400 B.C.
Hist.	*History of the Peloponnesian War* (*Historiai*)
Xenephon	Greek, philosopher, historian, soldier; 430–354 B.C.
Mem.	*Memorabilia*

Papyri

P.Cair.Zen.	*Zenon Papyri* (Liddel & Scott)
P.Flor.	*Papiri greco-egizii, Papiri Fiorentini*
P.Fouad	*Les Papyrus Fouad I*
P.Giss.	*Papyrus Collection of Giessen University* (*Griechische Papyri zu Giessen*)
P.Hib.	*The Hibeh Papyri*
P.Mich.	*Michigan Papyri*
P.Oxy.	*The Oxyrhynchus Papyri*
P.Ryl.Dem.	*Catalogue of the Demotic Papyri in the John Rylands Library, Manchester*
P.Tebt.	*The Tebtunis Papyri*
P.Zen.	*Zenon Papyri*
SIG	*Sylloge Inscriptionum Graecaru*

Qur'anic and Islamic Sources

Qur'an	
Ibrahim	Abraham

PERIODICALS

ABSA	Annual of the British School at Athens
AUSS	*Andrews University Seminary Studies*
BA	*Biblical Archaeologist*
BAR	*Biblical Archaeology Review*
BASOR	*Bulletin of the American Schools of Oriental Research*
BBR	*Bulletin for Biblical Research*
Bib	*Biblica*
BJRL	*Bulletin of the John Rylands University Library of Manchester*
BR	*Biblical Research*
BSac	*Bibliotheca Sacra*
CBQ	*Catholic Biblical Quarterly*
CJT	*Canadian Journal of Theology*
CSion	*Cahiers Sioniens*
CTJ	*Calvin Theological Journal*
DRev	*Downside Review*
DSD	*Dead Sea Discoveries*

ETL	*Ephemerides Theologicae Lovanienses*
FM	*Faith and Mission*
HTR	*Harvard Theological Review*
HUCA	*Hebrew Union College Annual*
JAOS	*Journal of the American Oriental Society*
JBL	*Journal of Biblical Literature*
JETS	*Journal of the Evangelical Theological Society*
JJS	*Journal of Jewish Studies*
JNSL	*Journal of Northwest Semitic Languages*
JSJ	*Journal for the Study of Judaism in the Persian, Hellenistic, and Roman Periods*
JSNT	*Journal for the Study of the New Testament*
JSOT	*Journal for the Study of the Old Testament*
JTS	*Journal of Theological Studies*
Mus	*Muséon: Revue d'études orientales*
Neot	*Neotestamentica*
NovT	*Novum Testamentum*
NTS	*New Testament Studies*
PEQ	*Palestine Exploration Quarterly*
RB	*Revue Biblique*
ResQ	*Restoration Quarterly*
RevExp	*Review and Expositor*
RevQ	*Revue de Qumran*
RHPR	*Revue de l'histoire et de philosophie*
RTR	*Reformed Theological Review*
ST	*Studia Theologica*
SwJT	*Southwestern Journal of Theology*
TJ	*Trinity Journal*
TynBul	*Tyndale Bulletin*
TZ	*Theologische Zeitschrift*
TZT	*Tübinger Zeitschrift für TheologieI*
USQR	*Union Seminary Quarterly Review*
VT	*Vetus Testamentum*
WTJ	*Westminster Theological Journal*
ZAW	*Zeitschrift für die alttestamentliche Wissenschaft*
ZNW	*Zeitschrift für die neutestamentliche Wissenschaft und die Kunde der älteren Kirche*

SERIES

AB	Anchor Bible
AmCNT	American Commentary on the New Testament
ANTC	Abingdon New Testament Commentaries
ANTF	Arbeiten zur neutestamentlichen Textforschung

BECNT	Baker Exegetical Commentary on the New Testament
Bishops	Bishops' Bible
BZNW	Beihefte zur Zeitschrift für die neutestamentliche Wissenschaft
CBC	Cambridge Bible Commentary
CBSC	Cambridge Bible for Schools and Colleges
ConBNT	Coniectanea Biblica: New Testament Series
DJD	Discoveries in the Judaean Desert
Ebib	Études bibliques
EC	Epworth Commentary
EKKNT	Evangelisch-katholischer Kommentar zum Neuen Testament
FRLANT	Forschungen zur Religion und Literatur des Alten und Neuen Testaments
Geneva	Geneva Bible 1599
HNT	Handbuch zum Neuen Testament
HNTE	Handbook for New Testament Exegesis
ICC	International Critical Commentary
JSJSup	Supplements to the Journal for the Study of Judaism
JSNTSup	Journal for the Study of the New Testament Supplement Series
JSOTSup	Journal for the Study of the Old Testament Supplement Series
JSPSup	Journal for the Study of the Pseudepigrapha Supplement Series
KCB	Kregel Charts of the Bible
KEK	Kritisch-exegetischer Kommentar über das Neue Testament (Meyer-Kommentar)
KNT	Kommentar zum Neuen Testament
NAC	New American Commentary
NCBC	New Cambridge Bible Commentary
NIBC	New International Biblical Commentary
NICNT	New International Commentary on the New Testament
NIGTC	New International Greek Testament Commentary
NTD	Das Neue Testament Deutsch
NTL	New Testament Library
NTM	New Testament Message
PCNT	Paideia: Commentaries on the New Testament
PNTC[1]	Pelican New Testament Commentaries
PNTC[2]	Pillar New Testament Commentary
RCRD	Rule of the Community and Related Documents
SBLDS	Society of Biblical Literature Dissertation Series
SBLMS	Society of Biblical Literature Monograph Series
SBLSS	Society of Biblical Literature Supplement Series
SD	Studies and Documents
SP	Sacra Pagina
TBC	Torch Bible Commentaries
THNTC	Two Horizons New Testament Commentary
TNTC	Tyndale New Testament Commentaries
WBC	Word Biblical Commentary

WC	Westminster Commentaries
WUNT	Wissenschaftliche Untersuchungen zum Alten und Neuen Testament

REFERENCE

ABD	Freedman, D. N., ed. 1992. *Anchor Bible Dictionary*. 6 vols. New York: Doubleday.
BAGD	Bauer, W., W. F. Arndt, and F. W. Gingrich, and F. W. Danker. 1979. *Greek-English Lexicon of the New Testament and Other Early Christian Literature*. 2nd ed. Chicago: University of Chicago Press.
Bateman[1]	Bateman IV, H. W. 2010. "Psalm 110: A Psalm of Assurance in the Midst of Change." In *Interpreting the Psalms for Preaching and Teaching*, ed. H. W. Bateman IV and D. B. Sandy, 150–61. St. Louis: Chalice Press.
Bateman[2]	Bateman IV, H. W. 2010. "Second Temple Exegetical Practices: Extra-Biblical Examples of Exegesis Compared with Those in the Book of Hebrews." *SwJT* 53 (1): 26–54.
BDAG	Danker, F. W., W. Bauer, W. F. Arndt, and F. W. Gingrich. 2000. *Greek-English Lexicon of the New Testament and Other Early Christian Literature*. 3rd ed. Chicago: University of Chicago Press.
BDF	Blass, F., A. Debrunner, and R. W. Funk. 1961. *Greek Grammar of the New Testament and Other Early Christian Literature*. Chicago: University of Chicago Press.
deSilva[1]	deSilva, D. A. 2000. *Honor, Patronage, Kinship and Purity: Unlocking New Testament Culture*. Downers Grove, IL: InterVarsity Press.
deSilva[2]	deSilva, D. A. 2000. *Perseverance in Gratitude: A Socio-Rhetorical Commentary on the Epistle "to the Hebrews."* Grand Rapids: Eerdmans.
EDNT	Balz, H., and G. Schneider, eds. 1990–1993. *Exegetical Dictionary of the New Testament*. Schneider. ET. 3 vols. Grand Rapids: Eerdmans.
EDSS	Schiffman, L. H. and J. C. VanderKam, eds. 2000. *Encyclopedia of the Dead Sea Scrolls*. 2 vols. New York: Oxford University Press.
ISBE	Bromiley, G. W., ed. 1979–1988. *International Standard Bible Encyclopedia*. 4 vols. Grand Rapids: Eerdmans.
MM	Moulton, J. H., and G. Milligan. 1997. *The Vocabulary of the Greek Testament: Illustrated from the Papyri and Other Non-literary Sources*. Peabody, MA: Hendrickson. First published 1930 by Eerdmans (Grand Rapids).
NIB	Keck, L. E., ed. 1994–2004. *New Interpreters Bible*. 12 vols. Nashville: Abingdon.
NIDNTT	Brown, C., ed. 1975–1978. *New International Dictionary of New Testament Theology*. 4 vols. Grand Rapids: Zondervan.
NIDOTTE	VanGemeren, W. A., ed. 1997. *New International Dictionary of Old Testament Theology*. 5 vols. Grand Rapids: Zondervan.
OEAGR	Gagarin, M., ed. 2010. *Oxford Encyclopedia of Ancient Greece and Rome*. 7 vols. New York: Oxford University Press.

PG	Migne, J.-P., ed. 1857–1886. *Patrologia Graeca*. [= *Patrologiae Cursus Completus*: Series Graeca]. 162 vols. Paris: Imprimerie Catholique.
TDNT	Kittel, G., and G. Friedrich, eds. 1964–1976. *Theological Dictionary of the New Testament*. Trans. G. W. Bromiley. 10 vols. Grand Rapids: Eerdmans.
TDOT	Botterweck, G. J., H. Ringgren, and H.-J. Fabry, eds. 1974–2006. *Theological Dictionary of the Old Testament*. Trans. J. T. Willis et al. 8 vols. Grand Rapids: Eerdmans.
TLNT	Spicq, C. 1994. *Theological Lexicon of the New Testament*. Trans. and ed. James D. Ernest. 3 vols. Peabody, MA: Hendrickson.
UT	Gordon, C. H. 1965. *Ugaritic Textbook*. Rome: Pontifical Biblical Institute.
Wise et al.	Wise, M., M. Abegg, and E. Cook. 1996. *The Dead Sea Scrolls: A New Translation*. San Francisco: HarperSanFrancisco.

BIBLE TRANSLATIONS

ASV	American Standard Version
CEB	Common English Bible
CEV	Contemporary English Version
CNT	Comprehensive New Testament
ESV	English Standard Version
KJV	King James Version
LXX	Septuagint
NAB	New American Bible
NASB	New American Standard Bible
NET	New English Translation
NIV	New International Version
NKJV	New King James Version
NLT	New Living Translation
NRSV	New Revised Standard Version
RSV	Revised Standard Version
WEB	World English Bible

INTRODUCTION

OVERVIEW OF INTRODUCTORY ISSUES

Author: Barnabas

Provenance: Written from a country within the Roman Empire other than Italy

Date: A.D. 63–66

Readers: Jewish Christians in Rome

Historical Setting: Nero's dislike of Jews culminated with Judaea's national unrest and rise of messianic fervor.

Occasion: Misunderstanding, questioning, and doubting Jesus's messiahship

Genre: Mix homily/midrash/letter

Theological Emphasis: Jesus is God's divine royal-priest through whom God has spoken and through whom God has fulfilled his promises.

AUTHORSHIP OF HEBREWS

Notably, there is no ascription of authorship for Hebrews. From the earliest formation of the church, the authorship of Hebrews has baffled church leaders and commentators (Koester, 2001, 19–46; Bateman et al., 2012, 19–25). No less than nineteen options have been offered for Hebrews's authorship (cf. Ellingworth, 1993, 3–21; cf. Bateman et al., 2012, 17–18). While a majority of commentators agree with Origen, who claims the author is unknown (D. Guthrie, 1990, 682; Carson and Moo, 2005, 604), a large number agree with Martin Luther, who argued that Apollos wrote Hebrews (G. Guthrie, 2001, 41–56). Yet several good reasons exist for suggesting that Barnabas wrote the letter.

First and foremost, there is the early testimony of several Western church leaders. On the one hand, Tertullian (d. 220), a North African apologist from Carthage, assumed that Barnabas wrote Hebrews. He considered Barnabas to be a man of equal stature to Paul and offered the Epistle of Barnabas as supporting evidence. On the other hand, Gregory (d. 392), Bishop of Elvira (southern Spain) and defender of the Nicene Creed, quoted Hebrews and attributed it to Barnabas (*Tractatus Origenis*). Finally, Philastrius (d. 397; also known as Filaster), Bishop of Brescia, Italy, considered Barnabas to be the author of Hebrews (*De Haeresibus*, 89). Yet, it must be acknowledged that Jerome (A.D. 345–419), best known for his translation of the Latin Vulgate and ministry in Rome, mentioned Barnabas as just one of several possibilities along with Luke and Clement of Rome (*De Viris Inlustribus*, 17). The Eastern Church, however, tended to favor Pauline authorship, a view still held by a few commentators today (cf. Black, 2001, 1–26).

Authorship Options

1. Barnabas
2. Barnabas translated by Luke
3. Voice of Barnabas written by Luke
4. Barnabas with a closing greeting by Paul
5. Paul
6. Paul translated by Luke
7. Luke
8. Clement of Rome
9. Apollos
10. Silas
11. Peter
12. Phillip
13. Priscilla and Aquila
14. Aristion
15. Stephen
16. Jude
17. Mary
18. Epaphras
19. Timothy
20. Unknown

Second, the Jewishness of the letter, personal awareness of those to whom he had written, and the description of the author's purpose seem to support Barnabas as the author of Hebrews. *As to Jewishness*, Barnabas was a Levite born in Cyprus and acquainted with the Jewish cultic system (Acts 4:36). The author of Hebrews was also aware of Judaea's cultic ritual practices (i.e., 7:11; 9:15; 13:11–13) and customs (i.e., 7:11; 9:15; 13:11–13). *As to personal awareness* of those to whom he wrote, he knew his readers (13:19, 23), identified with his readers (2:1, 3; 3:1, 14; 6:4; 10:19–25; etc.), and expressed his disappointments with his readers (5:11–6:4). He asked for prayer (13:18), gave them news of their friend Timothy (13:23), and recalled their "earlier days" in the faith (10:32; cf. 2:3–4). He knew of the persecutions they endured (10:32; 12:4), of their generosity to fellow believers (6:10; 10:32–34), and of their attitude toward their leaders (13:17). Naturally, this awareness enabled the author to encourage them (Heb. 13:22), which in turn appears to fit the description of Barnabas whom Luke described as "a good man, full of the Holy Spirit" (Acts 11:24), an apostle (Acts 14:14; 1 Cor. 9:6), and nicknamed "son of encouragement" (Acts 4:36).

Tertullian said, "For there is also extant a book entitled *To the Hebrews*, written by Barnabas a man well accredited by God since Paul associates him with himself in the observance of continence: *'Or is it only Barnabas and I who have not the right to do this?'* And surely the epistle of Barnabas has wider acceptance among the churches than has that apocryphal *Shepherd* of the adulterer." (*On Purity*, 20 [trans. Le Saint])

Finally, Barnabas *may have been* among those who "heard the message" from the apostles Peter and John (Acts 2:5–11; 4:4). The author of Hebrews tells us: "It [= the gospel] was first communicated through the Lord and was *confirmed to us by those who heard him*" (2:3 NET, emphasis added). We know that Barnabas was associated with the leaders of the Jerusalem church (Acts 4:36–37; 9:27; 11:27–30). He was part of the group of Hellenistic Jews who sold property and gave the proceeds to the apostles in Jerusalem (Acts 4:36–37). He served as a mediator for Paul before the apostles (Acts 9:27), took Paul with him to Antioch (Acts 11:25–26), and like Paul, persuaded people to believe the message about Jesus (Acts 13:43, 46). Barnabas seems, then, to be an orator of sorts with some rhetorical skills of persuasion. He also witnessed signs and wonders of the Holy Spirit (Acts 5:12; 11:8–11; 14:8–12; 15:12; Heb. 2:3–4).

Advocates for a Barnabas Authorship[1]		
Proponent	**Date**	**Source**
Tertullian	ca. 150–220	*De pudicitia*, 20; *On Purity* in Ancient Christian Writers vol. 28, trans. William P. Le Saint (New York: Newman Press, 1959), 115, 277.
Gregory of Elvira	ca. 375	*Tractatus Origenis*, eds. Pierre Batiffol and André Wilmart (Parisilis: A. Picard, 1900), 108.
Philastrius (or Filaster)	d. ca. 397	*De Haeresibus* (Basileae: Apud Henricum Petrum, 1939).
Caméron, John	1628	*Praelectiones in selectiora N.T. loca* (n.p.).
Wieseler, Karl G.	1848	*Chronologie des apostolische Zeialters bis zum Tobe der Apostel Paulas und Petrus: En Versuch* (Göttingen: Banbenhoeck und Ruprecht), 504.
Ritschl, Albrecht	1866	"Über die Leser des Hebrâebriefes," *Theologische Studien und Kritien* 39:89–102.
Keil, Carl Friedrich	1885	*Kommentar über den Brief an die Hebrëer* (Leipzig: Dorffling and Franke).
Salmon, George	1888	*Introduction to the New Testament* 3rd ed. (London: John Murray), 425.
Weiss, Bernhard	1897	*Der Brief an die Hebräer* (Göttingen: Vandenoeck & Ruprecht), 18; cf. *Manual of Introduction to the New Testament*, trans. A. J. K. Davidson in 2 vols. (New York: Funk & Wagnalls, 1889), 2:16–17.
Bartlet, J. V.	1902	"Barnabas and His Genuine Epistle," *Expositor* Sixth Series, 5:409–27.
Blass, Friedrich	1903	*Der Brief an die Hebräer: Text mit Angabe der Rhythmen* (Halle: Verlag von max Niemyer).
Gregory, Caspar René	1907	*Canon and Text of the New Testament* (Edinburgh: T&T Clark), 223ff.
Endemann, K.	1910	"Ueber den Verfasser des Hebräerberiefes," *Neue Kirchliche Zeitschrift* 21:102–16, esp. 121–22.
Wickham, E. C.	1910	*The Epistle to the Hebrews* (London: Methuen), xii.

1 The chart builds upon, completes entries, and expands information found in several sources: Spicq, 1952, 1:199 n. 8; Bruce, 1964, xxxvii n. 62; Hughes, 1977, 25 nn. 46–55; Attridge, 1989, 3 n. 26; D. Guthrie, 4th ed. 1990, 675 n. 2.

Advocates for a Barnabas Authorship[1]		
Proponent	**Date**	**Source**
Dibelius, Franz	1910	*Der Verfasser des Hebräerbriefes: Eine Untersuchung zur Geschichte des Urchristentums* (Strassburg: J. H. Ed. Heitz [Heitz & Mündel]).
Edmundson, George	1913	*The Church in Rome in the First Century* (London: Longmans, Green), 102–26.
Riggenbach, Eduard	1922	*Der Brief an die Hebräer*, 2nd ed., Kommentar zum Neuwn Testament 14 (Leizig: Deichert), xl–xli
Cadoux, Cecil John	1922	"The Early Christian Church in Egypt," *Expository Times*, 33:536–39.
Bornhaüser, Karl B.	1932	*Empfänger und Verfasser des Briefes an die Hebräer,* Beiträge zur Förderung christlicher Theologie 35, no. 3 (Gütersloh: Bertelsmann), 371–76
Loisy, Alfred	1935	*Remarques sur la littérature épistolaire du Nouveau Testament* (Paris: É. Nourry).
Badcock, F. J.	1937	*The Pauline Epistles and the Epistle to the Hebrews in Their Historical Setting* (New York: Macmillian), 198–99.
Strathmann, Hermann	1937	*Der Brief an die Hebräer*, Das Neue Testament Deutsch 9 (repr.; Güteringen: Vandenhoeck & Ruprecht, 1963), 75ff.
Snell, Anthony	1959	*New and Living Way: An Exposition of the Epistle to the Hebrews* (London: Faith), 17.
Robinson, J. A. T.	1976	*Redating the New Testament* (Philadelphia: Westminster), 200–20.
Hughes, Philip E.	1977	*A Commentary on the Epistle to the Hebrews* (Grand Rapids, Eerdmans), 25–29.
Hodges, Zane	1983	"Hebrews" in *Bible Knowledge Commentary*, eds. Roy B. Zuck and John F. Walvoord (Wheaton, IL: Victor Books), 779–80.
Pixner, Bargil	1992	"The Jerusalem Essenes, Barnabas and the Letter to the Hebrews," in *Intertestamental Essays in Honour of Jézef Tadeusz Milik*, Qumranica Mogilanensia, vol. 6; ed. Zdzislaw J. Kapera (Kraków: Enigma), 177–78.
Vanhoye, Albert	2015	*The Letter to the Hebrews: A New Commentary*, trans. Leo Arnold (New York: Paulist), 9–10, 12.
Bateman IV, Herbert W.	2020	*Hebrews*, Kerux Commentary (Grand Rapids: Kregel), 43–48.

Admittedly, there is no explicit connection between the description of Barnabas's character in Acts (4:36) and the statement in Hebrews concerning the author's encouraging words (13:22). Furthermore, there is no definitive evidence that distinguishes Barnabas as the *absolute* author of Hebrews. Nevertheless, Barnabas appears to rise above the other options. Hodges (1987, 777–78) claims, "While we cannot be absolutely certain of Barnabas as the author of Hebrews, it appears to me to be by far the best guess we can make." And though Donald Guthrie (1990, 674–75) makes a stab at refuting the Barnabas option by saying that "the data for determining that he did produce it are practically non-existent," he nevertheless presents enough evidence to suggest Barnabas as his second choice. Yet, from our perspective, Barnabas is the best option, a view held for centuries by many commentators. Nevertheless, Origen's statement is worth repeating: "But who it was that really wrote the epistle, God only knows" (Eusebius, *Hist. eccl.* 6.14 §3 [trans. Oulton]).

PLACE OF WRITING

While Barnabas may not have revealed from where he wrote Hebrews, he did provide a clue to ponder: "Those *from Italy* send you greetings" (13:24 NET, emphasis added). The phrase "from Italy" (ἀπὸ τῆς Ἰταλίας) seems to indicate the group's geographical origin (BDAG, s.v. "ἀπό," IV1b, p. 87). Nevertheless, the ambiguity of the phrase may refer to Italian Christians who lived in Italy or to Italian Christians who lived elsewhere in the Roman Empire. Wherever these Italian Christians lived, their geographical location generally serves to identify the place of origin for Hebrews.

Oxyrhynchus Papyri

The Oxyrhynchus Papyri is a collection of Greco-Roman letters discovered in an ancient rubbish dump near Oxyrhynchus, Egypt, a town that flourished during the Roman period in Middle Egypt about 125 miles south of Cairo. Excavations at the Oxyrhynchus dump began as early as 1882. The finds include the writings of Euripides, Sophocles, Menander, OT texts, OT Apocrypha, NT texts, NT Apocrypha, etc. Yet, 90 percent of the finds are public and private letters, public and private records, and public and private deeds written by or about ordinary people of antiquity who lived between 301 B.C. (Ptolemaic period) and A.D. 400s (Roman-Byzantine period). They are very helpful texts for understanding the NT era (Davis, 1933).

Italian Christians Living in Italy

Several lines of evidence suggest that these Italian Christians lived in Italy. First, it is possible that "those *from Italy* send you greetings" (13:24 NET, emphasis added) referred to Italian Christians who lived somewhere on the Italian peninsula. So, the phrase "from Italy" (ἀπὸ τῆς Ἰταλίας) could name the place where the Italian greeters were living, namely, Italy. Thus "from" (ἀπό) has the sense of "in" (ἐν) as it does in the Oxyrhynchus Papyri (1.81.5). The inhabitants "of Oxyrhynchus" (ἀπ᾽ Ὀξυρύγχων) meant the inhabitants "in Oxyrhynchus" (Moffatt, 1924, 246). This then may imply that the Italians as well as Barnabas were in Italy.

Second, there are subscriptions in some Greek manuscripts that underscore Italians who lived in Italy. Whereas a fifth-century Codex Alexandrinus (A) reads "Written from Rome" (Ἐγράφη ἀπὸ Ῥώμης), a sixth-century Codex Euthalianus (H) reads "From Italy" (ἀπὸ Ἰταλίας). Hughes (1977, 16) points out that while the subscription is an editorial addition, it may reveal a tradition or belief that Rome or the Italian peninsula was the place of origin.

Finally, two English translations appear to pinpoint Italy as the origin of Hebrews. William Tyndale's 1526 translated edition of the NT and the 1611 edition of the King James Version end this work "To the Hebrews" with "Written to the Hebrewes, from

Italy, by Timothie" (cf. 'Εγράφη ἀπὸ 'Ιταλίας διὰ Τιμόθέου; Nestle, 1936). Yet, current NT Greek texts (Nestle-Aland[28]) and English translations exclude the subscription (NASB, NRSV, ESV, NIV, NET). Nevertheless, Vanhoye (2015, 14) still argues that Barnabas wrote from Italy.

Italian Christians Living Elsewhere

It is also possible that the phrase "those *from Italy* [ἀπὸ τῆς 'Ιταλίας] send you greetings" (13:24 NET, empahsis added), referred to Italian Christians living elsewhere in the Roman Empire. Moffatt (1924, 247) points out that a similar phrase appears in Acts: "the Jews from Asia" (οἱ ἀπὸ τῆς Ἀσίας 'Ιουδαῖοι; 21:27). Several other examples appear in Acts all of which speak of people residing in a place other than their respective homeland.

People "from" (ἀπὸ) Geographical Regions

Acts 2:5	"devout people *from* every nation" (ἄνδρες εὐλαβεῖς ἀπὸ παντὸς ἔθνους)
Acts 10:23	"some of the brothers (and sisters) *from* Joppa" (τινες τῶν ἀδελφῶν τῶν ἀπὸ 'Ιόππης)
Acts 10:38	"Jesus *from* Nazareth" ('Ιησοῦν τὸν ἀπὸ Ναζαρέθ)
Acts 17:13	"Jews *from* Thessalonica" (οἱ ἀπὸ τῆς Θεσσαλονίκης 'Ιουδαῖοι)
Acts 21:27	"Jews *from* the [province] of Asia" (οἱ ἀπὸ τῆς Ἀσίας 'Ιουδαῖοι)

These were people "from" (ἀπό) geographical locations other than from where they lived.

While Moffatt (1924, 247), Strathmann (1937, 70–71), and Hiebert (1977, 85) are of the opinion that the Italian Christians and the author were somewhere other than the Italian peninsula, others are a bit more specific: Riggenbach (1922) suggests Cyprus, Hodges (1987, 777–78) argues for North Africa or Judaea, and Buchanan (1972, 263) specifies Judaea. Yet, Wikenhauser (1958, 464–45) confesses that pinpointing where the Italian Christians reside as well as its destination seems impossible to determine.

Westcott (1984), however, is a bit more emphatic. "'From the Italians' (ἀπὸ τῆς 'Ιταλίας)" he says, "contributes nothing of the solution to the question" (Wescott, 1984, 452) even though he argues that the Greek wordings chosen throughout the book "seem to favour a place of writing in Asia, Syria, or Egypt" (xliv). So, while many contemporary commentators choose not to suggest a place of origin (Carson and Moo, 2005, 604–05), we somewhat ambiguously conclude that "those *from Italy*" (ἀπὸ τῆς 'Ιταλίας) referred to Italians living in a country within the Roman Empire and thereby suggest the Hebrews' place of origin to be a country other than Italy.

ORIGINAL READERS

Admittedly, the recipients of Hebrews could be one of three possibilities: (1) a mixed group of Jew and Gentile Christians (Scott, 1936, 200–201; Cockerill, 2017, 20), (2) Gentile Christians (Moffatt, 1968, xv–xvii; Käsemann, 1984, 195–217) or (3) Jewish Christians (Bateman, 2012, 39). Most commentators, however, ascribe the recipients of Hebrews to be Jewish Christians (Spicq, 1952, 1:226–31; 1959, 390; Bruce, 1964, xxix; G. Guthrie, 1998, 19). Initial support for the Jewish Christian perspective began with Clement of Alexandria ca. A.D. 180 (Hypotyposes in Eusebius, *Hist. eccl.* 6.14.3–4), Tertullian ca. A.D. 220 (*De Pudicitia,* 20), and Jerome in A.D. 419 or 420 (*De Viris Inlustribus,* 17, 53). Yet, "to the Hebrews" (πρὸς 'Εβραιους) could be understood simply as a way to distinguish Jews from Gentiles (Westcott, 1984, xxxv–xxxvi). Or it could be descriptive for Jewish people living in Judaea in contrast to the Jewish people of the diaspora (Acts 6:1). So, the real debate here concerns whether the recipients of Hebrews were Jewish Christians who lived in Judaea or to the Hellenistic Jewish Christians who lived somewhere in the Roman Empire, presumably Rome.

The Ebionites according to Eusebius

"The first Christians named Ebionites—appropriately, in view of their poor and mean opinions about Christ. They regarded him [Christ] as a plain, ordinary man, born of intercourse between a man and Mary, who gained righteousness through character growth. They observed every detail of the Law and did not think that they would be saved by faith in Christ alone and a corresponding life." (Maier, 1999, 116)

Jewish Christians of Judaea

Some argue that Hebrews was written to Jewish followers of Jesus who lived in Judaea (Buchanan, 1972, 256; Gleason, 2007, 158–61). Others are more specific. Baur (1838, 123, 141–43), a German theologian of the Tübingen School of Theology, specifies the recipients to be of an Ebonite character. Spicq (1959, 390), a French professor of NT exegesis at the University of Friborg, redirects his efforts from proving a Hellenistic Jewish view to prove that the recipients were Essene Christians because of the discovery of the Dead Sea Scrolls (cf. also Braun, 1955, 37, 55; Kosmala, 1959, vii–xi; Fensham, 1971, 19). Still others maintain they were second-generation Christians located near Sychar (Samaria) influenced by those who lived at Qumran (Bowman, 1962, 9–16) or they were converted Jewish priests (Sandegren, 1955, 221–24; Daniélou, 1958, 111–24). Badcock (1937, 185–86) argues that they were Hellenistic Jewish Christians living in Judaea. Others consider the call to go "outside the tent" (13:13) to be a call to leave Jerusalem (Walker, 1994, 39–71; Mosser, 2009, 383–404).

Several lines of argument may support a Judaean Jewish view. Judaean Jewish Christians were more inclined to remain in Judaism (13:13) due to the location of the temple and its sacrificial system. Furthermore, there was a crisis in Hebrews that seemed imminent (1:2; 3:13; 10:25; 12:27) and thereby could be an allusion to the rising tensions between the Judaeans and Romans that eventually erupted into war in A.D. 66 (see "Date of Writing" below). Or the reader's suffering (10:32, 12:4) could be related to the persecution of the Judaean Church described in Acts (4:1–3; 5:20–21; 7:54–60; 12:2). Furthermore, there is no Gentile-Jewish controversy evident in Hebrews as there was in Paul's letter to the Romans (14:1–15:13). Finally, Judaean believers were acquainted with the OT and Jewish forms of exegesis[2] comparable to that evident in the scrolls discovered in the region of the Dead Sea (cf., Bateman, 1995, 11–27; Bateman, 1997, 9–116; Bateman et al., 2012, 163–66).

Yet the Judaean Jewish view has some problems. First, the generosity of the Christian community testified to in Hebrews (6:10; 10:32–34) does not fit a Judaean situation because they themselves were frequently in need of support from other churches. After Judaean churches sold their property to care for the needy in A.D. 33 (Acts 4:32–35), the church of Antioch assisted Judaean believers in the autumn of A.D. 47 (Acts 11:27–30), and Paul later collected money for them during his third missionary journey in A.D. 53–57 (Acts 18:23–21:17; 1 Cor. 16:1–3). Moreover, Barnabas drew attention to the fact that they had yet to suffer martyrdom (Heb. 12:3–4). Naturally, this does not fit the Judaean church. The Judaean church suffered several martyrs: Stephen in A.D. 35 (Acts 7:54–60); James, brother of John in A.D. 44 (Acts 12:2); and James, brother of Jude in A.D. 62 (Josephus, *A.J.* 20.9.1 §§200–204) just

2 H. W. Bateman IV, "Second Temple Exegetical Practices: Extra-biblical Examples of Exegesis Compared with Those in the Book of Hebrews," *Southwestern Journal of Theology* 53 (Fall 2010): 26–54.

to name a few (cf. Maier and Linnenbugel, 2016, 29–35).

Second, Jewish exegesis in Hebrews, parallel to that found in the Dead Sea Scrolls, need not be restricted to a Judaean Christian audience. Similar forms of exegesis appear in Paul's letter written to a mixed audience of Jew and Gentile Christians in Rome (cf. Heb. 1:5–13 with Rom. 3:9–18). Third, one would not expect a Jew-Gentile controversy in a work addressed solely to a Jewish-Christian congregation. Many Mediterranean cities had Jewish communities in them (Barkley, 1996, 414–18). Fourth, if the leaders of the Judaean Church were in mind, the expectation to honor leaders in Hebrews 13:7 may seem strange when the leadership was established and resolved rather early in the Judaean Church (Acts 4:33, 5:1–11; 6:1–6; 15:1–22; cf. Gal. 2:9). However, one might argue that the death of James in A.D. 62 may warrant an exhortation (Bateman, 2015[17], 51–80). In fact, the growing pressure to join the Jewish revolt in Judaea was confronted and discouraged by James's brother, Jude, who wrote to Judaean Jewish believers sometime between A.D. 62 and A.D. 66 (Bateman, 2015[17], 51–80).

Jewish Christians of Rome

The most widely accepted perspective is that Hebrews was written to Hellenistic Jewish followers of Jesus who lived in Rome (Bateman et al., 2012, 37). Hebrews seems to have been known in Rome first because Clement of Rome was the first to quote from Hebrews (A.D. 96; Hagner, 1973, 179–95). Additionally, the phrase in Hebrews 13:24, "those from Italy" (οἱ ἀπὸ τῆς Ἰταλίας), described those who are away from Italy sending greetings home to the church in Rome (see "Place of Writing" above). The mention of Timothy (Heb. 13:24) appears to support the Roman view because it assumes that this was "the Timothy" who was Paul's traveling companion and that Roman Christians knew him (Col. 1:1; Philem. 1). Furthermore, the leaders, as described in Hebrews (13:7, 17, 24), appear similar to the description found in 1 Clements 1:3. Moreover, the Hellenistic-Jewish Christians in Rome, like the Jewish Christians in Judaea, would have been familiar with Jewish exegesis used throughout Hebrews. Finally, the generosity of the readers (6:10 and 10:32) seems to match that which was true of other saints in Rome (Rom. 15:24b; Acts 28:14–16; 30–31). So, while a Judaean Jewish-Christian readership may be possible, it seems more probable that the people to whom Barnabas wrote was a group of Jewish followers of Jesus who lived in Rome (Bruce, 1964, xxx; Lane, 1991a, 22–26; Brown, 1997, 684; Cockerill, 2012, 40).

DATE OF WRITING

Arriving at a date for Hebrews begins with a very wide date range, namely, the death and resurrection of Jesus in A.D. 33 (Hoehner, 1977, 45–63) and the earliest quotation of Hebrews in Clement of Rome's first epistle to the Corinthians written in A.D. 96 (Bateman et al., 2012, 41–42). This extremely broad dating of Hebrews, however, can be narrowed based upon the mention of Timothy's joining Barnabas (Heb. 13:23). What is known about Timothy begins with Paul's second missionary journey (A.D. 50; Acts 16:1) and his being summoned to come to Paul just prior to Paul's martyrdom (A.D. 68; 2 Tim. 4:9; Maier, 2016, 35). And though we do not know when Timothy died, it seems reasonable to narrow the dating of Hebrews to A.D. 50 to A.D. 96.[3] Yet, this task of narrowing the dating of Hebrews continues with a discussion of the ritual cultic practices in Jerusalem's temple.

The silence about the temple's destruction in A.D. 70 often serves as a reason for a

3 See D. B. Wallace on "Date" in "Hebrews: Introduction, Argument, Outline," accessed October 15, 2018, https://bible.org/seriespage/hebrews-introduction-argument-and-outline.

pre-70 dating for Hebrews. Naturally, Barnabas's description of the Mosaic covenant "growing obsolete and aging is about to disappear" (τὸ παλαιούμενον καὶ γηράσκον ἐγγὺς ἀφανισμοῦ; 8:13) seems to indicate that the sacrificial system was still in operation (cf. 8:4, 13; 9:6–9; 13:11; esp. 10:1–2). Emphasis, however, must be placed on the ritual practices of the tabernacle and not Herod's temple itself because Barnabas's focus was on the cultic system initiated with the exodus generation in conjunction with the tabernacle (9:1–10). Nevertheless, the sacrificial system was in effect during the time of Barnabas and practiced in Jerusalem's temple. Thus, the date range for the writing of Hebrews may be A.D. 50 to 70.

The task of narrowing the dating of Hebrews continues with an acknowledgement of the rising tensions between Rome and Judaea during the time of Nero (see "Historical Setting" below). Some who argue for a Judaean destination consider the hard times in Hebrews 12:4 to be a reference to a time just prior to the total outbreak of war between the Judaeans and Romans in A.D. 66 (Gleason, 2007, 158–61). Those who argue for a Roman destination suggest that Hebrews 12:4 references a date prior to Nero's persecution of Jewish Christians in A.D. 64 (Hiebert, 1977, 89). The emperor was also said to have committed suicide in A.D. 68 (Suetonius, *Nero* 49, 57). As a result, many date Hebrews as A.D. 65–67 (Cadoux, 1922, 538; cf. Spicq, 1952, 1:257–61), A.D. 64–68 (Lane, 1991a, lxvi; cf. Allen, 2010, 78), or A.D. mid-60s (G. Guthrie, 1998, 22).

So, taking in consideration the practice of cultic sacrifices in Judaea, Nero's persecutions of Christians in Rome, and the rising tensions in Judaea between Judaeans and Romans (Bateman, 2015[17], 40–42), it seems reasonable to suggest that Hebrews was written either *just before* Nero began his persecution of Christians in Rome in A.D. 64 or *just before* the Judaean war with Rome in A.D. 66.

HISTORICAL SETTING

Establishing the historical setting for Hebrews involves at least four issues: the spread of Christianity to Rome, the Jewish people in Rome, the emperor Nero and the Jewish people in Rome, and finally Judaea during the A.D. 60s. All four play a role in understanding, interpreting, and applying the letter to the Hebrews for today's readers, teachers, and preachers of the book.

The Spread of Christianity to Rome

The historical setting for this work addressed "to the Hebrews" (πρὸς Ἑβραιους) must begin with the spread of Christianity to the city of Rome. In Luke's retelling of the beginning of the church in Acts 2, he recorded how the Holy Spirit enabled the apostles to speak to Jews and proselytes from all over the Roman Empire. Jewish people from numerous cities and countries were in Jerusalem to celebrate Pentecost (vv. 9–11).

Luke recalled how the apostles, filled with the Holy Spirit, spoke of the recently resurrected Messiah to all those celebrating the feast of weeks (Acts 2:12–41). As a result, many diaspora Jews came to faith. However, "a complaint arose on the part of the Greek-speaking Jews against the native Hebraic Jews, because their widows were being overlooked in the daily distribution of food" (Acts 6:1 NET). It appears, some of these Greek-speaking Jewish believers remained in Jerusalem until the stoning of Stephen at which point Luke recorded: "Now on that day a great persecution began against the church in Jerusalem, and all except the apostles were forced to scatter throughout the regions of Judaea and Samaria," and "those who had been forced to scatter went around proclaiming the good news of the word" (8:1, 4 NET). As a result, churches rose up throughout Judaea and the Roman Empire.

This historical fact is important when considering Christianity in Rome for at least three reasons. First, there is one Gospel and two letters written to Christians living in Rome: Mark's Gospel, Paul's letter to the Romans, and

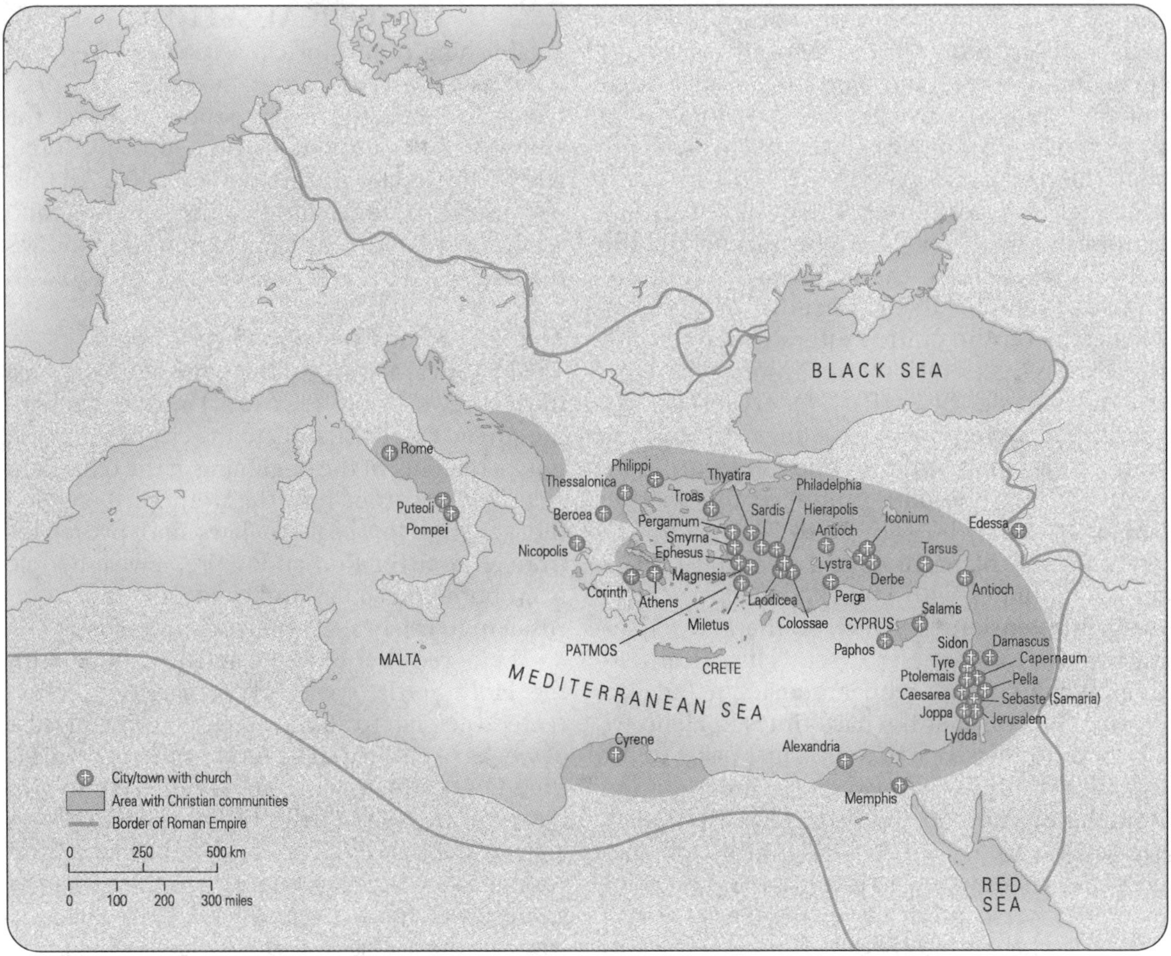

The Spread of Christianity by A.D. 100

Barnabas's "message of encouragement" (13:22). Second, the founders of these churches to whom Mark, Paul, and Barnabas wrote are unknown. While Mark's Gospel may be a reproduction of Peter's sermon, according to Papias, Bishop of Hierapolis, there is no clear indication that Peter founded the church in Rome. Similarly, Paul said that he did not plant the church (Rom. 15:20–22). Barnabas said that he and his readers received and accepted the message about Jesus from the apostles (2:3–4). So, who took the gospel to these Roman churches? They were probably Jewish worshippers from Rome, who on the day of Pentecost heard the message about Jesus from the apostles. Finally, the churches, to whom Mark and Paul wrote, were a Jew and Gentile group of followers. Hebrews was not (see "Place of Writing" above). So, there appears to be a multiple number of churches in Rome (cf. Acts 28:14–16; Koester, 2001, 73–76).

The Day of Pentecost

The Day of Pentecost, often referred to as *Succoth* (שָׁבֻעוֹת) is spoken of in several ways in the OT: "Feast of Harvest" (חַג הַקָּצִיר; Exod. 23:16), "Festival of Weeks" (חַג שָׁבֻעוֹת; Deut. 16:9), "Day of First Fruits" (יוֹם הַבִּכּוּרִים; Num. 28:26). It was fifty days after the day of Passover Sabbath. The word "Pentecost" is the Greek word for fifty (BDAG, s.v. "πεντηκοστή," p 796). In the books of the Apocrypha, the "Feast of Weeks" is referred as "Pentecost": ". . . so they came to Jerusalem, the feast of the weeks approaching. And after the feast, called Pentecost (πεντηκοστήν) . . ." (2 Macc 12:31–32; cf. Tob 2:1).

The Jewish People in Rome

The historical setting for Hebrews continues with the Jewish people who lived in Rome. First, they were Hellenistic Jews who were part of the Jewish dispersion (or "Jews of the Diaspora"). The Jewish Diaspora began when the Assyrians invaded Northern Israel (732, 734, 722 B.C.) and when Babylon invaded Judah (605, 597, 586 B.C.). And despite the many Jewish people who returned to Judah (539, 457, 444 B.C.), many others chose to live or migrate to other Gentile-governed nations (cf. Acts 2:5–11). Yet, often the Jewish Diaspora expanded due to forced migration to geographical areas like Lydia, Phrygia, and Laodicea. Laodicea was a Greek city that King Antiochus II built sometime between 261 and 253 B.C. to honor his wife Laodice (Josephus, *A.J.* 12.3.4 §§147–53). Nevertheless, the Roman magistrates protected the religious rights of the Jewish people living in Lydia, Phrygia, and elsewhere in Roman providences (Josephus, *A.J.* 14.10.1–26 §§185–267).

The Hellenistic Jewish Church Begins

Now there were devout Jews from every nation under heaven residing in Jerusalem. When this sound occurred [= the coming of the Holy Spirit], a crowd gathered and was in confusion, because each one heard them [= apostles] speaking in his own language. Completely baffled, they said, "Aren't all these who are speaking Galileans? And how is it that each one of us hears them in our own native language? Parthians, Medes, Elamites, and residents of Mesopotamia, Judaea and Cappadocia, Pontus and the province of Asia, Phrygia and Pamphylia, Egypt and the parts of Libya near Cyrene, and ***visitors from Rome, both Jews and proselytes***, Cretans and Arabs—we hear them speaking in our own languages about the great deeds God has done!" (Acts 2:5–11; NET, additions/emphasis added)

As to the Jewish population in Rome, there is evidence of an early political relationship with Roman senators beginning with Judas Maccabee and his brothers from 167 to 143 B.C., maintained by Hasmonean leaders from 143 to 63 B.C., and later nurtured by Herod the Great from 31 to 4 B.C. So, some migration to Rome may have occurred due to political relations with Judaean leaders, especially once Judaea became part of the Roman province of Syria in 63 B.C.

After Pompey subdued Judaea in 63 B.C., he took captive a large number of Jewish people to Rome as slaves (Plutarch, *Pomp.* 5.45.1–5; Josephus, *A.J.* 14.4.5 §79). In fact, many Jews living in the city of Rome were initially slaves who later became Roman citizens (Philo, *Leg.* 156). Consequently, Jewish people in Rome during the first century may be divided into three categories: slaves, some free, and Roman citizens (Rutgers, 1994, 60; cf. Barkley, 1996, 289–92). Josephus (*B.J.* 2.1 §80) estimated that eight thousand Jews lived in Rome during the reign of Augustus.

Judaea, Not Palestine

In 539 B.C. when the exiles began their return to Jerusalem (Ezra 1–2), they occupied only the geographical area of Judah.

In 164 B.C. when Judas Maccabee reestablished religious freedom to Judaea, subsequent nephews expanded Judaean influence to include Idumea, Samaria, Galilee, the coastal plains, and the Transjordan.

In 63 B.C. when Pompey brought Judaea under Roman control as a client kingdom, it was known as the province of Judaea.

In A.D. 135, after the Romans had subdued the Jewish revolts of A.D. 66–70 and 132–135, Rome renamed Judaea Palestine.

Thus Herod, Jesus, and his disciples lived in the province of Judaea, not Palestine.

In his article titled "Roman Policy towards the Jews: Expulsions from the City of Rome during the First Century C.E.," Rutgers argues that relations with and decisions regarding the Jewish people in Rome and throughout the Roman Empire was not based upon "a standard policy toward the Jews: *Roman magistrates responded to situations*" (1994, 59, emphasis added). They were "often guided by purely pragmatic concerns rather than by an ideology of tolerance" (1994, 71). He takes issue with ancient sources that say Jewish expulsions from Rome by Tiberius in A.D. 19 and Claudius in A.D. 49 were based upon religious reasons (1994, 60–66; cf. Suetonius, *Tib.* 25; *Claud.* 25.4; Josephus, *A.J.* 18.3.5 §§81–84.). Furthermore, he argues that Roman leadership was "not influenced by pro- or anti-Jewish sentiment but must rather be seen within the larger framework of the ruling of the empire" (1994, 72). He concludes, "Rome readily acknowledged the distinctiveness of the Jewish people . . . because they had no reason to hinder the free exercise of Jewish religious practices" (1994, 73; cf. Barkley, 1996, 282–319).

Rutgers's argument may be underscored with various historical actions of Augustus and Claudius. Augustus guaranteed the Jewish people's position in Rome. He honored their Sabbath and permitted them to send their temple tax to Jerusalem. He granted Roman citizenship and allowed the study of Jewish law (Philo, *Embassy* 156–58; Barclay, 1996, 292–95, cf. 76–77, 238, 267–68, 310). He also admired Herod's loyalty and appreciated his ability to rule. Herod's success contributed to Augustus's *Pax Romana*, assisted in the spread of Roman culture by way of comprehensive building projects (e.g., Caesarea, Sephoris, Jerusalem temple, etc.), provided Rome with a reliable ally on the eastern fringes of the empire, and prepared his sons in the ways of Rome with a Roman education (Richardson, 1996, 197–202; 226–34; 239–40). Furthermore, Claudius issued an edict that guaranteed Jews in Rome and throughout the empire the right "to practice the customs of their fathers without hindrance" (τὰ πάτρος ἔθη ἀνεπικωλύτως φυλάσσειν; Josephus, *A.J.* 19.5.3 §290). So, it seems Jewish people in Rome were accepted and protected as long as they did not disrupt the peace of Rome.

Pax Romana

Pax Romana, which means "peace of Rome," was inaugurated with Augustus in 27 B.C., and lasted 207 years, until Marcus Aurelius died in A.D. 180.

It was a period of relative peace, minimal Roman expansion by military force, and a period of expansion of the arts and architecture. Augustus was the first to help Rome realize they could live in peace without warring with those surrounding them.

Augustus established border security via the active role of Roman legions, which involved building Roman roads for military movement. This is not to suggest that Rome did not address with military force territories that were still on the fringes of the Roman Empire (e.g., the Balkans and Germania). With the exception of Claudius's invasion of Britain and Trajan's expansion efforts, Rome's foreign policy was to live at peace.

This is not to say, however, that Jewish people in Rome were not at times a problem. It seems that in 139 B.C., they were expelled from

Rome for undermining Roman values (Valerius Maximus, *Facta et dita memorabilia* 1.3.3). In A.D. 19, they were expelled from Rome for proselytizing (Dio, *Hist. of Rome* 57.18.5). In A.D. 41, it seems they were prohibited or restricted from holding open meetings due to their growing number in Rome (Dio, *Hist. of Rome* 60.6.6). In A.D. 49, it seems there were disruptive riots by followers of Christ (*Chrestus*; Suetonius, *Claud.* 25) that resulted in the expulsion of the Jews and Jewish Christians from Rome (Rutgers, 1994, 64, 66; Witherington, 1998, 539–44). It's even been suggested that the persecutions of Jewish Christians in Rome were "private Jewish antagonisms" (Moule, 1950, 41; cf. Acts 17:5; 19:23–41). Yet, it seems possible that the events in Judaea may have precipitated some angst in Rome that may have been a contributing factor behind Nero's persecution in A.D. 64.

Nero and the Jewish People in Rome

Relationships between Nero and the Jewish people in Rome were tenuous during the 60s because of Nero. Nero, who was emperor from A.D. 54 to 68, plays a rather significant role in understanding Hebrews. After the death of Claudius (13 October 54), Nero was "acclaimed *imperator*" and honored by the Senate (Suetonius,[4] *Nero* 8). "Barely emerged from boyhood and holding the empire in consequence of a crime," Nero was now Emperor of Rome (Tacitus,[5] *Ann.* 13.1 [trans. Jackson]). As Nero grew into his role as Caesar, "his insolence, lust, extravagance, greed, and cruelty" were at first perceived as "youthful mistakes" that were later determined "faults of his character" (Suetonius, *Nero* 26 [trans. Graves]). Tacitus and Suetonius, just to name two of many historians and biographers, recorded Nero's many horrendous deeds and depraved doings, which included but was not limited to the execution or murder of most of his family. He slept with his mother, murdered his mother, married one stepsister and eventually executed her, executed his other stepsister, raped and murdered his stepbrother, kicked his pregnant wife to death, castrated and married a freedman, and engaged in many other degrading activities (Chaplin, 2003, 36–37).

As to Nero's relationship with Jewish people, it was strained. And yet in all fairness to Nero, "he despised all religious cults except that of the Syrian Goddess, and one day he showed that he had changed his mind even about her by urinating on the divine image" (Suetonius, *Nero* 56 [trans. Graves]). His actions, however, were in keeping with his character. "Nothing could restrain Nero," according to Suetonius, "from murdering anyone he pleased, on whatever pretext" (*Nero* 37 [trans. Graves]). Yet his disdain for Christians was evident after the fire of Rome. Although the great fire of Rome may have been an accident (Tacitus, *Ann.* 15.38–39), Suetonius accused Nero as having "brazenly set fire to the city," watched its burning, and "sang *The Fall of Troy* from beginning to end" (*Nero* 38 [trans. Graves]). Regardless, Nero blamed the fire on the then-known Jewish sect called "Christians" (Dando-Collins, 2010). Again, his actions were in keeping with his character.

So in light of Rutgers's (1994, 59) observations that "*Roman magistrates responded to situations*" and Nero's propensity for murdering people for any reason, it is not *too* much

4 Suetonius (ca. A.D. 69–122) was a Roman historian during the imperial era of the Flavian dynasty. His most important work is his work entitled *The Twelve Caesars* (*De Vita Caesarum*).

5 Tacitus (ca. A.D. 56–120) was a senator and a historian of the Roman Empire. Two notable works are *Annals* and the *Histories*. While the *Annals* focuses attention on Roman Empire from the death of Augustus (14 B.C.) to those who ruled during Rome's civil war (A.D. 69), *Histories* covers the Flavians and the first Judaean war (A.D. 70).

of a stretch to suggest that when the chaotic, disparaging, and life-threatening events were escalating throughout Judaea (A.D. 57–66), many Jews and Gentiles who had converted to Christianity in Rome paid the price. It seems that Romans did not distinguish between Jews and Christians at the time (Boccaccini, 1991, 17; cf. "Figure 3," p. 20; con. Barkley, 1996, 283). Hengel (1985, 30) even suggests that more should be made of the connection between the Neronian persecution in Rome and the Judaean revolt, a connection that we entertain and endorse below.

Nero's Governor Appointees to Judaea

Felix (A.D. 52–60)
Porcius Festus (A.D. 60–62)
Albinus (A.D. 62–64)
Gessius Florus (A.D. 64–66)

Albinus and Florus were governors in power around the time Barnabas and Jude wrote their respective letters and when Mark wrote his Gospel. All of Nero's appointees contributed to the growing hostility between the Romans and Judaeans.

Judaea during the A.D. 60s[6]

Although Hebrews was written to Jewish believers in Rome, the events in Judaea are also important to this historical backdrop because information about what was happening in Judaea did not remain in Judaea. Two factors warrant some understanding of the sociopolitical happenings in Judaea. First Nero, like other emperors, followed the guidelines for foreign affairs established by Caesar Augustus in A.D. 6. Nero appointed several Roman procurators or governors to govern Judaea. They were responsible to combat the attacks of "robbers" or revolutionaries so as to maintain the *Pax Romana*, exercise judiciary functions, and administrate the financial affairs of foreign territories under Roman jurisdiction. Nevertheless, the political ambitions, incompetence in dealing with Jewish cultural concerns, and personal greed were factors that eventually led to Judaea's war with Rome. Tacitus (*Hist.* 5.9.3–5; 5.10.1) attributed Judaea's religious turmoil, which finally erupted into war, to two cruel and irresponsible Roman governors: Felix and Festus. Yet, Nero appointed four irresponsible Roman governors.

Nero's first governor appointee to Judaea was Felix. Felix was a Gentile, who married a Jewess—Drusilla, the fourteen-year-old daughter of Agrippa I. Naturally, the marriage was against Mosaic law and raised the ire of the Jewish Zealots who forbade sexual intercourse or the marriage union of any Jew and Gentile. Felix also crucified numerous Zealots and punished those who followed them. Riots in Judaea were a commonplace. The most famous localized revolt occurred during Felix's governorship, which was led by an Egyptian (Josephus, *A.J.* 20.8.6 §§169–72; *B.J.* 2.13.5 §§6–63; Acts 21:37–36). Finally, Felix mismanaged a social issue concerning the equality of citizenship in Caesarea, which resulted in Caesarean Jews having their homes plundered. These actions forced Nero to replace Felix with Porcius Festus (A.D. 60–62). Consequently, the issue concerning Syrians and Jews living in Caesarea fell onto Festus, which ended with Judaeans deprived of social equality with Syrians. Furthermore, Syrians were regarded as masters of the city. Unfortunately, Festus could not undo his predecessor's abuse of power. As a result, numerous Judaeans joined the Judaean Zealot movement for freedom. Their ruthless activities grew more intense under Festus, who

6 For a fuller discussion about Judaean events, see "Occasion of Jude's Letter" in *Jude* (Bateman, 2015[17], 44–80) and M. Hengel, *The Zealots: Investigations into the Jewish Freedom Movement in the Period from Herod I until* A.D. *70*, translated by D. Smith (Edinburgh: T&T Clark, 1997).

eventually died in office only to be replaced with Albinus (A.D. 62–64).

Albinus was incorrigible when it came to money. He robbed, accepted bribes, and practiced extortion. He triangulated one Judaean faction against another for money and in the end escalated the Judaean and Roman animosity. When Nero recalled Albinus to Rome, Albinus executed major criminals and released the remaining prisoners—many of whom were revolutionaries—before he left. Although all prisons were empty, the task of Gessius Florus (A.D. 64–66) was made more difficult. Yet when it came to greed, Florus was worse than Albinus. His plundering escalated from robbing individuals to plundering entire villages, towns, and cities. The Judaean revolt broke out two years into Florus's governorship, triggered by his attempt to relieve Jerusalem's temple of its treasury.

So, Tacitus rightly attributed the Judaean war with Rome to two cruel and irresponsible Roman governors, Felix (A.D. 52–60) and Festus (A.D. 60–62), but certainly Albinus (A.D. 62–64) and Florus (A.D. 64–66) were equal contributors to the problem. In fact, it seems more appropriate to conclude that under Felix, Festus, and Albinus the relationships between the Romans and Judaeans were deteriorating rapidly, but total collapse occurred under Florus.

The second factor that warrants some discussion concerns the Jewish leaders over Judaea. To begin with, the *Tosefta Menahot*, a rabbinic supplement to the Mishnah, described Judaea during the A.D. 60s as a place of social hostility, a culture lacking moral values, and a society consumed with materialism driven by greed that at times erupted into hostile behavior (13:22; *Babylonian Gittin* 55b–56a). Judaea's social hostility toward Rome was recorded in several pieces of Jewish literature written prior to the Jewish war (Pss. Sol. 17:21–32; 4Q161 f8 10.1–8, 11–21; 4Q285 5:1–6 [frag. 7, 1–6]). The disregard for moral societal values is evident among Judaea's Herodian leaders: murder, incest, divorce, and marriage to Gentiles plagued the Herodian household (Richardson, 1996, 43–51). Materialism driven by greed and hostility in Judaea permeated even the ruling priesthood (Bateman, 2015[17], 70–75). As a result, Jewish dissatisfaction frequently erupted into local revolts throughout Judaea just prior to the total outbreak of war with Rome. These three forms of social decay generated numerous sociopolitical events. Each tended to be turbulent, intrusive, and life-threatening for anyone living in the country. For Josephus (*B.J.* 1.9–10), Jerusalem fell because *a Jewish civil war*, created by the Zealots, provoked God to purge and punish Judaeans. "Josephus was convinced," says Hengel (1989, 10), "that God himself had ordained the downfall of Jerusalem and the Temple, because of the sins that had been committed in it—particularly by the Zealots."

What Is the Mishnah and the *Tosefta Menahot?*

The Hebrew verb "mishnah" (שנה) means "to study and review." The noun "Mishnah" is the name of a major collection of Jewish oral traditions (or "Oral Torah") compiled in written form around A.D. 189 (according to tradition).

The literary work known as "Mishnah" consists of six orders or *sedarim* ("seder," סדר), and each order contains several tractates.

- *Zeraim* ("Seeds") deals with prayers and blessings, tithes, and agricultural laws (eleven tractates).
- *Moed* ("Festival") deals with the laws of the Sabbath and Festivals (twelve tractates).
- *Nashim* ("Women") deals with marriage and divorce as well as some oaths of the Nazirite (seven tractates).
- *Nezikin* ("Damages") deals with civil and criminal law, the courts, and other oaths (ten tractates).

- *Kodashim* ("Holy Things") deals with sacrificial rites, the temple, dietary laws (eleven tractates).
- *Tohorot* ("Purities") deals with the laws of purity and impurity (twelve tractates).

The *Tosefta Menahot* is a supplemental work to the Mishnah. Whether there was a pre-Tosefta recession or a latter compendium of the Mishnah is debated.

In conclusion, the messianic message about Jesus was introduced and churches were planted in the city of Rome sometime after the day of Pentecost (A.D. 33; Hoehner, 1997, 95–105), but it was perceived to be just another sect of Judaism. Due to his neurotic behavior, Nero tended to be hostile to Judaism in general and thus contributed to the increasing hostility between Rome and Judaea through his appointment of irresponsible governors. Yet, the moral decay of the Jewish political and religious leaders, the increase of messianic expectations (Bateman et al., 2012, 253–329), and the Zealot rebellion against Roman authority in Judaea (Bateman, 2015[17], 51–80, esp. 76–80) are some important historical factors for interpreting and then applying Hebrews to the twenty-first-century follower of Jesus.

OCCASION FOR WRITING

Commentators often suggest that the book of Hebrews was written to Jewish believers who were considering a return to Judaism. Yet, Bruce (1990, 376) suggests that something more than just a relapsing into orthodox Judaism was creating doubts. While we can only offer a historical occasion for the writing of Hebrews, it seems reasonable to propose that whatever occasion is offered for Hebrews, there must be a recognition of the sociopolitical turmoil in Judaea. Jewish people throughout the Roman world, especially those who practiced Judaism, were strongly linked with their Judaean homeland. They traveled to Judaea regularly, celebrated Passover in Jerusalem, and faithfully paid their temple tax (Barclay, 1996, 418–24). Furthermore Barnabas, along with Paul, was sent from Antioch of Syria with monies to assist the Jewish Christians in Judaea (cf. Acts 11:27–30). Later, other Jewish-Gentile churches sent money to Judaeans to meet their needs (1 Cor. 16:1–4; 2 Cor. 8:1–5; 10–12; 9:1–5). So, there can be little doubt that the followers of Jesus living in Rome were attuned to their kinsfolk: their dissatisfaction with Roman governors, the lack of morality among the Herodian leaders, and the corruption of Jewish religious leaders. Furthermore, they were more than likely attentive to the Zealots and their self-proclaimed "messiahs" that were stirring Judaeans to rise up against Rome during the mid-60s. Finally, Rome's heightened concern and eventual military response to Judaea's disruption of Roman peace must be considered as a *possible* underlying factor behind the persecutions mentioned in Hebrews 10:32 and 12:4.

Judaea's Discontent of Rome

Feelings about Judaea's political and religious atmosphere appear in numerous literary works. Discontentment concerning the political control of Judas Maccabee's nephews (often referred to as the Hasmoneans; 125–75 B.C.) as well as Herod the Great's rule (40–4 B.C.) resonates in at least seven Dead Sea Scrolls (1Q28, 1Q28a, 1Q28b, 4Q175, 4Q266, 4Q285, 4Q521).

When Rome was intruding in Jewish affairs (75–30 B.C.), negative attitudes appear to escalate in at least seven other Jewish texts (4Q161, 4Q382, 4Q458, Pss. Sol. 17:21–23; 1QM, 4Q246, 4Q376).

Relief was anticipated to come from a messianic figure (1Q28a; 1QM) as prophesied in the OT, interpreted in their literature, and applied to their historical situations (Bateman et al., 2012, 253–329).

It also seems reasonable to suspect that the happenings in Judaea had an impact on the beliefs of Christians in Rome as well as contributed to their doubts about Jesus. Perhaps they began to think the prophets and the later interpretations of the prophets that anticipated a warring "messiah" to defeat Judaea's enemies were right after all (cf. 1:1). Perhaps they began questioning the message they heard about Jesus (cf. 2:3b–4). Perhaps they began entertaining doubts about their confession of Jesus (cf. 3:1–2). Perhaps, due to a lack of clarity, they were questioning teachings about Jesus's messiahship (cf. 5:5–6:3). Perhaps the Jewish followers in Rome began to think that there might be something to this national movement happening in Judaea (cf. 13:14).

As a result, Barnabas reassured his Hebrew Christian readers in Rome about Jesus who was God's appointed messianic Son of promise (cf. 1:2–13; 3:2; 7:28), stressed Jesus's preeminence over angels (1:4–14), emphasized the inauguration of God's new covenant through Jesus (cf. 9:15–17), revealed the inadequacy of the Levitical priesthood (7:11–16, 23–24), and underscored the obsolete nature of the Mosaic sacrificial system (10:1–4). Barnabas also warned his readers, rather sharply, against the dangers of lapsing back into Judaism and thereby committing apostasy (drifting away, 2:1–4; falling away, 3:7–4:13; being dull of hearing, 5:11–6:20; and failing to retain boldness and patience until the end, 10:19–39). He wrote, "bear with my message of encouragement, for in fact I have written to you briefly" (ἀνέχεσθε τοῦ λόγου τῆς παρακλήσεως, καὶ γὰρ διὰ βραχέων ἐπέστειλα ὑμῖν; 13:22).

Thus, it seems more than reasonable to suggest that the occasion for Barnabas's writing of Hebrews was due to the instability of Nero and the intense sociopolitical situation in Judaea during the early to mid-60s. As messianic movements grew in Judaea during the mid-60s, they not only disrupted the peace of Rome; they may have raised questions and doubts about Jesus's messiahship among the Jewish Christians in Rome. The residual results were threefold: confusion, doubt, and persecution.

LITERARY GENRE

Although the genre of Hebrews has been referred to as a riddle ("*das literarische Rätsel*"; Wrede 1906, 1–5), at least three views have been proposed: (1) an early Jewish Midrash or Midrash-pesher, (2) a letter, (3) or a sermon. Yet in reality, aspects from all three views contribute to the description of Hebrews as a sermonic-midrashic-*like* letter.

The Midrash View

The Midrash or Midrash-pesher view argues that Hebrews has affinities with Qumran literature such as the pesher text that interprets the book of Habakkuk (1QpHab) and the midrashic text that speaks of the future temple built by a future Davidic king (4Q174; Bateman, 1995, 11–27). On the one hand, Buchanan (1972, xix) considers Hebrews a homiletical midrash that is centered around Psalm 110. On the other hand, Kistemaker (1961, 11) argues that "the *Midrash pesher*, peculiar *e.g.* to the commentary on Habakkuk, *is the method adopted* by the author of the Epistle to the Hebrews." Although Kistemaker (1961, 74, 141) falls short of calling Hebrews a *Midrash-pesher*, he contends that Hebrews "reveals the peculiar features of the *Midrash pesher*." Both Buchanan and Kistemaker, however, correctly distinguish the difference between Midrash as a genre and the features of midrashic exegesis (cf. Bateman, 1997, 47–77). Both also recognize that Hebrews exhibits aspects of early Jewish midrashic exegesis (Bateman et al., 2012, 163–66; Bateman, 2010, 26–54).

What Is *Midrash*?

The term *midrash* comes from *darash*, which means "to search," "to seek," "to examine," "to investigate."

For some (e.g., Wright, 1966, 105–38, 417–57), *midrash* is literature about the Bible, that is, a literature on literature—literature that attempts to make Scripture understandable and useful as well as show its relevance to a later generation—and literature that is predominantly creative in its handling of biblical material.

For others (e.g., Le Déaut, 1969, 395–413; 1971, 259–82), *midrash* is an indefinable Jewish way of thinking and interpreting Scripture that utilizes whatever methods are needed so that Scripture remains a living, breathing book relevant for everyday life.

Yet it seems more appropriate to define *midrash* as both a literary genre and exegetical process (Bloch, 1957, 5:1263–81; 1978, 29). So, while Hebrews may exhibit midrashic forms of early Jewish exegesis, it is not a literary work to be confused with rabbinic midrash.

The Epistolary View

Hebrews has at least two affinities with epistolary literature. First, Barnabas made several personal allusions to the readers (3:1, 14; 6:4; 10:19–25; etc.; cf. Dickie, 1913, 374–75; Lindars, 1989, 383n2). Second, Hebrews has a typical Greco-Roman postscript. It concludes with a benediction (13:20), personal remarks (13:22–24), and a farewell (13:25). Yet, the lack of a prescript is problematic. Greco-Roman letters tended to include: a salutation, sender, and addressees (Bateman, 2013, 20–34). Although some have argued that Hebrews does not follow the Greco-Roman epistolary composition but Asiatic-Judaean composition (Spicq, 1952, 1:24), some Judaean letters found in the Dead Sea region of Judaea demonstrate that Judaeans also used an opening prescript (Yadin, 1978, 126–36). Suggestions that the prescript was removed for canonical acceptance are unconvincing (Westcott, 1987, xxx; Spicq, 1952, 1:24–25; Moffatt, 1924, xxviii). There is no textual evidence supporting a missing prescript for Hebrews. Finally, it's been argued that "The author's concluding remark, 'I have written [ἐπέστειλα] to you briefly' (13:22), does not necessarily imply that the writing should be classified as a letter in the strict sense" (Holladay, 2017, 698; cf. Trudinger, 1972, 128–30). Nevertheless, there is no escaping the fact that Hebrews has characteristics of an ancient Greco-Roman letter.

What Is a Letter?

Since internet use exploded in the late 1990s, seldom have we needed to send a handwritten or typed letter through our postal system. We use electronic mail. Our emails typically consist of the message *header* and the message *body*. The message *header* generally includes the following fields, though the order may vary:

- From: The e-mail address and perhaps the name of the author(s)
- To: The e-mail address indicates primary recipient (multiple allowed), and for secondary recipients indicated below with Cc and Bcc.
- Subject: A brief summary of the topic of the message
- Date: The local time and date when the message was written

The message *body*, that larger box where a message is typed, is where our one-way communication occurs. Our e-mail message, however, may or may not end with a person's *closing* or signature block of information.

Somewhat like our electronic email, Greco-Roman and Jewish letters from antiquity tend to follow the same structure. A typical letter consisted of three component parts: (1) the letter's opening address and greeting or *header*, (2) the letter's *body*, and (3) the letter's *closing* or salutation. Yet a greeting or closing salutation may or may not have been included (Bateman, 2013, 20–48).

The Homily or Sermon View

First advocated by J. Berger in 1797 (Feine, Behm, and Kummel, 1963, 287), those who hold the homily view suggest that Hebrews has several affinities with first-century homilies (Stegner, 1988, 51–69). Barnabas referred to his work as a "word of encouragement" (τοῦ λόγου τῆς παρακλήσεως; 13:22), which parallels the terminology used to describe Paul's synagogue speech in Pisidian Antioch (Acts 13:15–16; cf. Swetnam, 1969, 261–69; Lane, 1991a, LXX). Furthermore, Paul's presentation to those attending the Pisidian Antioch synagogue reverberates with OT Scripture that reflects early Jewish midrashic-*like* practices that parallel those found in Second Temple literature.

Who Was Aristotle?

Aristotle was an ancient Greek philosopher and scientist. While little is known about his early life, it seems he was born (384 B.C.) and raised in Stagira, Chalkidki before moving to Athens (ca. 367 B.C.). He was taught by Plato and served in the Athenian academy before moving to Mecedonia (348 B.C.), where he taught Alexander the Great and other Macedonian kings.

Between 335–323 B.C., Aristotle wrote many works. One of those works was *Rhetoric* where he outline three types of rhetoric: (1) *forensic* or judicial, (2) *deliberative* or political, and (3) *epideictic* or ceremonial oratory

Who Was Cicero?

Cicero was a well-known, wealthy, and respected Roman statesman, orator, lawyer and philosopher (106–43 B.C.). He refused Julius Caesar's invitation to join in a ruling partnership with Pompey and Crassus (1st Triumvirate). In 63 B.C., he was elected consul. Unfortunately, he was placed on a list of political enemies of Octavian and Antony (2nd Triumvirate). In 43 B.C., he was beheaded.

His writings were in keeping with Hellenistic philosophy and rhetorical traditions. The discoveries of his writings were instrumental during the Renaissance period and admired by Erasmus, Luther, and Locke. His writings would later inspire John Adams and other founders of the United States.

There are those who see parallels in Hebrews with Hellenistic rhetorical style. For instance, Attridge (1989, 20–21) underscores the various rhetorical speech patterns in Hebrews that parallel those evident in classical Greek sources such as Aristotle's *Rhetoric* and Cicero's *Otator*. Although suggestions of rhetorical-like outlines modeling a classic Greek format exist (cf. Koester, 2001, 83–86), none really conform to the types of rhetoric defined in the extant handbooks from the Greco-Roman era (Lane, 1991a, lxxv–lxxx). Yet the rhetorical elements are undeniable.

Many acknowledge Hebrews as a sermonic-letter (Hagner, 1990, 13; Pfitzner, 1997, 20–22; Cockerill, 2014, 15–16). It seems, however, more accurate to refer to Hebrews as a sermonic-letter with midrashic-*like* methods of interpretations. Although a bit cumbersome of a description, the postscript evidences a letter-*like* format, the sermonic-*like* rhetorical devices reverberate throughout the writing, and the use of the OT parallels midrash-*like* practices commonly employed in Second Temple literature during the time of Jesus and his disciples (cf. Longenecker, 1999). All three depictions warrant recognition in describing the genre of Hebrews. Thus, it seems more than reasonable to conclude that Barnabas wrote a sermonic-midrashic-*like* letter.

Direct Quotations in Hebrews					
Hebrews Reference	Old Testament Quotation	Hebrews Reference	Old Testament Quotation	Hebrews Reference	Old Testament Quotation
1:5	Ps. 2:7	4:3, 5	Ps. 95:11	10:30	Deut. 32:35
	2 Sam. 7:14	4:4	Gen. 2:2		Deut. 32:38
1:6	Deut. 32:43	4:7	Ps. 95:7–8		Ps. 135:14
1:7	Ps. 104:4	5:5	Ps. 2:7	10:37–38	Hab. 2:3–4
1:8	Ps. 45:6–7	5:6	Ps. 110:4	11:18	Gen. 21:12
1:10–12	Ps. 102:25–27	6:14	Gen. 22:17	12:5–6	Prov. 3:11–12
1:13	Ps. 110:1	7:17, 21	Ps. 110:4	12:20	Exod. 19:12–13
2:6–8	Ps. 8:4–6	8:5	Exod. 25:40	12:21	Deut. 9:19
2:12	Ps. 22:22	8:8–12	Jer. 31:31–34	12:26	Hag. 2:6
2:13	Isa. 8:17–18	9:20	Exod. 24:8	12:29	Deut. 4:24
3:7–11	Ps. 95:7–11	10:5–9	Ps. 40:6–8	13:5	Deut. 31:6, 7
3:15	Ps. 95:7–8	10:16–17	Jer. 31:33–34	13:6	Ps. 118:6

GOD REVEALS HIS DIVINE PLAN PROGRESSIVELY THROUGHOUT HISTORY

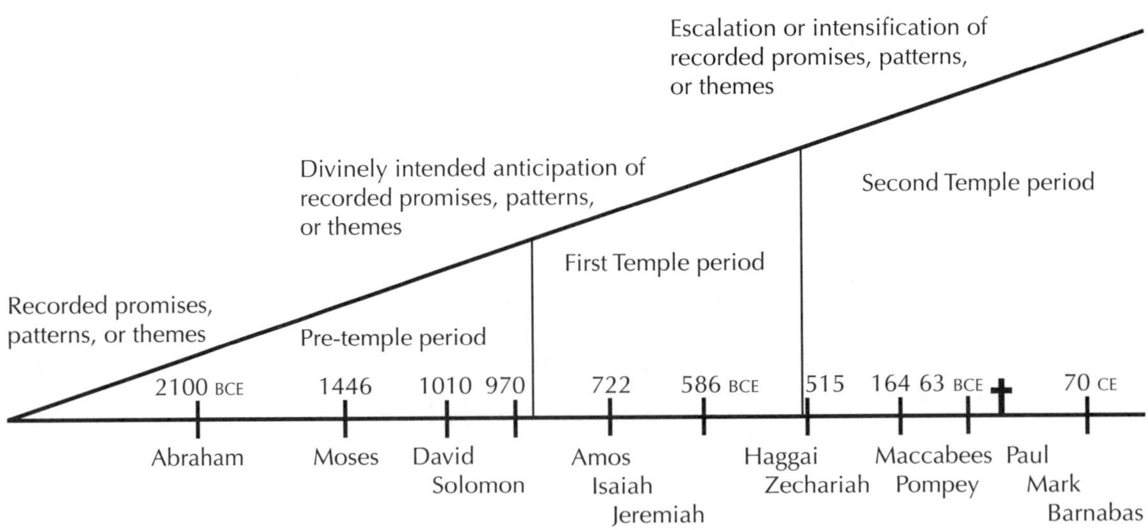

Literary Genres: Pentateuch | Historical Books, Prophetic Books, Poetic Books | Apocrypha, Dead Sea Scrolls, Pseudepigrapha | Gospels, Paul's Letters, General Letters, Revelation

HERMENEUTICAL APPROACH

Barnabas appealed to the OT (or Hebrew Scriptures) throughout his entire sermonic-midrashic-*like* letter. In the more than three hundred verses in Hebrews, at least fifty-four verses (ca. 18%) contain direct quotations from the Hebrew Scriptures and an equally significant number of allusions (cf. Bateman et al., 2012, 72–74). Barnabas drew from the Pentateuch, historical and prophetic books, and the poetic books. In essence, he drew from every portion of our current OT canon.

As a result, an important part of interpreting Hebrews is how Barnabas used Hebrew Scriptures. On what basis did he choose his passages and historical examples? What methods did he employ when he linked texts together or developed his argument? What theological points was he making by way of his quotes, allusions, and appeals to personalities from the Hebrew Scriptures?

To answer these and similar questions, a threefold hermeneutical reading strategy is applied throughout this commentary. This strategic reading traces the use of the Hebrew Bible, the Septuagint translation of the Hebrew Bible, noncanonical Jewish literature, and the NT by means of observing historical patterns, the development of divine promises, and the escalation or intensification of those patterns, promises, or themes (cf. Foulkes, 1958, 35; Goppelt, 1982, 17–18; Beale, 2012, 13–18). In other words, the threefold reading strategy traces the progressive understandings of God's promises, patterns, theological themes, and their escalations evident in Jewish literary works that span three periods of Jewish history: pre-temple period, First Temple period (first temple built ca. 963 B.C.), and Second Temple period (second temple built ca. 515 B.C.).[7]

Naturally, divine promises, historical patterns, and theological themes have a particular referential meaning in their original historical and literary context. Yet, many of these are not static but dynamic in their gradual historical interpretation and development, particularly those interpreted within Scripture. Consequently, the progress of biblical revelation, as presented in this commentary, takes into consideration the development of theological thinking in Jewish literature composed across time and throughout Jewish history in both canonical and noncanonical works. The starting point, however, is always the Scriptures and its historical and literary context. Then, consideration is given to any development, expansion,

THREEFOLD HERMENEUTICAL READING STRATEGY

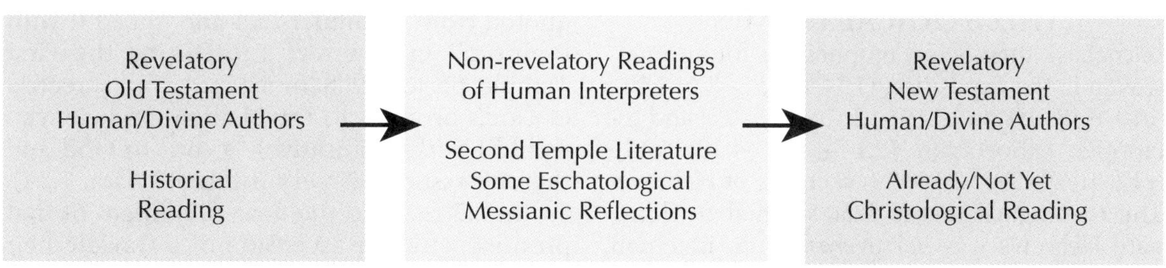

7 For a similar discussion but with an emphasis on various theological dispensations, see H. W. Bateman IV, *Interpreting the General Letters: An Exegetical Handbook* in Handbooks for NT Exegesis, ed. J. D. Harvey (Grand Rapids: Kregel, 2013), 89–125.

EARLY AND LATTER STAGES OF THE SECOND TEMPLE PERIOD

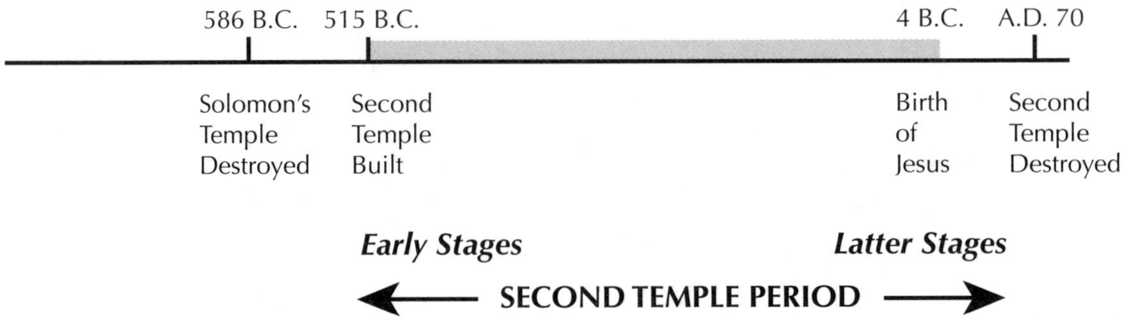

and application of divine promises, historical patterns, and theological themes in Second Temple, noncanonical Jewish literature, while at the same time being alert to their methods of interpretation (Bateman, 2010, 26–54). Finally, attention is given to Barnabas's usages of OT texts, themes, and personalities in Hebrews. In essence, this commentary manifests a threefold reading strategy, which has also been put into practice in several other works (Bateman et al., 2012, 17–36; Bateman, 2015[17], 90).

Consequently, the theological themes in Hebrews are evaluated from the perspective of a wider Jewish historical and literary context that finds its ultimate fulfillment in Jesus (Bateman et al., 2012, 26–35). This threefold reading strategy is exemplified and its significance is evident in the theological emphasis of Hebrews.

THEOLOGICAL THEMES

Barnabas's theological emphasis is found interwoven in the exposition (1:1–14; 2:5–3:6; 4:14–5:10; 6:13–10:28; 10:19–12:13; 13:1–25) and the emotive exhortation (2:1–4; 3:7–4:13; 5:11–6:12; 10:29–39; 12:14–29) sections of Hebrews. The theological theme that seemed to dominate Hebrews was *perseverance* (cf. Bateman, 2013, 119–20). Barnabas provided the reason why believers were to *persevere* in their faith. It was because Jesus was God's divine messianic Son of promise through whom God spoke and fulfilled his OT promises. Nobility in perseverance involved maintaining a confidence in Jesus—a confidence that included the certainty that Jesus was God's divine Son (1:1–14), the assurance of Jesus's eternal royal-priesthood (5:5–10; 7:1–28), and the acceptance that Jesus was God's morally excellent (4:14–15; 5:7; 7:28) and ultimate sacrifice (2:14–15; 9:11–18; 12:2) that inaugurated God's new covenant (8:8–13).

Persevere in Jesus

Believers were expected to maintain their believing faith in Jesus because of his divine sonship, his eternal royal-priesthood, and his inauguration of God's new covenant.

Jesus's Divine Sonship

Barnabas opened his sermonic-midrashic-*like* letter with a discussion about "sonship." He quoted from 2 Samuel 7:14 and linked it with Psalm 2:7 in Hebrews 1:5. During the First Temple period, 2 Samuel 7:14 was a record of God's promise to David about an heir who would be *like* (figurative) "a son" to God and thereby assume David's throne (2 Sam. 7:14). Psalm 2:7 recalled the near-fulfillment of that promise with the ascension of a Davidic heir (cf. 1 Kings 1:46–48; 9:4–5; 1 Chron. 28:5–7; 2 Chron. 13:8). Thus, a historical pattern began. Israel was to be ruled by a Davidic heir according to God's promise to David (1

Kings 11:43; 14:31; 15:18, 24; etc.). This pattern, however, was to be broken for a time (Jer. 22:24–30; 34:2–5). Prior to the dismantling of David's dynasty in 586 B.C. and destruction of the first temple, prophets spoke of a forthcoming Davidic heir by way of a metaphor, "the branch of David" (Amos 9:11; Isa. 1:1–5; Jer. 22:24–30; 33:14–17).

During the early stages of the Second Temple period, the anticipation of a forthcoming "branch of David" was reinforced in the Hebrew Bible (Zech. 3:8; 6:12–14; cf. Ps. 89:2–3, 19–52). Many Jewish authors of nonrevelatory Jewish literature recognized this historical pattern of a Davidic kingship based upon God's promise to David and God's subsequent promise to restore David's dynasty as a means for hope during Judaea's undesirable Roman subjugation. Consequently, passages from the Hebrew Scriptures about a future Davidic heir were linked together, underscored, and interpreted in noncanonical literature to anticipate a forthcoming Messiah, some with an emphasis to thwart the Roman occupation of Judaea (Pss. Sol. 2:1–3; 8:2–22; cf. 4Q252 5:1–5; 4Q174 3.2–13).

This anticipation of a Davidic heir (= Messiah) in the latter stages of the Second Temple period was affirmed in NT revelations about Jesus (Matt 1:5–16; Mark 1:9–11, etc.). Jesus was the ultimate fulfillment of God's promise to David (Matt. 12:42). Like his Jewish contemporaries, Barnabas linked together 2 Samuel 7:14 and Psalm 2:7 in Hebrews 1:5 by way of a typical midrashic method (*gezarah shewah*; Bateman et al., 2012, 163–64). However, the historical pattern of God's promise to David was applied to Jesus (cf. Heb. 1:2). Barnabas affirmed Jesus as the Messiah, the one anticipated by the latter prophets and many contemporary Judaean religious leaders. Yet, when Barnabas applied the figurative language "*like* a son" in 2 Samuel 7:14 and Psalm 2:7 to Jesus, the language was escalated to mean far more than when it was applied to Solomon, subsequent Davidic kings, and the anticipated Messiah (cf. Matt. 22:41–45). The Second Temple manner of Jewish exegesis by which Barnabas linked these two verses with Deuteronomy 32, Psalms 45, 104, 102, and 110 revealed this "son" or "heir" to be a divine royal-priest. Jesus was not just figuratively *like* God's "son" (2 Sam. 7:14; Ps. 2:7), but Jesus quite literally shared God the Father's divine nature (Heb. 1:3; cf. vv. 2b, 2c, 10–12; Bateman, 2001, 3–21).

Jesus's Eternal Royal-Priesthood

Barnabas also quoted Psalm 110 in his opening chapter. During the First Temple period, Psalm 110 was a psalm of assurance for a newly appointed Davidic king (Bateman, 2010, 150–61).[8] Whereas verse 1 presented the Davidic royal as divinely appointed with a promise of domination and rule over his enemies, verse 4 was God's irrevocable promise that sanctions the Davidic royal as "priest" *for as long as the royal-priest lived* (figurative: "forever"). Yet, the Hebrew Scriptures never emphasized the king's role as priest. However, a close examination of Davidic royals' activities in the OT revealed a pattern of priestly functions performed by Davidic kings. They blessed people (2 Sam. 6:18; 1 Kings 8:14–14), offered sacrifices (2 Sam. 6:13, 17–18; 2 Sam. 24:18–25; 1 Kings 8:62–66; 1 Chron. 21:18–28), exercised authority over the priesthood (2 Sam. 6), built and maintained the temple (2 Chron. 3:1–2: 5:7; 7:1–3; 29:1–35; 34:8–12a), and were called priests (2 Sam. 8:18; Ps. 110:4). Nevertheless, a Davidic king's priestly function was not to

8 For a preaching outline and preaching ideas for Psalm 110, see "Psalm 110: A Psalm of Assurance in the Midst of Change," in *Interpreting the Psalms for Preaching and Teaching*, eds. H. W. Bateman IV and D. B. Sandy (St. Louis: Chalice Press, 2010), 76–85.

The Prophet Jeremiah, Museum of Byzantine Culture, Thessaloniki, Greece. Unknown author; public domain.

be confused with the Levitical priest's function (cf. 2 Chron. 26:16–21 of Uzziah).

During the early stages of the Second Temple period, when Jewish exiles returned to rebuild the temple (539 B.C.), the functions of the anticipated Davidic heir become blurred. Confusion surfaces in Hebrew Scriptures when a Levitical high priest was granted royal authority and built the temple (Zech. 6:12–13; cf. Bateman et al., 2012, 196–200). Later descendants of Judas Maccabee, a Levite, eventually merged these two roles together. This merger began when the role of ruler was added to the role of the high priesthood (1 Macc 14:41–49; ca. 141 B.C.). In time, the ruler was elevated to a king and fused together as a Levitical royal-priesthood, and Judaea was declared a Jewish kingdom (Josephus, *J.A.* 13. 11. 1 §301). But some Jewish sects stood against this seemingly less than biblical union of a Levitical royal-priest. They argued for the coming of two Messiahs: a Messiah king and a Messiah priest (CD 12:23–13:1; 14:19; 19:10–11; 20:1). Yet there was a range of competing messianic portraits in the noncanonical Jewish literature. Nevertheless, their various portraits of a forthcoming messianic figure tended to share several features: humanity (lineage), authority (leadership), relationship with God (chosen), and royal warrior (military).

During the latter stages of the Second Temple period, clarity emerged about the Messiah's royal-priesthood. NT authors recalled Jesus's appeal to Psalm 110:1 when his messianic authority was being challenged (Mark 12:35; Luke 22:66–71). In Hebrews, however, Barnabas underscored and escalated the priestly functions of Jesus as a royal-priest. Jesus's function as royal-priest was greater than those exercised during the First Temple period. Barnabas linked Psalm 110:4 with Psalm 2:7 (Heb. 1:5, 13; 5:5–6) and with Genesis 14:17–20 (Heb. 7:1–2; 8:1). He drew unique attention to Jesus's role as royal-priest after the order of Melchizedek. Barnabas's presentation of Melchizedek without any ancestor escalated the interpretation of "forever" in Psalm 110:4. Jesus's rule was not metaphorically "forever" (Ps. 110:4; cf. 45:6; 102:27), nor was he metaphorically "seated at God's right hand" (Ps. 110:1). Jesus was quite literally exalted in God's presence (Heb. 1:5, 11; 3:6; 5:5–6; 8:1), ruling with God (1:3, 13; 8:1), and interceding as royal-priest on the behalf of believers (4:14–16; 8:1–2; 10:19–22) eternally. The "son's" love for righteousness (Ps. 45:7) was not hyperbolic language but rather reflective of reality because Jesus actually ruled in righteousness (Heb. 1:3d; 1:8–9), and his rule would one day exercise eternal control over all (1:3b; cf. 2:8) (Bateman, 2001, 3–21).

Jesus's Inauguration of God's New Covenant

Barnabas quoted Jeremiah 31 in Hebrews 8. During the First Temple period, Jeremiah prophesied a message of judgment and restoration. Originally, Jeremiah was a priest, from a priestly family, who was called by God to be a prophet in 627 B.C. during the reign of King Josiah (Jer. 1:2–3). Jeremiah's message was twofold: judgment and restoration. God was going to judge Judah because the Mosaic covenant was meant to be obeyed (11:1–8), but there was a conspiracy against the Mosaic covenant that was leading to their ruin (11:9–17). The consequence for disobeying the Mosaic covenant was God's judgment (17:1–4). Nevertheless, Jeremiah preached a parallel message of restoration. The Lord would restore his people to the land (29:10–14; cf. 31:1–14), restore the city of Jerusalem (30:18–22), restore David's dynasty (33:14–18; cf. 29:1–8), and make a new covenant with Israel (31:31–34).

During the latter part of the Second Temple period, the new covenant was perceived to be a mutual covenant between God and his people. For some Jews of Jesus's day, it was a renewal and an updated version of previous covenants that God had entered into with Jewish ancestors (Jub. 6, 15, 21, 30). For others, the new covenant was considered inaugurated and entered into by way of repentance and by taking an oath of obedience (CD 8:18–21). If new covenant oaths were abandoned, it would be with consequences (CD 8:18–21; 19:29–30; 32–34). In Hebrews, however, Barnabas corrected these misunderstandings of Jeremiah's direct prophesy about Jesus's inauguration of a new covenant. In Hebrews 8:13, he explained, "When he [God] speaks of a *new* covenant, he makes the first obsolete. Now what is growing *obsolete* and aging is about to disappear" (emphasis added). Barnabas capitalized on the words "new" and "obsolete." Jeremiah's mention of the new covenant spoken of was totally "new," which in turn meant the first covenant (e.g., the Mosaic covenant) was "treated as obsolete" and thereby outdated. During Jeremiah's day the Mosaic covenant was "growing old." For Barnabas, it was a done deal due to the sealing of the new covenant with the blood of Jesus (9:11–10:18).

Other Themes

Barnabas explored several other theological themes in Hebrews: he clarified Jewish beliefs about angels in comparison to the messianic Son, revisited the history of Jewish apostasy, and warned against God's judgment for disbelief.

Angels

Barnabas opened his sermonic-midrashic-*like* letter with a distinction between the messianic Son of promise and "angels." During the First Temple period, angels appeared somewhat

Archangel Gabriel by Gerard David (c. 1450).
Courtesy of Pharos.

sparingly with appearances to Abram (Gen. 18:2; 19:1, 15), Jacob (Gen. 28:12; 32:1), and in the Psalms where the psalmists charge angels to praise God (103:20; 148:2). Nevertheless, an angel of the Lord frequently appeared to people: Hagar (Gen. 16:7–14), Abraham (Gen. 22:11–15), Moses (Exod. 3:2–4), Balaam (Num. 22:22–38), Gideon (Judg. 6:11–23), Manoah and his wife (Judg. 13:3–22). Yet an extensive theology of angels emerged during the Second Temple period.

During the early stages of the Second Temple period, an angel of the Lord appeared before God on behalf of Jerusalem and Joshua the high priest (Zech. 1:12; 3:4). Two angels were actually named: Michael (Dan. 10:13, 21; 12:1; cf. Jude 1:9; Rev. 12:7) and Gabriel (Dan. 8:16; 9:21; cf. Luke 1:19, 26), both of whom are archangels. Yet, far more archangels are identified in later noncanonical literature: Raphael (Tob 12:15), Uriel (2 Esdr 4:1; 5:20), Jerahmeel (2 Esdr 4:36), and Sarqael (1 En. 20:7, 8), just to name a few.

Furthermore, there was a scroll found among the Dead Sea Scrolls called the "War Scroll" (1QM). On the one hand, a multitude of angels were presented as dwelling with God in the heavens (12:1; cf. 4Q493 1v–vi:1:1) and battling alongside people referred to as "the sons of light" (1:10–11; 7:6; 12:1; 15:14; cf. 4Q493 1i, ii, iii: 1, 3). Their commander was Michael, along with Gabriel, Sariels, and Raphael (9:15–16). On the other hand, Belial was named as a demonic angelic being that stood against God's people (1Q28 iii 13–iv. 26). He was the "prince" of the kingdom of wickedness (1QM xvii. 5–6). He reigned over his demonic forces, and his reign was one of injustice (1Q28 i. 16–18; iv. 19–20). People who followed after Belial were "the sons of darkness" that make up an army loyal to Belial (1QM 1:1, 5; 3:6, 9; 4:2; 15:2; 16:11; Jub. 14:31–33; cf. Eph. 2:2) and the enemies are the Kittim (= Rome: 1:2, 4, 6, 9, 12; 11:11; 15:2; 16:3–6, 9; 17:12, 14, 15; 18:2, 4; 19:10).[9] The NT reflects some of these developments: Gabriel (Luke 1:19, 26), Satan's kingdom (Mark 3:22–26; Eph. 2:2), demons (Mark 1:23–26; 5:1–13), and heavenly worship (1 Cor. 7:10; 10:19–22). Yet, Barnabas made it clear that Jesus was no angel (Heb. 1:4–14).

Apostasy

God's people have always wrestled with leaving the God they claimed to love. During the First Temple period, God's people rebelled at Mount Sinai (Exod. 32:1–33:6) and Kadesh Barnea (Num. 14; cf. Ps. 106:7–27a). Ezekiel paralleled the wilderness community's *turning away* from God with that of the first temple (966–586 B.C.) when Judah departed from the living God (Ezek. 20:8, 38; cf. Jer. 2:5; Dan. 9:5, 9; *Barn.* 3:8). Likewise, during the early part of the Second Temple period, Jewish communities departed from God through "abandoning the religion of their fathers" (1 Macc 2:19) and through the actions "of the lawless who had rebelled against God" (1QpHab 8:11, 16). To turn away from God, then, was deliberate rebellion against God: "Far be it from us that we should rebel against the LORD and turn away [ἀποστῆναι] this day from following the LORD" (Josh. 22:29 LXX, NRSV; cf. Wis 3:10). Similarly, during the latter part of the Second Temple period, God's people were warned about not repeating the rebellion of the exodus community (1 Cor. 10:1–8; CD 3.5–9). Barnabas frequently discussed the heart condition that might result in forsaking the living God (3:12; cf. Jer. 17:5; Sir 10:12). He weaved emotively driven cautions ("take care" or "see to it," Βλέπετε) about a hardened heart (Heb. 3:8, 15) or evil heart (3:12) that could affect one's relationship with the living God. According to Barnabas, God desired that all followers of

9 See J. Duhaime, "Light and Darkness," in *Encyclopedia of the Dead Sea Scrolls* (2000), 1:495–96; M. Mach, "Demons," in *Encyclopedia of the Dead Sea Scrolls* (2000), 1:189–91.

Jesus "hold fast" (κρατέω, 4:14; 6:18; κατέχω, 3:6, 14; 10:23) to their confession of Jesus as God's divine royal-priest.

Judgment

Judgment for disobedience appeared throughout the First Temple period and has been exemplified several times above. Likewise, during the Second Temple period, rebellion within the church was a frequent problem (Rom. 7:21–25; 3 John 10–12). As a result, NT authors made appeals to previous rebellions and divine punishment as a warning for followers of Jesus (Jude 5–16; 2 Peter 2). Likewise, Barnabas focused attention upon the pattern of judgment surrounding the exodus generation. He spoke of the rejection of God's revelation and subsequent punishment (Heb. 2:2–3a). He spoke of the rejection at Kadesh Barnea and God's punishment (3:7–11). He spoke the "shaking of the earth" at Sinai (Exod. 19:18) that appeared in subsequent Jewish literature (Judg. 5:4–6; Pss. 18:7; 68:7–8; Isa. 13:13; 64:2–4; Jer. 10:10; Hag. 2:6–7, 21; 1 En. 60:1–6; Barn 32:1–6) and quoted from Haggai 2:6 in Hebrews 12:26. In each and every case, Barnabas drew attention to a future judgment (2:3b; 4:1; 12:26).

Conclusion

Caird (1959, 45) has rightly described Hebrews as "one of the earliest and most successful attempts to define the relation between the Old and New Testaments." Barnabas capitalized and underscored these new and at times escalated revelations about Jesus, the messianic Son of promise, and subsequent applications to Jesus. Jesus was not just figuratively *like* God's "son" (2 Sam. 7:14; Ps. 2:7), but Jesus quite literally shared God the Father's divine nature (Heb. 1:3; cf. vv. 2b, 2c, 10–12). His rule was not metaphorically "forever" (Ps. 45:6) nor was he metaphorically "seated at God's right hand" (Ps. 110:1), but Jesus has been exalted for all eternity to rule alongside God the Father (Heb. 1:3d, 8–9, 12). Finally, the "son's" love for righteousness (Ps. 45:7) and God's subduing of his enemies (Ps. 110:1) was not hyperbolic language but rather reflective of reality because Jesus actually ruled in righteousness (1:3d; 1:8–9), and his rule would one day exercise complete control over all (1:3b; cf. 2:8) (Bateman, 2001, 3–21).

CONCLUSION

While comments like "admit our ignorance," "less certain," "one cannot decisively rule out," and "as good a guess as any" tend to undermine introductions to Hebrews (Carson and Moo, 2005, 604–9), it has been our desire to draw some conclusions to the many preliminary discussions that often appear in NT introductions and opening discussion within most commentaries on Hebrews. As a result, we have argued that Barnabas wrote this sermonic-midrashic-*like* letter from somewhere in the Roman Empire to a group of Jewish Christians living in Rome in order to encourage them to maintain their faith in Jesus, the divine royal-priest and messianic Son of promise, in spite of their persecutions and the national messianic eruptions that were happening in Judaea sometime between Nero's persecution in A.D. 63 and the eventual outbreak of the Judaean war with Rome in A.D. 66. Consequently, we will interpret and apply Hebrews based upon these introductory humble conclusions.

OUTLINE

While Hebrews could be divided into forty-plus exegetical units, such a lengthy preaching series may not be feasible for most twenty-first-century audiences. Therefore, we've chosen to divide Hebrews into five major divisions with twenty preaching units.

INTRODUCING GOD'S "MESSIANIC SON OF PROMISE": HIS RELATIONSHIP WITH GOD, ANGELS, AND THE HOUSEHOLD FAMILY OF FAITH (1:1–2:18)

- God's Final Spokes*man*: Divinely Appointed, Divinely Related, and Divinely Authoritative (1:1–4)
- God's Distinctions between "a Son" and "the Sons of God": What God Says about the Messianic Son of Promise (1:5–14)
- God's Recent Revelation: Reason for Concentrating on and Listening to It (2:1–4)
- God's Plans for the Messianic Son of Promise: Past, Present, Future (2:5–9)
- God's Equipping of the Messianic Son of Promise: The Leader of the Family Household of Faith (2:10–18)

GOD'S HOUSEHOLD FAMILY OF FAITH: MEMBERSHIP PRIVILEGES AND RESPONSIBILITIES (3:1–4:13)

- Distinctions between Jesus and Moses: A Call for a New Allegiance (3:1–6)
- Heeding and Avoiding Stubbornness: A Historical Lesson about People Who Rebel (3:7–19)
- The Fear Factor: Fearing Failure While Striving for Success (4:1–13)

THE ROYAL HIGH PRIESTHOOD OF JESUS: DISTINCTIONS, REPRIMAND, AND ARCHETYPE (4:14–7:28)

- God's Regal High Priest: Qualification and Appointment of Jesus (4:14–5:10)
- Reprimand for Apathy: A Call to Be Discernable Thinkers (5:11–6:12)
- God's Sworn Promise: Unalterable Purpose, Unchangeable Certainties (6:13–20)
- Melchizedek, a Royal-Priest of the Past: A Model of Priesthood, Guaranteed, Unchangeable, Sinless (7:1–28)

GOD'S NEW COVENANT: A CONTRAST OF SERVICE, SANCTUARIES, AND EFFECTIVENESS (8:1–10:39)

- Jesus's Heavenly Ministry: A Contrast of Ministries, Sanctuaries, and Covenants (8:1–13)
- God's Prescribed Sanctuary: Its Description, Regulations, and Shortcomings (9:1–28)
- Judaism's Blood Sacrifices: Their Descriptions, Shortcomings, and Replacement (10:1–18)
- Assurances of Jesus's Royal-Priesthood: Responsibilities, Limitations, and Expectations (10:19–39)

APPLICATION: EXAMPLES, ENDURANCE, AND ENCOURAGEMENTS (11:1–13:25)

- Triumphs of Faith: Israel's Impressive Story (11:1–40)
- Endurance and Discipline: The Endurance of an Athlete and the Instruction of a Child (12:1–13)
- Refusing God: The Dangers and the Penalties (12:14–29)
- A Call to Persist in Loving One Another: Encountering Real-life Situations (13:1–25)

Four comments may help to underscore our reason for our sermon series. First, it may seem odd that chapters 1 and 2 appear somewhat belabored. Yet, these opening chapters are foundational for Barnabas's subsequent material. So, we open the series slowly, knowing that these initial chapters are essential for the preaching of the entire book. Second, chapters 8, 9, and 10 share many of the same themes, so we've chosen to preach these chapters in four sermons because of the repetition of material. Third, chapter 11 could be broken into four preaching units. Yet, we've suggested one sermon for the chapter, with options for a more lengthy sermon series on Hebrews if desired. Finally, we realize that there is no single best way to preach any given text in Hebrews. We merely offer suggestions to consider, knowing that you are more familiar than we are with the specific needs of your people to whom you preach.

FOR FURTHER READING

Barclay, John M. 1996. *Jews in the Mediterranean Diaspora: From Alexander to Trajan.* Edinburgh: T&T Clark.

Bateman IV, H. W. 2012. "Three Obstacles to Overcome, and Then One." In *Jesus The Messiah: Tracing the Promises, Expectations, and Coming of Israel's King*, 211–52. H. W. Bateman IV, D. L. Bock, G. H. Johnston. Grand Rapids, Kregel.

Bock, D. L. 2008. "Single Meaning, Multiple Contexts and Referents." In *Three Views on the New Testament Use of the Old Testament*, 105–68. S. N. Gundry, series editor. Grand Rapids: Zondervan.

Champlin, E. 2003. *Nero.* Cambridge, MA: Harvard University Press.

Fanning, B. M. 1994. "A Theology of Hebrews." In *A Biblical Theology of the New Testament*, 369–416. Edited by R. B. Zuck and D. L. Bock. Chicago, IL: Moody Press.

Hengel, M. 1997. *The Zealots: Investigations into the Jewish Freedom Movement in the Period from Herod I until 70 A.D.* Edinburgh: T&T Clark.

ADDITIONAL RESOURCES FOR STUDYING HEBREWS

Bateman IV, H. W. 2012. *Charts on the Book of Hebrews.* Kregel Charts of the Bible. Grand Rapids, Kregel.

Bateman IV, H. W. (editor). 2007. *Four Views on the Warning Passages in Hebrews.* Grand Rapids: Kregel.

Bateman IV, H. W., D. L. Bock, G. H. Johnston. 2012. *Jesus The Messiah: Tracing the Promises, Expectations, and Coming of Israel's King.* Grand Rapids, Kregel.

Metzger, B. M. and Roland Murphy, eds. 1991. *The New Oxford Annotated Apocrypha: The Apocryphal/Deuterocanonical Books of the Old Testament.* New York: Oxford University Press (1965, 1977).

Schiffman L. H., and J. C. VanderKam, eds. 2000. *Encyclopedia of the Dead Sea Scrolls.* 2 vols. Oxford: University Press.

Wise, M., M. Abegg Jr., and E. Cook. 1996. *The Dead Sea Scrolls: A New Translation.* San Francisco: HarperSanFrancisco.

INTRODUCING GOD'S "MESSIANIC SON OF PROMISE" (1:1–2:18)

Barnabas's introduction centered around the identity of "a son." In it, he underscored the son's distinct relationship with God, angels, and people. First, Barnabas introduced the son's prominent eternal ruling relationship with God as both the messianic Son of promise and Creator of the world (1:2c–3; 1:6, 10–12). Second, this son had a ruling relationship over angels who worshipped and served him (1:6, 14). Third, this son had a familiar relationship with his followers due to his incarnation (2:11–14a). Fourth, this son's physical death had broken Satan's power, liberated people from the fear of death, and made atonement for the sins of all people (1:3; 2:9, 14b–15, 17). Finally, although the divine messianic Son of promise currently ruled, he awaited the day when all things would be subjugated to him (1:13; 2:8).

This first division may be divided into five preaching units. The first introduces and identifies "a son" as God's final spokes*man,* whose as messianic Son of promise and divine Creator has inherited a superior name to that of angels or "sons of God" (1:1–4). The second underscores God's distinctions between the messianic Son of promise and celestial sons of God by way of God's three statements to and about the messianic Son of promise (1:5–14). The third is Barnabas's warning to concentrate on and listen to God's new revelation about the messianic Son of promise (2:1–4). The fourth reveals God's plan for the messianic Son of promise (2:5–9). The final unit concludes with God's equipping the messianic Son of promise to be the leader of his household family of faith (2:10–18). At the very end of this section is a list of books and articles for further reading that may be helpful in understanding these preaching units.

Hebrews 1:1–4

EXEGETICAL IDEA

Unlike in times past when God spoke through many prophets, God had spoken in this new era through a single divinely appointed, divinely related, and divinely authoritative spokes*man*, "a son," to whom had been given a name superior to even that of the celestial sons of God.

THEOLOGICAL FOCUS

In this new era, God speaks to people through a new and superior spokes*man*, Jesus.

PREACHING IDEA

Tuning out the many makes it possible to hear the one and only voice that *really* matters.

PREACHING POINTERS

While Hebrews 1:1–4 is at once elegantly simple and brutally complicated, the message is quite simple: God spoke through his messianic Son of promise. The language of these beautiful verses, as will be seen in the exegetical section, was unveiling the NT motif of Jesus as the messianic Son of promise in both explicit and nuanced ways. Obviously, the original readers knew Jesus as Messiah, but did they know him as God's ultimate spokes*man*, his final word? Their challenge was the many prophetic voices—and, we might even add, the competing Jewish interpretations of those voices—that detracted from the one voice that really mattered.

Today, we too struggle with competing voices. There are the voices at work demanding our attention. There are the community voices like Big Brothers and Big Sisters of America entreating our participation in mentoring youth. There are voices at church appealing for our commitment, time, and money. There are also the family voices at home. Do you ever feel as though you are just drowning in a sea of voices? Prioritizing the important from the not-so-important voices is difficult to do. Yet there are times we need to tune out some of these voices. This passage appeals to our need to tune out the many, so that we can hear the voice that *really* matters.

GOD'S FINAL SPOKES*MAN* (1:1–4)

LITERARY STRUCTURE AND THEMES (1:1–4)

Barnabas's introduction to "a son," in verses 1–4, was an elegantly designed and well-proportioned sentence grammarians refer to as a period.[1] Although a distinct unit, these verses were an integral part of chapters 1 and 2 (Cockerill, 2015, 86–87). This single sentence introduced the original Roman Jewish readers to God speaking about his final spokesman for this new era (vv. 1–2a), whom Barnabas describes as divine royalty (vv. 2b–3c) and whom Barnabas revealed as having a unique position with God (vv. 3d–4).

Barnabas's major theme was that God communicates with people through one spokesman, his Son.

- ***God's Final Spokesman (1:1–2a)***
- ***The Son's Description as Divine Royalty (1:2b–3c)***
- ***The Son's Unique Position (1:3d–4)***

EXPOSITION (1:1–4)

Approaching Hebrews 1:1–4 must begin with understanding the original Jewish reader's array of spokes*men* that demanded their attention. The original readers were well aware of the Hebrew Bible prophets (Isaiah, Jeremiah, Amos, etc.) as well as several well-developed teachings about angels who also functioned as messengers of God (1 En.; 4Q400–07; 11Q17).

Songs of the Sabbath Sacrifice (4Q400–07 or 11Q17)

The *Songs of the Sabbath Sacrifice* were found in caves four and eleven among numerous scrolls at Qumran and may be referred to as 4QShirShabb (4Q400–07) or 11QShirShabb (11Q17). The manuscript begins with an invitation to consider "the mysteries of an angelic priesthood" (Wise et al., 1996, 365). The songs were not only recited as a liturgy for thirteen Sabbath celebrations, but they were also intended "to unite the worshipper with the angels worshipping in heaven" (Wise et al., 1996, 365). The idea that angels were involved in human worship also appears in 1 Corinthians 11:10. For a translation of the *Songs of the Sabbath Sacrifice*, see Wise et al., 1996, 365–78) under "Ancient Sources" and Newsom in *EncDSS* under "Songs of the Sabbath Sacrifice" (2000, 2:887–89).

Jesus as "The Messiah," however, was still a new phenomenon. The diverse anticipations of a messianic figure based upon the prophets often competed with what was true about Jesus's messiahship (Bateman et al., 2012, 253–329). This was clearly evident among the voices of the Jewish religious leaders employing the people of Judaea to revolt against Roman occupation, many of whom presented themselves as messiah (Bateman, 2013, 62–72). So, while the original readers of Hebrews believed in Jesus as Messiah, there were some uncertainties and misunderstandings about his messiahship. Barnabas seemingly helped to move

1 Although admittedly "the period, i.e., the organization of a considerable number of clause and phrases into a well-rounded unity, is rare in the NT" (BDF, 242 §464), they appear frequently in the NT. Three NT books open with periods (Luke 1:1–4; Heb. 1:1–4; 1 John 1:1–4; cf. Eph. 2:1–8). Yet they are found throughout Hebrews. Some of the more notable and lengthy periods are 2:2–4; 3:12–15a; 4:12–13; 5:7–10; 9:2–5; 14–16; 18–21; 22–24 10:19–25; etc. and others are OT citations (2:6–8; 3:7–11; 9:16–17).

his readers along in their beliefs about Jesus, their Messiah. He made it clear that unlike in times past when *God spoke* through many prophets, *God had spoken* in this new era through a single divinely appointed, divinely related, and divinely authoritative spokes*man*, "a son," to whom had been given a name superior to even that of the celestial sons of God.

God's Final Spokesman (1:1–2a)

In contrast to the many human agents in the past through whom God spoke to the people of Israel, God had most recently spoken to believers through a single agent, "a son."

1:1. Barnabas opened with a simple statement of fact: God communicated (λαλήσας, "he spoke") with his people. The phrase "many times and many ways long ago" (πολυμερῶς καὶ πολυτρόπως πάλαι) conveyed that throughout Israel's history and by many methods, the prophets were God's spokes*men*. It was "through the prophets" (ἐν τοῖς προφήταις) that God proclaimed "to our fathers" (τοῖς πατράσιν) monotheistic beliefs while living in a world of polytheism. Moses appeared to be the first biblical prophet, who heard directly from God, embraced what God said, and proclaimed what God had spoken. God's revelations to Moses through a burning bush (Exod. 3:4–4:17, 28–31) and from the mountain (Exod. 19:1–24:4) were given to the people of Israel. Later, God "spoke" (λαλήσας) through other prophets by means of dreams (Dan. 2–4, 7–8), visions (1 Sam. 3:10–15), and celestial beings (Zech. 1:9–15) who then conveyed that message to God's people. So from the preformation and formation of the nation to the exilic and postexilic time periods in Israel's history, leaders and the people of Israel had heard from God by way of many spokes*men*.

1:2a. Barnabas's implicit contrast (note there is no contrastive Greek conjunction) suggested that God's most recent revelation "through *a son*" (ἐν υἱῷ) was superior to that given previously "through the *prophets*." "The force of the expression in Hebrews," according to Lane, "is to characterize the son as the one through whom God spoke his final and decisive word" (Lane, 1991a, 1, 10). Thus, there was one final and ultimate spokes*man*.

> *TRANSLATION ANALYSIS:* "A son" (1:2a)
> Translating the prepositional phrase as "through a son" (ἐν υἱῷ) rightly reflects the absence of the Greek article (NET, NRSV), which is contrary to many translations that suggest "his son" (KJV, ASV, NASB, ESV, NIV, NLT, WEB*)*. The lack of the article underscores the fact that Barnabas has a single person in mind and not an entire group, as might be the case when speaking of the "sons of God" (Job 1:6; 2:1; 38:7; Pss. 29:1 [28:1 LXX]; 89:7 [88:7 LXX]; cf. 11Q13 2.14).

Lane's view is reinforced with the phrase "during these end of days" or "these last days" (ἐπ' ἐσχάτου τῶν ἡμερῶν τούτων). The phrase served to contrast a former era with a *final* era or time period (cf. Luke 7:27–28). Furthermore, there was but one spokes*man*, *"a son"* (ἐν υἱῷ) not many as in the past. Finally, God "has spoken to us" (ἐλάλησεν ἡμῖν) and not merely "to our fathers" of the past. And though God's current message about the son is an important theme throughout Hebrews,[2] there remained continuity between God's word in the past and the present: (1) it echoed warnings (Ps. 95:7–11 in Heb. 3:7–11) and exhortations (Prov. 3:11–12 in Heb. 12:5–7) that were to be heeded by believers living "in these days"; (2) it revealed promises fulfilled in the Son (Gen. 22:17 in Heb. 6:13–20); and (3) it provided vehicles for understanding the nature and salvific work of the Son (cf. Attridge, 1989, 38; Koester, 2001, 184). Thus, unlike the previous era when God spoke by way of *many*

2 Hebrews 1:1, 2:2, 4:12–13; cf. "he said" or "has said" in 1:5, 13; 3:10, 4:3–4; 5:5–6; 7:21; 8:8; 10:9, 30; 13:5.

prophets, in this final era God had spoken by way of a single person, "a son" (υἱος). At this point in the introduction, the meaning of "son" was not yet defined. "Son" (υἱος) could have been descriptive for Adam (Luke 3:38), for celestial "sons of God" (Job 1:6; 2:1; 38:7), and Davidic monarchs (2 Sam. 7:14; Ps. 2:7, 11–12). Only as these opening verses were unwrapped was this Son's identity clarified to the original readers of Hebrews.

The Son's Description as Divine Royalty (1:2b–3c)

The Son was described as God's divinely appointed royal-priest and divinely related spokes*man*.

1:2b–c. Barnabas's description drew attention first to this son's *divinely appointed* heirship: "*whom he* [God] *appointed* [ὃν ἔθηκεν] heir of all *things*" (chiastic structure line B). This opening clause alluded to Psalm 2:7 and stands in chiastic parallel with another clause later in verse 3e (line B') that echoed Psalm 110:1, "he sat down at the right hand of the Majesty on high." Both were purposely inserted excerpts from royal psalms that originally referred to a Davidic king. The heavenly exaltation revealed this Son's honored position as God's ultimate messianic Son of promise (Heb. 5:6, 10; 6:20; 7:1–25) through whom God offered an inheritance to all those who persevered in their belief in his messianic Son (cf. 1:14; 6:12, 17; 9:15). Yet astonishingly, this messianic successor was not just an heir who ruled over Israel. There was an escalation of this Davidic king's rule. He was "the heir of all *things*" (κληρονόμον πάντων) due to Barnabas's second description as Creator (chiastic structure line C). He was the one "*through whom also he* [God] *created* the worlds" (δι' οὗ καὶ ἐποίησεν τοὺς αἰῶνας; cf. 11:3). "The worlds" (τοὺς αἰῶνας) of which Barnabas spoke were of our temporal universe (vv. 10–12; Vanhoye, 1969, 52–54; Vanhoye, 2015, 55). So, this son was presented as both the messianic Son of promise and Creator of the universe.

Chiastic Structure for Hebrews 1:1–4

The presentation of Hebrews 1:1–4 in a chiastic structure identifies the focus of Barnabas's description of "a son" to be located at the center of the structure.

- A The son's superiority: The son is superior to former prophets (1:1–2a).
  - B The son's *appointment*: He is heir of all things (1:2b).
    - C The son's *relationship with the universe*: He created the created order (1:3a).
      - D The Son's relationship with God: He is the reflection of God's glory (1:3b).
    - C' The son's *relationship with the universe*: He sustains the created order (1:3c).
  - B' The son's *appointment*: He is exalted (enthroned) at God's right hand (1:3d–e).
- A' The son's superiority: The son is superior to angels (1:4).

While the heart of Barnabas's description (line D) is the son's relationship with God through whom God both created and sustains the universe (lines C and C'), the son's portrayal as royal-priest (lines B and B') is predominate and central in Hebrews (4:14–10:31) and a theme to which Barnabas returns (5:5–6; 7:1–28). Yet Barnabas frames these verses with a contrast (lines A and A') that draws specific attention to this son's preeminence (Ebert, 1992, 163–79; Meier, 1985, 168–79; Bateman, 1997, 2013, 191–92).

Excursus on Psalm 2

While Barnabas recontextualizes Psalm 2 as an application to Jesus (Heb. 1:3, 5; 5:5), it helps to understand the psalm in its original context.

Psalm 2: A royal psalm. References to "king" (v. 6), "his anointed one" (v. 2), "scepter" (v. 9), and father-son imagery (vv. 7, 12) support a royal psalm motif.

Overview: Four major sections are evident: the rebellious plans of the nations (2:1–3), the response of the divine king (vv. 4–6), the reiteration of Yahweh's promise by the Davidic king (vv. 7–9), and the rebuke to the rebellious nations (vv. 10–12).

Message: The psalm's message is a twofold message to the nations. It exhorts the nations to abandon any plans of rebellion against the Lord and his anointed (vv. 2–3). It also exhorts the nations to submit to authority of the ordained Davidic king who will rule them (vv. 6–7) and who will smash their rebellion (vv. 8–9, 12). Thus, the psalm is an encouragement to the Israelite nation because it emphasizes that her king is God's viceregent.

Central Point: The central point occurs in Psalm 2:7. It specifically refers to the special or unique relationship between Yahweh and his viceregent when the Davidic viceregent had formally been given theocratic rights (2 Sam. 7:14; Ps. 89:27–28). Subsequent Davidic heirs may have used the psalm to legitimize their rule and authority over the nations. The usage was in keeping with Yahweh's dynastic promise to David and passed on to each Davidic heir (2 Sam. 7:14). In fact, Psalm 2 anticipates a victorious, sovereign king (Ps. 2:11–12) who has a unique relationship with Yahweh.

Ambiguities of the Psalm: Although associated with a Davidic king's coronation, Psalm 2 fails to identify a specific life situation or referent. Parallel language in 2 Samuel 7:12–16 and NT testimony of Davidic authorship (Acts 4:25–26) may suggest that the psalm was initially used for the coronation of David's son, Solomon (1 Chron. 28:1–8; 29:20–25). Even if Psalm 2 is not a coronation psalm, it is a royal psalm designed to show God's support for a Davidic viceregent (Ps. 2:2, 6, 7), God's anointed son.

Applications to an Eschatological Messiah: The ambiguities of the psalm lend themselves to be applied to an eschatological Messiah figure. The conceptual sense of Psalm 2 concerning the Davidic king's unique relationship with (vv. 1–2, 7) and support of Yahweh (vv. 1–2, 9) is maintained in Second Temple literature. Nevertheless, verses 1, 2, 7, and 9 are reinterpreted to speak of a future (eschatological) Messiah figure. In the Dead Sea Scrolls, 1Q28a 2:11 and 4Q174 1:18–19 emphasize the future Messiah's special relationship with God. However, 1Q28a 2:11 focuses on the future messiah's authority from God to rule and bless those whom he rules over, whereas 4Q174 1:18–19 focuses attention on God's divine protection of his people through the future messiah. *The Psalms of Solomon* emphasizes the future Davidic Messiah who will come in military power and establish his kingdom. If Psalm 2 is conceptually tied to 2 Samuel and applicable to Davidic heirs of the past, it is more than reasonable to expect these verses from the psalm to be applicable to an eschatological Messiah figure.

1:3a–c. The focal point of Barnabas's third description (chiastic structure line D) was in two depictions of this son as *divinely related* to God: "*who is* [ὃς ὢν] the radiance of God's glory" (ἀπαύγασμα τῆς δόξης), which was linked (καί) with "the imprint of God's nature" (χαρακτὴρ τῆς ὑποστάσεως αὐτοῦ). The word "radiance" (ἀπαύγασμα) occurs only here in the NT and can be translated "reflection" (NASB) and "reflects" (RSV, NLT). Yet, these latter two renderings are less than compelling because this son was more than just a reflection of God. He was the manifestation of God, the "radiance" (ESV, NIV) or "the brightness of his glory" (KJV). In the past, references to God's glory occurred when God hovered over Mount Sinai (Exod. 24:16–17), over the tabernacle (Exod. 40:34–35; cf. 1 Sam. 4:22), and within the temple (1 Kings 8:11–12; cf. Ezek. 10:18–19). Here in verse 3a, the son was uniquely identified as "God's glory" (Cockerill, 2012, 94; Hagner, 2002, 24).

"The radiance of God's glory" may be interpreted as synonymous with "the imprint of God's nature" (NASB; cf. *TDNT*, 9:421–22; *EDNT*, 1:118). Inserting the elliptical "who is" (ὃς ὢν) accentuated the fourth description that underscored the radiance of God's glory. The word "imprint" (χαρακτήρ) gave emphasis to this son's deity that revealed God's power, presence, and faithfulness (Koester, 2001, 180). Thus, the son was not only perceived as "the radiance of God's glory" but also "the exact representation of God's being." This divine relationship continued (τε) as Barnabas's final description of the son underscored his function as creator: "who *continually* sustains all things" (φέρων τὰ πάντα). The description parallels that of God (cf. Pss. 104 [103 LXX]; 102 [101 LXX] with Heb. 1:2c, 7, 11–12) and thereby describes this messianic Son of promise, who was uniquely identified with Yahweh, as divine.

Important Dependent Clauses (1:2b–3)

There are five dependent clauses in Hebrews 1:1–4 that are important descriptions about the son, which might be considered the son's credentials:

1. *whom he* [God] *appointed* (ὃν ἔθηκεν)
2. *through whom also he* [God] *created* (δι' οὗ καὶ ἐποίησεν)
3. *who is the radiance* (ὃς ὢν ἀπαύγασμα)
4. *and [who is] the imprint* (καί χαρακτήρ)
5. *who sustains* (φέρων)

The Son's Unique Position (1:3d–4)

As the divine messianic Son of promise, he shared a *divinely appointed position of authority* with God as he ruled over the entire universe in God's presence.

TEXTUAL ANALYSIS: Conflicting Text Critical Reading: 1:3

Grammatical Issue: The phrase "through himself" (δι' ἑαυτοῦ or δι' αὑτοῦ) appears to have been added to clarify the meaning of the ambiguous middle voice "he made for himself" (ποιησάμενος). The text is the preferred reading (cf. Metzger, 1994, 592).

txt. "he made purification for sins" (καθαρισμὸν τῶν ἁμαρτιῶν ποιησάμενος) (ASV, ESV, NASB, NET, NIV, NRSV)

var. "**through himself** he made purification for sins" (**δι' ἑαυτοῦ** καθαρισμὸν τῶν ἁμαρτιῶν ποιησάμενος) (KJV)

1:3d. Shifting emphasis to the installation of "a son" as the messianic Son of promise, Barnabas united two messianic concepts: priest and king. The clause "*after he made* [ποιησάμενος] purification of sins" had an explicit temporal connection with what happened next. The messianic Son of promise "sat" (ἐκάθισεν) next to God. Whereas the "cleansing of sins" (καθαρισμὸν τῶν ἁμαρτιῶν) was a priestly function and symbolic of this son's work of redemption (cf. 9:11–14), the description of "a son" "seated at the right hand" (ἐκάθισεν ἐν δεξιᾷ) of God was a depiction of the inauguration of this son's ruling authority in God's heavenly court, a repeated phrase throughout Hebrews that echoed God's endorsement of this son's messiahship (cf. 1:3, 13; 8:1; 10:12). Both phrases underscored the appointment of this son's royal-priestly role whereby he had a *divinely appointed position of authority*.

"Seated at the Right Hand"

In ancient Near Eastern culture, the depiction of a king sitting at the right hand of a god symbolized a king's honored position with a particular god as well as his divine power to rule. In Canaanite literature, King Keret sat at the right hand of Baal in "The Palace of Baal" (Gibson, 1977, 61–62); and in Egyptian literature, Pharaoh Horemheb sat at the right hand of Horus (Keel, 1978, 263). Similar symbolism was used to describe the OT Davidite's honored position and divine authority to rule over the nation of Israel (Pss. 2, 72, 110; cf. 1 Chron. 17:4; 28:5; 2 Chron. 9:8; 13:8), a rulership that was totally dependent upon Yahweh (Pss. 80:17; 89:21). Whereas Yahweh was literally enthroned in heaven (Pss. 2:4; 9:7; 29:10; Isa. 6:1), the depiction of a Davidic king sitting at Yahweh's right hand (figuratively speaking) symbolized his honored position with Yahweh as well as his divine power to rule.

The one with whom the royal-priest sat, according to Barnabas, was "the Majesty on high" (τῆς μεγαλωσύνης ἐν ὑψηλοῖς). Barnabas's description of God as "Majesty" (μεγαλωσύνη) was somewhat unique, occurring only three times in NT writings (Heb. 1:3; 8:1; Jude 1:25). Yet in the Septuagint, "Majesty" served as a common designation of Yahweh's grandeur: his "Majesty" (Tob 13:9; Wis 18:24; Sir 2:18; 44:2), his "greatness" (Deut. 32:3; Pss. 144[145]:3, 6; 150:2; 1 Esdr 4:46; Tob 13:4), and "the greatness" of his deeds or power (2 Sam. 7:21; 1 Chron. 17:19; cf. Sir 18:5). Later in Hebrews 8:1 when "the Majesty on high" was restated and expanded, the presence of an "appointed" (καθίσταται) royal-priest at the Majesty's right hand revealed a significant implication (8:2–3). Here in verse 3d, however, Barnabas merely foreshadowed a theme to be developed about this messianic Son's exaltation as royal-priest (cf. 4:14–16; 6:19–20; 7:17, 26; 10:19–22).

TEXTUAL ANALYSIS: Conflicting Text Critical Reading: 1:4

Stylistic Issue: Although the variant has minimal manuscript support ($\mathfrak{P}^{46}$ B), whenever "angel" (ἀγγέλος) is used in the body of the text, it is anarthrous (2:2, 5, 16; 12:22; 13:2). Only when introducing OT quotes does the author use an article (1:5, 7, 13). It seems a scribe added the article due to the similar appearances in the immediate context. The variant is the preferred reading (Bateman, 1997, 215–16).

"Baal with Thunderbolt" stele preserved in the Louvre Museum, Paris, France. Courtesy of Jastrow (public domain).

txt. "by becoming so much better than **the** angels" (τοσούτῳ κρείττων γενόμενος **τῶν** ἀγγέλων) (ASV, KJV, NET, NIV, NRSV)
var. "by becoming so much better than angels (τοσούτῳ κρείττων γενόμενος ἀγγέλων) (ESV, NRSV)

1:4. In correlation (τοσούτῳ) with this son's inaugurated rule as royal-priest, there came an inherited messianic title. As messianic "heir" (κληρονόμον, v. 2b), this son "inherited a name" (κεκληρονόμηκεν ὄνομα, v. 4b). Not only was he an "appointed heir of all things," but he had inherited a name unlike any celestial being in God's heavenly court (Bateman, 1997, 360 n. 35; Bateman, 2012, 124). Though there is a somewhat abrupt shift to angels (e.g., celestial "sons of God"), this was a rather significant differentiation for the first-century Jewish reader because angels also spoke for God (Dan. 10:1–12:13; Zech. 1:9–15; Tob 12:11–15; Jub. 1:27, 29; 2:1; Luke 1:11–13, 28–33). Yet, unlike the description "sons of God," the word "son" (υἱος) had been a messianic depiction in 2 Samuel 7 and Psalm 2 and later a messianic title in Second Temple texts (Bateman et al. 2012, 303–29). Barnabas's parallel lines (chiastic structure A and A') underscored the Son's superiority in a twofold manner. Whereas he was described as God's superior spokes*man* in verse 2a, here in verse 4 his inherited name was "distinctive" (BDAG, s.v. "διάφορος" 1, p. 239) from that of the "sons of God" who also spoke for God. This Son was without equal (Bateman, 1997, 361 n. 37). In the next preaching unit, Barnabas employed the use of "son" (υἱος) as a title for God's messianic Son of promise as a way to distinguish him from the celestial "sons of God." Eventually, the messianic Son of promise would be described as a royal-priest *after* the order of Melchizedek (cf. 5:6, 10; 7:17, 21). Yet here, Barnabas drew attention from times past when God spoke through many prophets, to a new era where God spoke through a single divinely appointed, divinely related, and divinely authoritative spokes*man* to whom had been given a name superior to even the celestial "sons of God."

Royal-Priest

The designation "royal-priest" is in keeping with the theological contribution of Hebrews—namely, that Jesus is a royal-priest in the order of Melchizedek (5:5–6; 7:1–28). Yet the aspect of this royal-priesthood during this present era differed from royal-priests in the previous era. Prior to 586 B.C., Davidic kings functioned primarily as a king over Israel, though they also performed some functions of a priest (Merrill, 1993, 50–61; Merrill, 1987, 263–67). So, while David and his decedents performed some priestly functions, their predominate role was that of ROYAL-priest. In this present age, however, the messianic Son of promise rules as king but functions primarily as priest. Thus, he is a royal-PRIEST. This is not to suggest that Jesus has no authority (see Heb. 1:5–14; 3:2–6; cf. Eph. 5:23; Col. 1:18–20). The designation, however, distinguishes the different emphasis between the First Temple period and this present age. Kurianal (2000, 158) argues that in Hebrews 7:26–28, "the two titles of Jesus, High Priest and Son are inseparably connected as the identity of the new High Priest." The Son will rule eventually as ROYAL-PRIEST.

Excursus on Psalm 110

While Barnabas recontextualizes Psalm 110 as an application to Jesus (Heb. 1:3, 13; 5:6; 7:17, 21; 8:1), it helps to understand the psalm in its original context.

Psalm 110: Like Psalm 2, Psalm 110 (109 LXX) is a royal psalm. References to "my Lord" (v. 1), and the kingly diction—"sit at my right hand" (vv. 1, 5), "a footstool for your feet" and "scepter" (v. 2)—support a royal psalm motif. Thus, the two psalms are linked conceptually.

Overview: Three major sections are evident: David spoke of Yahweh's oracle to his lord giving him authority to rule and a promising of victory over his enemies (vv. 1–2); David prophesied his lord's marching into a holy war, leading his army as priest-king (vv. 3–4); and David prophesied his lord's victory in battle against his enemies (vv. 5–7).

Message: The psalm's message is one of assurance to Israel's king. Yahweh assured his vice-regent (vv. 1a, 5) that when he, as appointed priest-king (vv. 1–2, 4), is in the midst of holy war (110:3), Yahweh would procure for him victory over all his enemies (v. 1b, 5–7).

Central Point: The royal psalm's central point is to show God's support for his Davidic viceregent, David's lord. Psalm 110:1 captures the essence of the entire psalm. Yahweh gave David's lord authority to rule and a promise of victory over his enemies. Yet Psalm 110:4 identifies the nature of this Davidite's kingship. His kingship would be one of a royal-priest in the order of Melchizedek.

Ambiguities of the Psalm: Since Psalm 110 is quoted or alluded to at least twenty times in the NT, many automatically classify the psalm as directly prophetic, especially since this is the traditional view. Thus, the traditional view limits the referent to Jesus Christ. However, several historical options exist concerning the psalm's time frame, speaker, and recipient. The most viable option is that David spoke the psalm (Mark 12:36; Luke 20:42–44; Acts 2:34–35; Matt. 22:43–44) to Solomon when David freely handed over his kingship to Solomon (1 Kings 1:32–35, 43–45; 1 Chron. 28:1–8; 29:20–25). It seems reasonable to suggest that the psalm may have been initially used for the coronation of David's son, Solomon. Certainly, if Psalm 110 is applied to a Davidic king like Solomon, it would seem even more reasonable to apply the psalm to one who is greater than Solomon, a great and long-awaited Davidic Messiah.

Applications to an Eschatological Messiah: Psalm 110 is not quoted in Second Temple literature. It is, however, alluded to in 11QMelchizedek and *The Testament of Job*. Both appear to retain the conceptual sense of the psalm concerning a king's rule and a royal-priest's victory over his enemies. Unlike the original sense of meaning for Psalm 110, both elevate rulership to include the cosmic realm. While 11QMelchizedek emphasizes Psalm 110's concept of a warrior king-priest who is victorious over his cosmic enemies, *The Testament of Job* emphasizes the authority of Job to rule on earth as well as in the heavenlies. Although neither source explicitly speaks of a Davidic messiah, 11QMelchizedek alludes to a Davidic king through the conceptual use of Psalm 110 as well as the symbolic use of the Melchizedek figure.

THEOLOGICAL FOCUS

The exegetical idea (unlike in times past when God spoke through many prophets, God had spoken in this new era through a single divinely appointed, divinely related, and divinely authoritative spokes*man*, "a son," to whom had been given a name superior to even that of the celestial sons of God) leads to this theological focus: In this new era, God speaks to people through a new and superior spokes*man*, Jesus.

In terms of theological themes in this preaching unit, the core point has a twofold emphasis. First, God communicates with people. And while his manner of communication has varied through various people throughout the ages, in this new era he has chosen to communicate through one person, the messianic Son of promise. And while the continuity between the past and current era is God's voice being heard through many good spokes*men*, God's one and only spokes*man* in this new era has a heightened sense of relevance (1:1–2a; 2:2a, 4; cf. 3:7–19). Second, there is a tremendous and unmistakable christological emphasis in these verses about God's one and only spokesman. There is no mistaking Barnabas's descriptive stress on Jesus as having a divine appointment, a divine relationship, and a divine authority as God's spokes*man*.

PREACHING AND TEACHING STRATEGIES

Exegetical and Theological Synthesis

What is clear in Hebrews 1:1 is that even though God had spoken in the past through many good people, in this new era God speaks through a superior spokesman, Jesus. Throughout the Roman Empire, orators were abundant. In Judaea, Jewish religious leaders were arguing for independence from Rome, while in Rome, political leaders demanded Jewish subjugation. But in Hebrews 1:1, Barnabas makes it perfectly clear: Jesus is better than all other orators.

What is more nuanced is Jesus's *description,* or perhaps we might say his *credentials.* His identity is expressed in one of the most robust christological sections in all of Scripture, a passage that can only be understood against the backdrop of his messianic role as royal-priest as appointed by his Father. He is God's messianic heir (v. 2a) and messianic royal-priest (v. 3). So, the challenge in preaching verses 1–4 is to make much of Jesus's superiority and identity while making some explicit application.

Let us think for a minute about this phrase in verse 2: "in these last days he has spoken to us." The shocking emphasis is that God *has* spoken. However, God's single spokes*man* differs from his previous spokes*men* because the one through whom he has spoken these days is superior to everyone else. This emphasis that God has spoken through Jesus allows for some distinct advantages due to his credentials as God's divinely appointed, divinely related, and his divinely authoritative ruling role in God's presence.

Preaching Idea

Tuning out the many makes it possible to hear the one and only voice that *really* matters.

Contemporary Connections

Is it true?

Is it true that there are many voices in our world today that tend to drown out Jesus? Yes, it seems so. Stop and think about the many voices demanding our attention today. Many are well-intended voices. For instance, we have voices expressing concern for our physical well-being such as dentists and hygienists saying we must brush our teeth twice a day and floss at least once a day. There are physicians and nutritionists challenging traditional medicine for a more food-based approach to treating preventable diseases and for a healthier lifestyle. We have political voices challenging our cultural and societal ideals and way of thinking and living. We have social media voices demanding our attention.

As followers of Jesus, we have many voices expressing concern for our spiritual well-being. These concerns may come in the form of worship musicians. Spiritual concern certainly comes in the form of sermons. Turn in to Christian radio, podcasts, or videos online today and it's like going to an all-you-can-eat spiritual restaurant. Our lists could be unending.

Now what?

So, what are we to do? Should I turn off our favorite Christian radio station? Should I discontinue listening to Christian worship music? Should I tune out my favorite radio preacher? No. That is not what is being suggested. Yet it's important that we be discerning about the voices to which we give an ear.

Throughout the twentieth and now twenty-first century, many people have claimed to speak for God. While some have been good, others have not been so good. We might agree that the founder of the Peoples Temple, Jim Jones, was a not a good spokesman for God because he eventually led 918 people to mass murder-suicide in November 1978 at Jonestown, Guyana. Yet we might agree that the American evangelist Billy Graham, who ran crusades from 1947 to 2005, was a good spokesman for God who eventually led an estimated 3.2 million people to respond to an invitation to follow Jesus. Yet even good evangelical speakers can drown out God's ultimate voice for today's follower of Jesus. Hebrews 1:1–4 drives home a simple truth about God's ultimate spokesman worthy of our attention today. Discernment of twenty-first-century preachers, teachers, and musicians is important. Do they represent God's one spokesman who *really* matters?

Remember that the exaltation of Jesus is itself an application. There are some passages of Scripture to which the immediate response is simply to fall on one's face in ever-loving wonder and awe. This, along with passages such as John 1:1–5, Colossians 1:15–18, and Philippians 2:5–11, is that kind of passage. The application is simply to trust Jesus more than everything else because he is exalted above all things as God's appointed royal-priest, the Messiah. In other words, if Jesus really is to be exalted, if this is *real*, then it is not impractical to call people to exalt Jesus. Those who do not exalt Jesus are avoiding reality, even if they don't know it. They are living delusional, fake lives.

Extend the thought of Barnabas to include all things. The idea is that Jesus is better than prophets and angels. Notice that his "betterness" extends to all things (vv. 2–3). Jesus, our messianic royal-priest is better than everything else. This truth has great application in so much as we have a tendency to daily place our trust in so many things other than Christ Jesus.

Remember that the application of chapter 1 is in chapter 2. Sermons on 1:1–4 and 1:5–14 set up a coming application in Hebrews 2. In Hebrews 1:1–4, Jesus is God's ultimate spokesman. As chapter 1 is preached, people should be drawn to listen to messages, teachings, and music about Jesus by virtue of his exalted position as one who is divinely appointed, divinely related, and divinely authoritative rule in God's presence.

Creativity in Presentation

One suggestion for using the example under "Preaching Pointers" would be to show a movie trailer for *A Beautiful Mind* (directed by Ron Howard, 2001). In this film, a mathematician named John Nash (played by Russell Crowe) struggles with hearing voices. As the story unfolds, you begin to catch a glimpse into the life of John Nash, his private drowning in a world of voices, and his struggle to discern the voice of reality amidst the voices in his head. Dr. Nash had to learn to tune out the many voices so as to listen to the relevant one. Another suggestion might be the use of YouTube videos that focus attention on how to get people to listen. Hebrews 1:1–4 reveals what God has done to get his people to listen to his son, Jesus.

Often our concern is with a person's credentials. When introducing a speaker, it's not unusual to present the person's credentials. If the speaker is a lecturer, the introduction often includes the degrees earned, the schools attended, the current profession, books written, etc. Present a sample of a person's credentials and then compare those with the credentials of the son in verses 2b–3. Finding credentials for an individual can be quickly located on a Wikipedia page, like the Wikipedia page for Chuck Swindoll (see below).

Perhaps a personal illustration might be used. My (Herb's) wife, Cindy, has given her ear to a credentialed nutritional doctor and favors reading experts who work in the area of nutrition regularly. In the past, she listened to her more traditional physician, but today she's quite intent on hearing what the nutritional doctors have to say in order to rid her life of prescription drugs—so much so that it has affected what she eats and how she lives. God gets our attention about the one and only voice that matters today by giving a somewhat thorough introduction to the Son. You might even ask: What does it take to get your attention?

The point you want to get across is simply this: God speaks to us today through a superiorly credentialed spokes*man*. Tuning out the many makes it possible to hear the one and only voice that *really* matters.

- Tune in to God's divinely appointed son (vv. 1–3a).
- Tune in to God's divinely related son (v. 3b).
- Tune in to God's divine authority figure (v. 4)

Charles Rozell Swindoll	
Born	Charles Rozell Swindoll October 18, 1934 (age 81) El Campo, Wharton County Texas, USA
Pen name	Chuck Swindoll
Occupation	Pastor, author, educator
Nationality	American
Genre	Inspirational, Christian living
Notable works	*The Grace Awakening* (1990), Swindoll's New Testament Insights commentary series
Notable awards	Evangelical Christian Publishers Association's Jordon Lifetime Achievement Award, 1997
Spouse	Cynthia Ann Parker (m. 1955)
Children	Curt, Charissa, Colleen, and Chuck Jr.

DISCUSSION QUESTIONS

1. What does it mean that Jesus is the "heir of all things"?

2. What do these verses teach us about the relationship of the Father to the Son?

3. Does this passage remind you of other passages that deal with the exaltation of Jesus?

4. What does it mean that Jesus "sat down"? What does that suggest about what he is doing now? (See Rom. 8:34.)

5. Based on the fact that God has spoken, is there a natural responsibility on our part? Does this passage imply that we are guilty of willfully ignoring the voice of God as he has spoken through Jesus?

Hebrews 1:5–14

EXEGETICAL IDEA

In explaining the distinction between "a Son" and "the sons of God" (e.g., angels), God spoke of the Son's prominent relationship with him, contrasted the Son's royal and creator status with that of the celestial sons of God, and promised the Son—whom angels served—a future absolute authority over all creation.

THEOLOGICAL FOCUS

The messianic Son of promise has been exalted to a prominent relationship with God, with a superior status to that of angels, and with a promise of absolute authority over all of creation that distinguishes him from all celestial sons of God.

PREACHING IDEA

Distinctions make a difference.

PREACHING POINTERS

Whereas Hebrews 1:1–4 underscored Jesus as God's superior spokes*man*, verses 5–14 provided the reason why he was God's preferred spokes*man* over the angels. The first-century Jewish community had a high regard for angels as powerful beings (Dan. 12:1; 1 En. 6:1–4a; 7:1–6; 1QM). Angels also delivered messages to people from God (Dan. 9:21; Luke 1:11, 26). Yet, Jesus was not an angel. So, distinguishing Jesus from the angels was important. Jesus was not to be confused with angelic beings, even though he too was sent by God.

In Hebrews 1:1–4, the emphasis for today addresses the question, what voices do we listen to that are inferior to the Son of God? However, in Hebrews 1:5–14 the emphasis is a cosmic hierarchy. Prophets spoke with God's authority, angels spoke with God's authority, but in this era Jesus speaks with God's authority. He is the new and developed thought of God. Or, to say it more precisely, the prophets were leading to Jesus who affirmed and completed their message (Matt. 5:17). Do we exhibit a hierarchy of spokesmen or spokeswomen when it comes to preachers and teachers? Who are the current or recorded voices to whom we might listen? Alistair Begg? Tony Evans? Timothy Keller? Thomas Long? Otis Moss III? John MacArthur? John Piper? Andy Stanley? Chuck Swindoll? Barbara Brown Taylor? Today's "celebrity" preachers are endless. But in Hebrews 1:5–14, the general assumption is a high view of God's voice by way of Scripture in order to establish the authority of the messianic Son of promise, Jesus. Barnabas defers to Scripture to reinforce Jesus as God's one and only exalted Son. There is no other. Distinctions make a difference.

DISTINCTIONS BETWEEN "A SON" AND "THE SONS OF GOD" (1:5–14)

LITERARY STRUCTURE AND THEMES (1:5–14)

In Hebrews 1:5–14, Barnabas explained why the messianic Son of promise's inherited name was unequaled among the celestial "sons of God" by way of three divinely spoken statements. First, God spoke about the Son's prominent relationship with God (vv. 5–6). Second, God spoke about his prominent relationship with the Son in contrast to that of the angels, whereby on the one hand angels are created servants, while on the other hand the Son was divine creator (vv. 7–12). Finally, God had spoken about his prominent relationship with the Son in connection with God's promise of an absolute ruling authority over all things, while celestial "sons of God" (e.g., angels) served the messianic Son of promise (vv. 13–14).

Barnabas's major theme was about the messianic Son of promise who ruled in God's presence, who had created the universe, whose rule and existence was eternal, and who had been declared to be God by God the Father.

- ***The Son's Prominent Relationship with God (1:5–6)***
- ***The Son's Prominent Relationship with God Contrasted (1:7–12)***
- ***The Son's Prominent Relationship with God as Promised (1:13–14)***

EXPOSITION (1:5–14)

Before, during, and after the time of Herod the Great (ca. 73–4 B.C.), expectations of a coming messianic figure were undeniable, as was the belief in a structured celestial world of angels. Yet, details about an anticipated Messiah figure[1] and the role of angels were sketchy. On the one hand, some Jews believed that the "son of David" *par excellence* would be like Solomon in that he would have the power to cast out demons (cf. 11Q11; 11QApPs[a]), be a leader of a future war (1Q28b 5:20–29; 4QM), and rule over the nations with priestly assistance (4Q161 ff7–10iii 11–15). On the other hand, angels were a featured subject in 1 Enoch. Not only was the fall of angels presented but also a hierarchy of the angelical world (Bateman et al., 2012, 102–04; cf. Bateman, 2015[17], 19–24). Another favorite book in the Jewish Apocrypha that features angels was Tobit. Tobit was a man who was visited by, protected by, and guided by the archangel Raphael (cf. Luke 1:11–20; 26–35). So, angels were important messengers who spoke and acted on behalf of God and were significant figures of the Jewish theistic worldview.

In Hebrews 1:5–14, Barnabas cleared up his readers' sketchy understanding of the Messiah and angels. He eliminated any confusion that may have existed between angelic messengers ("sons of God") and the messianic spokes*man* ("a son") for God. Despite the fact that Scripture (HB and LXX) and other nonbiblical Jewish literature never presented the Messiah as the creator of angels or as divine (Bateman et al., 2012, 322–25), Barnabas

1 For a presentation of what Jewish people believed about the coming Messiah, see "Expectations of a King" (Bateman et al. 2012, 211–330).

underscored the distinctions between "a son" and the "sons of God." God spoke of the Son's prominent relationship with him, contrasted the Son's royal and creator status with that of the celestial sons of God, and promised the Son—whom angels served—a future absolute authority over all creation.

The Son's Prominent Relationship with God (1:5–6)

Unlike the way in which he addressed angels, God spoke explicitly of the Son as his chosen messianic Son of promise with whom he had entered into a prominent relationship and to whom angels paid homage.

1:5. Barnabas's opening reason (γάρ, "for") for why "a son" and the name "Son" he inherited (vv 14) was superior to angels came from God himself. God "spoke" (εἶπέν) of this son as his messianic Son of promise (chiastic structure line A). The content of this divine proclamation was found in two quotes from Hebrew Scripture: Psalm 2:7 and 2 Samuel 7:14. God said to the son, "You are my son" (Υἱός μου εἶ σύ, ἐγὼ σήμερον γεγέννηκά σε) from Psalm 2:7. Psalm 2 spoke originally of a king's entrance into a unique relationship with God at his enthronement as King over Israel (cf. vv. 2, 6, 11–12; cf. Futato, 2007, 182; Ross, 2011, 1:197–214). Barnabas's linking (καί) of Psalm 2:7 with 2 Samuel 7:14, however, revealed God's fulfillment of a promise he made with David that underscored the permanency of David's future heir (cf. 2 Sam. 7:15–17; Bateman et al. 2012, 59–74, 76–83). During the Second Temple period, Jews believed a human successor to David's throne would arise (Bateman *e*t al., 2012, 211–329; Bateman, 2012, 93). Yet the superiority of the name or title "Son" (υἱός) was not limited to one's ordination to rule, because angelic beings were also granted ruling authority (cf. Deut. 32:8; Dan. 10:13; Jude 9; 1 En. 20:1–8). Rather, the superiority of the name "Son" (υἱός) resided in the fact that it was a designation or title that pointed to the fulfillment of God's promise to David. This "son" was God's ultimate messianic Son of promise.

VARIOUS PORTRAITS OF THE MESSIAH IN SECOND TEMPLE LITERATURE
(Bateman et al., 2012, 211–329; Bateman, 2012, 93)

	Hasmonean Period			Herodian Period				
Humanity (lineage)	Early 150–125 B.C.	Mid 125–75 B.C.	Late 75–50 B.C.	Pre 50–30 B.C.	Early 30–1 B.C.	Mid A.D. 1–30	Late A.D. 30–68	Post A.D. 68–135
Davidic Scion	*Jubilees*, *T. Judah*	1Q28 1Q28a 4Q266 = CD	4Q161 *PssSol*	1QM 4Q246 4Q376	4Q174 4Q252 4Q285		4Q369	*4 Ezra* *2 Baruch*
Human	*Jubilees*, *T. Judah*	1Q28 1Q28a 1Q28b 4Q266 = CD 4Q521	4Q161 4Q382 4Q458 *PssSol*	1QM 4Q246 4Q376	4Q174 4Q252 4Q285		4Q369 4Q423	*4 Ezra* *2 Baruch*
Offspring			*PssSol*		4Q174 4Q252		4Q369	

VARIOUS PORTRAITS OF THE MESSIAH IN SECOND TEMPLE LITERATURE (Bateman et al., 2012, 211–329; Bateman, 2012, 93)								
Hasmonean Period				**Herodian Period**				
Authority (Leadership)	Early 150–125 B.C.	Mid 125–75 B.C.	Late 75–50 B.C.	Pre 50–30 B.C.	Early 30–1 B.C.	Mid A.D. 1–30	Late A.D. 30–68	Post A.D. 68–135
Military Leader	*Jubilees,* *T. Judah*	1Q28a 1Q28b 4Q266 = CD	4Q161 4Q382 4Q458 *PssSol*	1QM 4Q246 4Q376	4Q174 4Q285			*4 Ezra* *2 Baruch*
Political Leader	*Jubilees,* *T. Judah*	4Q266 = CD 4Q521	4Q161 4Q382 *PssSol*	4Q246	4Q174		4Q369 4Q423	*4 Ezra* *2 Baruch*
Righteous Leader/Judge	*Jubilees,* *T. Judah*	1Q28 1Q28b 4Q266 = CD	4Q161 4Q458 *PssSol*		4Q252 4Q285 *1 Enoch*		4Q369 4Q423	*4 Ezra* *2 Baruch*
Relationship with God (Chosen)	Early 150–125 B.C.	Mid 125–75 B.C.	Late 75–50 B.C.	Pre 50–30 B.C.	Early 30–1 B.C.	Mid A.D. 1–30	Late A.D. 30–68	Post A.D. 68–135
Endowed with God's Spirit	*T. Judah*	1Q28b	4Q161		4Q174			
Unique Relationship with God		1Q28a	*Pss Sol*	4Q246	4Q174		4Q369	
Interpreter of the Law	*Jubilees,* *T. Judah*	4Q266=CD			4Q252			*4 Ezra* *2 Baruch*

1:6. Barnabas continued (δέ, "and") his discussion about the messianic Son of promise by drawing specific attention to the Son's prominent relationship with God. The Son was God's "firstborn" (πρωτότοκος). "Firstborn" may reflect the literal idea of firstborn in time or it may speak figuratively of God's unique and honored relationship with the nation Israel or Davidic king. Here it identified the unique and honored relationship between God and the messianic Son of promise (lines A and A'). In Hebrews, this unique relationship began at the messianic Son's exaltation in the heavens (1:3, 5; cf. 8:1; 10:21).

Literal and Figurative Use of "Firstborn"

For the literal use of "firstborn" in Scripture, see Exodus 22:28, Luke 2:7, Colossians 1:18, Hebrews 11:28, and Revelation 1:5; the LXX genealogies; and Psalms of Solomon 18:4.

For the figurative use of "firstborn" as a description of God's unique relationship with Israel, see Exodus 4:22; Numbers 11:12; Hosea 2:1; 11:1, 3–4; Jeremiah 31:9; Sir 17:17–18; Romans 8:29; Colossians 1:15; Hebrews 1:6; and perhaps Hebrews 12:23.

This prominent relationship was underscored with God speaking (λέγει, "he says") once again. This time God spoke of angels worshipping. "Let them worship" (προσκυνησάτωσαν) expressed an attitude or gesture of one's complete dependence on or submission to a high authority (BGAD, s.v. "προσκυνέω," p. 882). "Worship" appears twice in Hebrews solely because of two citations: Deuteronomy 32:43 and Genesis 47:31 in Hebrews 1:8 and 11:21, respectively. In Hebrew Scripture, to "bow down" or "prostrate oneself" reflected a person's attitude when in the presence of someone who was in a position of honor or authority. For example, Abraham bowed before three guests (Gen. 18:2), Joseph and Moses bowed before father figures (Gen. 48:12; Exod. 18:7), Joseph's brothers bowed before him as ruler over Egypt (Gen. 42:6; cf. 2 Sam. 14:4, 22), and Balaam bowed down before an angelic being (Num. 22:31). It was most common, however, with worshipping (1) foreign gods (Exod. 32:8; Deut. 8:19, 29:26, 30:17) and (2) Yahweh (Gen. 22:5, 24:26, 47:31; Exod. 4:31, 33:8, 34:8; Deut. 26:10, 32:43 [cf. 4Q44]). In both the Septuagint and the Dead Sea Scroll version of Deuteronomy 32 (4QDeutq), verse 43 concluded Moses's song that exhorted the celestial "sons of God" (Hebrew: אֱלֹהִים ; Greek: υἱοὶ θεοῦ) to bow down in homage before Yahweh based upon his future vengeance and deliverance of Israel (Hebrew: בֵּן; Greek: υἱός) (Bateman, 1997, 142–44). Here in Hebrews 1:6, "angels" (ἄγγελοι) bowed down in homage to the messianic Son of promise (part of line B). Another portion of line B that undergirded the divinity of the Son appeared in the next contrast between the messianic Son of promise and the angels.

The Son's Prominent Relationship with God Contrasted (1:7–12)

In contrast to what God said to and about celestial sons of God, God spoke to the messianic Son of promise as his divine royal-priest, who ruled righteously, who created and now sustained creation, and who was eternal unlike angels.

1:7. God continued (καί, "and") speaking (λέγει, "he says") of his prominent relationship with the messianic Son of promise when he underscored angels doing the Son's bidding. This contrast (μὲν . . . δέ; vv. 7–8) was between the divine messianic Son of promise who ruled the celestial sons of God who served the Son. "On the one hand" (μέν) God spoke about celestial beings as inferior to their creator by means of a descriptive praise psalm, Psalm 104 (Averbeck, 2010, 141–46; Ross, 2016, 225).

> *GRAMMATICAL ANALYSIS:* "On the one hand" (μέν) and "On the other hand" (δέ)
> The construction "on the one hand" (μέν) and "on the other hand" (δέ) is a contrastive parallelism that distinguished what God said about the "sons of God" (= angels, v. 7) and what he said about the messianic Son of promise (vv. 8–9 and 10–12). Yet translations tend not to translate μὲν . . . δέ as "on the one hand" (μέν) and "on the other hand" (δέ) due to appearance of πρὸς before μέν and δέ. Consequently, πρὸς μέν and πρὸς δέ merely indicates a point of reference (BDAG, s.v. "πρός" 3eα, p. 875) and thereby seemingly ignored in English translations. Yet, the μὲν . . . δέ construction occurs some eighteen times in Hebrews (1:7–9; 3:5–5; 7:2, 5–6, 8, 18–19, 20–21, 23–24; 8:4; 9:1–5, 6–7, 23; 10:11–12, 33; 11:15–16; 12:9, 10, 11) with various meanings depending on what particle appears with the μὲν . . . δέ construction.

Originally, the psalmist praised Yahweh as the one who both created and provided for his created order. Verse 4 spoke specifically of Yahweh's active involvement as sovereign King in administrating the universe. However, in Hebrews 1:7, God redirected this verse to his messianic Son of promise as the creator and administrator of the universe (chiastic structure line B) and thereby underscoring once again the Son's deity (cf. 1:2c, 3 a, c). So, "on the one hand" (μέν) unlike in the

Hebrew Scripture where angels were described as "ministers" of Yahweh, here God spoke about celestial sons of God (e.g., angels) as belonging to the messianic Son of promise and who were commissioned for the Son's service (cf. 1:14; Bateman, 1997, 226–27).

Chiastic Structure for Hebrews 1:5–13

Barnabas validated each of God's statements through an artfully designed grouping of seven passages from the Hebrew Scriptures. Whereas the initial referent for four citations was a Davidic king (2 Sam. 7:14; Pss. 2:7, 45:6–7, 110:1), the initial referent for three others was Yahweh (Deut. 32:43; Pss. 102:25–27; 104:4). By means of this chiastic pattern, Barnabas conveyed a theological statement about the Son: he was God's divine messianic Son of promise.

A The Son's status as Davidic royal-priest (Ps. 2:7, 2 Sam. 7:14) (1:5)

B The Son's status as divine (Deut. 32:43, Ps. 104:4) (1:6–7)

C The Son's status as divine Davidic royal-priest (Ps. 45:6–7) (1:8–9)

B' The Son's status as divine (Ps. 102:25–27) (1:10–12)

A' The Son's status as Davidic royal-priest (Ps. 110:1) (1:13)

Verses 5 and 13 (lines A and A') presented one conceptual image to explain (γάρ) why this son was unequaled among the angels—he was Israel's ultimate Davidic royal-priest. Verses 6–7 and 10–12 (lines B and B') presented the other reason—he was divine. And though verses 6–7 conveyed conceptually the divine activities of the son, grammatically the "on the one hand . . . on the other hand" (μὲν . . . δέ) construction in verses 7–8 was emphasized below to contrast the angels with the messianic Son of promise. Yet the focal point of the chiastic structure occurs in verses 8–9 (line C) where the concept of Davidic sonship and deity unite into one figure (Bateman, 1997, 149–206; 1995, 11–27). Thus verses 5–13 provided God's reasons (γάρ) why the inherited name "Son" was superior to that of the celestial sons of God by underscoring the Son's prominent relationship with God, contrasting the Son's royal and creator status with that of celestial beings, and promising a future absolute authority over all things.

TEXTUAL ANALYSIS: Conflicting Text Critical Reading: 1:8

Theological/Exegetical Issue: Moving beyond the manuscript support *(𝔓[46] ℵ B),* αὐτοῦ appears to be the last of several deliberate interpretive changes to Psalm 44:8 (LXX) by the author of Hebrews, and it is the more difficult reading (Bateman, 1997, 130–35). Furthermore, in Hebrews 2:7, 3:2, 8:11, and 9:19, a scribe appears to have altered the text to bring it into conformity with the LXX. Although most translations prefer the text, as it is with Hebrews 11:4 and 12:3 below, there is strong evidence for questioning the decision and for favoring the variant.

txt. "and the righteous scepter is the scepter of **<u>your</u>** kingdom" (καὶ ἡ ῥάβδος τῆς εὐθύτητος ῥάβδος τῆς βασιλείας **<u>σου</u>**) (ASV, ESV, KJV, NET, NIV, NRSV)

var. "and the righteous scepter is the scepter of **<u>his</u>** kingdom" (καὶ ἡ ῥάβδος τῆς εὐθύτητος ῥάβδος τῆς βασιλείας **<u>αὐτοῦ</u>**) (NASB)

1:8–9. Barnabas continued his contrast (δέ, "but"; NET) that began in verse 7 with a focus on the manner in which God spoke about the Son. "On the other hand" (δέ, contra NET rendering), unlike what God had said about the angels, here God spoke about the Son (πρὸς δὲ τὸν υἱόν, "but of the son"). These verses are the focal point (chiastic structure line C) of Hebrews 1:5–14 (Bateman, 2001, 3–21). Barnabas heightened God's relationship with the Son over the angels from a royal wedding psalm, Psalm 45 [44 LXX]. Originally, the psalmist directed attention to a Davidic king (vv. 1–8) about to be married (vv. 9–15). Verses 6–7 of the psalm, addressed to the king, drew attention to two symbols of royalty. "Your throne" (ὁ θρόνος σου) typically symbolized a king's rule (2 Sam. 7:16; 1 Chron. 17:12, 22:10; 2 Chron. 7:18; 1 Kings 9:5), his authority (Ps. 122:5; cf. Prov. 20:8), and his right to *execute* judgment and to *maintain* justice (1 Kings 10:9, 2 Chron. 9:8). "Scepter of justice" (ἡ ῥάβδος τῆς εὐθύτητος ῥάβδος) symbolized protection of his subjects, prosperity, and relationship to God. It too symbolized the king's function as judge and administrator of his people (Olivier, 1979, 47–49). Just as God judged the people justly (Ps. 67:5; cf. Isa. 11:4), the Davidic king was also expected to judge justly. Here in Hebrews 1:8, the two phrases reinforce (1) the prologue's statement that "a son" had entered into his inheritance as viceregent (Heb. 1:2b, 3d), (2) his active rule as royal-priest over his kingdom, and (3) his function as a righteous judge over the people of his kingdom. These symbols of royalty appear elsewhere in Hebrews ("throne": 4:16, 8:1, 12:2; "scepter": 9:4, 25; 11:21).

While the idea of a messianic Son of promise may have been an expectation of many Jewish people during Barnabas's day, the idea that he would be divine was not. Calling a Davidic king "God" rarely occurred in Israel. Yet, here in this ancient poem, the psalmist spoke figuratively to a Davidic prince on his wedding day and referred to him as "O God" and "God, your God" (vv. 1, 7). Yet, is anyone in the Hebrew Scriptures referred to as "God"? Yes, it seems God said to Moses: "See I made you 'God' [אֱלֹהִים] to Pharaoh" (Exod. 7:1; cf. 4Q374 frag. 2.2.6).[2] Not that Moses was God but rather God-like before Pharaoh (NRSV, NIV, NET; cf. NASB). Similarly, the psalmist honored the Davidic viceregent as Yahweh's man through whom he received his authority to rule over Israel in a manner in keeping with how Yahweh himself ruled over the universe (Harris, 1984, 65–89; Ross, 2013, 57–80). Thus, Moses and the Davidic king were ideally to be God-*like* in their leading and ruling God's chosen people (cf. 3:1–6). Here in Hebrews 1:8, however, this messianic Son of promise was not merely metaphorically God-*like* but rather quite literally hailed as God in how he ruled. Furthermore, the "son's" love for righteousness (Ps. 45:7) was no longer hyperbolic language but rather reflective of reality. Jesus actually ruled in righteousness (1:3d; 1:8–9), and he would one day exercise that righteous rule over all creation (1:3b; cf. 2:8; Bateman, 2001, 3–21).

Messianic Surprises

While a human messianic military figure was anticipated, there is nothing in nonbiblical Jewish texts about
his virgin birth,
his suffering death,
his immediate resurrection,
his being literally eternal,
his ruling presence with God,
his cosmic rule, and
his literal divinity.

Another new attribute of the messianic Son of promise was his eternality. "Forever and ever" (εἰς τὸν αἰῶνα τοῦ αἰῶνος) occurs fifteen times in Hebrews (1:2, 8 [twice]; 5:6; 6:5, 20; 7:17, 21, 24, 28; 9:26; 11:3; 13:8, 21 [twice]). Originally, the phrase spoke of the temporal duration of a royal-priest's ruling authority or of a worshipper. For instance, "May the king live forever" was used of David (1 Kings 1:31) and of the Persian king Artaxerxes (Neh. 2:3). The phrase also appears for a worshipper, "I will sing forever" means "as long as I live" in Psalms 52:9; 115:18; 145:1 (Sandy, 2002, 98–101, cf. 42, 44, 45–46). Thus, "forever and ever" was a figurative expression that initially spoke of the

2 Whereas Exodus says, "I will make you God (אֱלֹהִים) to Pharaoh," 4Q375 provides a comparison: "and he made him like a God (הים לו לא) over the powerful ones, and a cause of reeling for Pharaoh" [Martínez and Tigchelaar, 2000, 2:741].

longevity of a monarch's life but perpetuated by the promise of children (2 Sam 7:11b–12, 14a, 16; 1 Par. [1 Chron.] 17:11–14; Ps. 132:11–12). So when David died, his body was buried and decayed (1 Kings 2:10; 2 Par. [2 Chron.] 29:26–28) as did David's successors. Yet, in Hebrews 1:8, the concept of "forever and ever" was no longer hyperbolic language but rather reflective of a literal reality. Psalm 45, when linked with Psalm 102 served to speak of the *eternal duration* of the messianic Son of promise (cf. Heb. 7:24–25; 13:8; cf. Acts 2:29–36; 13:36).

These contrasts became Barnabas's reason (an anaphoric διὰ τοῦτο) for God's anointing the messianic Son of promise "above his companions" (παρὰ τοὺς μετόχους). "Companions" (μετόχος) occurs five times in Hebrews (1:9; 3:1, 14; 6:4, 12:8) and once in Luke 5:7. It may refer to an everyday acquaintance or it may speak of a partner in the legal or moral sense. Although translated as "fellows" (KJV), "comrades" (RSV), "companions" (NASB, NIV, ESV), and "more than anyone else" (NLT), the term should not be understood to speak of an everyday acquaintance (cf. Eccl. 4:10 LXX). Here in Hebrews, the messianic Son of promise had been assigned a superior office as God's royal-priest over his angelic companions, who in response paid homage (1:6) to him and served (1:7, 14) him.

TEXTUAL ANALYSIS: Conflicting Text Critical Reading: 1:12

Exegetical Issue: As in verse 8, the author made interpretive an change to Psalm 44:8 (LXX) to both balance and heighten the transitory character of creation in contrast to the son. The text is preferred (Metzger, 1994, 593).

txt. "and **like clothing** they will be changed" (**ὡς ἱμάτιον** καὶ ἀλλαγήσονται) (ASV, ESV, KJV, NASB, NET, NIV, NRSV)

var. "and they will be changed" (καὶ ἀλλαγήσονται)

1:10–12. Barnabas continued (καί, "and") his reasoning with another quote from Scripture (HB LXX). God's prominent relationship with the messianic Son of promise over the angels (chiastic structure line B') was reinforced from a lament psalm, Psalm 102 [101 LXX] (Ross, 2016, 205–24). Originally, the psalmist spoke of the reassurance he found in Yahweh's sovereignty. Verses 25–27 reflected the particular comfort of the psalmist because he recognized that Yahweh's ruling authority was permanent and immutable. Here in Hebrews 1:10–12, Barnabas reapplied the psalm to the messianic Son of promise to underscore, once again, the Son's deity (cf. 1:2c, 3a, c, 7).

The phrases "you Lord laid the earth's foundation" and "the heavens are the works of your hands" were purposely place in parallel to draw attention to the simple fact that the Son was the creator of the world (cf. Heb. 1:2–3). Specific attention was given to the world's temporary condition. It "will grow old" (παλαιωθήσονται) referred to physical aging or "to declare or treat as obsolete." Similar language appears in Luke 12:33 and Hebrews 1:11 and 8:13. In the Septuagint, "to grow old" spoke literally of clothing that had lost its usefulness (Josh. 9:5, 13). In Psalm 102 [101 LXX], the verb was used comparatively of the earth that "will become old" or "will wear out" *like* a garment (cf. Isa. 51:6; 11QPsa frag. C 2:1–11). Whereas creation had a fleeting existence, Yahweh did not. The earth, unlike Yahweh, would grow old. Barnabas's reapplication of Psalm 102:25–27 (101:25–27 LXX) shifted the referent from Yahweh to the messianic Son of promise. The contrast (δέ, "but") in these verses between the anointed son (v. 9) and created order were unmistakable to the original readers in Rome. Whereas the earth "will fade away" (NLT), "will become old" (KJV, NRSV), "will grow old" (RSV, NET), or "will wear out" (NIV, NRSV, ESV), the divine messianic Son of promise would not. The Son was quite literally eternal, just like God (cf. 13:8).

The Son's Prominent Relationship with God as Promised (1:13–14)

Unlike angels, God announced the present authority of the messianic Son—whom angels served—and promised him a future absolute authority over all creation.

1:13. In his concluding statement, in which he quoted God, Barnabas made a final contrast (δέ, "but") between the messianic Son of promise and celestial "sons of God," based upon one more passage from the Scripture (HB LXX). He closed this string of quotations (chiastic structure line A') with another royal psalm, Psalm 110 (109 LXX). This psalm was first alluded to in Hebrews 1:3e. The quoted phrase "sit at my right hand" (κάθου ἐκ δεξιῶν μου) once again asserted the messianic Son's superior ruling authority comparable to that of the angels as well as to that of any previous Davidic monarch. His superiority manifested itself in that he was God's messianic Son of promise who quite literally ruled in God's presence (1:3b, 8:1, and 10:12) while at the same time alluded to this Son's future absolute rule (cf. 2:5–9).

The messianic Son's future role as royal-priest appeared in the latter part of Psalm 110:1 (109 LXX). The clause "until I make your enemies a footstool for your feet" underscored, for Barnabas, the messianic Son's patient rule. "Until I make your enemies" (ἕως ἂν θῶ) anticipated a future event (cf. Heb. 2:8–9). The figure of speech, "a footstool for your feet" (ὑποπόδιον τῶν ποδῶν σου), in Scripture (HB LXX) symbolized the complete subjugation of a conquered people (cf. Isa. 51:23; Josh. 10:24). Although the "enemies" were yet to be defined, Barnabas would address who they were in Hebrews 2 (e.g., the fallen angel Satan and death, vv. 14–15) where he once again underscored this tension between the messianic Son's current and future rule (vv. 8b–9a). Nevertheless, here in verse 13 Barnabas focused attention on the divine messianic Son of promise who ruled patiently while anticipating a future and complete subjugation of all things in this temporal universe to him (cf. 1:2).

> *TRANSLATIONAL ANALYSIS:* The preposition "until" (ἕως)
>
> Robertson (1934: 975–76, 643) points out that "most examples of ἕως deal with the future." And though ἕως may be used either as a conjunction (Matt. 2:9, 14:22, 5:25) or a preposition (Matt. 11:23, Acts 8:40), here in Hebrews 1:13 it introduced a conjunctive dependent clause (cf. Moule, 1984: 85). Syntactically, ἕως modifies the verb "sit" (κάθου). Though Jesus had a place of authority as God's messianic Son of promise sitting at God's right hand, there remained an aspect of that ruling authority yet to be handed over to him. Thus, the preposition drew attention to an already / not yet aspect of the messianic Son of promise's rule.

1:14. Barnabas concluded with a rhetorical question about angels that expected an affirmative answer (emphatic negative "not," οὐχί). Angels were indeed ministering spirits. The adjective, "ministering" (λειτουργικός) was part of a significant and favored word group that means "servant," "minister" or "one commissioned for service." Barnabas used this group of terms throughout Hebrews (cf. 1:7, 14; 8:2, 6; 9:21; 10:11). In fact, "ministering" (λειτουργικός) and "minister" (λειτουργός) were frequently used for both angels and people who had been commissioned for service on behalf of a superior. For instance, Moses (Josh. 1:1), Solomon (2 Chron. 9:4) Elisha (2 Kings 6:15), Ptolemy (3 Macc 5:5), Paul (Rom. 15:16), cultic priests serving in a temple (Josephus, *B.J.* 2.17.4 §417; *A.J.* 13.2.3 §55; cf. Dionysius Halicarnassus, *Ant. rom.* 2.22.2), and the archangel Michael (T. Abram 15:1; Philo, *Virt.* 72, 74) were all ministering agents on behalf of a superior (cf. *TDNT,* 4:229–31; *TLNT,* 2:378–84). Here in verse 14, "ministering" (λειτουργικά) described celestial "sons of God" as "ministers" for their superior: the messianic Son of promise (cf. 1:7; λειτουργός). The recipients of this angelic service, however, were those in Rome who followed Jesus.

THEOLOGICAL FOCUS

The exegetical idea (in explaining the distinction between "a Son" and the "sons of God" [e.g., angels], God spoke of the Son's prominent relationship with him, contrasted the Son's royal and creator status with that of the celestial sons of God, and promised the Son—whom angels served—a future absolute authority over all creation) leads to this theological focus: the messianic Son of promise has been exalted to a prominent relationship with God, with a superior status to that of angels, and with a promise of absolute authority over all of creation that distinguishes him from all celestial sons of God.

In terms of a theological theme in this preaching unit, the christological emphasis of this passage is unsurpassable. God has proclaimed "a son" as his messianic Son of promise (vv. 5–13). He is God's exalted messianic Son of promise who reigns eternally in God's presence (vv. 5, 7–8, 13). He is the one through whom God created the celestial sons of God who currently worship and serve the messianic Son of promise (vv. 6, 10–11, 14). So, he is God's messianic Son of promise who rules in God's presence, who has created the universe, whose rule and existence are eternal, and who has been declared to be God by God.

The outcome of this overwhelming Christology in verses 5–14 is the unmistakable contrast between "a son" and the "sons of God" often referred to as angels. Their description as "sons" is not to be confused with or linked to "the messianic Son of promise." The "sons of God" are not eternal gods but created beings who *worship* God the eternal messianic Son of promise, who *serve* the eternal messianic Son of promise, and who *are inferior* to the messianic Son of promise. This distinction between the messianic Son of promise and the celestial "sons of God" makes for a rather significant theological difference.

PREACHING AND TEACHING STRATEGIES

Exegetical and Theological Synthesis

Hebrews 1:1–4 underscores the authority of "the son." He is the last word. He is the one who is God's final authority on all things. Therefore, he has gained superiority to the angels (v. 4). The simple statement of the son's superiority in verse 4 is explained in the next section of verses 5–14 with the use of eight OT quotations: Psalm 2:7, 2 Samuel 7:14, Deuteronomy 32:43; Psalms 104:4: 45:6–7; Psalm 102:25–27, and finally Psalm 110.

At first blush, this long list of OT quotations in Hebrews 1:5–14 may seem odd. Yet, they are critically important. First, they are a wonderful example of the NT's use of the OT. At some point early in the sermon series, it will be critical to explain how the NT writers used and applied the OT. (See the list of options under "For Further Reading" at the end of this first division.) This will allow you to explain a bit of biblical theology regarding the compositional nature of Scripture or how all Scripture is wrapped in a divine drama that envelops the history of salvation. This would be a wonderful opportunity to teach people how Scripture relates to itself.

Second, the significance of these passages is what they say about Jesus himself. The string of passages begins with Psalm 2:7, a remarkable passage about the Lord putting his anointed above his enemies. The final passage is another use of Psalm 110, where all the enemies of Christ are on his footstool. So again, the spirit of the text is triumphal. No matter what people may think of Jesus of Nazareth, He is now the ruling King, with all the enemies at His feet. Thirdly, the texts between these two messianic bookends show how much superior "the Son" is to the angelic "sons of God." This, of course, will be the point of the sermon. However, be sure to capitalize on this opportunity to teach the nature of Scripture and the exaltation of "the Son," Jesus, who is the Christ.

Preaching Idea

Distinctions make a difference.

Contemporary Connections

What does it mean?

What does it mean that distinctions make a difference? The distinction in this text is not the originator of the message. In the case of the angels and of Jesus, the message comes from God. However, the distinction is authority. The message from Jesus is more authoritative than the angels for the reason that he is God's final word, not just a messenger. We move from messengers (plural) to one messenger (singular). This distinction makes a huge difference.

In the 1990s, a new technology was invented for home phone service called caller ID. Whenever the phone rang, this simple feature allowed you to look at the small screen on the handset and see who was calling. As hard as it is to imagine, before this feature was invented you simply would always have to answer the phone. It didn't matter if it was your mother or a salesperson, the first person you'd want to talk to or the last, your best friend or an annoying neighbor—you had to pick up the phone because you had no way to make a distinction. Fast-forward to today: we cannot conceive of not having this technology. What drives technology is human nature. In this case, before we answer the phone, we expect we can make a distinction between someone we want to talk to and someone we don't.

Is it true?

Is it true that distinctions make a difference? Yes. Back to our illustration: if there is someone we really don't want to talk to, we can always block the call. This not only ensures that we don't talk to them in that moment, but that we never have to take their call again! Again, what drives technology is human nature. We believe we have a right to know who is calling us. In fact, we probably wouldn't buy a phone that didn't have this technology. In the same way, rare as it may be today, if we received a letter from a trusted friend, we would open it. If the letter was from the IRS, we would open it. But if the letter was "junk mail," we would toss it. The letters could be of the same material—in theory, they could even have the same content—but we handle them differently based on the return address. Likewise, we open or delete an email or text message based on who sent it. The difference is the source. The source makes it authoritative or valuable.

Now what?

We know that in this life, distinctions make a difference. Now, what we must do is filter out all the messages that we hear and take note of the message that comes from God alone? In the United States alone, depending on the research source, more than 6 billion text messages are sent every day. That totals more than 2.27 trillion text messages a year! We receive many messages. Add to these social media feeds and email and we are constantly engaging messages. The challenge for a believer in this age is to listen to the voice of Jesus amid the noise of so many messages. How do we do this? Let's start with the obvious. We listen to the voices that are louder and the voices that are constant. A constant "news feed" of information is very powerful. We have to find creative ways to allow the Word of God to be "louder."

We can make the Word of God "louder" in any number of ways.

- Listen to Scripture. When we are driving, taking a walk, or working out, there is always time to listen to Scripture. There are dozens of apps that read the Word to us.
- Expose our children to Scripture. Our children are bombarded with information that they process. They will only think of the Word of God as one thing among the many if we do not work to

show them that the voice of God is distinct.

- Sing Scripture back to God on a regular basis.
- Memorize Scripture. Again, for those with a smart phone, there are great Scripture memory apps that help us do this. But writing verses on cards or purchasing a set of Scripture memory verse cards works too.
- Listen to great preachers. Preachers and teachers who teach and preach Scripture help us hear God's Word.
- Pray for your pastor. This one may seem less helpful, but the reality is that the pastor is responsible to God for what he teaches us. When we pray for him, we will find that when he steps into the pulpit, we are more sympathetic, more attentive, and more eager to hear what God has to say to us through him.

Creativity in Presentation

One way to show that distinctions make a difference is to exemplify differences with everyday household items. For instance, women in the audience will identify with the distinction between a kitchen whisk and an electric mixer or a broom and a vacuum cleaner. On the other hand, men might connect with the difference between an auger and a power drill or a hammer or power hammer. While some teenage girls will make the distinction between cool and not-so-cool clothing, teenage boys may focus attention on cars. Then, direct attention to how to choose a brand for clothing or cars or whatever we buy. What authoritative voice or sales pitch motivates a person's decision-making process?

Another way to show that distinctions make a difference is to have an older elementary or preteen student on the stage and blindfold the child. Then invite his mother along with five other women his mother's age on the stage. Then ask each women to say the child's name, starting with the other mothers and ending with the child's mother. The child will instinctively recognize his mother's voice. Remove the blindfold and, with just the mother and the child on the stage, press the metaphor a bit. Those in the audience will get a little emotional when you say that this child has heard his mother call his name hundreds of times. We could line a hundred other women up and have them call his name, but he would recognize his own mother's voice. Her voice is distinct to him, and in fact it carries more authority. The distinction is the relationship. In the same way, Jesus alone is ours. He is the one who has called us to himself and he alone carries the authority of the Father.

The point you want to get across is simply this: distinctions make a difference between Jesus and the angels. One approach to an outline for this text would be as follows:

- Jesus is worshipped; the angels are worshippers (vv. 5–6).
- Jesus is Creator; the angels are created (vv. 7–12).
- Jesus is the promised Son; angels are servants (vv. 13–14).

DISCUSSION QUESTIONS

1. How many OT passages did Barnabas use in Hebrews 1:5–13 to demonstrate Jesus's superiority over angels? Can you list them?

2. What does Hebrews 1:5–14 say about angels?

3. What reasons does God provide in Hebrews 1:5–13 to support the distinction between Jesus and angels?

4. How do angels serve Jesus in Hebrews 1:14?

5. How does knowing about this distinction between Jesus and angels change or affect your thinking about angels?

Hebrews 2:1–4

EXEGETICAL IDEA

In his warning to concentrate on and listen to God's revelation about the messianic Son of promise, Barnabas recalled the physical punishment the exodus generation received when they defied God's revelation given through a myriad of celestial "sons of God," as a form of comparison about God's future punishment for those who would reject God's most recent revelation about the messianic Son of promise through whom God had spoken, eyewitnesses confirmed, and whose message God endorsed.

THEOLOGICAL FOCUS

God will punish any person who defies his revelation, especially those who reject his recent revelation about his messianic Son of promise through whom God has spoken, whom eyewitnesses confirmed, and whose message God endorsed.

PREACHING IDEA

Our focus determines our future.

PREACHING POINTERS

Hebrews 2:1–4 represents the conclusion to Hebrews 1. If Jesus was both superior to the prophets and to the angels, Barnabas needed to warn his readers not to lose sight of the message about Jesus. This was Barnabas's first of several stern warnings. How this passage is approached sets the tone for the other warning passages that follow. In order to drive the point home, Barnabas used a word picture of "slipping away." However, as we will see, he was not commanding them to keep from slipping; he was commanding them not to lose focus that will cause them to slip away. This was a significant difference. It was Jesus who kept them from slipping away, therefore Barnabas focused on him. The original audience would appreciate the strong historical precedent for focusing on the words of angels and of prophets. They would have understood how God kept people accountable for listening to their words. Now, God's greater spokes*man* had spoken. Therefore, the Roman followers of Jesus were expected to focus on what God said about Jesus.

Today, people may or may not listen to what a preacher is saying. In many people's minds, the preacher may or may not have authority. One reason is that we preachers have, perhaps unwittingly, presented ourselves as one voice among many that can demand attention. This, coupled with the reality that those who consider themselves "active" in the faith attend church only part-time, gives them the impression that focusing on Jesus is optional. This compounded indifference to the spoken word makes the warning of 2:1–4 more relevant today than ever. If we lose focus we will slip away. Our focus determines our future.

GOD'S RECENT REVELATION (2:1–4)

LITERARY STRUCTURE AND THEMES (2:1–4)

Like Hebrews 1:1–4, the opening verses (2:2–4) are a skillfully constructed sentence (a period). This statement, however, compares the message delivered through the angels (e.g., Mosaic covenant) to the new one delivered through the messianic Son of promise (e.g., new covenant, cf. 8:7–13; 9:15). The basis for Barnabas's warning is the message about the messianic Son of promise written about in chapter 1. People who professed to know the messianic Son of promise were first warned to concentrate on and listen to the messianic Son of promise (v. 1). As the basis of comparison, Barnabas recalled the exodus generation's rejection of God's revelation given at Mount Sinai, with God's future eternal punishment if anyone were to reject God's most recent revelation about the messianic Son of promise (vv. 2–3a). Finally, Barnabas drew attention to the verbal confirmation and divine endorsement about the messianic Son of promise (vv. 3b–4).

Barnabas's major themes in Hebrews 2:1–4 stressed God's dealings with disobedience and God's communication with his people.

- ***The Warning to Concentrate and Listen (2:1)***
- ***Recalling the Exodus Generation's Rejection (2:2–3a)***
- ***Verbal Confirmations and Divine Endorsements (2:3b–4)***

EXPOSITION (2:1–4)

When Barnabas wrote to the Jewish Christians in Rome during the mid-60s, there was a rebellion against Rome germinating in Judaea, one about which Jude warned believers to avoid (Bateman, 2015[17]). Needless to say, the OT wreaks of rebellion and God's punishment of the disobedient. So, there was a pattern clearly established in Scripture (HB LXX) and Jewish writings about rebellion and divine punishment that Barnabas wished to pause and underscore before advancing his discussion about the messianic Son of promise.

Rebellion in the Old Testament

Numerous examples of rebellion and punishment appear in the OT: the antediluvian events (Gen. 6:5–7), the tower of Babel (Gen. 11:1–9), the worship of the golden calf at Mount Sinai (Exod. 32:1–35), the disbelief and rebellion at Kadesh Barnea (Num. 13:26–14:35), the disobedience of Achan at Jericho (Josh 7:1–26), the repeated disobedience during the period of the Judges (Judg. 3:12–14; 4:1; 6:1–6; 10:6–9; 13:1), the rebellion of the northern kingdom of Israel (Hos. 10:1–2; 11:1–2, 5–7; Amos 2:6–8; 3:1–2, 10–15), and the rebellion of the southern kingdom of Judah (Hab. 1:1–11).

Here in Hebrews 2:1–4, Barnabas interrupted his exposition about "the Son" with this pastoral application (2:1–4). It was Barnabas's first of five emotive warning passages in Hebrews.[1] He warned his readers to concentrate on and listen to God's revelation about the messianic Son of promise (v. 1) by recalling the physical punishment the exodus generation received when they defied God's revelation given through a myriad of celestial "sons of

1 H. W. Bateman IV, "Introducing the Warning Passages in Hebrews: A Contextual Orientation" in *Four Views on the Warning Passages in Hebrews*, 23–85; ed. H. W. Bateman IV (Grand Rapids: Kregel, 2007).

God" as a form of comparison about God's future punishment for those who rejected God's most recent revelation about the messianic Son of promise (vv. 2–3a) while underscoring God's message spoken by the messianic Son of promise, confirmed by eyewitnesses and endorsed by God (vv. 3b–4).

Warning Passages in Hebrews
Hebrews 2:1–4
Hebrews 3:7–4:13
Hebrews 5:11–6:12
Hebrews 10:19–39
Hebrews 12:14–29

For other views, see Bateman, 2012, 149.

The Warning to Concentrate and Listen (2:1)

Barnabas warned his readers to concentrate on and listen to God's message about his messianic Son of promise.

2:1. Barnabas's opening statement "for this reason, it is necessary . . . to pay attention" (διὰ τοῦτο δεῖ . . . προσέχειν ἡμᾶς) was rather significant. The typical formulaic phrase "for this reason" (διὰ τοῦτο; NASV) or "therefore" (KJV, RSV, NET) referred back to and thereby drew a deduction from Hebrews 1. The quasi-impersonal subject "it is necessary . . . to pay attention to" (δεῖ . . . προσέχειν) conveyed a logical necessity for all followers of Jesus. They must *concentrate on* what God had spoken through the Son (1:2a), about the Son (1:2b–4), and to the Son (1:5–13). Thus, Barnabas created a logical response to the fact that the divine royal-priest was God's appointed messianic Son of promise to whom angels offer worship and service (Westcott, 1984, 36; Pfitzner, 1997, 56–58; Attridge, 1989, 63; Lane, 1991a, 36–37).

There is, however, a phrase unique to Hebrews worthy of some discussion: "lest we slip away" (μήποτε παραρυῶμεν (KJV) or "lest we *drift* away" (NASB, RSV, NIV, ESV, NET, NLT). The latter understanding was frequently understood as having a nautical sense (Westcott, 1984, 37; Bruce, 1964, 27; Pfitzner, 1997, 56–58). The alternative rendering "slip away" (KJV), however, is more fitting in light of a parallel in Proverbs 3. Immediately following twenty verses of instruction in Proverbs 3:1–20, the teacher in Proverbs exhorted: "Son, let not my words of wisdom *escape* from your sight, but pay attention to my counsel and understanding" or "Son, let not [my words of wisdom] *slip away* from your eyes" (v. 21; cf. Prov. 4:21; *TDOT*, 7:478–79; Spicq, 1952, 66–67). Thus, it seems a similar expectation occurred here in Hebrews 2:1 for followers of Jesus: do not lose sight of or defy the teaching about the messianic Son of promise—a theme to which Barnabas would return in Hebrews 5. Or to say it positively: *listen to* what God has spoken through and revealed about the divine messianic Son of promise (cf. 3:12; 6:4–6; 10:35; 12:25).

Recalling the Exodus Generation's Rejection (2:2–3a)

Based upon the exodus generation's rejection of God's initial revelation, which ended in physical punishment, Barnabas's logical assumption was that those who reject God's recent revelation about the messianic Son of promise would suffer an even greater judgment.

2:2. Barnabas then began a logical argument (εἰ γὰρ, "for if") about the exodus generation (v. 2a), their rejection of God's initial revelation delivered through a myriad of angelic beings, and his exacting a physical punishment for their disobedience. Barnabas assumed (εἰ, "if"; first class condition clause) for the sake of the argument that "the word spoken through the angels was established" (ὁ δι' ἀγγέλων λαληθεὶς λόγος ἐγένετο βέβαιος). The "word" (λόγος) referred to God's revelation or the Law given to Moses. Although angels or celestial sons of God were not mentioned in Exodus 19–20, Deuteronomy 33:1–5 recalled the theophany at Mount Sinai and how Moses declared that God "came from the midst of ten thousand holy ones" (NASB). The Septuagint added that "angels were with him at his right hand" (ἐκ δεξιῶν αὐτοῦ ἄγγελοι μετ' αὐτοῦ).[2] Barnabas also presented celestial beings mediating the Law from God to Moses (the aorist passive voice λαληθείς implied that God spoke the Law through angelic beings). Yet the importance was not through whom the Mosaic covenant was spoken but its binding nature.

The word "legally binding" (βέβαιος) when linked with "the word" (λόγος) or God's revelation (e.g., the Law) suggested that something was "valid" (RSV), "unalterable" (NASB), "steadfast" (KJV), "reliable" (ESV), "proved true" (NLT), "binding" (NIV), or a legal guarantee. In this case, the revelation of the Mosaic law was God's "legally binding" contract or covenant with Israel (cf. Exod. 19:3–20:21). Thus, the first assumption was that the Law, mediated *through angelic beings*, was a legally binding covenant. Later in Hebrews, this Law would be described as replaced (cf. 7:11–12, 18–19; 8:7, 13; 9:1–10).

Barnabas added (καί, "and") to his assumption (v. 2b) a focus on "all those" (πᾶσα) in the past who disobeyed God's legally binding word (= Law). They received a "just punishment" (ἔνδικον μισθαποδοσίαν). On the one hand and in conjunction with the legally binding (βέβαιος) nature of the Mosaic covenant, the word "just" (ἔνδικον) stressed the legal recompense for failure or refusal to obey God's Law (cf. Heb. 12:25; BDAG, s.v. "ἔνδικος," p. 332). On the other hand, the word "punishment" (μισθαποδοσίαν) signified a "penal reward" or "to receive a just penalty" (TDNT, 4:702; BDAG, s.v. "μισθαποδοσία," p. 653). Throughout Israel's history, the Law proved painful if disobeyed. God enforced physical penalties repeatedly on Israel for disobedience. Thus, the second assumption was that every past failure and deliberate refusal to hear (= obey) God's *legally* binding revelation (e.g., the Mosaic law) received a deserved punishment.

Israel's National Disobedience

There are numerous examples of the consequences of national disobedience in the Hebrew Scriptures. Of particular significance was the deportation of God's people, destruction of the temple, and the dismantling of the Davidic dynasty (e.g., Jer. 11:1–14 with 25:1–11; 29:1–23; 37:1–17, 39:1–10). Although a bit vague at this point, the disobedience to which Barnabas would draw specific attention is the disobedience of the exodus generation (Heb. 3:2–3, 7–11, 15–17; 8:5; 9:1–10; 11:23–29; 12:20–21).

2:3a. Barnabas drew his historical recollection about the exodus generation to a logical but heightened conclusion (*qal wahomer*)[3] applicable to followers of Jesus. Barnabas asked, "how shall we" (πῶς ἡμεῖς), who *disregard* God's recent revelation through and about the messianic Son of promise, *escape* God's eternal punishment? The word translated "disregard" or "ignore" (ἀμελέω) could speak of neglecting or not caring for people or ignoring or disregarding some spiritual matter. In his wedding banquet parable (Matt. 22:5), Jesus told of a king who sent his servants for a second time to those who had been invited to "come to the wedding banquet." Yet, those who heard the invitation "*paid no attention* and went off—one to his field, another to

2 Similarly, *Jubilees* (1:27–2:1), Josephus's recount (*A.J.* 15.5.3 §136; cf. 3.5.4 §89–90), and Stephen's speech (Acts 7:2–53) share the same perspective about the angels serving as God's messengers through whom God gave the Law to Moses (Walton, 1955, 255–57).

3 *Qal wahomer* is an argument of logic. Arguments begin with a less significant situation to something more significant. Thus, what applies in a less important case will certainly apply in a more important case (cf. Bateman, 2012, 163–64).

his business." Here in verse 3, as it was the case in Jesus's parable, God's message or summons could be ignored, but with dire consequences.

The dire consequence here in Hebrews 2 was no "escape" (ἐκφεύγω) from judgment. Speaking literally, "escape" (ἐκφεύγω) referred to individuals who fled an enemy while in battle (Josephus, *A.J.* 2.16.3 §341; *B.J.* 1.2.7 §65) or indicated a person's opportunity to break out of prison (Acts 16:27). In Sirach 16:13, "escape" (ἐκφεύγω) was used figuratively of the righteous and the criminal's inability to avoid eschatological penal punishment they deserve in the age yet to come (cf. Heb. 12:25; BDAG, s.v. "ἐκφεύγω" 2a, p. 247). Here, as in 1 Thessalonians 5:3, "escape" (ἐκφεύγω) described the inescapable and eternal danger that would come to those who disregarded God's recent message delivered through the messianic Son of promise (cf. Heb. 8:6–13; 10:5–18). The pattern of physical reprimand was escalated to something eternal. Thus, God's recent revelation about the messianic Son of promise was greater than the revelation given and received at Mount Sinai so too will be divine judgment for ignoring God's most recent revelation.

Verbal Confirmations and Divine Endorsements (2:3b–4)

Confirmation of God's most recent revelation was proclaimed by the messianic Son of promise, testified to by eyewitnesses, and endorsed by God.

2:3b. Barnabas purposely paralleled the phrase "through the Lord" (διὰ τοῦ κυρίου) with the phrase "through the angels" (δι' ἀγγέλων) in 2:2a. Whereas God revealed his old covenant *through angelic beings* (= sons of God), God recently spoke a new covenant "through the Lord" (= the messianic Son of promise in 1:2a; cf. 12:25). Hughes (1977, 78) points out that "the idea conveyed by the preposition 'through' (διά) in both cases is that of mediation, a concept of considerable importance in this epistle." Thus, God's recent revelation, mediated *through* the messianic Son of promise, superseded the previous revelation mediated *through* celestial sons of God (cf. Heb. 7:11–12, 18–19; 8:7, 13; 9:1–10).

The Son's message was "confirmed to us by those who heard" (ὑπὸ τῶν ἀκουσάντων εἰς ἡμᾶς ἐβεβαιώθη). For Barnabas, the verb "confirm" (βεβαιοω) echoed the legal testimony of verse 2a. Just as the connection of "the word" (ὁ λόγος) with "confirm" (βέβαιος) proved its certainty and was thereby legally binding, so too did the connection of "after it was first spoken" (ἀρχὴν λαβοῦσα λαλεῖσθαι) with "confirmed" or "guaranteed" (ἐβεβαιώθη) proved, for Barnabas, that "the saving message was guaranteed to us." Thus, the emphasis was both the accuracy and the legally confirming nature of the message.

Unfortunately, the meaning of "salvation" (σωτηρίας) is not clear here. Barnabas's use of the terms "salvation" (σωτηρίας) and "save" (σῴζω) may have spoken of physical rescue (σῴζω of Jesus in 5:7; σωτηρίας of Noah in 11:7), or they may have expressed the salvific work of the messianic Son of promise (σωτηρίας in 5:9; 6:9; 7:25; σῴζω in 9:28). Elsewhere in Hebrews, salvation would speak of deliverance from God's future eternal judgment (6:8–9). Yet here, the rejection of God's revelation meant *no deliverance* from God's future judgment (cf. 10:28) and thereby *no inheriting* of salvation (1:14) and *no everlasting life* (5:9; cf. 4:1).

Naturally, "the ones who heard" (ὑπὸ τῶν ἀκουσάντων) were eyewitnesses of Jesus's teaching who passed the message on to both Barnabas and his contemporaries (εἰς ἡμᾶς, "to us"). Thus, Barnabas was not an eyewitness or disciple of Jesus (Acts 2:5–11; 4:4). However, Attridge (1989, 67) correctly notes, "The emphasis is on the divine initiation and sustentations of the proclamation of the saving message." Furthermore, "our author," according to Bruce (1964, 29–30), "puts himself on the same level as his fellow-Christians who heard the gospel from those 'who from the beginning were eyewitnesses and ministers of the word' (Luke 1:2)."

2:4. God provided corroborating evidence to endorse the trustworthiness of the eyewitness testimonies. The English phrase "at the same time verified" (συνεπιμαρτυρέω) reflected a legal nuance in keeping with verses 2–3. Thus, God also "testifies" (NIV) or "verifies" (NLT) the eyewitness testimony about the new revelation (or "the new covenant") that was first spoken through "a son," or the "messianic Son of promise," or "the Lord" (Heb. 1:2a; 2:3).

> *LEXICAL ANALYSIS:* Hebrews 2:4: "At the same time verified" (συνεπιμαρτυρέω)
> The verb "at the same time verified" (συνεπιμαρτυρέω) appears in several classical Greek sources as (1) a legal term of someone who "joins in attesting" (Aristotle de Mundo 400a 15), (2) as a term to verify a statement to be true (Polybius, Hist. 25.6.42), or as (3) a term to concur with self-praisers (Plutarch, *Mor.* 7.539d; *TDNT*, 4:508–10). Yet it never occurs in the LXX and appears only here in the NT. As a result, it is rendered several ways: "God also bearing witness" (KJV), "God also bore witness" (RSV, ESV), "while God added his testimony" (NASB), "God also testified to it" (NIV), and "God verified" (NLT), "testifies at the same time" (BDAG, s.v. "συνεπιμαρτυρέω," p. 969), or "attests at the same time" (*EDNT*, 3:303).

According to Barnabas, the way God testified or verified the eyewitness accounts was by signs and wonders, various powers, and gifts of God's spirit that were "distributions of the holy spirit" (πνεύματος ἁγίου μερισμοῖς). The term, "distributions" (μερισμός) occurred twice in Hebrews (2:4; 4:12). Although "distributions" could speak of apportioning or distributing one's finances (Aristotle, *Ath. pol.* 48.2; *SIG* 364.81), here in Hebrews 2:4 it spoke of the "*distributions of the Holy Spirit*" (BDAG, s.v. "μερισμός" 2, p. 633) or the "*apportionment of the Holy Spirit*" (*EDNT*, 2:409). God's spirit served as his endorsement of the apostolic message (cf. Acts 2:1–4, 12–38; 10:44–45). And though translations made specific reference to gifts proceeding from the Holy Spirit (cf. KJV, RSV, NASV, NIV, ESV, NLT), the point here *was not* the cessation of the spiritual gifts nor was it an endorsement for the Trinity but rather the trustworthiness of God's new revelation through the divine messianic Son of promise verified by means of divine activities: signs and wonders, powerful deeds, and the distribution of spiritual gifts. Thus, the testimony to God's new revelation was threefold: (1) the origin of God's new revelation via the messianic Son of promise (2:3b), (2) the subsequent testimonies about God's new revelation via eyewitnesses (2:3c), and (3) the divine endorsement of God's new revelation via signs and wonders, various powers distributed by his spirit (2:4).

THEOLOGICAL FOCUS

The exegetical idea (in his warning to concentrate on and listen to God's revelation about the messianic Son of promise, Barnabas recalled the physical punishment the exodus generation received when they defied God's revelation given through a myriad of celestial "sons of God" as a form of comparison about God's future punishment for those who would reject God's most recent revelation about the messianic Son of promise through whom God had spoken, eyewitnesses confirmed, and whose message God endorsed), leads to this theological focus: God will punish any person who defies his revelation, especially those who reject his recent revelation about his messianic Son of promise through whom God has spoken, whom eyewitnesses confirmed, and whose message God endorsed.

Two theological themes stand out in this preaching unit. The first theological theme is God's dealings with disobedience. Regardless of the revelation a generation has, people who reject God's revelation can expect to experience God's judgment. Knowing this clearly established pattern in the OT, Barnabas underscored that God's reproof for rejecting his past revelation would also come to those who reject his recent and final revelation about the messianic Son of promise. However, judgment is no longer limited to physical discomfort, ruin, or defeat by enemies. There is a heightening of God's punishment in this new era. It will be an eternal punishment unknown in the OT. So, to reject God's recent revelation about the messianic Son of promise is to expect an eternal judgment that is far more severe.

The second theological theme is that God communicates with his people, a theological point evidenced in Hebrews 1:1–4. Just as God revealed himself to Moses and the exodus community through a myriad of celestial sons of God, he also revealed himself through the messianic Son of promise. In both cases, God's revelation is not to be rejected (2:2–3).

PREACHING AND TEACHING STRATEGIES

Exegetical and Theological Synthesis

The warning not to slip away began with "Therefore," meaning that 2:1–4 is the application of chapter 1. Because of the accountability given to those who heard the prophets and the angels, we are more highly accountable to God's singular spokes*man*. The angel's words were not simply reliable in the sense that they would come true; they were reliable in the sense that they were "legally binding" (βέβαιος). The reasoning is that God *held* people accountable for disobedience to his spokesmen; therefore, God *will hold* people accountable for disobedience to his spokesman.

This warning was given, of course, in the backdrop of the rebellion of the wilderness generation. The "every transgression or disobedience" that "received a just retribution" referred to those who were punished by God for their rebellion in the wilderness.

Barnabas concluded by appealing to their immediate historical experience. It was declared by the Lord, it was affirmed to them by those who heard it, then it was later affirmed by attesting miracles (v. 4). This validation added weight to the warning: God will hold you accountable like he held our forefathers accountable, and this has been attested to us by God himself.

Preaching Idea

Our focus determines our future.

Contemporary Connections

What does it mean?

What does it mean that our focus determines our future? Several textual questions will need to be explained. In the application section of the sermon, it will be important to unpack exactly what it means to pay attention. First, Jesus and the Father are mentioned. This combined mentioning makes the message weighty. This message was delivered by Jesus, affirmed by the Father with signs and wonders confirming Jesus, the Son. Thus, it is explicitly clear, how could anyone escape if they neglected this? Second, for many, "so great a salvation" has become a part of our church vernacular. However, this is not simply an adjective that Barnabas was floating out there. The greatness of salvation is tied to the logic of the text; it was first given by Jesus and affirmed through signs and wonders.

Is it true?

Is it true that our focus determines our future? Yes! Consider Olympic athletes who know that they will compete in four short years. On some training days, this may seem like an eternity. But in light of what needs to be done, the next forty-eight months will go by quickly. They do not have any margin for error. They must make every training day count. They watch video after video of the world's best athletes. They put in their bodies only what will make them top performers, discipline their bodies past what they thought was possible, and do all this for one reason: they are fixated on a future prize. What they are doing in this moment is dictated by what they want in the future. Their future will be determined by their present focus, and so will ours.

This is a difficult text to preach. There is no way around it. However, what must be clear is that if people do not focus on Christ, they will determine to have a future without him. "Slip away" is tied to focus. This passage is not giving us a robust doctrine of eternal security or challenging the idea of eternal security; rather, the immediate focus is spiritual slipping or drifting. It is a warning, and so it must warn. When this passage is preached, our desire to be traditional, intellectual, or trendy is now subservient to our desire to warn. The text warns, so we warn. The preacher who reads this text at face value is determined not to leave the listener with any ambiguity. This is life or death, heaven or hell. If they want a future with Jesus, they must focus on Jesus.

This is a huge issue for the reason that, ironically perhaps, the church itself is providing much of the background noise to our life. If someone is actively involved in church, it is very possible for them to be absorbed with church activity without focusing on Christ.

What we focus on will influence our future. That is a truism. However, the appeal to authority is coming from chapter 1—namely, the authority of the angels when they were speaking for God.

Now what?

The application of this text for today is really embedded within its expectation to pay attention. Ask, rhetorically, how does our present-day focus determine our future? Think about one's focused attention to buy a car. That focus, if carried out, will determine your budget for the next four or five years. Similarly, why it is important to focus or pay attention when attending small group meetings or listening to the sermon? In Romans 1:18–32, Paul says that all the world will be called to give account for not paying attention to how God has revealed himself. Consider the opposite of the warning in Hebrews 2, which we find in the Bereans of Acts 17:10–11 who searched the Scriptures diligently. In other words, they were paying attention. While these are explicit examples from Scripture, there are implicit examples as well. In Proverbs 8, there is the personification of wisdom. God is speaking to us all the time. His call to pay attention or to focus our attention on him is all around us. The person who does not focus on what God is saying will find that they have slipped away or drifted, and they will face God's wrath.

Since our focus determines our future, reading Scripture more regularly may serve to keep us focused. Perhaps getting involved in a small group will stimulate greater focus on spiritual things that will ensure our future.

Creativity in Presentation

There is a built-in metaphor here of "slip" and lots of ways to play off the metaphor. The idea is not slipping away or drift as much as it is "losing focus." Imagine wading in the shallow part of the ocean and casually talking to a friend. Standing in chest-high water in the surf is not a passive activity. In a few moments, without doing anything at all, you have lost sight of where you originally started. What did you do to slip or drift? Nothing at all. This is the point: if you do not intentionally focus on Jesus, you will slip or drift away. We might even say, water moves us even if we perceive that we are standing still. Therefore, to stand still is to drift!

In this way, ignoring focus on Jesus has the same result as rejecting Jesus. People who do not focus on Jesus consider their distraction a little trickle. In reality, they will be swept away. The undertow of rejection always takes out those wading in the waters of neglect. Those who ignore focus on Jesus are not innocent; they are simply pre-drifters who will, with absolute certainty, be caught in the undertow.

Although slipping or drifting are very helpful metaphors and can be used well, the idea of focus is perhaps a better one. Or to say it more precisely, the emphasis in verse 1 is not on the slipping or drifting as much as the paying attention. Refusing to pay attention is the cause for the slipping or drifting effect. The idea of slip or drift makes one think of something that happens as a matter of incident. However, this is not the best way to express the concept. The idea is this: slipping or drifting is taking place as a result of a refusal to focus. There is something passive going on called spiritual slipping, yet that passive activity is a result of the refusal to focus.

The passage has what may be called a "mitigated imperative." While there is not technically an imperative, it is strongly implied by the question, "How shall we escape . . . ?" The effect of this is that the author is saying, "Don't slip away or drift! You won't escape, so don't slip!" Whatever creative elements are used, it is always important to make sure that the creative elements do not become an end in themselves. The goal is to make the text live. While this is always true, it is especially true in the warning passages. The metaphors used should make the warning bite and sting, because it is the best representation of the text at hand.

Finally, for those who prefer tight outlines, it might be tempting to deal with verse 1 as one of three points. However, verse 1 is the driving idea modified by the following verses. It might be a better idea to preach verse 1 as the initial stand-alone idea. Perhaps you might just jump into the warning as an introduction, and then show how the following verses give teeth to the warning.

The point you want to get across is simply this: Our focus determines our future. One approach to an outline for this text could be as follows:

- Focus! (v. 1).
- Focus because God punished people who lost focus (vv. 2–3a).
- Focus because salvation is so great (vv. 3b–4).

DISCUSSION QUESTIONS

1. What is the real warning behind the warning passage?
2. How do you ensure that you do not take the teeth out of the text?
3. How is the metaphor of drift influencing the passage?
4. Are there other passages of Scripture that address the issue of focus?
5. How does this passage relate to the one immediately preceding it?

Hebrews 2:5–9

EXEGETICAL IDEA

God's plan for his messianic Son of promise—and *never* the angels—was that the Son's authority be expanded to an absolute ruling authority over all of creation, even though his Son, Jesus, existed ever so briefly as a man, died a gruesome death on behalf of all people, and then was exalted to his currently partial rule.

THEOLOGICAL FOCUS

God's plan for the messianic Son of promise to rule with absolute authority begins with Jesus's life as a man, his death for all people, and his exaltation as God's messianic Son of promise.

PREACHING IDEA

Great plans require perceptive thinking and time.

PREACHING POINTERS

The anticipation of a messiah was part of Jewish theological thinking ever since Jeremiah and Ezekiel prophesized the demise of Judah at the hands of Nebuchadnezzar. It was part of God's plan. As a result, most of the Jewish people of the first century made *conjectures* about a future messiah and were at times misguided and driven by current social, religious, and political affairs (Bateman et al., 2012, 211–49). And despite their misunderstandings, the Messiah came according to God's plan. This passage hints at what would be further explained in chapter 3, namely, God's plan. Jesus was faithful to fulfill the plan of God. Yet, God's plan was expanded to fulfill far more than what was anticipated in Jesus.

Even today, when people think of God's plan, they often do not see it as active but static. They understand creation, Christmas, and Easter, but beyond that they might wonder if the plan of God has stalled out. Yet, God is active today in fulfilling his plan. This is the flow of the text: Jesus is the means by which the plan will be executed because he has an expanded but hidden role and because of his dying on behalf of all people. Thus, we should be encouraged that people today can actually be active in God's plan by making much of Jesus. And so, these verses have the feel of encouragement—we are encouraged to be aggressively waiting for Jesus to fulfill his plan. Great plans require perceptive thinking and time.

GOD'S PLANS FOR THE MESSIANIC SON OF PROMISE (2:5–9)

LITERARY STRUCTURE AND THEMES (2:5–9)

Hebrews 2:5–9 resumed Barnabas's exposition about the messianic Son of promise that he began in Hebrews 1. In these five verses, Barnabas revealed God's past, present, and future plan for Jesus. More specifically, Barnabas clarified God's promise to the messianic Son about his future absolute rule first mentioned in Hebrews 1:13.

Continuing the discussion that distinguished between angels (= the sons of God) and the messianic Son of promise, Barnabas first identified that God's plan was not for the "sons of God" to control the world to come (= the kingdom) but rather for the messianic Son of promise, as God testified in Psalm 8:4–6 (vv. 5–8a). Then Barnabas interpreted Psalm 8:4–6, whereby he underscored the result of the messianic Son's absolute rule and admitted that God's final plan for the messianic Son's rule was not yet seen, but that only a portion of his rule was realized, namely, the Son's exaltation because of his gruesome death (vv. 8b–9a). Finally, Barnabas revealed God's intention behind the messianic Son's gruesome death, namely, that the messianic Son of promise would die for all people (v. 9b).

Barnabas drew attention to two theological themes: God's plan and Jesus's humanity.

- ***What God's Plan Is Not and What It Is (2:5–8a)***
- ***God's Plan Interpreted as Partially Executed (2:8b–9a)***
- ***God's Intention (2:9b)***

EXPOSITION (2:5–9)

Before and even during the time of Barnabas, many Jewish people (but not all) anticipated the coming of a messiah. Since the very beginning of the Second Temple period (515 B.C.), they pondered who he might be, when he might come, and what he might do. Yet, *their conjectures* about the Messiah were incomplete and *their plans* for the Messiah were at times misguided and driven by current social, religious, and political affairs (Bateman et al., 2012, 211–49).

Returning to God's promise spoken to the messianic Son of promise introduced in Hebrews 1, Barnabas revealed with more precision God's plan for the messianic Son of promise as presented in Psalm 8. Any inadequate understandings about the ruling authority of angels were corrected (Heb. 2:5–8a). Any conjectures that his Roman readers may have had about the extent of God's messianic Son's kingship were purged (vv. 6–8a). Any doubt about the messianic Son's ruling authority was eliminated by distinguishing between what is yet to come and what was partially realized in Jesus's ever-so-brief existence as a man (i.e., incarnation), his suffering and death for all people, and his exaltation (vv. 8b–9). Thus, God's plan for his messianic Son of promise—and *never* angels—was for the Son's partial authority be expanded to an absolute authority over all of creation, even though the Son, Jesus, existed ever so briefly as a man, died a gruesome death on behalf of all people, and then was exalted to rule.

What God's Plan Is Not and What It Is (2:5–8a)

God never planned for the sons of God (e.g., angels) to rule over the coming kingdom, but rather to award complete control to the messianic Son of promise.

2:5. Barnabas resumed (γάρ, "now") his argument from Hebrews 1 (Lane, 1991a, 45; Ellingworth, 1993, 145; Cockerill, 2012, 126–27), more specifically from verse 13. He underscored this fact: God had not subjected his coming kingdom to celestial beings but to the messianic Son of promise. During the First Temple period, angels were entrusted with the administration of the present world (Deut. 32:8; Dan. 10:13, 21; 21:1), but during the Second Temple period Jewish theology expanded the role of angels in the affairs of the world (1 En., Tob, 4QM; cf. Sir 17:17; Eph. 6:12).[1] Yet, Barnabas made it clear that it was the messianic Son of promise who would have dominion over "the world about to be" (τὴν οἰκουμένην τὴν μέλλουσαν), not the created celestial beings. On the one hand, the world (τὴν οἰκουμένην) was the temporal universe (= the kingdom) over which the messianic Son of promise currently has authority (cf. 1:3e, 6, 13a; cf. Eph. 1:20–22), a universe that eventually would be shaken (cf. 12:26–27). On the other hand, Barnabas drew attention to "the coming inhabited earth" (cf. 1:2b, 13b–14). The expression had its equivalence in "the age to come" (6:5) and the "city to come" (13:14). After a divine shaking (12:26–28), the remains of this "temporal universe" would be inherited by followers of Jesus, namely, God's future kingdom (cf. 12:28). Thus, God never intended nor did he ever plan for "the temporal universe" and its inhabitants to be ruled by angels (cf. Gen. 1:28–30; Bateman, 2013, 89–120).

TEXTUAL ANALYSIS: Conflicting Text Critical Reading: 2:6

Theological/Exegetical Issue: Manuscript support is strong for the text (𝔓[46] C* P 81 104 1881). It seems more likely that a scribe would have changed the text to bring it into agreement with the Septuagint (Lane, 1991a, 42). The text is the preferred reading (Metzger, 1994, 593).

txt. "**<u>what</u>** is man that you take thought for him" (**<u>τί</u>** ἐστιν ἄνθρωπος ὅτι μιμνῄσκῃ αὐτοῦ) (ASV, ESV, KJV, NASB, NET, NIV, NRSV)

var. "**<u>who</u>** is man that you take thought for him" (**<u>τίς</u>** ἐστιν ἄνθρωπος ὅτι μιμνῄσκῃ αὐτοῦ)

2:6. In contrast (δέ; "but," NET) to "a world" (= a kingdom) ruled by angels, Barnabas revealed that God reserved control over "the world to come" (= God's future kingdom) for the messianic Son of promise as God testified (διεμαρτύρατο) in Psalm 8. Although Barnabas merely said, "but there is a place where someone has testified" (διεμαρτύρατο δέ πού τις λέγων), the statement from Psalm 8:4–6 (8:5–7 LXX) served as his authoritative source. "The indefiniteness with which the citation is introduced," says Attridge (1989, 70–71), "probably reflects a common homiletic practice, whereby the expositor does not dwell on what is commonly known or presupposed." Regardless as to why no citation was provided, Barnabas quoted from a psalm where the psalmist marveled that Yahweh, the Lord of heaven (vv. 1a, 9), granted humans (ἄνθρωπος, "man") dominion over the earth (vv. 5–6; Ross, 2013, 2:287–98).

---

1 H. W. Bateman IV, "The Role of Divine Beings in Jewish Theology," in *Charts on the Book of Hebrews* (Grand Rapids: Kregel, 2012), 102–105.

Excursus on Psalm 8

While Barnabas recontextualized Psalm 8 as an application to Jesus, it helps to understand the psalm in its original context.

Psalm 8: The single motif of creation identifies this psalm as a creation psalm: Yahweh, the Lord of heaven, had created the moon and stars (v. 3), created humanity (vv. 4–5), and created animal life (vv. 7–8).

Overview: The psalmist's declaration of praise for Yahweh (v. 1a and v. 9) helps distinguish the psalm's structure. Thus three major sections exist: the psalmist praised the excellency of the nature of the Lord (v. 1a), the psalmist marveled at the Lord's greatness and grace who used children to confound the mighty and who entrusted men and women with his creation (vv. 1b-8), and finally the psalmist praised the grandeur of the Lord's character (v. 9).

Message: The psalmist expressed his awe of Yahweh and his amazement that not only would the Lord of heaven even think about mankind but also that he granted men and women dominion over his creation.

Ambiguity of the Psalm: There is no ambiguity about the psalm's single motif of creation. The psalm is identified along with several creation psalms, including 19, 29, 104, and perhaps 139 (cf. Sabourin, 1974, 177–78; Westermann, 1981, 139; Ross, 2011, 289). There is, however, ambiguity about the psalmist's use of "man" (ἄνθρωπος) in the singular, the appearance of "gods" (אֱלֹהִים), and the lack of connection in later Second Temple Jewish literature with a messianic figure.

Central Point: The central point of the psalm appears in verses 3–8 where mortal men and women are granted power and authority over God's created order. Of particular significance is verses 5–6 where the psalmist observed that Yahweh, the Lord of heaven, made men and women a little lower than heavenly beings, crowned them with honor, and gave them authority of his creation.

Yet, Barnabas applied the psalmist's somewhat ambiguous reference to a plurality of humans ruling over creation in Psalm 8:4 (8:5 LXX) to speak of one person: the messianic Son of promise (Mitchel, 2007, 65). So, when Barnabas quoted "man" (ἄνθρωπος) and "son of man" (υἱὸς ἀνθρώπου), he did not use the term "man" in a collective or inclusive sense because he was applying the ruling authority to God's messianic Son of promise. The referent was no longer a general reference to mankind but rather to the incarnate Jesus.

The Interpretation of "Man" (אֱנוֹשׁ)

In Psalm 8, the psalmist's use of "man" (אֱנוֹשׁ) and "son of man" (וּבֶן־אָדָם) in the singular is ambiguous. On the one hand, "man" (אֱנוֹשׁ) and "son of man" (וּבֶן־אָדָם) in the psalm's historical and literary context were understood collectively for "human beings" (CEB; cf. NRSV), the "human race," and "mankind" (NET). On the other hand, some translations provide a literal rendering for the Hebrew word "man" (KJV, ASV, ESV, NIV; cf. LXX, ἄνθρωπος). Nevertheless, the literal rendering "man" or "son of man" does not necessarily eliminate the collective interpretation of the word in Psalm 8's original context. Similarly, it's not unusual for English renderings for "man" (ἄνθρωπος) in the NT to be understood with an inclusive sense for a human being (BADG, s.v. "ἄνθρωπος" 1, p. 18. 1a; Bateman, 2013, 146–48). The appearance of "Son of man" (וּבֶן־אָדָם) should not be conflated with Jesus's title "Son of man" in the Gospels.

TEXTUAL ANALYSIS: Conflicting Text Critical Reading: 2:7

Theological/Exegetical Issue: The additional material in the variant reading probably represents a scribe's desire to complete the quotation from Psalm 8:7 (LXX). The text, however, is supported with less manuscript evidence (𝔓[46] B D[c] K L). Nevertheless, the shorter reading of the text is the preferred reading (Lane, 1991a, 43; Metzger, 1994, 593–94).

txt. "you crowned him with glory and honor" (δόξῃ καὶ τιμῇ ἐστεφάνωσας αὐτόν) (ASV, ESV, KJV, NET, NIV, NRSV)

var. "you crowned him with glory and honor, **and you set him over the works of your hands**" (δόξῃ καὶ τιμῇ ἐστεφάνωσας αὐτόν, **καὶ κατέστησας αὐτόν ἐπὶ τὰ ἔργα τῶν χειρῶν σου**) (NASB)

2:7. Two contrasting points were highlighted in Psalm 8:5 (8:6 LXX). On the one hand, the phrase "you made him lower *than the angels* [τι παρ' ἀγγέλους] for a little while [βραχύ]" referred to someone's *humble status* in comparison to that of angels. For the psalmist, it referred to every human in general. For Barnabas, it referred to a specific human being's brief time on the earth, namely, the messianic Son of promise, Jesus. So, Barnabas underscored the messianic Son's status as being somewhat less than "heavenly beings" or "angels" (cf. G. Guthrie, 1998, 98). Yet, this status was somewhat "brief" or for only "a little while" (BDAG, s.v. "βραχύς" 2, p. 183; NASB, NRSV, ESV, NET; deSilva, 2000, 109).

The Interpretation of "Gods" (אֱלֹהִים)

The independent Hebrew clause in Psalm 8:5 [8:6 HB] literally means "you make them lack a little from *gods*" (וַתְּחַסְּרֵהוּ מְּעַט מֵאֱלֹהִים). Not only is this one-for-one rendering awkward, but there are conflicting interpretations for the word "gods" (אֱלֹהִים). Some translations interpret "gods" (אֱלֹהִים) as "heavenly beings" (NE,T ESV, NIV; Kraus, 1988, 183), others as "God" (NRSV, NLT; cf. CEB; Ross, 2011, 296), and still others as "angels" (KJV LXX, ἀγγέλος; Comfort, 2009, 53). Nevertheless, Barnabas tends to follow the Septuagint's rendering of "gods" (אֱלֹהִים) as "angels" (ἀγγέλος; cf. Westcott, 1984, xxxiv, 476–80; Kistemaker, 1962, 57; Mitchell, 2007, 64).

On the other hand, the phrase "you crowned him with glory and honor" (δόξῃ καὶ τιμῇ ἐστεφάνωσας αὐτόν) referred to someone's *exalted status*. For the psalmist, it spoke of human beings in general as "crowned" (תְּעַטְּרֵהוּ) and thereby underscored the royal status of human beings as God's viceregents (plural) over creation (Gen. 1:26–30). For Barnabas, it spoke specifically of the Son of promise who had been exalted (cf. Heb. 12:2–3) and who reigned as God's sole viceregent (singular).

2:8a. The psalmist closed Psalm 8:7 with a metaphor similar to the one observed in Hebrews 1:13. One phrase served to link Psalm 8 with Psalm 110: "under his feet" (ὑποκάτω τῶν ποδῶν αὐτοῦ) from Psalm 8:6 (8:7 LXX) joined "a footstool for your feet" (ὑποπόδιον τῶν ποδῶν σου) from Psalm 110:1 (109:2 LXX). In Scripture (HB and LXX), both metaphors indicated complete subjugation to an authority figure. For the psalmist of Psalm 8, Ross (2011, 297) says "every human was given the commission and the capacity to rule over life on this planet" (Gen. 1:28). Yet, for Barnabas, the referent was no longer human beings plural but rather the singular messianic Son. The metaphor spoke specifically of the messianic Son's "authority" (NLT), "control" (NET), or "subjection" (NRSV, ESV; cf. NASB, NIV). It was the messianic Son of promise, Jesus, who had been granted "the commission and the capacity to rule" over "the world" (= the kingdom; cf. Heb. 1:2b, 13b; Glen, 1982, 39–51).

God's Plan Interpreted as Partially Executed (2:8b–9a)

While the messianic Son of promise is to have absolute rule, admittedly God's final plan for the messianic Son is not yet seen, and only a portion of it is currently realized, namely, Jesus's exaltation after his gruesome death.

2:8b. Barnabas offered an interpretation or explanation (γάρ, "now") for Psalm 8:4–6 whereby he underscored three points from God's testimony. The first underscored God having placed "all things under his feet." As explained above, the metaphor spoke of the messianic Son's "authority" (NLT), "control" (NET), or "subjection" (NRSV, ESV; cf. NASB, NIV). Thus, the result of the messianic Son's authority (ἐν τῷ ὑποτάξαι, "in control" or "in subjection"; Wallace, 1996, 593 n. 12) was that God's given authority to the messianic Son of promise was without boundaries. "All things" were interpreted by Barnabas to mean that God "left" (ἀφῆκεν, aor.) nothing outside of the Son's absolute authority.

The second point Barnabas underscored from God's testimony in Psalm 8 was the current reality (νῦν δέ, "at present," ESV) of the Son's ruling authority. Barnabas admitted that God's final plan for the messianic Son's authority was "not yet seen" (οὔπω ὁρῶμεν). So, while God's plan for the messianic Son of promise was an authority without limitations (ὁρῶμεν αὐτῷ τὰ πάντα ὑποτεταγμένα, 2:8c; cf. 1:13b), it had yet to be realized in its entirety at the time Barnabas wrote to the Jewish followers of Jesus in Rome.

TEXTUAL ANALYSIS: Conflicting Text Critical Reading: 2:9
Theological Issue: The appearance of χωρίς may be due to a scribe's misreading of χάριτι, or it may reflect a theological point that expresses the spatial distance of Jesus from God due to his now being lower than the angels. The text is preferred (Metzger, 1994, 594).

txt. "so that **by the grace** of God he might taste death for everyone" (ὅπως **χάριτι** θεοῦ ὑπὲρ παντὸς γεύσηται θανάτου) (ASV, ESV, KJV, NASB, NET, NIV, NRSV)

var. "so that **without** God he might taste death for everyone" (ὅπως **χωρὶς** θεοῦ ὑπὲρ παντὸς γεύσηται θανάτου)

2:9a. The final point Barnabas underscored from God's testimony in Psalm 8 was the position of the incarnate messianic Son of promise in relation to the angels. This was the first time Barnabas referred to the messianic Son of promise as Jesus because the discussion drew specific attention to the divine messianic Son's humanity. The phrase "for a while lower than the angels" (βραχύ τι παρ' ἀγγέλους ἠλαττωμένον; 2:9a) spoke of the incarnate Jesus's status. By placing "for a little while" (βραχύς) before "we see" (βλέπομεν), Barnabas stressed the momentariness of Jesus's humble position (cf. Pfitzner, 1997, 62).

Yet, the following clause, God "has crowned *him* with glory and honor" (δόξῃ καὶ τιμῇ ἐστεφανωμένον), stressed Jesus's exaltation. Figuratively speaking, "he has been crowned" (ἐστεφανωμένον) may distinguish publicly the service of a high priest (Sir 45:12) or the performance of an athlete (1 Cor. 9:25; BDAG, s.v. "στεφανόν," p. 944). Here Barnabas highlighted the distinguished service for which God had awarded Jesus as viceregent, namely, his gruesome death (cf. Heb. 12:2–3). Thus, the reason (διά + an accusative noun) Jesus had been exalted was "*because* he suffered death" (διὰ τὸ πάθημα τοῦ θανάτου; 2:9c). The Son's suffering, along with his incarnation and exaltation, were vital for his glorification (12:2; cf. 1:3; 10:12–14). The presentation of Jesus as having been "made lower" and "has been crowned" (ἠλαττωμένον and ἐστεφανωμένον; perf. ptc.) emphasized God's past act with continuing results in the present. Barnabas, according to Cockerill (2012, 133), "is affirming the continued humanity of the exalted and eternal Son as the representative of the people of God" (cf. Heb. 4:14–15).

God's Intention (2:9b)

God's intention for Jesus's ever-so-brief existence as a man was so that he might die a violent death on behalf of all people.

2:9b. God's intention for Jesus's incarnation was "so that" (ὅπως) he "might taste" (γεύσηται) death on "behalf of everyone" (ὑπὲρ παντός, 2:9d; cf. 6:20; 7:25; 9:24). In other words, Jesus's gruesome death was God's plan. The metaphor "tasted death" (NLT) was Barnabas's first explicit reference to Jesus's physical death (though his death is implied in 1:3). It served as a graphic expression of a grievous event Jesus experienced: Jesus "would experience death" (NET). Yet, God's plan that Jesus die a gruesome death on behalf of all people was God's generous and beneficent intention (χάριτι θεοῦ; "by God's grace"; cf. NLT, NET). It was an act whereby God volunteered to do something he was not obligated to do (BDAG, s.v. "χάρις" 2a, p. 1079). "God gave Jesus up," says Koester (2001, 218), "to die for others out of divine favor" (cf. 7:1–10:25). Thus, the humanity of Jesus was linked with his ultimate human-exalted state because of his death "on behalf of all *people*" (ὑπὲρ παντός; cf. 1:3a; 10:5–10), all of which was part of God's beneficent intention.

THEOLOGICAL FOCUS

The exegetical idea (God's plan for his messianic Son of promise—and *never* the angels—was that the Son's authority be expanded to an absolute ruling authority over all of creation, even though his Son, Jesus, existed ever so briefly as a man, died a gruesome death on behalf of all people, and then was exalted to his currently partial rule) leads to this theological focus: God's plan for the messianic Son of promise to rule with absolute authority begins with Jesus's life as a man, his death for all people, and his exaltation as God's messianic Son of promise.

Two theological themes stand out in this preaching unit. The first theological theme is God's plan (vv. 5–8a). He plans to eventually award the divine messianic Son of promise absolute ruling authority over all of creation. There are no surprises. It was part of God's beneficent intention. The second theological theme is the humanity of Jesus. The messianic Son of promise came as a man, died a gruesome death as a man, and was exalted as a representative for all people for whom he died (vv. 8b–9a). Yet we'd be remiss if no attention was given to what appears to be Jesus's unlimited substitution atonement in that he died "on behalf of all *people*" (ὑπὲρ παντός; cf. 1 John 2:2). Thus, the death of Jesus was for all people whether they are men or women from North America or South America, Asia or Asia Minor, Eastern Europe or Western Europe, Eastern Australia or Western Australia. It does not matter about the person's skin color or wealth. Jesus died for all people and all sorts of people make up his kingdom.

PREACHING AND TEACHING STRATEGIES

Exegetical and Theological Synthesis

In 2:5–9, Barnabas developed the idea of authority that he began developing in chapter 1 and applying in 2:1–4. The messianic Son of promise has more authority because the world was subjected to the Son, *not* to the angels (v. 5). For verification that God has given all authority to Jesus, he recontextualized Psalm 8 and applied it to the Son. The conclusion that he drew is quite compelling: *nothing* was left out of the Son's control (v. 8).

This of course raises a question: If all things are under the Son's control, why don't we see it that way? Anticipating this response, he observed that we currently do not see this, but what we do see is the substitution of the Son for us. Therefore, we live in a broken world, but not with a broken plan. The execution of the plan includes a temporary hiding of the authority of the Son; the Son will be later crowned with glory and honor (vv. 8, 9).

Preaching Idea

Great plans require perceptive thinking and time.

Contemporary Connections

What does it mean?

What does it mean that great plans require perceptive thinking and time? Anything that we do of value takes planning and time. Raising a great family, having a great marriage, growing a business, succeeding in college—none of these great tasks are done without taking time. Each of these are only done if someone is willing to put in the effort over an extended period of time.

Someone said the heart cannot embrace what the mind does not believe. Simply stated, if we have a great ambition that demands all of us, we have to the think the thoughts that will help us achieve the goal. Without the right thinking, we will eventually break. Thus, the greatest challenge for a marathon runner is to "get his/her mind right." No one can run a long-distance race without the correct frame of mind. This is what makes this text so encouraging. God's guarantee for us is that he will execute the plan through the person of Jesus. This knowledge gives us the hope to carry on and to persevere.

Is it true?

Is it true that great plans require perceptive thinking and time? One of the best illustrations to demonstrate this truth is the incredible story of Sir Ernest Shackleton and the voyage of his ship *Endurance*.

Ernest Shackleton set out to cross the Antarctic on foot. In early August of 1914, his ship sailed from England with twenty-seven men. However, by mid-January of 1915, they got locked in an island of ice, or what was called an "ice floe." The boat literally was stuck in the ice and was simply carried along. For ten months, it drifted before the ship was locked in place and could no longer move. They removed what they could, and they began to walk on foot across the frozen ice. They made camp miles away. At one point, they sent back for supplies to find that the boat was being crushed by the ice, and it eventually sank. They took their dog sleds and pulled everything until they finally got back to the ocean. Once they established camp, Shackleton took three men and got in a small boat to find the closest inhabited island, which was Elephant Island. The captain reached safety and had multiple failed attempts to reach his men. However, he finally launched a boat that was successful. On August 30, 1916, ten months after their boat sank, they were all rescued. They were rescued because their captain was persistent in coming back for them. They had the right frame of mind to wait until the plan could be executed. The fact that one of the camps Shackleton set up on the ice floe was named Patience Camp illustrates the need for maintaining the right frame of mind.

Now what?

Since great plans require perceptive thinking and time, we have to ask ourselves a question about our own state of mind. The focus of the text is really upon Jesus. The focus of the text is that Jesus has an expanded yet invisible role to ultimately be a perfect sacrifice for us. So as we preach the sermon, as a whole we will make much of the glorious role of Jesus in God's plan. This makes the application of the text somewhat challenging. After all, the genre here is not hortatory; it is expository. Barnabas is simply advancing the truth that Jesus executes God's plan in three ways.

However, the reality of this situation is that the great plan is not fully executed. This means that there will be a period of waiting. Which leads us to a question: What do we do until Jesus comes back? The answer is that we must have the right state of mind.

If we believe that our captain is coming back to rescue us and make all things right, then how does that effect our demeanor? It seems we should have the attitude of patience and the attitude of peace. We are peace in a world of disruption because we know that Jesus will make all things right. It is not that we don't get upset but rather that we are not rattled. We have our minds right. We know that Jesus will come back to make all things right.

This helps us, in a very practical way, with the problem of evil. We know that there is much that goes on in the world that is not right. There is so much injustice, hatred, and abuse. Yet, none of this escapes the eyes of Jesus. He sees all and knows all. Therefore, having the right frame of mind means fixating and focusing on Him.

Creativity in Presentation

One way to communicate that great plans require perceptive thinking and time is to actually show pictures of the ship *Endurance* mentioned above. The excellent documentary titled *The Endurance: Shackleton's Legendary Antarctic Expedition* (directed by George Butler, narrated by Liam Neeson, 2000) gives the scope of the mission. However, and this is important, be sure to note the significant difference between Jesus and the captain. It was a wonderful thing that the captain came back to save all of his men. However, the reason he came back was due to the original plan failing. On the contrary, God's plan has not failed! We live in a broken world, but we do not live with a broken plan.

Another idea would be to show the clip of the famous Olympic marathon race in 1968. In this race, John Stephen Akwari ran for his home country of Tanzania. Due to a practice injury, he ran the race hurt. In fact, he was so slow that he came into the arena after a lot of fans had already left. He finished not only last, but hours after every other runner. When asked why he finished the race, he said, "My country did not send me 5,000 miles to start the race; they sent me 5,000 miles to finish the race." Clips of this race are readily available online. He was able to finish through very daunting odds because he had his mind right. He had the right thinking.

The point that should be communicated is that great plans require perceptive thinking and time. Here is a simple outline to clarify:

- An Envisioned Plan: In the future, Jesus has expanded authority (vv. 5–8a).
- A Partially Revealed Plan: The authority of Christ is unknown to us (v. 8b).
- A Fully Executed Plan: In the plan of God, we see that Jesus is substituted for us (v. 9).

DISCUSSION QUESTIONS

1. Read Proverbs 16:9. How does this passage relate to Hebrews 2:5–9?

2. Why is it comforting to know God is actively carrying out his good and perfect will?

3. Where do we see God's grace in Hebrews 2:5–9? Is it possible for us to be at peace in the times of the most misunderstanding?

Hebrews 2:10–18

EXEGETICAL IDEA

Whereas the result of Jesus's gruesome death was God's way to equip him to be the leader of the family household with whom he worshipped and trusted God, Jesus's incarnation created a human connection that defeated Satan, eliminated the fear of death, and qualified him for service as high priest—one who was able to aid members of the household family of faith in their physical, emotional, and spiritual struggles.

THEOLOGICAL FOCUS

God equips Jesus perfectly to lead the household family of faith with whom he worships and trusts God and for whom he defeated Satan, conquered death, and currently serves as a high priest who is able to identify with the physical, emotional, and spiritual struggles of all family members.

PREACHING IDEA

Jesus is a better leader.

PREACHING POINTERS

During the Greco-Roman period, the family unit was an essential element to society: husband, wife, children, and slaves. They were the household family unit. It was a microcosmic unit of the Roman Empire over which Caesar ruled as the head of all family units. The family was crucial in the Greco-Roman world.

Even today, the family is critical to society. However, what makes the family different in today's society is the acceptability of wrong behavior among our leaders that trickle down into our families. We tend to assume that leaders will lie, steal, cheat, and even manipulate the law in their favor. We recognize that many are not respectable. Whether they be our bosses, political leaders, or church leaders, integrity is lacking, the love of money abounds, and immoral behavior is blatantly flaunted in public and on television. Yet, the leadership of Jesus is radically different. He is our "founder," or, we might say, our "captain." Jesus is our better leader. He is a trustworthy leader over the numerous household families of faith that make up God's kingdom.

GOD'S EQUIPPING THE MESSIANIC SON OF PROMISE (2:10–18)

LITERARY STRUCTURE AND THEMES (2:10–18)

In 2:10–18, Barnabas explained God's beneficent intention introduced in verse 9b. More specifically, he accentuated God's divine favor by drawing attention to God's equipping the messianic Son of promise to be the head of a family household to which followers of Jesus belonged and with whom he could identify. In his explanation about *God's beneficent plan* for the messianic Son of promise, Barnabas underscored that Jesus's gruesome death equipped him to be the leader God intended him to be. Furthermore, Jesus's suffering for all people featured his shared humanity with those for whom he died (vv. 10–11a). Based upon Jesus's shared humanity, Jesus declared his relationship with his followers. He was not embarrassed to refer to his followers as family and thereby willing to affirm publicly his relationship with the household family of faith by joining together with them in their praise of and trust in God (2:11b-13). Barnabas concluded with the accomplishments and limitations of Jesus's incarnation. He identified a twofold intention of Jesus's incarnation and death: the defeat of Satan and the elimination of the fear of death. Yet, Barnabas clarified that these accomplishments were not for angels but rather limited to people (vv. 14–16). Barnabas ended with one final intention about Jesus's incarnation, namely, to stress Jesus's qualification to be a merciful, faithful high priest who was able to understand and aid people (vv. 17–18).

Barnabas's twofold theme stressed in this unit was God's divine favor and the messianic Son of promise's relationship with his family of followers and accomplishments.

- ***God's Beneficent Plan Explained (2:10–11a)***
- ***Jesus Declares His Relationship with Believers (2:11b–13)***
- ***Accomplishments and Limitations of Jesus's Incarnation (2:14–16)***
- ***Jesus's Qualifications (2:17–18)***

EXPOSITION (2:10–18)

Living as a family and belonging to a family household unit was an important part of the Greco-Roman world. Whether a person was Jewish or Roman, a person's status began with their ancestral family's origin, lineage, and reputation (deSilva, 2000, 155–97). The household was a family unit that consisted of *husband* and wife, *master* and slave, and *father* and children (Aristotle, *Pol.* 1.3; cf. 1 Esdr 5:1). Naturally, the *husband*, *master*, and *father* are descriptive for the head of the household unit. In fact, Plato in his *Republic* (384–370 B.C.), Xenophon (430–355 B.C.) and Aristotle (384–322 B.C.) in their respective works entitled *Discourse on Estate Management* (or *Oeconomica*), Plutarch in his *Advice to Bride and Groom* (A.D. 46–120), and Seneca in his *Moral Epistles* (A.D. 40–112) provided household instructions concerning slaves to masters, wives to husbands, and children to father. It was believed that disorder in the household was a threat not only to the Greco-Roman family but also the Greco-Roman society, namely, the Roman Empire (Bateman, 2013, 81–84). Barnabas believed the same

Barnabas shifted from the messianic Son's relationship with angels to the Son's family relationship with his followers. The shift was rather significant for his Jewish readers in Rome. So, while Jesus's gruesome death was God's way to equip him to be the leader of the household family of faith with whom he worshipped and trusted God, Jesus's incarnation created a human connection that defeated Satan, eliminated the fear of death, and qualified him for service as high priest, one who is able to aid his family in their physical, emotional, and spiritual struggles.

God's Beneficent Plan Explained (2:10–11a)

God's desired objective that Jesus suffer for all people was to equip him as the founder and leader of the household family of faith.

2:10. Expanding upon verse 9b, Barnabas explained (γάρ, "for") God's beneficent favor (χάριτι θεοῦ, "God's grace") "on behalf of all *people*" (ὑπὲρ παντός). God (αὐτῷ, "he") regarded it "fitting" (ἔπρεπεν) or "appropriate" that Jesus die. While uncommon in Jewish theology to associate God with a world of suffering, Barnabas was not concerned about Jewish theological "propriety" but rather with "human needs and the salvific action that meets those needs" (Attridge, 1989, 82). After all, God was the one "for whom" (δι' ὃν) and "through whom" (δι' οὗ) creation existed (G. Guthrie, 1998, 107; cf. the relative clauses in 1:2b–3c). So, the reason why God's beneficial favor (χάριτι θεοῦ, v. 9b) corresponded with Jesus's violent death "on behalf of everyone" (ὑπὲρ παντός, 2:9b; cf. 1:3d) was because this divine favor permitted people entrance into God's kingdom ("bring many sons to glory"). The "sons of glory" was a specific reference to people of faith who were heirs with Jesus, shared in his kingdom, and inherited salvation (1:14; 6:12, 17; 9:15; Koester, 2001, 227).

"Perfection" (τελειόω, τέλειος, τελειότης) Language in Hebrews (Adapted from Bateman, 2012, 131)		
Background of the Term: "Perfection"	**Perfection of Christ in Hebrews**	**Perfection of Believers in Hebrews**
Barnabas used the language of "perfection" (τελειόω, τέλειος, τέλειότης, etc.). They appear in verb forms (2:10; 5:9; 7:19, 28; 8:8; 9:9; 10:1, 14; 11:40; 12:23), in other forms (5:14; 6:1; 7:11; 9:11; 12:2), and in a related synonymous term (καταρτίζω ["to make complete"] in 13:21).	Hebrews applies the language of perfection to Jesus three times: 1. "who is perfected through sufferings" (2:10); 2. "perfected" so as to become the "source of eternal salvation" (5:9); and 3. "perfected forever" in contrast to the Levitical priests, who continued to have weakness (7:28). Finally, Jesus is the "perfecter of faith" (12:2).	In terms of perfection and maturity, believers are urged to progressively advance from infancy to adulthood (τελειότητα, "perfection" or "maturity") in 5:14–6:2.

Furthermore, it was within God's propriety (ἔπρεπεν γὰρ αὐτῷ) to equip the messianic Son of promise to be a "pioneer" or "leader." The concept of a "pioneer" or "leader" (ἀρχηγός) in Josephus appeared to speak of a person who authored something (*A.J.* 7.9.4 §207; *C. Ap.* 1.29 §270) or to speak of someone who was a founder of a city (*C. Ap.* 1.19 §130). Jesus, as messianic Son of promise, was God's leader or founder who was perfected through his sufferings. The gruesome sufferings[1] of Jesus as incarnate Son "completed," "perfected" (τελειῶσαι), or more appropriately "equipped" him to be what God intended for him to be (cf. 4:14–16). Thus, Barnabas contrasted "pioneer" (ἀρχηγὸς) with the term "to make perfect" (τελειῶσαι) to signify that Jesus began and finished perfection for his followers during his earthly suffering, which culminated in death (2:10). Jesus was a "pioneer" in that he was both the "founder" (cf. ESV) of salvation, and as founder "led" his followers forward in their salvation. "Hebrews' argument that Jesus' passion was morally congruent ('fitting') with God's character and aims is," according to Koester (2001, 226), "distinctive within the NT."

2:11a. For Barnabas, the grounds (τε γάρ, "for indeed") for bringing "many sons to glory" (πολλοὺς υἱοὺς εἰς δόξαν) occurred by way of linking "the one [Jesus] who consecrates" (ὁ ἁγιάζων) with "those whom [followers] he consecrates" (οἱ ἁγιαζόμενοι), thereby stating that they were "all of one" (ἐξ ἑνὸς πάντες; KJV Tyndale). Although ambiguous, the phrase "all of one" (ἐξ ἑνὸς πάντες) recognized Jesus as the one who shared in the humanity (anthropomorphically) of people in general as well as acknowledged his solidarity with family members of faith in accordance with God's planned program (theologically). So while some translations interpret "all of one" (ἐξ ἑνὸς πάντες) as "all from one source" (ESV; Lane, 1991a, 58), "all are the same origin" (NET; Mitchell, 1989, 78), or "all are from one Father" (NASB, NRSV, NLT), they detract from verse 11b where the Son declared his relationship with the household family of faith. So, "all of one" is better rendered and understood as "are of the same family" (NIV; Pfitzner, 1997, 65–66; G. Guthrie, 1998, 108). Thus, for Barnabas, Jesus shared in the humanity of all people but consecrated and led only those who were Jewish members of the family household of faith in Rome.

The Consecration of Believers

While it is true that the word "holy" (ἁγιάζω) when referring to objects meant "set apart," when used with people it meant "consecrate" or "dedicate" in both a cultic and moral sense (BDAG, s.v. "*ἁγιάζω*" 2, p. 9). Here followers of Jesus were "those being consecrated" (οἱ ἁγιαζόμενοι; 2:11), Barnabas later spoke of followers as "those who are consecrated" (τοὺς ἁγιαζομένους; 10:14; cf. 10:29) and still later of the need of followers to "pursue consecration" (διώκετε τὸν ἁγιασμόν; 12:14). So, the idea of "consecration" (ἁγιάζω) in Hebrews was something that was happening (2:11), had happened (10:14), and was to be pursued (12:14). Jesus, who was consecrating, and those he had consecrated captured his work as royal-priest introduced in 1:3 and expanded on it in 4:14–16.

Jesus Declares His Relationship with Believers (2:11b–13)

The messianic Son of promise declared his relationship with believers by referring to them as family, by praising God together with his family, and by trusting God together with his family.

2:11b. Barnabas explained (δι' ἣν, "so"; NIV, NET; cf. ESV, NLT) why Jesus did not

1 Crucifixion was a disgrace in the Greco-Roman world and a curse among Judaeans. See M. Hengel, *Crucifixion: In the Ancient World and the Folly of the Message of the Cross* (London: Philadelphia: SCM/ Fortress, 1977).

hesitate to call his followers "brothers *and sisters*" (ἀδελφοὺς αὐτοὺς καλεῖν). In the Greco-Roman world of the first century, the term "brothers" tended to be reserved for people of the same social status. Yet when used of a person belonging to another level of society, social status gave way to a relational unity and bond (Koester, 2001, 230). In Hebrews, Barnabas's portrait of those who follow Jesus moved from "sons" (υἱούς, v. 10), to "brothers *and sisters*" (ἀδελφούς, v. 11; cf. 17), and then to "children" (τὰ παιδία, v. 13). Thus, while Jesus was God's divine messianic Son of promise, that royal-priest status gave way to a relational bond with all those within the household family of faith. Barnabas underscored the astonishing relationship between the divine messianic Son of promise and those who were part of his family.

Translation of "Brothers" (ἀδελφός)

Several translations render "brothers" (ἀδελφός) as "brothers and sisters" (e.g., NRSV, NET, NLT). The Greek word "brothers" (ἀδελφός) has considerable evidence in nonbiblical sources for the plural form to be a reference to "brothers and sisters" (BDAG, s.v. "ἀδελφός," p. 16). Similarly, the context here in Hebrews appears to indicate a broader understanding, particularly when followers are viewed as "children" (τὰ παιδία) in verse 14. For a more complete discussion on this and similar gender-inclusive terms, see Bateman (2013, 145–48) and Straus (1998).

2:12–13. Barnabas stressed his portrayal of Jesus speaking to his followers directly through two passages from the Septuagint: Psalm 22:22 and Isaiah 18:17–18. First, Jesus spoke through a lament psalm, Psalm 22:22 (21:22 LXX). Originally, Psalm 22 portrayed the suffering of a righteous person, namely, his frustration of unanswered prayer and yet his resolve to praise God in an assembly of people for his deliverance (Ross, 2013, 521–51). Here in Hebrews, Jesus, as the speaker who had suffered a horrific death but was now exalted and in God's presence, offered praise to God: "I will proclaim your [= God's] name to my brothers" (ἀπαγγελῶ τὸ ὄνομά σου τοῖς ἀδελφοῖς μου). The fact that Jesus praised God "in the midst of the congregation" (ἐν μέσῳ ἐκκλησίας) may reflect the Jewish perspective that worship on earth somehow mirrored that which occurred in heaven (4Q400–07, 11Q17; cf. Anderson, 2001, 993–94). Naturally, the parallel between "brothers and sisters" (τοῖς ἀδελφοῖς) and "congregation" (ἐκκλησίας) had the contextual understanding of an assembled Jewish group of Jesus's followers (Bruce, 1990, 82). Thus, Jesus created immediate commonality with his household family of faith in that he understood human suffering and yet still praised God (cf. 4:15; 10:32–38).

Second, Jesus seemingly spoke Isaiah 18:17 as though they were his own words: "I will be confident in God [him]" (ἐγὼ ἔσομαι πεποιθὼς ἐπ' αὐτῷ). The unmistakable conceptual link between Psalm 22 and Isaiah 18 was, for Barnabas, a significant proof of confidence in God. Jesus had placed total confidence or trust in God.

Third, Jesus spoke the words of Isaiah 18:18 to his followers, saying, "Here I am with the children God has given to me" (Ἰδοὺ ἐγὼ καὶ τὰ παιδία ἅ μοι ἔδωκεν ὁ θεός). Originally, Isaiah was speaking of his offspring (Shear-jashub, 7:3; Maher-shalal-hash-baz, 8:1, 3) given by God as signs of his sovereign presence. Here in Hebrews, not only did Jesus's humanity create solidarity with people who followed him, but also with God's sovereign act of handing people over to Jesus as his children, as members of his household family of faith. It too was a sign of God's promise. Thus, Jesus praised God together with his family and trusted God together with the family God had given him.

Accomplishments and Limitations of Jesus's Incarnation (2:14–16)

The messianic Son's physical death resulted in the defeat ("render powerless") of Satan and the elimination of the fear of death for people but not for angelic beings.

2:14. Barnabas concluded (οὖν, "therefore") by way of Isaiah 18:18 where Jesus had referred to his followers as "children God has given to him." Jesus, like his children, shared in their humanity: "because *the children* share in blood and flesh" (τὰ παιδία κεκοινώνηκεν αἵματος καὶ σαρκός). "Blood and flesh" was a typical metaphor indicating the humanity Jesus shared with people (cf. Matt. 16:17, 1 Cor. 15:50; Gal. 1:16; Eph. 6:12) and thereby "he also shared the same *things*" (καὶ αὐτὸς παραπλησίως μετέσχεν τῶν αὐτῶν). The intended result (ἵνα, "so that") of the messianic Son's shared humanity, more specifically the death he suffered as a man (διὰ τοῦ θανάτου), was twofold: that he would render Satan powerless and that he would set people free from the fear of death.

The first result was that "he might render powerless" (καταργήσῃ; NASB) Satan. Although a common phrase in Paul, it appears only two other times in the NT. In Luke 13:7, it spoke of something becoming unproductive (e.g., a tree). But here in Hebrews, Barnabas spoke of something losing its power or effectiveness. Jesus, the messianic Son of promise, successfully battled Satan, "the lord of death" (Attridge, 1989, 92), and reinforced the presence of God's kingdom.

2:15. The second result was that "he might set free" (ἀπαλλάξῃ) people. More specifically, Barnabas spoke of being freed from something that tended to control all people. In Luke 9:40, "set free" (ἀπαλλάσσω) was used to describe a person who had been set free from an evil spirit (BDAG, s.v. "ἀπαλλάσσω" 1a, p. 96). Here in Hebrews, the result of Jesus's death freed people who were once enslaved to the fear of death (cf. Job 4:12–21, Sir 40:1–9). Death was Satan's instrument that generated fear (Koester, 2001, 232). Granted, people still died (9:27), but the removal of sin had disarmed Satan from using death as an instrument against the household family of faith. And though "the lord of death" had not been annihilated (see Rev. 12:7–12, 20:10, 14), Satan's tyranny and the subsequent fear of death were "condemned to inactivity or ineffectiveness" (cf. 2 Tim. 1:10; *TDNT*, 1:453). Thus, the death of Jesus had rendered Satan "powerless" (καταργήσῃ; v. 14) and thereby "liberated" or "set free" (ἀπαλλάξῃ; v. 15) followers of Jesus who had a lifelong fear of dying (cf. 1 Cor. 15:53–55).

2:16. Barnabas's assumed assertion which his readers could have deduced on their own (γὰρ δήπου, "for surely"; cf. BDAG, s.v. "δήπου," p. 223) was, once again, about the angels. Here, however, Barnabas addressed those for whom Jesus had a concern ("concerned about," ἐπιλαμβάνεται), namely, people who followed him (1 Tim. 6:12; BAGD, s.v. "ἐπιλαμβάνομαι" 2c, p. 295; Attridge, 2001, 94; Lane, 1991a, 64). The concern was further underscored by way of a contrast (ἀλλά, "but"). Unlike the previous contrast that addressed the distinction between the messianic Son of promise and "sons of God" (= angels), here the contrast was between angels and humans. Barnabas identified those to whom the Son's redemptive work was extended (Johnson, 2006, 101). In contrast (ἀλλά, "but") to the angels, Jesus, the son of human Jewish descent, helped all those who were of the family of faith (2:16b; cf. Isa. 41:8–10). Angels needed no liberation from the fear of death. They were spiritual beings. Thus, the messianic Son of promise did not provide salvific help for angelic beings (2:16a; cf. 1:14).

Jesus's Qualifications (2:17–18)

The messianic Son's shared humanity qualified him for his present work as one who was able to act as a merciful and faithful high priest.

2:17. Deemed as the "nerve center" of the epistle (Ellingworth, 1993, 179), "therefore" (ὅθεν)[2] introduced Barnabas's summation in verses 17–18. Admittedly, these verses foreshadow the topic of priesthood in 4:14–16. The opening clause, "he was obligated to be made according to all his brothers *and sisters*" (ὤφειλεν κατὰ πάντα τοῖς ἀδελφοῖς ὁμοιωθῆναι), once again identified Jesus as a member of the human family of faith (2:17a). Jesus was morally "obligated" (ὤφειλεν) to become *fully human* (ὁμοιωθῆναι, "like"; Heb. 5:3, 12; cf. Phil. 2:5–7). It was an inescapable necessity.

The purposed result (ἵνα, "so that") of the Son's shared humanity was his qualifications to "become" (γένηται) a merciful and faithful high priest (Heb. 2:17b; cf. 4:16). This point was rather significant for these first-century readers because at the time (A.D. 59–66) there was a chain of self-absorbed and morally corrupt high priests serving in Jerusalem (VanderKam, 2004, 463–87). So unlike Judaea's priests, Barnabas portrayed Jesus as one who mirrored God. Just as God was merciful (cf. Exod. 34:6), so too was the messianic Son of promise. As a "merciful" (ἐλεήμων) royal high priest, Jesus was able to cleanse the sins of people and bring them into God's presence (Heb. 1:3a; 4:16; 5:7–10; 10:5–10, 19). Just as God was faithful (cf. Ps. 145 [144 LXX]), so too was the messianic Son of promise. As "faithful" (πιστός) royal high priest, Jesus was both loyal to God and those who followed him (Heb. 3:2; cf. 5:7–10; 7:25–26; 10:5–10; 12:2). And just as high priests made atoning sacrifices in the past, Jesus as royal high priest had made an atoning (τὸ ἱλάσκεσθαι) sacrifice on behalf of all people, which was once for all (8:3; 7:27). Thus, Jesus was able to help (δύναται βοηθῆσαι) the Jewish followers of Jesus in Rome who were tempted.

LEXICAL ANALYSIS: "An Atoning Sacrifice" (ἱλάσκεμαι*)*

The Greek word ἱλάσκεμαι is interpreted one of three ways. One way is "the *propitiation* for the sins of the people" (ASV, ESV). During the Classical Greek period, "propitiation" referred to an offering made by worshippers to pacify an offended deity (BDAG, s.v. "ἱλάσκεμαι" 1, p. 374; Hughes, 1977, 122–23; Bruce, 1964, 53). Another way is "the *expiation* for the sins of the people" (RSV; BDAG, s.v. "ἱλάσκεμαι" 2, p. 374). During the Hellenistic period, "expiation" concerned a removal of a ritual or moral defilement by way of prescribed rituals that may or may not have included animal sacrifice. In the OT, the word came to mean "cleanse from defilement" (Ellingworth, 1993, 189). The final way is "the *atonement* for the sins of the people" (NRSV, NET, NIV). Origen connected the Day of Atonement with 1 John 2:2 (αὐτὸς ἱλασμός ἐστιν) because the Septuagint (Lev. 25:9) rendered the Hebrew (בְּיוֹם הַכִּפֻּרִים) as "the Day of Atonement" in Greek (τῇ ἡμέρᾳ τοῦ ἱλάσμοῦ). Like John, Hebrews 2:17 also envisioned the Day of Atonement with the shared description of blood, cleansing, an innocent victim, and the idea that the one who atones was himself in heaven, having made atonement for sinners (Koester, 2001, 241; Mitchell, 2007, 76–77; Cockerill, 2012, 150–51). So, rather than propitiation (which implies a sacrifice that turns away the wrath of God) or expiation (which implies that the offender is purified of the sin that causes offense), *atonement* best reflects the sense of the OT conceptual linkage evident in 2:14 and later in Hebrews 9–10.

2:18. Barnabas explicitly underscored the Son's shared humanity by accentuating causally (ἐν ᾧ γὰρ; NRSV, ESV, NIV) the messianic Son's solidarity with people: "because he himself suffered" (ἐν ᾧ γὰρ πέπονθεν αὐτὸς). More pointedly, the sufferings suffered were when Jesus

2 The Greek word "therefore" (BDAG, s.v. "ὅθεν" 2, p. 692) is a frequently used inferential conjunction in Hebrews (3:1; 7:25; 8:3; 9:18; 11:19).

was tempted (πειρασθείς; 2:18a). The affirming effect of the Son's temptation was that he would be able to help those who were tempted (2:18b; cf. 4:15–16; Ellingworth, 1993, 190). In other words, Jesus may have suffered while being tempted, but he passed the test! This was clearly evident in Luke's Gospel. Luke's genealogy of Jesus began with Jesus, followed by a long list of people, but ended with Jesus being "the son of Adam" (Luke 3:23–38). And while the genealogy identified Jesus's human connection, what's rather significant appeared in what follows. Jesus, a son of Adam, was tempted and yet Jesus (the second Adam; cf. Rom. 4) passed the test (Heb. 4:1–13), after which Jesus launched his ministry (4:14–15; cf. Bock, 1994, 383–84). What a contrast! Barnabas made a similar contrast to the exodus generation who were tested in the wilderness, but they failed their numerous tests (cf. Exod. 15:25; 16:4; 17:2, 7; 20:20; Num. 14:22)—a theme Barnabas would pick up later in Hebrews 3:7–4:13. In the meantime, believers could know that when God tested the household family of faith, Jesus was there to intercede and help them with their temptations because he too was tempted and actually passed the test.

THEOLOGICAL FOCUS

The exegetical idea (whereas the result of Jesus's gruesome death was God's way to equip him to be the leader of the family household with whom he worshipped and trusted God, Jesus's incarnation created a human connection that defeated Satan, eliminated the fear of death, and qualified him for service as high priest—one who was able to aid members of the household family of faith in their physical, emotional, and spiritual struggles) leads to this theological focus: God equips Jesus perfectly to lead the household family of faith with whom he worships and trusts God and for whom he defeated Satan, conquered death, and currently serves as a high priest who is able to identify with the physical, emotional, and spiritual struggles of all family members.

Several theological themes appear in this preaching unit. The first theological theme is about God's divine favor (χάριτι θεοῦ). Though first introduced in verse 9b, Barnabas explained that God's favor or God's grace was to be seen in his plan for Jesus to suffer a gruesome death for all people. It was part of God's divine favor that Jesus die in order to equip him to be the leader of a household family. The second theological theme is about the messianic Son of promise. Not only did Jesus's physical death equip him to be the leader God intended for him to be over his family household, but Jesus's physical death broke Satan's power and liberated his family from the fear of death. Finally, Jesus's physical death parallels the sacrifice offered on the Day of Atonement in the OT and yet escalates its significance. The sacrifice shares the description of and the need for blood, cleansing, and an innocent victim. And yet the sacrifices offered in the past were limited to the nation of Israel. Jesus's atoning work is escalated as an atonement for the sins of all people (1:3; 2:9, 14b–15, 17).

PREACHING AND TEACHING STRATEGIES

Exegetical and Theological Synthesis

Barnabas expanded on the idea that Jesus "tasted death for everyone" by explaining that it was appropriate that Jesus be made "perfect through suffering." He also recognized Jesus as the leader/founder of the faith. The rest of the text works out why Jesus was our brother and our victory. He was our brother because Jesus identified with us and because we have the same "source" (v. 11). To explain this claim, Barnabas repurposed two OT passages, Psalm 22:22 and Isaiah 18:17–18.

The children of God share in the same material substance with each other, and therefore Jesus partook of the same material substance in his incarnation. This sharing and his subsequent death had two dramatic effects. First, it allowed Jesus to render the devil powerless in his ability to use the weapon of death against us eternally. Second, Jesus could take those of us who fear death and deliver us. As he ended the passage, Barnabas told us explicitly that all of this was possible because he was tempted as we were and because he was our high priest (vv. 17–18). The significance of this textually is that this was the earliest hint of the theme that would be developed throughout the rest of Hebrews.

Preaching Idea

Jesus is a better leader.

Contemporary Connections

What does it mean?

What does it mean that Jesus is a better leader? The evidence of the leadership in the text is threefold: Jesus has an expanded role, a hidden role, and a role as our substitute. What this means for us is something quite remarkable. Because of this, he can "help those who are being tempted."

According to one study, the weight loss industry garnered $68.2 billion in 2017.[3] The harsh reality is that we do not need an industry to lose weight. No one is stopping us from doing so. However, the industry is attractive and effective for the reason that it offers help. Someone can identify with our problem and lift us out of the situation. In the same way, Jesus is our leader. He is not only our pioneer, but he provides the empathy and genuine help we really need.

Jesus is a remarkable leader for the reason that he understands exactly what we are going through, and he is committed to lifting us out of this situation.

Is it true?

As human leaders at home and in our places of influence, our natural reflex is not identification. Our natural reflex is pontification. We have a bias for edicts. I want everyone to do what I say. Things would go much smoother if everyone would do what I want. What shocks me as a leader is unresponsiveness.

Each of us has this internal compass that tells us that our opinion is true north. This makes perfect sense to us, doesn't it? *Because we see that tendency in ourselves, we might project that idea on Jesus.* However, we do not see that exasperation in the teaching of Jesus. Why? Because he knew our failures. He knew we were by nature unresponsive. Jesus has such a deep love for us that he calls us brother. He fights for us, and he suffers with us, which all goes to the heart of the gospel: Jesus did not teach "Do this and your life will be better." He did not merely teach the moral standard and our inability to live up to it. Instead, he decided to be the leader who anticipates our needs for us. Jesus in essence says, "So *I* will live with you, *I* will fight for you, and *I* will suffer with you."

The heart of the gospel is not that Jesus makes me better. The heart of the gospel, and the point of Hebrews, is that Jesus *is better*.

- We have a family—because *he* calls us his brother.
- We have a future—because *he* fights for us.
- We have empathy—because *he* suffers with us.

He is a better brother. He is a better fighter. He is a better priest. He is a better leader.

Now what?

This passage, like so many in Hebrews, is explanatory not hortatory. Barnabas was teaching us something about Jesus. The effect it should have on us is confidence. Our application is that to trust the plan of God is to trust the person of God. This means that we have confidence in

3 J. LaRosa, "Top 6 Trends for the Weight Loss Industry in 2018," MarketResearch.com, https://blog.marketresearch.com/top-6-trends-for-the-weight-loss-market-in-2018.

God's overall plan because we trust the one who is responsible for executing the plan.

Therefore, reflecting on verse 18, we should have confidence in God's plan and accept the help that comes when we are tempted. Ironically, part of accepting the reality of God's plan is coming to grips that we will be tempted to sin in this life. Sin is never God's will, but since he does not remove temptation, we have to say, in a broad sense, temptation is part of the plan . . . and so is God's help. So, the question this text pushes on is simple: Do we accept the help of Jesus when we are tempted?

Jesus helps (v. 18). He helps us by providing the life-giving Word of God. He helps us by providing prayer as a means of comfort and leadership, and he provides us with friends who understand and empathize with our troubles. God can never be blamed for sin (James 1:13–15) for the reason that God has done so much to keep us from sinning. God has designed a kingdom that propels us to victory and not defeat. So, are we laying hold of the means of grace that our leader so graciously gave us? Are we praying and fasting for victory over sin? Are we memorizing verses that deal with our weakness?

Creativity in Presentation

Imagine that a child is being bullied in school. However, the child's brother attends the same school, and tells his younger brother that if he ever got in trouble to simply call him. However, while his brother could help him, the child never takes advantage of that resource. What good is a big brother if we never call on him? Why do we not call on the name of Jesus when we know the depth of how much we need him?

It might be effective to have two brothers up front or on the stage: one who is small and one who is large. As you are explaining the illustration, be sure to talk about the depth of the relationship between brothers. Perhaps you could include personal illustrations if you have brothers. While brothers bicker often, they have an undeniable commitment to be there for each other no matter the circumstance. Faithful brothers will always help each other get out of trouble.

Similarly, the analogy can only somewhat compare to how Jesus intercedes for us in our weakness. He sympathizes and fights for and with us in our weakness, but we must also be willing to call on him for help. What good is a brother who fights for us without us ever calling on him? In the case of Jesus being a better brother, we realize *how much* he has already been fighting for us when we call on him.

The point you want to get across is simply this: Jesus is a better leader. One approach to an outline for this text would be as follows:

- Jesus is our brother (vv. 11–13).

- Jesus is our victory (vv. 14–18).
  - He defeats our enemy and fears (vv. 14–15).
    He destroyed the devil. He set us free from the fear of death.
  - He goes to God for us (v. 17).
    He identifies with us like brothers.
    He is not ashamed of us.
  - He comes alongside us (v. 18).
    He fights for us.

DISCUSSION QUESTIONS

1. Although Jesus is leading us with divine sovereignty, what is our human responsibility?

2. How has Jesus played an active role in your life amidst pain or suffering?

3. How does understanding the character and leadership of Jesus change your perspective on human leadership?

FOR FURTHER READING

Bateman IV, Herbert W. (editor). 2007. *Four Views on the Warning Passages in Hebrews*. Grand Rapids: Kregel.

_________. 2001. "Psalm 45:6–7 and Its Christological Contributions to Hebrews," *TJ* 22NS: 3–21.

__________. 2013. "The Theology of the General Letters." *Interpreting the General Letters: An Exegetical Handbook*, 89–120. Edited by John D. Harvey. HNTE Grand Rapids: Kregel.

deSilva, David A. 2000. "Kinship: Living as a Family in the First-Century World." *Honor, Patronage, Kingship & Purity: Unlocking New Testament Culture*, 157–97. Downers Grove, IL: InterVarsity Press.

Glen, Donald R. 1982. "Psalm 8 and Hebrews 2: A Case Study in Biblical Hermeneutics and Biblical Theology." *Walvoord: A Tribute*, 39–52. Edited by Donald K. Campbell. Chicago: Moody Press.

Mach, Michael. 2000. "Angels." *Encyclopedia of the Dead Sea Scrolls*, Volume 1, 24–27. Edited by Lawrence H. Schiffman and James C. VanderKam. New York: Oxford University Press.

Newsome, Carol S. 2000. "Songs of the Sabbath Sacrifice," Volume 2, 887–89. *Encyclopedia of the Dead Sea Scrolls*. Edited by Lawrence H. Schiffman and James C. VanderKam. New York: Oxford University Press.

Nickelsburg, George W. E. 2000. "Enoch, Books of." *Encyclopedia of the Dead Sea Scrolls*, Volume 1, 249–53. Edited by Lawrence H. Schiffman and James C. VanderKam. New York: Oxford University Press.

GOD'S HOUSEHOLD FAMILY OF FAITH (3:1—4:13)

While Barnabas further developed the theme of Jesus's faithfulness in the opening verses of Hebrews 3, the thematic unity of this second major division (3:1–4:13) centered around the household family of faith. On the one hand, there were household privileges. Family members had received a heavenly calling (3:1); they had an allegiance with those who were part of the community of faith as well as with Jesus, the messianic Son of promise (3:1, 14a). They also had the opportunity to eventually participate in God's Sabbath celebration (4:3, 9). On the other hand, these privileges warranted several household responsibilities: a persistent commitment to the teachings about the messianic Son of promise (3:1, 6b, 14b), an avoidance of stubborn unbelief (3:12, 15; 4:7b, 11b–12), and a balance between a fear of failing to take part in God's Sabbath celebration with a striving to succeed in joining in it (4:1, 6a, 11a).

This second division may be divided into three preaching units. The first underscores the distinctions between Jesus and Moses that calls for the household family of faith to adhere to their confession about and allegiance to Jesus as God's sent spokesman and high priest (3:1–6). The second is a series of exhortations and expectations directed to members of the household family of faith about heeding and avoiding stubborn unbelief with a lesson from history (3:7–19). The third is Barnabas's call for the household family of faith to fear failure while striving for the successful crossing of the threshold into God's heavenly place of rest and avoiding the historical pattern of rebellion and divine judgment (4:1–13). At the very end of this section is a list of books and articles for further reading that may be helpful in understanding these preaching units.

Hebrews 3:1–6

EXEGETICAL IDEA

Members of the household family of faith were to give careful consideration to the confession about Jesus as God's sent spokes*man* and high priest, who deserved greater honor than even Moses as well as their persistent allegiance.

THEOLOGICAL FOCUS

Persistent allegiance to Jesus as God's sent spokes*man* and high priest that exceeds all other loyalties is both urged and expected.

PREACHING IDEA

Loyalty involves careful deliberation, deserved respect, and steadfast commitment.

PREACHING POINTERS

No matter where they lived in the world, Jewish people of all ages tended to be loyal to their Jewish homeland, their Jewish law, and their Jewish celebrations. This was certainly the case during the time of Barnabas. Jewish people throughout the Roman world believed God had called them, established them in Judaea, and would act on their behalf to execute divine justice in Judaea. This sense of *nationalism* began in the Sinai desert under the leadership of Moses, who was their national hero. He was well known, his service respected, and his name venerated. A Jewish person's national connection to Judaea was generally strong and his or her sense of loyalty profound.

We too exhibit loyalties. Loyalties are often evident in our choices of a particular sports team whether they be at the high school, college, or professional level. Where we work, worship, and window-shop may expose our loyalty to a particular place or product. Oftentimes, however, loyalty to people such as our bosses, friends, and family are unmistakable. As we shall see, Barnabas is going to emphasize that the features of loyalty to Jesus involve careful deliberation, deserved respect, and steadfast commitment.

DISTINCTIONS BETWEEN JESUS AND MOSES (3:1–6)

LITERARY STRUCTURE AND THEMES (3:1–6)

Although in some respects these verses were a continuation about Jesus's faithfulness mentioned in 2:17, the word "therefore" indicated that Barnabas was beginning a new section that addressed directly the household family of faith. Barnabas opened with an appeal to the household family of faith, namely, that they consider carefully their confessions about Jesus as God's sent spokes*man* and high priest whom Barnabas compared with their national hero, Moses (vv. 1–2). He then explained why Jesus, in comparison to Moses, deserved greater honor as the one with ruling authority "over" the household family of faith that Jesus himself established (vv. 3–6a). Barnabas closed the unit with the family's responsibility to maintain their allegiance to the teachings about Jesus (v. 6).

There were three themes Barnabas underscored: God's provision, Jesus's faithfulness, and the believer's responsibility.

- ***An Appeal for Careful Consideration (3:1–2)***
- ***Jesus Deserves Greater Honor Than Moses (3:3–6a)***
- ***Maintain the Allegiance to Jesus (3:6b)***

EXPOSITION (3:1–6)

Most practicing Jews living during the latter part of the Second Temple period (167 B.C. to A.D. 70) preserved a threefold set of core beliefs: monotheism, election, and eschatology. N. T. Wright (1992, 279) summarizes these beliefs as follows: "There is one creator god, *who has chosen Israel to be his people*, giving her his Torah and *establishing* her in his holy land. He will act for her and through her *to re-establish* his judgment and justice, his wisdom and his shalom, throughout the world" (emphasis added). Thus, Barnabas was writing to a Jewish household family of faith in Rome whereby *every* Jewish person believed *they* were "the called" or more pointedly "chosen of God." Yet this *national calling* began in the Sinai desert under the leadership of Moses. Long after his death, Moses remained their national hero. He was well-known, his service respected, and his name venerated.

In Hebrews 3:1–6, Barnabas made several important distinctions between Jesus and Moses that redirected the Jewish believer's calling, presented a new hero, and underscored their need to follow God's new leader. Thus, Barnabas accentuated the necessity to focus attention on Jesus (v. 1) as part of the household family's responsibility (v. 6b). As God's faithful messenger and high priest, Jesus superseded their national hero, Moses (vv. 3–6a). In essence, members of the household family of faith in Rome were to give careful consideration to the confessions about Jesus as God's sent spokes*man* and high priest, who deserved greater honor than even Moses as well as their steadfast allegiance.

An Appeal for Careful Consideration (3:1–2)

As members of the household family of faith that had been summoned together, they were urged to give careful consideration to their confessions about Jesus, who had proven himself faithful to his divinely appointed task, as had Moses.

3:1. For Barnabas, this section, while new (ὅθεν, "therefore"), was a continuation of the faithfulness of Jesus and the household family of faith. Barnabas, for the first time, addressed his readers as "holy brothers *and sisters*" (ἀδελφοὶ ἅγιοι). The mention of "holy brothers *and sisters*" emphasized the household family of faith who were "set apart" (ἅγιος) and thereby shared together in spiritual realities as "sons *and daughters* of God" (2:10–13), as members of the same family (2:11), and privy to the forgiveness of sin through Jesus, the high priest (2:17; *TLNT*, 490). Thus, Barnabas drew attention to the ideal character of the household family of faith as a whole and did not single out people individually (Westcott, 1984, 73). They were a community, a family of faith.

As "brothers *and sisters*," they were also "partners of a heavenly calling" (κλήσεως ἐπουρανίου μέτοχοι). Throughout Hebrews, the term "partners" (μέτοχος) was used to describe the household family's allegiance to one another in a technical and moral sense (cf. Ps. 119:63 [118:63 LXX]).

> *LEXICAL ANALYSIS:* "Partners" (μέτοχος)
> Unlike in Hebrews 1:9 where μέτοχος is translated "companions," here it meant "partakers" (KJV, NASB), "sharers" (RSV, NIV) or "you who share" (ESV), "friends" (NLT), and more pointedly "partners" (NRSV, NET; BDAG, s.v. "μέτοχος" 1, p. 643, *TDNT*, 2:830–32, *TLNT*, 2:478–82). The term "partners" (μέτοχος) later appears in Hebrews 3:14 in reference to the community's allegiance with Jesus, who is their royal-priest, and again in Hebrews 6:4 where there is an appeal regarding the family's allegiance with God.

More importantly, the household family of faith was joined together due to their "heavenly calling" (κλήσεως ἐπουρανίου). The term "heavenly" (ἐπουρανίου) is an important term in Hebrews (6:4; 8:5; 9:23; 11:16; 12:22). Here it described the calling of the household family of faith as a heavenly one. For the Jewish household family of faith in Rome, the call distinguished that of the Jewish nation at Mount Sinai from the summons Jesus made during his earthly life, and from the one currently made from heaven (cf. 1:3; 2:10; 3:1b). It was an appeal to a Jewish household family of faith to differentiate their call from all others. They were "fellow Christians" with an allegiance to one another, and not "fellow Jews" with a duty to Jerusalem, its temple, or its priests. Thus, followers of Jesus were considered to be in partnership or aligned with one another due to their heavenly call from Jesus, the messianic Son of promise (cf. 2:11–12).

Based upon their allegiance (= partnership) and their shared calling from God via Jesus, Barnabas made his appeal: "think carefully about Jesus, the apostle and high priest whom we confess" (cf. 2:1). The expectation to "think carefully," "consider" (κατανοήσατε) or "fix one's eyes on Jesus" (*EDNT*, 2:265; cf. BADG, s.v. "κατανέω" 3, p. 415) conveyed the idea of becoming absorbed in Jesus. In Job's reply to Eliphaz, he said: "When *I ponder* [or *consider*; ἐφρόντισα] the many plans God still has in store, I fear Him" (Job 23:15; cf. Isa. 57:1). Here in Hebrews, Barnabas wanted the household family of faith to not only consider Jesus but to ponder him, to come to know him, to grasp him, to understand him (*TDNT*, 4:974). More specifically, they were to ponder their "confession" (τῆς ὁμολογίας) of Jesus as an "apostle" and "high priest."

Barnabas specifically underscored their twofold confession of Jesus. To begin with, Jesus was an "apostle" (τὸν ἀπόστολον). Apostles were often *messengers sent* from God with extraordinary status (BDAG, s.v. "ἀπόστολος" 2b, p. 122). The prophet Ahijah was an apostle *sent* to deliver a divine message to the wife of king Jeroboam when she came and asked about her sick son (1 Kings 14:6 [3 Kgdms. 14:6 LXX]; cf. *TDNT*, 1:413–14, 423). They were God's sent spokes*men*. Although it is only here in Hebrews where in the NT Jesus was called an "apostle," Jesus often identified himself as one *sent* by God to deliver God's message (Hebrews 2:12's quotation of Psalm 21:23 [22:22 LXX]). Jesus was, after all, God's final spokes*man* (cf. 1:2). Thus, their confession included a simple fact: Jesus was sent by God.

Jesus, the Apostle (ἀπόστολος)

Throughout the Synoptic Gospels, Jesus was presented as one sent by God (Mark 9:37; Matt. 10:40; 15:24; Luke 10:16), who spoke God's message (Mark 1:21–22; Luke 4:31–32), and who acted with God's authority (Mark 1:23–28; Luke 4:33–37). In John's Gospel, Jesus was sent by the Father (5:23–24, 36–38; 6:29, 44, 57; 7:27–29; 8:16, 18, 26, 29, 42; 9:4; 11:42; 12:44–45; 20:21; 13:20; 14:24; 15:21; 16:5, 17:3, 8, 18, 21, 25; 20:21; cf. 16:27–28; cf. Heb. 3:1). As one who was Spirit-led (3:34), Jesus knew things that others did not (1:48; 2:24–25; 5:52; 6:6, 61, 64; 7:29; 8:14, 55; 11:42; 12:50). Jesus had authority and power (5:17–23, 10:37–38, 14:10–11, 17:4–8) over temporal or physical needs (2:1–11, 6:3–15), nature (6:16–20), sickness (4:46–54, 6:1–2, 9:1–34), and death (11:1–47). His authority testified or witnessed to Jesus having been sent by the Father. As one sent by the Father, it was Jesus who had been given authority to judge all things (5:22–23, 26–27, 30; 8:14–18, 26; 12:47–48). Together, these pictures served to testify of or witness to his oneness of mission with the Father (5:16–23; 10:30, 38; cf. 14:10–11, 20; perhaps 8:19).

Not only did their confession focus attention on Jesus as one who had been sent as God's spokes*man*, their confession also included Jesus being God's "high priest" (ἀρχιερέα; cf. 1:3a, 13; 5:5–6; 7:17). "The combining of the two roles," says Bruce (1964, 56), "is not common in the OT." Nevertheless, Barnabas expected the household family of faith to give careful consideration to two confessions about Jesus: he was God's sent spokes*man* (cf. 1:2), and he was God's high priest (cf. 2:17).

TEXTUAL ANALYSIS: Conflicting Text Critical Reading: 3:2

Exegetical Issue: External evidence (p13 B) supports the omission of "all" (ὅλῳ). Yet, a scribe may have deliberately added "all" (ὅλῳ) to conform more closely with Numbers 12:7, which the author quotes directly in Hebrews 3:5. The variant is the preferred reading (see NET note).

txt. "just as Moses also was faithful in **<u>all</u>** God's [his] house" (ὡς καὶ Μωϋσῆς ἐν **<u>ὅλῳ</u>** τῷ οἴκῳ αὐτοῦ) (ASV, ESV, KJV, NASB, NIV, NRSV)

var. "just as Moses also was faithful in God's house" (ὡς καὶ Μωϋσῆς ἐν τῷ οἴκῳ αὐτοῦ) (NET)

3:2. Barnabas's attention returned to Jesus's faithfulness and to his appointment by God. Here the faithfulness of Jesus ("by being faithful," πιστὸν ὄντα) repeated 2:17, especially since Jesus's faithfulness was already established in 2:5–18 (Lane, 1991a, 76). Furthermore, Jesus's appointment (τῷ ποιήσαντι) reiterated Barnabas's previous point about God's plan that equipped Jesus as leader of the household family of faith (cf. 2:10). Yet, Jesus was not the first to receive an appointment from God: "The Lord appointed Moses and Aaron" (κύριος ὁ ποιήσας τὸν Μωϋσῆν καὶ τὸν Ααρῶν; 1 Sam 12:6 [1 Kgdms. 12:6 LXX]). Later Jesus "appointed" (ποιῆσαι) twelve to be sent out (Mark 3:14). Here in Hebrews, Jesus also had a divine appointment. As God's spokes*man* and high priest, Barnabas described Jesus as having proved himself faithful to his appointed task, a point he would develop further in 5:5.

To drive home his point here, however, Barnabas made a comparison (ὡς) between Jesus and Moses. The phrase "as Moses was *in* his house" alluded to Numbers 12:7 (LXX) where it was said of Moses, "he is faithful in all *my* [= God's] house" (ἐν ὅλῳ τῷ οἴκῳ μου πιστός ἐστιν; Ellingworth, 1993, 201;

Cockerill, 2012, 163–64). Although Barnabas changed "my" (μου) to "his" (αὐτοῦ) in Hebrews 3:2b, the "house" still referred to God's house. Most commentators consider "in the house" (τῷ οἴκῳ) to be a metaphor for God's people (Bruce, 1964, 56–57; Ellingworth, 1993, 201; Cockerill, 2012 163–64). Moffatt (1968, 42) made the assertion more pointedly when he says, "Moses is *part of* the House" and "Moses *belonged to* the house in which he served so faithfully" (emphasis added). Thus, in the midst of discussing Jesus's faithful service as an apostle and high priest, Barnabas reflected back to Israel's national hero, Moses, who too was deemed *faithful*.

Was Moses Ever Referred to as an Apostle or High Priest in Hebrew Scripture?

In Exodus 3:10, Moses was described as one whom God sent to Pharaoh (LXX: "And come now, 'I will send' [ἀπόστολω] you to Pharaoh, king of Egypt"). In Psalm 99:6, Moses was designated a priest. However, his Levitical background (Exod. 2:1–10), his ministry of the word and privileged vision of God (Exod. 33:12–34:35; Num. 12:7–8), his plea for pardon of guilty people (Exod. 32:11–14, 31–35; Num. 14:13), and his service at the altar (Exod. 24:4–8) clearly associated him with priestly functions. Philo (*Mos.* 2.1.2–3) presented Moses as having fulfilled the roles of prophet, high priest, king, and legislator. Thus, Moses was considered to be one sent by God who performed priestly acts. And though known primarily for his role as the law-giving prophet, he was the one who led the people of Israel out of exile. His ministry was rather broad and yet seemingly similar to that of Jesus.

Jesus Deserves Greater Honor Than Moses (3:3–6a)

The household family of faith was to focus their attention on their confession of Jesus as God's sent spokes*man* and high priest because

Moses Smashing the Tablets of the Law by Rembrandt (1606–1669). Public domain. Courtesy of DcoetzeeBot.jpg

Jesus deserved more honor than even Moses and had been given even greater authority.

3:3. The expectation to focus attention on their twofold confession of Jesus as God's final spokes*man* and high priest was not without reason (γάρ, "for"). God had deemed Jesus his messianic Son of promise (οὗτος, "this one") "worthy" (ἠξίωται) of "more glory" (KJV, NIV ESV, NET, etc.) when compared to what was extended to Moses (3:3a). At the time, "glory" (δόξης) was an enhanced honor, a recognition of status or performance, and therefore would be better defined as fame, recognition, renown, honor, or prestige (BDAG, s.v. "δόξης" 3, p. 257). Granted, God had spoken with Moses through angels (Deut. 33:1–5), and Moses had seen the radiance of God's glory (LXX Num. 12:8)—even if in a limited sense (Exod. 33:18, 22)—it still resulted in causing his face to shine (Exod. 34:29–30, 35; 2 Cor. 3:12–18). Yet, Moses's experiences and achievements paled in comparison to the messianic Son of promise. Jesus was, after all, the incarnate Jesus who after his death was exalted at God's right hand (1:3c, 13), who shared God's radiance (1:3a), who brought people into the household family of faith (2:10), with whom members of the household in Rome had an intimate family relationship (2:12–13), and about whom they had confessed as God's apostle and high priest (3:1).

Yet, Barnabas underscored Jesus as having "more *honor* than Moses" (πλείονος . . . *δόξης* παρὰ Μωϋσῆν) with a proverbial statement: "the one who establishes the house has greater honor [τιμὴν] than the house" (3:3b). The proverb served "to describe a parallel relationship: The messianic Son of promise is to Moses as the builder of a house is to the house" (Cockerill, 2012, 165). Thus, in comparison (καθ') to the esteem or honor Moses received, the preeminence of the messianic Son of promise over Moses was analogous to the predominance of a builder who built a house.

Moses, Israel's Venerated Hero

Respect for Moses appears often in the NT (esp. Jesus's transfiguration: Mark 9:2–5). It's also evident in nonbiblical material as well. His *notoriety* as lawgiver (CD; 1Q28), spokesman (Jub. 1:1–29), and prophetic voice (T. Mos.) permeated Second Temple literature (cf. Falk, 2000, 576–77). His intercessions on behalf of God's people were not only *respected*; they were presented as a model for prayers of confession (Jub. 1:19–21; 4Q493). Finally, Josephus (*B.J.* 2.8.9 §145), in his comments about the Essenes, revealed their *veneration* of Moses: "After God, they hold in awe the name of their lawgiver, any blasphemer of whom is punished with death" (trans. Thackeray). And though he was never "anointed" or called "anointed one" in the Bible, Moses was called "anointed one" in a nonbiblical Jewish text: "Cursed be the man who fails to preserve and carry out all the commandments of the Lord as spoken by Moses His anointed . . . ." (4Q377 2.2; trans. Wise et al., 1996, 338).

3:4. From a common truism about houses, Barnabas inserted (γάρ, "for") a theological theme. He began with an everyday agreed upon assumption: every house has a builder (3:4a). He then drew a theological truth recognizable by any good Jew: the builder (ὁ κατασκευάσας) of all things was God (3:4b; cf. 2:10). Jewish people of the Second Temple period believed that "there was one creator god, *who had chosen Israel to be his people*, given her his Torah, and established her in his holy land. He would act for her and through her to re-establish his judgment and justice, his wisdom and his shalom, throughout the world" (Wright, 1992, 279, emphasis, tense, and punctuation changes added). Yet, here the identity of God as the builder of all things recalled the description of God equipping Jesus to be a *new leader* over a *new household*. Jesus, the divine messianic Son of promise, was the one through whom God spoke (1:2) and through whom high priestly service was rendered (cf. 1:3; 2:9–10, 17) for those who were members of the household of faith, and others (cf. "on behalf of all," ὑπὲρ παντός; 2:9).

3:5. Returning to his comparison between Moses and Jesus (cf. 3:3), Barnabas provided the final element of the messianic Son's ascendancy over Moses. "On the one hand" (μέν), Moses—recognized as "faithful *in* all God's house" as quoted from Numbers 12:7—was also deemed "as a servant" (ὡς θεράπων) *in* God's house. Moses was one of many within the fledgling Jewish nation. His service was recognized in a very broad sense and thereby was not to be limited to priestly functions. God declared Moses to be his servant in a very broad sense (Num. 12:7, Josh.

1:2), Moses recognized himself as God's servant in a very broad sense (Exod. 4:10, 14:31; Num. 11:11; Deut. 3:24), and God's people honored him as God's servant in a very broad sense (LXX: Josh. 9:2, 1 Chron. 16:40 adds "through the hands of Moses, God's servant," Wis 10:16; Philo, *Sacr.* §12 [allusion to Exod. 4:10]). Moses was also a reliable witness (μαρτύριον) with regard to speaking on behalf of God, leading God's people, relaying and establishing a bilateral (conditional) covenant between God and his people, instituting a sacrificial system that made it possible for people to approach God, and laying a foundation for Israel to become a theocratic Jewish nation (Bateman, 2013, 90–102).

TEXTUAL ANALYSIS: Conflicting Text Critical Reading: 3:6a
Theological Issue: Manuscript support is strong for both readings: text (𝔓[13] ℵ A B C I K P 044 0278 33 81 1881) and variant (𝔓[46] D* 0121b 0243 6 88 1739). A scribe may have altered the text from οὗ to ὅς for clarification and thereby affirm more exactly that Christians are God's house and not Christ's house. The text is the preferred reading (Metzger, 1994, 595).

txt. "**whose** house we are" (**οὗ** οἶκός ἐσμεν ἡμεῖς) (ASV, ESV, KJV, NASB, NET, NIV, NRSV)

var. "**which** house we are" (**ὅς** οἶκός ἐσμεν ἡμεῖς)

3:6a. "On the other hand" (δέ), Barnabas quite emphatically presented "Christ" (Χριστός) as "a son" (the messianic Son of promise; cf. 1:1–14) *over* God's house (= household family of faith). The lack of a verb has generated at least two English renderings: "Christ *is* faithful" (NET) or "Christ *was* faithful" (NRSV). Yet more significantly was the presentation of the messianic Son of promise "over" (ἐπί) God's house whereby Barnabas underscored his authority over the household family of faith (cf. 2:8b; 3:1b). Whereas Moses was presented as "*in* God's house" (= Jewish nation), the divine messianic Son of promise was presently *over* God's house (= multiethnic household family). As the one who built or founded the household family of faith, Jesus had been granted authority over the household family as "The Messiah" (= the Christ). Moses was never considered God's anointed, nor did God or the people of Israel ever recognize Moses as a king. Jesus, however, was God's messianic Son of promise, God's viceregent, God's "right hand" exalted man (cf. 1:3).

"Christ" (Χριστός)

The noun "Christ" (Χριστός) was *not* Jesus's last name but rather an epithet. The Hebrew equivalent was "Messiah" (מָשִׁיחַ), which meant "anointed" (with oil) or "Anointed One." During the First Temple period, prophets, priests, and kings were "anointed" figures. The prophet Elisha (1 Kings 19:15–16), the high priest Aaron (Exod. 40:13; cf. Lev. 7:36), subsequent priests and high priests (Exod. 40:14–15, Lev. 16:32; Num. 35:25; cf. Sir 45:15), and kings were all anointed figures. As to kings, Samuel anointed Saul (1 Sam. 10:1, 15:10) and David (1 Sam. 16:12–13; cf. Sir 46:13). Nathan the prophet and Zadok the priest anointed Solomon (1 Kings 1:45, cf. 1 Chron. 29:22). Elijah anointed Hazael over Syria and Jehu over Israel (1 Kings 19:15–16). Furthermore, Israel's kings were called "the Lord's anointed": David of Saul (1 Sam. 26:9, 11, 23), hymnwriters of David and his descendants (2 Sam. 22:51, Pss. 2:2, 18:50; cf. Lam. 4:20), and the psalmists of the Davidites (Pss. 84:9; 89:38, 51; 132:10, 17). During the Second Temple period, the word "Messiah" (מָשִׁיחַ) became just one of several designations or epithets for a future Messiah figure. The others were "the branch of David," "the prince," "the Son" or "Son of God" (Bateman, 2012, 253–329).

Epithets for Expectant Messianic Figures

	Messiah, Anointed, Anointed One	Branch, Shoot, Root	Prince, Chief, Leader	Son, Son of God, Firstborn, Son of Man
Old Testament Sources	1 Samuel I Kings 1 Chronicles Psalms Zechariah	Isaiah Jeremiah Zechariah	Ezekiel	2 Samuel 7 Psalm 2 Psalm 89 Daniel 7
Qumran Sources	CD 1Q28 1Q28a 4Q252 4Q266 4Q382 *4Q458 4Q52 1*	4Q161 4Q174 *4Q252* 4Q285	CD 1Q28b 1QM 4Q161 4Q266 4Q285 4Q376 4Q423 4Q496	1Q28a 4Ql74 4Q246 4Q369
Pseudepigrapha Sources	*Psalms of Solomon*	*Testament of the Twelve Patriarchs: T. Judah*	*Jubilees*	*Psalms of Solomon* *1 Enoch* *4 Ezra*

Maintain the Allegiance to Jesus (3:6b)

Membership in the household family of faith depended upon maintaining an allegiance to Jesus, God's messianic Son of promise.

TEXTUAL ANALYSIS: Conflicting Text Critical Reading: 3:6b
Theological/Exegetical Issue: Although the majority of manuscripts support the longer reading (א A B C D K P 044 0243 0278 33 81 629 1739 1881 Byz), it appears reasonable to suspect that a scribe inserted "until the end" (μέχρι τέλους βέβαίαν) to imitate Hebrews 3:14. The lack of concord between βέβαίαν and καύχημα may further support the preferred text rendering (p13 p 46 B). The text is the preferred reading.

txt. "if we hold fast the confidence and the pride of hope" (ἐὰν τὴν παρρησίαν καὶ τὸ καύχημα τῆς ἐλπίδος κατάσχωμεν) (ASV, ESV, KJV, NET, NIV, NRSV)

var. "if we hold fast the confidence and the pride of hope **until the end**" (ἐὰν τὴν παρρησίαν καὶ τὸ καύχημα τῆς ἐλπίδος **μέχρι τέλους βέβαίαν** κατάσχωμεν) (NASB)

3:6b. Followers of Jesus were, according to Barnabas, "his house" (οὗ οἶκός ἐσμεν ἡμεῖς; lit., "whose house we are"). "House" (οἶκός) was a metaphor for members who made up the household family of faith. Yet, retaining one's membership in the household family of faith was conditioned upon (ἐάν, "if") household family members "holding fast" or "holding firmly" (κατάσχωμεν) to "our confidence." The expectation to "hold fast" echoed "the necessity to pay attention" (δεῖ . . . προσέχειν) to Jesus as mentioned in Hebrews 2:1, namely, that followers of Jesus were to heed what God had spoken through the Son (1:2a), about the

Son (1:2b–4), and to the Son (1:5–13). Here in Hebrews 3:6, Barnabas emphasized the necessity "to hold fast" or "to retain faithfully the traditions, convictions, or beliefs" (BDAG, s.v. "κατέχω" 2b, p. 532) about Jesus's rule as "The Messiah" (= "Christ"). These teachings were described as "our confidence." The house (= household family of faith) was ruled *over* by the messianic Son of promise (3:6a) whose function was that of God's final spokes*man* (1:2; 3:2) and God's divine royal high priest (1:2–3; 5–13; 2:10, 17; 3:1). Thus, family members were expected to *retain, keep in their memory*, or *maintain* these things that they had been taught and had confessed about Jesus.

What the members of this household family of faith were taught and confessed in verse 1 (cf. 3:14) were described as their "confidence and boast" (τὴν παρρησίαν καὶ τὸ καύχημα). Although "confidence" (τὴν παρρησίαν) appears in most translations (KJV, NASB, NRSV, ESV, NET), the context suggests a *conviction*, a *resolve*, or a *determination*. The member's *conviction* was a form of "boldness" (ESV) or "courage" (NIV). It was a *resolve* about Jesus that Barnabas described in terms of a family member "taking possession of" this teaching and confession about Jesus and thereby remaining within the household family of faith ("whose house we are"). It was to be a *steadfast allegiance* to the teachings about Jesus (cf. 10:23) as God's messianic Son of promise, who created a household family of faith (cf. 10:24). Thus, "*hold firmly* to our *confidence*" might also be rendered as "*retain* your *resolve* about the Christ" (cf. Cockerill, 2012, 92) or "*maintain* your *conviction* about Jesus."

THEOLOGICAL FOCUS

The exegetical idea (members of the household family of faith were to give careful consideration to the confession about Jesus as God's sent spokes*man* and high priest, who deserved greater honor than even Moses as well as their persistent allegiance) leads to this theological focus: Persistent allegiance to Jesus as God's sent spokesman and high priest that exceeds all other loyalties is both urged and expected.

Three theological themes appear to rise the surface in this preaching unit: God's provision, Jesus's faithfulness, and the believer's responsibility. First, God's provision was evident in his having sent Jesus as an apostle, God's spokesman (v. 1). It was a reminder that God communicates with people (cf. 1:2). Furthermore, God appointed Jesus, which recalls God's plan (v. 2; cf. 2:10). Second, Jesus's faithfulness was viewed in conjunction with his appointment *over* the household family of faith and thereby he deserved greater honor than even Moses (v. 2; cf. 2:8b–11a). Third, the believer's responsibility was emphasized, namely, Barnabas urged believers to persevere in their allegiance to Jesus. Members of the household family of faith were to think carefully about and maintain their resolve about Jesus as God's sent spokesman, high priest, and messianic Son of promise (vv. 1, 6a).

PREACHING AND TEACHING STRATEGIES

Exegetical and Theological Synthesis

The household family of faith was confronted with a different calling, a new hero, and the need to adjust their previous commitment to Judaism. In essence, they were at a theological crossroad. Barnabas appealed to the household family of faith to consider carefully the confessions about Jesus as God's sent spokes*man* and high priest, whom Barnabas then compared with their national hero, Moses. The reason why Jesus deserved greater honor than Moses was because he ruled "over" the household family of faith (= church). Consequently, the household family of faith had the responsibility to maintain their allegiance to the teachings about Jesus.

Preaching Idea

Loyalty involves careful deliberation, deserved respect, and steadfast commitment.

Contemporary Connections

What does it mean?

What does loyalty or allegiance mean? What does it look like? To be loyal tends to mean to be trusting of another person, to be reliable, to be dependable. So, a loyal person is someone who is trustworthy, reliable, and dependable. The Navy Seals have a code that defines what careful deliberation, deserved respect, and steadfast commitment means for them (see https://navyseals.com/nsw/seal-code-warrior-creed):

- Loyalty to Country, Team and Teammate
- Serve with Honor and Integrity On and Off the Battlefield
- Ready to Lead, Ready to Follow, Never Quit
- Take responsibility for your actions and the actions of your teammates
- Excel as Warriors through Discipline and Innovation
- Train for War, Fight to Win, Defeat our Nation's Enemies
- Earn your Trident everyday

Is it true?

Is it true that loyalty involves careful deliberation, deserved respect, and steadfast commitment? Yes, it is particularly true of our military forces. The above code of the Navy Seals exemplifies their deserved respect. It's also true about allegiances to sport teams. My (Herb's) wife is an avid Philadelphia Eagles fan who faithfully watches their games, records their games to watch again (especially their 2018 Super Bowl LII victory), and collects Eagles paraphernalia like Eagles throw blankets, Eagles flags, and Eagles jerseys, sweatpants, and hats. She even has a replica of the Eagles' stadium. She is what we might call a loyal Philadelphia Eagles fan who exemplifies steadfast loyalty. It's likewise true about allegiances to one's alma mater. My (Herb's) neighbor converted his eight-hundred-square-foot basement into a Purdue University "man cave" with walls painted with Purdue's colors and Purdue paraphernalia scattered throughout the basement. It's not unusual to see high school loyalty at wrestling matches, woman's basketball and softball games, and football games.

There are other sorts of loyalties as well. Loyalty to a product is another example. Apple computer owners tend to be committed to the Apple brand due to the computer's reliability and multifaceted capabilities. Homeowners who do repairs around the home may favor going to Lowe's or Home Depot because of their respected service or their variety of tools, home repair items, and landscaping options. Men may favor Men's Warehouse because their range of suit and sport coat options that can be tailored to fit or retailored to expanding waistlines. We all tend to give careful deliberation, deserved respect, and steadfast commitment to something or someone.

Now what?

What should we consider, in light of this call to a loyalty that involves careful deliberation, deserved respect, and steadfast commitment? Perhaps consideration could be given to priorities. When we consider to whom or to what we are loyal, how do those feelings or those loyalties compare to our loyalty to Jesus? How do our loyalties to country, sport teams, and merchandise compare to that of Jesus? For instance, when we consider our stewardship of time and money invested in corporate worship, how does it measure up compared to the amount of time and money devoted to entertainment? Is worship part of our weekly schedule and giving based upon convenience? Careful deliberation would warrant a faithfulness to weekly worship in both time and money.

Perhaps consideration could be given to how we respect one another, pray for one another, and care for one another. We are, after all, members of the same household family. Our steadfast commitment to Jesus should warrant a pattern of behavior that is in keeping with expectations of a kingdom saint. Lying and gossiping, cheating and stealing, coveting and bankruptcy, lusting and adultery ought not to characterize or be patterns of our behavior. Are we listening and hearing what Jesus desires of us? Perhaps we might take some time, take a walk, and ponder our confession of Jesus anew.

Creativity in Presentation

To involve the congregation in the sermon, some people may own and may be willing to loan you sports paraphernalia of their favorite local high school, college, or professional sports team. Identifying congregants' team or alma mater loyalties may be a fun interactive way to introduce the sermon. Or perhaps, if your congregation is about fifty to 150 people, you might pass out three-by-five cards to everyone the week before you preach your sermon on Hebrews 3:1–6 and ask these questions: "To whom or to what do you consider yourself loyal? Why? What is it about that person, place, or thing that warrants your loyalty"? If your congregation is larger than 150 people, you may want to contact your congregation by email or perhaps survey a group of people on Facebook asking the same questions.

A display of loyalty might be viewed in a clip from the heartfelt Christmas movie *It's a Wonderful Life* (directed by Frank Capra, 1946) where George Bailey (played by Jimmy Stewart), owner of the Bailey Bros. Building & Loan Association, discovers that he has very loyal friends and is declared the richest man in Bedford Falls. You might share how the movie gives careful consideration to George Bailey's character, the earned respect of the community, and the community's commitment to George Bailey. A display of loyalty might also be viewed from *White Christmas* (directed by Michael Curtiz, 1954). It opens and closes with the U.S. Army 151st Division sings Irving Berlin's "The Old Man." It's a heartfelt example of loyalty to a person who deserved respect. While these are older movies, it may be that congregants still view them yearly at Christmastime. If not, *Christmas with the Kranks* (directed by Joe Roth, 2004), starring Tim Allen and Jamie Lee Curtis, might be another movie that demonstrates neighborhood loyalty.

To differentiate between "in God's house" from "over God's house," another military example might be used. In *White Christmas*, Major General Waverly was "in" the army during World War I, while President Franklin D. Roosevelt was "over" all the armed forces at the time. Perhaps, if you know an officer in one of the branches of our armed forces, you might highlight his rank and branch "in" which he or she served. Then identify the U.S. president in office at the time who was "over" him.

Finally, if it doesn't offend people in the congregation, the Apostles' Creed could be adjusted to reflect commitment, loyalty, and dedication by replacing the repeated beginning words "I believe in" as follows:

> *I will commit myself to* God, the Father almighty,
> creator of heaven and earth.
>
> *I will be loyal to* Jesus Christ, God's only Son, our Lord,
> who was conceived by the Holy Spirit,
> born of the Virgin Mary,
> suffered under Pontius Pilate,
> was crucified, died, and was buried;
> he descended to the dead.
> On the third day he rose again;

he ascended into heaven,
he is seated at the right hand of the Father,
and he will come to judge the living and the dead.

I will dedicate myself to the Holy Spirit,
the holy catholic Church,
the communion of saints,
the forgiveness of sins,
the resurrection of the body,
and the life everlasting. Amen.[1]

The point you want to get across is simply this: loyalty involves careful deliberation, deserved respect, and steadfast commitment. One approach to an outline for this text would be as follows:

- Loyalty to Jesus involves careful consideration (vv. 1–2).
- Loyalty to Jesus involves deserved respect (vv. 3–4).
- Loyalty to Jesus involves steadfast commitment (vv. 5–6).

DISCUSSION QUESTIONS

1. When was the Jewish nation called (i.e., established), and how does that calling differ from the one the household family of faith received?
2. What was God's plan for Jesus and how did Jesus fulfill that plan?
3. Why does Jesus deserve greater honor than Moses?
4. What are the two confessions about Jesus we need to consider carefully?
5. What confessions should still be held today?

1 "The Apostles' Creed," in *Praying Together*, May 2007 electronic ed. (London: English Language Liturgical Consultation, 1988), 22, https://irp-cdn.multiscreensite.com/a42fbdb2/files/uploaded/praying.pdf; also available at https://www.englishtexts.org/the-apostles-creed. English translation of *The Apostles' Creed*, adapted © 1988 English Language Liturgical Consultation (ELLC), and used by permission. www.englishtexts.org.

Hebrews 3:7–19

EXEGETICAL IDEA

While God exhorted the household family of faith to resist stubborn unbelief as evidenced in the exodus community, Barnabas expected believers to take heed of any potential stubbornness as well as take steps to avoid it because of the family's allegiance with Jesus, the messianic Son of promise, and because of the stubborn unbelief of the exodus generation that infuriated God.

THEOLOGICAL FOCUS

Vigilance in heeding, avoiding, and resisting stubbornness against God is based upon the household family of faith's present relationship with Jesus and the historical willful unbelief of God's people in the past.

PREACHING IDEA

Stubborn unbelief leads to straying.

PREACHING POINTERS

The Roman household family of faith was well aware that stubborn disbelief was an obstacle to overcome. Historically, stubborn unbelief resulted in Jewish people straying from God that had devastating consequences for the exodus generation, especially at Mount Sinai (Exod. 32:1–33:6) and again at Kadesh Barnea (Num. 14; cf. Ps. 106:7–27a). Consequently, Barnabas not only exhorted the household family of faith about stubborn disbelief; he also explained why it was a problem before issuing his warning about it.

Even today, we struggle with disobedience that leads us to *straying* from God rather than *staying* with God. Many ministries fly a banner about security (= eternal security) in Jesus. However, this sort of security preached, to the neglect of a call for obedience, oftentimes leads to spiritual lethargy. We are all prone to wander and prone to leave the one we love. Therefore, we need the warnings in Hebrews to motivate us to stay close to Jesus when, in reality, we want to wander. We too need to be warned about stubborn unbelief that leads to straying.

HEEDING AND AVOIDING STUBBORNNESS (3:7–19)

LITERARY STRUCTURE AND THEMES (3:7–19)

Barnabas connected his expressed concern for the household family of faith (v. 6) with God speaking directly to them (3:7a). Through a somewhat modified version of Psalm 95:7b–11, God exhorted members the household family of faith by saying, "if you hear" him speaking, "don't harden" your heart like the infuriating exodus generation (vv. 7–9). God's exhortation was followed by God's explanation about his irritation with the exodus generation, namely, their stubborn unbelief that led to rebellion (vv. 10–11). Barnabas then posed an expectation and an exhortation. He expected the Jewish followers of Jesus in Rome to take heed of any stubborn unbelief within their household family, but also exhorted them to take steps to remind one another about the dangers of stubborn unbelief. Yet, the reason for his exhortation was because of their partnership with the messianic Son of promise (vv. 12–14). Barnabas closed with a historical motivation from the past for avoiding stubborn unbelief that provokes God (vv. 15–19).

Barnabas's major theological theme was for the household family of faith to avoid the danger of stubborn unbelief that would lead to their rebellion.

- ***God's Exhortation about Stubborn Unbelief (3:7–9)***
- ***God's Explanation about Stubborn Unbelief (3:10–11)***
- ***Exhortation to Heed Stubborn Unbelief (3:12–14)***
- ***Motivation from History (3:15–19)***

Barnabas's Second Warning in Two Parts and Four Old Testament Texts

Barnabas moved from the household family of faith's need to persist in believing in Jesus (3:1–6) to his second of five warnings (3:7–4:13). His second warning was presented in two parts. Part one opened with the failure of the exodus generation. They were unfaithful and disobedient (3:7–19). Part two expressed two expectations: to fear failure and to strive for success (4:1–13). Barnabas underscored his warning with quotations of Psalm 95:7b–11 and Genesis 2:2 as well as allusions from Exodus 17:1–7 and Numbers 13–14. Barnabas appealed to these texts in order to parallel the household family of faith's current situation with that of the wilderness community at Kadesh Barnea.

EXPOSITION (3:7–19)

Stubborn unbelief was problematic for all God's people and was an obstacle to overcome even for the best of God's people. Historically, stubborn unbelief resulted in rebellion that had devasting consequences for the exodus generation, especially at Mount Sinai (Exod. 32:1–33:6) and again at Kadesh Barnea (Num. 14; cf. Ps. 106:7–27a). When Barnabas penned Hebrews, a Zealot rebellion against Roman officials was gaining momentum in Judaea. Their *loss of freedom* underscored the basis for several skirmishes with Rome. Hengel (1989, 113n200) contends that "the theme of freedom runs through Josephus's accounts of the fourth sect [= Zealots] and the later insurrectionary movement up to the end of the Jewish War like a scarlet thread." Yet, Judaean believers were directed, in Jude's letter, to steer clear of the Judaean revolt against Rome (Bateman, 2015[17]).

And though the events were happening in Judaea, news about the turmoil traveled to Rome. Barnabas's readers maintained their ties with their Judaean homeland by way of sending a yearly temple tax and attending Jewish celebrations in Jerusalem (Acts 2:1, 8–11; Barclay, 1995, 418–24). No doubt the Zealot's call for the liberation of Judaea from Roman occupation, stubborn aspirations to reclaim Judaea as God's independent national kingdom, intense desires for a Messiah figure to lead them, and the growing momentum of the movement throughout Judaea would weigh on members of the Jewish household family of faith in Rome and perhaps even give them pause to reconsider their confessions about Jesus and return to Judaism's cultic way of life.

So, Barnabas directed God's exhortation in Psalm 95 to the members of the Jewish household family of faith in Rome to resist any sympathies they might have for Judaism (Heb. 3:7–11) and reinforce God's perspective about stubborn unbelief, their partnership with Jesus, and the historical stubbornness of the exodus generation of the past (vv. 12–19).

God's Exhortation about Stubborn Unbelief (3:7–9)[1]

God exhorted members of the household family of faith to listen and avoid stubbornness.

3:7. By inserting "therefore" (διό), Barnabas connected his concern for the household family of faith's maintaining their resolve about Jesus (v. 6) with Psalm 95. Thus, Barnabas presented God speaking (λέγει) to the household family of faith through his "holy spirit" (τὸ πνεῦμα τὸ ἅγιον; 3:7a). Linking the "holy spirit" with God's voice was a typical first-century way of God revealing information through the prophets with no *explicit* Trinitarian theistic intent (cf. 1Q28 8:16; 4Q25 8 6:8; Bateman, 2012, 113–14). Barnabas's reference of the "holy spirit" merely underscored that God spoke. What God said were several verses taken from Psalm 95. Originally, Psalm 95 was a summons for Jewish people to praise and pay homage to the Creator-King as well as an exhortation to obey God and avoid stubborn unbelief. The verses Barnabas cited here in Hebrews were from Psalm 95:7b–11. They underscored the psalmist's gnomic call for obedience. It was a call that transcended all time, all generations, and all cultures. Thus, members of the household family of faith were exhorted to obey God's voice (v. 7c).

Excursus on Psalm 95

While Barnabas recontextualized Psalm 95 as an exhortation to his readers, it helps to understand the psalm in its original context.

Psalm 95: The psalm appeared to be a descriptive praise psalm. There was a call to praise (vv. 1–2), a motivation to praise (vv. 3–7a), and an emphasis on God's greatness and grace (vv. 5–7a; Ross, 2016, 114). Although the psalm was probably used for the festivals of unleavened bread, harvest and ingathering at the end of the year in Jerusalem (Exod. 23:14–19), its gnomic nature would seem to fit numerous worship occasions: "Today, if you hear my voice."

Overview: The psalm began with praise to the Creator and King (vv. 1–7a), but it shifted to an exhortation for worshippers not to "harden their hearts" (= be stubborn) and thereby forfeit their opportunity to enter God's safe and secure place, namely, the Promised Land (vv. 7b–11).

1 For various perspectives on Hebrews 3:7–14, see H. W. Bateman IV, ed., *Four Views on the Warning Passages in Hebrews* (Grand Rapids: Kregel, 2007), 94–108; 195–96; 262–72; 350–53.

Message: The congregation was summoned to praise and pay homage to Yahweh their King-Creator-Shepherd, but also exhorted to obey and not rebel against God.

Ambiguity of the Psalm: There is some ambiguity about the psalm's type. Is it an enthronement psalm (Mowinckel, 2014, 1:179), a prophetic exhortation (Sabourin, 1974, 104; Kraus, 1989, 244–55), or a prophetic liturgy (Gunkel, 1998, 317)? More significantly, there is ambiguity involved with dating the psalm. While we may not know when the psalmist actually composed Psalm 95, its gnomic character is undeniable: "Today, if you hear my voice" lends itself to be recontextualized to another historical setting.

Central Point: It seems the central point of the psalm centered around the congregation's regard for God by way of praising him (vv. 1–2), worshipping him (v. 6), and obeying him (vv. 7c–11).

3:8–9. God's exhortation to the household family of faith was a straightforward prohibition (μή; Wallace, 1996, 469): "do not hardened your hearts" (μὴ σκληρύνητε τὰς καρδίας ὑμῶν). The term "hardened" (σκληρύνητε)had the metaphorical sense of stiffening one's neck, which conveyed an attitude of stubbornness. It was a term used to describe Zedekiah (2 Chron. 36:13), the exodus generation (Exod. 32:9, etc.), the predynastic Jewish tribes (Judg. 2;19), the dynastic kingdoms of Israel and Judah (2 Kings 17:14, Ezek. 2:4, 3:7, etc.), Jewish ancestors (4Q504 4:7), and as a characteristic *not to be observed* among the members of the Essenes at Qumran (1Q28 5:5, 26). Thus, God's spirit warned the household family of faith in Rome not to be stubborn and thereby provoke God, as the exodus generation did at Kadesh Barnea.

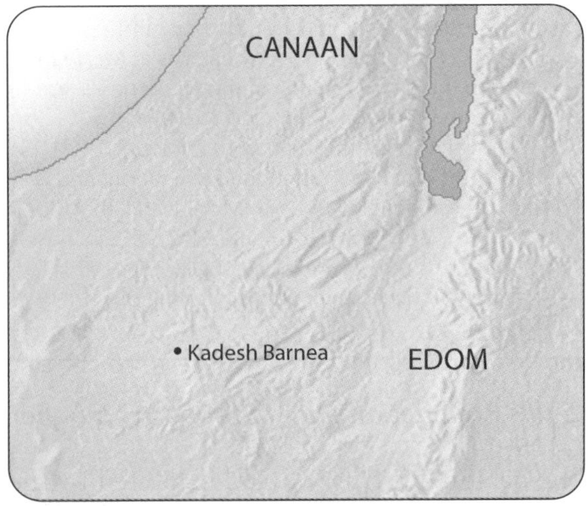

The psalmist called his readers to obey God's voice, namely, to resist stubbornness (= harden heart). He appealed to the failure of the exodus generation that lead to rebellion, the testing of God for forty years, and God's subsequent judgment. They were the three key focal points of Psalm 95:7b–10. Although the place names of "Meribah" and "Massah" were cited in the psalm (cf. Exod. 17:1–7), Barnabas changed the names to reflect their actual meaning: "rebellion" (παραπικρασμῷ) and "testing" (πειρασμοῦ).[2] The change then underscored an event to which the psalmist actually alluded: the stubborn unbelief that led to their rebellion at Kadesh Barnea recorded in Numbers 14:1–45. The household family of faith was not to be like the exodus generation who, while at Kadesh Barnea, stood at the threshold of Canaan and yet refused to trust God.

2 Derived from its verb form "I rebel" (παραπικραινω), the noun "rebellion" (παραπικρασμῷ) is not found prior to the LXX and even then, it occurs only once (Ps. 94 [HB 95]:8). Its usage is equally sparse in the NT, occurring only twice when Barnabas quotes Psalm 94 (HB 95):8 in Hebrews 3:8 and 3:15.

Editorial Differences between Psalm 95:7b–11 and Hebrews 3:7–11	
Psalm 95:7–11	**Hebrews 3:7–11**
Today, if only you would obey him! [8]He says, "Do not harden your hearts as at ***Meribah***, as in the day at ***Massah*** in the wilderness, [9]where your fathers tempted me, tried me, even though they had seen my work. [10]For forty years I disgusted that generation, and I said, "These people have wayward hearts; they do not obey my commands." [11]So I swore in my anger, "They will never enter into my resting place."	Therefore, just as the holy spirit says, Today, if only you would obey his voice! [8]He says, "Do not harden your hearts as in the ***rebellion***, in the days of ***testing*** in the wilderness. [9]There *your fathers* tested me by trial and they saw my works for forty years. [10]Therefore, *I became provoked* at that generation and *I said*, "Their hearts are always wandering and they have not known my ways." [11]So *I swore* in my anger, "They will never enter my resting place."

God's Explanation about Stubborn Unbelief (3:10–11)

The habitual distrust of God exhibited by the exodus generation was the reason why God became upset and thereby denied them entrance into the land of Canaan.

3:10. By inserting a second "therefore" (διό) into the psalm, Barnabas not only shifted the emphasis of the psalm, he also drew specific attention to the reason why God "became angry" (προσώχθισα; NIV, NRSV, NLT) or "became provoked" (ESV, NET). First, the shifted phrase "for forty years" in Hebrews 3:9b qualified "and they saw my works." Thus, the clause "and they saw my works *for forty years*" stressed the number of years the exodus generation saw God work on their behalf. Second, it underscored why God was "very upset" (BDAG, s.v. "προσοχθίζω," p. 884) with the exodus generation. They habitually (ἀεί) wandered and lacked knowledge about God's ways (οὐκ ἔγνωσαν τὰς ὁδούς μου). In other words, they did not trust God, and therefore, they disobeyed God repeatedly.

3:11. The habitual distrust of God did not end well for the exodus generation. God "swore" (ὤμοσα) "in anger" (τῇ ὀργῇ) against them. To swear or to take an oath was a common cultural custom of the ancient Near East and in Second Temple Judaism. In the Bible, oaths had significant judicial value and were to be taken seriously (Pss. 15:4; 63:11; Eccl. 5:4–5; Matt. 23:16–22). And though some Jewish writers warned against oath taking (Sir 23:9–11; Philo, *Spec. 1,2,3,4.* 2.1–2), people of the Jewish Essene sect in Judaea swore oaths for community initiation purposes (Josephus, *B.J.* 2.139–42). The phrase "observe what comes out of your lips" (Deut. 23:24) was interpreted to mean that every binding oath a person promised with regard to the Law could not be broken, even if it meant death (4Q270 frag. 9 col 2.16:6–8; cf. Wise et al., 1996, 66). Here in Psalm 95:11 (94:11 LXX), God took an oath against the exodus generation that drew attention to their stubborn disbelief that led to their rebellion at Kadesh Barnea (Num. 14:1–4, 10), their punishment (vv. 11–12), Moses's intercession and God's forgiveness (vv. 19–20), and God's honoring his oath (vv. 40–45).

The phrase "into my rest" (εἰς τὴν κατάπαυσίν μου), is readily debated among commentators due to its ambiguity in Psalm 95:11 (94:11 LXX). In the psalm, the psalmist may have spoken of the land as Israel's "resting-place" (Deut. 12:9; cf. Isa. 11:10, 32:18's promise of a "secure resting place"), or he may have referred to the temple as Yahweh's resting-place (Ps. 132:14; cf. Isa. 66:1 with 2 Chron. 6:41). The latter option, however, speaks indirectly to the land as Israel's resting-place as well, in that, the temple symbolized the place where Yahweh mediated "rest" to the faithful Jewish community throughout the land (cf. 1 Kings 8:27–53; 9:1–9; Jer. 7:1–15). The abstract idea of "rest" indicated blessings of a *safe and secure life* (= rest) in the land (BDAG, s.v. "κατάπαυσις" 2, p. 523).

Second Temple Jewish literature captured this OT connection when Jewish texts spoke of the future Davidite to and through whom Yahweh would bestow rest (4Q174 2:18–3:13, 4Q504 4; cf. Ps. 132, Isa. 66:1). Thus, "the oath [in Ps. 95:11] summed up covenantal blessings promised to God's people—*blessings of a secure life in the land*—which were connected with God's [temple] presence among them" (Laansma, 1997, 41–45, 67–75). Later in 4:4, the expression "place-of-rest" in the land via the temple shifted to a "place-of-rest" that belonged to God. Thus, "*my* resting-place" would eventually evidence an escalation of meaning from a *physical* earthly place of rest to a *heavenly* one. But here in verse 11, Barnabas motivated the household family of faith by recalling how the rebellion of the exodus generation infuriated God and as a result was denied a *safe and secure life* (= rest) in the land of Canaan.

Exhortation to Heed Stubborn Unbelief (3:12–13)

Barnabas expected the household family of faith to take heed of any potential stubborn disbelief among themselves and exhorted them to take steps to avoid it and its subsequent relational breakdown with God.

3:12. At this point, every family member was given fair warning about the dangers of stubborn unbelief and abandoning God: "Keep your eyes open, brothers *and sisters*" (βλέπετε, ἀδελφοί; BDAG, s.v. "βλέπω" 6, p. 179). While several alternative translations exist ("take care brothers *and sisters*," NRSV; "see to it, brothers and sisters," NET; or "be careful brothers *and sisters*," NLT), this was, for Barnabas, a rather sharp summons to the entire family household of faith in Rome.

The expressed threat was that family members within the household (μήποτε ἔσται ἔν τινι ὑμῶν, literally, "lest there will be in any of you") might have "an evil, unbelieving heart." Naturally, the "heart" (καρδία) spoke of the moral decisions, the moral life, or vices and virtues (BDAG, s.v. "καρδία" 1bδ, p. 508). Here the "heart" was clearly qualified as "evil, unbelieving" (πονηρὰ ἀπιστίας). Jeremiah made similar observations about the heart. The Jewish people of his day followed the inclination of their stubborn and wicked heart that was even more wicked than their Jewish ancestors (11:8; 16:12; cf. 7:24–26). Whereas "evil" denoted a person's morally corrupt decisions (BDAG, s.v. "πονηρά" 1aβ, p. 851), "unbelieving" (ἀπιστίας) referred to a person's "unwillingness to commit" (BDAG, s.v. ἀφίστια 1, p. 103), ignore God's voice, or simply to disobey God (Num 14:9; cf. v. 11). Thus, every member in the household family of faith who was unwilling to commit or align themselves to Jesus was accused of making decisions that were morally corrupt and unethical.

For Barnabas, the result (ἐν τῷ + inf., ἀποστῆναι)[3] of moral corruption and unbelief was apostasy. An "unwillingness to commit" (ἀφίστια) led to "falls[ing] away" (NASB, RSV, ESV), "turn[ing] away" (NIV, ESV, NET, NLT, etc.), "forsak[ing]" (NET), or "departing" (KJV). The idea was that

3 While Spicq (1952, 2:75) and Wallace (1991, 593 n. 12; cf. RSV, TEV) interpret ἐν τῷ + the infinitive ἀποστῆναι as result, others view it as epexegetical and thereby defining "an evil, unbelieving heart" (Ellingworth, 1993, 222; Cockerill, 2012, 184).

uncommitted people were more prone "to distance themselves" from God (BDAG s.v. "ἀφίστημι," 2a, p. 158) or withdraw from God. Joshua reflected a similar concern when he said, "Far be it from us that we should rebel [ἀποστῆναι] against the LORD and turn away [ἀποστῆναι] this day from following the LORD . . ." (Josh. 22:29 LXX). Here in Hebrews 3:1, 12, to have a morally corrupt and unbelieving heart resulted in withdrawing from God (cf. Jer. 17:5; Sir 10:12). Or we might say, there was a relational breakdown with God whereby family members were prone to leave the household family of faith (cf. 10:25). Bruce (1990, 376) suggests something more than just a relapsing into orthodox Judaism was creating doubts. Similarly, Hengel (1985, 30) believes that more should be made of the connection between the Neronian persecution of believers (A.D. 64–65) in Rome and the Jewish revolt when interpreting Mark's Gospel, also written to Roman followers of Jesus. Thus, Barnabas cautioned ("take care" or "see to it") about stubbornness (3:8, 15) or the lack of commitment to Jesus (3:12) that could and would affect one's relationship with the living God. So, any sympathies for or desires to support the Zealot political upheavals in Judaea or any desires to return to Judaism were clearly discouraged here.

The Heartbeat of Psalm 95

Psalm 95:7–11, as it was quoted in Hebrews 3:7–10, reverberated the heartbeat of the wilderness community. They *turned away* from God (Num. 14:9, 32:9; cf. 13:1–14:45). Ezekiel paralleled the wilderness community's *turning away* from God with those of the first temple (966–586 B.C.), namely, the Jewish community's departure from the living God (Ezek. 20:8, 38; cf. Jer. 2:5; Dan. 9:5, 9; Bar 3:8). Likewise, Second Temple (514 B.C.–A.D. 70) Jewish communities departed from God through "abandoning the religion of their fathers" (1 Macc 2:19) and through the actions "of the lawless who had rebelled against God" (1QpHab 8:11, 16; *TDOT*, 9:1–5).

3:13. In contrast (ἀλλά, "but") to his warning about a relational breakdown with God, Barnabas made a positive appeal: "exhort one another" (παρακαλεῖτε ἑαυτούς; KJV, ASV, NRSV, NET).[4] This act of exhorting was to be done daily (καθ' ἑκάστην ἡμέραν) as Barnabas underscored with the phrase "as long as it is called 'Today'" (ἄχρις οὗ τὸ σήμερον καλεῖται). "Today" (σήμερον) pointed back to the Psalm 95 quotation (v. 7). Its gnomic sense once again transcended time. Thus, Barnabas reapplied the psalm to the era of the Roman Empire during the time in which the Jewish household family of faith lived (cf. 1:2a).

Barnabas's intention (ἵνα, "that") for exhorting one another regularly was in order that followers of Jesus might avoid a hardened (μὴ σκληρυνθῇ) heart or stubbornness brought on by sin's deception (3:13c). Whereas "hardened" or stubborn unbelief in verses 8 and 15 referred to the ten spies whose negative report discouraged an entire exodus generation (Num. 13:32–14:4; 32:9), here the expectation for a daily practice of exhortation within the household family of faith in Rome was intended to prevent any stubbornness (= a hardened heart; cf. 4:7) against God. Thus, exhorting one another repeatedly (= daily) was intended to avoid stubborn unbelief against "the living God."

4 Ellingworth (1993, 223) links the concept of comfort with exhortation and may be reflected in the translation "encourage" (NASB, NIV). Cockerill (2012, 185 n. 49), however, points out that Ellingworth's understanding of "comfort" in light of the broader context of Hebrews (cf. 6:18; 10:25; 12:5; 13:19, 22) and the LXX's preferred use of παρακαλεῖτε misses the urgency of the immediate context.

"Do Not Harden" (μὴ σκληρυνθῇ)
As in the previously occurrence (v. 8), "do not harden" (μὴ σκληρύνητε) was from Psalm 95 [94 LXX]. The Septuagint rendered the Hebrew word *qsh* in Psalm 95:8 as "stiff-neck" or "harden" (σκλερύνω). Although rare in secular Greek, many occurrences in the Septuagint had a moral and religious connotation. Of particular interest was the word's use to describe Israel, who stiffened their neck / hardened their heart to Yahweh's divine desires and thereby refused to follow his ways (Deut. 10:13–16, 2 Kings 17:13–14, 2 Chron. 30:6b–8, Neh. 9:16). Philo (*Leg.* 3:136) noted that when an ass or the horse refused to move, it tightened and stiffened its neck because efforts to resist were localized in their neck. So metaphorically speaking, "stiff-neck" or "harden" (σκλερύνω) meant stubborn disobedience or deliberate resistance to move (= obey; cf. *TLNT*, 3:260–61). Thus, the point Barnabas made was not to be *like* an obstinate or stiff-necked ass or horse.

3:14. The reason (γάρ, "for") for exhorting each other was because of the relationship the household of faith in Rome had with the messianic Son of promise: "we have become partners with Christ" (μέτοχοι γὰρ τοῦ Χριστοῦ γεγόναμεν). Unlike in 3:1 where the emphasis was upon the partnership or allegiance (μέτοχος, "partnership") within the community, here the emphasis was upon the present reality (γεγόναμεν) of the family's partnership or allegiance with the messianic Son of promise (τοῦ Χριστοῦ), which in turn joined them with God (1:3a). This present allegiance, however, had continuing effects (intensive perf.).

Nevertheless, the partnership, allegiance, or relationship was conditional (ἐάνπερ, "if"). The repetition of the phrase "if we hold firm" (ἐάνπερ . . . βεβαίαν κατάσχωμεν) from verse 6 underscored Barnabas's concern for the household family of faith as well as betrayed the family's genuine need to maintain their confession or resolve about Jesus as God's sent spokes*man* and high priest (cf. 3:6, cf. 10:23). Any partnership or allegiance involved an obligation (βεβαίαν). Here in Hebrews, the Jewish household family of faith in Rome was expected or even obligated to "remain firm" (κατάσχωμεν) or "to *adhere* firmly" to what they had been taught and confessed about Jesus (BDAG, s.v. "κατέχω" 2b, p. 532). The duration of their faith in Jesus was "until the end" (μέχρι τέλους), more specifically until they died. Thus, avoiding stubborn unbelief about God's Messiah not only revealed their loyalty or allegiance to their confessions about Jesus, it also reinforced the household family's obligation to be loyal to the messianic Son of promise. Thus, family membership had both privileges and responsibilities.

LEXICAL ANALYSIS: "Firm" (βεβαίαν)
Although "firm" (βεβαίαν) is clearly translated and understood with a judicial sense in 2:2 (cf. 6:19; 9:17), here the legal sense seems less clear. Some English Bibles obscure the term's significance altogether (see NIV). Translations like "*steadfast* until the end" (KJV), "*faithful* till the end" (NLT), and "*firm* until [to] the end" (NASB, RSV, ESV, NRSV, NET). It seems that the term "firm" had the sense of maintaining continuity, being unwavering, or being persistent in one's original commitment to Jesus (BDAG, s.v. "βεβαίος" 2, p. 172). So, the household family of faith was to be committed to their original confession about Jesus (cf. 3:6, 14), and yet, the presence of "firm" (βεβαίαν) inadvertently stressed the community's obligation to maintain their partnership with or their allegiance with "The Messiah" (= Christ). Thus, partnership with the divine royal Son had both privileges and obligations. Here the partners' obligation involved loyalty to Jesus.

Motivation from History (3:15–19)

Recalling a historical rebellion of the exodus

generation reinforced the household family's need to avoid stubborn unbelief.

3:15–18. "While it is said" (ἐν τῷ λέγεσθαι, temp. inf.) introduced Barnabas's reiteration of Psalm 95:7. The restatement of Psalm 95:7 set the stage for several rhetorical questions and drew attention to varying aspects of the exodus generation and the themes of "hearing" (= obeying), "today" (= anytime), and "hardening" (= stubbornness) already applied to the household family of faith (Johnson, 2006, 118).

Here, however, the rhetorical form of questioning recalled the rebellion (παρεπίκραναν) of the exodus generation who were led out of Egypt under Moses's leadership (v. 16). Barnabas evoked their provoking of God and his subsequent punishment, namely, physical death (v. 17). And he reminded them that God denied his chosen exodus generation entrance into the land of promise due to their deliberate *disobedience* (v. 18). In other words, God withheld his *safe and secure life* (= rest) for them in the land of Canaan because of their rebellion.

LEXICAL ANALYSIS: "The rebellion" (παρεπίκραναν)
English interpretations about "rebellion" vary. Some supply *"him"* to indicate God's being made angry or provoked: "For who provoked *Him* when they had heard?" (NASB; in keeping with the LXX). Other translations do not insert the direct object *"him"* and thereby emphasize the wilderness community's rebellion: "Who were they that heard and yet were rebellious?" (RSV, NRSV) or "who were those who heard and yet rebelled" (ESV), and most simply put, "who rebelled [against God]" (NLT, NET cf. BDAG, s.v. "παραπικρασμός," p. 770, *TDNT*, 6:125–27). The LXX's reflection of the exodus events (Ps. 77:17 [78:17 HB], 40, 56; Ps. 105 [106 HB]: 7; Ezek. 20:13, 21), as it was alluded to here in Hebrews 3:12b, favored the latter English rendering. Thus, Barnabas appealed to the Israelite wilderness community as a negative example, an example of an unfaithful community that was not to be followed or imitated.

What Is an Inclusio?

An inclusio is a literary device that brackets verses. Typically, the same set of words appear at the beginning and end of a group of verses. Barnabas sometimes bracketed verses or entire sections by way of an inclusio. For example, he bracketed verses by way of an inclusio in Hebrews 1:3 and 1:13, 3:12 and 3:19, 4:14 and 5:10, and 8:7 and 10:16–17. Barnabas was known for bracketing sections of thought by way of inclusion: Hebrews 1:1 and 4:13 as well as 4:14 and 10:23. The following examples are adopted from Bateman, 2012, 192.

Hebrews 1:3 and 1:13	the repeated presentation of the Son positioned at the right hand of God
Hebrews 3:12 and 3:19	the repeated presentation of the unfaithfulness of the wilderness generation
Hebrews 4:14 and 5:10	the repeated presentation of Jesus as regal priest
Hebrews 8:7 and 10:16–17	the repeated presentation of the new covenant

Two Major Sections:

Hebrews 1:1 and 4:13	the similar periodic sentence on God's Son and the periodic sentence on God's Word
Hebrews 4:14 and 10:23	the repeated exhortation to hold fast

3:19. Barnabas then drew his conclusion (καί, "so"; cf. NET) from the argument he presented in verses 15–18. Yet, the words "*we see* that" (βλέπομεν ὅτι) actually served as a bracket (= an inclusio) to the words that began this rather lengthy sentence in verse 12, "*beware*, brothers *and sisters*" (βλέπετε, ἀδελφοί). And though verses 12–19 are a bracketed group of verses, Barnabas closed and reinforced his message that appeared toward the end of this bracket, namely, verses 15–18. He concluded his point based upon Jewish history ("we see," βλέπομεν) or as "history teaches" (Ps. 106:24–26; Spicq, 1952, 2:79). Jewish history about the exodus generation's failure to experience God's *safe and secure life* (= rest) in the land of Canaan was because of (δι' + accusative) their deliberate refusal to believe or trust God, which was "apostasy" (ἀπιστίαν). Thus, God prevented them from crossing over Canaan's threshold to enjoy a *safe and secure life* (= rest) in the Promised Land (cf. Num. 14:28–35; 40–45).

THEOLOGICAL FOCUS

The exegetical idea (while God exhorted the household family of faith to resist stubborn unbelief as evidenced in the exodus community, Barnabas expected believers to take heed of any potential stubbornness as well as take steps to avoid it because of the family's allegiance with Jesus, the messianic Son of promise, and because of the stubborn unbelief of the exodus generation that infuriated God) leads to this theological focus: Vigilance in heeding, avoiding, and resisting stubbornness against God is based upon the household family of faith's present relationship with Jesus and the historical willful unbelief of God's people in the past.

The major theological theme of this preaching unit is the real and present danger of stubborn unbelief that leads to rebellion, which is addressed in three ways. The first is in the form of a call to avoid it. The household family of faith is to listen to and obey God (vv. 7, 13). The second is a warning. The household family of faith is warned about stubborn unbelief evidenced within the exodus generation (vv. 8–9, 12–13). The third is an historical example. The household family of faith is to be aware of the divine reaction to stubbornness that leads to rebellion (vv. 10–11, 15–18).

PREACHING AND TEACHING STRATEGIES

Exegetical and Theological Synthesis

This passage began with words from God. This was a significant turn of a phrase as it established that the words of the OT specifically were given by God's holy spirit. The quotation was from Psalm 95 and called the household family of faith not to harden their heart against God. As noted above, Barnabas inserted "therefore" in verse 10, which highlighted the reasons God became angry. The motivation to avoid rebellion was so that the listener would enter into God's rest. The theme of rest was then developed through the rest of the passage through two specific admonitions.

First, they were warned not to have an unbelieving heart (v. 12). Second, they were to hold fast their confidence that they shared in Jesus (v. 14). Third, the concluding motivation was from history. Their own nation's history of rebellion, and God's consistent response to it, should motivate them not to fall into unbelief (v. 19).

Preaching Idea

Stubborn unbelief leads to straying.

Contemporary Connections

What does it mean?

What does it mean that stubborn unbelief leads to straying? Theologically, there's a strong focus on being vigilant. As Herb noted above, "Vigilance in heeding, avoiding, and resisting stubbornness against God is based upon the household family of faith's present relationship with Jesus and the historical willful unbelief of God's people in the past." Yet, there will be a real theological challenge in this text for those who have a strong sense of God's security. In fact, some may be troubled by the apparent warning to those who are in the congregation, if not at least in the crowd, who are given this strong warning. Nevertheless, this passage recalls Psalm 24,

> Who shall ascend the hill of the LORD?
> And who shall stand in his holy place?
> He who has clean hands and a pure heart,
> who does not lift up his soul to what is false
> and does not swear deceitfully.
> (vv. 3–4 ESV)

It seems that the only ones who are allowed to worship are those who have perfect purity and perfect integrity, yet the psalmist said something that was suspiciously messianic, starting in verse 7:

> Lift up your heads, O gates!
> And be lifted up, O ancient doors,
> that the King of glory may come in.
> Who is this King of glory?
> The LORD, strong and mighty,
> the LORD, mighty in battle!
> Lift up your heads, O gates!
> And lift them up, O ancient doors,
> that the King of glory may come in.
> Who is this King of glory?
> The LORD of hosts,
> he is the King of glory! (vv. 7–10 ESV)

The psalmist progressed from the qualification to worship to the ultimate object of our worship—the King of glory. Hebrews 3:7–19 is a call to vigilance. The implication is that people who reject clear warnings, who are not vigilant, are in danger of being found astray from Jesus. Warnings, in and of themselves, are not punishment or judgment, but they are a means for avoiding impending trouble. They reveal what is best for us.

Is it true?

Is it true that stubborn unbelief leads to straying? While we do not want to believe it, we are all prone to wander away from God. And not only do we feel it, we do it. We may want to believe that disobedience is static and that it does not move or effect anything around us, but it does. We forget that disobedience, even if not exposed, has a detrimental effect on all those around us. It's never stationary. It's not static, it's dynamic; it's a living death. It can lead to disobedience, which leads to hardening, and hardening leads to unbelief. (v. 8)

We might liken disobedience to pancreatic cancer. It is one of the worst forms of cancer because of the location of the pancreas. This organ is embedded so far into the abdominal cavity that it is hard to detect the cancer. What often happens is that the cancer starts in the pancreas but then migrates and metastasizes until it is all over the body. Not only is the cellular composition of the cancer different from other forms of cancer, but there is simply no warning of the impending danger.

If we knew we had cancer cells inside of us, we would address it. We would be aggressive in going after it. We know that cancer, by its very nature, migrates and moves. Like cancer, sin acts the same way. Although not all of us may have cancer, we each have sin inside of us. Sin is more dangerous than cancer, and it literally lives in us. Why would we not heed the warning and do anything we could to avoid the effects of cancer?

Now what?

Living in stubborn unbelief that leads to straying is a clear and present danger to everyone. This is why God gave us the warnings. When a car dashboard shows a warning light, we ignore it to our peril. We may even find a way to make the light go off. However, that does not make the warning go away!

The way to make the warning go away is to heed the warning. This is the application of the passage: self-examination. Is there any evidence of disloyalty to Jesus in my life for which I need to repent? Or more specifically, is there sin in my life I do not want to repent of? If that is the case, we must ask why. Why would I risk the outcome of not heeding the warning? Why would I want to jeopardize all that I love? Why is this sin so important to me?

When viewed this way, it helps us to see how similar we are to the nation of Israel. All throughout their history, they were plagued with a love for idols. They wanted to worship something other than the one true God. And yet, as Calvin said, our hearts are idol factories, creating things that we can love more than God.

Creativity in Presentation

This is an important time to remember that creativity in communication must be faithful to the text. If someone uses a visual illustration that is physical, it will be important that it does not take attention away from the text. This is always true; however, it is especially true with this sobering text.

One approach would be to have the congregation think of warning signs. Some warning signs could be placed on the stage. These could be road signs, or they could be signs that say "DANGER" or "KEEP OUT." It would be effective if you could display the large signs used in construction zones. Talk through each of the signs on the stage and describe where they might be found.

Then, ask the question about motivation. Why would someone hang or set up a warning sign? How often have we seen a sign that says, "WET PAINT"? Our propensity is not to avoid the alleged painted wall or bench but rather to reach out and touch it to see if the warning sign is true. Yet warning signs are not used to irritate us; they are used because someone was motivated to protect us. Although the danger is real, we may not feel like it is. Now, be sure to explain the significant difference between the motivation behind human warnings and divine warnings. The threat level that motivated these warning signs is assessed by people. It may or may not indicate a real threat. However, the warnings placed by God are there due to a very real threat. God is perfect, and his motivation for warning us is to protect us from a very real danger.

Therefore, this is the good news. Since the warning is real, we must heed the warning to avoid the divine impending danger. The security that comes from receiving the warning is the reality that God will protect those who heed the warning!

The point you want to get across is simply this: Stubborn unbelief leads to straying. One approach to an outline for this text would be as follows:

- God's warning against stubborn unbelief (vv. 7–11)
- Don't stray from God (vv. 12–13).
- Don't stray from God, or you won't share in Christ (v. 14).
- Don't stray from God and forfeit his rest (vv. 15–19).

Time must be taken with verses 7–11 to establish the motivations found in verses 12–19.

DISCUSSION QUESTIONS

1. If sin leads to straying, and sin starts with the belief of a lie, what lies are we believing that cause us to fall into sin?

2. What steps are necessary to take in order to combat the lies we believe with the truth of God's Word?

3. Sin breeds selfishness, and we often do not see who all we are hurting by our choices to sin. When we give ourselves over to a lifestyle of sin, who suffers?

4. Who are the people in your life that help you deal with your sin? Who challenges you to repent when you are deliberately living in sin?

Hebrews 4:1–13

EXEGETICAL IDEA

The household family of faith was expected to fear failure because of the historical stubborn unbelief of the exodus generation, and yet, based upon God's invitation for a future Sabbath celebration, the household family of faith was expected to strive to be successful in not repeating the historical failures of the past.

THEOLOGICAL FOCUS

God's promise of a future celebration with him is available to all those who do not take their future with God for granted and thereby do not cease striving to succeed in joining God in his future celebration.

PREACHING IDEA

People who fail to learn from the past are guaranteed to repeat it.

PREACHING POINTERS

Time and again, Jewish leaders and Jewish people throughout the Roman Empire rejected Jesus, the message about Jesus, and his messengers. The kingdom Jesus proclaimed was turned down. Yet, Judaeans living during the mid-60s assumed they could rebel against Rome, declare their independence, and exist apart from the Roman Empire as "God's Jewish kingdom." They displayed repeatedly a fearless audacity that threatened Rome's revered *Pax Romana* (= Roman peace). Their stubbornness led to a rebellion that revealed self-assurance, feelings of fearlessness, and defiant activities, whether they be aggressive or passive-aggressive behavior. The Jewish family of faith in Rome was well aware of the Judaean revolt in much the same way as those who had been taken captive to Babylon in 605 and 597 B.C. were aware of the happenings in Jerusalem during the time of Jeremiah. From beginning to end, Barnabas addressed the original readers' current story by showing connecting points between the Jewish rebellion against Rome in Judaea with the exodus rebellion against God at Kadesh Barnea. Thus, Barnabas recalled a similar sort of rebellion against God's plan for his people.

Even today, we too wrestle with rebelling against God's plan. The plan God has for my life is impacted by Jesus's words in the Sermon on the Mount and aspects echoed in Hebrews 13. Jesus demonstrated life in the kingdom by painting a picture of people who love their enemies, divest in this world to invest in the life to come, and to not worry about what tomorrow might bring. All those kingdom virtues are very counterintuitive. I want to dispose of my enemies, hoard in this life, and fret over tomorrow. We all tend to rebel against God's plan. This passage addresses a rebellion that has eternal consequences. It's the type of rebellion that can lead to a failure to enter the rest of God. Thus, when we fail to learn from the past we are guaranteed to repeat it.

THE FEAR FACTOR (4:1–13)

LITERARY STRUCTURE AND THEME (4:1–13)

As a form of application, Barnabas challenged the household family of faith to fear failure yet strive for success (4:1–10). He opened with the expectation to fear failure because the exodus generation was divided between those who did and did not listen to God. Nevertheless, Barnabas inferred that the household family of faith were paying attention to God, believing God, and thereby safe and secure with God just as God said (vv. 1–5). Based upon what God said in verse 5, Barnabas determined that God's invitation to the exodus generation remained open by God's repeated invitation spoken through David by offering a reasonable explanation for God to have spoken about another invitation and by concluding that a future Sabbath celebration remained available for the household family of faith (vv. 6–10). Barnabas closed with an intentional expectation to strive for success in order to avoid the historical pattern of disobedience because God's revelatory message probes and issues divine judgment—judgment that penetrated, separated, and judged the innermost thoughts and attitudes of all living creatures (vv. 11–13).

Barnabas's theme was simple: persevere in faith in Jesus or suffer divine judgment.

- ***The Fear of Failure (4:1–5)***
- ***God's Invitation Remains Open (4:6–10)***
- ***Strive for Success (4:11–13)***

EXPOSITION (4:1–13)

Stubborn unbelief that leads to rebellion tended to involve self-assurance, feelings of fearlessness, and defiant activities, whether they be aggressive or passive-aggressive behavior. For Judaeans living during the mid-60s the assumption that they could rebel against Rome, declare their independence, and exist as "God's Jewish kingdom" apart from the Roman Empire required a great deal of chutzpah. The vigorous rhetoric of Judaea's rebellious leaders was a repeated display of their fearless audacity that threatened Rome's revered *Pax Romana* (= Roman peace). "Anyone might make himself *king* [βασιλεύς] as the head of a band of rebels," according to Josephus, "and then would press on to the destruction of the community, causing trouble to few Romans . . ." (*A.J.* 17.10.8 §285 [trans. Marcus]). Barnabas addressed the original readers' current story that revealed connections between the Jewish rebellion against Rome with the exodus rebellion against God at Kadesh Barnea. Barnabas recalled a similar sort of rebellion against God's plan for his people. Judaeans were repeating history.

Not only was there rebellion against God's plan, like the people at Kadesh Barnea, the Jews living in Judaea during the 60s were divided. At Kadesh Barnea, some were listening to God (e.g., Moses, Joshua, Caleb), and others were not (ten spies who swayed an entire nation to rebel). In Judaea, the Zealots were promoting, recruiting, and swaying Judaeans to join their cause, namely, to reestablish the nation of Israel on their terms, not God's. There were, however, those who stood against the revolt like Josephus (*Vita,* 1.4 §§17–20) and Jude (Bateman, 2015[17], 51–80). Yet, the news about Judaea's rebellion, did not remain in Judaea. After all,

Judaea was still the beloved homeland of all Jewish people and the location of their place of worship, the temple, which they supported financially by way of their annual temple tax.

So, while disruptive events in Judaea were not occurring in Rome, the household family of faith in Rome was aware of and perhaps even sympathetic to the Zealot cause. Any empathy they may have had for those wreaking havoc in Judaea may in turn have raised questions about Jesus, his messiahship, and God's messianic promise. Subsequently, Barnabas interjected an emotional factor: fear. He expected the household family of faith to fear failure because of the historical failure of the exodus generation (vv. 1–5); and yet, based upon God's repeated invitation for a future Sabbath celebration (vv. 6–10), Barnabas expected the family of faith to strive for success and not repeat the historical disaster of the past (vv. 12–13).

The Fear of Failure (4:1–5)

As a household family of faith in Rome, members were to fear failing to cross the threshold into God's heavenly "place-of-rest" and thereby avoid repeating the disaster of the exodus generation.

4:1. Barnabas opened his application (οὖν, "therefore") with the expectation to fear, "let us fear" (φοβηθῶμεν; NASB, ESV). Whereas "fear" as it pertained to death was eliminated in 2:14, "fear" here was an expectation. Unfortunately, some translations soften the sense of becoming frightened (BDAG, s.v. "φοβέω" 1, p. 1060) with renderings like "we must be weary" (NET) or "let us be careful" (NIV; cf. NRSV). Yet, when the exodus generation saw Pharaoh chasing them, "they feared greatly" (וַיִּירְאוּ מְאֹד; LXX: ἐφοβήθησαν σφόδρα) or "they were terrified" (NET; Exod. 14:10). The NLT captures the truest sense of Barnabas's concern: "so we ought to tremble with fear." The household family of faith was to "fear" (φοβηθῶμεν). What was to be feared was failure.

Unfortunately, some translations soften this failure with "should *seem* to come short of it" (KJV; cf. NRSV), "may *seem* to have failed" (ESV), or "may *seem* to come short of it" (NASB, NET; cf. *TDNT*, 2:232–33; Westcott, 1986, 93; Ellingworth, 1993, 239–40). Others rightly recognize a real and present danger of failing: "*be found* to have fallen short of it" (NIV), "*be discovered* to have failed to reach it" (RSV; cf. Attridge, 1989, 124). Even though the temporal phrase "while a promise remains of entering his rest" *may* support a softer rendering, a comparison of this verse with verse 11 favors a translation that evidences a real threat. Barnabas contemplated a real and present danger of "failure" or "fall" (ὑστερηκέναι) that would have eternal ramifications (cf. 6:6; Laansma, 1997, 285). Thus, this particular Roman household family of faith was at risk of failing to enter God's place of rest, namely, "that some of you *might fail* (δοκῇ . . . ὑστερηκέναι) to experience it" (NLT; cf. BDAG, s.v. "δοκεω" 2, p. 255, and s.v. "ὑστερηκέναι" 1, p. 1043). The events happening in Judaea may have caused them to question their *allegiance* to Jesus and *awakened* a desire to return to Judaism because loyalty to Moses, the Law, and Judaism was entrenched in their DNA.

So, Barnabas drew attention to the current availability of God's promise of rest. Before dealing with the concept of rest, attention must be given to the two types of divine promises (ἐπαγγελίας) in Hebrews: fulfilled (realized) and unfulfilled (unrealized). In 4:1, the promise of "rest" was a promise yet to be fully realized, "while it remains" (καταλειπομένης; BDAG, s.v. "καταλείπω" 4, p. 521). Thus, the household family of faith were *potential* recipients of God's promises (cf. 1:14; 6:12, 17; 9:15). What was to be feared here in verse 1 was a failure to enter God's promise of "rest" (κατάπαυσις), a theme of great theological import in Hebrews (noun: 3:11, 18; 4:1, 3 [twice], 5, 10, 11; verb: 4:4, 8, 10).

TEXTUAL ANALYSIS: Conflicting Text Critical Reading: 4:2
Exegetical Issue: Both the manuscript evidence (𝔓[13] 𝔓[46] A B C D* 0243 0278 33 81 1739 2464) and the possibility that a scribe altered the case ending of "unite" (**συγκεράννυμι**) from **ους** to **ος** strongly supports the text rendering and thereby draws attention to Kadesh Barnea and *the community's unwillingness to listen to Joshua and Caleb*. The text is the preferred reading.

txt. "because **they were not united** by faith with those who listened" (**μὴ συγκεκερασμένους** τῇ πίστει τοῖς ἀκούσασιν) (ASV, ESV, KJV, NASB, NET, NRSV)

var. "because those who heard **did not combine it** with faith" (μὴ **συγκεκερασμένος** τῇ πίστει τοῖς ἀκούσασιν) (NIV)

4:2. Barnabas's rather strong expectation continued (καὶ γάρ, "for") with a comparison (καθάπερ κἀκεῖνοι, "just as also") with the exodus generation. Like the exodus generation, the household family of faith had God's "good news" (εὐηγγελισμένοι). For the exodus generation, the "good news" centered around the land of Canaan. For the household family of faith in Rome, however, the "good news" centered around the messianic Son of promise. Barnabas drew attention to the fact that they had that "good news" (ἐσμεν εὐηγγελισμένοι, "we have good news") about the messianic Son of promise with ongoing benefits (intensive perf.). Yet (ἀλλ', "but"), Barnabas recalled that the exodus generation never profited from hearing their good news in that they failed to unite with those (namely, Moses, Aaron, Joshua, and Caleb) who believed and trusted that God could and would fulfill his promise (v. 2b–c; cf. Num. 13:30; 14:5–19).

When Jesus was alive, Jewish political leaders, high priests, and Judaeans rejected God's messianic Son of promise (Luke 22:66–71; 23:6–23), his message (Luke 4:16–30; 9:51–56; 13:31–35; 19:47), and later his messengers (Acts 4:1–22; 5:17–42). That rejection continued with their angst against Rome. Zealots were known for their stubborn unwillingness to call anyone master or lord (Hengel, 1989, 229–30). God was the "sole ruler" over Judaea, the only one to be called Master and Lord (Josephus, *B.J.* 2.8.1 §§117–118). "They think little of submitting to death in unusual forms," according to Josephus (*A.J.* 18.1.6 §§23–25), "and permitting vengeance to fall on kinsmen and friends if only they may avoid calling any man master" (trans. Feldman). They rejected Jesus as their Master and Lord. They never benefited from God's "good news." Yet, there were those in Judaea, like Jude, who believed that Jesus was the messianic Son of promise. Jude wrote to Judaean believers, underscored the disbelief of the Zealots (v. 4), called to memory how throughout history God dealt with those who rejected his message (vv. 5–7), and warned of God's future judgment for all those who rejected God's message (vv. 14–16; Bateman, 2015[17]).

The household family of faith in Rome was also aware of Judaea's past rejection of Jesus (cf. Mark's Gospel) as well as Judaea's current willful disbelief. The historical parallels between the Kadesh Barnea revolt and the current Judaean revolt were similar. They both reflected a rejection of God's "good news." So, Barnabas called attention to those of the exodus generation who did not listen to those who had accepted God's good news. He made it clear that because of the exodus generation's lack of unity (μὴ συγκεκερασμένους) to trust God, entering "God's rest" (= God's *safe and secure* place) ended more specifically in God's judgment. Barnabas would return to this theme of being united later when he expressed his expectation for the household family of faith to live in harmony with one another (13:1). Yet here, Barnabas's point was that God's safe and secure place remained open (v. 1) in accordance to God's promise (v. 2). He clarified what and where this place of rest was in verses 3b–5 with an escalated interpretation.

> *TEXTUAL ANALYSIS:* Conflicting Text Critical Reading: 4:3
> Syntax Issue: Both the manuscript evidence (𝔓[13] 𝔓[46] B D K P 044 33 614) and the consecutive use of "for" (γάρ) in the immediate context (vv. 2, 3, 4) support the text rendering. The variant may be an unintentional error due to verses nearby that use "therefore" (οὖν; cf. vv. 1, 11, 16). The text is the preferred reading (Metzger, 1994, 595–96).
>
> *txt.* "**for** we who have believed enter that rest" (εἰσερχόμεθα **γὰρ** εἰς [τὴν] κατάπαυσιν οἱ πιστεύσαντες) (ASV, ESV, KJV, NASB, NET, NIV, NRSV)
>
> *var.* "**therefore** we who have believed enter that rest" (εἰσερχόμεθα **οὖν** εἰς [τὴν] κατάπαυσιν οἱ πιστεύσαντες)

4:3–5. Barnabas's stern call to fear failure, however, was followed with an inference of hope. The conjunction "for" (γάρ) linked "those who believed" (οἱ πιστεύσαντες) God's message and were currently entering into "the rest" (τὴν κατάπαυσιν) in verse 3a with those of the past who heard God's message in verse 2 (namely, Moses, Aaron, Joshua, and Caleb). Though the message itself differed, the emphasis was belief in or trust in God about his message and his ability to fulfill his promise. Barnabas underscored the need to remain attached to those in the household family of faith who trusted in God's messianic Son of promise and subsequent benefits of doing so.

Barnabas built his affirmation on Psalm 95:11 and Genesis 2:2. The word "rest" (κατάπαυσις) that appears in both verses served as Barnabas's basis for linking them together (*gezerah shawah*; Bateman, 2012, 164).[1] Thus, what applied to one verse applied to another. Furthermore, the two passages reflect an "orderly chiastic pattern" that functioned as a "bridge" from 4:3a to 4:6.

Ps. 95	oath prohibition entrance (3b)
Gen. 2	connection to creation (3c)
Gen. 2	connection to creation (4)
Ps. 95	oath prohibition entrance (5)

Together these two OT texts underscored that "*my* resting place" was the one associated with God's first Sabbath, which was a heavenly one (Laansma, 1997, 288–89; cf. Attridge, 1989, 126–28). Thus, Barnabas escalated the *physical* place of rest in Canaan to be an entrance or opening into God's place of rest in *heaven*. We might even suggest that the land of Canaan as a place of rest was a mere shadow of God's heavenly one in much the same way as the tabernacle was a mere shadow of the heavenly tabernacle (cf. Heb. 8:5). Barnabas frequently paralleled the earthly to future heavenly realities: "the coming world" (2:5), the heavenly city (11:10, 16; 12:22; 13:14), the heavenly fatherland (11:14), and the unshakeable kingdom (12:28).

> **God's First Sabbath**
>
> The clause "*God rested* on the seventh day from all his works" (*κατέπαυσεν ὁ θεὸς ἐν τῇ ἡμέρᾳ τῇ ἑβδόμῃ ἀπὸ πάντων τῶν ἔργων αὐτοῦ*) as quoted from Genesis 2:2, spoke specifically of "God's creation Sabbath." Albeit a conclusion to the creation account, this concept had implications for the institution of Sabbath law, namely, the humanitarian concern that *all* Israel *rest from work* and be refreshed *on the seventh day* and seventh year (human, beast, and land alike; Deut. 5:12–15, Lev. 25:1–13). Thus, the divine and human Sabbaths were closely related in Judaism (Exod. 20:11; 31:15–17). Yet, the OT saint *never* participated in "God's creation Sabbath" in that

---

1 H. W. Bateman IV, "Second Temple Exegetical Practices: Extra-biblical Examples of Exegesis Compared with Those in the Book of Hebrews" in the Dead Sea Scrolls issue of *SWJT* 53.1 (Fall 2010): 26–54.

God's place of rest differed from Israel's. It appears that God, since creation's completion, enjoyed an ongoing Sabbath or "seventh day of rest" elsewhere (hence "*my* rest" in 3:11). The two terms for "rest" (noun: κατάπαυσις; verb: κατάπαυω) verbally linked together Psalm 94:11 [95:11 HB] and Genesis 2:2 in Hebrews 4:3–5. Together they stressed "God's creation Sabbath" or "creation rest" that should not be confused with a local "resting place" (= land of Canaan) because God's place of rest was not a physical place of rest but a heavenly one (*EDNT*, 2:265–66).

As God's promise of rest spanned the ages (cf. 4:7), the household family of faith looked forward to entering into God's *heavenly* resting-place with him. It was a heavenly primordial Sabbath rest that was currently available but not yet totally realized. This heavenly Sabbath rest, according to Barnabas, was for "those who believed" (οἱ πιστεύσαντες) in the messianic Son of promise and was available pending one's perseverance in that belief (cf. 3:14). Consequently, the exodus generation once again served as a paradigm of unfaithfulness to be avoided.

- God swore that the exodus generation would *never* enter his place of rest (4:3b).
    - Regardless of the exodus generation's failure, God's works were complete at the time of creation (4:3c).
    - God entered into his place of rest from all his works on the seventh day (4:4).
- God barred the exodus generation entrance into his place of rest (4:5).

As members of the household family of faith, Jewish believers in Rome were to fear failure of entering God's heavenly "place-of-rest" and avoid repeating the historical failure of the exodus generation.

God's Invitation Remains Open (4:6–10)

The twofold reason for pursuing God's rest was that the exodus generation had rejected God's offering and that another remained available to all who chose to accept God's open invitation.

4:6. In this rather long sentence that spans verses 6–7 (a Greek period; cf. 1:1), Barnabas offered a twofold reason (ἐπεὶ οὖν, "since therefore"; cf. NASB, NRSV, ESV) that explained the availability of God's *heavenly* place of rest (4:1, 3a). On the one hand, speaking theologically, divine rest was reserved for people who fulfilled the conditions attached to it, namely, faith (cf. 3:6b; 14b). "It remains" (ἀπολείπεται) tended to be a technical term used in a will for "leaving" property to someone (MM, s.v. "ἀπολείπω"). Yet in Jude as well as here in Hebrews, it's used to describe a "departure" from a place or a "reservation" somewhere (BDAG, s.v. "ἀπολείπω" 2 and 3, p. 115). In Jude 6, it was used of the angels who "left" their domain (= place in heaven). In Hebrews 4:6, there was "reserved" for the household family of faith a future "place-of-rest." On the other hand, speaking historically, the initially invited guests (i.e., the exodus generation) rejected God's invitation and *failed* to enter God's *safe and secure place* (= God's rest) reserved for them in Canaan due to unbelief (cf. 3:19; Matt. 22:1–14). So according to Spicq (1952, 83), "the resting place is still vacant, and it is for Christians. This is obvious since centuries long after Moses, David renewed the divine promise." Thus, God had not annulled his promise about a place of rest. There was reserved a future "place-of-rest" for all people who fulfill the conditions attached to it, namely, faith in God's promise.

4:7. Centuries later, long after the unfaithful and disobedient exodus generation, God "again" (πάλιν) established another "day" of opportunity whereby people were invited to hear God, obey God, and enter a place of rest. Barnabas specified that God's invitation was later made "through David." It was through David that God made another offer. David was God's spokesman (cf. 1:1a) through whom his spirit spoke Psalm 95. Taking advantage of the gnomic sense of the word "today," Barnabas applied Psalm 95 to the current Jewish household family of faith in Rome (cf. 3:7). Thus, this other occasion offered during the time of David was applicable for Barnabas's readers. God's renewed invitation to enter a place of rest, however, was escalated to be an entrance into God's *heavenly* place of rest.

Study of King David, by Julia Margaret Cameron, public domain. Courtesy of Dcoetzee.

4:8. The final reason (γάρ, "for") for pursuing God's invitation to enter this *heavenly* place of rest was because of Joshua. Barnabas anticipated a potential objection or perhaps even misunderstanding. So, he assumed an untruth for the sake of the argument (εἰ + aor. verbs), namely, that Joshua's conquest of Canaan some forty years after the Kadesh Barnea event had established God's "rest" (κατέπαυσεν).[2] Though it was true, for the initial exodus generation never entered into the land, what about Joshua? Did he not lead the next generation into the land of rest (Deut. 12:9–10, Josh. 21:43–45)? Obviously, another rest was in view because some five hundred years after the time of Joshua, David raised once again the topic of rest in Psalm 95. Taking advantage of the gnomic sense of "today," Barnabas appealed to Psalm 95 to verify that entrance into the land of Canaan was not God's final resting-place and that another existed. Once again, perhaps the land of Canaan as a place of rest was a mere shadow of God's heavenly one in much the same way as the tabernacle was a mere shadow of the heavenly tabernacle (cf. Heb. 8:5; 9:24).

4:9. Barnabas drew his conclusion (ἄρα, "so then"; cf. ESV, NRSV, CNT) for verses 6–7. He summarized the argument that he began in verse 3, which was this: there remained for the people of God a Sabbath rest. Naturally the "people of God" (τῷ λαῷ τοῦ θεοῦ) were those who were part of God's household family of faith in Rome (= God's house; cf. 3:6), namely, those who maintained their confession about Jesus as God's sent spokesman, high priest, and messianic Son of promise.

Unfortunately, the term "Sabbath rest" (σαββατισμός), at times, is presumed to be synonymous with "rest" (κατάπαυσις) or that the word "Sabbath rest" (σαββατισμός) is interchangeable with "rest" (κατάπαυσις) in Hebrews 3:11, 18; 4:1, 3, 5, 10–11. As a result, "Sabbath rest" in Hebrews 4:9 is *wrongly limited* to a "rest from works" (KJV, RSV, NASB, NIV, ESV, NET; "special rest" NLT). Yet, for Barnabas, "Sabbath rest" (BDAG, s.v. "σαββατισμός," p. 909) and "rest" (κατάπαυσις) reflected two different ideas. Whereas "rest" (κατάπαυσις) conveyed

2 The "if" (εἰ) plus the aorist tense verb in both the protasis (i.e., κατέπαυσεν) and the apodosis (i.e., ἐλάλει) is a second class conditional clause, more specifically a past contrary to fact clause (Wallace, 1996, 694–95, 451)..

the idea of no work to take place on the Sabbath, "Sabbath rest" (σαββατισμός) more appropriately spoke of a "Sabbath celebration," *which included* a cessation of work, but more specifically, it spoke of a Sabbath celebration of salvation whereby members of the household family of faith joined in God's Sabbath celebration along with a myriad of angelic beings (12:22–24; cf. Rev. 4:1–11; Attridge, 1989, 131; Laansma, 1997, 276–77). Thus, there was yet to be experienced a Sabbath celebration for all God's people.

The Jewish Theology of "Sabbath Rest"

"Sabbath rest" (σαββατισμός) not only referred to a cessation from work (Exod. 20:8–10, cf. 26:29–30; Isa. 58:13; Neh. 13:15–22) but also of festive celebration of God. During temple visits, special foods and Sabbath songs united human and angelic worshippers (Isa. 56:2, 7; Jer. 17:19–27; Jub. 50:8–11; 4Q403; 11Q17; *DJBP*, 538–39). In the *Songs of the Sabbath Sacrifice*, instructions were provided for a Sabbath rest: "The *song accompanying the sacrifice* on the seventh Sabbath. . . . Rejoice, you who exult in knowing Him, with a song of rejoicing among the wondrous godlike. . . . Laud, all you confessing divine beings, the King of praise" (4Q403 [trans. Wise et al., 1996, 371]). Another Second Temple Jewish text read, "For great is the honor which the Lord gave to Israel to eat and to drink and to be satisfied on [the Sabbath] day of festival and to rest in it from all work" (Jub. 50:10 [trans. Wintermute], cf. 2:21–22). In yet another text, "when they had collected the arms of the enemy and stripped them of their spoils, they kept the sabbath, giving great praise and thanks to the Lord, who had preserved them for that day and allotted it to them as the beginning of mercy" (2 Macc 8:27 [NRSV]; cf. Attridge, 1989, 131).

4:10. The reason (γάρ, "for") why a "Sabbath rest" remained for the household family of faith was twofold. On the one hand, the implied subject of this verse were members of the household family of faith in Rome (Koester, 2001, 271–73; G. Guthrie, 1998, 164). So for Barnabas, a member of the family is "the one who has entered [ὁ εἰσελθών] God's rest had also rested from his works" (cf. NET). "Rest from his works" (εἰς τὴν κατάπαυσιν αὐτοῦ) referred to works associated with the Mosaic law. For a Jewish member of the household family of faith in Rome, keeping the Mosaic law was still practiced (Acts 3:3–11; 5:20–25, 42; 15:19–21; 18:18; 21:23–26). It was a way for all Jewish people at the time to express their covenantal loyalty to God (Holmén, 2001, 37–87). It was, once again, part of their DNA. Barnabas would eventually make it clear that the Mosaic law was ineffective and obsolete (cf. 8:13; 10:1, 3–4).

Barnabas then compared (ὥσπερ, "as") the family members resting with God. Unfortunately, God resting "from his own" (ἀπὸ τῶν ἰδίων ὁ θεός) is difficult to interpret. Although "God's rest" was a rest from his creativity (Gen. 2:2 in v. 4), Koester (2001, 273) does not presume a complete inactivity on God's part. God remained active even on the Sabbath (John 5:16–18; *Exod Rab* 30:9; *Gen Rab* 11:10). God's activity was clearly evident during the exodus by way of God's provision of water (Exod. 15:22–25a; 17:1–7; Num. 20:2–13), the provision of manna (Exod. 16:14–18; Num. 11:7–9), and the provision of quail (Exod. 16:12–13; Num. 11:31–33). It was also evident in Hebrews in that the messianic Son of promise sustained all things (cf. 1:3) and interceded for the household family of faith 24/7 (cf. 4:16; 7:25).

Strive for Success (4:11–13)

As a household family of faith, members were to strive for success, because God's revelatory message was able to penetrate, separate, and judge the innermost thoughts and attitudes of all people.

4:11. Barnabas ended his application of Psalm 95 in the same manner in which he began, with an exhortation: "let us make every effort" (σπουδάσωμεν, NRSV; cf. NET), "let *us* strive"

(ESV; cf. KJV), or "let us give diligence" (ASV; cf. NASB). Every member of the household family of faith was to strive for success, even for Barnabas ("let *us*"). Just as Paul "sought strenuously" to honor the Apostolic Council's concern for the poor (Gal. 2:10) and exhorted Timothy to "make every effort to come" to Rome before his death (2 Tim. 4:9), so too were those of the Roman household family of faith to be "especially conscientious," to be "applying oneself diligently," or to be "zealously engaged" for success (BDAB, s.v. "σπουδάζω," p. 939).

The objective was "to enter *that* rest" (εἰς ἐκείνην τὴν κατάπαυσιν). Two terms were significant here. First, in Hebrews the term "to enter" (εἰς) spoke exclusively of entrance into a local reality or to cross over a threshold. Barnabas frequently referred to entering local realities: the inner shrine behind the curtain (6:19, 20), the holy place (9:12, 25), the sanctuary (9:24), the world (10:5). Second, "*that* rest" (ἐκείνην τὴν κατάπαυσιν; RSV, NASB, NIV, ESV) served to link Psalm 95:11 and Genesis 2:2 in Hebrews 4:3b–5. Yet, there was an escalation of the *physical* place of rest in Canaan to a *heavenly* "place-of-rest" (NET, NLT). Thus, entrance into "that rest" was crossing over the threshold into God's *heavenly* place of rest, where members of the household family of faith would join in the ongoing Sabbath celebration of God "at the day of their salvation" (*EDNT*, 2:266).

God's Place of Rest

As in other Jewish literature, the place-of-rest concept was not merely a state of mind but "resting places without number" and "dwelling places of the holy ones and their resting-places" (1 En. 45:3, 39:4; cf. 2 En. 61:2–3 [J] with John 14:2; 4 Ezra 7:36; 8:48–52; perhaps Jos. Asen. 15:7). Likewise, there existed a place of eternal torment for communities of people who rejected God (4 Ezra 7:26–44). Like his Jewish counterparts, Barnabas concerned himself with a heavenly "place-of-rest" *prepared for the faithful community* (cf. 4 Ezra 7:88–99). He too addressed an event that remained outstanding, namely, the household family of faith crossing over into a future resting-place, an entrance into that world to come, an event that had yet to be realized (cf. Rev. 21:1–22:5). Perhaps the contrast to *not* striving to succeed to enter God's heavenly place of rest was the flipside of rebellion.

Barnabas's intended result (ἵνα, "so that") for every member of the household family of faith was for them to strive and successfully pass over into God's rest so that they would "not fall" (μὴ . . . πέσῃ) "by following the same pattern" (ἐν τῷ αὐτῷ ὑποδείγματι) of the disobedient exodus generation. In 3:17, those who "fell" (ἔπεσεν) spoke of those who died in the desert due to stubborn unbelief that led to rebellion. Here in 4:11, "will not fall" (μὴ . . . πέσῃ) spoke of avoiding the same pattern of stubborn misbehavior. Thus, the members of the household family of faith were expected to take steps "to avoid both the cause and effect" evidenced in the failure of the exodus generation to cross over the threshold into God's heavenly place of rest. It was not unusual to find the exodus generation employed as an example to avoid (2 Cor. 10:11; Jude 5). Their rebellion or disobedience was not to be repeated (Attridge, 1989, 132).

4:12. Barnabas closed this section with another rather long sentence (a Greek period; cf. 1:1–4) that provided the reason (γάρ, "for") for striving to succeed in entering God's *heavenly* "place-of-rest." It was "God's word" (ὁ λόγος τοῦ θεοῦ). The appearance of "God's word" was another way of speaking about God's revelatory message (cf. 2:3). Occurring twice in Hebrews (4:12, 13:7), it not only drew closure to Barnabas's second warning (3:7–4:11), it redirected attention to God, whose revelatory message had been recorded (1:1, 3:7, 4:8) and whose judgments against the exodus generation for their stubborn unbelief had been remembered (2:1–2, 3:16–19).

Described in metaphorical language, God's revelatory message (= word) was first personified as a "life-breathing being" (ζῶν) and quite "active" (ἐνεργής). Like the divine speaker (Heb. 3:12, 9:14, 10:31, 12:22), God's word was "living" or "alive" (cf. Ps. 147:15; Prov. 8:1–9:6). Second, God's word was "active" (RSV, NASB, NRSV, ESV, NET), "effective" (Lane, 1991a, 1993), or "powerful" (KJV; cf. BDAG, s.v. "ἐνεργής," p. 335). Thus, the personification of "the word of God" as a "living power" (NLT) explicated the relevance of God's revelatory message even if that divine word was spoken decades ago (cf. Isa. 55:11; 1QH 5:13b–25).

Then Barnabas compared God's revelatory message (= word) with an inert object: a "sharp double-edged sword" (τομώτερος μάχαιραν δίστομον). This strikingly powerful visual employed a traditional image of God's written message as a sword (Isa. 49:2, Wis 18:15–16, Eph. 6:17) as well as revealed the powerful function of God's revelatory message. It had "piercing" (διϊκνούμενος) and "dividing" (μερισμοῦ) capabilities. "The word of God" probed ("piercing") like a sharp knife and posed divine judgment ("able to judge") like a sword as in the case of Israel's physical judgment after the Kadesh Barnea event (Num. 14:43–45) that rendered the people totally defenseless (cf. 1QH 14:29–33; Rev 19:15; Ellingworth, 1993, 262). Together they served to speak figuratively about "the word of God," which was able to meticulously infiltrate the innermost attitudes, thoughts, and motives of a community.

"Piercing" (διϊκνούμενος) and "Dividing" (μερισμοῦ)

"Piercing" (διϊκνούμενος) and "dividing" (μερισμοῦ) were a strikingly powerful visual. While "piercing" (διϊκνούμενος) occurs in the NT only here, "dividing" (μερισμοῦ) occurs twice (Heb. 2:4, 4:13). On the one hand, God's word had "piercing" (διϊκνούμενος, KJV, RSV, NASB, RSV, NET; BDAG, s.v. "διϊκνέομαι," p. 245), "deep cutting" (NLT; Pfitzner, 1997, 83), or "penetrating" (BDAG, s.v. "διϊκνέομαι," p. 245, Attridge, 1989, 133) capabilities. Josephus employed the term literally to describe "great boulders" used to "penetrate" Rome's military offensive at Jotopata (*B.J.* 3.7.8 §167; cf. *A.J.* 13.4.4 §96) and to speak of great flames that did not "penetrate" the interior of Jerusalem's temple in A.D. 70, which gave Titus reason to believe he might rescue the temple from utter destruction (*B.J.* 6.4.7 §261). On the other hand, "dividing" (μερισμοῦ) meant to "separate" or "divide" (BDAG, s.v. "μερισμός" 1a, 633). It had been used to speak positively of David's literal divisions of the priests (*A.J.* 7.14.7 §366; cf. 1.6.4 §146), neutrally of God's literal divisions of the nations (Philo, *Post* 90), and negatively of the literal "divisions" threatening the early church (Ignatius, *Phld* 2:1; *Smyrn* 7:2). Together, they were two coordinate words that expresses a single concept (= a hendiadys), namely, that God is able to dismember with great precision people's genuine thoughts and motives.

4:13. Barnabas continued (καί) his presentation about God's written message by shifting to creation. Barnabas's simple declaration that "no creature is hidden" (οὐκ ἔστιν κτίσις ἀφανὴς) from God is a clear assertion that shouts: no one escapes God. For Barnabas, God showed no favoritism. The people of Israel believed it (Ps. 139:11–12), the people of the Greco-Roman world believed it (Seneca, *Epistles* 83), and Jewish people of the latter part of the Second Temple period believed it (Sir 16:17; 1 En. 9:5). No created thing was hidden from God (Attridge, 1989, 136 nn. 48, 49; Lane, 1991a, 103; Koester, 2001, 274; Cockerill, 2012, 217 n. 16).

Instead (δέ), God uncovered everything in an uncompromising and confrontational manner. Unfortunately, the expression "naked and exposed" (γυμνὰ καὶ τετραχηλισμένα) is difficult to interpret. Yet, the term "exposed" (τετραχηλισμένα; ESV, NET, NLT), when used in parallel with "naked" (γυμνά) or "laid bare" (NIV, NASB, RSV; BDAG s.v. "γυμνός," p. 208), spoke of the bending back of the neck of sacrificial animal, bared for the knife, before slaughter (BDAG, s.v. "τραχηλίζω," p. 1014; cf. Attridge, 1989, 136). Yet, another option is that the terms spoke of being gripped by the neck as in an athletic competition. Philo (*Praem* 290) used the term to speak of a person's ability to reason. Reason was personified as one who "grapple[s] with the vast number of particular subjects . . . grows exhausted and collapses just as an athlete 'with his head gripped in a neck-hold' [ἐκτραχελιζομενος] by superior power" [trans. Colson]. Although both options have merit, it seems Barnabas shifted the metaphor to an athletic competition. God's revelatory message was like a wrestler who gripped his opponent in an incapacitating neck-hold and laid his rival prostrate before the divine referee. So, all of creation laid disrobed and prostrated before the personified revelatory word of God. And as if nakedness was not enough, God's discomforting grip on peoples' souls left them defenseless before him, the one to whom all of creation must give an account (cf. Jude 14–15).

THEOLOGICAL FOCUS

The exegetical idea (the household family of faith was expected to fear failure because of the historical stubborn unbelief of the exodus generation, and yet, based upon God's invitation for a future Sabbath celebration, the household family of faith was expected to strive to be successful in not repeating the historical failures of the past) leads to this theological focus: God's promise of a future celebration with him is available to all those who do not take their future with God for granted and thereby do not cease striving to succeed in joining God in his future celebration.

There are at least two theological themes in this preaching unit: perseverance and divine judgment. On the one hand, the theme of perseverance is evident in two expectations: to fear failure to enter heaven (vv. 1, 3–5) and to strive to succeed in participating in the future celebrations of God with the angels (v. 11; cf. v. 9). On the other hand, divine judgment appears in God's dealings with the exodus generation (vv. 2, 6–7) and God's revelatory message as being active and able to penetrate and separate the innermost thoughts and attitudes of a person (4:12) and thereby create a great deal of discomfort on judgment day (4:13).

PREACHING AND TEACHING STRATEGIES

Exegetical and Theological Synthesis

This text was the second of five warning passages in Hebrews. It's a strong warning for the household family of faith. It warned that members of the household family of the faith may not be able to "enter God's rest." Barnabas wove two story lines into one. The story line of creation (God's work) was presented alongside the story line of migration (God's people). Like a novelist dealing with multiple story lines, Barnabas wove them together to form another story line—invitation. This was not a history lesson, but it was an invitation to avoid the same mistakes as the children of Israel. From beginning to end, this passage pulled the listener into the story by showing connections with Israel's story and our story. In fact, they are the same story. The theological issue addressed was the nature of rest. Does rest represent entering into God's peace as a believer, thus agreeing with God's work of sanctification? Or, does it mean entering God's rest initially by his work of justification?

Preaching Idea
People who fail to learn from the past are guaranteed to repeat it.

Contemporary Connections

What does it mean?
What does it mean that people who fail to learn from the past are guaranteed to repeat it? We know this from every aspect of our lives. We bemoan the fact that we forget the simple lessons in life that cost us time and money down the road.

Perhaps the most tragic of all is when we have a loved one, perhaps a son or daughter, who keeps making the same mistakes again and again. They keep sticking their hand on the same hot burner, but they expect it not to burn them the second or third time. If we do not learn from the story line of ancient Israel, we will become like them. In fact, the very reason we have a record of Israel and their failures is to teach us that God has a better plan for us.

Consider for example the life of Marie Curie, the acclaimed French physicist. She was the first woman to win a Nobel Prize. However, her untimely death at the age of sixty-six was the result of overexposure to radiation. Learning from that mistake, doctors, x-ray technicians, and patients today wear lead vests for protection when being exposed to radiation.[3]

Is it true?
Is it true that people who do not learn from past mistakes, will repeat them? The second battle George Washington fought was a precursor to the French and Indian War (1754–63). He was attached to a British general who had never fought on American soil. In the European theatre of war, armies would fight in lines. It was all very gentlemanly. However, on the American continent, the Native Americans fought with a stealth ambush. They would hide, ambush, and retreat.

Knowing this strategy, Washington warned his general not to advance too far into enemy territory. After all, Washington had been beaten badly the first time he fought these native warriors and was glad to escape with his life.

The general thought he knew better, and he refused to change his tactics. In the end, he lost most of his army and was routed in a bitter defeat. He was unwilling to learn from the past mistakes of others.

Now what?
The point in this text is not that we learn from our own history but that we learn from the history of Israel. As it has been said, a good man learns from his mistakes, but a wise man learns from the mistakes of others.

This passage is challenging us to learn from the mistakes of others. So, what is our response? Will we follow the pattern of the nation that would not listen, or will we heed the warning and enter into God's rest?

What is required of us is self-diagnosis. Imagine that we could take an MRI of our soul. We would see inside all the good and bad. Any hidden sin and every secret motive. Perhaps if we really saw this, we would wince. We would be surprised that we could be so calloused about such sin for so long.

Creativity in Presentation
Using the illustration of the MRI, we could show the progression of radiology. It really is fascinating. Yet, the original x-ray photographs were crude. Technology advanced and medical professionals could see more and more that includes the latest technology of MRI and CAT scans. This technology

3 "Marie Curie," Wikipedia, https://en.wikipedia.org/wiki/Marie_Curie (accessed March 31, 2020).

allows the doctor to do a full body scan and see everything going on in the internal organs. Doctors can even do a close up of the heat and note where blockage to the heart or colon may potentially be located. The technology is so advanced that radiologists can warn of disease long before it actually affects the patient. This is what is happening in this passage. Using the light and heat of Scripture, we are to examine ourselves to ensure that we have no blockage—and in so doing, apply the cure that God provides.

Another illustration would be showing a one-minute clip from the film *The Lion King* (codirected by Roger Allers and Rob Minkoff, 1994, https://www.youtube.com/watch?v=dZfGTL2PY3E). In this scene, the mandrill monkey Rafiki helps the young lion Simba overcome the pain from his past by teaching him a lesson. Simba has been running from the pain in his past for a long time because it would be too hard for him to deal with it. However, Rafiki hits him with a stick to explain how the past can hurt, but it is not wise to let the pain define who we are. The second time Rafiki goes to hit him, Simba gets out of the way. Rafiki explains that we can either continue to be hurt by the past, or we can learn from it and move forward. This can be done by either not repeating the same mistake twice, or perhaps responding in a more Christlike way when the challenges of life come.

The point you want to get across is simply this: People who fail to learn from the past are guaranteed to repeat it. One approach to an outline for this text would be as follows:

- Story Line One—Migration: the Israelites fail to enter rest (vv. 1–2).
- Story Line Two—Creation: God entered his rest (vv. 3–5).
- Story Line Three—Invitation: God's invitation remains open (vv. 6–13).

The outline is composed of three potential "story lines" in the text: that of God's people in the wilderness, creation, and our own story line.

DISCUSSION QUESTIONS

1. How important is the application of humility in Hebrews 4:1–11? What would happen if we continued to live in prideful arrogance?

2. What are some examples of repetitive sin struggles we have? Is it possible to overcome a repetitive sin struggle or addiction?

3. In order to stop repeating the cycle of sin, what do we need to learn?

4. What are some current challenges you are facing right now?

5. Are we able to glorify the Lord completely with our lives if we never deal with the pain from our past mistakes or difficulties in life?

FURTHER READING

Aharoni, Yohanan, Michael Avi-Yonah, Anson F. Rainey, and Ze'ev Safrai. 2002. *The Carta Bible Atlas*, Fourth Edition, 186–97. Jerusalem: Carta Publishing.

Bateman IV, Herbert W. (editor). 2007. *Four Views on the Warning Passages in Hebrews*. Grand Rapids: Kregel.

__________. 2013. "The History of the General Letters." In *Interpreting the General Letters: An Exegetical Handbook*, 57–72. Edited by John D. Harvey. HNTE Grand Rapids: Kregel.

deSilva, David A. 2000. "Entering God's Rest: Eschatology and the Socio–Rhetorical Strategy of Hebrews." *Trinity Journal* 21NS (2000), 25–43.

__________. "Kinship & The 'Household of God' in the New Testament" In *Honor, Patronage, Kingship & Purity: Unlocking New Testament Culture*, 199–239. Downers Grove, IL: InterVarsity Press.

Falk, Daniel K. 2000. "Moses." In *Encyclopedia of the Dead Sea Scrolls*, Volume 1, 576–77. Edited by Lawrence H. Schiffman and James C. VanderKam. New York: Oxford University Press.

___________. 2000. "Moses, Texts of." In *Encyclopedia of the Dead Sea Scrolls*, Volume 1, 577–81. Edited by Lawrence H. Schiffman and James C. VanderKam. New York: Oxford University Press.

Levine, L. I. 1992. "Jewish War." In *Anchor Bible Dictionary*, 839–45. New York: Doubleday.

THE ROYAL HIGH PRIESTHOOD OF JESUS (4:14—7:28)

Many commentators have suggested that this third division about the royal-priesthood of Jesus is "the long-anticipated exposition" of Psalm 110:4 (Cockerill, 2012, 293; Attridge, 1989, 187; Spicq, 1952, 2:205; Weiss, 1889, 371–71). Yet, we shouldn't overstate the importance of the exposition of Psalm 110 as though Barnabas was concerned solely with the exegesis of Psalm 110 (Caird, 1959, 48) or that Hebrews was "a homiletical midrash based on Ps 110" (Buchanan, 1972, xix).

While Barnabas's central theme was the royal high priesthood of Jesus (4:14–5:10; 7:1–28), a sub-theme was an expressed concern about biblical apathy. On the one hand, Barnabas expanded his initial allusion to Jesus's royal-priesthood (1:2 parallel with 1:3) and his two direct statements (2:17; 3:1). Barnabas's appeal (5:11–6:20) to Jesus's royal high priesthood after the order of Melchizedek is of great theological import because he thereby reinforced that Jesus was God's promised, effective, and eternal regal high priest who superseded the Levitical system (vv. 5:5–6, 10; 6:20; 7:1–28). On the other hand, there was an emphasis to advance in understanding about Jesus's role as God's regal high priest in order to prevent a rejection of Jesus.

Structural Observation

Despite the division suggested here, namely 4:14–7:28, many rightly argue that 4:14–10:25 is the heart of Hebrews (G. Guthrie 1994, 80–82; Cockerill 2012, 218). Hebrews 4:14 and 10:21 bracket the unit with similar wording: "since we have a great high priest who has passed through the heavens" (4:14) and "since we have a great priest over the house of God" (10:21). Thus, 4:14–16 and 10:19–25 are overlapping transitions for Hebrews. Nevertheless, while agreeing with this "inherent unity" (G. Guthrie 1994, 81), we have divided Hebrews a bit differently for peaching purposes. Attention is drawn here to Barnabas's introduction to Jesus's royal high priesthood (4:14–5:10; 7:1–28), his confronting the community's biblical apathy (5:11–6:12), and the reassurance of God's promise (6:13–20).

This third division may be divided into four preaching units. The first identifies God's royal-priest for the household community of faith, his qualifications, and his divine appointment (4:14–5:10). The second is a reprimand against apathy that calls the household family of faith to be discerning thinkers (5:11–6:12). The third presents God's sworn promise that has an unalterable purpose with two unchangeable certainties for the household of faith (6:13–20). The fourth tackles Melchizedek, a regal priest of the past who served as a model for Jesus's royal-priesthood as guaranteed, unchangeable, and sinless (7:1–28). At the very end of this section is a list of books and articles for further reading that may be helpful in understanding these preaching units.

Hebrews 4:14–5:10

EXEGETICAL IDEA

Jesus, the household family of faith's high priest to whom they were to cling and through whom they had safe access to God in order to experience God's compassion, met the qualifications for the high priesthood in keeping with his divinely appointed tasks as regal high priest.

THEOLOGICAL FOCUS

Clinging to Jesus, God's appointed regal high priest, makes it possible for the household family of faith to approach God in safety in order to experience his compassion.

PREACHING IDEA

Everyone needs compassion, but where do we get it?

PREACHING POINTERS

For the Jewish household family of faith in Rome, access to God was initially by way of the Levitical priesthood. A priest's eligibility for priesthood was based upon his descent from Aaron's male line (e.g., patrilineal descendants), being chosen by God, and being officiators of temple sacrifices on behalf of God's people. Unfortunately, not all priests, particularly the high priest, were God's chosen nor were they ethical and willing to be compassionate. The truth of this passage for the original readers of Hebrews was that Jesus, God's chosen high priest, made it possible for the followers of Jesus in Rome to have access to God and experience God's compassion without going to the temple in Jerusalem.

Even today, there are many charlatans who preach, "Thus sayeth the Lord," but lack in demonstrating compassion. But like the believers in Rome, we too need to experience compassion. Whether it be at work when we make a mistake and the boss says, "It's OK. I too have made mistakes"; at school when we don't seem to be getting it and the teacher says, "It's OK, let's meet after school and see if we can improve your understanding of the course material"; or at home when we crash the car and Mom and Dad say, "It's OK, I'm just glad you're not hurt"—everybody needs to experience compassion.

GOD'S REGAL HIGH PRIEST (4:14–5:10)

LITERARY STRUCTURE AND THEMES (4:14–5:10)

Having introduced Jesus as high priest (2:17; 3:1; cf. 1:3), Barnabas resumed his discussion about Jesus's priesthood. After his simple declaration about Jesus's position as the household family of faith's royal high priest, Barnabas issued a two-fold expectation for them. They were to cling to Jesus because Jesus understood them, and they were to approach God in safety in order to experience his compassion (4:14–16). Barnabas then explained the qualifications of a high priest: "appointed," "able to deal gently" with people, "obligated to sacrifice," and "called" by God (5:1–4). Barnabas closed with the appointment of Jesus as a royal high priest whom God declared to be his royal-priest, "who offered up" prayers to God, who "learned" obedience, who "became" the source for delivering people from wrongs committed, and who "was designated" by God as his royal high priest (5:5–10).

Barnabas's themes were the regal priesthood of Jesus and the household family of faith's responsibilities regarding Jesus's position.

- ***Jesus, the Royal High Priest (4:14–16)***
- ***Qualifications of a High Priest (5:1–4)***
- ***The Appointment of Jesus as Royal High Priest (5:5–10)***

EXPOSITION (4:14–5:10)

Typically, a person's eligibility for the Jewish high priesthood was based upon his descent from Aaron's male line (e.g., patrilineal descendants), being chosen by God, and being officiators of temple sacrifices on behalf of God's people. And while it may seem odd that Barnabas would take the time to describe the qualifications of a high priest to a group of Jewish people, not all high priests during the latter part of the Second Temple period were God's chosen nor were they ethical. High priests during the time of Barnabas tended to purchase the honor of being high priest, extorted wealth from the Jewish populists, and stole from other priests. They created a "have and have-not" society and a multiplicity of divisive and greedy Jewish factions. For instance, a wealthy and former high priest (48–59 B.C.) Ananias, son of Nedebaeus, was notorious for his corruption within the temple precincts (VanderKam, 2004, 455–63). Throughout the early 60s, Ananias maintained a swaying influence over the Judaean people and subsequent Judaean high priestly families.He was so greedy that his servants would enter the threshing floors and forcefully steal the tithes of the priests or beat those who refused to hand over their tithe. Other high priests were guilty of the same practices. Josephus (*A.J.* 20.9.2 §§205–07) at one point explained how "priests who in olden days were maintained by the tithes now starved to death" (trans. Feldman).[1] So, it was relevant for Barnabas to draw attention to this fact: Jerusalem's priesthood was corrupt. Yet, Barnabas made it clear that the members of the household family of faith had a high priest, Jesus, to whom they were to cling and through whom they had safe access to God in order to experience God's compassion. Jesus met the qualifications for the high priesthood

1 R. Bauckham, "Josephus' Account of the Temple in Contra Apionem 2.102–109," in *Contra Apionem: Studies in Its Character and Context with a Latin Concordance to the Portion Missing in Greek*, eds. L. H. Feldman and J. R. Levison, AGAJU 34 (Leiden: Brill, 1996), 327–47.

and had been divinely appointed as God's regal high priest.

Who Was Ananias, Son of Nedebaeus?

Except for the high priest Caiaphas, the priest before whom Jesus stood trial, Ananias held the position of high priest longer than any other (A.D. 48–59). Herod Agrippa I, grandson of Herod the Great, appointed Ananias, son of Nedebaeus, as high priest. Early in his appointment as high priest, Ananias had to answer to Claudius, the emperor of Rome, for his mismanaging a situation in Samaria. However, he was exonerated and kept his high office. Ananias appears in the NT in Acts 23 and 24 when Felix was Roman governor over Judaea (A.D. 52–60). Paul appeared before Ananias and the Sanhedrin in Jerusalem (23:1–5) and again when Paul appeared before Felix in Caesarea (24:1–21). Fortunately, Ananias lost his high priest position when Herod Agrippa I replaced him with Ishmael, son of Phiabi. Nevertheless, Ananias maintained his influence with the high priests who followed him. While the circumstances surrounding his death are less than clear, it seems he was killed (August/September A.D. 66) like many others who fell victim of the Jewish revolt that erupted in A.D. 66 (VanderKam, 2004, 455–63).

Jesus, the Royal High Priest (4:14–16)

Jesus was the household family of faith's royal high priest to whom they were expected to cling and through whom they were to approach God in safety so that God's compassion might be experienced.

4:14. Concluding (οὖν, "therefore") his theme about Jesus as high priest (1:3; 2:17; 3:1), Barnabas declared that the household family of faith had (ἔχοντες, "since having") Jesus as their high priest (cf. 8:1; 10:19) who was both "great" (μέγαν) and "the Son of God" (τὸν υἱὸν τοῦ θεοῦ). Referring to a high priest as "great" was not unusual and was simply "part of the traditional language" (Attridge, 1989, 139; cf. Lev. 21:10; 1 Macc 13:42). And though referring to Jesus as a "great high priest" parallels a traditional pattern, Jesus's having passed "through the heavens" escalated his greatness above all other high priests before him (cf. 1:3, 13; 2:9–10). Furthermore, the description of Jesus as "the Son of God" echoed God's declaration of Jesus as his messianic Son of promise in Hebrews 1:5–13. The "Son of God" was one of several epithets used for an expectant Messiah (4Q246; 4 Ezra 7:26–36; Bateman, 2012, 305–08; 316–20) and a familiar epithet in Mark.[2] Thus, Barnabas reaffirmed that Jesus was God's exalted royal high priest who ruled in God's presence (cf. 1:3, 13; 2:8b; 3:6a).

Based upon Jesus's authority as regal priest, Barnabas expected the household family of faith to "hold fast" (KJV, NASB, RSV, NRSV, NET, ESV), "hold firmly" (NIV), or "adhere strongly" (BDAG, s.v. "κρατέω" 6a, p. 656) to the confessions about Jesus as God's sent spokes*man* and high priest (1:2; 2:17; 3:1). Although similar to his previous appeal to "hold fast" (κατέχω) in 3:6 and 3:14, the verbs differ with a slightly different emphasis. On the one hand, the earlier emphasis of "hold fast" (κατέχω) was for the original readers to adhere to, retain, or maintain the personal confessions about Jesus (3:6, 14). On the other hand, "hold fast" (κρατέω) in 4:14 was an expectation to "adhere strongly to" the community's confessions or teachings about Jesus (2:1). Yet, both verbs addressed how the household family of faith was to respond to what they "confessed" (BDAG, s.v. "ὁμολογία," p. 709; cf. Rev. 2:25, 3:11; *TDNT,* 3:910–12). The household family of faith was to *maintain* as well as *adhere strongly* to their confessions about Jesus as God's sent spokes*man* (1:2, 3:1) and high priest (1:3; 2:17; 3:1). There was no wiggle room. They were to persevere in their confession about

2 H. W. Bateman IV, "Defining the Titles 'Christ' and 'Son of God' in Mark's Narrative Presentation of Jesus," *Journal of the Evangelical Theological Society* 50.3 (September 2007): 537–59.

Jesus. Thus, here in 4:14, members of the household family of faith in Rome were urged to *adhere strongly to* or *cling to* their confession.

4:15. The reason (γάρ, "for") for persevering or *clinging to* their confession about Jesus was twofold. On the one hand, Jesus was not incapable (μὴ δυνάμενον) of "sympathizing" (BDAG, s.v. "συμπαθῆσαι," p. 958) with people. The word "sympathizes" often revealed a sense of tenderness between family members: mothers with children (4 Macc 14:13–14, 15:4; Josephus, *B.J.* 6.3.4 §211) and brothers with brothers (4 Macc 13:23). This deep affection of family relationships intensified during times of suffering: mothers with children (4 Macc 15:7, 11–15) and sons with mothers (Josephus, *A.J.* 13.8.1 §233). Jesus's sympathy for people was evident in his compassion for people as well. When Jesus saw five thousand people, "he had compassion on them, because they were sheep without a shepherd" (Mark 6:34). Barnabas linked tenderness or affection with human weaknesses. By "weakness" (NIV, NASB, RSV, NET), Barnabas meant a "lack of confidence or feeling of inadequacy" (BDAG, s.v. "ἀσθένεια" 3, p. 142). Jesus witnessed the lack of confidence and inadequacy in his disciples: they feared him (Mark 4:41; 6:50), they misunderstood him (Mark 9:32; cf. 5:36), and they kept silent about him (Mark 16:8). Thus, due to his human experience with his disciples, Jesus "understands" (NLT) human feelings of uncertainties and perhaps even timidities about the household family's confessions about him.

The Gospel of Mark

The lack of confidence and feelings of inadequacy mentioned in Hebrews parallel Mark's presentation of the disciples as they wrestled with who Jesus was and their frequent failure to understand what following Jesus entailed (8:33; 9:32; 10:35–40). Mark's Gospel was seemingly written to address similar misunderstandings and failures among Roman Christians (ca. mid-60s). Mark's message was written to followers of Jesus who confessed Jesus as Messiah on the basis of his mighty deeds and words (1:1–8:30) but did not seem to understand that to follow Jesus was the "way" of suffering (8:31–16:8). It may be that they did not fully grasp that a call to discipleship was a call to suffering. Hengel (1985, 30) suggests that when considering Mark's Gospel, more should be made of the connection between the Neronian persecution in Rome and the Judaean revolt, a connection endorsed for Mark as well as a parallel concern for Barnabas in Hebrews. Both texts were written during the mid-60s.

In contrast (δέ, "but") to other high priests, Jesus "has been tested" (πεπειρασμένον), in a painful sense by God, to reveal Jesus's character (BDAG, s.v. "πειράζω" 2b, p. 792). Jesus passed his tests (2:17–18; cf. 5:8), showed himself to be faithful (2:17, 3:1–2, 6), and completed God's divine plan (2:10; cf. 5:9). Thus, he was "without sin" (χωρὶς ἁμαρτίας) in that *Jesus obeyed God totally* (Koester, 2001, 283; Cockerill, 2012, 227). Jesus knew the challenges and difficulties that came with trusting God.

4:16. Barnabas concluded (οὖν, "therefore") with a climatic expectation (Ellingworth, 1993, 269). The household family of faith was to "approach" (προσερχώμεθα; NET, NRSV, NIV) or "draw near to" (ASV, NASB, ESV) God with a sense of "confidence" (παρρησίας). Barnabas frequently mentioned God's throne in Hebrews (cf. 8:1; 12:2). And while to "approach the throne of grace" has royal imagery (Isa. 6:1; 66:1; cf. 16:5), there was no literal throne in heaven. The metaphor merely underscored God's ruling authority (see Heb. 1:8–9). Nevertheless, people of the Roman Empire would often approach a king's throne in person with petitions concerning justice, civic disputes, and rewards, which may have felt like approaching a god (Koester, 2001, 284–85). Paul stood before Roman governors to petition for justice (Acts 24:10–21; 26:1–23, 25–27, 29) and to settle civil disputes (Acts

18:12–16; 22:30–23:5). Yet, Barnabas emphasized that approaching the supreme ruler of the universe (= God's throne) was possible only through Jesus, the one who ruled alongside God (cf. 1:3, 13). Jesus made it possible to approach God with "confidence" (παρρησίας) or more specifically in "safety" or "security." The previous emphasis about the messianic Son's relationship with people (2:11–18) and recent emphasis on his ability to sympathize with human frailties (vv. 14b–15) provided a sense of "safety" or "security" in approaching God's throne.

"Confidence" (παρρησία)

Most translations render παρρησία as "confidence" or "boldness" (3:6, 4:16, 10:19, 35). Yet, it is unlikely that παρρησία meant "fearless" (cf. Prov. 20:9, 10:10; Wis 5:1; 1 Macc 4:18; 3 Macc 7:12). Such a meaning would be out of place because it counters the expectation to "fear" (4:1; cf. 10:30–31; 12:29). It is also unlikely that παρρησία conveyed the idea of speaking openly with God. In Proverbs, Wisdom spoke "openly" (παρρησία) in the public square (1:20). Similarly, a citizen in the Greco-Roman world had the right to speak "openly" in the midst of a gathering of people (see *TDNT*, 5:871–75) and to express oneself "openly" in public (3 Macc 4:1). It seems more than likely that in Hebrews 4:16, "confidence" (παρρησία) spoke more of a person's "safety" or "security" when approaching God. In the LXX, "safety" existed for the poor (Ps. 11:5 [12:5]) and for the repentant (Job 22:26; 1 John 3:21) before God. When discussing human relations, it expressed "security" in the mutual confidence between two brothers (*P.Mich.* 502.9, 12) and between a husband and wife (Josephus, *A.J.* 2.4.4 §52). In Hebrews, a relationship with the messianic Son of promise (2:11–18) enabled members of the household family of faith in Rome to "approach the throne of grace in safety" (*TLNT*, 3:62).

The intentional result (ἵνα, "so that") in approaching the reigning sovereign God of the universe in safety was so that household family members of faith might experience God's "mercy" (ἔλεος) and know God's "grace" (χάριν). God's "mercy and grace" (ἔλεος *καὶ* χάριν) were so close in meaning that they may have expressed to the household family of faith in Rome a single "activity of God, from which human being's benefit" (Ellingworth, 1993, 270). That single activity conveyed God's compassion (cf. Pss. 103:8; 111:4; 116:5). Together they "powerfully picture the total adequacy of the benefits God's people receive when they enter God's presence through this 'merciful' (2:17) High Priest" (Cockerill 2012, 228). Finally, Jesus provided help to the household family of faith in a timely manner (εἰς εὔκαιρον βοήθειαν). Unlike human Judaean priests and kings, the messianic Son of promise was available 24/7.

Qualifications of a High Priest (5:1–4)

Jewish high priests were divinely chosen men, put in charge to represent God to people, and to perform priestly duties for themselves as well as for others.

5:1. Barnabas paused to explain (γάρ, "for") the qualifications of a high priest (BDAG, s.v. "γάρ" 1d, p. 189). The phrase "from among men" (ἐξ ἀνθρώπων) could be understood in a generic sense of humanity rather than maleness (NET nn. 23–25). Yet, the specificity to men was due to the historical practice of choosing Jewish men for the office, even after the return from exile (cf. VanderKam, 2004, 491–93; Bateman, 2012, 84–91). So, high priest appointments were from among the Jewish male population of Aaron/Zadok lines from the tribe of Levi. They were charged with representing people before God through various priestly duties. The verb "appointed" (καθίστημι) spoke of their twofold divinely appointed charge (divine pass.; cf. 5:4): to serve as an intermediary between God and people ("represent them before God," cf. 5:2a) and to act on their behalf ("to offer gifts and sacrifices," cf. 5:3). Thus, "appointed" (καθίστημι) underscored the fact that every human high priest was *ordained.* More specifically (epexegetical ἵνα), high priests were divinely placed in mediatory roles to represent God to people through their various priestly duties.

5:2. Barnabas added (καί, "and") that high priests were representatives for men and women "able to [can] deal gently" or perhaps "able to moderate one's passions" (μετριοπαθεῖν δυνάμενος). Moderating one's passions was not to eliminate personal emotions, but rather to control them. For instance, after the death of his lifelong partner, Sarah, Abraham was presented as one who exercised a moderation of feelings that was neither overly grievous nor indifferent as though nothing painful had occurred (Philo, *Abr.* 255–57, cf. *Ios.* 26). The reason why a high priest was able to moderate his passions with "those who are the ignorant and misguided" (τοῖς ἀγνοοῦσιν καὶ πλανωμένοις) was twofold. The first was because (ἐπεί) he himself (αὐτὸς) suffered the same "weakness" (BDAG, s.v. "ἀσθένειαν" 2, p. 142; *TDNT,* 1:492). In fact, he was "bound" or "weighed down" (BDAG, s.v "περίκειμαι" 2, p. 801) by the same inadequacies. He was aware of his own propensity to err (cf. 9:7) caused by his own weakness of faith. "Weakness" here differed from that in 4:15 where it spoke of Jesus understanding human weakness. Here "weakness" spoke of a Levitical priest's weakness as it pertained to his own unwitting propensity to sin (cf. Num. 15:22–29). Thus, as a millstone or as a chain around one's neck weighs a person down, so the high priest was "burdened" (περίκειται) with his own inadequacies of faith and thereby "moderated his passions" toward other offenders (BDAG, s.v. "περίκειμαι," p. 801; Attridge, 1989, 143–44; Kurianal, 2000, 53–55).

5:3. Barnabas continued (καί, "and") with the reason why a high priest offered sacrifices. It was "because *he himself*" (διά + intensive accusative *αὐτήν*) was obligated to offer sacrifices for himself and other people (Lev. 4:3–21). During the First and Second Temple periods, the larger body of Levites served in various temple roles: singing, music, preparations for sacrifices, or custodial care of the temple. So, not every Levite performed the sacrificial rituals (1 Chron. 24:29–31; 11Q21.2–4; 1QM 2.1–2; CD 14.3–6). Yet, those Levitical priests who traced their lineage from Aaron and Zadok were legally "obligated" (ὀφείλει) under the Mosaic law to perform sacrificial rituals and were to serve as administrators in the temple (Ezek. 40:45–46, 44:15, 48:11; Sir 50:12–17; 11Q22.2–4, 1QM 7.9–11).[3] Although "obligated" (ὀφείλει) was often a technical term for fiscal responsibility (Philem. 18), here in Hebrews it conveyed the judicial duties of a priest to make sacrifices and serve in the temple. Zechariah, John the Baptist's father, was of the priestly division of Abijah, a descendent through Aaron's son Ithamar (1 Chron. 24:1, 6, 10). He was chosen from his priestly division to enter the temple and burn incense (Luke 1:8–9). Due to a priest's own "weakness" (ἀσθένειαν), namely, his human propensity to disbelieve or disobey God (Philo *Spec* 1.114; cf. Spicq, 1952, 2:109; Ellingworth, 1993, 278), the judicial charge of the high priest was to make sacrifices *for himself* and *for people* (Lev. 4:3–35). The most significant sacrifice he performed was a yearly one on the Day of Atonement (Lev. 16:1–34).

5:4. As Barnabas continued (καί, "and") his discussion about the high priest, he shifted to distinguishing between illegitimate and legitimate priesthoods. Speaking negatively, Barnabas made it clear that no high priest could assume or "take *the honor* upon himself" (οὐχ ἑαυτῷ τις λαμβάνει *τὴν τιμήν*). This emphasis would have resonated with the household family of faith in Rome. They would have been aware of the corruption that plagued Jerusalem's high

3 Jeremias, *Jerusalem in the Time of Jesus: An Investigation into Economic and Social Conditions during the New Testament Period,* translated by F. H. and C. H. Cave (Philadelphia, PA: Fortress, 1969), 147–221.

priesthood since the time of Judas Maccabee (167–164 B.C.). Jason and Menelaus *paid* for the honor, Aristobulus and Alexander Jannaeus *expanded and established the power* of the office into a Levitical royal-priesthood, and Aristobulus II and Antigonus *usurped* the position of royal high priest (VanderKam, 2004, 197–393; Bateman et al., 2012, 234–48).

High Priests: Name and Dates	Historical Issues and Literary Sources	High Priests: Name and Dates	Historical Issues and Literary Sources
Jason 175–172 B.C.	… purchased the high priesthood from a Gentile king but eventually forced out 2 Maccabees 4:7–23 (cf. 1 Maccabees 1:11–15); Josephus, *A.J.* 12.5.1 §§240–41 →	Menelaus 172–162 B.C.	… purchased the high priesthood from a Gentile king: Antiochus IV 2 Maccabees 4:24–50; 11:27–33; 13:3–8; Josephus, *A.J.* 12.9.7 §§383–85
Alcimus 162–160 or 159 B.C.	… was appointed high priest by a Gentile king: Nicanor → 1 Maccabees 7:12–16, 21–25, 54–57; 2 Maccabees 14:1–4; Josephus, *A.J.* 12.9.7 §385; 12.10.6 §413	Jonathan 152–142 B.C.	… was the brother of Judas Maccabee and was appointed high priest by a Gentile king: Alexander Balas 1 Maccabees 9:23–10:66
Simon 142–134 B.C.	… was the brother of Judas Maccabee and acquired national recognition as high priest, leader, governor, ethnarch, and protector of the Jewish people → 1 Maccabees 10:67–14:45	John Hyrcanus 134–104 B.C.	… assumed the high priesthood after the murder of his father, Simon, and expanded the Hasmonean kingdom 1 Maccabees 16:11–22; Josephus, *A.J.* 13.8.1 to 9.1 §§230–58
Aristobulus 104–103 B.C.	… assumed the high priesthood after the death of John Hyrcanus, declared himself king and priest, and expanded the Hasmonean kingdom → Josephus, *A.J.* 13.11.1–3 §§301–19; *B.J.* 1.3.1–6 §§70–84	Alexander Jannaeus 103–76 B.C.	… assumed the royal-priesthood from his brother and expanded the Hasmonean kingdom Josephus, *A.J.* 13.12.1 to 15.5 §§320–405; *B.J.* 1.4.1– §§85–106; 4Q Pesher Nahum 3–4 i 1–9
Hyrcanus II 76–67 B.C.	… was appointed to the high priest position by his mother, Alexandria, and eventually assumed the royal-priesthood → Josephus, *A.J.* 13.16.2 §408; 14.3.3–4 §§46–57; *B.J.* 1.5.1 to 6.5 §§109–137	Aristobulus II 67–63 B.C.	… usurped the royal-priesthood from Hyrcanus II, was defeated by Pompey in 63, and was carried off to Rome and eventually murdered Josephus, *A.J.* 14.3.4 to 4.3 §§46–67; *B.J.* 1.7.2–6 §§142–152
Hyrcanus II 63–40 B.C.	… was appointed as high priest by a Roman: Pompey Josephus, *A.J.* 13.16.2 §408; → 14.3.3–4 §§46–57; *B.J.* 1.5.1 to 6.5 §§109–137	Antigonus 40–37 B.C.	… usurped the royal-priesthood from Hyrcanus II, was defeated by Herod the Great, was carried off to prison and died Josephus, *A.J.* 14.8.4 to 16.4 §§140–491; *B.J.* 1.10.1 to 18.3 §§195–357

Many Jews considered these high priesthoods as illegitimate (Pss. Sol. 2:1–3; 8:2–22) and others referred to one of them in their writings as a "wicked priest" (1QpHab 8.14–9.12). While debates abound about the exact identity of this "wicked priest," the description was applicable to more than one priest.[4]

Even later, priestly families—Ananus, Boethus, and the Phiabi families that supplied the high priesthood position—were corrupt and problematic during the reigns of Herod the Great, his sons (Archelaus, Antipas, Philip), and grandsons (Agrippa I, Agrippa II; cf. VanderKam, 2004, 394–490, 493). So, underscoring the contrast (ἀλλά, "but") between legitimate and illegitimate high priests would have resonated with the Jewish people in Rome because they would have been aware of the corruption among Jerusalem's priests, a corruption that Mark underscored in his Gospel, particularly among the experts of the Law (12:38–40) and at the trial of Jesus (14:55–65).

So, in contrast to illegitimate high priests, there was Aaron. Speaking positively, Barnabas made it clear that Aaron was a legitimate high priest due to his divine appointment (Exod. 29:7–9). Those who have been divinely appointed ("when called by God," καλούμενος ὑπὸ τοῦ θεοῦ), like Aaron and his sons (1 Chron. 6:50–53; 24:1–19), were Israel's legitimate priests (Exod. 28:1; 29:7; Lev. 8:1–2; Num. 17:5; 18:1; 2 Sam. 8:17; Ps. 105:26). Thus, God's pattern for assuming the honored position of high priest was to be by divine appointment and not self-appointed.

The Appointment of Jesus as Royal High Priest (5:5–10)

Jesus was God's appointed regal high priest who had experientially learned obedience and was fully equipped for the high priestly service as God's royal high priest similar to that of Melchizedek.

5:5. By way of comparison (οὕτως καί, "so also") with Aaron in verse 4, "the Messiah" (ὁ Χριστός) did not elevate himself to the office of high priest, "but" (ἀλλά) rather God gave the honored position to Jesus. The clause "*God* said to him" (ὁ λαλήσας πρὸς αὐτόν) echoed Hebrews 1:5. God said, "Today I have begotten you" (ἐγὼ σήμερον γεγέννηκά σε). The repeated quote from Psalm 2:7 reminded the household family of faith of Jesus's divine appointment (1:5–13 and 3:6). It also served to transition and expand the household family of faith's understanding about the *royal* high priest that Jesus "became" (γεγέννηκά, or "begotten"; 2:17, 5:5, 6:20, 7:16).

> **"Begotten" (γεγέννηκά)**
> The term "father" was not used in Psalm 2:7, but rather a verb, "begotten" (KJV, RSV, NASB, ESV, NRSV). It conveyed, however, the concept of "fathering" (NIV, NET, NLT). Speaking metaphorically, "I have fathered you" sometimes served to identify God's initiation of his unique relationship with the nation Israel (Deut. 32:18–19; cf. Exod. 4:22, Hos. 11:1) or, as it was the case in Psalm 2:7, with the anointed Davidite (cf. 2 Sam. 7:14, Ps. 89:27–28). Whereas a human father-son relationship began at physical birth or adoption, for God the father-son relationship with a royal Davidite began the day of his coronation/exaltation (Bateman, 1997, 323 n. 39, 219).

5:6. Barnabas accentuated the status of Jesus's high priesthood by linking Psalm 2:7 with Psalm 110:4 and stressed three central themes. First, "you are a priest." The force of "you are a priest" cannot be overstated. Barnabas alone ascribed the title of priest, more specifically high priest, to Jesus (cf. 2:17; 3:1; 4:14). "You are a priest" in its original literary context

4 A. S. van der Woude, "Wicked Priest or Wicked Priests in the Habakkuk Commentary," *Journal of Jewish Studies* 33 (1982): 349–59.

conferred a divine promise and title of priest to a Davidic king of Israel, perhaps Solomon.[5] Thus, "you are a priest" underscored the mission of Jesus by using cultic terminology reserved for priests and their temple activities (cf. Kurianal, 2000, 11). Second, "forever" (εἰς τὸν αἰῶνα, lit., "for the ages") described the eternality of both his position and priestly service (6:20, 7:17; cf. 1:8, 10–12). While initially employed as a figure of speech for the longevity of the life of a human Davidic king, "forever" here was escalated to a literal sense for eternity (cf. 1:7, Sandy, 2002, 98–101). Third, "after the order of Melchizedek" distinguished Jesus's priesthood from all Levitical priesthoods as well as the Levitical royal-priesthood created by Judas Maccabee's family. Barnabas's recollections of Melchizedek occurred only in Hebrews (5:6, 10; 6:20; 7:1, 10, 11, 15, 17). The infrequent yet distinct reference to Melchizedek from Scripture (Gen. 14, Ps. 110), coupled with the unparalleled descriptions of Melchizedek and his regal priesthood in Hebrews, made Melchizedek profoundly important for Barnabas's argument.

Did Davidic Kings Ever Perform Priestly Duties?

Although Scripture *emphasized* a Davidic king's royal functions over priestly ones, Davidic kings were often presented as performing priestly duties. They were known for having blessed people (2 Sam. 6:18; 1 Kings 8:14–14), for having offered sacrifices (2 Sam. 6:13, 17–18; 2 Sam. 24:18–25; 1 Kings 8:62–66; 1 Chron. 21:18–28), and for having exercised authority over the priesthood (2 Sam. 6), and they were at times called priests (2 Sam. 8:18, Ps. 110:4). Yet, there were limitations placed on a Davidic king. Certain priestly functions were reserved for the Levitical priesthood (cf. Uzziah, 2 Chron. 26:16–21; Isa. 6:1). So, while the Davidic king performed priestly functions, in Hebrews Jesus's royal high priestly functions were expanded and thereby further underscored his superior rule as messianic Son of promise (cf. Matt. 12:42), as well as stressed how his royal-priesthood, like Melchizedek's, was superior (7:15–17, 20–22, 24–27, 28b) to that of any Levitical high priest (7:11–14, 23, 28a) or any royal high priest after the order of the Hasmoneans.

5:7. This rather long sentence in Greek that ends in verse 10 (a Greek period, cf. 1:4) further developed Jesus as "the Messiah" (ὁ Χριστός). While "who" (ὅς) might refer back to "son" (υἱός) in Psalm 2:7, commentators generally consider Jesus to be the subject of the sentence (Ellingworth, 1993, 284; Cockerill, 2012, 240). "In the days of his flesh" (ἐν ταῖς ἡμέραις τῆς σαρκὸς αὐτοῦ, v. 7; cf. 2:14) was a figure of speech for Jesus's incarnation or rendered "during his earthly life" (NET). It was during his earthly life that Jesus made anguished appeals to God (perhaps an allusion to Gethsemane, Mark 14:32–42; cf. Attridge, 1989, 148). Barnabas highlighted an aspect of Jesus's anguished prayers not found in the Gospels, namely, that "he was heard because of his reverence" (καὶ εἰσακουσθεὶς ἀπὸ τῆς εὐλαβείας; NET). "His reverence" (εὐλάβεια; ESV, NLT, NIV) may be rendered as "fear" (KJV, CNT) or "piety" (NASB; cf. BDAG, s.v. "εὐλάβεια," p. 407; *EDNT,* 2:78–79). Yet, Barnabas used a similar word to speak of Noah's showing a reverent regard of God in his constructing of an ark for the deliverance of his family (11:7; BDAG, s.v. "εὐλαβέομαι" 2, p. 407). Luke used it of devout Jews (2:25; Acts 2:5, 22:12). In Hebrews 12:28, the household family of faith gave thanks and offered worship to God in reverence and awe. Here in Hebrews 5:7, the pious prayer of Jesus, namely, the petitions and supplications, done with strong cries and tears,

5 H. W. Bateman IV, "The Use of Psalm 110:1 in the New Testament," *Bibliotheca Sacra* 149 (Oct–Dec 1992): 438–53.

was heard "because of his reverence" for God's sovereignty over his life situation (2:9–10). Thus, in his deeply felt human cries and his human reverence for God's sovereignty over his life, Jesus learned experientially what obedience entailed.

5:8. Even though (καίπερ, "although") he was "a son" or the messianic Son of promise (cf. 1:1–15), Jesus "learned obedience" (ἔμαθεν . . . τὴν ὑπακοήν, v. 8; cf. 3:2). How he learned it was "through the things he suffered" (ἀφ' ὧν ἔπαθεν; cf. Heb. 2:18). The phrase "learned from what he suffered" (ἔμαθεν ἀφ' ὧν ἔπαθεν τὴν ὑπακοήν) was a common Greek proverbial play on words that was used negatively of people who learned from their mistakes (Philo, *Mos.* 2.55). Yet, Barnabas was not indicating any failures of Jesus. Jesus learned as a result of physical sufferings (2:10; 12:1–3; cf. Mark 15:16–39). So even though Jesus was God's messianic Son of promise (ὢν υἱός; cf. ὃν ἔθηκεν κληρονόμον, "whom [God] appointed heir," 1:2), he was accused, mocked, scorned, and killed for no fault of his own (Mark 15:16–39). The sufferings he suffered were part of God's plan to equip him to be the head ("pioneer") of the household family of faith (2:9–10, 18).

5:9. Continuing (καί, "and") his development of Jesus (ὅς clause) as "the Messiah" (ὁ Χριστός), Barnabas explained why Jesus "was made perfect" (τελειωθείς): "he became" (ἐγένετο) the source of salvation (cf. 2:10, "the pioneer"). During the First Temple period, when a Levitical high priest died, those who were guilty of unintentional manslaughter were set free from cities of refuge (Num. 35:25; Josh. 20:6). The high priest's death served as their source for atonement. And while Jesus was not to be confused with a Levitical high priest, as God's regal high priest, his death was a source for freedom or a form of atonement. Whereas in 2:9, the messianic Son of promise was described as suffering death "on behalf of all" (ὑπὲρ παντός), here Barnabas qualified the beneficiaries as "those who obey him" (τοῖς ὑπακούουσιν αὐτῷ). As in 2:10, "the Messiah" (ὁ Χριστός) was again presented as the one who "completed" (τελειῶσαι, or "perfected") God's plan. Thus, Jesus was the "source of eternal salvation" (αἴτιος σωτηρίας αἰωνίου)—a theme Barnabas would further develop in 8:1–10:18.

5:10. In concluding this long Greek sentence, which began in verse 7, Barnabas declared once again that Jesus was a royal high priest. Yet here, God, in an unambiguous manner, designated Jesus as a regal high priest (cf. 1:5–13). The term "designated" or "called" (προσαγορεύω) was unique to Hebrews in that Jesus was given a rank similar to that of Melchizedek, a rank never linked by God to the ancestral call of any Levitical high priest (5:1–4). Even though some Levitical high priests (Aristobulus and Alexander Jannaeus) later expanded the office to include a royal element, the expansion was rejected particularly by a group of Essenes who resided at Qumran (1QpHab 8.14–9.12). Thus, unlike the Levitical high priests of the First and Second Temple periods, God designated Jesus as the messianic Son of promise, a "high priest" according to the royal-priestly rank of Melchizedek.

"Call" (προσαγορεύω)

The verb "called" (KJV) or "designated" (NASB, RSV, NIV, ESV, NRSV, NLT, NET) only occurs here in the NT. It's typically used as an address to an individual (as in a cultural greeting according to one's rank: Herodotus 1.134; 2.80; as an epistolary greeting: *POxy* 3.526.2; as a friend: 1 Macc 14:40). Other usages included the identification of a person or a thing: Antiochus was called Epiphanes (2 Macc 4:7, 10:9); Nicanor was called father of the Jews (2 Macc 14:37); God's title was Lord (Philo, *Abr* 121); and the ark's cover was called a mercy seat (Philo, *Mos.* 2.97). Its use also included the giving of a name to someone or something: of God naming the heavens as firmament (Philo, *Opif.* 36), of kings granting titles to subordinates (Philo, *Opif.* 148), and of Nehemiah naming the place of holy fire as naphtha (2 Macc 1:36). Here in Hebrews 5:10, God gave the name "high priest" to *the* Christ (note the previous reference to Christ as the Son: vv. 5–6; cf. 1:5–13, 3:6, 4:14).

THEOLOGICAL FOCUS

The exegetical idea (Jesus, the household family of faith's high priest to whom they were to cling and through whom they had safe access to God in order to experience God's compassion, met the qualifications for the high priesthood in keeping with his divinely appointed tasks as regal high priest) leads to this theological focus: Clinging to Jesus, God's appointed regal high priest, makes it possible for the household family of faith to approach God in safety in order to experience his compassion.

The major theological themes of this preaching unit are twofold: the regal priesthood of Jesus and the responsibility of the household family of faith. On the one hand, there is the development of Jesus as high priest (4:14; cf. 3:1). His high priesthood is a regal high priesthood (4:14; 5:5–6, 10) and not to be confused with the Levitical priesthood (5:5–6; 10). Yet like a Levitical priest, Jesus was chosen from among people (4:16; 5:4), appointed to represent people (4:16; 5:1, 5–6), and capable of understanding people (4:15; 5:2). Yet unlike the Levitical priests, Jesus learned obedience through his suffering (4:15; 5:7–8), the source of salvation (cf. 5:3 with 5:9), and yet managed to do so without any wrongdoing or disobedient acts (4:15).

On the other hand, there is the development of the household family of faith's responsibility. Unlike earlier in Hebrews where the household family of faith was expected to *maintain* their confessions about Jesus as founder and high priest of the community (3:6, 14), here the expectations were heightened. Based upon the simple fact that Jesus was God's appointed regal high priest for the household family of faith, members of the household were to cling to Jesus (4:14). Furthermore, the household family of faith was expected to approach God with a sense of safety through Jesus so that family members might experience God's compassion (4:16).

PREACHING AND TEACHING STRATEGIES

Exegetical and Theological Synthesis

The immediate exegetical significance of this section was something that Barnabas had been hinting about previously in 5:10 and 6:20, namely, the superiority of Jesus's priesthood. This was the exegetical and theological trajectory of the book to this point. After setting up the superiority of Jesus to the angels and the prophets in chapter 1, the stern warning of chapter 2, the superiority of Jesus over Moses in chapter 3, the warnings of chapters 4 and 6, and the introduction of the idea of Jesus as high priest here in chapter 5; the stage was now set to show next in chapter 7 how Jesus was a super high priest.

The soteriological importance of Hebrews 4:14–5:10 is hard to overstate. Through this we understand Stephen's exclamation of seeing the heavens opened and the Son of Man standing at the right hand of the Father in Acts 7:56. This also ties up the theological ideas that Paul develops in Romans 8:31–34. In a sense, we can fold into this the idea presented in Philippians 2:1–11.

In sum, Jesus has received his high place of exaltation due to his humiliation on this earth (Phil. 2). And yet, in this high and exalted state his work continued (Rom. 8). He was still at the Father's right hand, and he was praying for the Roman household family of faith in Rome. Why? The answer would be unfolded in what would follow in Hebrews 7. Jesus is at the Father's right hand, because he is a super high priest. The shadowy figure of Melchizedek in the OT existed to give followers of Jesus a sense of the full and completed work of Jesus. Hebrews 7 can only lead to worship.

Preaching Idea

Everyone needs compassion, but where do we get it?

Contemporary Connections

What does it mean?

What does it mean that everyone needs compassion? We need a high priest that not only makes it possible for us to have access to God, but to make it possible for us to experience God's compassion. Throughout Scripture, God has extended his compassion to numerous people: God gave compassion to Adam and Eve by allowing them to live, albeit outside the garden (Gen. 3). God gave compassion to the Ninevites by sending Jonah (Jonah 1). God demonstrated his compassion Naaman by healing him from leprosy (2 Kings 5). The presence of Jesus as our high priest is an extension of the compassion that we find all through Scripture.

Every year, there is a new batch of superhero movies. As of this writing, the trend is to recapture superheroes created decades ago by weaving new storylines and concepts into the various film series. What is remarkable about each of these superheroes is that they have two things in common. First, they are human (or humanlike). We understand their feelings. They have wins, losses, fears, and failures, and they experience many of the same problems we do and demonstrate compassion toward those they rescue. Second, however, they are not like us in some distinct way. They can fly, have incredible strength, or possess something that makes them quite remarkable. So, they are both like us and not like us.

We need both access to God and the opportunity to experience God's compassion. Jesus is the only one with complete access to God. And, gloriously, the one who gave us access to God is the one who knows us more intimately than anyone. This is why we praise Jesus: he is very much like us and very much not like us.

Is it true?

Is it true that that everyone needs compassion? Yes! We all make mistakes. We are painfully aware that we do things that do not please others. Husbands and wives need compassion as we try to communicate with one another. Children need compassion from their parents as they attempt the awkward transition to adulthood. We need compassion in our workplace as we may not hit the goals we have established for ourselves. However, in each of these circumstances, we should find empathy. After all, every parent has been a child, every employer has or is an employee, and every spouse knows what it is like to miss the mark in marriage. Our compassion with others is rooted in our identification with others.

Many Christians live in a passive state with God, blandly assuming that God has no interest in them. And yet, Jesus provides all the empathy we need from God *and* all the access we need to God. If the people in our congregation cannot relate to being in a courtroom, they can at least relate to a courtroom drama. Our people can understand the idea of a defendant, a prosecutor, and a judge. Imagine that someone is guilty of a crime. That person cannot approach the judge, but needs someone to go between them. He needs someone who has access to the judge, like a defense attorney. While it is true that the defendant can defend himself and thereby grant himself access to the judge, in almost all cases one's defense would be access in name only. In other words, the "access" is limited because the defendant representing himself does not really speak the judge's language or have the legal finesse to present a proper defense.

However, even if the defendant has a lawyer with access, the person must also have one who has empathy. After all, if the lawyer has no compassion for the defendant or the case, the defendant will not be represented. What Jesus provides us is enough empathy that he can understand us, and enough access that he can go to the Father.

Now what?

What can we expect from a compassionate God? First, we can expect forgiveness. We can approach God in prayer with boldness, repent, and ask forgiveness. It ought not to be a matter of can I forgive myself but of trusting in God's great compassion to forgive all those who confess their wrongdoings to God and others. Do our prayers reflect this type of boldness? Jesus told two parables on prayer. The parable of the friend at midnight (Luke 11:5–13) and the parable of the persistent widow (Luke 18:1–8) both have a theme of shameless persistence. What Jesus encouraged his followers to do in prayer makes more sense when we understand that he actually is there (Rom. 8:34), making a way for us as our royal high priest! So, the application of this passage is to pray like we mean it; pray like it is real because Jesus, who understands us, is making a way for us to do so.

Creativity in Presentation

It would be possible to test the congregation's ability to identify superheroes. Start with an easy one. Talk about Superman and how he can fly, how he has super strength, and how he can produce heat from his eyes. Perhaps on the screen there could be a picture of Superman with all his powers listed to the right of the picture. For lists of powers, see the Marvel and DC Comics websites. Then go through each of the superheroes and note their superpowers, note especially those who have the word "man" or "woman" in their name (e.g., Iron Man, Wonder Woman, Spider-Man, Ant-Man, etc.). Demonstrate that each of these has a unique power.

Yet each of them also has something unique. They are, at their core, human (or humanlike). What makes some of them unique is that they are alien (e.g., Superman, Captain Marvel, Thor, etc.). What makes others unique is that they have special powers or abilities, even though they are not alien (e.g., Batman, Black Widow, Black Panther, etc.). They are very much human!

These of course are creations of our imaginations. They do not exist! We created them. Therefore, their creation says so much about their creators. Now ask this question, "So, what is it about *us* that makes us create these people?" We have created a whole race of superhuman people. Evidently, we enjoy the idea of someone who is greater than us but has empathy with our individual situation. We did not create humans in these stories, nor did we generally create mere aliens with power. We created superhumans. They have enough power to help, but enough humanity to empathize.

The text has two imperatives: hold on and draw near. There is an explanatory "for" (γάρ) in 5:1 that supports the reason we draw near. What follows in 5:1–10 is a comparison of Jesus and the priesthood. In sum, we draw near because, while the priest is qualified, Jesus was enthroned by God himself!

The point you want to get across is simply this: Everyone needs compassion, but where do we get it? One approach to an outline for this text would be as follows:

- We have God's compassion, so hold on (vv. 4:14–15).
- We have God's compassion, so draw near (vv. 5:1–10).

DISCUSSION QUESTIONS

1. Who is your hero? Obviously, Jesus is. However, do you have an earthly hero? Perhaps a father figure or a mentor? Why is this person your hero?

2. We would not have access to God without the life of Christ. What specifically about the life of Jesus grants us access to the Father? Be specific.

3. Do we realize our deep need for Jesus? We obviously realized our need for him at our point of salvation, and we know we need him for the culmination of our salvation at the end—but what about in the here and now? Why do we need Jesus daily?

4. What does it mean that Jesus gives us access but also shows us empathy?

Hebrews 5:11–6:12

EXEGETICAL IDEA

The household family of faith in Rome, reprimanded for their inability to advance in their understanding of Jesus as regal high priest and in discerning life situations, was exhorted to press on in their understanding about the messianic Son of promise in conjunction with a motivational word of encouragement.

THEOLOGICAL FOCUS

Everyone who claims to be a follower of Jesus must understand the details of Jesus as God's messianic Son of promise.

PREACHING IDEA

The mind is a terrible thing to neglect.

PREACHING POINTERS

During the Greco-Roman period, the literate person was in the minority. Very few could afford an education; even fewer could read and write. This was not because they were incapable of learning; they just learned differently. They learned orally. Naturally, this could lead to stagnation in advancing in knowledge and understanding of new subjects. In this unit, Barnabas expressed his disappointment in the Roman Jewish household family of faith about their inability to advance in their understanding of Jesus as regal high priest. So, he reprimanded them and exhorted them to press on in their orally taught understanding about the messianic Son of promise, to move from their ruts and stop neglecting their need to advance in their understanding.

Even today, as literate as our society is, it's very easy to stagnate and become apathetic about advancing in our understanding about issues. It's a common leadership maxim that people within an organization will do anything in the world to keep from thinking. The temptation in an organization is simply to execute our roles without thinking about how our work affects the larger picture. We find this temptation in our adolescence, where academic pursuits simply become checking boxes and a means to the end of getting a degree. We, perhaps unwittingly, are programmed to check boxes and not to think outside of them. The spiritual danger is that we treat our relationship with God like a relationship with other organizations. We simply want to check boxes. However, the mind is a terrible thing to neglect.

REPRIMAND FOR APATHY (5:11–6:12)

LITERARY STRUCTURE AND THEMES (5:11–6:12)

Having introduced Jesus as God's appointed regal priest, Barnabas wanted to expand his discussion, but there was a problem. Hebrews 5:11–6:20 was another digression similar to the one in Hebrews 2:1–4. Hebrews 5:11–6:20 was also a warning passage, like Hebrews 2:1–4 (Bateman, 2012, 143–48). In this first half of the warning (5:11–6:12), Barnabas issued a reprimand for apathy because the household family of faith had become indifferent about advancing in knowing more about Jesus as evidenced by their need of a teacher and their unskilled ability to discern between good and evil (5:11–14). Barnabas advanced his reprimand with an expectation for them to press on to developing into discerning thinkers by moving beyond theological ruts in view of the harsh reality for anyone who rejected God's benefits (6:1–8). Barnabas closed with a motivational word of encouragement based upon past expressions of love and service toward others (6:9–12). The second half of the warning (6:13–20) will be addressed in the next preaching unit.

The two themes Barnabas focused on were expressed in his expectation for the household family of faith to develop understanding of Jesus as God's messianic Son of promise and not to get stuck in theological ruts that diverted attention away from Jesus.

- ***A Reprimand for Apathy (5:11–14)***
- ***An Expectation to Press On (6:1–8)***
- ***A Motivational Word of Encouragement (6:9–12)***

Barnabas's Third Warning

Barnabas moved from his desire to speak more about Jesus's regal priesthood (5:1–10) to his third of five warnings (5:11–6:12). His third warning was presented in three parts. Part one opened with a reprimand (5:11–6:12). Part two was an expectation (6:1–8). Part three was a motivation (6:9–12). Barnabas underscored his warning with quotations of Psalm 95:7b–11 and Genesis 2:2, as well as allusions from Exodus 17:1–7 and Numbers 13–14. Barnabas appealed to these texts in order to parallel the readers' current situation with that of the wilderness community at Kadesh Barnea.[1]

EXPOSITION (5:11–6:12)

Organized education was rare throughout the Greco-Roman world. Receiving learned instruction was generally reserved for those who could afford to pay a tutor or pay tuition to attend a private school. Despite the lack of historical records, it has been estimated that literacy rates during the first-century Greco-Roman world were no more than twenty percent (Chiappetta, 1953, 149–56; Harris, 1989, 3–24; Walton et al., 2013, 111–20). So educated people, as we might think of an educated person, were few in number. A person who was able to write letters (called an amanuensis) was considered a learned person, able to perform an acknowledged professional skill and linked with scribes throughout the Greco-Roman society (Bateman, 2013, 49–51).

For instance, the apostle Paul came from the city of Tarsus where people, who could afford it, applied themselves to the study of philosophy and "the whole round of learning

---

1 For various views on this warning passage, see H. W. Bateman, *Four Views on the Warning Passages in Hebrews* (Grand Rapids: Kregel, 2007), 108–18, 192–205, 272–80, 352–58.

in general" (Strabo, *Geogr.* 14.5.13 [trans. Jones]). He was an educated Jewish person who was trilingual, trained in Jerusalem, and studied the Mosaic law under Gamaliel (Acts 22:1–3). The fact that he was sent to Jerusalem to be educated appears to indicate that he came from a somewhat wealthy Hellenistic Jewish family. And though Paul was able to write his own letters, he employed an amanuensis for five of them: 1 Corinthians, Galatians, Philemon, Colossians, and 2 Thessalonians. This is not to insinuate, however, that people did not learn or advance in learning, but rather that their methods of learning differed as did their reading and writing capabilities. People still learned; they just learned orally (Walton et al., 2013, 121–66). The Bereans, after they *heard* Paul's message, searched the Scriptures for themselves (Acts 17:11), which probably meant that the Scriptures were read orally in order to hear and validate Paul's message for themselves. They advanced in their learning about Jesus, God's messianic Son of promise. Here in Hebrews, Barnabas expressed his disappointment in the Roman Jewish household family of faith about their inability to advance in their understanding of Jesus as regal high priest. So, he reprimanded them and exhorted them to press on in their orally taught understanding about the messianic Son of promise. And yet, he provided a motivational word of encouragement based upon past expressions of love and service toward others.

Roman portraiture fresco of a young man with a papyrus scroll from Herculaneum, 1st century A.D. Public domain. Courtesy of Soefm.

A Reprimand for Apathy (5:11–14)

Teaching about Jesus as regal high priest was hampered due to the household family of faith's apathy for and deficient level of understanding about Jesus as God's divinely appointed messianic Son of promise.

5:11. Barnabas wanted to enter into deeper discussions about Jesus as the messianic Son of promise likened to that of Melchizedek, but speaking candidly, it was a difficult topic (περὶ οὗ, "about this") to develop "because" (ἐπεί, or "since") the household family of faith had become "dull of hearing" (KJV, RSV, NRSV, ESV), "slow of hearing" (NIV), "sluggish in hearing" (NET), or perhaps "hard of hearing" (BDAG, s.v. "νωθρός," p. 683). While "hard of hearing" may indicate a form of deafness, most translations suggest "dull of hearing." On the one hand, this figure of speech sometimes spoke of aptitude: a donkey as "the dullest among living creatures" (Philo, *Post.* 161; *Abr.* 266) or a person as "dull-minded" (Philo, *Sacr.* 32; *Deus.* 63). Plutarch used the term to speak of a person's ability in study: Cato was "sluggish of comprehension and slow" (*Cat. Min.* 1.3 [Perrin]; cf. *TLNT,* 2:552–54). On the other hand, Pfitzner (1997, 95) suggests that "dull of hearing" spoke of "mental dullness as failure to listen properly" as underscored elsewhere in Hebrews (cf. 2:1; 3:7, 15; 4:1–2). Yet, the household family of faith in Rome may have become dull-minded due to indifference or apathy. They neglected their responsibility to listen with a willingness to advance in their learning and thereby unable to teach or share about Jesus with others (cf. 2:3). When "dull of hearing" (νωθροὶ . . . ταῖς ἀκοαῖς) was linked with "milk" in verse 15, Barnabas drew attention to the household of faith's indifference about advancing in their confessions about Jesus (cf. 3:1). They were experiencing apathy toward moving beyond what they already thought they knew and understood about Jesus (cf. 6:12).

TEXTUAL ANALYSIS: Conflicting Text Critical Reading: 5:12
Grammatical Issue: The difficulty of this issue surrounds the lack of accents in the earliest manuscripts. Consequently, contemporary translators discern, based upon context, which is the more appropriate form. Thus, the editorial committee felt "someone" (τινά) gave a more accurate contrast: a teacher versus a set of teachings. The text is the preferred reading (Metzger, 1994, 596).

txt. "you need **someone** to teach you again the basic elements of the oracles of God" (πάλιν χρείαν ἔχετε τοῦ διδάσκειν ὑμᾶς **τινὰ** τὰ στοιχεῖα τῆς ἀρχῆς τῶν λογίων τοῦ θεοῦ) (ESV, NASB, NET, NIV, NRSV)

var. "you have need that one teach you again **which are** the basic elements of the oracles of God" (πάλιν χρείαν ἔχετε τοῦ διδάσκειν ὑμᾶς **τίνα** τὰ στοιχεῖα τῆς ἀρχῆς τῶν λογίων τοῦ θεοῦ) (KJV, ASV)

5:12. Barnabas offered evidence (καὶ γάρ, "for indeed") to support his claim about their apathy to learning (BDF, 236 §452; Attridge, 1989, 158; Ellingworth, 1993, 302): "Although *you* ought to be" (ὀφείλοντες εἶναι) a community of "teachers" (διδάσκαλοι), they were not. In Hebrews 5:3, "ought" (ὀφείλω) addressed the judicial duty of a priest to offer sacrifices on behalf of others. Here, however, Barnabas's concern was not with a priest's cultic responsibility but rather the household family of faith's responsibility to communicate or teach their confessions about Jesus to others (3:1). Perhaps, they were questioning their confession about Jesus. Barnabas pointed out that they needed to be taught "all over again" (NIV) or "again" (ASV, NASB, NRSV, ESV, CNT, NLT). The word "again" (πάλιν) stressed the household family's need of someone "to teach" (διδάσκειν) them the basics (cf. 6:1).

Barnabas drew attention to their educational deficiencies with the use of "milk" (γάλα). While "milk" (γάλα) could stand for real milk (1 Cor. 9:7; LXX: Gen. 18:8, Exod. 23:19, Judg. 4:19), it was often used figuratively (a meronomy). For instance, "a land flowing with milk and honey" symbolized the Promised Land's rich food-procuring abilities (Exod. 3:8, 17; Num. 13:27; Deut. 26:15; Joel 3:18; cf. *NIDOTTE,* 2:136). During the first century, food imagery came to symbolize levels of learning. Philo (*Agr.* 9) argued, "But seeing that for babes milk is food, but for grown men wheaten bread, there must also be soul-nourishment, such as is milk-like suited to the time of childhood, in the shape of the preliminary stages of school learning, and, such as is adapted to grown men, in the shape of instruction leading the way through wisdom and temperance and all virtue" ([trans. Colson et al.]; cf. Philo, *Congr.* 19; *TDNT,* 1:646). Similarly, here in Hebrews, "milk" (γάλα) referred to the basic elements of instruction. In this context, it concerned matters of Jesus's regal priesthood (5:5–6, 10). Barnabas drew attention to the fact that the household family of faith was floundering in the "basic teachings" (= elementary level) about their faith rather than engaging more "advanced teachings" (= collegiate level) about the messianic Son of promise. Thus, rather than being a community of collegiate-level teachers, they remained a community of elementary-level learners.

Metaphors of Hebrews 5:11–6:10		
Metaphors	**Primary Referent**	**Secondary Referent**
Children	Beginning learners	Novice inquirers
Milk	Elementary education	Basic teachings
Adults	Advanced learners	Mature inquirers
Solid food	Discerning learners	Critical thinkers

5:13–14. The reason (γάρ, "for") the household family of faith was revisiting basic elementary-level teachings was because they were "unskilled" (KJV, RSV, ESV, NRSV), "inexperienced" (NET), "not accustomed" (NASB, NIV), or "unacquainted" (BDAG, s.v. "ἄπειρος," p. 100) with developing their thinking. While "unskilled" (ἄπειρος) may refer to any number of things, here it was associated with learning that affected discernment in thinking and living rightly (δικαιοσύνης). The household family of faith in Rome lacked the learning needed to make discerning decisions necessary for everyday life situations. The NLT captures this well: "And a person who is living on milk *isn't very far along in the Christian life and doesn't know much about doing what is right*" (emphasis is mine). We might even suspect that they were lacking in discernment about the Judaean happenings and the increasing hostility to Rome for independence and thereby an increased desire to return to Judaism was enticing them to question Jesus's messiahship.

Barnabas underscored his concern with a contrast (δέ, "but") between an "infant's" (νήπιος) consumption of "milk" (= easy instruction) and an "adult's" (τελείος) ability to digest more "solid food" (= significant teachings). The metaphor of "solid food" (ἡ στερεὰ τροφή) drew attention to the capability of digesting tougher material that would enable the household family of faith to value and discern between the good and bad events that were happening around them in Rome as well as those happening in Judaea.

An Expectation to Press On (6:1–8)

The household family of faith was expected to advance in their understanding of Jesus because no repentance existed for the household family member who abandoned Jesus, God's messianic Son of promise.

TEXTUAL ANALYSIS: Conflicting Text Critical Reading: 6:2
Stylistic/Theological Issue: Although support for the text (א A C I K P 33 81 614 1739) and the variant is strong ($\mathfrak{P}^{46}$ B 0150), a scribe may have changed "instruction" (διδαχήν; acc.) to "of instruction" (διδαχῆς; gen.) to *agree* with the series of genitives in the text, or he changed "of instruction" (διδαχῆς; gen.) to "instruction" (διδαχήν; acc.) to *avoid* the string of genitives. Yet, the agreement of διδαχὴν with θεμέλιον (v. 1) has theological significance. The variant is the preferred reading (Lane, 1991a, 132).

txt. "**of instruction** about baptisms, of laying on of hands" (βαπτισμῶν **διδαχῆς**, ἐπιθέσεώς τε χειρῶν) (ASV, KJV, NASB)
var. "**instruction** about baptisms, of laying on of hands" (βαπτισμῶν **διδαχὴν**, ἐπιθέσεώς τε χειρῶν) (ESV, NET, NIV, NRSV)

6:1–2. Barnabas advanced (διό, "therefore") his candid reprimand with an expectation: "let us press on" (NASB), "let us leave [behind]" (KJV, ESV, NIV; BDAG, s.v. "ἀφίημι" 3b, p. 156), or "we must progress" (NET). The "sense of 'move on' was one of progression in spiritual growth or development" (Mitchell, 1989, 118). Naturally, Barnabas included himself: "let us." Yet, he did not expect something without providing some direction. Speaking positively, he told how to advance: "by leaving" (ἀφέντες) "*the* early *teaching* about Messiah" (*τὸν* τῆς ἀρχῆς τοῦ Χριστοῦ *λόγον*). Not that the household family of faith was to forget "the . . . teachings" (τὸν . . . λόγον), but rather advance in them. "Let's stop going over the basic teaching about Christ" (NLT). Barnabas wanted the household family of faith in Rome to advance in their messianic understandings of Jesus as God's appointed regal priest (cf. 5:5–6, 10).

Speaking negatively, Barnabas explained how *not* to advance: "by not rehashing *again*" (μὴ *πάλιν* . . . καταβαλλόμενοι) the basics (lit., "not again laying down the foundation"). The emphatic "not again" (μὴ πάλιν) spoke volumes. Barnabas wanted to eliminate reruns and to move people out of their theological topical ruts. He identified six teachings to stop rehashing: (1) "repentance [μετανοίας] from dead works," which may reference things done in Judaism that demonstrated covenantal loyalty (circumcision, burying the dead, honoring the Sabbath, etc.; cf. Holmén, 2001, 74-–79); (2) "faith in God" that excluded the divine messianic Son of promise (1:5–13); (3) "teaching of baptism" that focused attention on one's identity with Jesus (Col. 2:12) and not necessarily a ceremonial cleansing (Mark 7:4; 4Q514 1.i.5–7)[2] and/or John's baptism (Acts 19:1–7; Josephus, *A.J.* 18.5.2 §117); (4) "laying on of hands," which may have been some sort of confirmation of the Spirit's indwelling (Acts 8:17–18; 9:17; 19:6); (5) "resurrection of the dead," which may have been a reference to the bodily resurrection of Jesus and all members of the household family of faith (cf. 1 Cor. 15:3–4, 12–22; 1 Thess. 4:14–18); and (6) "eternal judgment," which may have dealt with the resurrection and subsequent eschatological judgment for those who did not accept Jesus as God's messianic Son of promise (Attridge, 1989, 164–65). Perhaps these were the community's set of theological pet peeves that prevented a more holistic approach to learning about Jesus as God's appointed regal high priest (cf. 5:11).

Textual Analysis: Conflicting Text Critical Reading: 6:3
Grammatical Issue: Manuscript support ($\mathfrak{P}^{46}$ ℵ B I K L 0122 0278 6 33 88 614 629 630 1241 1739 1881) and flow of thought to the subsequent phrase "if God permits" argues for the text reading. Yet, it is also easy to explain a scribe's orthographic confusion between "we will do" (ποιήσ**ομεν**) and "let us do" (ποιήσω**μεν**). The text is the preferred reading (Metzger, 1994, 596).

txt. "and **we will do** this" (καὶ τοῦτο **ποιήσομεν**) (ASV, ESV, KJV, NASB, NET, NIV, NRSV)

var. "and **let us do** this" (καὶ τοῦτο **ποιήσωμεν**)

6:3. Barnabas continued (καί, "and") with an explicit desire: "this we intend to do" (τοῦτο ποιήσομεν). "This" (τοῦτο) referred back to his initial expectation in verse 1: "let us press on." Barnabas intended to move beyond the six basic topical and theological ruts in verses 1 and 2. Barnabas intended to entertain more advanced teaching about Jesus as regal priest, which he eventually does in chapter 7. Although Barnabas used an "authorial 'we'" (Cockerill, 2012, 267), he cushioned his statement by making it conditional (ἐάνπερ, "if"). Furthermore, he did

2 For further discussion on Jewish ceremonial baptism, see Hermann Lichtenberger, "Baths and Baptism" in *Encyclopedia of the Dead Sea Scrolls*, eds. L. H. Schiffman and J. C. VanderKam (New York: Oxford University Press), 1:85–89.

not presume upon God. There was an evident submission to God (cf. James 4:15). It was a serious sentiment that stressed the household family of faith's need to advance in their understanding about Jesus as God's appointed regal priest that could only come through the appropriation of God's grace (Attridge, 1989, 165; Cockerill, 2012, 267).

6:4. The reason (γάρ, "for") for Barnabas's intention was well-founded because no repentance (εἰς μετάνοιαν "to repentance") existed for the apostate. His perspective was presented with the statement that it was "impossible" (ἀδύνατον) "to renew again to repentance" (πάλιν ἀνακαινίζειν εἰς μετάνοιαν). Although Barnabas highlighted several "impossibilities" throughout Hebrews (6:4, 18; 10:4; 11:6), here he claimed that it was impossible to lead a person to repent after he or she turned away from God. With as much time spent on the topic of repentance as a basic foundation of faith (v. 2), it is interesting that the community needed to be taught this aspect of repentance. Yet, Barnabas was quite descriptive about those for whom repentance no longer existed.

SYNTACTICAL ANALYSIS: "it is impossible . . . to renew to repentance"
Some translations follow the Greek order and begin the clause in verse 4 ("It is impossible . . .") and end the clause in verse 6 (". . . to renew them again to repentance"; NET; cf. NIV, NLT). Others translate the clause as a unit either at the beginning of verse 4 ("it is impossible to restore again to repentance"; RSV, NRSV, ESV) or verse 6 ("It is impossible to renew them again to repentance"; NASB). What tends to rattle the twenty-first-century reader, however, is not the English rendering of the clause but its meaning, particularly as it concerns the impossibility (an absolute) "to bring to conversion again" those who have turned away, whether they be the teachers and fellow-teachers of the community (*TDNT*, 3:451–52), a group within the community (Gordon, 2008, 92), or the entire Jewish Christian community (Attridge, 1989, 170–71, Lane, 1991, 1:135). It is impossible for God to restore an apostate.[3]

Barnabas's description of those for whom repentance no longer existed revealed a common thread of spiritual experiences by his original readers. First, they were "once enlightened" (τοὺς ἅπαξ φωτισθέντας), which implied a *divinely directed experience* (pass. ptc.). The term "once" (ἅπαξ) conveyed an unrepeatable event. "Those who have been enlightened" (τοὺς φωτισθέντας) described the initial experience of the gospel that set the convert's life in a new direction (10:32; cf. Bartimaeus: Mark 10:46–52). The image of light suggested both new knowledge and a new way of life (cf. 2 Cor. 4:6; Eph. 1:18; 1 Tim. 1:10; 1 John 1:5–10; Pfiztner, 1997, 97).

6:5. Second, they *experienced* the gift of salvation. On the one hand, "tasted" (γευσαμένους) literally meant to "eat" or "drink" as in the case of the Lord's Supper (Acts 20:11) or of eating of manna (Wis 16:21, John 6:31–58). On the other hand, the figurative usage was that of "experiencing something [to the full]" or "to experience something" whether it was cognitive or emotional (BDAG, s.v. "γεύομαι" 2, p. 195). Philo frequently applied this metaphor to real spiritual experiences (of divine love: *Som.* 1:165; of virtue: *Abr.* §89; of holiness: *Mos.* 1:190) in contrast to those who were spiritually inexperienced. So, as it was the case in Hebrews 2:9, "taste" (γεύομαι) maintained a metaphorical sense. Whereas in 2:9, the verb's graphic imagery conveyed Jesus's having experienced death, here in Hebrews 6:4–5 the metaphor conveyed people having encountered

3 For various views on the word "impossible" in this warning passage, see H. W. Bateman, *Four Views on the Warning Passages in Hebrews* (Grand Rapids: Kregel, 2007), 108–18, 192–205, 272–80, 352–58.

something spiritual (cf. a person's encounter with Yahweh: Ps. 33:9 LXX [34:8]). It was not a matter of tasting and not consuming. Thus, *having experienced* ("tasted") the heavenly gift directed attention to *experiencing* God's grace (cf. Rom. 5:15; 2 Cor. 9:15; Eph. 3:7, 4:7). The gift of the holy spirit spoke of a relationship with God (cf. Acts 2:38, 10:45). Both expressions were privy to people who were members of the household family of faith (*TDNT,* 1:676, Attridge, 1989, 170).

Finally, they *have been given* a "partnership" (μέτοχος), they were "partakers of" (KJV, RSV, NASB, NET) or "shared in" (NIV, NLT, NRSV, ESV) the holy spirit. As in 3:14, "partnership" (μέτοχος) once again emphasized the household family of faith's allegiance. Here that allegiance was with God. Unlike 3:14, it was not with the divine messianic Son of promise, but with the divine spirit (= God's spirit):[4] "we have become partners with God's spirit." Thus, through various salvific activities and experiences, the household family of faith "have become" (γενηθέντας) aligned with *God himself.* They have *experienced* God's "good word."

6:6a. Perhaps a small group of individuals within the larger household family of faith had rejected, "turned away from" (NLT), or "fallen away" (NASB, NRSV, NIV; cf. KJV, ESV) from God. They "committed apostasy" (NET; cf. RSV). Typically, "turn away" (παραπεσόντας) spoke of "a failure to follow through on a commitment" (BDAG, s.v. "παραπίπτω," p. 770). If terms of a contract *with a person* "should be broken," it was rendered invalid (*POxy* 1.95:34; emphasis mine, cf. MM, 488–89). Similarly, if terms of the covenant *with God* were broken "by acting faithlessly," the contract was broken (Ezek. 14:13; 22:4; cf. Exod. 19:1–20:21; Deut. 11:26–29, 28:58–68; CD 1:3; 4Q266f2i:8). Here in Hebrews, according to Barnabas, "turned away from" (παραπεσόντας) would have been a warning to people who considered rejecting their allegiance with or commitment to Jesus (cf. 3:14). Thus after "having been enlightened" and having experienced (1) the "heavenly gift," (2) "the word of God," and (3) "the miracles of the coming age," an impending danger existed for them or anyone who may be swayed to turn away (cf. Origen, *In John* 28.7; Andrews, 1873, 28.51–56). Barnabas was concerned about a segment of apostates who threatened to sway the entire household family away from God, similar to what had occurred at Kadesh Barena (cf. Heb. 3:8–11).

A crucial word in this discussion was "renew" (ἀνακαινίζω). Barnabas warned candidly and unequivocally: renewal or restoration did not exist for those who turned away from the divine royal-priest (cf. 1:1—2:4). It was "impossible" (ἀδύνατον). A close parallel may exist in Philo (*Praem.* 49) where he wrote "to educate a *disbeliever* [ἀπιστοῦντα] was difficult or rather *impossible* [ἀδύνατον]" ([trans. Colson]; cf. 6:18). Although it would appear "quite unnatural for anyone to let go again the heavenly gift" (*TDNT,* 1:382), Barnabas feared that some members of the household family of faith considered turning away from their belief in Jesus, the messianic Son of promise. It was a real concern that threatened the household family of faith. Thus, they would subsequently face the impossibility of their restoration. Abandoning the only foundation there was for repentance and faith ended in eternal destruction.

6:6b. For Barnabas, the reason why no repentance existed for those who rejected God's messianic Son of promise was "because [=

4 For an understanding of God's spirit in Second Temple texts, see H. W. Bateman IV, "Portraits of God's Spirit in Hebrews Compared with the Dead Sea Scrolls" in *Charts on the Book of Hebrews* (Grand Rapids: Kregel, 2012), 113–14.

since] they are crucifying again" (NET n.; cf. NIV) or "since they are crucifying once again" (ESV cf. NRSV) Jesus to his or her own hurt (ἑαυτοῖς). While it may be true that "crucify" tended to speak of a literal crucifixion, "the context seems to require the figurative meaning crucify again" (BDAG, s.v. "ἀνασταυρόω," p. 72) or "re-crucify" because a second literal crucifixion could not be had. Such a literal rendering was an unsettling paradox. Barnabas insisted that Jesus's death was "a once for all" unique sacrifice (cf. 9:25–28). Metaphorically, it may mean a *continual* crucifixion (pres. tense) of the Son (Tertullian, *Pudic.* 9.11; Origen, *In John* 20.12, Andrews, 1873, 89–90). Or it may mean to "crucify *again*" as rendered in the NLT: "they themselves are nailing him to the cross once again" (cf. Heb. 9:25–28). Yet, Barnabas's point was that the act of turning away from Jesus was a *visible display of hostility*, unbelief, and rejection that was acted out when Jesus initially and quite literally was crucified (Heb. 9:25–28; cf. *TLNT,* 3:12). Since the crucifixion was a historical event that happened once and could not be repeated, Barnabas's point was that apostates were *like* the crowd that mocked Jesus, scourged Jesus, and killed Jesus that day at Golgotha (read Mark 15:14–32). Thus, they displayed the same hostility, unbelief, and rejection that was acted out when Jesus initially and quite literally was crucified.

Crucifixion of Jesus

Described as "the most pitiable of deaths" (Josephus, *B.J.* 7. 6. 4 §203), crucifixion was the literal act of binding, nailing, or impaling of a person, whether they be dead or alive, to a cross, a stake, or a tree for execution or for exposing the corpse of that individual. "Crucifixion" appears in several ancient sources as a means of punishment (cf. *EncDSS* 1:158–59). The chief baker was crucified by Pharaoh just as Joseph predicted (Josephus, *A.J.* 2.5.3 §73). Haman wished to punish Mordecai, Esther's uncle, by means of crucifixion (Josephus, *A.J.* 11.6.10 §246). King Xerxes of Persia impaled the head of a Spartan Greek king on a stake (Herodotus, *Hist.* 7.238; cf. Thucydides, *Hist.* 1.110; *POxy* 5.842.18.22). Yet, it was possible to survive a crucifixion (Josephus, *Vita* 420). Nevertheless, it became Rome's way of quelling the Spartacus slavery revolt in Rome and the Jewish revolting in Judaea (Josephus, *B.J.* 2.14.9 §306, 5.2.4 §449).

Crucifixion was not only a horrific death, it was also a public shame (παραδειγματίζω). While speaking of the king of Tyre (v. 12) who was likened to a guardian cherub (v. 16), Ezekiel says, "I (= God) exposed you before kings to make a 'spectacle' (παραδειγματισθῆναι) of you" (Ezek. 28:17; cf. Esth. 14:11 [LXX]).. In the Psalms of Solomon 2:14, "Before the face of the sun their criminal deeds have been revealed" (this seems to be similar to Numbers 25:4; cf. 3 Macc 7:14 (*TDNT,* 2:32).

In addition (καί, "and") to "re-crucifying" the messianic Son of promise, they also insulted him or put Jesus to "shame publicly" (παραδειγματίζοντας). Thus, the second reason why no repentance existed for those who rejected God's promise was because they were holding Jesus up to "public disgrace" (NIV), "public shame" (NLT; cf. NASB, CNT, KJV), or "in contempt" (NET, NRSV; BDAG, s.v. "παραδειγματίζω," p. 761). This concept "to shame publicly" or "hold in contempt" denoted an event (often punishment) that caused great public humiliation and usually served as a warning to others (Num. 25:4; Jer. 13:22; Polybius, *Hist.* 2.60.7). In other words, to repudiate the messianic Son of promise was to reject their confessions about him and their allegiance with Jesus (cf. Peter in Mark 8:27–29; 14:54, 66–72). Thus, they too would have taken part and shared in the public scorn hurled at Jesus during his trial, on his way to Golgotha, and while hanging on the cross (cf. Matt. 26:67–68; 27:38–43; *TLNT,* 3:12).

6:7–8. Barnabas linked (γάρ, "for") verses 7–8 to verses 4–6 with an appeal to an agricultural image. Like other Jewish authors before him, Barnabas compared the household family of faith to plants (Isa. 5:1–10; Ezek. 15:1–8; John 15:1–8) to illustrate his point. Speaking positively, the ground that absorbed the rain produced food or useful plants and received a blessing from God (Gen. 1:11–12). Thus, a faithful and obedient commitment from the household family of faith was to bear a useful harvest. In this context, being a useful harvest may be related to their ability to teach others (cf. Heb. 5:12).

In contrast (δέ, "but") and thereby speaking negatively, the same ground that produced thorns and thistles or worthless plants were worthless and close to being cursed. Barnabas was not contrasting two different fields but rather the same field with different results. The ground that produced thorns and thistles was subject to burning or divine judgment (Matt. 13:30, 42; 25:41; John 15:6.). The theme of divine judgment throughout the OT was well known to Jewish people (Ps. 18:8 [17:9 LXX]; Isa. 30:27; Jer. 4:4; 21:12).[5] Thus, any household family member that turned away from Jesus would bear no harvest and would be subject to divine judgment (cf. Heb. 6:4–5).

A Motivational Word of Encouragement (6:9–12)

Based upon the household family of faith's expressions of love for one another, Barnabas was confident about their future.

6:9. In contrast (δέ, "but") to those who had rejected or were considering abandoning the faith and whose end would be destruction, Barnabas concluded with a motivational word of encouragement. He was confident about the overall future of the household family of faith. Despite the prospect of turning away, which occasioned Barnabas's earlier warning (6:1–8), he now affirmed the household with "we are convinced . . . of better things" (πεπείσμεθα . . . τὰ κρείσσονα). Although translated numerous ways—"persuaded" (KJV, ASV), "confident" (NRSV, NIV, NLT), "convinced" (NET), or "we feel sure" (ESV; BDAG, s.v. "πείθω" 4, p. 792)—the rhetorical use of the plural "we are convinced" (πεπείσμεθα) was an intense expression of Barnabas's personal confidence in them. In addition, his reference of his readers as "dear friends" (NIV, NET) or "beloved" (KJV, NASB, RSV, NRSV, ESV) used only here in Hebrews reinforced Barnabas's encouragement rather than discouragement. Together, the rhetorical use of "we are" and "dear brothers" served as a powerful expression of certitude. An assumed confidence that the community would experience the "better things" of salvation (i.e., "the blessing of God"; cf. 6:7). Nevertheless, Barnabas conceded his displeasure of dealing with the harsh reality concerning those who abandoned Jesus, namely, that a curse and destruction existed for all who turn away from Jesus, the one who was the only foundation for repentance and faith.

6:10. The basis (γάρ, "for") for Barnabas's confidence in the future for the household family of faith was that God was not unjust. God would not forget their works and expressions of love on behalf of others. Theologically, "to forget" (ἐπιλαθέσθαι) spoke of God's inability to ignore good deeds (cf. Sir 3:14; 44:10), the sacrifice of the righteous (cf. Barnabas 35:6), and communities of servants (cf. Isa. 44:21, 49:15). The idea that God would not "overlook" (RSV, NRSV, ESV) or "forget" (KJV, NASB, NIV, NLT, NET) was a Jewish traditional motif of God's faithfulness (Attridge, 1989, 174; Ellingworth, 1993, 330). Here in Hebrews 6:10, the idea that God would not "forget"

5 See Hebrews 10:27. A verbal allusion exists with Genesis 3:17 and may recall Psalm 95 spoken of in Hebrews 3:12–4:11 (cf. 1 En. 27:1).

(ἐπιλαθέσθαι; KJV, NET, NLT) spoke of his constant fidelity (*EDNT*, 2:30) or God's righteousness (*EDNT*, 1:31). God's constant righteousness, his faithfulness, and his fairness, would not allow him to forget the household family of faith's works of loving service extended toward other believers that were done in his name (Heb. 10:32–34). Thus, Barnabas affirmed the household family of faith concerning their present spiritual life and yet lent credence to his subsequent admonition that "brotherly love must continue" (13:1; 1 John 2:29; 5:1; James 2:8, 14–18; cf. Rom. 2:6–7; 1 Cor. 3:12–13). Barnabas's confidence in the household family of faith's works and particularly their love was evident in the way they had assisted one another (6:10b; cf. 10:32–34).

6:11. Once again, Barnabas's rhetorical use of the masculine plural "we" was an intense expression of his personal confidence in the household family of faith. Although at times translated "we desire" (KJV, NASB, RSV, ESV) or "we want" (NIV, NRSV), such renderings minimize Barnabas's earnest and reassuring desire for this group of "dear friends." The verb "we desire" (ἐπιθυμέω) often communicated strong passions, whether they be sexual (Matt. 5:28; 4 Macc 2:5), coveting of things (Acts 20:33, 1 Macc 4:17), or cravings for nourishment (Deut. 14:26; Luke 15:16, 16:21). So, Barnabas's desire was rather strong (BDAG, s.v. "ἐπιθυμέω" 2, p. 371). His affection for the household family of faith was best conveyed in English translations with "our great desire" (NLT) or "we passionately want" (NET). The desire here was for there to be an intense yearning, an urgent longing, a passionate striving that every individual ("that each of you," ὑμῶν τὴν αὐτήν; cf. 3:12, 13; 4:1, 11; 10:25; 12:15) progress toward (πρός) something. Barnabas desired that his Jewish recipients in Rome maintain their confidence in God and his promises until the very end of their lives (cf. Koester, 2001, 317).

6:12. The intended result (ἵνα, "so that") of this passionate desire was twofold. The first result was that each member of the household family of faith revert from their apathetic behavior about learning (μὴ νωθροί, "not dull minded"). This repeated occurrence of the adjective "sluggish" or "dull" (5:11) recalled Barnabas's initial critique in 5:11–14, which preceded his exhortation (6:1–3) and warning (6:4–8). In verses 9–12, however, Barnabas expressed his confidence and "passionate desire" that the household family of faith would continue on with purpose—not as indifferent, lazy, or unwilling to learn, but as imitators of those who faithfully persevered and thereby inherited what God had promised.

The second result (δέ, "but") contrasted the first. It was so that each family member might imitate (μιμηταί) those who through faith persevered and inherited God's promise (6:13; 11:1–40; cf. Philo, *Sacr.* 123; *Mos.* 1.158). Barnabas would develop this thought in the next unit.

THEOLOGICAL FOCUS

The exegetical idea (the household family of faith in Rome, reprimanded for their inability to advance in their understanding of Jesus as regal high priest and in discerning life situations, was exhorted to press on in their understanding about the messianic Son of promise in conjunction with a motivational word of encouragement) leads to this theological focus: Everyone who claims to be a follower of Jesus must understand the details of Jesus as God's messianic Son of promise.

The primary theological theme in this preaching unit is the household family of faith's responsibility. First, they are to develop in their understanding of Jesus as God's messianic Son of promise (5:11, 13–14; 6:3). Family members should be aware, understand, and teach others about Jesus, who is God's messianic Son of promise. Second, the household family of faith is not to get stuck in theological ruts that essentially divert attention away from Jesus (6:1–2, cf. 6:7). The inability to move beyond theological pet peeves (e.g., baptism vs. sprinkling, Calvinism vs. Arminianism, premillennialism vs. amillennialism, inerrancy vs. errancy, etc.), not only stagnates the household family of faith; it opens the door to apostasy (6:4–6; cf. 8). Thus the expectations as to how shall we then live creates apathetic people.

PREACHING AND TEACHING STRATEGIES

Exegetical and Theological Synthesis

Hebrews 5:11–6:12 was a transition. Barnabas had just completed a massive theological comparison of Jesus to the high priest (5:1–10), and was about to launch into another warning (6:4–8). This transition was helpful for the one who was preaching sequentially through the book in so much as it gave a needed pastoral moment between these two heavy sections. Also, it contained provocative metaphors that were so clear, they almost preach themselves.

Barnabas begins with an observation and reprimand for apathy. This is the chief critique that drives the passage. They had become dull of hearing. Notice that the "you" in 5:11 was plural. The idea was that this was written to a group of people and not to an individual. As a whole, there were some within the household of faith who had grown spiritually dull.

He then moved to an expectation to press on (6:1–8). This was a strong warning not to fall away. Yet, the warning was couched in an imperative for them to press on and keep going. The significance of the idea of not being renewed can't be overstated (v. 6). They could not be renewed for the reason that they were expressing the same hostility as those who were crucifying Jesus.

He then closed with a motivational word of encouragement. Barnabas was confident about their future. His confidence rested in the justice of God. Because of God's remembrance of them, he hoped for better things. He envisioned them moving away from their sluggishness and persevering in God's promise (6:12).

Preaching Idea

The mind is a terrible thing to neglect.

Contemporary Connections

What does it mean?

What does it mean that the mind is a terrible thing to neglect? Every child has this innate desire to grow up. To be more than they are. One of the worst things a child could say to another child on the playground is, "You're such a baby!" The implication behind that statement is regression: you are not growing up, you're going backwards. And no child wants to go backward—they naturally want to grow up!

It is so heartbreaking when someone grows mentally but not physically, or physically but not mentally. Our heart breaks for such situations. Medical doctors can guess at the situation to see what the cause is. Yet as leaders, we see people who have stunted spiritual growth. Some Christians grow in physical years but do not grow spiritually. Tragically, some have no aspirations to grow spiritually.

This text is to a spiritual anomaly what a doctor is to a physical anomaly. Barnabas had thus diagnosed the problem: they were dull. But note he said they had *become* dull (5:11). This is a spiritual regression by the willful act of neglecting the mind. They were childish by choice.

As a result, this choice had affected their learning; they were students who should be teachers (5:12). This had also affected their eating: they were infants who should be adults (5:12d–13).

Is it true?

Is it true that the mind is a terrible thing to neglect? Water, if left alone, will stagnate. This is a major health hazard in developing countries. The worst problem with stagnant water is that it can facilitate the spread of diseases like malaria. The water becomes a breeding ground for mosquitos that can transmit the disease. If water is not flowing, all kinds of parasites and bacteria can grow. All of this is caused simply because the water is not flowing. It is sitting with no movement.

The illustration that has often been used is the Dead Sea. It is a sea in Israel, more like a large lake, into which water flows in but none flows out. As a result, it is rich with salt and mineral deposits. You can swim in it, but the water is so thick with minerals, that you will float. If you open your eyes, they will burn. The salt deposits make the water extremely dense. This is why it is called "dead." Aside from a limited number of algae, bacteria, and fungi that tolerate the extremely salty environment, there is no plant or animal life because there is no flow.

One of the most dangerous positions to be in is that a Christian who is not growing. This is someone who is a student but should be teaching by now. The stagnation is not just neutrality but regression! This willful neglect of the mind is a choice to go backward and not forward spiritually.

Now what?

If we agree that the mind is a terrible thing to neglect when it comes to understanding Jesus as our royal high priest, what are we to do? Notice that Barnabas is writing to the "you" (5:11). Who is the "you"? It was this group. No one is isolated here. What happens when a group of people of spiritually stunted people get together: The answer is, we don't have any expectation of each other. We are comfortable with our lethargy. Many churches have made a passive ascent to a mutual mediocrity.

It's true that we simply don't take time to think through our faith, and we neglect this truth. Families get caught in the inertia of busyness. Churches get caught in the inertia of institutionalism. The result with both of these is that both families and churches prioritize activity over maturity. What do we do if we prioritize activity over maturity? Here are three applications.

First, we need to commit to a group; commit to a Sunday school, life group, or discipleship group. This group should have clearly defined goals to reach spiritual maturity. If possible, be involved in both an open group and a closed group. An open group welcomes new members, has an indefinite end date, and serves as a catalyst to reach others. A closed group is smaller, has a definite end and start date, and no one is added. An open group can draw others in for breadth, a closed group can push you to depth.

Second, we need to celebrate spiritual growth. We do this with our own children. We mark everything. If we are a parent there is the expectation and the joy of marking every milestone. And we dutifully mark every milestone on social media. It is the joy of parents to watch their children grow.

Third, intentionally fight apathy. The best way to do this is with regular church attendance. While this might sound like a banal application. The truth is that church attendance among those who consider themselves regular church attenders has fallen sharply. It is deceptive to think that we can be inconsistent in our fellowship but consistent in our growth. The one serves the other.

Impossibilities Matter

Fighting apathy is a continual challenge today. Another way of addressing apathy might be to preach a four part series on the impossibilities in Hebrews. The series might be titled "Impossibilities Matter": (1) It's impossible to please God without trust and faith in God (11:1–2, 6). (2) It's impossible for sacrifices to take away sin (10:1–4). (3) It's impossible for God to lie (6:18). (4) It's impossible for the restoration of apostates (6:4–6).

Creativity in Presentation

One way to illustrate the problem of the neglected mind is to play off the word *neutral.* When say we are "neutral" in our opinion of something, perhaps we mean that we do not have a strong opinion. Many people approach their faith this way, and especially their thinking about their faith. They do not want or expect to grow in their faith, but they do not want to go backwards. They do not want to regress, but there is no proactive plan for growth.

When a car is in neutral, we assume it is not going forward or in reverse. The implication is that by not being in drive or reverse, it is in a motionless state.

You could demonstrate this with a prerecorded video shoot of a car on a hill in neutral or find on old clip. Another option would be to have a track on the stage, much like the pinewood derby cars tracks. As you hold the car on the track you could demonstrate the car going down the track.

Now, imagine that you take a car to the top of a hill (track). You do not put the car in park, but you leave it in neutral with no emergency brake. What happens next? Demonstrate this by placing the car on the track and letting go. It is neutral, but it is going backwards.

The car goes backwards! The problem with staying spiritually neutral is that we assume that we are on level ground. We assume that the world, the flesh, and the devil are not against us. With all of this uneven land in front of us, to be neutral is to regress!

The point you want to get across is simply this: the mind is a terrible thing to neglect. One approach to an outline for this text would be as follows:

- Don't be apathetic, but learn (5:11–14).
- Don't fall away, but press on (6:1–8).
- Don't forget God's promises (6:9–12).

DISCUSSION QUESTIONS

1. What does "dull of hearing mean" (Heb. 5:11)?
2. What is the antithesis of falling away, as expressed in Hebrews 6:1–8?
3. What is the significance of this being a corporate passage written to a local body of believers?
4. Why are the participles in Hebrews 6:4–5 important to the interpretation of the passage?
5. What is the significance of the personal encouragement and confidence expressed in Hebrews 6:10–11?

Hebrews 6:13–6:20

EXEGETICAL IDEA

God's pledge to Abraham about heirs, conferred to Abraham by way of his perseverance, was certified by way of God linking his vow to his pledge, which had unchangeable certainties about Jesus as God's royal-priest.

THEOLOGICAL FOCUS

Followers of Jesus can trust that God will fulfill his pledge to those who persevere because of his trustworthy word about Jesus, his royal high priest.

PREACHING IDEA

God's promises are not like human promises—they are guaranteed.

PREACHING POINTERS

For the first-century Jew, Abraham was the recognized forefather of God's theocratic nation of Israel, whose existence was traced back to early Mesopotamia and the times of the Egyptian Pharaohs. "Abraham is often mentioned," according to Evans (2001, 2), "as the ideal example of Jewish piety and orthodoxy." In fact, he was considered God's friend, because he observed God's commandments. He was recognized as faithful to God. Here in Hebrews 6:13–20, Barnabas focused attention on *God's pledge to Abraham*, namely, that he would be a "father of a multitude." Abraham believed God, and God kept his pledge.

Today, verbal pledges or commitments are part of everyday life. We make pledges to our spouses during wedding ceremonies. We make commitments to volunteer in community organizations like Big Brothers Big Sisters, the Boy Scouts, or the Girl Scouts. We make pledges to provide monthly donations to World Vision, St. Jude Children's Research Hospital, and the church. We sign contracts for services to be completed within a timely manner. Unfortunately, obligations to an agreement is an endangered expectation. We don't always believe them. We don't always fulfill them. How does the everyday reality that not everyone keeps their promises, affect us? Is it true that God's promises are not like human promises—that they are in fact guaranteed?

GOD'S SWORN PROMISE (6:13–20)

LITERARY STRUCTURE AND THEMES (6:13–20)

Barnabas expanded his statement in Hebrews 6:12 about those who, through perseverance, "inherit the promises." Barnabas opened with God's pledge made to Abraham, which God confirmed with a divine oath whereby Abraham by way of perseverance became heir of God's promise (vv. 13–15). Barnabas then clarified the value of God's vow to certify God's unalterable pledge so that the household family of faith in Rome would adhere strongly to Jesus (vv. 16–18). Barnabas closed with two unchangeable certainties that the household family of faith have with Jesus: safety and his intercession as God's regal high priest (vv. 19–20).

Barnabas's foremost theme of this unit for members of the Jewish household family of faith was God's reliability.

- ***God's Pledge (6:13–16)***
- ***God's Unalterable Pledge (6:17–18)***
- ***Unchangeable Certainties (6:19–20)***

EXPOSITION (6:13–20)

Abraham, whose name means "father of a multitude," is a respected figure in three world religions: Judaism, Christianity, and Islam. He is recognized as the biological ancestor for both the Jewish people (Gen. 21:1–7; 22:1–18: "our father Abraham") and people of Islam (Gen. 16:1–16; Quran, *Ibrahim*). Yet Islam, under Muhammad's leadership, was founded much later (A.D. 610). Nevertheless, for the Jewish people of Rome in the first century, Abraham was the forefather of God's theocratic nation of Israel, whose existence could be traced back to early Mesopotamia (Gen. 12:1) and the times of the Egyptian Pharaohs (Exod. 2:24; Ezek. 33:24; Mic. 7:20).

While aspects of Abraham's story were found in Genesis 12–25, his story was retold in several Second Temple nonbiblical texts (CD, 1Q20, 4Q225, 4Q252, Jub., and Josephus, *A.J.* 1.6.5–17.1 §§148–256) and for good reason. "Abraham is often mentioned," according to Evans (2001, 2), "as the ideal example of Jewish piety and orthodoxy." In fact, "Abraham . . . was considered God's friend, because he observed the commandments of God and he did not choose to follow the will of his own spirit" (CD iii.2–3 [trans. Wise et al., 1996, 53]; cf. 2 Chron. 20:5–7). He "was recognized as faithful to God . . . that he might be accepted. And the Lord blessed him . . . one hundred and seventy-five years" (4Q226 frag 7.1–2 [trans. Wise et al., 1996, 264]).

So, like his Jewish counterparts, Barnabas quite often drew attention to Abraham (2:16; 6:13–20; 7:1–10; 11:8–19). Yet here in Hebrews 6:13–20, Barnabas focused attention on God's pledge to Abraham about heirs and Abraham's perseverance in God's unalterable pledge provided unchangeable certainties about Jesus as God's royal priest for the household family of faith.[1]

God's Pledge (6:13–16)

God's pledge to Abraham was realized by way of Abraham's patience.

1 For an overview of God's promises, beginning with Abraham but ultimately fulfilled in Jesus, see H. W. Bateman IV, *Charts on the Book of Hebrews* (Grand Rapids: Kregel, 2012), 128.

6:13–14. Barnabas transitioned ("now"; NET, BDAG, s.v. "γάρ" 2, p. 190) the ambiguous statement of verse 12 about those who "inherited the promises" with a specific example: Abraham. Barnabas recalled God's "promise" (BDAG, s.v. "ἐπαγγέλομαι" 1b, p. 356) or pledge made with Abraham. As mentioned in 4:1, two types of promises existed in Hebrews: fulfilled and unfulfilled. Whereas the promise in 4:1–11 presented to the household family of faith was an unfulfilled promise (i.e., entrance into God's heavenly place of Sabbath celebration of rest), here all who faithfully persevered in Jesus—the one through whom God's promises to Abraham were fulfilled (6:20)—were considered the realized heirs of Abraham ("heirs of the promise," 2:16; 6:17–18; cf. Rom. 4:13–22; Gal. 3:29).

Barnabas once again presented God as having "sworn" (ὤμοσεν) an oath (or "he made a vow"). The earlier appearance of "sworn" was made about the people at Kadesh Barnea (3:11; 4:3). It was a sworn oath of judgment. Here, the phrase "he swore by himself" (NET, NASB, NRSV, ESV) or he "took an oath in his own name" (NLT) called special attention to God's vow to Abraham. It was a sworn oath of blessing. This was one of several passages whereby Barnabas spoke of the trustworthiness of God's pledge. How God swore was demonstrated with a paraphrase of Genesis 22:17. While the promises to Abraham may have included land, heirs, and kings (Bateman et al., 2012, 37–40), Barnabas restated only *one* aspect of God's promise to Abraham: "in blessing I will bless you and in multiplying I will multiply you" (v. 14). What God promised Abraham was that he would be the father of a great nation (cf. Gen. 12:2–3, 15:5, 17:5). This appeal to God's sworn promise to Abraham revealed the Jewish cultural and theological foundations, namely, that God made promises to people, and Abraham received one of those promises (Mic. 7:20; Bar 2:34; Odes Sol. 9:73; cf. Pss. Sol. 9:9–11).

6:15. Barnabas continued (καί οὕτως, "and so") verse 14 by revisiting how ("in this way"; BDAG, s.v. "οὕτω," "οὕτως" 2, p. 742) Abraham inherited God's promise. Abraham became an heir of God's pledge to him "by persevering" (NET), by "having patiently waited" (NASB, ESV), or by "having patiently endured" (NRSV). It was by way of his "patience" (BDAG, s.v. "μακροθομέω" 1, p. 612) that Abraham obtained God's promise. More specifically, he waited twenty-five years for God to fulfill his promise about his heir, Isaac (Gen. 12:2, 4; 21:5; cf. Johnston, 2012, 38–52).

Unlike Hebrews 4:1 where the promise was something to look forward to, here in Hebrews 6:15 God's pledge to Abraham was realized. Abraham did not merely obtain a "confirmation" of God's promise (Lane, 1991a, 151); God's pledge to Abraham was fulfilled (Koester, 2001, 326; Cockerill, 2012, 285; Bateman et al., 2012, 39–40). God fulfilled his promise through the birth of Isaac (Gen. 15:1–6; 21:1–5; Heb. 11:11) and his living in the land (Gen. 15:7–21; Heb. 11:8–9). This was the first occurrence in Hebrews where Abraham was mentioned as one who inherited God's promise. He served not only as an example of one who inherited the promise (6:12, 15; 7:6), but also of *how* he inherited it (Ellingworth, 1993, 338–39). He was patient. He trusted God. He persevered in his everyday life circumstances. As it was in Hebrews 4:1, so it was here. God's promises were available to people who trusted God and waited patiently.

Who Was Philo?[2]

Philo (ca. 15 B.C.–A.D. 50) was a Greek-speaking Jewish philosopher who lived in one of the largest Jewish communities in the Roman Empire: Alexandria, Egypt. Josephus

2 D. R. Schwartz, "Philo, His Family, and His Times," in *The Cambridge Companion to Philo*, ed. Adam Kamesar (Cambridge, NY: Cambridge University Press, 2009): 9–31.

(*A.J.* 18.8.1 §259) described him as being "no novice in philosophy" (trans. Feldman). Due to the fact that organized education was rare and reserved for the wealthy throughout the Greco-Roman world, Philo no doubt came from a respected Jewish family with means. He was also a Roman citizen recognized as a political leader (*Spec. 1,2,3,4.* 3.1–6; Josephus, *A.J.* 18.8.1 §257–60). His Roman citizenship was due to Julius Caesar granting it to either his father or grandfather. Jerome (Schaff et al., 1979, 365) claimed that Philo came from a priestly family. So, like the Jewish historian Josephus (*Vita* 1.1–6 §2), it seems that he too may have had ties to the Hasmonean dynasty, though like many living at the time was not a person who took on responsibilities of the priesthood (Schwartz, 2009, 11). Philo, however, was known for his writings: expositions of the Mosaic law (*Abr.; Jos.; Virt.; Praem.*) and exegetical commentaries (*Leg.; Cher; Sacr.; Det.; Post.; Gig; Deus.; Agr.; Plant; Ebr.; Sobr.; Conf.; Migr.; Her.; Congr.; Fug.; Mut.; Somn.*; cf. Borgen, 1992, 334). Naturally, Philo's interactions and interpretations of the text reveal his methods of exegesis. While many people underscore Philo's use of allegory, he was on record as one who had criticized Jews who employed allegory to such an extent that they distorted the text along with Jewish customs, while at the same time recognizing the validity of a literal interpretation of the text (*Migr.* 89–93).

6:16. Barnabas clarified (γάρ, "for") God's "swearing" (ὀμνύουσιν). As noted in Hebrews 3:11, 18, to swear or to take an oath was a common cultural custom of the ancient Near East and Second Temple Judaism. Some people would swear by something greater as a witness to the veracity of their statement (cf. Matt. 23:16–22; *POxy* 3:482.37–38). Yet, here in verse 16, translations differ. Some suggest "by something" (ESV, NET), while others say, "by someone" (NASB, NRSV, NIV, NLT, CNT). It seems "by someone" (κατὰ τοῦ μείζονος) was more consistent with Barnabas's previous reference of God's swearing to those who disobeyed (3:18). "For our concept of an oath," said Philo (*Sacr.* 91–93), "is an appeal to God as a witness on some disputed matter. But nothing is uncertain or open to dispute with God. . . . Truly He needs no witness, for there is no other God to be His peer" (trans. Colson; cf. Gen. 31:53; Num. 30:3–4; Ps. 132:2; BDAG, s.v. "ὀμνύουω," p. 706).

God confirmed his oath by appealing to himself since he was without a superior. Unlike people who took oaths, "there is nothing amiss," according to Philo's comments on Genesis 22:16, "in God bearing witness to himself. For who else would be capable of bearing witness to him?" "He alone shall affirm anything regarding himself, since he alone has unerringly exact knowledge of his own nature. God alone therefore is the strongest security first for himself, and in the next place for his deeds also, so that he naturally swore by himself when giving assurance regarding himself, a thing impossible for anyone else" (Philo, *Leg.* 3.205–07 [trans. Colson et al.]).

God made such an oath so that in Abraham's "mind [it] might be established more securely and firmly even than it was before" (Philo, *Abr.* 273 [trans. Colson]). God's oath pointed to his unequivocal capability in and of himself to uphold his promise (6:17–18; cf. Ps. 89:35). God's oath was his bond. It was a universal confirmation that guaranteed the certainty of a transaction Thus, God's spoken bond of promise not only provided a guarantee to Abraham (cf. 6:15 with 11:12, 17–19), it provided security to Abraham's heirs of promise, namely, the Jewish household family of faith in Rome.

God's Unalterable Pledge (6:17–18)

God's unalterable pledge to Abraham was the basis for Abraham's heirs of promise to adhere strongly to Jesus, the object of their hope.

6:17. Barnabas extended (ἐν ᾧ, "in the same way") God's pledge with Abraham to the heirs of Abraham. The appearance of "even more clearly" (BDAG, s.v. "περισσότερος" c, p. 806) underscored a truth about the household family of faith, namely, that they were the "heirs of the promise." God guaranteed (BDAG, s.v. "μεσιτεύω," p. 634) his promise with a description of his purpose. Unfortunately, translations vary: "immutability of his counsel" (KJV), the "unchangeable character of his purpose" (RSV, NRSV, ESV), or the "unchangeableness of his purpose" (NASB; BDAG, s.v. "ἀμετάθετος" 1, p. 53). Regardless of which translation is used, the point was that God's purpose did not change (2:10) and that God's concern had been for Abraham's descendants (2:16). The NLT translates it well: "God . . . would never change his mind." It might be said that God was like an *inflexible* king (cf. 3 Macc 5:1) with an *inflexible* plan (cf. 3 Macc 5:12) who exhibited an "*unflinching* determination" (Josephus, *C. Ap.* 2.22 §189). This description of God's purpose foreshadowed Barnabas's citation of Psalm 110:4, "The LORD has sworn and will not change his mind" (7:21; Koester, 2001, 327). We might even say that God's spoken bond of promise to Abraham was like God himself, *unchangeable*.

6:18. God's intended result (ἵνα; "so that") for intervening with both a pledge and an oath was to provide certainty for the household family of faith. "The blessings that God promised to Abraham foreshadow the blessings that the listeners—his heirs—hope to receive" (Koester, 2001, 328). Barnabas stressed this certainty that God's pledge and oaths were "unchangeable" or "unalterable" (BDAG, s.v. "ἀμετάθετος" 1, p. 53) with a reason: "because [ἐν οἷς] it is impossible [ἀδύνατον] for God to lie [ψεύσασθαι; NLT]." The word "impossible" (ἀδύνατον) appeared here in Hebrews for a second time. The first time it spoke of the impossibility of God restoring an apostate (6:4–8). In this context, it spoke of the trustworthiness of God's promise. It reflected the overwhelming Jewish conviction that God cannot lie (1 John 1:10, 5:10; *TDNT*, 9:600–603), and thereby created an absolute truth about God. A church father, Clement of Rome, put it this way: "for nothing is impossible with God *except* [save] to lie" (*1 Clement* 27:2 [trans. Goold]). But we might add the impossibility "to restore an apostate." Together they stress "the threat of judgment and the reality of hope" (Koester, 2001, 331). Here in 6:18, the absolute impossibility of God making a false assertion had the intended result of certainty in order to create a desire for the household family of faith to persevere.

So, based upon the absolute certainty of God's pledge, members of the household family of faith who had found "refuge" in Jesus were "to be greatly encouraged" (BDAG, s.v. "παράκλησις," p. 766). More specifically they were once again encouraged "to hold fast." As in Hebrews 4:14, the expectation was "to adhere strongly to someone" (BDAG, s.v. "κρατέω" 6a, p. 565). Here it was their "hope" (ἐλπίδος). This hope, however, was not a human subjective wishful way of thinking, but rather was objective (Lane, 1991a, 153). Thus, the household family of faith was to adhere strongly to an objective hope. Jesus, God's messianic Son of promise, was the object of their hope (2:10; Attridge, 1989, 183).

Unchangeable Certainties (6:19–20)

Security, firmly fixed, and presence before God were unchangeable certainties for the household family of faith because Jesus had entered God's presence as regal high priest.

6:19. Barnabas advanced his discussion about the "hope" (ἐλπίδος) that the household family of faith "had" (ἔχομεν) with a threefold description. First, hope was compared (ὡς) to an "anchor" (ἄγκυραν) for the soul. Only here in the NT does a metaphorical use of "anchor" occur (literal occurrences: Acts 27:29, 30, 40). Nevertheless, Philo often depicted in figurative language the pious soul as one securely anchored in a vision of God (*Cher.* 12–13) and in virtue (*Sacr.* 90; cf. *Leg.* 2:90). Thus, "hope" was depicted as grasping the person's soul securely.

Greco-Roman Ship Anchors

Originally, anchors were merely a weighted piece of wood (probably with a rock or bundle of rocks) with an empty barrel on top to slow the ship down and keep it on course (Dixon, 1911, 947). Over time, the Greeks and Romans improved their ship's anchors. Often, a ship would have several anchors used not only to anchor a ship but also to slow it down for maneuvering purposes (Josephus, *B.J.* 3.10.1 §469; cf. Acts 27:17). Before the time of Jesus, "flukes" began to appear on Roman anchors to help them dig into the sea bottom. At first, they were merely wooden anchors with flukes, but eventually the anchor's flukes were furnished with iron tips (cf. Pliny the Elder, *Nat.* 7.09; Heliodorus, *Aeth.* 8.6.9).

Anchor from Roman Ship. Primo piano dell'ancora in legno con ceppo in piombo. Public domain. Courtesy of Marco Chemello (Museoscienza).

Second, Barnabas described hope as "sure" (ἀσφαλῆ) and "unshifting" (βεβαίαν). These two terms, however, are typically translated as "sure and steadfast" (KJV, NASB, RSV, NRSV, ESV, NET) or "firm and secure" (NIV). While sometimes used to *modify* "anchor" (RSV, NRSV, NLT), it seems that the two terms better serve to *clarify* the metaphor "hope" (NASB, NIV, NET). Unlike Hebrews 2:2, where "unshifting" (βεβαίαν) emphasized the certainty of the Mosaic law whereby it served as God's legally binding contract with Israel over a long period of time (BDAG, s.v. "βεβαίος" 3, p. 172), here "unshifting" (βεβαίαν) was linked with "sure" (ἀσφαλῆ) to speak of "hope" as something that was "fixed firmly."

Third, hope was personified. Moving beyond "hope's" security ("as an anchor") and being "fixed firmly ("sure and binding"), Barnabas also described "hope" (= God's spoken promise) as something that reached inside the inner sanctuary "behind the veil" (KJV, NASB) or "curtain" (RSV, NIV, NRSV, ESV, NET) or a "curtain of heaven" (NLT). The reference to the "veil" or "curtain" was a figure of speech for heaven (BDAG, s.v. "καταπέτασμα," p. 524) and yet an assertion that implied a comparison (a hypocatastasis). Historically, the veil was the second inner curtain of the tabernacle/temple (Exod. 26:31–33; 37:3–5 [36:35–37 HB], 40:3, 21–27; 2 Par [2 Chron.] 3:14; cf. Philo, *Mos.* 2:95; Josephus, *B.J.* 5.5.4 §212). Whether the tabernacle, Solomon's temple, Haggai's temple, or Herod's temple of Jesus's day, all were structures of worship in Jewish history. All were considered the abode of God's presence. All had veils to separate people from God's Holy of Holies. Here "hope" was personified as having reached inside and behind the curtain of God's heavenly abode where Jesus himself had also entered (v. 20; 9:12, 24).

6:20. Jesus had already "entered" (εἰσῆλθεν) beyond a metaphorical veil. He did not, however, enter as an angel (recall 1:4–13) nor as a Levitical priest (recall 5:5–10). Jesus entered behind the veil as a "forerunner" (πρόδρομος). While sometimes used of "first fruits" of a harvest (Num. 13:20; Isa. 28:4), the Greek historian Herodotus (*Hist.* 1.60; 7.203), who wrote about the Greek wars against the Persians, used "forerunner" to speak of a messenger. The latter usage was similar to Barnabas's reference to Jesus as an "apostle" (Heb. 3:1). Yet, a "forerunner" was most frequently used to speak of those who were first to enter into a battle (Wis 12:8; Josephus, *A.J.* 12.9.4 §372) and similar to Barnabas's reference to Jesus as a "pioneer" who paved a path for others to follow (2:10). Here in Hebrews, the "forerunner" (πρόδρομος) also referred to Jesus who had gone before those who followed after him as both God's messenger (3:1) and "pioneer" (ἀρχηγός; 2:10). Jesus was "the forerunner of his followers" (BDAG, s.v. "πρόδρομος," p. 867). The reason why he was "the forerunner of his followers" was because (γενόμενος) Jesus entered behind heaven's curtain as God's regal high priest, a regal high priest similar to that of Melchizedek's order.

The reappearance of Melchizedek recalled Psalm 110:4 when Barnabas linked it to Psalm 2:7 in Hebrews 5:5–6. Here Jesus was once again referred to as regal high priest (5:5; cf. 2:17; 3:1; 4:14) to stress Jesus's mission, by using cultic terminology reserved for priests and their activities associated with offering sacrifices. "Forever" (εἰς τὸν αἰῶνα; lit., "for the ages") once again described the duration of both Jesus's position and priestly service (5:6; cf. 1:8, 10–12; 6:20; 7:17). The phrase "after the order of Melchizedek" once again distinguished Jesus's priesthood from the Levitical priesthoods established by God and the Levitical royal-priesthood usurped by Judas Maccabee's family (i.e., Aristobulus, 103 B.C.; Alexander Janneus, 103–76 B.C.; John Hyrcanus, 76–30 B.C.; cf. Dowley, 2003, 60–61). The reemergence of Melchizedek at this point served as Barnabas's way to resume his discussion about Jesus as a regal priest (5:1–10), a discussion that was put on hold (5:11). The return to the subject of Jesus as regal high priest after the order of Melchizedek served as a transition to his more developed discussion about Melchizedek in chapter 7 where it would be pointed out that Melchizedek was elevated above Abraham and Levi.

Historical-Theological Paradigm Shift

During this period of the early church, Jewish people who placed their faith in Jesus as their Messiah were being challenged with a new way of thinking about God and God's ways. Historically, the Messiah was a human Davidic heir who ruled over the nation of Israel (Bateman et al., 2012, 211–329). The anticipated Messiah was, in their eyes, expected to reestablish Israel as an independent nation. Furthermore, the Levitical priesthood was the means to God through sacrifices. Yet, God expanded the priestly functions of the Davidic heir to include high priestly functions. Jesus, then, became God's appointed regal high priest of promise.

THEOLOGICAL FOCUS

The exegetical idea (God's pledge to Abraham about heirs, conferred to Abraham by way of his perseverance, was certified by way of God linking his vow to his pledge, which had unchangeable certainties about Jesus as God's royal-priest) leads to this theological focus: Followers of Jesus can trust that God will fulfill his pledge to those who persevere because of his trustworthy word about Jesus, his royal high priest.

The foremost theological theme and point of this preaching unit is God's reliability. Earlier in Hebrews, an emphasis was placed on God's willingness to communicate with people (1:2).

Here the emphasis was on the reliability of God's communication. This reliability began with his unalterable pledge to Abraham and was fulfilled in Jesus (vv. 13–14, 17–18). Confirmation of God's message about Jesus was already noted in 2:4. Yet, an underlining theme here is a person's responsibility with regard to God's unalterable pledge, namely, to persevere. Just as Abraham persevered in belief in God's promise (v. 15), the household family of faith could persevere in the certainties of God's promise fulfilled in Jesus as God's regal high priest (vv. 17–20).

PREACHING AND TEACHING STRATEGIES

Exegetical and Theological Synthesis

The structure of the text moved from the promise God made to Abraham to the promise he made to the household family of faith in Rome. The notable shift was that while God made a promise to Abraham (6:13–16), that promise was fully explicated as unalterable because it was double-pledged both with the original covenant and the reality that God swore by his own name (6:17–18). The point, however, was not a historical one. The point was that God's double promise functioned as "strong encouragement" to the followers of Jesus in Rome to hold fast. Barnabas ended this section with the brilliant and hopeful metaphor of an anchor of hope—an anchor that went into the very holy place of God!

God had always kept his promises. During this section of Hebrews, there was a healthy tension given to the promises of God: that they were given to save members of the household family of faith, and the reality that those who were saved would walk in obedience and endure until the end. While the focus of the first part of chapter 6 was on our ability to endure, the emphasis on the last part was on God's promises. The theological idea that was at stake was the character of God. He, by his very nature, was a God who kept his promises.

Preaching Idea

God's promises are not like human promises—they are guaranteed.

Contemporary Connections

What does it mean?

What does it mean that God's promises are not like human promises—they are guaranteed. There is a sense in which our word is not our bond. Our culture at large does not honor the bonds of an agreement. The amount of litigation necessary to do business nowadays is testimony to the reality that we do not trust people to keep their word. Someone who is faithful to their word is indeed rare. In an age of entitlement and individual rights, we no longer feel obligated to keep an agreement with someone. This is especially true if the obligation to the agreement has or develops a cost associated with it that is not to our advantage.

Is it true?

Is it true that God's promises are not like human promises—they are guaranteed? It is not difficult to establish in people's minds that human promises are not guaranteed. All of us have experienced circumstances where people did not keep their word. Rarely today would someone enter into contractual work without some written expectation of the work that is to be done.

Then there are the large-scale breaches of trust such as the Enron scandal where 4,500 people lost jobs due to top executives willfully misrepresenting the company's actual losses. The scandal exposed a corporate culture where a few people risked the well-being of many others and broke their pledge to work for the good of the company.

Of course, there are examples that are closer to home. All of our lives have been touched by divorce in some way, and we have to some extent experienced how difficult, and even hostile, life can become when people live with the implications of a broken pledge.

Now what?

What is so significant about the lost art of keeping a promise? Few things in this life are really secure. The anchor that is holding us to the throne of God is a brilliant reality that calls us to have both hope and confidence in God. Perhaps the most obvious application of this passage is that we should have hope in the one who will always keep his obligation toward us.

On the one hand, it is extremely affirming to know that God keeps his promises. The question then is this: "How much do you trust God?" The point of this passage is to take comfort in the promises of God.

On the other hand, what are we to do about the obligations we make with others? Since it is true that God keeps his pledges to us, we too ought to keep our promises to others. We can count on God's word, but can the people with whom we make promises count on us to keep our word. Are our spouses disappointed because we have not met an obligation we promised, implied or otherwise? Have we fulfilled obligations to employees for strong leadership and a good work environment? Have we fulfilled our obligation to our employers by giving all that we promised we would fulfill in the ethical completion of our work? These are all questions pressed on us by this text.

Creativity in Presentation

The idea of a lost sign for keeping one's word may be portrayed with the History Channel's show *American Pickers* (2010–). This is a reality television series about two men, Mike and Frank, who with the assistance of Danielle travel as antique archeologists throughout the United States to explore people's homes, barns, sheds, and large lots to buy antiques and collectibles. With every deal, it's sealed with a handshake. They reflect a lost sign of a pledge between two people, a handshake.

Another possibility might be to paint the mental picture of a court room or perhaps even have a mock court room set up, or at least a witness bench, on the platform. You could ask what it would feel like if you were asked to come on the stage, place your hand on the Bible, and give a testimony. If so, your heart would race much more than if you were engaged in casual conversation in the hallway. Why is that?

When you place your hand on the Bible, the idea is that the Bible is a higher authority. And so, since our own word may be suspect, we swear on something—the Bible—that is greater than ourselves. This seems odd since many people in court rooms don't believe the Bible, but nonetheless we take it seriously. Legally, it is not a crime to lie. But if we lie "under oath," it is a crime called perjury. There are two wrongs—lying *and* doing it under oath. Just the opposite of this is God, who gives us two things: his word, and his word under an oath of his name. There is no higher authority than this. God not only delivered but he swore an oath that he would do what he said (this is referred to in v. 14). God's word was unbreakable. He did not need to do this, but he did it to give us confidence in the future promise!

Why did God even swear an oath to begin with? Isn't his word enough? Yes, it is. But the answer is found in our need, not his (Bateman, 2012, 128). God did not need to swear an oath to shore up his character. We need an oath to shore up our doubt. He does not need to strengthen his integrity; we need to strengthen our hope. It is not any need of his to be accountable, but it is our need to be assured.

The point you want to get across is simply this: God's promises are not like human promises—they are guaranteed. A way to simplify the outline would be in two simple points:

- God made a pledge to Abraham (vv. 13–15).
- God made a pledge to you (vv. 16–20).

DISCUSSION QUESTIONS

1. What is the significance of God swearing an oath (Heb. 6:13)?

2. What are the "two unchangeable things in which it is impossible for God to lie" (Heb. 6:18)?

3. What is the significance of the metaphor of the anchor mentioned in Hebrews 6:19?

4. What is implied in our hope being "sure and unshifting" (Heb. 6:19)?

5. In what sense is Jesus our "forerunner" (Heb. 6:20)?

Hebrews 7:1–28

EXEGETICAL IDEA
Scripture's silence about Melchizedek and Abraham's encounter with Melchizedek served to underscore the imperfection of the Levitical system and exalt the status of Jesus as regal priest.

THEOLOGICAL FOCUS
Jesus's exalted status as royal high priest permanently supplants the cultic system of Judaism.

PREACHING IDEA
Jesus is permanently for us.

PREACHING POINTERS
The Jewish household family of faith in Rome was no doubt aware of interpretive stories about biblical figures that were part of Jewish tradition. According to these stories, the "sons of God" left heaven to have intercourse with women (1 En. 6:1–7:6), Sarah's beauty was embellished (1Q20), Manasseh's penitential prayer was a proposed theological supposition (Pr Man), and the Letter of Jeremiah was an embellishment of Jeremiah 10 about idols. Similarly, there were embellished stories about Melchizedek. Yet, Hebrews 7 recalled, interpreted, and applied the biblical encounter between Abraham and Melchizedek in Genesis to underscore the imperfection of the Levitical system, and its replacement by way of the exalted status of Jesus as regal priest in the order of Melchizedek.

Even today, when a novelist wants to explain something, he or she will release a "prequel." A prequel is a story released after the original story but concerns events that took place before the original. This is the sense of Hebrews 7. Hebrews 7 is the prequel to the life of Jesus. The book of Hebrews was written after Jesus went back to heaven but contains events that led up to this coming. In a similar way, when we encounter Jesus, we can hardly imagine the amount of backstory there is. Hebrews 7 explains that the backstory to Jesus is the Levites, and the backstory to the Levites is Melchizedek. A good prequel will help the reader appreciate the original. In this case the prequel—the story of the Levites and Melchizedek—is not a better or embellished story, but a story that helps us appreciate even more our engagement with Jesus. Jesus is permanently for us.

MELCHIZEDEK, A ROYAL-PRIEST OF THE PAST (7:1–28)

LITERARY STRUCTURE AND THEMES (7:1–28)

Hebrews 7, according to Attridge (1989, 187), "serves to elaborate the importance of his [= Jesus's] exalted status in language that markedly contrasts the earthly, temporal, and fleshly with the heavenly, eternal, and spiritual, the realm to which Jesus [Christ] has been raised." Barnabas accomplished this by continuing his discussion about Melchizedek (cf. 5:10–11; 6:20; 7:1). He opened with a summary of Melchizedek's meeting with Abraham from whom Melchizedek received a tithe, after which Barnabas offered several interpretations about Melchizedek and Abraham's encounter to demonstrate how it was that Melchizedek was greater than Abraham and how his regal priesthood was loftier than that of the Levitical priesthood (vv. 1–10). Barnabas continued by underscoring the imperfections of the Levitical priesthood that warranted God's changing of both the Levitical priesthood as well as the religious legal system ("the law") whereby Jesus emerged as God's better priest from the tribe of Judah, namely, a royal-priest who was *like* Melchizedek (vv. 11–19). Barnabas closed with the regal high priesthood of Jesus in contrast with the Levitical priesthood: whereas Levitical priests had no direct promise from God, Jesus had a direct promise; whereas Levitical priests died regularly, Jesus was resurrected; whereas Levitical priests were sinners in need of sacrifice, Jesus was sinless (vv. 20–28).

Barnabas's theme focused on the Levitical priesthood and how Jesus's regal high priesthood differed from that of the Levitical priesthood.

- ***Melchizedek's Meeting with Abraham (7:1–10)***
- ***Imperfections of the Levitical Priesthood (7:11–19)***
- ***The Regal High Priesthood of Jesus (7:20–28)***

EXPOSITION (7:1–28)

Undaunted by the household family of faith's lack of understanding (5:11), Barnabas resumed his teaching about Jesus as God's appointed royal high priest by retelling the story of Melchizedek and offering an interpretation and an applicable application to Jesus. While there is limited information about the Roman household family of faith's knowledge about Melchizedek, there is a range of understandings about Melchizedek in nonbiblical Jewish literature. Some Jewish traditions recognized Melchizedek as a human figure in history (Josephus, *B.J.* 6.10.1 §§438–39; *A.J.* 1.10.2 §§179 – 81; 1Q20 23:12–17). For instance, Philo (*Abr.* §235) presented a historical retelling of the meeting of Abraham and Melchizedek in such a way so as to elevate Abraham while minimizing Melchizedek's reception of a tithe. Philo wrote,

> When the high priest of the most high God [= Melchizedek] saw him [= Abraham] approaching with his trophies, leader and army alike unhurt, for he had lost none of his own company, he was astonished by the feat, and, thinking, as indeed was natural, that such success was not won without God's directing care and help

to their arms, he stretched his hands to heaven and honored him with prayers on his behalf and offered sacrifices of thanksgiving for the victory and feasted handsomely those who had taken part in the contest, rejoicing and sharing their gladness as though the success were his own; and so indeed it was, for "the belongings of friends are held in common," as the proverb says, and this is far more true of the belongings of the good whose one end is to be well-pleasing to God. (trans. Colson)

Yet, Philo did emphasize Abraham's tithe elsewhere (*Congr.* 99). Other Jewish traditions, based upon some scanty information, elevated Melchizedek to angelic status (4Q546 frag. 3:2; 4Q401; perhaps 4Q280, 4Q286, 11Q13). Still other sources appeared to exalt Melchizedek as priestly figure (cf. 4Q491 with 11Q13; cf. Eskola, 2001, 84).

Melchizedek in Jewish Sources		
Jewish Sources	**Jewish Traditions**	**Reference**
Philo (ca. 15 B.C. to A.D. 50)	**Historical Figure**: "God made Melchizedek, the king of peace [i.e., the city of Salem] . . . and he was worthy of his priesthood. For he is called a just king . . . because he is the interpreter of law." "Melchizedek defined the Most High, from his conceiving of God not in a low and groveling spirit, but one of exceeding greatness and sublimity. . . ." "Melchizedek was a self-instructed and self-taught high priest."	*Leg.* 3.79 *Leg.* 3.79 *Congr.* 99
Dead Sea Scrolls (ca. 100 B.C.)	**Future Priestly Figure**: "Melchizedek will issue a day of Jubilee whereby he returns inheritances and releases people from the debt of all their sins." "Atonement will be made for the sons of light and those predestined to Melchizedek." "It will be decreed for 'the year of Melchizedek's favor' [Isa. 61:2, modified], and by his might he will judge God's holy ones and so establish a righteous kingdom. As it is written about Melchizedek 'a godlike being has taken his place in the council of God in the midst of the divine beings he holds judgement.'" "Melchizedek will prosecute the vengeance required by God's statutes. He will deliver all the captives from the power of Belial [the devil], and from the power of all the spirits predestined to him."	11Q13 2:2–6 11Q13 2:7–8 11Q13 2:9–11 11Q13 2:13, 25
Josephus (ca. A.D. 37 to 100)	**Historical Figure**: "Melchizedek means the righteous king; and he was without dispute . . . thus, he was made the priest of God." "Melchizedek supplied Abram's army in a hospitable manner . . . when Abram gave him the tenth part of his prey, Melchizedek accepted of the gift."	*A.J.* 1.10.2 §180 *A.J.* 1.10.2 §181 (cf. 1Q20 23:12–17)

Perhaps one of these various Jewish traditions about Melchizedek was influencing or confusing the Roman household family of faith. Due to Barnabas's emphasis on angels in chapter 1, it seems the Jewish members of the household family of faith in Rome were aware of the traditions about a celestial Melchizedek, and that was what baffled their thinking. Perhaps the idea of a future Melchizedekian priestly figure who would make atonement for sins was mystifying to the household family of faith. Whatever their confusion about Melchizedek, Scripture's silence about Melchizedek, and Abraham's encounter with Melchizedek, served Barnabas's purpose in order to stress the imperfection of the Levitical system and contrast to the permanently exalted status of Jesus as regal high priest.

Melchizedek's Meeting with Abraham (7:1–10)

The selected, interpreted, and applied events about Melchizedek's predominance over Abraham and the Levitical priesthood underscored Jesus's supremacy over the Levitical priesthood and subsequently the Mosaic law.

7:1. As a way of advancing (γάρ, "now") his discussion about Melchizedek (BDAG, s.v. "γάρ" 2, p. 189), Barnabas first summarized the brief historical encounter between Melchizedek and Abraham in Genesis 14:18–20. After defeating four kings from Mesopotamia and rescuing his nephew Lot, Abraham met Melchizedek, a Canaanite royal-priest of Salem. Like other Jewish authors (Josephus, *B.J.* 6.10.1 §§438–39; *A.J.* 1.10.2 §179–81; Philo, *Abr.* §235), Barnabas accepted the historicity of Melchizedek's kingship and priesthood but with particular stress placed on his blessing of Abraham.

The History of Salem

Salem was a Canaanite city inhabited as far back as 2100 B.C. Josephus credited Melchizedek to be the city's founder and first royal-priest (*B.J.* 6.10.1 §438). But unlike other Canaanite royal-priests, he served the "Most High God" (*El Elyon* meant "one sovereign God who created the universe"). Although this divine epithet appeared in the Ebla tablets, we do not know to what extent the inhabitants of Salem worshiped Yahweh as the Most High God (cf. *UT*, 126: III:5–5). We only know of Melchizedek's service to him.

In 1011 B.C. when David was crowned king over Judah in the city of Hebron (1 Chron. 11:1–3), he realized his need to relocate his base of operation from Hebron, a Levitical city of refuge in Judah (Josh. 21:11–13), to another city that might unite Israel. The best location was Melchizedek's Salem, which was then occupied by the Jebusites (Judg. 1:21). Its fortified walls and underground shaft that led to the city's water supply made it difficult to conquer. Yet, the city was an ideal location for several reasons. It was not associated with any Jewish city of any particular tribe. It was not a designated Levitical city but a Jebusite city. It was located in the center of the county. Thus, due to its neutrality and strategic location it was the best city to serve as Israel's capital. David captured Jerusalem from the Jebusites (cf. 2 Sam. 5:6–10; 1 Chron. 11:4–9; Josephus, *B.J.* 6.10.1 §439) and was crowned king over Israel in 1004 B.C. (1 Chron. 12:38–40).

Later in Jewish literature, the ancient city of Salem was linked with Jerusalem. In Psalm 76:2, Salem and Zion appeared in a parallel construction indicating that they were one and the same city. Josephus also linked Salem with Jerusalem and the City of David (*A.J.* 7.3.2 §65–68).

Eventually, David built himself a palace in 976 B.C. (2 Sam. 5:11) and brought the ark to Jerusalem in 977 B.C. (2 Sam. 6:1–21; 1 Chron. 15:1–29). Solomon was made coregent around 973 B.C., just prior to David's death. In 971 B.C., Solomon was anointed king over Israel (1 Kings 1:32–40; 1 Chron. 29:22b–23). It seems David composed Psalm 110 as well as Psalm 2 to be recited during Solomon's formal coronation in 971 B.C. Thus, David made the first connection between the former and perhaps even the first royal-priest over Salem, Melchizedek. His son,

Solomon, was now to rule as royal-priest just as Melchizedek once did over the city of Salem, but Solomon's rule from Jerusalem, the City of David extended over all Israel (Merrill, 1987, 243–48; 273–84).

7:2. Furthermore (καί, "also"), it was Melchizedek "to whom Abraham paid" (ᾧ . . . ἐμέρισεν) a "tithe" or a portion "from the spoils of war" (BDAG, s.v. "δέκατος" 2b, p. 216). Commenting briefly on Melchizedek as king, Barnabas interpreted his name, "king of righteousness" (מֶלֶךְ = "king"; סְדֹם = "righteousness") and described the sort of king he was, a king of peace (cf. Josephus, *A.J.* 1.10.2 §180). Barnabas would later describe Rahab as one who welcomed Jewish spies in peace (11:31) and would exhort the household family of faith to live in peace (12:14). These selected facts about Melchizedek from Genesis 14 were restated and interpreted by Barnabas to serve as the foundation upon which to advance the household family of faith's knowledge about what it meant to be a regal high priest "according to the order of Melchizedek" (τὴν τάξιν Μελχισέδεκ). Barnabas expanded an OT theological concept within Psalm 110 initially applied to Solomon by David in 971 B.C. (Bateman et al., 2012, 91–100).[1] Yet, Barnabas was not so interested in recounting the historical record of Melchizedek. His concern was with what Melchizedek had come to symbolize theologically.

7:3. Paramount for advancing an understanding about Melchizedek was Barnabas's observations and subsequent interpretations drawn from Scripture's silence in Genesis 14. First, "without father, without mother" meant Melchizedek lacked ancestors, and "without lineage" meant he lacked descendants. This silence distinguished his royal-priesthood from the Levitical order of priests because a Levitical descent was requisite to Israel's priesthood (Exod. 28:1; 40:12–16; Ezek. 44:15–31; 1 Chron. 23:2–5 with 23:28–32). Furthermore, silence about Melchizedek's birth ("he has no beginning of days") as well as his death ("nor end of life") portrayed him as totally void of human relationships and thereby someone who was beyond history. Consequently, "by having" (ἔχων) no Scriptural evidence about his birth, genealogy, and death, Barnabas developed a twofold theological contrast (δέ, "but") about him. First, he "is similar to" or "like" (ἀφωμοιωμένος; BDAG, s.v. "ὁμοιότης," p. 707) the messianic Son of promise. Second, his priesthood was eternal ("he remains a priest for all time"). Scripture's silence about Melchizedek's origins, descendants, and epitaph provided Barnabas with a "picture" about Melchizedek, namely, that he was a figure beyond history and even eternal. Not that Melchizedek was a christophany but rather a historical figure, who *resembled* the Son of God due to Scripture's silence that perpetuated him as an eternal royal high priest (cf. Heb. 1:3–13).

7:4. Barnabas transitioned (δέ, "but") from recalling a historical accounting about Melchizedek to an expectation from his readers: "observe" (θεωρεῖτε). They were to "observe" or "perceive" Melchizedek's significance, particularly his greatness (BDAG, s.v. "θεωρεῖτε" 1, p. 454; Lane, 1991a, 167). His greatness manifested itself in his ever so brief encounter with Abraham—the patriarch of the Jewish race—who paid Melchizedek a tenth "out of his spoils" (ἐκ τῶν ἀκροθινίων) taken in battle (repeating v. 2a). The noun "spoils" (KJV, ASV, NASB, NRSV, ESV) or "plunder" (NET) referred to the "topmost or *best* part of the heap" and thereby was symbolic of the firstfruits typically

1 H. W. Bateman IV, "Psalm 110: A Royal Psalm of Assurance in the Midst of Change," in *Interpreting the Psalms for Teaching and Preaching*, eds. H. W. Bateman IV and D. B. Sandy (St. Louis: Chalice Press, 2010), 150–61.

reserved for the gods (BDAG, s.v. "ἀκροθίνιον," p. 40). "Plunder" often included human captives (Herodotus, *Hist.* 1.86). In Abraham's case, Lot and his family were rescued captives who had become part of another king's spoils of war (Gen. 14:14–16). Although Scripture says that Abraham rescued Lot and his family, it says very little about Abraham's spoils of war. Whatever the plunder, he gave a portion to Melchizedek.

7:5. Continuing (καί' "and") his interpretation about Melchizedek's greatness, Barnabas directed attention to the collection of tithes. "On the one hand" (μέν), "those belonging to the sons of Levi" who served as priests collected "a tithe" (NET) or "a tenth" (KJV, ASV, NASB, NRSV, NIV, ESV) did so "according to the Law" (κατὰ τὸν νόμον). When the phrase "according to the law" was used in the context of priesthood and sacrifice in Hebrews, it denoted a religious cultic system and thereby best rendered "according to the Levitical religious system" (Cockerill, 2012, 309).

As noted earlier (5:3), not everyone who was born a Levite entered the "priestly office." Unlike his father, Zechariah, who served as priest, John the Baptist was not a priest (cf. Luke 1:5, 8–9; 2:59–80). So, the emphasis was on those Levites who actually entered the priestly office and who performed their duties in accordance with God's ordinance. Furthermore, Levitical priests were expected to collect a tithe or a tenth from Jewish followers of Yahweh ("their fellow countrymen," NET). It was an expectation of all Jews that was reinforced by Hezekiah, reinstated after the return from exile, and practiced throughout the Greco-Roman world (cf. Num. 18:21–24; 2 Chron. 31:2–12; Neh. 10:32–39; 12:44–45; Tacitus, *Hist.* 5.5.1). Thus, a Levitical priest's authority to collect a tithe was based solely upon a priest's physical descent, governed by a legal ordinance, and limited to collecting tithes from Abraham's heirs (and perhaps God-fearers).

7:6. "On the other hand" (δέ), Melchizedek's greatness was linked to his reception of a tenth from Abraham's spoils. Unlike verse 2 where stress was placed on Abraham "paying a tithe," verse 6 emphasized Melchizedek's collecting a tithe (δεδεκάτωκεν). But more significant was that Melchizedek "blessed" (εὐλόγηκεν) Abraham. Melchizedek's blessing of Abraham was yet another (καί, "and") indication that Melchizedek was elevated above Abraham. His superior position was further underscored by the fact that Abraham was "the one who had *the* promise" (τὸν ἔχοντα τὰς ἐπαγγελίας). In Hebrews 6:15, Abraham served as an example of one who had inherited "*the* promise" (τῆς ἐπαγγελίας; cf. Bateman, 2012, 37–40). In both cases, the article "the" (τῆς) identified the promise as something well known to the readers (Wallace, 1996, 225). So, the content of that promise needed no further explanation. What was emphasized, however, was the explicit contrast with the Levites. Whereas Levitical priests had a "command" from God, Abraham had "a promise" from God (Attridge, 1989, 196). Thus, the greatness of Melchizedek was underscored in Barnabas's contrast between Levitical priests who were expected to collect tithes and Melchizedek who received a tithe from Abraham.

The Old Testament Tithe

Corresponding closely to the Hebrew noun "tenth part" or "tithe" (מַעֲשֵׂר), a "tithe" implied giving a tenth of one's property, produce, or currency. Scripture (HB LXX) ordained three different tithes: (1) a tithe to the Levites and the temple (Lev. 27:30–33; Num. 18:21–32; Neh. 10:34–39), (2) a tithe to the poor (Deut. 14:28–29), and (3) a tithe to oneself to be consumed by the tither in Jerusalem (Deut. 14:22–26). Josephus (*A.J.* 4.8.22 §240) later echoed the existence of these prescribed tithes: "In addition to the two tithes which I have already directed you to pay each year, the one for the Levites and the other for the banquets, you should devote a third every third year to be distribution of such things as are lacking to widowed women and orphan children" (trans. Thackeray). Thus, tithing was a well-defined practice in Judaism, especially during the Second Temple period when tithing was expressly conveyed as "an ordinance forever" (Tob 1:6; Jub. 13:25–27, 32:10; cf. Sir 35:9; 11Q19 43:2–17, 60:6–11). Throughout the Roman world, Jewish people were expected to pay a "half-shekel" to Jerusalem's temple, which Gentiles viewed as a temple tax (Tacitus, *Hist.* 5.5.1). Although Jesus's concern for justice, love, mercy, and faith devalued meticulous tithing as a form of covenantal loyalty and devotion to God (Matt. 23:23 // Luke 11:42; Luke 18:9–14; cf. Jdt 11:13), Barnabas made a profound point about this revered practice of tithing that resonated in Jewish tradition and the household family of faith in Rome (*NIDOTTE*, 2:1035–55; Barclay, 1996, 417–19; Holmén, 2001, 106–28).

7:7. Barnabas then linked (δέ, "now"; NET) another interpretation about Abraham's encounter with Melchizedek. As in previous recollections about this meeting between Melchizedek and Abraham, the content of Melchizedek's blessing was of no importance to Barnabas. The fact that Melchizedek blessed Abraham underscored Barnabas's description of Abraham as "the lesser" and thereby described Melchizedek as Abraham's "superior" (cf. Bateman, 2012, 123). The act, however, revealed Melchizedek's superiority to Abraham as well as all subsequent siblings, including those of the tribe of Levi who officiated as priests. Thus, a superior *blessed* an inferior, which implied that Melchizedek's priesthood was grander than the Levitical priesthood.

7:8. Barnabas added (καί, "and") to his interpretation with an emphatically marked difference between the Levitical priests and Melchizedek. "In the one case" (ὧδε μέν), Levitical priests were "mortal men" (ἀποθνήσκοντες ἄνθρωποι). The adjective "mortal" (ἀποθνήσκοντες) highlighted the certainty of their demise: Levitical priests died. As mortal people, they eventually ceased to have any vital priestly or authoritative functions on earth (BDAG, s.v. "ἀποθνήσκω" 2, p. 111). "In the other case" (ἐκεῖ δὲ), Melchizedek, who had neither beginning nor end in Scripture, was "attested" or "affirmed" (μαρτυρούμενος) to be alive ("because he lives," ὅτι ζῇ). So, while Levitical priests died, Melchizedek lived on in Scripture's silence.

7:9–10. Barnabas's interpretation continued (καί, "and") seemingly with a qualification or conjecture ("so to speak" or "it could be said," ὡς ἔπος εἰπεῖν). Josephus said that "the Romans, who are, *so to speak* (ὡς ἔπος εἰπεῖν), the masters of the world, are (my) loyal friends" (*A.J.* 15.11.1 §387 [trans. Marcus]). Similarly, Barnabas said "it could be said" that even though the Levites were to collect tithes according to their religious cultic system, Genesis indicated that Levi paid a tithe to Melchizedek through Abraham because (γάρ, "for") Levi was, like all Jewish people, "in the loins" (ἐν τῇ ὀσφύϊ) of father Abraham." "Of father" was an alternative expresion to "the patriarch" in verse 4. "In the loins" meant that Levi was in "the reproductive organs" of Abraham (BDAG, s.v. "ὀσφῦς" 2, p. 730). Thus, all Jewish people were present in Abraham in an unborn state ("so to speak"). When Abraham paid a tithe to Melchizedek, "it could be said" that all of Israel had paid a tithe to the superior royal-priest, Melchizedek.

Imperfections of the Levitical Priesthood (7:11–19)

The imperfections of the Levitical priesthood and the Law that supported its cultic system warranted a change of the priesthood from the tribe of Levi to the tribe of Judah fulfilled in Jesus.

7:11. Barnabas continued (μὲν οὖν, "so" or "now") his explanation about Melchizedek (BDAG, s.v. "μὲν οὖν" 2e, p. 630) by underscoring

God's promise of a different kind of priesthood. He framed the central theme of priesthood with a contrary-to-fact or an unreal condition (εἰ + ἦν): if "through Levitical priesthood" perfection was to occur (but it cannot), would there be the need for a promise of a different sort of priest (but there is)? The Levitical priesthood did not bring perfection. For Barnabas, the concept of "perfection" (τελείωσις) referred to a person's relationship with God (cf. 5:19; Moffatt, 1968, 96; Attridge, 1989, 200; Bateman, 2012, 131–32). Thus, the ineffectiveness of the Levitical priesthood was expressed in its inability to provide adequately for a person's bonding with God, which in turn warranted the need for a "different" priest (cf. 5:6). Barnabas's word choice of "different" (ἕτερον) instead of "another" (ἄλλος) was rather significant. For Barnabas, a "different *kind*" of priest was a royal-priest similar to Melchizedek and thereby non-Aaronic. Jesus was not just "another" Levitical priest. So, a notable change had occurred in priesthoods.

7:12. Barnabas provided a twofold reason (γάρ, "for") for the "change" (μετατιθεμένης). The first recalled the change of priesthoods mentioned in verse 11. The second expanded the parenthetical statement in verse 11. Since the Law served as the basis for the Levitical priesthood, when a change of priesthoods occurred, "out of a necessity" (ἐξ ἀνάγκης) it produced a change in the Law (Mitchell, 1989, 146; cf. NET). Koester (2001, 354), however, pointed out that such a change counters OT texts (Exod. 40:15; Num. 18:19; 25:13). Even Josephus (*A.J.* 20.10.1 §26), in his accounting about high priests, said, "Wherefore it is also a tradition that none should hold God's high priesthood save him who is of Aaron's blood, and that no one of another lineage, even if he happened to be a king, should attain to the high priesthood" (trans. Feldman). Yet changes did occur.

When the high priesthood was changed from one Levitical household to another (1 Kings 2:35), no one really complained until Menelaus purchased the high priesthood in 171 B.C. (1 Macc 4:23–50; cf. Josephus, *A.J.* 12.5.1 §§237–41). Even the Hasmoneanswho eventually established themselves as royal-priests were from the tribe of Levi and had a mix of supporters (e.g., Sadducees) and dissenters (e.g., Essenes; cf. Bateman, 2012, 211–52; Bateman, 2013, 57–88). Yet, these changes within the Levitical priestly system always involved a person from the tribe of Levi. Barnabas, however, stressed that with the coming of Jesus there was now an entirely different priesthood, one that had absolutely no connection with the tribe of Levi. His reasoned observations about the priesthood warranted "change." The change from the Levitical order to a Melchizedekian order had profound ramifications for the Jewish members of the household family of faith in Rome. It required that a simultaneous change occurred from one covenant (Mosaic law; Exod. 20:1–17; Deut. 6:1–25) to another (a new covenant; Jer. 31:31–34)—a point Barnabas would develop fully in chapters 8 and 9.

> *Textual Analysis:* Conflicting Text Critical Reading: 7:13
> Literary Issue: Manuscript support is strong for both readings: text (ℵ B D 044 0278 1881) and variant ($\mathfrak{P}^{46}$ A C 33 81 1739). The wordplay in verse 3 between "belonged" (μετέσχηκεν, first clause) and "served" (προσέσχεν, second clause) appears to support the author's style for phonetic effectiveness evident in 1:1. The text is the prefered reading (cf. Lane, 1991a, 174; Towner, 99).
>
> *txt.* "from which no one **has ever served** at the altar" (ἀφ' ἧς οὐδεὶς **προσέσχηκεν** τῷ θυσιαστηρίῳ) (ASV, ESV, NASB, NET, NIV NRSV)
>
> *var.* "from which no one ever **served** at the altar" (ἀφ' ἧς οὐδεὶς **προσέσχεν** τῷ θυσιαστηρίῳ) (KJV)

7:13. Barnabas made two inferences (γάρ, "for") about verse 12 in the form of an application. The first appeared here in verse 13 and the second in verse 14. First, "the one about whom [ἐφ' ὃν] these things were spoken" referred *not* to Melchizedek but to Jesus. Melchizedek was never described as a member of a tribe (Koester, 1989, 354). Thus, the "different priest" (ἕτερον ἀνίστασθαι) of verse 11 was Jesus who not only came from a "different tribe" (φυλῆς ἑτέρας), but he was the one whom Barnabas had *likened* to Melchizedek (cf. v. 4). Admittedly, the idea that no one from Judah "has ever officiated at the altar" reflected a general cultic prescription. There were exceptions (1 Sam. 6:12–21; 8:18; 2 Sam. 24:18–25; 1 Kings 8:1–5; 8:62). Nevertheless, cultic duties of sacrifice were the basic and divinely prescribed duties of a Levitical priest (Num. 18:1–7; 1 Cor. 9:13).

7:14. Barnabas made a second inference (γάρ, "for") when he said, "*it is* quite clear" (πρόδηλον; TNT; cf. NASB, ESV) that Jesus "descended" (ἀνατέταλκεν) from Judah. Attridge (1989, 201) suggests that Barnabas's use of "descended" evoked messianic prophecies of the "branch" and the "star" that would arise as Yahweh's agent.[2] Yet, there was no explicit connection here with the line of David (cf. Matt. 1:2–17; Luke 3:33). Perhaps "descended from Judah" was another phrase in need of no further explanation due to the culture of Barnabas's Jewish audience as well as the emphatic placement of "*it is* quite clear" (πρόδηλον) in the clause. What stood out, however, was Barnabas's somewhat negative comment: Moses said nothing about priests from the tribe of Judah (cf. Deut. 33:7 as opposed to the priestly lots described in Deut. 33:8–11 for Levi).

7:15. Barnabas added to (καί, "and") as well as expanded his application in verse 14 with "even more clear" (περισσότερον ἔτι κατάδηλόν). Speaking positively, Barnabas offered an assumed to be true statement ("if," εἰ + ind.) that brought clarity to verse 14. Jesus was declared to be that "different priest" (cf. v. 11) who "arises" (BDAG s.v. "ἀνίσταται" 7 & 9, p. 83). The verb "arise" could be used of a person assuming a position of a prophet, priest, or king (Num. 24:17; Zech. 6:12; cf. Moffitt, 1968, 97; Koester, 2001, 355) as well as Jesus's resurrection (Mark 16:5–8). In fact, the idea of "arise" reinforced Barnabas's argument spoken of previously in Hebrews about Jesus's exaltation as royal-priest (1:2, 3, 13; 2:9; 3:1; 4:14; 5:5–10; 6:19–20). Thus, "arise" (ἀνίσταται) served a dual purpose. It spoke of Jesus's resurrected presence as well as God's exalted royal-priest in the *likeness* of Melchizedek. Barnabas's use of the Greek word "likeness" (τὴν ὁμοιότητα) was a mere stylistic change from the "order of Melchizedek" (cf. 5:6, 10; 6:20; 7:11, 17; cf. "similar to" in v. 3).

7:16. Barnabas further clarified what he meant by "different priest" with another contrastive observation that intensified his argument. Jesus was priest not by law "but [δέ] by the power of an indestructible life" (NET, ESV, NIV). The choice of the rare word "indestructible" (BDAG, s.v. "ἀκαταλύτος," p. 35) as well as its position in the sentence accentuated Barnabas's theological thrust. Jesus had "a life that cannot be destroyed" (NLT). The expression "indestructible life" (NET) or "endless life" (KJV, ASV) served to foreshadow a discussion about Jesus's eternality in verse 17 while underscoring a point he made earlier (cf. 1:8–9). Thus, a new royal high priest arose in the *likeness* of Melchizedek. His name was Jesus. Jesus had become a priest not by the Mosaic legal regulation of physical descent but by his divinely exalted situation. His

2 The "branch" and the "star" were frequently understood in Jewish literature for an anointed one and later a messianic figure. Compare Numbers 24 (Bateman et al., 2012, 52–57), Isaiah 11 (Bateman et al., 2012, 149–52), Jeremiah (Bateman et al., 2012, 169–76), and Zechariah 3:8 and 6:12 (Bateman et al., 2012, 195–201) with Jewish expectations of the one called the branch and prince (Bateman et al., 2012, 275–302).

resurrection and exaltation allowed him to hold his position as royal-priest permanently.

7:17. Barnabas concluded (γάρ, "for") his application about Jesus's distinctive priesthood with a scriptural validation from Psalm 110:4 (cf. 5:6, 10; 6:20). "It is testified" or "it is attested" (μαρτυρεῖται) punctuated specific points about Jesus (cf. 10:15). First, he was a royal-priest *like* Melchizedek, or we might say a *type* (τὴν τάξιν) of Melchizedek. The phrase "according to the order of Melchizedek" throughout Hebrews (5:6, 10; 6:20; 7:11, 17) might be rendered better as "according to 'the type' (τὴν τάξιν) of Melchizedek" (Koester, 2001, 355), especially since Barnabas had already spoken about him comparatively ("similar to," v. 7; "likeness," v. 15). The idea that Jesus was a "type" of Melchizedek meant that the historical imagery of Melchizedek as a royal high priest was first linked by David to Solomon in Psalm 110 but now had an ultimate and heightened application to Jesus. There was both an emphasis on a pattern in history (typology) as well as an escalation and prophetic element assumed in Barnabas's typological-prophetic understanding of the psalm as it pertained to Jesus.[3] Second, he was eternal (εἰς τὸν αἰῶνα), a concept emphasized about the "Son" earlier in Hebrews (1:2–3, 1:5–13; cf. 5:6; 10:15; Bateman, 2012, 136). Thus, Psalm 110:4 served to accentuate that this was an entirely different royal high priest who held his position permanently.

7:18–19a. Barnabas summarized (γάρ, "for") the significance of Jesus as a royal high priest like that of Melchizedek with a contrast. There was, "on the one hand" (μέν), an "annulling" (ἀθέτησις) of a "former command," namely, God's command governing the Levitical religious system given to, recorded by, and ordained by Moses—the person who had already been described as God's faithful servant "*in* God's house" (3:5). Important for understanding this abrogation of the law was the cultural belief that the person who initiated a bilateral covenant could annul it at a later time, and if he so chose, replaced it with another one. And despite the fact that a Jewish person may have been aware that it was sinful to abrogate God's laws (Isa. 24:16 LXX; Ezek. 22:26), here in verse 18, the annulment of the Mosaic covenant had occurred in a judicial and officiating sense. In other words, God, who had initiated a covenant whereby the Aaronic priesthood was to serve God's people was replaced with Jesus's royal-priesthood (cf. 7:11–12, 15–17, 19b, 21–22, 24–25, 27). Furthermore, God terminated his old covenant (7:11; 8:13; cf. Gal. 2:21; 3:23–24; 5:1–4) as he promised he would do through the prophets (Jer. 31:31–34; Ezek. 36:26–30; 37:12–14). The reason (διὰ τὸ αὐτῆς, "because of its") was because the law was "weak" (ἀσθενές) and "useless" (ἀνωφελές). This weakness and uselessness was explained (γάρ, "for") in a parenthetical remark—it made nothing "perfect" (*ἐτελείωσεν;* cf. v. 11). Barnabas once again underscored the inability of the Levitical religious system to fix a person's relationship with God or "complete God's design for humanity" (Koester, 2001, 356).

7:19b. "On the other hand" (δέ), God introduced "a better hope." At this point Barnabas merely made known a "better hope." He would later define this "better hope" (κρείττονος ἐλπίδος) in verse 22 to be a "better covenant" (κρείττονος διαθήκης), a concept Barnabas expanded later in chapter 8. In the meantime, "hope" here was an objective reality. Elsewhere

3 See H. W. Bateman IV, "The Use of Psalm 110:1 in the NT," *Bibliotheca Sacra* 149 (Oct–Dec 1992): 438–53 and W. E. Glenny, "The Israelite Imagery of 1 Peter 2" in *Dispensationalism, Israel, and the Church: The Search for Definition*, eds. C. A. Blaising and D. L. Bock (Grand Rapids: Zondervan, 1992), 156–58.

in Hebrews, Barnabas spoke of holding firmly to our confessed hope (= Jesus; 3:6; 10:), to be eager for hope (= promise realized hope in Jesus; 6:17–18). In 6:18–19, hope was personified as someone who reached inside the tabernacle's Holy of Holies. That someone was Jesus. Here in 7:19, the better hope was the ability to enter into God's presence. Barnabas also underscored hope's benefits, namely, access to God. "Hope" was that "through which" (διὰ + genitive) the household members of faith were able to "draw near" (ASV, NET, ESV, NIV, etc.) or "approach" (NASB) God. On the one hand, the idea of "approach" echoed approaching God's throne as in acceptable cultic service (4:16; cf. BDAG, s.v. "ἐγγίζω" 1aα, p. 270). On the other hand, here in verse 19 "draw near" to God had more of a relational emphasis (James 4:8; Attridge, 1989, 204).

The Regal High Priesthood of Jesus (7:20–28)

Jesus's royal-priesthood had divine confirmation, unchanging permanence, and eternal effectiveness established apart from the Law.

7:20a. Barnabas continued (καί, "and") his discussion with further proof of Jesus's superior royal-priesthood with a rather long and complex sentence that begins here in verse 20a (καθ' ὅσον, "by as much as") and ends in verse 22 (κατὰ τοσοῦτο, "by so much as"). Barnabas developed an elaborate comparison or contrast between Jesus's priesthood with the Levitical priesthood. Although this comparison began in verses 18–19, special attention was now given to God's sworn oath. Verse 20a picked up a twofold discussion from verse 15 whereby Barnabas presented Jesus as a royal-priest as well as from verse 19 whereby Barnabas introduced a "better hope." He opened with God's sworn affirmation about Jesus as royal-priest: it was "not without" (οὐ χωρὶς) God's "sworn oath" (ὁρκωμοσίας).

God's "sworn oath" recalled Barnabas's earlier discussion. As it was in 6:13, so it was here. As God's oath in 6:13–20 guaranteed his promise to Abraham, so too, God's oath in 7:21 was a bond of confirmation about the Son's royal-priesthood (cf. 1:2–3, 5–13). An even stronger statement existed in 7:20a with the double negative, "not without an oath." This affirmation "came after the law" in that historically, Psalm 110:4 echoed God's promise to David's son Solomon (2 Sam. 7:8–16; Bateman, 1992, 438–53). The coronation

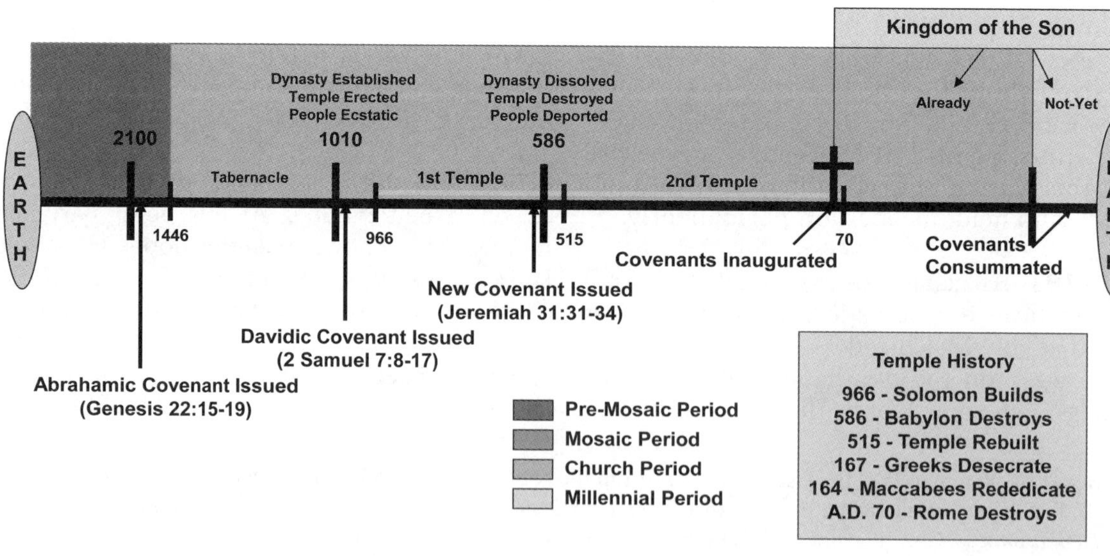

of Solomon (971 B.C.) was a subsequent historical event to the one at Sinai (1446 B.C.). Thus, unlike Levitical priests, God uttered this same oath with Jesus via Psalm 110:4 to confirm Jesus's royal-priesthood (cf. Ps. 89:35).

7:20b–21. These verses were parenthetical statements that accentuated Barnabas's important contrastive deduction (γάρ, "for"). "On the one hand" (μέν), "others" (οἱ), namely, the Levitical priests, "have become" priests without a divine oath. Earlier, Barnabas spoke of a priest's appointment to the position (cf. 5:1–4). "On the other hand" (δέ), Jesus (ὁ, "who") was a royal-priest who entered his position with a divinely sworn oath. Whereas in 5:5–6 Jesus's royal-priesthood was divinely confirmed and punctuated with a reference to Psalms 2:7 and 110:4, here Barnabas heightened his earlier point when he repeated Psalm 110:4 with the added phrase: "the Lord has sworn and will not change his mind." Granted there have been times in Scripture (HB LXX) where God did change his mind with regard to his anger toward Nineveh (Jonah 3:9–10), in his anger toward Israel (Amos 7:3, 6; Ps. 105:45), and in his decision about Saul's rule over Israel (1 Sam. 15:35).[4] However, Psalm 110 had already been linked to 2 Samuel 7:14 (cf. 1:5) and Psalm 2:7 (cf. 1:5, 5:5–6), both of which recalled God's lateral or unconditional covenant with David (Bateman et al., 2012, 59–87, 91–100).

Translation of Hebrews 7:20a, 22: "by as much as [καθ᾽ ὅσον] . . . by so much as [κατὰ τοσοῦτο]"

Translations vary as to how to begin the sentence in verse 20a as well as the second half of the sentence in verse 22a. For instance, verse 20a may be rendered "and to the extent that" (καί . . . ὅσον) with a corresponding comparison "to that extent" (κατὰ τοσοῦτο) in verse 22a. Other renderings are "and by as much as . . . by so much" (NASB), "and to the degree that . . . to that same degree" (NAB), "and since . . . accordingly" (NET). See BDAG, s.v. "ὅσος" 3, p. 729; s.v. "τοσοῦτος" 5, p. 1012. Regardless, it is an elaborate comparison.

7:22. Barnabas resumed the argument he began in verse 20a with a comparison. Yet now, it was not about Jesus's superior priesthood, but rather it was about Jesus as "the guarantor" of a "better covenant." "Guarantor" (ἔγγυος) is one of the many legal metaphors used throughout Hebrews to impress upon the household family of faith a significant theological point just as he did when he used "legally binding" (2:2), "he swore by himself" (6:13), and "annulled" (7:18). Here, Jesus who held his royal-priestly position based upon God's sworn promise became the guarantor of a "better covenant" (κρείττονος διαθήκης), a covenant that had replaced the Mosaic law (7:12, 18; cf. 8:6–7, 13). So, Jesus, as "the guarantor," not only reaffirmed the validity of God's Abrahamic, Davidic, and new covenants promised in Scripture (HB LXX), he guaranteed them. He is the one through whom God fulfilled God's promises.

7:23. Continuing (καί, "and") his string of comparisons, Barnabas stressed the issue of duration. "They, on the one hand" (οἱ μέν) referred to the "numerous" Levites who "were made" (γεγονότες or cf. "appointed," 5:1–3) to serve God over the centuries. Admittedly the exact number of Levitical priests appointed to serve God since the time of Aaron is impossible to determine. Nevertheless, Josephus (*A.J.* 20.10.1 §226–27) suggested that there were eighty-three high priests from Aaron to Phanasus (cf. Bateman, 2012, 84–91). Yet, Barnabas's point was not in the number of priests but in the reason for so many priests.

4 R. Chisholm, "Does God Change His Mind?" *Bibliotheca Sacra* 152 (Oct–Dec 1995): 387–99.

It was "because of death" (διὰ τὸ θανάτῳ). Priests were mortal. They died (7:8). Death prevented priests from perpetual service. When one priest died, another took his place. They held their positions in succession, one after another (Westcott, 1984, 191).

Translation of Hebrews 7:23 "and" (καί)
Some translations render καί with a transitional "now" (NIV), giving the impression that there is a change or new topic, or they merely eliminate any translation (NASB, ESV). Others render it as "because" (NLT) as though providing a reason, while yet others give the indication that Barnabas merely continues his discussion and thereby translate καί as "and" (Geneva, KJV, ASV, NET).

7:24. "He, on the other hand" (ὁ δέ) referred to Jesus whose priesthood was "unchangeable" (ἀπαράβατος). While some translations say "unchangeable (KJV, ASV), others say "permanently" (NIV, NET, ESV). Due to its lack of usage, however, the exact meaning is difficult to determine. Yet, it did not convey, as some have suggested, the idea that Jesus's royal-priesthood was "without successor" or "untransferable" (cf. Moffatt, 1968, 99; Spicq, 1952, 2.197; Hughes, 1977, 268). Similarly, Jesus as Son, when compared to creation was unchanging (1:12). Plutarch (*Def. orac.* 3) described the stars as having "unchanging" or "immutable" (ἀπαράβατος) movement. Barnabas presented Jesus's royal-priesthood as fixed, absolute, or immutable. The reason (διὰ . . . αὐτὸν) given for Jesus's immutable royal-priesthood was because he "remains forever" (μένειν . . . εἰς τὸν αἰῶνα). He continued to exist. Naturally, "he remains forever" recalled the "forever" of Psalm 110:4 in Hebrews 7:17 as well as Psalm 45:6–7 and Psalm 102:26–27 in the opening chapter of Hebrews (vv. 8, 12). The point that Barnabas made, somewhat relentlessly in chapter 7, was that Jesus, along with his royal-priestly position, was eternal (cf. Bateman, 2012, 136).

7:25. Barnabas now offered the implication (ὅθεν) concerning Jesus's eternal royal-priesthood. First, Jesus "is able to save." For Barnabas, this ability (δύναται, "he is able") was not a mere possibility. It was a certainty (cf. 2:18; 4:15; 5:7). Naturally, "to save" (σῴζειν) could refer to a person's physical deliverance or spiritual deliverance (Bateman, 2015[17], 127–31). For Barnabas, it spoke of a person's spiritual deliverance. Second, the spiritual deliverance had an unlimited duration. It was "forever" (εἰς τὸ παντελές). The translation "completely" (KJV, ASV, NET, ESVS, NIV; BDAG, s.v. "παντελής" 1, p. 754) addressed the degree to which Jesus saved an individual. It was complete or thorough (Bleek, 1828–40, 398; Riggenbach, 1922, 101). Yet, the translation "for all time" (NASB, NRSV, NLT; BDAG, s.v. "παντελής" 2, p. 754) stressed the unlimited duration of a person's salvation (Moffatt, 1968, 100; Ellingworth, 1993, 391). Nevertheless, it seems "for all time" spoke both of Jesus's ability to save completely as well as for an unlimited duration (Hughes, 1977, 269; Attridge, 1989, 210; Lane, 1991a, 176; Koester, 2001, 365). Barnabas's propensity for stylistic variation[5] favors the latter option. Thus, Barnabas underscored the spiritual deliverance that has an unlimited duration for all people who came to God "through Jesus" (δι' αὐτοῦ). The Jewish household family of faith in Rome no longer came to God through the Levitical priesthood but through God's royal-priest, Jesus (cf. John 14:6–7; 1 John 4:23; 5:1).

The reason Jesus was the one through whom the household family of faith was saved

5 For instance, the use of "similar to" (ἀφωμοιωμένο) in verse 3 and "likeness" (τὴν ὁμοιότητα) in verse 15 is a stylistic change from "order of Melchizedek" (τὴν τάξιν Μελχισέδεκ; cf. 5:6, 10; 6:20; 7:11, 17). Similarly, the rarely used adjective "endless" (ἀκαταλύτος) in verse 16, the frequently used phrase "for all time" (εἰς τὸν αἰῶνα) in verses 17 and 25, and the phrase "for all time" (εἰς τὸ παντελές) here in verse 25 suggest a stylistic change.

was because Jesus lived. For Barnabas, Jesus was always living (πάντοτε ζῶν). He was immortal. His eternality as royal high priest had an expressed purpose (εἰς τὸ + infinitive): to intercede on behalf of those who follow him. Whenever "intercession" (ἐντυγχάνειν) was used with "for" or "on behalf of" (ὑπέρ) in Paul's writings, it carried significant theological importance. In Romans 8:34, before a heavenly court, Jesus *interceded* on behalf of the Roman followers of Jesus to whom he wrote. Therefore no one could bring a charge against them. Here in Hebrews 7:25, Jesus as the royal high priest "*intercedes* on behalf of" those who come to God through him (7:25a, δι' αὐτοῦ τῷ θεῷ). Naturally, his intercession occurred before a heavenly court (cf. 1:3, 8–9, 13; 8:1) where he provided "the way" to God (cf. 2:10–12). Unfortunately, the theological concept of intercession has been "grotesquely misrepresented in popular Christian thought" in that "[Jesus] is not to be thought of 'as an ornate, standing ever before the Father with outstretched arms,' like the figures in the mosaics of the catacombs, and with strong crying and tears pleading our cause in the presence of a reluctant God; but as a *throned* priest king, asking what He will from a Father who always hears and grants His request" (Bruce, 1964, 155).

7:26. Barnabas concluded (γάρ, "for") his threefold list of comparisons with what has been described as a "rhapsody" (Moffatt, 1968, 101) about Jesus, the eternal royal high priest. Barnabas's enthusiasm began with Jesus's *personal traits* as "royal high priest" (ἀρχιερεύς). Barnabas readily connected decisive traits with Jesus as high priest: he was merciful (2:17), he sympathized with people (4:15), and good things were associated with him (9:11). He also resided in heaven (4:14), was exalted above the heavens (7:26; cf. 1:3), was enthroned at the right hand of God (8:1), and reigned over God's house (10:21; cf. 3:6). Here, Barnabas linked several decisive features with Jesus being "fitting" for those who follow him (Westcott, 1984, 195).

Previously, the term "fitting" (ἔπρεπεν) was used to speak of the appropriateness of God to perfect Jesus through suffering (2:10). Here "fitting" spoke of the eternal and perfect royal high priest as someone who was suitable for his followers. Jesus was "holy" (ὅσιος) signifying his devotion to God, "innocent" (ἄκακος) indicating an absence of guilt, and "undefiled" (ἀμίαντος) representing his place among the sacred sanctuary (Mitchell, 2007, 155–56). He was in fact "separate from sinners" (κεχωρισμένος ἀπὸ τῶν ἁμαρτωλῶν) and "exalted above the heavens" (ὑψηλότερος τῶν οὐρανῶν; cf. 1:2–3). It was this separation and exalted position that distinguished Jesus from Levitical priests. Why Barnabas shifted from Levitical "priests" in general to "high priest" here may be due to Barnabas wanting to use a "higher title" not found in Psalm 110:4 (Ellingworth, 1993, 393). Regardless of the reason, the emphasis was simply that the household family of faith in Rome, those who followed Jesus, had "such" (τοιοῦτος) a high priest, who was devoted, guiltless, undefiled, and suitable.

7:27. Barnabas's enthusiasm continued with Jesus's *work* as royal high priest. Unlike an ordinary Levitical high priest who was expected to offer sacrifice for his sins and then for the sins of the people (cf. 5:3), Jesus as the exalted royal high priest did not. However, Barnabas's linking of the double sacrifice of high priest with "daily" (καθ' ἡμέραν) sacrifices is problematic among commentators. Granted, Levitical priests offered daily sacrifices in the morning and evening (Exod. 29:38–42; Num. 28:3–8), but the high priest's double sacrifice was an act completed only once a year during the Day of Atonement (cf. 9:7). It seems Barnabas conflated the daily sacrifices with those offered on the Day of Atonement (Attridge, 1989, 213; Lane, 1991, 1:194; Koester, 2001, 368). In other words, Barnabas blurred the distinction between the two types of sacrifices. Yet, despite the ostensive problem, the point Barnabas emphasized was this: Jesus made but one sacrifice—himself—and it was sufficient. It was "once for all" (ἐποίησεν; cf. Bateman, 2012, 129). Thus, unlike the daily sacrifices of the Levitical priest and the double sacrifice of the Levitical high priest, Jesus's "once for all" sacrifice was both temporal (unrepeatable) and modal (thorough; cf. Mitchell, 1989, 156). His sacrifice need not be repeated.

7:28. Barnabas closed with a two-point summarization (γὰρ, "for") with a contrast. First, within the priesthood and the Levitical religious system, "appoint" (καθίστησιν) was used of men who had "weaknesses" (ἀσθένειαν; cf. 5:1). It spoke of a high priest's appointment to a position of authority. Yet, despite their position of authority, they had "weaknesses." As it did in 4:15, the mention of "weakness" here recalled Barnabas's explicit argument about Levitical priests in 7:8, 23, and 27. These contrasting concepts stretched back to 2:10–18 and 5:1–10. Thus, "weakness" once again stressed the fallibility and ineffectiveness of the men functioning as Levitical priests.

In contrast (δέ, "but") to a Levitical priest's appointment, Barnabas underscored God's appointment of "a son" (υἱόν), an appointment that echoed his previous statement whereby he described "a son" as God's "appointed heir of all things," namely, a Davidic heir with authority (1:2; cf. 3:6; 5:8–10). Jesus's appointment was undergirded with "the word of confirmation." The phrase recalled the divine oath from Psalm 110:4 in Hebrews 7:21. It also drew attention to Jesus's perfection mentioned in 2:10 and 5:9. So in chapter 7, according to Attridge (1989, 215), "Christ's perfection is intimately connected with his exaltation, his installation in the realm of the eternal" (cf. Bateman, 2012, 131). So, whereas the law established the Levitical religious system (7:11–12, 18–19, esp. v. 20), God's sworn oath established Jesus as a different kind of royal-priest who not only interceded for his people, he guaranteed a better covenant to those who followed him.

THEOLOGICAL FOCUS

The exegetical idea (Scripture's silence about Melchizedek and Abraham's encounter with Melchizedek served to underscore the imperfection of the Levitical system and exalt the status of Jesus as regal priest) leads to this theological focus: Jesus's exalted status as royal high priest supplants permanently the cultic system of Judaism.

The major theological theme of this preaching unit is twofold: the Levitical priesthood and the regal high priesthood of Jesus. First, the Levitical priesthood is an inferior priesthood in comparison to the historical regal priesthood of Melchizedek because they paid tithes to Melchizedek and were mortal (vv. 1–10, 23). Furthermore, the Levitical priesthood was inadequate in that permanent relationships with God were impossible to achieve through the Levitical cultic system (vv. 11, 27–28). Finally, the Mosaic legal system had been changed and replaced due to its ineffectiveness (vv. 12, 18–19, 22, 28).

Second, Jesus's regal high priesthood differs from that of the Levitical priesthood. To begin with, Jesus was from the tribe of Judah, not Levi (vv. 13–14), and likened to that of the regal high priest, Melchizedek (vv. 15–17). Furthermore, the regal high priesthood of Jesus was one of promise, unlike the Levitical priesthood (vv. 20–21). In addition, Jesus's sacrifice for sin was sufficient, never to be repeated (vv. 26–27). Finally, Jesus is a resurrected eternal royal high priest who lives for all eternity (vv. 3, 24–25).

PREACHING AND TEACHING STRATEGIES

Exegetical and Theological Synthesis

The immediate exegetical significance of this section was something that Barnabas had been hinting at previously in 5:10 and 6:20, namely, the superiority of Jesus's priesthood. The importance of this is the exegetical and theological trajectory of the book to this point. After setting up the superiority of Jesus, the messianic Son of promise to the angels and the prophets in chapter 1, the stern warning of chapter 2, the superiority of Jesus over Moses in chapter 3, the warnings of chapters 4 and 6, and the introduction of the idea of Jesus as high priest in chapter 5; the stage was set to show how Jesus was a super high priest.

The soteriological importance of this passage is hard to overstate. Through this we make sense of Stephen standing at the right hand of the Father in Acts 7:56. This also ties up the theological ideas that Paul develops in Romans 8:31–34. In a sense, we can fold into this the idea presented in Philippians 2:1–11 (cf. Moore et. al., 2019, 106–44).

In sum, Jesus had received his high place of exaltation due to his humiliation on this earth (Phil. 2). And yet, in this high and exalted state his work continues (Rom. 8). He is still at the Father's right hand, and he is praying for us. Why? The answer is unfolded here in Hebrews 7. He is at the Father's right hand, because he is a super high priest. The shadowy figure of Melchizedek in the OT existed to give us a sense of the full and complete work of Jesus. Hebrews 7 can only lead to worship.

Preaching Idea

Jesus is permanently for us.

Contemporary Connections

What does it mean?

What does it mean that Jesus is permanently for us? To answer that question, we need to first ask, how do you deal with the idea of Melchizedek? While there is no getting around the reference to Melchizedek, he is not the key to the passage. Jesus and his work is key. But if we do not deal with the OT context at all, we miss the point Barnabas was trying to communicate.

We have been reminded that the book of Hebrews is very intertextual, meaning it is dependent on OT texts such as Psalm 110. This is especially true in chapter 7. You could argue that all of chapter 7 is a sermon, and the text of the sermon is the quotation of Psalm 110 found in verse 17. This literary background gives us a creative idea as to how to shape the sermon.

Here are some key issues that will need explanation:

- Who is Melchizedek?
- What is the significance of a high priest, anyway?
- Was Melchizedek an OT appearance of Christ (christophany)?
- Why did Abraham give Melchizedek a tithe?
- Is this a NT encouragement to tithe?

Is it true?

Is it true that Jesus is permanently for us? Yes, Jesus is permanently for us. Yet, to answer this question in terms of the passage's extended comparison requires taking a trip into the past to better understand who Melchizedek was and how he prefigured Jesus. It may be difficult to thrust listeners into the world of first-century Judaea, but there is much to be gained in taking this interpretive journey, though you will need to be selective for the sake of time.

The original audience could mentally retrieve this context and perhaps make a more immediate comparison of Melchizedek to Jesus than we can. In our century, an instructive approach to reading Scripture that may be helpful and that many seem to use in their preaching is a theology of the "compositional nature" of the Bible. This approach is often referred to as a "canonical approach." By this approach, the key to understanding a passage is not just the immediate context, but how this text relates to the whole of Scripture. In other words, this approach is the working out of theology that believes the Bible is one literary unit, working itself out in various ways. Thus, the OT is as authoritative as the NT. So, applied to reading Hebrews 7, we might teach people to trust God's message in the OT found in the message expressed in the NT.

By way of argumentation, one might go to the requisite OT passages. Hebrews 7 as a whole becomes a weighty exposition as piece after piece of evidence is presented concerning Melchizedek and the Levitical priesthood in comparison to Jesus, our superior high priest. However, it could be helpful to turn to Romans 8:34, where the mediating work of Jesus is expressed most concisely.

Now what?

How should we respond to the reality that Jesus is permanently for us? The application, like so many passages, is to praise Jesus. This is a chapter of Scripture that clearly calls for the response of worship. A further application is to have confidence in Jesus because he is the permanent high priest.

In any way that we can, we should impress on the listener the practical confidence they should have in the security of salvation in Jesus, our superior high priest, by his atonement for our sins and perpetual intercession for those who follow him. The doctrine of eternal security is not expressly pressed here, but it is certainly the logical implication of the text. We have confidence because Christ is the permanent priest before the throne of God.

Creativity in Presentation

Most listeners will be familiar with the Star Wars movies. They are famous for the fact that, after the originally released movies, the ones that followed provided the long-anticipated backstory of the original trilogy, plus origin stories for many of our favorite characters. While some would argue that the prequels were better than the originals, most believe that the originals were better. And then there are the Disney sequels, which many liked better than the prequels but not as much as the originals. We might raise this discussion as a way of creating tension in the audience—which was really better? A transitional question might then ask the same of the Levitical priests, Melchizedek, and Jesus.

Another way is to approach this sermon's theme is with fashion. Who wore a leather jacket better: James Dean in *Rebel without a Cause* (1955), John Travolta in *Grease* (1978), or Henry Winkler in *Happy Days* (1974–84)? The truth is that the original was James Dean. Except for the first film, the later movie and TV series depict events in the past.

The truth is that each of these contemporary illustrations serve to highlight the reality that these are unanswerable questions. They depend on someone's age and preference. Yet, this is not so with Jesus. Many Jews over the centuries rejected Jesus as God's messianic Son and instead held fast to the original Levitical priesthood, at least until the temple was destroyed in A.D. 70. Yet, followers of Jesus from the first century on, Jew and Gentile alike, have subscribed to the argument in Hebrews that God's sequel in Jesus is superior in every way to the prequels. Hebrews 7 tells us that the prequels are important, but they are nothing compared to Jesus.

One creative way to preach the whole chapter in one single sermon is to show the unity of thought by suggesting that the chapter could be viewed as a sermon itself. Rhetorically, this works because the text has a clear beginning and two main structural points. The last part of the second main division is somewhat of a summary, and as such could be considered a conclusion of sorts to the sermon. The sermon sample below follows the idea that the main application is found in verses 23–25 with verse 25 being the main application: we are secure, because Christ is our permanent high priest. This is the singular application of this very didactic chapter.

The point you want to get across is simply this: Jesus is permanently for us. One approach to an outline for this text would be as follows:

- Introduction: Who is Melchizedek (vv. 1–10)?
- Jesus is permanent because he is indestructible (vv. 11–19).
- Jesus is permanent because God promised it to be so (vv. 20–25).

DISCUSSION QUESTIONS

1. What is the significance of Melchizedek?
2. Why is the comparison to Melchizedek helpful?
3. How is the comparison to Melchizedek seemingly unhelpful?
4. How do we best communicate that Melchizedek is both a comparison and a contrast to Jesus?
5. What is the relationship of Hebrews 8:1 to the rest of the passage?

FURTHER READING FOR DIVISION THREE

Aharoni, Yohanan, Michael Avi-Yonah, Anson F. Rainey, and Ze'ev Safrai. 2002. *The Carta Bible Atlas*, Fourth Edition, 142–62. Jerusalem: Carta Publishing.

Bateman IV, Herbert W. (editor). 2007. *Four Views on the Warning Passages in Hebrews*. Grand Rapids: Kregel.

__________. 2013. "The Theology of the General Letters." *Interpreting the General Letters: An Exegetical Handbook*, 89–120. Edited by John D. Harvey. HNTE Grand Rapids: Kregel.

Evans, Craig A. 2000. "Abraham." *Encyclopedia of the Dead Sea Scrolls*, Volume 1, 2–4. Edited by Lawrence H. Schiffman and James C. VanderKam. New York: Oxford University Press.

Lim, Timothy H. 2000. "Wicked Priest." *Encyclopedia of the Dead Sea Scrolls*, Volume 2, 973–76. Edited by Lawrence H. Schiffman and James C. VanderKam. New York: Oxford University Press.

Steudel, Annette. 2000. "Melchizedek." *Encyclopedia of the Dead Sea Scrolls*, Volume 1, 535–37. Edited by Lawrence H. Schiffman and James C. VanderKam. New York: Oxford University Press.

VanderKam, James C. 2004. "The High Priests in the Herodian Age (37 BCE to 70 CE)." *From Joshua to Caiaphas: High Priests after the Exile*, 394–490. Minneapolis: Fortress.

GOD'S NEW COVENANT (8:1–10:39)

Barnabas's theme for this fourth division centered around the old and new covenants. Having laid the groundwork in Hebrews 7:11–19, Barnabas had prepared the household family of faith for an extended discussion about a new covenant by way of distinguishing it from the numerous cultic facets of the first covenant. More specifically, chapters 8–10 differentiated the new covenant (8:8–13; 9:15–16; 10:29) from the first covenant (= Mosaic covenant; 8:7, 13; 9:18; 10:1, 28). He intertwined discussions about earthly and heavenly realities about sanctuaries, sacrifices, and ministries. He contrasted between *sanctuaries* whereby the earthly tabernacle was the place of worship (8:5; 9:1–5, 9–10, 21) that foreshadowed God's heavenly tabernacle (8:2, 5; 9:11, 24). He contrasted *sacrifices* whereby he stressed that the repetition of animal sacrifices had limitations (9:6–7, 9–10, 19–28; 10:1–4, 8–9, 11) in comparison with Jesus's efficacious sacrifice (9:11–16, 23–26; 10:5–7, 10, 12–14, 27–28). Finally, he contrasted between the *ministries* of priests and high priests who ministered in the tabernacle and were hindered by physical inadequacies (9:6–7; 10:11) in comparison with Jesus's royal high priesthood that had no constraints (8:13; 9:27–28; 10:5–10, 12–14, 19–20).

While preaching this division is a bit challenging, we have suggested four preaching units. The first introduces Jesus's heavenly ministry as a contrast between two sanctuaries and two covenants (8:1–13). The second underscores God's prescribed sanctuary, namely, its description, regulations, and shortcomings (9:1–28). The third addresses Judaism's blood sacrifices, more specifically their descriptions, shortcomings, and replacement (10:1–18). The fourth addresses a believer's responsibilities and expectations in terms of the assurances of Jesus as royal high priest (10:19–39). However, it may be possible to preach topically on Hebrews 8:1–10:39 by way of Barnabas's intertwining of themes: sanctuaries, sacrifices, and ministries. At the very end of this division is a list of books and articles for further reading that may be helpful in understanding these preaching units.

Hebrews 8:1–13

EXEGETICAL IDEA

Jesus's ministry as regal high priest in a heavenly sanctuary was of better quality than the ministries performed in earthly sanctuaries because the nature of the first covenant was incomplete and God's people were repeatedly breaking it, so God inaugurated a new internalized covenant that replaced the first one.

THEOLOGICAL FOCUS

Jesus's ministry as God's regal high priest is of better quality than those ministries performed on earth due to God's inauguration of his new set of covenantal promises.

PREACHING IDEA

What is perfect will not be obsolete.

PREACHING POINTERS

For Barnabas, Hebrews 8 was a significant turning point in his discussion. From 8:1 until 10:39, the tone changed from hard warnings, to discussions of Melchizedek. It was a long expository section on the superiority of Jesus, and the old or first covenant. For the Jewish person who was a member of the household family of faith, the Mosaic law was extremely important, even for those who were first-generation followers of Jesus. Yet, the transition to the new covenant was difficult (cf. Acts 15; Rom 7; Gal. 2; Eph. 2; etc.). The Jewish believers living in Rome wrestled with understanding God's plan expressed in Scripture (HB LXX) as it was accomplished through Jesus. Barnabas could have discussed in this section why Jesus was *supreme*, but instead he discussed why Jesus was *superior*. He did not use the superlative but the comparative.

Today, we accept and celebrate the new covenant during our communion services without much thought given to the old. There is the temptation to downplay the old covenant due to its imperfections. Yet the point of the new covenant is its superiority to the old because it is better than the first due to Jesus who inaugurated it. In a similar way, we accept new car models that are placed yearly on the market with improved shapes and often confusing new digital accessories. We give little thought to Ford's Model-T, which is the basis of the modern car. Like Ford's Model-T, the first covenant was magnificent. If we stop to appreciate the design of the old covenant (like Ford's Model-T), it makes the new covenant (or new cars) even more glorious. The problem is that its design had an internal expiration date built in leading to God's new covenant due to the perfection of Jesus who showcased the new covenant. Yet unlike new car models, the divine perfections of the new covenant will never expire due the perfection of the one who inaugurated. It will never become obsolete.

JESUS'S HEAVENLY MINISTRY (8:1–13)

LITERARY STRUCTURE AND THEMES (8:1–13)

Drawing upon the exaltation of Jesus first mentioned in 1:3, Barnabas shifted his emphasis about Jesus as God's royal high priest (cf. 5:5–6; 7:21) to his ministry in God's presence where he served as our royal high priest by underscoring Jesus's ineligibility to serve as a priest as prescribed in the Mosaic covenant when he was on earth (vv. 1–6). Barnabas then drew attention to the need for a new covenant. By way of a lengthy citation from Jeremiah 31:31–34 (38:31–34 LXX), Barnabas highlighted the flawed nature of the Mosaic religious system as well as the problem of perpetual lawbreakers whereby Barnabas punctuated the need for a different covenant (vv. 7–9) and God's resolution of the problem, namely, a new covenant (vv. 10–12). Barnabas concluded with the effect of this new covenant, namely, that it replaced the first one (v. 13).

Barnabas's major themes were Jesus's regal high priesthood, the new covenant, and God's interaction with his people.

- ***Jesus's Ministry in God's Presence (8:1–6)***
- ***The Need for a New Covenant (8:7–12)***
- ***The Effect of the New Covenant (8:13)***

EXPOSITION (8:1–13)

The bedrock of Jewish cultic rituals performed in earthly sanctuaries was the Mosaic covenant. The Jewish household family of faith in Rome was well aware of God's covenantal privileges and responsibilities. In general, covenants were agreements that served as a form of legal accountability between two or more people in order that each party would respectfully fulfill their stated obligations toward each other (Bock, 1999, 140–51; Weinfeld, 1970, 368–81). More specifically, biblical history revealed that God made rather significant covenantal promises with people. During the pre-Mosaic and Mosaic periods, God made five covenantal promises: the Noahic, Abrahamic, Mosaic, Davidic, and new covenants.

Unconditional Universal Covenants		Unconditional Covenants of Promise to the Nation Israel		Conditional Covenant to the Nation Israel	
Noahic	Genesis 6:8; 9:8–17 Consummated in Genesis 7:8–28; 9:12–16	**Abrahamic**	Genesis 12:1–4; 13:14–17; 15:1–7; 17:1–8 Confirmed in Genesis 21:2–7 (cf. Heb. 6:13–15)	**Mosaic**	Exodus 20:1–26 Confirmed in Exodus 24:1–18; Deuteronomy 28:1–62; 29:2–15
		Davidic	2 Samuel 7:4–17 Confirmed in 1 Kings 1:28–30, 39– 40, 45–48; 2:10–12; 1 Chronicles 23:1		
		New	Jeremiah 31:31–34; 33:33–34; Ezekiel 36:24–37:14 Confirmed in Daniel 9:20–27; Ezra 1:1–8; 2 Chronicles 36:22–23; Haggai 2:1–9		

These covenants consisted of sovereign pronouncements of God's promise that were often expressed in terms of God's "loyal" or "steadfast love" (*NIDOTTE*, s.v. "חסד"). Whereas the Noahic covenant was a universal promise for all people (and the animals), the other four were directed to God's chosen people. Only three, however, are unilateral (or "unconditional") covenants whereby God obligated himself with an "I will do" statement that was not dependent upon the success of the persons with whom God made covenants (Bateman, 2013, 95–102). They were irrevocable. Barnabas, however, drew attention to Jesus's ministry as God's regal high priest that was of better quality than the ministries performed in earthly sanctuaries due to the sinfulness of people and Jesus's inauguration of God's new set of covenantal promises.

Jesus's Ministry in God's Presence (8:1–6)

Jesus's current service as God's royal high priest in God's presence was of better quality to that of Levitical priests who ministered in the earthly sanctuary and to that of the Mosaic religious system regulating Jewish cultic activities.

8:1. Barnabas transitioned (δέ, "now") to his "chief point" or his "main point" (κεφάλαιον) about Jesus's eternal royal high priesthood. The opening statement "*such* a high priest" (τοιοῦτον . . . ἀρχιερέα) was a verbal link to "*such* . . . a high priest" (τοιοῦτος . . . ἀρχιερεύς) in 7:26. It served to connect the main theme of both chapters, namely, Jesus's eternal royal-priesthood that was like that of Melchizedek and not Levi. Yet, the connection also underscored Barnabas's advancement to the core of his exposition he began in chapter 7. The relative clause "who sat down (ἐκάθισεν) at the right hand (ἐν δεξιᾷ) of the throne of the Majesty in heaven" echoed the paraphrase of Psalm 110:1 in Hebrews 1:3. But unlike 1:3 where Barnabas's introduction of "a son" was enigmatic, the statement about an appointed "son" in 7:28 was unmistakably about Jesus and his royal-priesthood, which had been developed throughout chapter 7 and would continue on in chapter 8. And whereas in 5:5–6 Barnabas emphasized that Jesus was God's appointed royal high priest (= Son), here in 8:1, he drew specific attention to Jesus as the Jewish household family of faith's (ἔχομεν, "we have") royal high priest.

8:2. Barnabas continued (καί, "and") with what Jesus did as royal high priest. He was a "minister" (λειτουργός). Barnabas used similar terms to describe both worship and ministry throughout Hebrews (λειτουργικός, 1:14; λειτουργεω; λειτουργια, 8:6; 9:21). Thus, angels "worshipped" and "ministered" in heaven (1:7, 14), priests "ministered" in earthly sanctuaries (9:21; 10:11), and Jesus also "ministered" (8:2, 6). Yet, here in verse 2, where Jesus ministered was rather significant. He ministered "in heaven" (ἐν τοῖς οὐρανοῖς) in God's presence. As in 1:7, "minister" (λειτουργός) applied to one engaged in an administrative or cultic service. Unlike 1:7, however, angelic beings were not the subject. Here in 8:2, the focus was on Jesus's administrative function as a "minister" in the "sanctuary '*that is*' [καί] the true tabernacle." For Barnabas, "sanctuary" and "true tabernacle" were synonymous. He used a common connector (καί, "that is") to explain or expound on the meaning of "sanctuary" (Ellingworth, 1993, 402). It was the "true tabernacle." Throughout chapters 8–9, the "true tabernacle" was a metonymy, namely, another way for speaking of God's heavenly dwelling (see 8:5). Two items are worth noting here. First, Barnabas was not so concerned with Herod's temple in Jerusalem. Yet, there were times when he seemed to blur connections to it (8:3–5). Nevertheless, his repeated comparison to the wilderness generation was the foundation of his argument (2:2–3; 3:7–11, 16–19; 8:5; 9:1–10). Second, the "true tabernacle" (τῆς ἀληθινῆς) that was "set up" by the Lord served to distinguish between the two sanctuaries: one heavenly and one earthly (cf. v. 5). His statement "not man" (οὐκ ἄνθρωπος) alluded to the manmade wilderness tabernacle (Exod. 25–27; Josephus, *A.J.* 3.6.3 §§115–133; Bateman, 2012, 78). Barnabas shifted emphasis from Israel's historical and earthly tabernacle to God's "true tabernacle," namely, the heavens where God actually dwelt and was adored (see 8:5).

> *TRANSLATIONAL NOTE:* "Tabernacle"
> The term "tabernacle" (σκηνή, KJV, NASB, NIV, NET) may also be translated "tent" (RSV, NRSV, ESV, NLT) or "booth" (NRSV: Mark 9:5; Matt. 17:4; Luke 9:33). Of the twenty times σκηνή occurs in the NT, ten are in Hebrews (8:2, 5; 9:2, 3, 6, 8, 11, 21; 11:9; 13:10).

8:3. Barnabas recapitulated (γάρ, "for") a principle stated in 5:1, namely, that high priests were appointed to offer both gifts and sacrifices (Ellingworth, 1993, 403; Attridge, 1990, 218). So, as it was in Hebrews 5:1 and 7:28, so it was here. The term "appointment" (καθίσταται) spoke about assigning a person to the position of authority (BDAG, s.v. "καθίστημι" 2b, p. 492). In this case, it was his authority as high priest. The purpose (εἰς τὸ = infinitive) of "every" (πᾶς) high priest's appointment was to "*continually* offer" (προσφέρειν) a variety of gifts and sacrifices to God. Barnabas once again blurred distinctions. As it was the case with sacrifices (7:27) and the tabernacle/temple (8:2), Barnabas shifted back and forth between priests (7:5, 11–13; 8:4) and high priest (8:3; cf. 5:1–4) thereby blurring their diverse features. Yet, it was Barnabas's logical conclusion (ὅθεν, "so" NASB, NET; "and so" NIV, CNT) that was rather important. Like all Levitical priests, "it was necessary" (ἀναγκαῖον; NASB, NRSV, ESV, CNT) that Jesus as royal high priest "also" (καί) "offer" (προσενέγκῃ) something to God. So, just because Jesus's ministry occurred in God's presence (= "heavenly sanctuary"; 8:1–2) it did not exclude him from making an offering. Yet, his offering would be explained in more detail later in 9:12–15 and 10:5–10.

A History of the Tabernacle

The tabernacle's history began with its creation in the Sinai desert around 1446 B.C. Its construction was commanded by God and served as Israel's very first sanctuary (Exod. 25–27; Josephus, *A.J.* 3.6.3 §§115–133). People of the wilderness generation donated the materials needed for its construction (Exod. 36). Once it was built and set up, Moses consecrated it for worship (Exod. 40). During the wilderness wanderings, the tabernacle would be disassembled and transported to the Israelites next location and reassembled whenever they stopped to set up a new camp.

Once the people of Israel arrived in the semi-conquered land of Canaan, Joshua set up the tabernacle at Shiloh (Josh. 18:1; 19:51). Shiloh was Israel's religious center where legitimate sacrifices were to take place (Josh 22:19, 29). At one point, the Philistines captured the ark of the covenant but later, under pain of Yahweh's affliction, willingly returned it to the Israelites, at which time it was placed in the house of Abinadab at Gibeah (1 Sam. 5:1–7:1). While what happened next is unclear in Scripture, the tabernacle somehow came to be located at Gibeon (1 Chron. 21:29). Although the ark was eventually brought to Jerusalem, Davidic kings still offered sacrifices at the tabernacle even though the ark was in Jerusalem (1 Chron. 16:39–40; 21:28–30; 2 Chron. 1:3–6).

Eventually, the tabernacle was replaced with a permanent temple in Jerusalem (2 Sam. 7:8–17; 1 Chron. 17:3–15, 28:19; Wis 9:8). Once Jerusalem's temple was built, Solomon brought the ark to the temple as well as the tabernacle (2 Chron. 5:5; 1 Kings 8:4). Levitical priests served in the tabernacle until the temple was built (1 Chron. 6:32). Yet, the contents of the tabernacle were eventually incorporated within the temple precincts even during the time of Hezekiah's repairs of the temple (2 Chron. 29:5–7). Both the tabernacle and the temple were God's special sanctified dwelling places that demonstrated his desire to "meet" with his covenant people and manifest his glory among them (Exod. 29:43; 40:34–38; cf. 1 Kings 8:6–21; Josephus, *A.J.* 8.4.2 §§106–107). Yet, despite God's desire to meet with the Jewish people, ritual impurity and moral failings jeopardized the continuation of God's presence there (Exod. 32–33; Ezek. 8–10), and so his glory left the temple (Ezek. 10:1–19). Eventually, Nebuchadnezzar destroyed the temple in 586 B.C.[1]

Although Jerusalem's temple was rebuilt in 515 B.C when Jewish people returning from exile resettled the land of Judah (Haggai 1:14–1 5; Josephus, *A.J.* 11.4.1–3 §§75–82), nothing more was ever said in Scripture about the tabernacle until the writing of the NT. Nevertheless, the Essenes at Qumran believed the temple was the place of the tent of meeting [the tabernacle], and Jerusalem was the camp (4Q394 frag. 1.2:16–17a); and Josephus, in his description of the Sinai tabernacle, referred to it as "the whole temple." Yet, it was Herod's temple that eventually constituted an important link and symbolic value for Jewish people throughout the Greco-Roman world to which Jewish people made yearly pilgrimages (Acts 2:1, 5, 9–10; Philo, *Spec.* 1.69–70; Barclay, 1996, 418–21). Nevertheless, God's returned presence to the rebuilt temple was anticipated (Hag. 2:6–9; Zech. 2:8–13; 14:16–19).

Thus, Scripture (HB LXX) described the tabernacle's place in Jewish history beginning with Moses and ending with Nebuchadnezzar. It was constructed in the Sinai wilderness, transported and stationed at Shiloh, and then moved to Gibeon where it became and appeared to remain the center of ritual sacrifice until it was placed within Solomon's temple. The tabernacle remained there until the temple's destruction.

8:4. Barnabas resumed (οὖν, "now") his discussion from verse 2 with his proclivity for contrasts. He started his contrast here ("on the one hand," μέν) but concluded in verse 6 ("on the other hand," δέ). He opened his contrast with another contrary-to-fact or unreal condition (εἰ + ἦν; cf. Wallace 1996, 694–96). "On the one hand" (μέν), "if Jesus were on earth" (but he is not), "he would not be a priest" (but he is). The statement underscored how Jesus's role as a royal high priest did not fit the old Levitical religious system, especially because there were (ὄντων, "so" or "and so") earthly priests who currently offered sacrifices to God. In essence, the Mosaic law's explicit emphasis was on the earthly priesthood while remaining silent about any sort of heavenly priesthood. So, Jesus was "legally excluded from the earthly" tabernacle/temple (Ellingworth, 1993, 405). Yet, he was eligible to serve where God actually resided (= "heavenly tabernacle").

8:5. For Barnabas, "those who serve" (οἵτινες . . . λατρεύουσιν) referred to all earthbound priests presently preforming their service to God in an earthly sanctuary, namely, a "sketch *that is* [καί] a shadow of the heavenly one." "Sketch" and "shadow" were synonymous. As it was in verse 2 concerning the sanctuary and tabernacle, so it was here. The latter explained (καί, "*that is*") the former. Elsewhere in the NT, "shadow" (σκιά) referred to a mere "copy" or "representation" of something that was real (cf. 10:1; Col. 2:17). Here in Hebrews 8:5, the tent-sanctuary or tabernacle that Moses set up was a "copy" of the greater or God's "real" heavenly dwelling place (= "sanctuary"), a point Barnabas validated with a

1 There is the possibility that the tabernacle resided with the temple. See R. E. Freeman, "Tabernacle" in *Anchor Bible Dictionary* (New York: Doubleday, 1992): 242–300, esp. 293–94.

quote from Exodus 25:40 (cf. Acts 7:44). Yet, this sort of earthly-heavenly dichotomy was not unique in Jewish thinking.

In the Testament of Levi, the author wrote, "In the uppermost heaven of all dwells the Great Glory in the Holy of Holies superior to all holiness" where angelic priests conduct their services (3:4–6; [trans. Kee]). According to Philo (*Spec. 1,2,3,4.* 1.66), "The highest, and in the truest sense the holy, temple of God is the whole universe, having for its sanctuary the most sacred part of all existence, even heaven, for its votive ornaments the stars, for its priests the angels who are servitors to His powers, unbodied souls" (trans. Colson). Both reflected a shared tradition with other Jewish writers (4Q403 1.40–45; 4Q405 frag. 23 1.4; T. Lev. 3:4–7; 1 En. 14:8–23).

Similarly, for Barnabas, the heavenly sanctuary belonged to the celestial world (cf. Heb. 8:2 with 9:24), and its Holy of Holies was in the heavens (cf. 8:5 with 9:24–28). Yet, Barnabas interpreted and expanded this dichotomy to include the dichotomy that existed between Judaism (old) and Christianity (new) and thereby resumed his argument first presented in 7:11–12, 22–24. Thus, unlike the Levitical priests of the Aaronite order who served in the earthly sanctuary (8:4), God had appointed Jesus to serve within the celestial sanctuary as his royal high priest. Consequently, Barnabas distinguished the lesser earthly sanctuary (i.e., a copy) with the greater heavenly sanctuary (i.e., the real residential dwelling) where God was honored and surrounded by cherubim, seraphim, and other angelic beings (Isa. 6:1–4; Ps. 18:10; Ezek. 1:5, 22–28; Wood, 2008, 51; cf. 1 En. 14:20–23; 40:1–3).

8:6. Barnabas now completed or answered the contrast of verse 4. "On the other hand" (δέ), Jesus "has obtained [τέτυχεν] a different ministry." Jesus's ministry was "different" (διαφορωτέρας) in the sense that his ministry (λειτουργίας), to which had already been alluded in verse 2, was of greater value. So the phrase "as things are now" (νυνὶ), according to Barnabas, spoke of Jesus's ministry as superior to that of all earthly priests. This emphasis would resonate with the Jewish household family of faith who were familiar with the corrupt priesthood in Jerusalem (VanderKam, 2005, 455–90).

Furthermore, Barnabas tied Jesus's superior ministry as royal high priest to his service as a "mediator" (μεσίτης) of a better covenant (cf. better hope, 7:19; better covenant, 7:22). Employed in legal contexts, a "mediator" was a neutral person or a trusted arbitrator who could negotiate peace between contestants or parties to either remove a disagreement or to reach a common goal. For instance, Caesar Augustus was the "neutral" person who negotiated peace between Herod the Great and his sons Alexander and Aristobulus, whom Herod had accused of treason (Josephus, *A.J.* 16.4.3 §§118–19; cf. 16.2.2 §§24–26 Richardson, 1996, 25–40). Here in 8:6, Jesus mediated a "better covenant" (κρείττονός . . . διαθήκης) based entirely upon what God promised through Jeremiah. Thus, for Barnabas, Jesus's mediation was always in relation to what God had initiated and implemented. Jesus was a mediator of God's "better covenant."

The Jewish concept of a "covenant" (διαθήκη) denoted the special kind of relationship between God and Israel. "A covenant is," as Philo said, "a symbol of the grace which God has set between Himself Who proffers it and man who receives it. And this is the crowning benefaction, that there is nothing between God and the soul save the virgin grace" (cf. *Mut.* 6:52–53 [trans. Colson and Whitaker]). Thus, it was an *asymmetrical* relationship in that it was initiated, implemented, and governed by God alone. Barnabas, likewise, spoke of God's initiating and implementing a new covenant with one exception: God governed or mediated the new covenant through Jesus, his appointed regal high priest.

The Need for a New Covenant (8:7–12)

Due to the flawed nature of the first covenant being incomplete and the problem of God's people repeatedly breaking it, God promised a different covenant that would be internalized and not need to be taught.

8:7. Barnabas introduced his final point (γάρ, "for") by way of yet another contrary-to-fact or unreal condition (εἰ + ἦν; cf. Wallace, 1996, 694–96). "If that first one had been faultless" (but it was not), then "no one would have looked for a second one" (but they did). Barnabas's mention of a flawed "first one" and the need of "a second" has at least three challenges. First, what was the identity of "that first *one*" (ἡ πρώτη ἐκείνη)? Although the term "first" typically had a temporal sense, Barnabas was not referring to God's very first covenant initiated with Noah (Gen. 9:11). The covenant Barnabas spoke of here was the one God initiated with those whom he had rescued from Egypt. The Mosaic or Sinai covenant was alluded to in Hebrews 2 (vv. 2–3), chapter 7 (vv. 5, 11–12, 18–19a, 28), and chapter 8 (vv. 4–5; cf. v. 9). References to Moses and the tabernacle (8:4–5), the quotation from Jeremiah (8:8–12), and the tabernacle's function (9:1, 15, 18) provide further support. Thus, "that first *one*" referred to the Mosaic covenant that governed the Levitical religious system. It was "first" only in comparison with the now discussed "second one."

Second, "faultless" (ἄμεμπτος) normally applied to a person's spiritual condition whether of Abram (Gen. 17:1), of Job (Job 1:1) of priests (Josephus, *A.J.* 3.12.3 §278), or of Christians (Phil. 2:15; 3:6; 1 Thess. 3:13). But here it described a thing. Philo used the term to speak positively of things of beauty (*Leg.* 3:63), of relationships (*Post.* 181), of sacrifice (*Agr.* 127), of life (*Mut.* 47, 48, 51), and of marriages (*Spec.* 1:138). For Barnabas, however, it had a unique usage. He used "faultless" negatively of a thing, namely, the Mosaic law (cf. Heb. 7:11). The former Jewish religious system could not fully accomplish what was needed (cf. 7:12, 18). Nevertheless, the expressed negativity was not Barnabas's but God's (8:8; cf. Ezek. 20:25). At this point, Barnabas underscored the less than perfect Mosaic covenant or religious cultic system.

Third, to what did "a second one" (δευτέρας) refer? Having already introduced it in a somewhat enigmatic manner as a "better hope" (Heb. 7:19b) that was later described as a "better covenant" (7:22) and then mentioned as a covenant that Jesus mediated (8:6), Barnabas's subsequent reference here referred to God's new covenant (8:13; 9:15).[2]

> *TEXTUAL ANALYSIS:* Conflicting Text Critical Reading: 8:8
>
> Syntax Issue: Manuscript support is strong for both readings: text (א* A D* I K P 044 33 81 326 365 1505 2464) and variant (𝔓46 B 0278 614 1739 1881 Byz). However, the text is the preferred reading (see Lane, 1991a, 202; Metzger, 1994, 597).
>
> *txt.* "for when he found fault **with them**, he said" (μεμφόμενος γὰρ **αὐτοὺς** λέγει) (ASV, ESV, KJV, NASB, NIV, NRSV)
>
> *var.* "for when he found fault, he said **to them**" (μεμφόμενος γὰρ **αὐτοῖς** λέγει) (NET)

8:8. The basis (γάρ, "for") for the faulty law was compounded by the Jewish people themselves. The phrase "after finding fault with them" (μεμφόμενος . . . αὐτούς) referred to the

2 See conference video of H. W. Bateman IV and G. H. Guthrie, "Understanding the New Covenant as Presented in Jeremiah, Understood at Qumran, and Fulfilled in Hebrews" filmed during the Fifth Annual Let's Know the Bible Conference (Leesburg, IN: Cyber-Center of Biblical Studies, 2017), https://www.youtube.com/watch?v=Mz5qhEflouk&list=PLyaoTy8_0DgFIcTudaV6pYTHr8YteOZo6&index=4&t=969s.

perpetual disobedience of Judah just prior to the deportation, destruction, and dismantling of David's dynasty in 586 B.C. (Jer. 52:1–30). The speaker (λέγει, "he says,") was God. Returning once again to the theme of God's speech (Heb. 1:1), Barnabas quoted Jeremiah, one of Israel's greatest prophets. He was God's mouthpiece who preached Jerusalem's destruction and Israel's restoration. Just as Jeremiah had prophesied, King Nebuchadnezzar of Babylon destroyed Jerusalem with its temple (Jer. 5:1–6:30; cf. Hab. 1:1 –11). In time, Jewish people would return from exile to Jerusalem, rebuild the temple, and reestablish temple worship (Ezra 1:1–3:13; Hag. 1:14; 2:2–4, 14–18). Yet, they never experienced God's total plan of restoration spoken of in Jeremiah and other prophets such as Isaiah and Ezekiel.

Barnabas quoted from Jeremiah 31:31–32.[3] The opening expectation, "Look the days are coming," was a very common prophetic phrase used throughout Jeremiah (cf. Jer. 7:32; 9:25; 16:14; 23:5, 7). For Barnabas, those days had arrived (cf. 1:2). God said, "I will complete a new covenant." This was the first of six "I will" announcements that appeared in Jeremiah's citation (see related sidebar). The word "complete" (συντελέσω) recalled the theme of Jesus's perfection elsewhere in Hebrews (2:10; 5:9; 7:28) and was a key theme in Hebrews (cf. Attridge, 1989, 227; Koester, 2001, 386; Bateman, 2012, 131–32). Barnabas once again argued that only one aspect of God's restoration had occurred (cf. 2:5, 8b–9). This was evident in the next phrase. Jeremiah's isolating "the house of Israel" and "the house of Judah" was a figure of speech known as a hendiadys whereby the two phrases drew attention to the entire Jewish nation. Although Jesus had inaugurated the new covenant, there was yet a future aspect of that new covenant yet to be realized (Bateman, 2013, 113–16).[4]

8:9. God made it clear through Jeremiah 33:32 that the "new" covenant would be qualitatively (κατά) better and different from the former covenant made between God and Israel at Mount Sinai. The reason (ὅτι, "because"; KJV, NET, NIV) for the difference was twofold. First, the Jewish people "broke" (CEV) the Mosaic covenant (Jer. 7:1–29). God had promised to be their God (Exod. 19:1–20:17), and they promised to be his people (Exod. 19:5–8; Deut. 5:27–28). It was agreed that each party had a responsibility. If the Jewish people obeyed God, God would bless them (Deut. 28:1–14), but if they disobeyed God, God would punish them (Deut. 27:15–26; cf. Bateman, 2013, 98–99). Unfortunately, God's people repeatedly broke their agreement with God, which Jeremiah recorded, leading up to God's promise of a new covenant.

The second reason (assumed ὅτι) was because God "ceased to care" (CEV) about the Jewish people. The negated verb "did not care" (οὐκ ἠμέλησα) was used earlier in 2:3. Unlike in 2:3 where the verb was part of a warning to those who "ignored" the spiritual matter of God's great salvation message, here the negated verb "did not care" (οὐκ ἠμέλησα) was used in the more typical manner of neglecting or not caring for people. Because of the Jewish people's failure to "abide" by the first covenant (cf. 2:2–3 with 3:7–12; 15–18), God "did not care for them" (NASB), he "paid no heed to them" (RSV), he "had no concern for them" (NRSV, ESV), he "turned away from them" (NIV), or he "turned his back on them" (NLT). In essence, he rejected them (Jer. 6:30; 7:29; cf. Lam. 1:18–22; 2:20–22; 5:1–22). Barnabas

3 For Jeremiah 31:31–32 in the original language from the Hebrew Bible, Septuagint, and Hebrews, see H. W. Bateman IV, *Charts on the Book of Hebrews* (Grand Rapids: Kregel, 2012), 157.

4 D. Peterson, "The Prophecy of the New Covenant in the Argument of Hebrews 8:1–10:18," *Reformed Theological Review* 38 (1979): 74–81; R. L. Omanson, "A Superior Covenant: Hebrews 8:1–10:18," *Review and Expositor* 82 (1985): 361–73.

had already reminded the household family of faith of a previous historical situation of God's punishment after the Kadesh Barnea insurrection mentioned in Hebrews 3:7–19. Barnabas once again reminded the household family of faith about Israel's refusal to trust God.

The Six Divine "I Wills" of the New Covenant

1. I will make a new covenant with the house of Israel and the house of Judah, *not like* the covenant that I made with their fathers.
2. I will put my law within them.
3. I will write it on their hearts.
4. I will be their God, and they shall be my people.
5. I will forgive their iniquity.
6. I will remember their sin no more.

8:10. Within Barnabas's quote, Jeremiah transitioned (ὅτι, "for")[5] to a discussion about the new covenant. Positive characteristics were accentuated by way of several "I will" statements spoken by God. First, "I will establish with the house of Israel" directed attention to those with whom God would establish his new covenant, the people of Israel. Israel and Judah would not have meant "the church" to Jeremiah or Jeremiah's initial readers of his material (Bateman et al., 2012, 174–76; Bateman, 1999, 227–303). While Jeremiah was not privy to what the new covenant would mean for the entire world, he was aware that God would not forget his people and would restore them (Bruce, 1990, 187–93). Nevertheless, for Barnabas's Jewish audience in Rome, this promise would have resonated well with them as well as other Jewish people living elsewhere (cf. CD 6.17–21; 8:21; 20:12).

Second, "I will put my laws in their minds" and "I will inscribe them on their hearts" were two metaphors in parallel with each other that emphasized the internalizing of the law. Unlike the old covenant written on stone tablets (Exod. 32:15–16; 34:1, 4, 27–28) to be taught (Deut. 6:6–9), the new covenant would no longer be something external but would be internalized. Even in Proverbs 3:3, there was an emphasis on living out what was taught. Teachings were not only a part of the lifestyle of the religious person but part of their very nature (cf. 7:3; Pss. 40:8; 119:11). Having already warned his readers about the dangers of hardened hearts (or hearts of stone) that caused people to turn from God (3:8, 10, 12; cf. Ezek. 36:26–27), Barnabas highlighted God's desire for tender hearts that were more apt to obey God and be faithful to him.

Third, "I will be their God" and "they will be my people" was yet another parallel construction that served to underscore the personal relationship between God and those who follow him. It was reminiscent of previous discussions about partnership (of a heavenly calling, 3:1; of God's spirit, 6:4).

TEXTUAL ANALYSIS: Conflicting Text Critical Reading: 8:11

Lexical/Exegetical Issue: Moving beyond the manuscript support for the text (𝔓[46] א A B D K L 0278 33 1739 1881), it seems a scribe may have altered the reading to bring the verse into conformity to the LXX (Jer. 38:31–34). The text is the preferred reading.

txt.	"and each one shall not teach his **fellow citizen**" (καὶ οὐ μὴ διδάξωσιν ἕκαστος τὸν **πολίτην** αὐτοῦ) (ASV, NASB, NET, NRSV)
var.	"and each one shall not teach his **neighbor**" (καὶ οὐ μὴ διδάξωσιν ἕκαστος τὸν **πλησίον** αὐτοῦ) (ESV, KJV, NIV)

8:11. Continuing (καί, "and") his transition from discussing the old covenant to the new, Barnabas drew attention to yet another

5 The use of ὅτι here is a loosely connected conjunction rendered "for" but is transitional to the following comment about the new covenant (cf. BDF, 238 §456; BDAG, s.v. "ὅτι" 4b, p. 732).

characteristic about the new covenant with a rather strong emphatic reversal (οὐ μή, "not not"). A similar powerful double negative statement appears in Hebrews 8:12 and 13:5 (cf. Wallace, 1996, 468, 761). The formidable theological point emphasized here was that the new covenant was unlike the first covenant. The new covenant would not require people to teach each other: "they will *certainly not* teach" (NET). Barnabas did not mean there would be no need for teachers, because the household family of faith in Rome were obviously in need of teaching (5:11–14), and they were currently being taught by Barnabas (5:11–12; 6:1, 3; 7:1). Barnabas recognized that during the era of the first covenant, the emphasis was on a Jewish national knowledge of God (cf. 3:1–6; Wright, 1992, 279), typically generated and communicated through a privileged class of people, namely, those who were prophetic priests (e.g., Samuel), prophets (e.g., Moses, Isaiah, Jeremiah, etc.), and prophetic kings (e.g., David; cf. Westcott, 1984, 226). This was not, however, to suggest that people did not teach each other (Deut. 4:9–10; 6:7, 9; 11:19–20), but rather God spoke and drew people to himself through the prophetic voices of people (Heb. 1:1).

The way previous saints came to "know the Lord" was through the prophetic voice of various people (e.g., Moses: Deut. 4:5, 14: 6:1; Jer. 2:4; 4:5; 5:1, 20: 27; etc.). But in this new era the way people come to "know the Lord" was to be through "a son," Jesus (1:2). It was through Jesus and God's Spirit that made it possible to know God (John 6:45; 14:26; 1 John 2:27). As it was with the first covenant, so it was with the second, in that it involved a recognition of and obedience to God (Mark 12:28–34; 1 John 2:3–11; Koester, 2001, 387). Jeremiah made it clear that there were no limitations as to who might know God: "from the least to the greatest." While in his historical context, Jeremiah may have been thinking of the reuniting of the Jewish nation, the ambiguity of the statement allowed for a heightened fulfillment. This was not to suggest that Gentiles had no hope of knowing God (1 Kings 17:6–24; 2 Kings 4:4–37; Jonah 3:1–2, 5, 10). All people would know God through God's royal high priest (Matt. 28:19–20; Luke's Gospel), Jesus, and that the inadequate Jewish cultic system had been replaced with a new covenant.

8:12. The prophet Jeremiah stressed the basis (ὅτι, "for")[6] by which everyone could know God. God said, "I will be merciful toward their evil deeds," and "their sins I will remember no longer." Once again, the parallel construction conveyed a single theological concept: God forgave people. He would not hold past wrongs against his people (Ps. 103:12). Barnabas would explain this concept more fully in 9:1–10:18 when he discussed Jesus's atoning work. In the meantime, under the Mosaic covenant God's mercy was apparent. The Levitical religious system was incapable to fix a person's relationship with God or "complete God's design for humanity" (7:11). Nothing was in place that could perfect a person's relationship with God (cf. 5:19). The new covenant changed all of that through Jesus.

The Effect of the New Covenant (8:13)

The effect of the new covenant was its replacement of the first covenant.

8:13. In his closing comment on Jeremiah 31:34, Barnabas revealed the new covenant's effect on the first covenant (cf. 8:7). During Jeremiah's historical situation, "when" (ἐν τῷ λέγειν) he initially spoke of this new covenant, he indicated the antiquatedness of the first covenant. Barnabas's twofold description of the old covenant was rather important. First, "he [= God] has made old the first" (πεπαλαίωκεν

6 Some commentators view this ὅτι as reason. Thus, the clause explains the spiritual basis of the new covenant. It states why everyone will know God (cf. G. Guthrie, 1998, 282).

τὴν πρώτην). This idea about growing old first appeared in Hebrews 1:11 where Barnabas used Psalm 102 to create a positive contrast about "a son." Here the contrast spoke positively about the new covenant. And yet, in Hebrews 1:11 the earth was described as worn-out clothing, while here the first covenant was depicted as old. Thus, Barnabas stated a fact: "God has made the first *covenant* old (KJV), "obsolete" (NRSV, NIV, NET, ESV, NLT), or we might say, "God treated the first covenant as obsolete" (RSV).

Second, a rather important fact was the simple gnomic reality that "the thing growing old [παλαιούμενον] was near to disappearing" (ἀφανισμοῦ). Generally, the noun is translated "disappear" (NASB, NIV, NRSV, NET), "vanish away" (KJV, RSV, ESV), or "put aside" (NLT). Consequently, the reality was that the antiquated first covenant, a condition Jeremiah introduced, was to be replaced. Even though the Levitical priesthood was still in effect at the time Barnabas wrote to the household family of faith (ca. A.D. 65; cf. Bateman, 2012, 41–42), Barnabas revealed the condition of the first covenant. Barnabas once again used the verb "grow old" (cf. 8:13a). Yet, here the article "the" (τό) governed "growing old" (παλαιούμενον) and "disappearing" (ἀφανισμοῦ) whereby the latter explained (καί, "that is") the former. Thus, for Barnabas, the first covenant was *currently* growing old, *that is* (καί), it was *currently* disappearing (BGAD, s.v. "ἀφανισμός," p. 155). Together they served to underscore Barnabas's conclusion (δέ, "now") that the first covenant had passed its prime, its purpose was no longer valid, and thereby it was of no consequence (7:12, 18).[7] The idea was "out with the old" and "in with the new." The Mosaic law was "now out of date and will soon disappear" (NLT). Barnabas would devote greater attention to the inauguration and mediation of this new covenant in chapter 9:15–28.

THEOLOGICAL FOCUS

The exegetical idea (Jesus's ministry as regal high priest in a heavenly sanctuary was of better quality than the ministries performed in earthly sanctuaries because the nature of the first covenant was incomplete and God's people were repeatedly breaking it, so God inaugurated a new internalized covenant that replaced the first one) leads to this theological focus: Jesus's ministry as God's regal high priest is of better quality than those ministries performed on earth due to God's inauguration of his new set of covenantal promises.

The major theological theme in this preaching unit that resonates throughout this chapter is Jesus's regal high priesthood. Whereas Jesus is first presented as a divine regal high priest (1:1–15), here his regal priesthood is similar to that of Melchizedek but differs from the Mosaic Levitical priesthood (5:1–10; 7:11–28). Here, the emphasis is on the place where Jesus serves as a regal high priest (vv. 1–2; cf. 9), and on his inauguration of a new covenant (vv. 7–12) that replaces the inadequate and outdated Mosaic cultic system (v. 13). Another theological theme is God's desire to communicate with his people (vv. 5b, 8; cf. 1:2; 3:7; 6:13–14). Here the emphasis is God's desire to make and inaugurate relational promises with people.

PREACHING AND TEACHING STRATEGIES

Exegetical and Theological Synthesis

The section begins by developing the idea that Jesus is in heaven and not on earth. Since Jesus as a High Priest has been established, he now establishes that his ministry is in a different place, it is in God's presence.

From this Barnabas began to discuss the plan proper. The plan was the God would establish a new covenant proper which assumes

7 D. K. Lowery, "Christ, and the End of the Law" in *Dispensationalism, Israel and the Church: The Search for Definition*, eds. C. A. Blaising and D. L. Bock (Grand Rapids: Zondervan, 1992), 230–47.

that there is something wrong with the old covenant (v. 7). This point is developed with an application of Jeremiah 31:31–32, which Barnabas quotes. This New Covenant does not mean the old covenant was bad, but rather that is was incomplete, and in that way anticipatory. The New Covenant was always the plan. Yet, key words like "copy," "shadow." and "pattern" (v. 5) about the tabernacle embedded in the New Testament reveals the tabernacle's value. The tabernacle was a way that Old Testament saints were given access to God's forgiveness. However, they had a far deeper meaning as a pattern, a template, or a schematic of the work of Christ that would come later.

Finally, Barnabas explained the effect of the new covenant arrangement. Namely that the old is vanishing and ready to go away. It was Jeremiah who introduces the New Covenant, it is now here, and its presence demands that the old be rendered obsolete.

Preaching Idea

What is perfect will not be obsolete.

Contemporary Connections

What does it mean?

What does it mean that "what is perfect will not be obsolete"? The explanation of this passage establishes the significance of the old covenant. It provides specific implications of a covenant and the fact that God alone initiated the covenant. While the significance of God's initiation might not be fully appreciated, God is the driver in all of this: God will establish a new covenant (v. 8), God will put it in their hearts (v. 10), God wants people to be able to have access to him without a mediator (v. 11), and God will show mercy (v. 12). These are important patterns in God's plan.

While the qualities of the new covenant are straightforward, verse 11 needs some explanation. Barnabas is not suggesting that we do not need instruction. The book of Hebrews is clear that we are to remember the leaders who taught us (13:7) and to remain under the teaching authority of those who keep watch over your souls (13:17). What is remarkable about verse 11 is the intimacy that God envisions in the new covenant. Thus, Jeremiah prophesied that people would not need an intermediary to instruct them, but they could have God instruct them (Jer. 31:34). This glorious point is internal instruction. It is realized in so many passages in Scripture: in the Gospel of John, the metaphor of the branch *abiding* in the vine (John 15), the promise of the Holy Spirit who would teach us everything we need to know (John 14:15–31), and Jesus defining eternal life as knowing the Son (John 17:3)! The new covenant demonstrates its remarkable superiority in the fact that it is now an internal covenant. While we remain under the authority of a local church, we relate to God as individual believers.

Is it true?

Is it true that "what is perfect will not be obsolete"? How often do we describe a person as perfect? The word "perfect" tends to be used of something or someone who is flawless or has achieved supreme excellence. A perfect diamond is without defect. It is flawless. While the idea of a "perfect number" is today merely historic in nature it is not obsolete. Yet, there was a time when the numbers 6, 28, 496, and 8,128 were considered perfect numbers.

A good artist is someone is able to faithfully reproduce something and thereby produce something that is "picture perfect" of someone or something. A "perfect gentleman" is applied to a man who manifests ideal standards established or recognized by a particular society. The American cellist, Yo-Yo Ma, a Parisian born to Chinese parents, is often praised for having achieved perfection in playing the cello.

Alfred Nobel, an inventor of some 355 inventions, amassed a large fortune during the 1800s. In his last will he specified that a foundation be formed whereby ninety-four percent of his total assets be used to establish a foundation so that "Nobel Prizes" were awarded to people who served humanity. The recipients are those who had achieved supreme excellence in a field that contributed to society. Nobel Prize winners' contributions tend to never be out-of-date though they may be improved upon.

Here in Hebrews 8, the argumentation is of a new and more perfect covenant inaugurated by Jesus's perfection as royal high priest. Barnabas built his case on a long quotation from Jeremiah 31:31–34. This new covenant, this better covenant, exceeds any perfect cuts a jeweler might make to create a perfect diamond or the human perfection attributed in playing the cello or paint a portrait. The new covenant is so complete it has no expiration date or design flaws due to the one who designed it and the one who inaugurated it. God's promise of the restoration of his people during a time of significant bondage and persecution found its fulfillment in the person of Jesus Christ.

Now what?

If "what is perfect will not be obsolete," how do we realize and appropriate this perfection as believers? Chapter 8 details the importance of why Jesus is not on earth. This is a practical reality. According to John 16:4–7; 12–14, it was to our advantage that Jesus is not physically present with us. The absence of the Son means the presence of the Spirit. The Spirit is an internal enabling power that allows us to have an audience with God. It allows us to internalize the Word of God in our lives, which convicts us of wrong doing and illuminates the importance of the Son of God in our lives. Interestingly, Jesus leaves us his Spirit, but it guides us back to his presence. Thus, Jesus is very present even in His absence.

By way of application, this means we need to honor the work of the Son by cultivating the presence of the Spirit in our lives. The presence of the Spirit may be manifested as he enables us to love people that many in our society may consider less than perfect and difficult to love like the homeless, immigrant, and those racially different than us. Yet, due to the absence of any direct imperatives, this passage has a seemingly difficult application. However, Barnabas is not trying to get us *to do* something, but rather *to think* about something. If you are preaching through the book as a series, you will note there is a shift in tone from the warnings that have a specific application to this section that is purely expository. The application is thus implied: we are to love the regal Messiah for his completion that never expires and appreciate the work of the Spirit within us.

This first-century house church is filled with people who once based their entire hope on the old covenant. Now, Barnabas is clarifying for them it is now obsolete. It was an imperfect set up for a perfect covenant that will never expire. Their reactions, and ours, should be ever loving wonder and praise for what God has done; for his accomplished plan whereby, Jesus is God's eternal royal high priest. The immediate application to this section in general, and this passage specifically is wonder and praise. To let the more pressing things of life grow "strangely dim in the light of his glory and grace."

Creativity in Presentation

In presenting this preaching unit, an iPhone or smart phone might be used to demonstrate the point of the passage. Hold up an iPhone, or another smart phone, and describe how it was designed to communicate information. You could even tell an interesting story about how a smart phone was incredibly handy in finding directions or accessing information. If you want, you could do the entire presentation while using your phone as the controller. You might consider encouraging a parent and young person to talk about how they use their phones. You could even tell a compelling story of how a smart phone saved someone's life or helped rescue someone from danger. Then say something like the following:

The cell phones we carry in our pockets are called "smart phones." They are small but powerful computers that can give us directions, connect us to the internet, and track all of our daily activity. Yet, each one of them has an interesting, built in feature. They each have an embedded expiration date. Both the hardware and the software are intended to last about two years. That's it. Hundreds of dollars to buy, untold millions in research and development with some of the brightest minds are invested in a device that is completely disposable.

The point is that these devices are powerful, yet they are limited. They are designed to become obsolete. The reason for this is basic economics. The designer of the phone wants, in a few years, to turn your attention and money to something more exciting, newer, and better. They are not perfect and thus they will be obsolete.

In the same way, the Designer of the old covenant did something remarkable. The old covenant was a means for man to communicate with God. This is not insignificant. Think of the glory of the book of Exodus as God draws people to himself by covenant relationship and establishes this reality through the powerful symbolism of the work of priests in sacrifice and in the tabernacle. It was incredible and effective. And yet, from the very beginning of its beautiful design, it was supposed to become obsolete. The old covenant had a built-in expiration date. It was designed to turn your attention to something newer and better—the new and better Moses, Joshua, priest and prophet—Jesus. Jesus, however, will never be replaced. The point you want to get across is simply this: "What is perfect will not be obsolete." A simple outline for this passage might be:

- The perfect plan is for Jesus to minister in heaven (vv. 1–6).
- The perfect plan is for a new covenant (vv. 7–12).
- The perfect plan makes the old pattern obsolete (v. 13).

DISCUSSION QUESTIONS

1. Is it encouraging or discouraging that Jesus is in heaven and not on earth (Heb. 8:1)?
2. Why would Jesus not be a priest if he were on earth (Heb. 8:4–5)?
3. What is the significance of the lengthy quotation from Jeremiah (Heb. 8:8–12)?
4. What are the differences in this text between the pattern (the old covenant) and the new covenant?
5. What does it mean that the old covenant is obsolete (Heb. 8:13)?

Hebrews 9:1–28

EXEGETICAL IDEA

In contrast to the cultic regulations for the earthly tabernacle and the ineffectiveness of cultic rituals, the arrival of Jesus as God's regal high priest and his entrance into God's heavenly presence guaranteed an efficacious cleansing of a person's conscience, and as God's mediator of a new covenant, Jesus intended to establish an inheritance for the Jewish household family of faith.

THEOLOGICAL FOCUS

Jesus is the mediator of God's new covenant, and royal high priest whose self-sacrifice makes it possible to purge a person's conscience of guilt as well as experience God's promised inheritance.

PREACHING IDEA

Previews determine the plan.

PREACHING POINTERS

Since the time of Moses (ca. 1446 B.C.), the Levitical cultic system of sacrifice was intended to be front and center for God's chosen people of Israel. For more than 1,500 years, the cultic practice of animal sacrifice—first practiced in the tabernacle, then Solomon's temple, then Haggai's temple, and finally in Herod's rebuilt temple—had been part of Judaea's history. In this section, Barnabas developed the idea that Jesus's sacrifice was better than the Levitical cultic system of animal sacrifice. By way of a synopsis, Barnabas developed a brief picture of the tabernacle. Since the household family of faith in Rome knew it so well, they did not need a full review, just a synopsis. Consequently, Barnabas pointed out particular aspects for the purpose of his illustration, and he even used the term "parable" (*parabole*) in verse 9. The tabernacle was an illustration, a metaphor, or a picture.

Today, the church building is an illustration, a metaphor, or picture of God, particularly as it concerns Jesus. Some churches have stained glass windows, rather than curtains where cherubim were displayed. Rather than a place where burnt offerings were to take place in the tabernacle's courtyard, today's churches feature a cross. And rather than an ark of the covenant located in the Holy of Holies, churches today display a table with an inscription: "The Lord's Table" or "Do This in Remembrance of Me." Yet as was the case during Israel's history, today's tabernacle (= church building) where worship occurs conjures various perspectives, some good and some not so good. Nevertheless, the church is meant to exemplify something better. Previews determine the plan.

GOD'S PRESCRIBED SANCTUARY (9:1–28)

LITERARY STRUCTURE AND THEMES (9:1–28)

In developing his discussion about Jesus's heavenly ministry before God, Barnabas expanded his initial treatment about the covenants introduced in chapter 8 but with a greater emphasis placed on distinctions between the people and places where covenantal rituals were initiated and practiced. He opened with the cultic regulations for the earthly tabernacle with its furnished chambers where various types of priestly service and the ineffective cultic rituals took place (vv. 1–10). The imperfect service of the high priest was then contrasted with the arrival of Jesus as God's high priest and his entrance into God's presence with his efficacious offering to God that guaranteed the cleansing of a person's conscience (vv. 11–14). Barnabas closed with concluding remarks that focused attention on Jesus as the mediator of the new covenant where God actually dwelt and where Jesus served due to his eternally effective offering (vv. 15–28).

Barnabas's theme was a familiar one: God kept his promise about the new covenant through Jesus who mediated the new covenant in God's presence due to the effectiveness of Jesus's sacrifice.

- ***The Earthly Tabernacle (9:1–10)***
- ***The Arrival of Jesus into God's Presence (9:11–14)***
- ***The Mediation of Jesus as High Priest (9:15–28)***

EXPOSITION (9:1–28)

During the Greco-Roman period, Herod's temple in Jerusalem was *the center* of a great deal of Jewish religious activity. It was a temple revered by *most* Jews at the time. Although Herod began rebuilding the temple's edifice in 19/20 B.C., he saw only the temple's main building completed (Josephus, *J.A.* 15.11.1, 6 §§380–87, 421–23). Portions of the temple's construction were still in process when Jesus visited the temple during his first Passover in Jerusalem some forty-six years later (John 2:14–22). Nevertheless, by the time Barnabas wrote Hebrews (ca. A.D. 65), the temple's construction had been completed (A.D. 63). "The exterior of the building," according to Josephus (*J.A.* 5.5.6 §222), "wanted nothing that could astound either mind or eye" (trans. Thackeray et al.). Jewish people during the time of Herod's temple (20 B.C. to A.D. 70) came from all over the Greco-Roman world to worship God (Acts 2:5, 9–13). Yet, there were *some* Judaean Jews who believed that the temple was defiled and thus sought after another temple (11Q19/11Q20). Nevertheless, Herod's temple served as the repository of the Hebrew Scriptures, the place where Levitical priests served (Luke 1:8), a meeting place for the Sanhedrin, an important military stronghold for the city of Jerusalem (Josephus, *A.J.* 5.5.8 §§238–47), and the place where people came to worship (Mark 11:15–19; Acts 3:1–10; 21:26). Yet, Barnabas did not dwell on Herod's magnificent temple and the Levitical priests who ministered there; rather, he contrasted Israel's earliest place of worship where high priests performed ineffective cultic ritual practices of an old covenant (a time before the deep-seated corruption of Herod's temple worship) with Jesus's efficacious service as God's royal high priest who inaugurated as well as meditated a new covenant in heaven where God actually resided.

The Earthly Tabernacle (9:1–10)

The earthly tabernacle, built for worship, consisted of two furnished chambers where various types of priestly service took placed, though with limited cultic impact.

> *TEXTUAL ANALYSIS:* Conflicting Text Critical Reading: 9:1
> Stylistic Issue: Manuscript support is strong for both readings: text (א A D 0278 0285 33) and variant (𝔓[46] B 6 629 1739 1881). Yet the use of "on the one hand, now" (μὲν οὖν) without "even" (καί) is in keeping with the author's style and thereby denotes a continuation (cf. 7:11; 8:4). A scribe may have added "even" (καί) to parallel the old and new order when in fact the author wishes to contrast the two. The variant is the preferred reading (cf. Lane, 1991b, 214, with Metzger, 1994, 597–98).
>
> *txt.* "On the one hand, now **even** the first covenant had regulations for worship and an earthly sanctuary" (Εἶχε μὲν οὖν [**καὶ**] ἡ πρώτη δικαιώματα λατρείας τό τε ἅγιον κοσμικόν) (ASV, ESV, NASB, NRSV)
>
> *var.* "On the one hand, now the first covenant had regulations for worship and an earthly sanctuary" (Εἶχε μὲν οὖν ἡ πρώτη δικαιώματα λατρείας τό τε ἅγιον κοσμικόν) (KJV, NET, NIV)

9:1. Resuming (οὖν, "now") his discussion on the first covenant (8:7, 13), Barnabas recalled how "the first [*covenant*] had regulations" (εἶχε . . . ἡ πρώτη [*διαθήκη*] δικαιώματα). Translations add the word "covenant" because it's assumed in the text (KJV, NET, NASB, NRSV, ESV, NIV, NLT, CNT; cf. 8:7). The construction "on the one hand" (μέν; vv. 1–5) followed later with "on the other hand" (δέ; vv. 6–7) was yet another contrastive parallelism (Westcott, 1984, 243; Lane, 1991b, 222) that first drew attention to *where* worship happened before describing *what* happened during worship. The term "regulations" in verse 1 and again in verse 10 bracket these ten verses as a single unit (Attridge, 1989, 231 n. 11). And as he did in 3:1–6, Barnabas provided a neutral description of the Jewish cultic system under the first covenant (Ellingworth, 1993, 431). Naturally, the first covenant had numerous regulations. Although the term "regulations" (NASB, RSV, NRSV, NIV, NET, ESV, NLT) or "ordinances" (KJV) had a wide spectrum of usage in the Septuagint and nonbiblical material, the NT restricted "regulations" (δικαιώματα) to contexts concerning the requirements of the Mosaic law (BDAG, s.v. "δικαίωμα" 1, p. 249; *TLNT,* 1:343–45). This was, then, particularly evident in Barnabas's introductory statement of Hebrews 9:1. His use of "regulations" gave emphasis to the cultic rules or "legal statutes" prescribed in "the first *covenant*" (ἡ πρώτη [*διαθήκη*]) that was to govern "service *to God*" (BDAG, s.v. "λατρεία," p. 587; cf. 9:6–10) within the earthly sanctuary (cf. 9:2–5).

> *TEXTUAL ANALYSIS*: Conflicting Text Critical Reading: 9:2
> Theological Issue: A few manuscripts (like B) adds "and the golden altar of incense" (καὶ τὸ χρυσοῦν θυμιατήριον) in an attempt to bring concord between verses 2 and 4 and thereby remove the difficulty concerning the location of the golden altar of incense in the tabernacle. The text is the preferred reading (Metzger, 1992, 598).
>
> *txt.* "and the bread of presence" (καὶ ἡ πρόθεσις τῶν ἄρτων) (ASV, ESV, KJV, NASB, NET, NIV, NRSV)
> *var.* "and the bread of presence **and the golden altar of incense**" (καὶ ἡ πρόθεσις τῶν ἄρτων **καὶ τὸ χρυσοῦν θυμιατήριον**)

9:2–5. Barnabas began by clarifying (γάρ, "for you see") the "regulations" or "cultic rules" for the earthly "tabernacle" (KJV, NASB, NIV) or "tent" (RSV, NRSV, NET, NLT) *where* worship was to take place. Although the tabernacle was a single entity, it was divided into two sections or chambers: the Holy Place and the Holy of

Holies (Josephus, *J.A.* 3.6.4 §§124–26). The "holy place," or as Barnabas described it, "the first room" (NIV), "first section" (ESV), or "outer one" (NET), contained two pieces of furniture: the lampstand and the table on which the consecrated bread was placed.

In verses 3–4, Barnabas continued (δέ, "and") his description of the tabernacle *where* worship was to occur. Here he mentioned "the second curtain" (τὸ δεύτερον καταπέτασμα). This curtain or veil was first introduced in Hebrews 6:19 where hope was personified as having entered behind the veil of the innermost part of God's *heavenly sanctuary*, or more specifically having entered into God's presence (cf. 4Q400; 1 En. 14:14–22). Here Barnabas underscored the function of the veil that separated the Holy Place within the *earthly sanctuary* from the innermost part of the Holy of Holies where God's glory settled (cf. Exod. 40:34–38). Behind this "curtain" (NET, NRSV, ESV, NLT) or "veil" (KJV, ASV, NASB, CNT) were two pieces of furniture: the golden altar of incense and the ark. There was, however, a seemingly less than accurate description of the furniture's placement. Typically, the ark alone was in the Holy of Holies. Perhaps Barnabas desired literary balance: two tents (outer, v. 2a, and inner, v. 2b) each with two pieces of furniture (vv. 2b and 3b) (cf. Ellingworth et al., 1983, 178). More than likely, Barnabas reflected a later Jewish tradition (1 Kings 6:20; 2 Bar 6:7; cf. Lane, 1991b, 220). Despite the discrepancy, Barnabas's point centered on the "regulations" or "legal statutes" established for the place *where* worship occurred (Koester, 2001, 403; Bateman, 2012, 80–81).

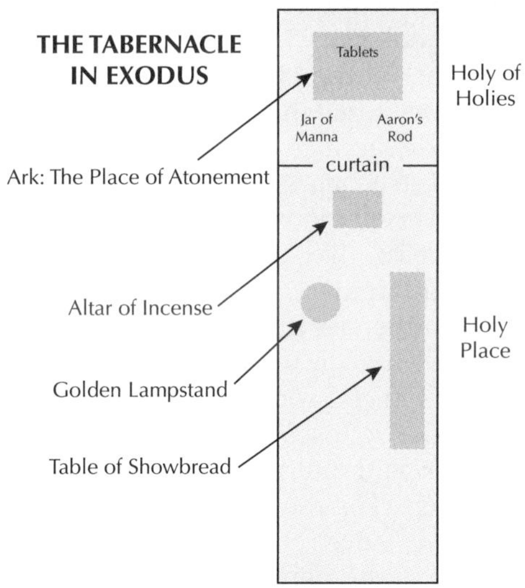

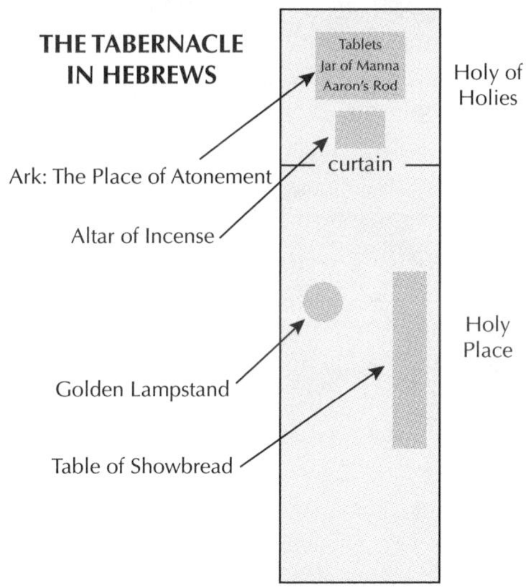

Scripture	Holy Place	Altar of Incense	Inner Curtain	Holy of Holies	Manna and Rod	Tablets	Ark
Exodus	26:33–34	30:1–10; 37:25–29; 40:5, 26–27	26:31–35; 36:35–38; 40:3b, 21	26:33, 35	16:32–34 (Num. 17:10)	40:20	25:10–22; 37:1–9; 40:3a, 20–21
Josephus, *Antiquities*, Book 3	§§122–33	§§144–46	§§139–43	§§126	§§122–26	§§147–50	§§134–38

In verses 4–5, Barnabas drew direct attention to the ark of the covenant. First, the ark contained three items: a golden urn of manna, Aaron's rod that budded, and the stone tablets of the covenant. Second, ornamental cherubim hovered over the ark and overshadowed the mercy seat. The prominence of cherubim as crafted ornamental figures over the ark and embroidered on the tabernacle curtain or veil mirrored the existence of real living beings who served God in heaven. Barnabas belabored these descriptions merely to emphasize the "earthly" nature of the tabernacle as opposed to the "true tabernacle" mentioned previously in Hebrews 8:2.

Cherubim

The term "cherubim" occurs only here in the NT. Yet, in the Septuagint and extrabiblical material, herubim (also referred to as "living creatures") were winged celestial beings of governance (cf. Ezek. 1:22–28 with 10:20; 1 En. 61:10) who appeared to possess both human and animal (lion, ox, and eagle) characteristics (Ezek. 1:5–10; 10:8, 14, 21; cf. Apoc. Ab. 18:3–13). Josephus contended, however, that "no one can say or imagine what they looked like" (Josephus, *J.A.* 8.3.3 §73). They served as God's guardians of the tree of life (Gen. 3:24; cf. 1 En. 20:7), as God's vehicle to move through the universe (2 Sam. 22:11, Ps. 18:10, cf. Ezek. 10:19–20), and as God's means of departing from Jerusalem's temple before its destruction (Ezek. 10:1–10). They also surrounded God's throne (Ps. 80:1, 99:1; 4Q405 frag 20–21–22, 6–9; 1 En. 14:18–20; 2 En. 21:1; Josephus. *A.J.* 3.6.5 §137). When mentioned in connection with the earthly tabernacle and the temple, they were prominent ornamental figures. Cherub figures were crafted from gold (Exod. 25:18, 37:7; Josephus, *J.A.* 8.3.3 §72) or of wood overlaid with gold (1 Kings 6:23–32; 2 Chron 3:10–13), which overshadowed the cover on the ark (Exod. 25:19–20, 37:8–9; 1 Sam. 4:4; 1 Kings 8:6–7; 1 Chron. 13:6; 2 Chron. 5:7–8; Philo, *Mos.* 2.97). Cherub figures were embroidered on the curtains or veil separating the Holy of Holies from the Holy Place (Exod. 26:1, 31–33, 36:35; 2 Chron. 3:14; and an allusion to cherubim in Josephus, *J.A.* 3.6.4 §126). Finally, carved engravings of cherubs appeared on the walls and doors of the temple (1 Kings 6:29, 32, 34–35).

9:6–7. Whereas the connector "on the one hand" (μέν) of verses 2–5 was to describe the "regulations" of *the where* of worship (e.g. earthly sanctuary), the connector here "on the other hand" (δέ) of verses 6–7 was to depict *the what* of worship. Barnabas highlighted the multiple priests who "*continually* perform *ritual* duties" (τὰς λατρείας ἐπιτελοῦντες) in the first or outer chamber, in contrast (δέ, "but") with the one and only high priest whose predominate place of service was within the second or inner chamber where God's glory had settled (Exod. 40:34–38). The duties of the high priest were well defined. He alone entered the inner chamber with an animal blood sacrifice for himself and the "*inadvertent* sin" (ἀγνόημα) or wrongdoing committed by the everyday Jewish person.

At least two points warranted attention. First and foremost, the phrase "once a year" referred to the great Day of Atonement, an event repeated annually in the life of a Jew (10th Tishri = Sept/Oct; cf. Exod. 30:10; Lev. 16:34; cf. Philo, *Leg.* 306–07; Josephus, *A.J.* 3.10.3 §240). The second was the term "once." This term was introduced in Hebrews 6:4. Yet, unlike in Hebrews 6:4 where "once" conveyed a unique and unrepeatable event, here in Hebrews 9:7 "once" also conveyed a numerical concept but one that was practiced annually. Thus, once every year, during the annual Day of Atonement (also referred to as *Yom Kippur*), the high priest entered into the Holy of Holies (3 Macc 1:11). This was the one and only day of the year the high priest was permitted to enter the "inner tent" of the tabernacle or "the heart of the sanctuary" (Philo, *Ebr.* 135–36). The high priest first entered to seek propitiation (to be ritually purified) for himself and a second time for his priestly family (Lev. 16:6, 11; cf. Heb. 5:3; 7:27; Josephus, *A.J.* 3.10.3 §243). He then entered a third time to seek propitiation for the entire community (Lev. 16:34; Josephus, *A.J.* 3.10.3 §241). One of the many important *symbolic* acts of the Day of Atonement was the use of a scapegoat that was sent into the wilderness, and with it, the sins of the community (Lev. 16:7–10, 20–22; Josephus, *A.J.* 3.10.3 §241). God's loving compassion must have appeared larger than life on this day, knowing that the event needed repeating year after year. The important observation, however, was Barnabas's contrast (δέ) with the continuous priestly activities in the Holy Place ("outer tent": 9:6) and the high priest's activity in the Holy of Holies ("inner tent," 9:7). Despite the contrast, the multiple offerings and the annual atonement sacrifice were conflated by Barnabas into one big ineffective regulation (9:25, 10:1–4).

The Religious Significance of "Blood" in Hebrews 9

"Blood" is used throughout Hebrews 9 as a figure of speech known as a metonymy. It served as a linguistic symbol for life. It is through "blood" (Lane, 1991b, 246) or the extinguished life (= a sacrifice) of an animal or person whereby defilement can be purged and thereby

. . . a person had access to God (v. 7).
. . . a person's conscience was purged (v. 14).
. . . the new covenant was inaugurated (v. 18).
. . . people were consecrated (v. 19).
. . . the tabernacle and cultic utensils were purified (v. 21).
. . . everything under the cultic system was purified (v. 22).

9:8. The appearance of the English phrase "by this" (NRSV, ESV, NIV, NLT; anaphoric τοῦτο) referred back to verses 6–7. Barnabas elaborated on the repetitive cultic sacrifices with an appeal to the Holy Spirit. Unlike in Hebrews 3:7–11 where God's spirit spoke through a specific scriptural passage (Ps. 95:7–11), here God's spirit was "clarifying" (δηλοῦντος), "making clear" (NET), "signifying" (KJV, ASV, NASB), or "indicating" (NRSV, ESV) that the cultic priesthood and all priestly acts were unable to fulfill God's purpose (7:11; cf. Ellingworth, 1993, 437; Mitchell, 2007, 176). In fact, *actual* access to God "had *yet* to become known" (BDAG, s.v. "φανερόω" 2a, p. 1048) or "had not *yet* been disclosed" (cf. NASB, NRSV, NIV). So as long as any cultic sanctuary with its cultic rules and rituals remained, genuine access to God for all people was restricted to one person, the high priest (Attridge, 1989, 241; Mitchell, 2007, 176; Lane, 1991b, 223).

9:9. Barnabas built on (ἥτις, "which"; BDAG, s.v. "ὅστις" 3, p. 729) his thoughts about the "first tabernacle" (τῆς πρώτης σκηνῆς) by way of referring to the earthly sanctuary as an "illustration" (παραβολή; cf. NIV, NLT) or "symbol" (NASB, NRSV, ESV, NET). Some commentators suggest that the "illustration" or "symbol" was limited to the activities that occurred in the "inner sanctuary" (= Holy of Holies) of the tabernacle (v. 8a; Moffatt, 1968, 118; Lane, 1991, 2:224). Others suggest that it referred to both chambers of the tabernacle and ultimately the entire cultic system of worship (v. 8b; Buchanan, 1972, 145; Attridge, 1989, 241). The immediate and closest referent, "the first tent" (τῆς πρώτης σκηνῆς), favors the entire tabernacle as Barnabas's illustration (Michelle, 1989, 177). Ambiguities, however, continue with various English translations of the phrase "for the present time" (εἰς τὸν καιρὸν τὸν ἐνεστηκότα). Some interpretively render the phrase as "the time *then* present" (KJV, AV, NET), while others suggest that "the present time" (NASB, NRSV, NIV, NLT, CNT) must be *now*. Whereas the former draws attention to the "old age" whereby *symbolic* access to God was limited and therefore coming to an end (8:13; Lane, 1991b, 224), the latter idea referred to the "present age" (ESV) when Barnabas was *now* writing and free access to God had been achieved through Jesus, the royal high priest (4:14–16; 10:19–25; Bruce, 1990, 209). Yet, it seems the two interpretations overlap. Whereas the "old age" was coming to an end at the time of Barnabas's writing, the "new age" was already present. The new covenant had been inaugurated, but the old covenant was in the process of "growing obsolete" (8:13) (cf. Michelle, 1989, 177). Furthermore, the household family of faith had experienced, according to Koester (2001, 398), "the powers of the age to come" (6:5) but had not received their "inheritance in the world to come" (1:14; 2:5).

Even though the old covenant was in the process of "growing obsolete" (8:13), gifts and sacrifices were still being offered in Herod's temple. Unfortunately, "when" (καθ'; NET; cf. BDAG, s.v. "κατά" 2a, p. 512) they were offered in accordance to cultic rituals, they had little effect on a person's inward being, namely, the moral consciousness that distinguishes right and wrong (BDAG, s.v. "συνείδησις" 2, p. 967). "Conscience [συνειδότος], established in the soul like a judge," said Philo (*Opif.* 128), "is never abashed in administering reproofs, sometimes employing sharper threats, sometimes gentler admonitions; threats, where the wrongdoing appeared to be deliberate; admonitions, to guard against a like lapse in the future, when the misconduct seemed unintentional and the result of want of caution" (trans. Colson, et al.). Yet, the cultic offerings were unable to "perfect" (KJV, NASB, NRSV, ESV, NET), "cleanse" (NLT), or "clear" (NIV) the conscience. The imperfect state of the worshipper's conscience was never ever freed from guilt (BDAG, s.v. "τελειόω" 2eα, p. 996), no matter how many ritual sacrifices were performed.

TEXTUAL ANALYSIS: Conflicting Text Critical Reading: 9:10

Grammatical Issue: Moving beyond the manuscript evidence (𝔓[46] א* A I P 0278 33 81 104 1739 1881 2464), a scribe may have changed the text from a nominative "regulations" (δικαιώματα) to a dative (δικαιώμασιν) and inserted an article "and" (καί) because of the string of datives that presided: "food and drink and ceremonial baptisms" (βρώμασιν καὶ πόμασιν καὶ διαφόροις βαπτισμοῖς). The text is the preferred reading (Metzger, 1992, 598).

txt. "and various baptisms, **regulations** for the body imposed until the time comes to set things right" (καὶ διαφόροις βαπτισμοῖς, **δικαιώματα** σαρκὸς μέχρι καιροῦ διορθώσεως ἐπικείμενα) (cf. ESV, NASB, NET, NRSV)

var. "and various baptisms, **and regulations** for the body imposed until the time comes to set things right" (καὶ διαφόροις βαπτισμοῖς, **καὶ δικαιώμασιν** σαρκὸς μέχρι καιροῦ διορθώσεως ἐπικείμενα) (KJV, Geneva, Bishops)

9:10. Unlike the cultic regulations in 9:1 about an earthly worship facility, verse 10 stipulated *what* was to take place within that facility, namely, prescribed matters about food and purification. For instance, the first covenant food "regulations" or "legal statutes" *distinguished* what animals and which portions of the harvest were permitted for sacrifice: burnt offering (Lev. 1:3, 10, 14), grain offering (Lev. 2:1, 4–8, 11), peace offering (Lev. 3:1, 6), and votive and freewill offerings (Lev 22:17–27; 23:15–20; etc.). It also *defined* basic requirements for animal and harvest presentations to the Lord: burnt offering (Lev. 1:4–9, 11–13, 15–17), grain offering (Lev. 2:2, 9, 12–16; 6:14–15), peace offering (Lev. 3:2–5, 7–17; 7:11–14), and votive and freewill offerings (Lev. 22:28; 23:10–13; etc.). Finally, it *dictated* regulations for eating priestly stipends and for worshippers consuming their portions in the tabernacle/temple: priest's grain offering (Lev. 2:3, 10; 6:16–180), peace offering (Lev. 7:15, 28–36), priestly stipends (Lev. 22:1–16, 29–30), worshipper's offering (Lev. 7:22–27), and votive and freewill offerings (Lev. 22:29–30; etc.). Even a segment of the Essenes who resided at Qumran used the phrase "according to the regulation" or "usual regulations" to govern their discussions about the cycle of festivals throughout the year with their corresponding sacrifices (11Q19; cf. 17.15; 19.4; 20:0 [twice]; 20.9; 21:0; 22.10; 23.5; 25.6, 15; 27.3; 28.5, 8).

Old Testament Feasts and Celebrations in Hebrews (Bateman, 2012, 82)

Feast	When	Regulations	Description	Hebrews
Sabbath (and Jubilee)	Every 7th day of the week	Exod. 23:10–12; Lev. 23:3	Patterned after God's six days of creation, all work stops on the seventh day of the week.	4:3–4
Passover	March/April	Exod. 12:1–20; Lev. 23:5; Num. 28:16	People celebrate the nation's escape from Egypt under the leadership of Moses.	11:28
Feast of Unleavened Bread	The week following Passover	Exod. 23:15; Lev. 23:6–8; Num. 28:17	For seven days, people eat bread without leaven as a reminder of women who had no time to let bread rise when they left Egypt.	not cited
Firstfruits	April	Exod. 23:16a; Lev. 23:9–14; Num. 28:26	Once the harvest season begins people are to bring the firstfruits of harvest to the priest.	not cited
Feast of Weeks (Pentecost)	June Fifty days after Passover	Exod. 23:16b; Lev. 23:15–21	At the end of the grain harvest, people bring their offerings to God as a reminder that God provides.	not cited
Feast of Trumpets	Sept/Oct 1st day of the month	Lev. 23:23–25; Num. 29:1–2	On the first day of the month of the New Year festival, a blast of trumpets sounded to mark the start.	not cited
Day of Atonement	Sept/Oct 10th day of the month	Lev. 16:1–34; Num. 29:7–11	The entire nation fasts, confesses their sin, and ask God's forgiveness.	9:7, 25
Feast of Tabernacles (Shelters)	Sept/Oct 15th day of the month	Lev. 23:33–43; Num. 29:12–40	For seven days, after arriving in Jerusalem, people build shelters of branches, as a reminder of desert living during the exodus.	not cited

Consequently, the tabernacle "regulations" that were carried over to Herod's temple were recognized as imposed externals for outward ritual purity until the new order came (Holmén, 2001, 275–86). The gifts and sacrifices offered in the tabernacle or Herod's temple did not rid the worshipper of a "guilty conscience" (τελειόω, "perfect"; v. 9). Unlike many of his Jewish contemporaries, Barnabas recognized that a new order had come through Jesus, the regal high priest according to the order of Melchizedek (7:11–12; 8:6, 13; 9:11, 15; Holmén, 2001, 328–43). Nevertheless, God had these old regulations "imposed" (ἐπίκειμαι) on his chosen people until a time of "reformation" (KJV, NASB, ESV) or "redemption" (NRSV, NIV, NLT, CNT), or until "the new order" came (NET; cf. BDAG, s.v. "διορθώσις," p. 251). So, the earthly tabernacle with its outer and inner chambers and their respective furnishings served as the place where earthly priests officiated cultic rituals until God shifted his paradigm: the old covenant for a new one.

The Arrival of Jesus into God's Presence (9:11–14)

The arrival of Jesus in heaven began with his entrance into God's presence and the presentation of himself as an efficacious offering that guaranteed the purging of a person's guilty conscience.

> *TEXTUAL ANALYSIS:* Conflicting Text Critical Reading: 9:11
> Theological Issue: Manuscript support exists for both readings: text (𝔓[46] B D* 1611 1739 2005) and variant (א A K L P 0142 0278 33 1881). Yet, it appears a scribe may have adjusted the text so that "things to come" (τῶν μελλόντων) in 9:11 would agree with "things to come" (τῶν μελλόντων) in 10:1. The text is the preferred reading (cf. Lane, 1991b, 229; Metzger, 1994, 598).
>
> *txt.* "a high priest of the good things **that have come**" (ἀρχιερεὺς τῶν **γενομένων** ἀγαθῶν) (ESV, NIV, NRSV)
>
> *var.* "a high priest of the good things **to come**" (ἀρχιερεὺς **τῶν μελλόντων** ἀγαθῶν) (ASV, KJV, NET, NASB)

9:11. Barnabas described the arrival of Jesus in heaven as God's appointed high priest (cf. 5:5) with two rather long Greek sentences (vv. 11–12 and vv. 13–14). The first contrasted (δέ, "but") the previously mentioned unenlightened period referred to as the "old age" during which time the earthly tabernacle and Herod's temple was in operation (vv. 1–10; esp. v. 10). Although some translations emphasize a temporal coming "when Christ appeared" (NRSV, ESV, NIV), the real thrust was the current reality of Jesus serving as regal high priest in God's presence. After Jesus arrived in heaven, "he entered" (εἰσῆλθεν) the greater, more perfect "heavenly tabernacle" (= God's residential presence) not made with hands whereby "Christ has now become" (NLT; cf. NET, ASV) God's royal high priest (cf. 1:3d, 5–13; 5:5) whereby he provided "the good things that have come," namely, eternal redemption (vv. 12, 15), purification of conscience (v. 22), a promise of eternal inheritance (v. 15), forgiveness of sins (v. 22), and deliverance (v. 28).

9:12. Barnabas continued (ellipsis: εἰσῆλθε) his contrast between "the tabernacles" with an observation about the earthly high priest and Jesus as the eternal high priest: "He [Jesus] did not *enter* by means of" (οὐδὲ [*εἰσῆλθε*] δι'; BDAG, s.v. "διά" 3a, p. 224; Spicq, 1952, 2:256) the blood of animals (9:12a). The earthly high priest practiced an old form of cultic service. In contrast to earthly high priests, Jesus entered God's residential presence (= heavenly tabernacle) "by means of" (διά) his own "blood" (9:12b). "Blood" (αἷμα) served as a double metonymy for both the physical death of Jesus and his atoning sacrifice (cf. 10:19; 12:24; 13:12). His physical death was a new sort of atoning self-sacrifice. Furthermore, in contrast to earthly high priests who entered yearly into God's symbolic presence, namely, the Holy of Holies yearly until he died, Jesus entered God's presence (= heavenly tabernacle) with his self-sacrifice executed only "once" and then remained in God's presence (9:12c). So, Jesus did not enter a human-made tabernacle with an animal blood sacrifice that needed to be repeated yearly. Jesus appeared before God and presented himself as a resurrected living sacrifice whom God then exalted (cf. 1:3c; 5–14; 5:5–10; 7:14–26).

> *TEXTUAL ANALYSIS:* Conflicting Text Critical Reading: 9:14
> Stylistic/Exegetical Issue: Manuscript support exists for both readings: text (A D* K P 365 1739*) and variant (א 0278 33 81 1881). The use of direct address seems equally mixed in the hortatory sections (cf. 3:7–19; 10:32–36 with 2:1–4;

4:1–14; as well as 5:11–6:12; 12:25–29), though most commentators prefer the text (cf. Lane, 1991b, 230; Metzger, 1994, 599).

txt. "**our** conscience" (τὴν συνείδησιν **ἡμῶν**) (ESV, NET, NIV, NASV)

var. "**your** conscience" (τὴν συνείδησιν **ὑμῶν**) (ASV, KJV, NASB)

9:13. In his second long sentence in the Greek, introduced with "for if" (εἰ γάρ), Barnabas moved from a lesser to greater argument (*qal wahomer*) to underscore the guarantee of Jesus's offering. Barnabas began a logical "for if" argument about cultic sacrifices and their inefficiency with an assumption (εἰ, "if"; first class condition). For the sake of his argument, he assumed sacrifices (= "blood") of goats, bulls, and the ashes of a heifer were sufficient for the "cleansing of the flesh" (τῆς σαρκὸς καθαρότητα). He adopted the cultic presumption that by way of an animal sacrifice, a person's "physical body" (BDAG, s.v. "σάρξ" 2a, p. 915) was "ritually cleansed" or purified (BDAG, s.v. "καθαρότης," p. 490). While a "bull" was not often used for sacrifice in the Pentateuch, they appeared in later Jewish practices (Judg. 6:25; Isa. 1:11; 1 Esdr 7:7; Philo, *Fug.*, 186; cf. Koester, 2001, 4:10). Similarly, the ashes of a heifer were typically limited to purify a person defiled by touching a corpse (Num. 19:9; Josephus, *A.J.* 4.4.6 §§78–81). However, by the time Barnabas wrote, purity laws were expanded whereby heifer ashes were used to purify more than a person, particularly at Qumran (11Q19 49.5–6; Philo, *Leg.* 262, 267–72; cf. Harrington, 2001, 726).

9:14. Barnabas then drew a logical but heightened conclusion about the atoning sacrifice (= "blood") of Jesus (v. 14). Barnabas asked, "how much more" (πόσῳ μᾶλλον) effective would be the atoning self-sacrificing death of Jesus? Jesus "offered himself" (ἑαυτὸν προσήνεγκεν) *like* a sacrificial gift without any defects to God (BDAG, s.v. "προσφέρω" 2a, p. 886). This offering was accomplished "by means of" (διά) "the eternal spirit" (πνεύματος αἰωνίου). While commentators tend to render "spirit" as the "Holy Spirit" (Lane, 1991b, 240; Koester, 2001, 410; Cockerill, 2012, 398), the word "spirit" (πνεύματος) typically referred to God's spirit in Philo, Josephus, and the Essenes who lived at Qumran. Granted, even though some may suggest that "the eternal spirit" was Jesus's own spirit (Johnson, 2006, 238), for Barnabas and his Jewish contemporaries, "spirit" merely referenced God's eternal spirit (Bateman, 2012, 113–14). So, Jesus's self-sacrificial offering was effective by means of God's eternal spirit. Jesus's self-sacrifice (= "blood"), offered once, guaranteed the cleansing of one's "conscience," namely, the moral consciousness that distinguishes right and wrong (BDAG, s.v. "συνείδησις" 2, p. 967; cf. 9:9 discussion) concerning relationships with God and neighbor (Mark 12:30–31).

The Mediation of Jesus as High Priest (9:15–28)

God's intention for Jesus's mediation of the new covenant was so that people might receive an inheritance established by means of the new covenant in fulfillment of God's requirements for Jesus's service as royal high priest in God's presence.

9:15. Building upon Hebrews 8:6 where Jesus was presented as God's royal high priest who was the mediator of a new covenant, here Barnabas underscored (καί διὰ τοῦτο, "and for this reason") his lesser to greater argument (*qal wahomer*) of verses 11–14 (cf. 1 Tim. 2:5–6). Jesus, God's royal high priest whose self-sacrificing death provided inner cleansing and the causal connection for Jesus as the mediator of the new covenant, is a more effective high priest.

For Barnabas, God's intention (ὅπως, "in order that"; BDAG, s.v. "ὅπως" 2, p. 718) for Jesus serving as mediator of the new covenant was in order that those "who are called" (οἱ κεκλημένοι) might receive "the eternal inheritance" (τῆς αἰωνίου κληρονομίας) as God "promised" (τὴν ἐπαγγελίαν). This theme of a promised inheritance was a resumption of Hebrews 4:1 whereby Barnabas spoke of a yet-to-be-realized "promise" (ἐπαγγελία). Unlike Hebrews 4:1, however, the promise was not as narrowly focused. Here Barnabas spoke more broadly of the household family of faith's "eternal inheritance" (τῆς αἰωνίου κληρονομίας). People who had been invited (οἱ κεκλημένοι, "who are called")—those who were partners of the heavenly calling (3:1)—would not only enter the heavenly place-of-rest where Sabbath celebration occurred in God's residential presence (4:1–11), but they would be entitled to much more. Later, when Barnabas once again resumed the theme of a promised inheritance, "the eternal inheritance" (τῆς αἰωνίου κληρονομίας) included an entrance into the eternal city (11:9–10, 13–16; 12:22–24), which was promised to Abraham (even though he did not know of Jesus) as a gift for all those who faithfully persevered in Jesus. Hence, people within the household family of faith who persevered were the realized heirs of Abraham (6:13–20; cf. Rom. 4:13–25).

Portraits of the Holy Spirit in Hebrews Compared with Portraits in Qumran Literature
(Bateman, 2012, 113–14)

Examples	Qumran Reference	Qumran Text	Parallel in Hebrews
God speaks through his spirit.	I Q28 VIII, 16 4Q266 II, 12 4Q258 VI, 8 1Q34 bis II, 7	. . . and by what the prophets have revealed by His holy spirit. No man belonging to the Covenant of the . . . . . . with their descendants. He taught them through those anointed by the holy spirit, the seers of truth. from age to age, and as the prophets have revealed by His holy spirit. And no man from men of the covenant Community who removes from any commandment . . . . Your holy spirit, by the works of Your hands and the writing of Your right hand, in order to declare to them the foundations of glory, and the eternal works . . .	Hebrews 3:7–11 10:15–17
God guides or encourages through his spirit.	1QH[a] IV, 38 1QH[a] VIII, 25 1QH[a] XVII, 32	I give thanks to You, O Lord, [for] You have spread Your holy spirit over Your servant [. . .] his heart . . . . . . encouraging myself by Your holy spirit, clinging to the truth of Your covenant serving You in truth and a perfect heart, and loving Your holy name. With a sure truth You have supported me, and by Your holy spirit You have delighted me; even until this day	Hebrews 3:7–11 9:8

Portraits of the Holy Spirit in Hebrews Compared with Portraits in Qumran Literature (Bateman, 2012, 113–14)			
Examples	**Qumran Reference**	**Qumran Text**	**Parallel in Hebrews**
God indwells or anoints through his spirit.	CD II, 12 4Q504 1–2 V, 15 4Q287 X, 13 4Q266 2 II, 12	. . . the surface of the earth with their descendants. He taught them through those anointed by the holy spirit, the seers of . . . Indeed, You have poured out Your holy spirit upon us, [. . .] against the anointed of [His] hol[y] spirit [. . . .] with [their] descendants. He taught them through those anointed by the holy spirit, the seers of truth.	Hebrews 1:1 2:4
God empowers through his spirit.	4Q444 I, 1	And I am among those who fear God, who opens his mouth aided by His veritable knowledge, and [. . .] empowered by His holy spirit. [. . .]	Hebrews 2:4
God illuminates through his spirit.	CD–A 2:12 1QH[a] 6:24 1QH[a] XX, 11–12 4Q427 2–3 II, 13 4Q266 II, 12	the surface of the earth with their descendants. He taught them through those anointed by the holy spirit, the seers of that by Your favor for m[an . . .] Your holy spirit, and thus . . . You bring me to Your understanding. As which You gave me, and I have listened faithfully to Your wondrous counsel by Your holy spirit. by Your holy spirit. (1QHab 20:16) You have opened within me knowledge in the mystery of Your insight, and a spring of Your strength and your . . . (1QHa 20:17). . . . with their descendants. He taught them through those anointed by the holy spirit, the seers of truth.	Hebrews 9:8 10:15–17
God saves or sanctifies through his spirit.	1QH[a] VIII, 20 1QH[a] XXIII, 13 4Q255 II, 1	Your mercy with Your servant forever, to cleanse me by Your holy spirit, and to bring me near by Your grace according to Your great mercy [. . .] in [. . .] [. . .] Your holy spirit You have spread out, atoning for guilt . . . . . . (1Q28 3:7) . . . and so be joined to His truth by His holy spirit purified from all]	Hebrews 9:14

As it turned out (γενομένου, "since"; BDAG, s.v. "γίνομαι" 4a, p. 197), those who were called had already received the eternal inheritance of promise due to Jesus's self-sacrificial death that "set them free" (ἀπολύτρωσις). Although rare, the noun "set free" had a consistent meaning of "setting free for a ransom" as it pertained to one's literal freedom from some sort of captivity or enslavement (BDAG s.v. "ἀπολύτρωσις" 2a, p. 117). For instance, captors exacted a ransom fee for the freedom of an individual (Plutarch, *Pomp.* 24; cf. Plato, *Leg.* 919a), or a king counted the cost of "setting free" a group of slaves, either of which could have been captured in war and later sold into slavery (Josephus, *A.J.* 12.2.3 §27). Here, however, the term "redeemed" (cf. KJV, RSV, NASB, ESV, NRSV) or "set free" (NET, NLT, NIV) spoke of "violations" or "sin" committed under the first covenant. Sin was perceived as a personified jailkeeper who kept people in need of liberation (cf. Rom. 3:24; 6:16). Thus, the idea of "cancellation" or "remission" of sin portrayed a person being set free from sin's captivity, namely, a captivity that could not be expiated completely under the first covenant (10:1–3, 11; cf. Col. 1:14; Eph. 1:7). Unlike the previous covenant that regulated priests and their performance of external rites for ritual purity day after day (9:13; 10:1–3, 11), the effectiveness of Jesus's self-sacrificing death guaranteed the effectiveness of God's new covenant that was introduced in Jeremiah 31:31–34. Thus, Jesus was the mediator of the new covenant because God had declared that Jesus's self-sacrifice was more effective than any animal sacrifice offered during the previous era under the Mosaic law (= "first covenant").

9:16–17. Barnabas then moved to clarify (γάρ, "for") this inheritance for God's people. The noun (διαθήκη) was not translated as "covenant" as it was in Hebrews 8:6. Here in Hebrews 9:17, as it was in nearly all secular Greek, "covenant" (διαθήκη) meant a person's last will and testament and thus justifiably translated "testament" (KJV) or "will" (RSV, NASV, NIV, ESV, NET, NLT). Josephus used the term to speak of Herod the Great's various last wills and testaments concerning his successors, wills that were eventually mediated by Caesar Augustus (*A.J.* 17.3.2. §53; 17.6.1 §146; 17.8.1–2 §§188–95; cf. BDAG, s.v. "διαθήκη" 1, p. 228).

Barnabas expanded (γάρ, "for") this connection to "a last will and testament" with a specific application about the new covenant. Sweetnam (1965, 389) rightly observes that the noun "covenant" (διαθήκη) "attains the perfection of a last will and testament in which the death of the testator results unequivocally in the bestowal of goods on the legatee."[1] Just as it was the case with a person's last will and testament, so it was with the new covenant. A will or testament meant little until the testator died, at which point the will or testament became "legally binding" or "legally sure" (βεβαία). As it was the case in 2:2 concerning the Mosaic law and in 6:19 concerning God's promise to Abraham, the term "legally binding" (βεβαία) continued to stress the judicial validity of God's new covenant. However, the new covenant when revealed by Jeremiah, remained a dormant "will" of promise "since" (ἐπεί) it was unable to provide an inheritance to beneficiaries without the death of the executor of the will and testament. It had "no force" (μήποτε ἰσχύει; BDAG, s.v. "ἰσχύω" 4, p. 484). The sacrificial death (= "blood") of Jesus activated the legatee's promise of inheritance (9:24–28; 10:10–18; cf. 2 Peter 1:17–19). Barnabas conflated Jeremiah's new covenant of promise with the concept of a last will and testament.

9:18. Barnabas drew his discussion about the new covenant to a conclusion (ὅθεν, "therefore") with a historical recounting about the inauguration of the "first [*covenant*]" (ἡ πρώτη [*διαθήκη*]). The insertion of "covenant"

1 J. Sweetnam, "Suggested Interpretations of Hebrews 9:15–18," *Catholic Biblical Quarterly* 27 [1965]:373–90.

(διαθήκη) by translators is once again a contextual assumption in that the noun "covenant" did not appear in the Greek text (NET, NASB, NRSV, NIV, ESV etc.; cf. 8:7, 9:1). Nevertheless, God's first covenant with his people was "dedicated" (KJV, ASV; Koester, 2001, 418), "put into effect" (NIV, NLT), "ratified" (CNT), or "inaugurated" (ἐγκεκαίνισται; NET, NASB, NASV) with an animal sacrifice (= "blood"). The reason for the various English renderings is because the verb occurs only in Hebrews (9:18; 10:20). Unfortunately, the Septuagint adds to its ambiguity. On the one hand, the verb could signify "to give newness to something," and thereby translated "renew" the kingdom (1 Sam. 11:14 [1 Kgdm. 11:14]), the temple (2 Chron. 15:8; 1 Macc 4:36, 54, 57; 5:1), or people (Ps. 50:12 [51:10]; Isa. 41:1). On the other hand, it could denote "the beginning of something" implying that something new was being "ratified" *like* a written agreement or "dedicated" *like* a temple (Deut. 20:5; 3 Kgdm. [1 Kings] 8:63; 2 Chron. 7:5; BDAG, s.v. "ἐγκαινίζω" 2, p. 272). Here in Hebrews 9:18, it referred to the "ratification" (Lane, 1991b, 243) or "inauguration" (Ellingworth, 1993, 466; Mitchell, 2007, 189) of God's written agreement with the wilderness generation.

TEXTUAL ANALYSIS: Conflicting Text Critical Reading: 9:19

Exegetical Issue: Manuscript support exists for both readings: text (A C D P) and variant (𝔓[46] K L 044 0278 81 1241 1505 1739 1881). Yet, the variant manuscript evidence is more strongly attested. Thus, it seems the shorter variant reading would have been expanded to conform to Exodus 24:5. The variant is the preferred reading (Lane, 1991b, 232).

txt. "the blood of calves **and goats**" (τὸ αἷμα τῶν μόσχων [**καὶ τῶν τράγων**]) (ASV, ESV, KJV, NASB, NET, NRSV)

var. "the blood of calves" (τὸ αἷμα τῶν μόσχων) (NIV)

9:19–20. In yet another long Greek sentence (vv. 19–20), Barnabas explained (γάρ, "for") the procedure for the new covenant's ratification. He recounted the sequence of events about the Mosaic covenant, but with a degree of historical license or "freedom" (cf. Moffatt, 1979, 129; Cockerill, 2012, 408). He began in verses 19–20 with Moses's encounter with God on Mount Sinai (cf. Exod. 24:1–3). After Moses disclosed God's covenant to the wilderness generation, "he took" (λαβών) animal blood (cf. Exod. 24:5), "sprinkled" (ἐράντισεν) the blood on the tablets and the people (cf. Exod. 24:6–8a), and made a pronouncement (λέγων): "This is the blood of the covenant that God has commanded you to keep" (cf. Exod. 24:8b). While it is true that the tabernacle had not been built when the Mosaic covenant was ratified (Koester, 2001, 420), Barnabas conflated the historical information (Mitchel, 2007, 196). As he did regarding the tabernacle and Herod's temple (cf. 8:2) and the ritual sacrifices of priests and high priests of the past (cf. 9:6–6), here he conflated the ratification of the Mosaic covenant with the dedication of the earthly tabernacle as though both were activated with an animal sacrifice (= "blood").

9:21. Barnabas continued his recollection about the beginning of the first covenant with a somewhat loose connection (καὶ ... ὁμοίως, "and . . . similarly") whereby an all-encompassing form of purification was extended to the tabernacle utensils such as the bronze pots, shovels, bowls for tossing blood, meat hooks, and firepans (Exod. 27:3) as well as the gold plates, ladles, pitchers, and bowls for pouring out blood (Exod. 37:16). And while Barnabas excluded the initial inauguration of the tabernacle and cultic utensils from his recounting of the Exodus 24 inauguration of the Mosaic covenant (Attridge, 1989, 258), Koester (2001, 420) contends it was echoed in other independent sources, such as Josephus (cf. Josephus, *A.J.* 3 §§206–06). Regardless, the point made by Barnabas was that things were purified with animal blood.

9:22. Regardless of Barnabas's liberties taken about the initial historical events surrounding the tabernacle's dedication, it was clear to Barnabas for the household family of faith that God had established a pattern of purification that involved the extinguishing of a life (= "blood," v. 22). But then Barnabas added (δέ, "and") this statement: without the taking of a life, there is no "forgiveness" (ἄφεσις). "Forgiveness" had multiple shades of meaning. On the one hand, it referred to the act of "liberating" Israelites from slavery (Lev. 25:10, 41; Jer. 41[34]:8, 15, 17; cf. Polybius, *Hist.* 1.79.12; 1 Macc 10:34; Josephus, *A.J.* 17.7.1 §185), the "release" or "return" of *property* held for debt (translated "Jublilee": Lev. 25:13, 28, 31, 33), and the "release," "remittance," or "discharge" of a *debt* (Deut. 15:1–2; 31:10). For instance, Demosthenes (*C. Andr.* 33.3) spoke of "a release and discharge from all the [*financial*] obligations exiting between us" (trans. Spicq, TLNT; emphasis added). On the other hand, it was at times employed in secular Greek to speak of the "forgiveness" of an offense (cf. Philo, *Her.* 6.30), "acquit" (Plato, *Leg.* 9.869; Josephus, *A.J.* 14.9.5 §182, *B.J.* 1.9.9 §214), or "pardon" (Josephus, *B.J.* 1.24.4 §481). Philo employed the term to speak of the "liberation" of one's soul (*Her.* 55:273) and "remission" of sins (*Mos.* 2:147; *Spec. 1,2,3,4.* 1:190, 215) in a manner similar to the NT (cf. Matt. 26:28; Mark 1:4; Luke 3:3, 12:47; Acts 5:31, 10:43, 13:38, 26:18; Col. 1:14; cf. Luke 1:77; Acts 2:38; Eph. 1:7; Heb. 10:18). Here in Hebrews 9:22, God forgave sins due to the self-sacrificial death (= "blood") *of Jesus* (*TDNT,* 1:509–12; *EDNT,* 1:181–83).

9:23. In yet another contrastive parallelism (μέν . . . δέ), Barnabas elaborated (οὖν, "indeed") on his discussion in verses 19–22. "On the one hand" (μέν), purification of the earthly tabernacle (e.g., book, people, tabernacle, utensils, etc.) with an animal sacrifice was "a necessity" (BDAG s.v. "ἀνάγκη" 1, p. 60). Naturally, the need for "a ritual purification" (BDAG, s.v. "καθαρίζω" 3bα, p. 488) or cleansing was necessary due to the sinful people who serviced and worshipped in Israel's earthly tabernacle (cf. 8:3). While the tabernacle and its paraphernalia were considered "copies" (ASV, NASB, NIV, ESV, NLT, CNT), "sketches" (NET, NRSV), or "patterns" (KJV) in our English translations, verse 9 would seem to suggest that "symbol" might be a better rendering (BDAG, s.v. "ὑπόδειγμα" 2, p. 1037).

"On the other hand" (δέ), purification of "the heavenly tabernacle" (= God's residential presence) required a sacrifice that was of "a higher status" or "more prominent" (BDAG, s.v. "κρείττω" 1, p. 566) than a mere animal sacrifice. While translations say "better sacrifice," the subsequent contrast (δέ, "on the other hand") between sancturaries warrants the idea of "a more prominent sacrifice," namely, a sacrifice of something higher on the food chain. Nevertheless, this contrastive parallelism (μέν . . . δέ; "on the one hand . . . on the other hand") is somewhat odd in that it insinuated that the "heavenly tabernacle" (= God's residence) was in need of "purification." Naturally, commentators have offered several suggestions as to what Barnabas meant here. Moffatt (1979, 131–32) suggests that heaven itself was in need of purification. Since sin affected all of creation (Rom. 8:19–22), there was a belief in a cosmic reality of sin (= "rebellion") in need of a purging event. Enoch's recollection of angelic sin (1 En. 6:1–4a; 7:1–6) and the Essenes who resided at Qumran believed in cosmic conflict between good and bad angels (4QM), which would appear to support Moffatt. Lane (1991b, 247) more pointedly says, "Sin as defilement is infectious" (cf. 1 Cor. 5:6–7; Koester, 2001, 427). Bruce (1990, 228), however, suggests that Barnabas was speaking of the spiritual household family of faith's consciences that were in need of a more prominent sacrifice (v. 14). Similarly, the ideal realities of the metaphorical symbols (i.e., tabernacle and Herod's temple) were part of the spiritual order in need of purification in order to approach and enter into God's presence (cf. Attridge, 1989, 262). Ellingworth (1993, 477) suggests that it was merely an "inaugural rite" (9:18, 28; 10:1; cf. Mitchell, 2007, 194). Just as the first covenant was activated with a sacrifice (e.g., of an animal), so too was the new covenant activated with a sacrifice (i.e., of Jesus). Due to Barnabas's conflation of material in verse 22, it seems more than likely that the parallelism was a combination of the need of the purification for cosmic sin by a blood sacrifice as well as a blood sacrifice that ratified the two covenants.

9:24. In yet another rather long Greek sentence, Barnabas developed (γάρ, "for") the need for "a more prominent" sacrifice mentioned in verse 23 (Ellingworth, 1993, 480; Cockerill, 2012, 417). Barnabas reiterated his discussion about "the true sanctuary" in which Jesus "appeared" (εἰσῆλθεν), namely, the place where God dwelt. Barnabas once again spoke of the "true sanctuary" as one not made with hands (cf. v. 11; "perfect tent") to reinforce what the "true sanctuary" or the "perfect tent" was not (NET renderings). It was not a symbolic replica. The earthly tabernacle was a mere "representation" (NET), "pattern" (ASV), or more commonly rendered a "copy" (NASB, NASV, ESV, NIV, NLT, CNT) of God's heavenly residence where he was honored and adored (cf. BDAG, s.v. "ἀντίτυπος" 2, p. 91). Barnabas then contrasted (ἀλλ', "but") the earthly tabernacle with the "true sanctuary." Unlike the earthly tabernacle where high priests offered sacrifices before a cloud symbolizing God's presence, Barnabas presented Jesus as one who "*now* appears" (*νῦν* ἐμφανισθῆναι) before God in his heavenly residence on behalf of the Jewish household family of faith. He described Jesus to be in the actual place where God dwelt (1:3d, 13; 8:1; cf. 10:12) and where God's Sabbath celebration took place (4:9–11).

Various Descriptions of the Tabernacle

Barnabas described the earthly tabernacle in various ways in Hebrews. In 8:5, it was a "sketch *that is a* shadow" (ὑπόδειγμα σκιά). In 9:9, it was an "illustration" or "symbol" (παραβολή). In 9:23, it was a "representation" or "copy" (ὑπόδειγμα). In 9:24, it was a "representation" (ἀντίτυπος). Despite the variety of terms, the point is this: the earthly tabernacle implied a resemblance of a heavenly reality, a physical counterpart where God symbolically dwelt (cf. Exod. 40:34–38; Lev. 16:2).

9:25. Barnabas continued (οὐδ' ἵνα, "and not"; NET, NLT; BDAG, s.v. "οὐδέ" 1, p. 723) his contrast between mere symbols and reality in verse 25. To begin with, Jesus did not "offer himself" (προσφέρῃ ἑαυτόν) to God "again and again" (NET, NRSV, NIV, NLT, CNT) or "often" (KJV, NASB; BDAG, s.v. "πολλάκις," p. 846). This reality offered a threefold contrast to that of the old era: (1) Jesus did not offer multiple offerings (πολλάκις, "many times") like previous high priests; (2) Jesus did not enter God's symbolic presence yearly (κατ' ἐνιαυτόν, "every year") like previous high priests (cf. 8:7); and (3) Jesus did not offer animal sacrifices (ἐν αἵματι ἀλλοτρίῳ, "with blood not his own") like previous high priests but offered himself (cf. 9:12).

9:26. Barnabas closed his extremely long Greek sentence with the reason (ἐπεί, "for"; BDAG, s.v. "ἐπεί" 2, p. 360) for the differences listed in verse 26. If Jesus was like other high priests (cf. 5:1–4), "it would be necessary" (ἔδει) to experience multiple sufferings (πολλάκις παθεῖν, "to suffer many times"). This suffering was not a general form of suffering, but rather a specific reference to Jesus's death by crucifixion (BDAG, s.v. "πάσκω" 3aα, p. 785). If the repetition of his physical death was a necessity, Jesus would have had to die over and over again from the very beginning of creation (cf. Cockerill, 2012, 422; Guthrie, 1998, 316). In an emphatic contrast (νυνὶ δέ, "but now"), Barnabas described

Jesus as appearing "once *for all*" (ἅπαξ). As in Hebrews 6:4, "once" underscored an unrepeatable event. Yet, Barnabas's use here of "once" emphasized a theological feature that was totally unique: the life Jesus lived was exclusively special. So, English translations underscore this matchless event with "once *for all*" (RSV, NRSV, NIV, ESV, NET). Barnabas punctuated the distinctive life of Jesus with a proverbial wisdom statement: people were "appointed to die once" (9:27). In the meantime, another exclusive aspect of his life was that Jesus ended a past era (ἐπὶ συντελείᾳ τῶν αἰώνων, "at the end of the ages"), reminiscent to "in these last days" that opened Hebrews (1:2). It was his self-sacrifice that brought closure to the Mosaic era of ritual cultic practices (8:13).

9:27. Barnabas continued (καί, "and") his reason with a parenthetical comparison (καθ' ὅσον, "just as") to punctuate Jesus's death. Barnabas appealed to a "post-mortem judgement that was, in traditional Greek mythology, the fate of the soul" (Attridge, 1989, 265; cf. Plato, *Rep*. 10.614b–621D). So, death was considered an ordained reality for all people even among Jewish authors: "Will you not reflect that if you disobey there is nothing in store for you but death with torments?" (4 Macc 8:11 [trans. Anderson]; Eccles. 3:2). For Barnabas, however, the emphasis was not that people died, but that people would be judged (μετὰ δὲ τοῦτο κρίσις, "and after that judgment").

9:28. Barnabas continued (οὕτως καί, "so also") his emphasis with a text from Scripture (HB LXX): "Christ was offered once *to bear the sins of many*" (Isa. 53:12). The scriptural allusion came from Isaiah's fourth servant song (52:13–53:12) where Isaiah defined the ultimate rejection of the suffering servant. The word "to bear" (ἀνενεγκεῖν; cf. KJV, NASB, RSV, NIV, ESV, NET) or "to take away" (NIV, NLT) appears twice in Hebrews. As it did in Hebrews 7:18 where it was rendered "set aside" (NET; BDAG, s.v. "ἀναφέρω" 4, p. 75), here too Barnabas stressed the judicial and official sense of the word. It was a strong expression that spoke to the legal removal or cancellation of human wrongdoing (= "sin") through the sacrificial death of Jesus, who had been presented clearly in Hebrews to be a royal-priest (cf. 1:3d; 5:5). The removal of sin was efficacious "of many" (πολλῶν) people, as is evident in Hebrews 10:12–14. Thus, the life Jesus lived was both exclusive and effective in that at the end of his human existence, many people could profit from it.

Isaiah's Suffering Servant[2]

Isaiah referred to exiled Israel as Yahweh's servant several times in chapters 40–55. Yet, despite Israel's special position as the Lord's servant, they were blind and deaf and failed to understand the Lord's purposes (42:19). Despite their sin, the Lord remained committed to them (44:21–22). There was, however, another servant in these chapters who, though addressed as "Israel" (49:3), was distinct from the sinful, exiled nation. His ministry was described in the four "servant songs" (42:1–7; 49:1–13; 50:4–11; 52:13–53:12). This "Israel" would deliver exiled Israel from bondage (49:5; cf. vv. 8–13) and would carry out God's ideal for Israel by bringing God's salvation to the nations (49:6). This ideal Israel would mediate a covenant on behalf of both Israel (cf. 49:8) and the nations (42:1–7). He would do this by bearing the sins of "the many," which included

2 R. Chisholm, "How to Read Isaiah's Servant Songs" in *Isaiah: How to Read, Understand, and Interpret the Prophet*, by R. Chisholm and H. W. Bateman IV (Leesburg, IN: Cyber-Center for Biblical Studies, 2016), 27; also "Let's Know the Bible" conference, available on YouTube at https://www.youtube.com/watch?v=wW4JqedtSUM&feature=youtu.be. For further reading, D. L. Bock and M. Glaser, *The Gospel according to Isaiah 53: Encountering the Suffering Servant in Jewish and Christian Theology* (Grand Rapids: Kregel, 2012).

both Israel and the nations (52:13—53:12). Though he would suffer the judgment of God on behalf of "the many" (53:4–6, 10–12; cf. 49:7; 50:10), the Lord would eventually reward him by elevating him to kingship over the nations (52:13–15; 53:11–12; cf. 49:7).

Some expectations of the Messiah (Greek: the Christ) involved his bringing an end to sin. "And he himself [will be] free from sin, [in order] to rule a great people," and "he will lead them all in holiness" (Pss. Sol. 17:36, 41). With the removal of sin, Christ Jesus was able to rule and lead a holy people. He was to wait, however, for that time when God would fully consummate his ruling authority over a truly holy people (1:13; 10:13).

Unlike people who were appointed to die, Jesus was appointed to die for the sins of many people and then return for those people who eagerly await his return. Jesus fulfilled the requirement of a better sacrifice because the heavenly tabernacle was not a symbolic replica but rather an undefiled heavenly residence where God actually dwelt and where Jesus now served due to his single and eternally effective sacrifice for sin.

THEOLOGICAL FOCUS

The exegetical idea (in contrast to the cultic regulations for the earthly tabernacle and the ineffectiveness of cultic rituals, the arrival of Jesus as God's regal high priest and his entrance into God's heavenly presence guaranteed an efficacious cleansing of a person's conscience, and as God's mediator of a new covenant, Jesus intended to establish an inheritance for the Jewish household family of faith) leads to this theological focus: With Jesus as the mediator of God's new covenant, members of the household family of faith have a royal high priest whose self-sacrifice makes it possible to purge a person's conscience of guilt as well as experience God's promised inheritance.

The major theological themes in this preaching unit are threefold. The first is that God keeps his promise about the new covenant (vv. 15–16; cf. 8:6; 10:20). The second is the presentation of Jesus as the mediator of God's new covenant (vv. 15, 24b). The third is the effectiveness of Jesus's sacrifice, able to cleanse a person's conscience of guilt (v. 14; cf. 10:2, 17–18). His sacrifice was done once (vv. 12, 26, 28; cf. 7:27; 10:10).

PREACHING AND TEACHING STRATEGIES

Exegetical and Theological Synthesis

This passage begins with an explanation of the earthly tabernacle in 9:1–10. However, the explanation is truncated, seemingly because the listener would have already had a grasp on the details of the tabernacle (v. 5). The point of discussing the tabernacle is to illustrate that in reality what they thought was the ultimate plan was simply the preview to the plan. The real plan was for Jesus to enter into God's presence and execute all that he was planning all along. The effectiveness of this plan was that, while the old covenant could not purity the conscience (v. 9), Jesus, in God's presence, could purify it (v. 14). The driving point is that this was the fulfillment of the prophesied new covenant (v. 15). Jesus mediates this new covenant as the permanent high priest.

Preaching Idea

Previews determine the plan.

Contemporary Connections

What does it mean?

What does it mean that previews determine the plan? Everything in life has a backdrop to it. There is always a preview to the overarching plan. In the context of whole Bible, God used the tabernacle to preview God's plan for salvation. The tabernacle was the backdrop for Jesus's atoning sacrifice. Jesus was the perfect, sacrificial lamb of God. Yet, what is interesting is that one of the best ways to understand God's plan of salvation is to look at the temple because it is the picture that represents it. Hundreds of years before Jesus came, the tabernacle and the temple gave us a graphic representation of God's holiness, sin's costs, and the atoning sacrifice of Jesus.

Is it true?

Is it true that previews determine the plan? Everything that we appreciate in life has a backdrop to it. When a diamond is purchased, the jeweler will set the diamond on a piece of black, velvet cloth. The blackness of the cloth will illustrate all the beautiful facets of the diamond. As the diamond is turned, its beauty will be illustrated, and the background will be forgotten.

Think for a moment about a famous painting. It will be hard for people to remember the backdrop of the *Mona Lisa*, the backdrop for one of Degas's ballerina dancers, or the backdrop for one of Monet's paintings in his *Water Lilies* series. We remember what is in the foreground, but we rarely remember what is in the background. This is exactly as the artist intended. The backdrop is there and exists, but its existence is present so you forget it and simply remember what is in the foreground. That is the very point of it.

In the same way God gave us an understanding of himself that was rich in detail. The instructions for the tabernacle were nothing less than exquisite. And yet, it is only when we see Jesus that we understand that the tabernacle was the background. This is what Paul meant when he said that what used to be glorious had no glory compared to the glory of the new covenant (2 Cor. 3).

Now what?

How do previews determine the plan? As noted previously, this entire section is without any imperatives. In Hebrews 8, Barnabas was not trying to lead us to *do* something but to *understand* something. We are being led to understand that the tabernacle was pointing us ultimately to Jesus. Therefore, the tone of this passage is still worship. The intent is that as we take a moment to understand the backdrop Jesus stepped into, we will love him more deeply and feel more confident in his work on our behalf.

The application must follow this trajectory in reverse: we worship Jesus because of all he has done for us, but what he has done for us cannot be understood apart from the tabernacle. You cannot appreciate the plan unless you appreciate the preview. An application could be this: the more fully you understand what Jesus has done for you, the more of a priority he will be in your life. We love him the more we understand him. This allows us to appreciate passages such as Hebrews 9 for more than just the Jewish history it presents. The preview to the plan is a portal to prioritizing Jesus.

If this first-century house church in Rome full of Jewish followers of Jesus was filled with people who once based their entire hope on the old covenant, Barnabas was now clarifying for them that it was just a setup, a pattern for the reality that would follow. Their reactions, and ours, should be ever-loving wonder and praise for all that God has done. The immediate application, then, to this section in general and this passage specifically, is wonder and praise; or to put it in the words of the hymn, to let the more pressing things of life grow "strangely dim, in the light of his glory and grace" ("Turn Your Eyes upon Jesus," Helen Howarth Lemmel, 1922).

Creativity in Presentation

We might open with a rhetorical question. Ask the congregation to think of their favorite work of art. Then show a few of the more famous ones on the screen. You could even show what are (arguably) the most famous works of art of all time. Take some time scrolling through the list and noting the significant features of each of the works of art.

When the slides are done, ask, "Now, which is your favorite background to the art?" The point is that people will be hard pressed to remember any of the backgrounds. As they are puzzling this, you might remind them that the background *was* there. These works of art are not like a child writing on a bulletin with pen on a white background. Each artist took careful attention to what was in both the foreground and background. Each were incredibly important, because the artist wanted you to really notice the foreground. The background was effective for the very reason that it was *less* memorable. The foreground and the background together make the work a masterpiece.

In the same way, all of the work of the tabernacle is not unimportant. We cannot throw away the old sacrificial system as if it is irrelevant! It is the background that, by the Artist's design, fades away so the glory of the foreground is seen. If we understand the preview, we understand the plan.

Working off the idea of how previews determine the plan, a simple outline might be as follows:

- The failure of the preview: it could not purify the conscience (vv. 1–10).
- The function of our high priest: Jesus's presence before God can purify the conscience (vv. 11–14).
- The fulfillment of the plan: the new covenant is here (vv. 15–28).

DISCUSSION QUESTIONS

1. Why would someone under the old covenant not have a pure conscience (Heb. 9:9)?
2. What is implied in the phrase "eternal redemption" (Heb. 9:12)?
3. Does Hebrews 9:11–14 imply that the old covenant system was bad?
4. How are the copies of things "purified" (Heb. 9:23)?
5. After reading Hebrews 9:23–28, explain how the idea of high priest, mentioned since Hebrews 3:1, is now brought to clarity and focus.

Hebrews 10:1–18

EXEGETICAL IDEA

The symbolic acts of Judaism's blood sacrifices offered through its inadequate covenantal system were replaced with Jesus's efficacious sacrificial death, which completed God's will, established a new covenant, and set into motion the household family of faith to be set apart for God as well as to experience God's forgiveness.

THEOLOGICAL FOCUS

Jesus, through his efficacious sacrificial death, fulfilled God's will, replaced symbolic acts of animal sacrifices, established a new covenant, and set into motion believers being set apart for God and experiencing forgiveness.

PREACHING IDEA

The shadow is irrelevant when the reality is here.

PREACHING POINTERS

As the Jewish household family of faith in Rome heard this portion of Hebrews read for the first time, they would have been very familiar with the Jewish cultic system of ritual sacrifices. Herod's temple had not yet been destroyed. So, there remained in place an active sacrificial system despite the religious corruption of the high priests. The ritual sacrifices and imagery were accessible to all who went to Jerusalem and worshipped. Thus, when Barnabas explained that these cultic systems were "shadows" and thus inadequate due to their repetitive nature, we can imagine how this passage resonated with the first-century listener. They would also identify with the inability of the sacrifices to make someone truly clean and pure before God. The idea of inadequacy was a perfect segue into the discussion of the complete adequacy of Jesus and his sacrifice.

Today people are largely unfamiliar with first-century cultic rituals. Yet, they are familiar with "shadow" realities. From early on, we develop dependence on certain "shadow" realities in our life. We become familiar with family and church structures that are "shadows" of biblical expectations. We engage financial systems that are mere "shadows" of security. We become dependent on federal and state government social services that are "shadows" of a standard of living. Yet, God makes it clear that all things, material or immaterial, are imperfectly represented in this life. Every imperfect thing in this life is a "shadow" to point us and to lead us to Jesus. The imperfect bodies in this imperfect world systems, including the church, are filled with imperfect people, and that makes us long to see Jesus, our regal high priest, and to see the kingdom of God. So, while the "shadows" we experience today are good, they are pale and incomplete representations of reality. "Shadows" are representations, not a reality on which to depend. The shadow is irrelevant when the reality is here.

JUDAISM'S BLOOD SACRIFICES (10:1–18)

LITERARY STRUCTURE AND THEMES (10:1–18)

In Hebrews 10:1–18, Barnabas recapitulated and closed his comments for 8:1–9:28 (Lane, 1991b, 257). Barnabas began by recalling earlier discussions about "symbols" and developing further their inadequacies within Judaism's cultic system (= the law) with specific attention given to animal sacrifices (vv. 1–4). He then validated the inadequacy of Judaism's cultic system with Jesus's quotation of Psalm 40 whereby Barnabas featured the adequacy of Jesus's self-sacrifice (vv. 5–10). After supporting the incapabilities of Levitical priests, Barnabas directed attention to the capacities of Jesus's self-sacrifice (vv. 11–14). He then closed with God's replacement of the covenantal cultic system with God's new covenant whereby every member of the household family of faith had been set apart for God (vv. 15–18).

Barnabas's major themes upon which he focused were the inadequacy of Judaism's cultic system and the need for and inauguration of a new covenant.

- ***Inadequacy of Judaism's Cultic System's Sacrifices (10:1–4)***
- ***The Adequacy of Jesus's Sacrifice (10:5–10)***
- ***The Capacities of Jesus's Sacrifice (10:11–14)***
- ***God's New Covenant Realized (10:15–18)***

EXPOSITION (10:1–18)

Sacrifices were an essential part of the Greco-Roman world during the A.D. 60s when Barnabas wrote to the household family of faith in Rome. On the one hand, sacrifices offered by the Greco-Roman Gentiles were viewed as gifts to the gods such as Athena, heroes such as Hercules, and emperors such as Caesar Augustus. Sacrifices could be food offerings, such as fruit, grains, milk, etc., or animal offerings. Male animals tended to be offered to male gods such as Apollo, and female animals were offered to goddesses such as Diana. The most frequent sacrifices offered were vow-related.

Roman relief depicting a scene of sacrifice, with libations at a flaming altar and the victimarius carrying the sacrificial axe. Wolfgang Sauber / CC BY-SA (https://creativecommons.org/licenses/by-sa/3.0)

On the other hand, Judaism's sacrifices were offered to the one and only God of Abraham, Isaac, and Jacob. It was a sacrificial system established during the time of Moses for "wrongs committed against one's neighbor and God" (= sin; cf. Lev. 19:18; Deut. 6:5; Mark 12:30–31). And though Judaism's cultic practices were still in force when Hebrews was written, some considered the cultic system contaminated due to Herod's temple and the corrupt priesthood. One Jewish writing from this time period anticipated a day when Judaism's sacrificial system would be practiced properly, when Jerusalem's temple would be built correctly, and the sacrificial system practiced accurately according to an approved religious calendar. For instance, burnt offerings would be consumed on a rebuilt outer altar for every day, the Sabbath, and the new moon (11Q19 12–14). Naturally, cultic regulations concerning animal sacrifices were often interpreted and innovations added, especially concerning the eating of meat slaughtered outside the temple precincts (11Q19 52.13–16, 19–21; 53.7–8) and sacrifices offered for purification (11Q19 18.4–6; 35.10–15; cf. Milgrom, 2001, 807–12). Like his contemporaries, Barnabas also took issue with Judaism's sacrificial system. The symbolic acts of Judaism's blood sacrifices offered through its inadequate covenantal system were replaced with Jesus's efficacious sacrificial death, which completed God's will, established a new covenant, and set into motion the household family of faith to be set apart for God as well as to experience God's forgiveness.

Inadequacy of Judaism's Cultic System's Sacrifices (10:1–4)

Judaism's cultic system (= the law) that regulated the symbolic acts of animal sacrifices were ineffective and never took away a person's imperfection.

TEXTUAL ANALYSIS: Conflicting Text Critical Reading: 10:1

There are two text critical issues for verse 1. The first is a theological/exegetical issue: Support of the text among the manuscripts (ℵ C 044 1739 1881) overwhelms the variant's support (p[46]). The variant treats "house" (σκιά) and "image" (εἰκόνα) as complementary terms rather than contrasting and perhaps reflects a scribe's having been influenced by a traditional Platonic concept (Lane, 1991b, 254; Metzger, 1994, 599). The text is the preferred reading by translators.

txt. "**not the true** form of these realities" (**οὐκ αὐτὴν** τὴν εἰκόνα τῶν πραγμάτων) (NRSV; cf. ASV, ESV, KJV, NASB, NET, NIV)

var. "**and** the form of these realities" (**καὶ** τὴν εἰκόνα τῶν πραγμάτων)

The second is a grammatical issue: Support for the variant (1241 1505) exists, but the lack of concord between "they make" (δύνανται, pl.) and "law" (νόμος, sing.), argues against it. Thus the text is the prefered reading by most translators (p[46] D* H K 0285 326 365 629 630 1739 1881; cf. Lane, 1991b, 254; Metzger, 1994, 600).

txt. "**it can never make** perfect those who approach" (**οὐδέποτε δύναται** τοὺς προσερχομένους τελειῶσαι) (ASV, ESV, KJV, NASB, NET, NIV, NRSV)

var. "**they can never make** perfect those who approach" (**οὐδέποτε δύνανται** τοὺς προσερχομένους τελειῶσαι)

10:1. Barnabas's propensity for long Greek sentences continued (vv. 1–2). He opened his discussion about sacrifices by restatements about earthly shadows or copies of heavenly realities introduced in 8:3–5 and 9:23–26 (Lane, 1991b, 260; Mitchell, 2007, 199). Yet, he developed (γάρ, "for") his initial thoughts with a description of the law as *possessing* "a shadow" (σκιά) of things to come. Unlike in Hebrews 8:5, where the earthly tabernacle was the "shadow" or "copy" of a heavenly reality, here "shadow" was a bit more ambiguous. "The law" itself was *not* a "copy" or "representation" of a heavenly reality, but rather an "imposed" cultic system (9:10b) that regulated the tabernacle (8:5; 9:1–5), priests (8:3–4; 9:6–7), sacrifices (8:3–4; 9:18–22), etc. In other words, the regulated cultic system (= "the law") *possessed* (ἔχων, "having") the "shadow" or a "preliminary sketch" (Morris, 1981, 12:94–95) foreshadowing something yet to come. The phrase "of the good things to come" recalled Barnabas's earlier description of Jesus who was the "high priest of the good things to come" (9:11), namely, eternal redemption (9:12, 15), purification of conscience (9:22), a promise of eternal inheritance (9:15), the forgiveness of sins (9:22), and deliverance (9:28). So, the cultic system (= the law) was "a dim preview" (NLT) of Jesus's achievements as high priest.

Judaism's cultic system (= the law), however, was not to be confused with "the true reality" (αὐτὴν τὴν εἰκόνα). While English translations offer other possible renderings such as "very image" (KJV) or "the true form" (NRSV, ESV, CNT), they may suggest a synonymous relationship with "shadow" (σκιά) oftentimes associated with Philo (*Mig.* 12) who equated the two terms. Yet, Barnabas clearly contrasted the "symbol" as "not" (οὐκ) an "image" (Mitchell, 2007, 199; Cockerill, 2012, 428). Barnabas's point was that the cultic system possessed symbols *like* the tabernacle and practiced symbolic acts *like* animal sacrifice year after year for purification. Unfortunately, these acts were merely symbolic and were "unable" (οὐδέποτε δύναται) to perfect those who came to worship God. In essence, Barnabas stressed its "futile repetitiveness" (Johnson, 2006, 249). Nevertheless, the regulated cultic practices articulated within the law were a shadow of a new reality, namely, Jesus's ministry as a high priest in God's presence.

10:2. As this long Greek sentence continued, Barnabas provided the reason (γάρ, "for") why the symbolic acts of purification needed repeating by way of a two-part rhetorical question that expects negative answers. First, would worshippers under Judaism's regulated cultic system offer animal sacrifices repeatedly if they were purified "once *for all*" (ἅπαξ). The expected answer was no. Unlike Hebrews 9:26, where "once *for all*" underscored the effectiveness of the unique sacrifice of Jesus, here in Hebrews 10:2, Barnabas underscored a repeated theme about the ineffectiveness of animal sacrifices (7:11, 18–19; 8:7; 9:9; 10:8–9, 11). Like other Jews who recognized the system's limited benefits (cf. Wis 2:2, 5:9; Philo, *Post.* 112, *Deus.* 177) or corruptions (11Q19), Barnabas articulated that there was no "once *for all*" effective form of purification in Judaism's religious system. "Worshippers" (τοὺς λατρεύοντας) were required to offer animal sacrifices repeatedly to achieve *outward* purity (9:13). Yet, due to the unique and unrepeatable sacrifice of Jesus (9:26), worshippers under the new covenant received *inner* purification (9:9, 14; 10:10, 14–18, 22). Thus, Barnabas underscored Judaism's lack of an effective sacrifice for "purification" (κεκαθαρισμένους), in contrast to Jesus's "once *for all*" sacrifice, which was unique, definitive, and eternally effective (cf. 7:27, 9:12).

The second half of Barnabas's rhetorical question that also expected a negative answer addressed the worshipper's "conscience" (KJV) or "consciousness" (NASB, RSV). Would worshippers under Judaism's regulated cultic system offer animal sacrifices repeatedly if their consciences were free of guilt? The expected answer was once again no. It was not unusual for the "conscience" (συνείδησιν) to refer to a person's awareness of God (1 Peter 2:19), of an idol (1 Cor. 8:7), of deliberate and abominable deeds against another (Josephus, *A.J.* 16.7.4 §212; Josephus, *B.J.* 4.3.11 §193; cf. P.Fouad 28, 15), or of an awareness or unawareness of a crime (PFlor 338, 17; Josephus, *A.J.* 16.4.2 §103). Philo (*Det.* 146) employed the term as follows: "Let us then, who are convicted by *an awareness* of our own acts of unrighteousness, beseech God to punish us rather than let us alone" (trans. Goold, emphasis mine). Here in Hebrews 10:2, Barnabas recognized that an animal sacrifice was unable to eliminate guilt felt by a person due to their awareness of wrongs against neighbor and God (= "sin"; cf. Lev. 19:18; Deut. 6:5; Mark 12:30–31) because the sacrifice (= "blood") of bulls and goats was an imperfect symbolic act. It was only the sacrifice of Jesus that was able to free a guilty conscience (cf. *TLNT,* 3:332–36; BDAG, s.v. "συνείδησις" 1, p. 967).

The Day of Atonement in Leviticus and Hebrews (Bateman, 2012, 83)		
Questions	**Leviticus 16**	**Hebrews**
Who officiates?	As the Levitical high priest, he alone entered a tabernacle made with human hands (16:2, 17; cf. Exod. 25–26).	As regal high priest, Jesus alone entered the heavenly tabernacle (9:12, 25–28; 10:1–3, 10:14).
What is needed?	1. A young bull was needed for a sin offering (16:3, 6, 11, 14, 18–19). 2. Two male goats were needed (16:5, 7–10): one as a sin offering (16:3, 15, 18–19), and one as a scapegoat (16:5, 8, 10, 20–22).	One sacrifice was needed, Jesus (9:11–14). Compare the concept of human atonement in Romans 9:3.
What happens to the animals?	1. The bull was sacrificed as a sin offering, and its blood was sprinkled on the atonement plate (16:6, 11, 14). 2. The sin offering goat was sacrificed, and its blood was sprinkled on the atonement plate (16:15). 3. The scapegoat was sent into the wilderness (16:10, 21–22).	Jesus's death on the cross serves as atonement in the heavenly Holy of Holies (9:12; 10:4–10). Some may argue that Jesus died and offered his own blood in the heavenly sanctuary.
Who benefits?	1. The blood of the sacrificed bull benefited the high priest and his household (16:6, 11–14). 2. The blood of the sacrificed goat benefited the people (16:15). 3. The blood of the sacrificed bull and goat benefited the tabernacle (16:18–19). 4. The scapegoat benefited the community (16:21–22).	1. The blood of Jesus benefited all who are called (9:15). 2. The blood of Jesus benefited all who eagerly awaited him (9:28). 3. Compare: The sufferings of Jesus benefited all who obeyed him (5:9).
How often is this to occur?	1. On the Day of Atonement, the high priest entered the Holy of Holies three times on behalf of himself, the people, and then the tabernacle (16:11, 15, 18–19, 33). 2. The Day of Atonement and its expectations were repetitious and needed to be practiced annually (16:29, 34).	1. Jesus entered the heavenly Holy of Holies *once* for all people (9:28). 2. Jesus entered the heavenly Holy of Holies *once* for all, never to be repeated (9:12, 25–28; 10:1–3, 10–14).

10:3–4. Barnabas drew specific attention to his twofold rhetorical question with a sharp contrast (ἀλλ', "but"). The expectation of an animal sacrifice year after year was a perpetual reminder of a Jewish person's wrongs committed against neighbor and God (= "sin"; cf. Lev. 19:18; Deut. 6:5; Mark 12:30–31) as well as the ineffectiveness of such ritual practices. The reason (γάρ, "for") why the symbolic acts of purification needed repeating was simply because exterminating the life (= "blood") of an animal was not sufficient. They were ineffective ritual practices. Barnabas's statement that "it is impossible" (ἀδύνατον) for the life an animal to effectively eliminate the consequences of wrongdoing, was stated as an absolute theological impossibility. It was Barnabas's third theological impossibility. In Hebrews 6:4, he highlighted the impossibility of repentance for an apostate. In Hebrews 6:18, he underscored the impossibility for God to make a false assertion. Here in Hebrews 10:4, he asserted the impossibility for animal sacrifices to take away wrongs against neighbor and God (= "sin"; cf. Lev. 19:18; Deut. 6:5; Mark 12:30–31). Philo (*Spec.* 1:282–83) concurred: "But as for the soul . . . what age long stretch of years can convert it to decent living? . . . only God, with Whom that is possible which is impossible with us. So, he who intends to sacrifice must consider not whether the victim is unblemished but whether his own mind stands free from defect and imperfection" (trans. Gould). Elsewhere Philo (*Mut.* 49) admitted, "Infinite indeed are the defilements that soil the soul, which it is impossible to wash and scour away altogether" (trans. Gould). Thus, it was understood, at least in first-century Judaism, that animal sacrifices never took away a person's or a community's sins, nor did they elevate a person's guilty conscience (cf. 9:9, 14).

The Adequacy of Jesus's Sacrifice (10:5–10)

The death of Jesus, according to God's will, replaced Judaism's covenantal cultic system with a new covenant through which God was in the process of setting apart members of the household family of faith.

10:5–7. Barnabas validated (διό, "so" or "therefore") his argument about the ineffectiveness of animal sacrifices with Scripture as quoted by Jesus. The temporal expression "when he came [εἰσερχόμενος] into the world" was "distinctly incarnation language" (Lane, 1991b, 262). It was Jesus who spoke verses 6–8 from Psalm 40 (cf. Heb. 1:2; 2:12).[3] To validate his arguement, Barnabas quoted two verses from Psalm 40.

The focus of the psalmist in Psalm 40:6–8 was on God's "lack of delight" (οὐκ ἠθέλησας) in animal sacrifices. The term "delight" (θέλω) spoke often of God's "delighting in," "being pleased with," or "approving of" things. For instance, he took delight in the land (LXX: Ps. 84:2 [85:1], in people's sacrifices (LXX: Ps. 50:18, 21 [51:16, 19], Jer. 14:12), in people's works (LXX: Eccl. 9:7; Jdt 15:10), in the rebuilding of the temple (LXX: Hag. 1:8; cf. 2 Macc 14:35), and according to Josephus, the coexistence of free will and fate (Josephus, *A.J.* 18.1.3 §13). But in Psalm 40:6–8 as quoted here in Hebrews 10:5–7, Barnabas made it perfectly clear that animal sacrifices, particularly whole burnt offerings, were of little value to God. They were powerless and ineffective to secure a proper relationship with God. Barnabas recaptured the psalmist's recognition about his own body and a willingness to present himself to God as a sacrifice to please God. This concept was then applied to Jesus's willingness to offer himself as a sacrifice. Jesus, as God's regal high priest (vv. 5, 9; cf. 1:2), recognized the imperfections of animal sacrifices the Law required in which God did not delight (cf. 10:1, 4), understood God's desires for him to be a more prominent sacrifice (cf. 9:13–14), and willingly accomplished God's desire by offering himself to be a sacrifice (cf. 2:9b–10).

10:8. Barnabas then explained what Jesus meant (λέγων, "when he says") in yet another very long Greek sentence that described two specific issues about sacrifices in Psalm 40.[4] The first concerned the weakness of Jewish sacrifices. Although Judaism's cultic system had regulations for six blood sacrifices, Barnabas drew attention to the weakness of two blood sacrifice: burnt offererings and sin

3 For Psalm 40:6–8 in the original languages from the Hebrew Bible, Septuagint, and Hebrews, see H. W. Bateman IV, *Charts on the Book of Hebrews* (Grand Rapids: Kregel, 2012), 160.

4 Barnabas frequently portrayed Jesus as speaking Hebrew scripture. In Hebrews 2:12–13, Jesus spoke Psalm 22:22 and Isaiah 17–18 and also applied those texts to himself.

sacrifices. God lacked delight in whole burnt and sin offerings. "Whole burnt offerings" (ὁλοκαυτώματα), as perscribed and regulated within Judaism's cultic system (= the law), required the entire animal to be consumed by fire with nothing remaining for the worshipper (Lev. 14:19–20; Num. 15:3; cf. BDAG, s.v. "ὁλοκαύτωμα" 1, p. 703). "Sin offerings" (περὶ ἁμαρτίας), as prescribed and regulated within the law, required that only the fat of an animal was consumed by fire while the meat was to be reserved for and eaten by priests (Lev. 4:1–5, 13; 6:26; cf. BDAG, s.v. "ἁμαρτία" 1a, p. 50). Yet, God took no delight in any ritual offerings while injustice prevailed among his people (cf. Mic. 6:1–9).

<table>
<tr><th colspan="6">Israel's Six Blood Sacrifices Differentiated
(Archer, 1974, 244)</th></tr>
<tr><th>Name</th><th>Purpose</th><th>Victim</th><th>God's Portion</th><th>Priest's Portion</th><th>Worshipper's Portion</th></tr>
<tr><td>Burnt offering</td><td>Offered for committing of general sins</td><td>Unblemished male ox, sheep, goat, or dove (according to a person's ability to pay)</td><td>The entire animal was to be consumed</td><td>Nothing</td><td>Nothing</td></tr>
<tr><td>Sin offering</td><td>Offered for committing specific sins where no restitution was possible</td><td>If a priest, a bullock; if a ruler, a he-goat; if a congregant, a she-goat</td><td rowspan="5">The fatty portions (e.g., fat covering the organs, kidneys, liver)</td><td>The remainder was to be eaten within the court of the tabernacle</td><td>Nothing</td></tr>
<tr><td>Trespass offering</td><td>Offered for sins where restitution was possible</td><td>Ram (only)</td><td>The remainder was to be eaten within the court of the tabernacle</td><td>Nothing</td></tr>
<tr><td>Peace offerings of thanks</td><td>Fellowship with God; a communal meal for unexpected blessing and deliverance</td><td>Unblemished male or female ox, sheep, or goat</td><td rowspan="2">Breast given to the high priest

Right foreleg given to the officiating priest</td><td>Remainder eaten in the court that same day</td></tr>
<tr><td>Peace offering associated with a vow</td><td>For blessing or deliverance already granted when a vow had been made in support of the petition</td><td>Unblemished male or female ox, sheep, or goat</td><td>Remainder eaten in the court the first or second day</td></tr>
<tr><td>Peace offering of one's freewill</td><td>To express general thanksgiving and love toward God, without regard to any specific blessing</td><td>Male or female ox, sheep, or goat (minor imperfections permitted)</td><td>The remainder was to be eaten within the court of the tabernacle</td><td>Remainder eaten in the court the first or second day</td></tr>
</table>

10:9. The second weakness explained (τότε εἴρηκεν, "then he says") concerned Jesus's willingness to do God's will. With a rather strong emphasis (Ἰδού, "behold"), Jesus said, "I have come to do your will." The statement not only echoed Jesus's sentiments in Gethsemane (Mark 14:36),[5] but recalled Barnabas's previous discussions about Jesus's willingness to be God's "pioneer" (2:9b–10). Jesus's willingness to obey God served to "remove the first [*covenant*]" (ἀναιρεῖ τὸ πρῶτον [*διαθήκη*]) with his intention (ἵνα, "in order that) "to establish the second" (τὸ δεύτερον στήσῃ). As it was earlier in Hebrews where "the first" (τὸ πρῶτον) was a reference to the entire Mosaic covenantal system (8:7, 13; 9:1), so it was here. Barnabas once again recalled the end of Judaism's cultic system when he described the first covenant as "obsolete" (παλαίω) in 8:13. Here Barnabas pointed out the system as "abolished" (NRSV) (ἀναιρεῖ), "cancelled" (NLT) (BDAG s.v. "ἀναιρέω" 1, p. 64). Naturally, "the second" (τὸ δεύτερον) was a reference to the new covenant (cf. 8:7). The law's inadequate animal sacrificial system was replaced with the adequate self-sacrifice of Jesus with the intention (ἵνα, "in order that") that a new covenant be put in place.

10:10. Barnabas ended this long sentence in verse 10 with the means "by which" (ἐν ᾧ) God's "will" (θελήματι) was fulfilled. The statement recalled Hebrews 2:9b–11b where Jesus was presented as the agent through whom God made the household family of faith "holy." It was not God's will for the regulated animal sacrifices in Judaism's cultic system, which was imposed on people, to exist forever. But rather, God's will was fulfilled when Jesus inaugurated a new covenant (τὸ δεύτερον, "the second") that replaced the first covenant through Jesus's self-sacrifice "once *for all*" (ἐφάπαξ; Lane, 1991, 2:265; Ellingworth, 1993, 505). The appearance of "Jesus Christ" (Ἰησοῦ Χριστοῦ) occurs only here in Hebrews. It spoke clearly of his humanity ("Jesus") and his messiahship ("Christ"; cf. "son" in 1:5–13). It was the new covenant whereby the household family of faith "have been made holy" or "have been dedicated" (ἡγιασμένοι; perf. pass.) through a human agent: "Jesus" (Ἰησοῦ, gen. of agcy.) "who is the Christ" (Χριστοῦ, gen. of ap.). So, in accordance with God's will, the newly established covenant, activated via the death of Jesus, was the one that made the Jewish household family of faith in Rome perfect (10:10).

The Capacities of Jesus's Sacrifice (10:11–14)

Unlike the work of the Levitical priests, whose everyday sacrifices were incapable of removing sin's guilt, the work of Jesus had the capacity to brand the family of faith as set apart.

> *TEXTUAL ANALYSIS:* Conflicting Text Critical Reading: 10:11
> Literary/Exegetical Issue: Manuscript support exists for both readings: text (𝔓[13] 𝔓[46] ℵ D K P 044 33 81 1739 1881) and variant (A C P 88 104 365 614 630). Yet, the variant may have been a scribal addition reflecting a desire to create literary conformity with Hebrews 5:1 and 8:3. The text is the prefered reading (Lane, 1991b, 254; Metzger, 1994, 600).
>
> *txt.* "and every priest stands day after day" (καὶ πᾶς μὲν ἱερεὺς ἕστηκεν καθ' ἡμέραν) (ASV, ESV, KJV, NASB, NET, NIV, NRSV)
> *var.* "and every **high** priest stands day after day" (καὶ πᾶς μὲν **ἀρχιερεὺς** ἱερεὺς ἕστηκεν καθ' ἡμέραν)

5 Mark's Gospel was one of three works written for the household family of faith in Rome. It may be that Barnabas's readers were well aware of Mark's Gospel, and Jesus's prayer in Gethsemane. Regardless, Jesus's prayer in Gethsemane to do God's will was a well-known part of the passion narrative (cf. Matt. 29:39; Luke 22:42).

10:11. Barnabas offered another (μέν . . . δέ) contrastive parallelism about everyday priests and Jesus as God's regal high priest. "On the one hand" (μέν), all Levitical priests of Judaism's cultic system constantly stood (ἕστηκεν, "stand") day in and day out, offering animal sacrifices repeatedly that never took away a person's sin—a reiteration of Hebrews 10:4. Of particular significance was the description of priests who stood at the altar and the contrast to Jesus who "sat" (ἐκάθισεν) next to God in the next verse (Deut. 10:8; Josephus, *A.J.*. 13. §372). Ellingworth (1989, 507) takes note of the difference between Solomon's "sitting on the throne of David" and "standing before the altar" of God.

> Now the LORD has fulfilled his promise that he made; for I have succeeded my father David, *and sit on the throne* of Israel, as the LORD promised, and have built the house for the name of the LORD, the God of Israel. (2 Chron. 6:10)

> Then Solomon *stood before the altar* of the LORD in the presence of the whole assembly of Israel and spread out his hands. (2 Chron. 6:12)

Whereas standing was a normal position for a priest or king exerting his cultic functions in the tabernacle (as well as angels in God's heavenly court) and thereby an honored position, the idea of Solomon sitting on David's throne was a symbol of authority (cf. Bateman, 1992, 438–53). Here Barnabas described Solomon as a regal priest in the order of Melchizedek (Ps. 110:1, 4; cf. 1 Kings 13:1 [3 Kgdms. 13:1]).

10:12. "On the other hand" (δέ), Jesus (οὖτος, "this one") offered his self-sacrifice once, a sacrifice that never needed to be repeated (cf. 9:26–28). The phrase "for all time" (εἰς τὸ διηνεκές) recalled the priesthood of Melchizedek in 7:3 where Barnabas linked Jesus with Melchizedek. Furthermore, Barnabas recalled Jesus's positioned authority with the requoting of a portion of Psalm 110:1, "*he sat down at the right hand* of God" (cf. Heb. 1:3d, 13; 8:1). Barnabas purposely repeated the description of the inauguration and ruling authority of Jesus in God's heavenly court in three distinct contrasts. First, Barnabas recalled 1:3 where he said previously, "so when he had accomplished cleansing for sins, *he sat down at the right hand of the Majesty on high*." Here in 10:12, Barnabas quoted Psalm 110 to contrast Jesus's "sacrifice for sins for all time" with the inadequacy of animal sacrifices. Second, Barnabas recalled Hebrews 1:13–14 where he quoted Psalm 110 to contrast Jesus's role as Davidic king with the role of angels as servants of the king. Finally, Barnabas recalled 8:1 and in 10:2, where he quoted Psalm 110 to contrast Jesus's efficacious role as royal-priest with the ineffective role of Levitical priests (cf. 1:3d).

10:13–14. Although he broke off Psalm 110:1 toward the end of verse 12, Barnabas picked up the quotation "*until his enemies are made a footstool for his feet*" and offered an interpretation. As it was in 1:13, "a footstool for his feet" was a figure of speech that spoke of a future subjugation of all things to Jesus, who was the Messiah (Χριστός). It was at the right hand of God where Jesus was now waiting for this future subjugation. As he did in Hebrews 1:13, Barnabas understood the psalm as anticipating a future event where everything would be placed under Jesus's control (cf. 2:8–9).

Barnabas summed up (γάρ, "for") the completed work of Jesus in verse 14 (Ellingworth, 1989, 511). "The one offering" (μιᾷ . . . προσφορᾷ) recalled the "once *for all*" (ἐφάπαξ) statement about Jesus in verse 10 and was in keeping and synonymous with "sacrifice" (θυσία; vv. 5, 8, 11) that distinguished animal sacrifices from Jesus's self-sacrifice (Attridge, 1989, 280n34). The effects of Jesus's self-sacrifice was permanent (εἰς τὸ διηνεκές, "for all time"), unlike the perpetually offered animal sacrifices by Levitical priests. So, members of the household family of faith, according to Barnabas, were in the process of "*being* made sanctified by God" (τοὺς ἁγιαζομένους, divine pass.). Not that the household family of faith was not sanctified (cf. KJV, NASB, NRSV, CNT), but it seems the emphasis here was on the process of *being* sanctified (NIV, ESV, NLT). Or perhaps we might say, the Jewish household family of faith in Rome was in the process of being set apart from others (BDAG, s.v. "ἁγιάζω" 2, p. 9). The work of Jesus as a Melchizedekian king-priest's one and only sacrifice was both sufficient and permanent for setting apart the household family of faith.

God's New Covenant Realized (10:15–18)

God's spirit testified to the replacement of the old covenant with God's new covenant that was part of every believer's very being and made believers blameless.

10:15. Barnabas transitioned (δέ, "and") to three proofs of the finality of Jesus's sacrifice. The first proof presented was that God's spirit testified to the efficacious self-sacrifice of Jesus (vv. 15b, 17a). Ellingworth (1989, 512) believes that though God's spirit was not a major theological emphasis, the spirit had appeared in Hebrews as a "speaker" (3:7) and "revealer" (9:8) of Scripture. Here, Barnabas noted that God's spirit "bears witness" (μαρτυρεῖ) for the third time in Hebrews (7:8, 17; 10: 15a). Yet, the emphasis here was on God's plan to replace Judaism's cultic system (2:9b–10; 5:8–10; cf. Cockerill, 2012, 454). Whereas Jesus himself testified to his establishing the new covenant by way of his self-sacrifice via Psalm 40:6–8 (quoted in Heb. 10:8–9), God's spirit was presented as testifying to its successful replacement.

10:16–17. The second proof occurred when Barnabas redirected his attention to Jeremiah 31:33–34, which was first quoted in Hebrews 8:7–12. His use of "this" (αὕτη) was cataphoric and therefore pointed forward to his discussion about Jeremiah 31:33–34. However, there was a difference in the manner by which Jeremiah was quoted (Lane, 1991b, 268). When Barnabas quoted Jeremiah in 8:7–12, it was from Jeremiah's perspective prior to 586 B.C. whereby the emphasis was on the obsolete nature of Israel's cultic system that *would soon* disappear (Heb. 8:13). It was presented as a future expectation for the nation of Israel under siege due to sin. Here in Hebrews 10:16–17, however, the text from Jeremiah 31:33–34 was "manipulated" in such a way so as to emphasize the application of the new covenant whereby it was a current reality for "the household family of faith" (πρὸς αὐτούς, "with them"; cf. Heb. 10:16) due to the self-sacrifice of Jesus (Attridge, 1989, 281; Mitchell, 2007, 204).

Hebrews 8:10, 12b	Hebrews 10:16–17
This is the covenant that	This is the covenant that
I will establish <u>*with the house of Israel*</u> [τῷ οἴκῳ Ἰσραὴλ]	I will establish <u>*with the them*</u> [πρὸς αὐτούς]
After those days, says the Lord:	After those days, says the Lord:
I will put my laws *into their mind,*	I will put my laws *on their hearts,*
I will inscribe them *on their hearts*	I will inscribe them *on their minds*
and I will not remember	and I will not remember
their sins	their sins
	and their lawless deeds
anymore	anymore

Thus, Jeremiah 31:33–34 was fulfilled and the new covenant was in full force for those who were members of the household family of faith (cf. 9:15, 28). Koester highlights an additional phrase that Barnabas added: "and their lawless deeds." "Adding these words to the quotation," says Koester (2001, 435–36), "emphasizes the scope of God's grace. Since the Son of God hates 'lawlessness' (1:9), he purges it from the people of God."

10:18. Barnabas concluded (ὅπου δέ, "now where") with a further interpretation about "forgiveness" (ἄφεσις), which he introduced in 9:22. As noted in chapter 9, "forgiveness" (ἄφεσις) was an "act of freeing a person from an obligation, guilt, or punishment" (BDAG, s.v. "*ἄφεσις*" 2, p. 155). Yet unlike in 9:22, where Barnabas underscored that under Judaism's covenantal cultic system "forgiveness" was impossible to be had without extinguishing life (= "blood"), here forgiveness was a matter of fact and thus the ineffective sacrificing of animal blood (10:4, 11) had now ended.

THEOLOGICAL FOCUS

The exegetical idea (the symbolic acts of Judaism's blood sacrifices offered through its inadequate covenantal system were replaced with Jesus's efficacious sacrificial death, which completed God's will, established a new covenant, and set into motion the household family of faith to be set apart for God as well as to experience God's forgiveness) leads to this theological focus: Jesus, through his efficacious sacrificial death, fulfilled God's will, replaced symbolic acts of animal sacrifices, established a new covenant, and set into motion believers being set apart for God and experiencing forgiveness.

At least two major theological themes stand out in this preaching unit. On the one hand, there was the emphasis of the Jewish religious cultic sacrificial system regulated by the Mosaic law. First, the cultic system (= Mosaic law) was a shadow of future realities (10:1) much like the tabernacle (8:5). Whereas the tabernacle was a mere "shadow of a heavenly sanctuary," Judaism cultic system (= law) *possessed* a "shadow" of a future reality. Second, the "shadow" emphasis within the cultic system was animal sacrifice. Animal sacrifices were deemed ineffective in that they never took away a person's sin (vv. 1, 3–4, 11) evident by the fact that they were repeated yearly (vv. 1, 3, 11; cf. 9:13). Finally, the cultic system of animal sacrifice had been done away (v. 9), which was a reiteration of previous statements (8:13).

On the other hand, there was the inauguration of the new covenant, the covenant that had replaced the Mosaic covenant by way of the once-for-all self-sacrifice of Jesus. First and foremost was the emphasis on the established new covenant (vv. 16–17), which was a reiteration of former declarations (8:7–13; 9:15). Second, Jesus clearly established the new covenant in accordance with God's will (v. 9), which was a reiteration of former statements about God's will for Jesus (2:9b–10). Naturally, an emphasis on the new covenant's viability occurred by way of a blood sacrifice, namely, that of Jesus (vv. 12–14), which was also a reiteration of previous statements (9:15). Finally, this new covenant inaugurated with Jesus's blood provided the forgiveness of sins (vv. 17–18), which was another theological theme peppered throughout Hebrews (1:3d; 2:11, 17; 9:14, 28; etc.).

PREACHING AND TEACHING STRATEGIES

Exegetical and Theological Synthesis

Barnabas began by explaining that the current Judaic system of sacrifices was inadequate (10:1–4). The insufficiency laid in the fact that these sacrifices were limited in time. They were a shadow not the reality, and as a shadow they could never perfect those who drew near. The only hope was the "true form of these realities . . ." found in the person and work of Jesus.

This led to a discussion of the adequacy of the sacrifice of Jesus (10:5–10). The focus of this discussion was Psalm 40:6–8, which the writer put in the mouth of Jesus. Jesus made it clear, using the psalm, that God did not delight in animal sacrifices. The reason the animal sacrifices were not pleasing was that in the execution of the will of the Father, Jesus rendered useless the old shadow. The shadow gave way to the symbols.

The sacrifice of Jesus had the capacity to set apart the faith family (10:11–14), and it established his royal authority, which Barnabas attested to by the use of Psalm 110:1. Finally, this authority led to the institution of a new covenant with believers. Barnabas concluded this section with a discussion of the proofs of Jesus's authority: the testimony of God's spirit, the fulfillment of Jeremiah 31:33, and the fact that he was the life taken so that forgiveness could be offered.

Preaching Idea

The shadow is irrelevant when the reality is here.

Contemporary Connections

What does it mean?

What does it mean that the shadow is irrelevant when the reality is here? There are all types of shadows of reality. Plato taught that the intangibles we experience (love, peace, fulfillment) are representations of the true forms that existed somewhere beyond our ability to see. He was partially correct. All of the qualities of life, love, joy, peace, goodness, happiness, and fulfillment that we experience are shadows that point us to the greater reality.

A mental way to think of this is that long ago the plan was enacted. From the very moment that there was an earth, Jesus stepped out to enter into it. Yet between the time he leaned out of heaven to the time he stepped on the earth, the light of the glory of God was behind him so that his shadow was cast over all the events that proceeded him. Thus, the reason that the OT seems so explicitly to point to Christ is that in the economy of God, he was almost here. The shadow of Jesus announces his presence. And, since the shadows God gave us in the OT always pointed to reality, we should not be surprised that what is in the OT so clearly points to Jesus.

Is it true?

Is it true that the shadow is irrelevant when the reality is here? We see this with anything that we love. Imagine that a child loves to collect baseball cards. If the child had the opportunity to go to a major league game with his favorite players, he would not be looking at his cards! In the same way, we could not go to a concert and put on sound reducing headphones to block out the noise and listen to a recording of our favorite album. If we have a picture of a family member in our home, we would not stare at the picture if that person came to see us. We certainly would not chide the family member if they blocked the view of their own picture!

In the context of the original hearers, there were some who did not like reality because it was blocking their view of the shadow. What a twist! It would seem complete asinine foolishness except for the fact that we see this in our own lives. We often want the blessing more than the source of the blessing. We want the shadow, not the reality.

Now what?

The most immediate application may be to those in the faith family who love the faith family more than they love Jesus. This sounds strange when we say it out loud, but the truth is that our affection for the tangible can draw our affections more to the buildings, the programs, the people, and the relationships as much as what, or rather *who* they ultimately lead us to. The question is not, do I love the organization of the church? But rather, do I love Jesus? All of this that we know and love in local bodies are earthly expressions of eternal realities that we will experience one day.

At the same time, there are some outside of the faith family who love the "good" of this world without realizing that all that good comes from one source. Without acknowledging this, they become inadvertent idolaters who worship a shadow and not the reality. The application to them is simple: the reality is here; the shadows only function is to show us what is real. We don't reject the shadow, but we want to draw so close to the reality of Jesus that he is the focus and not the shadow.

Creativity in Presentation

One way to illustrate this would be to use the illustration of a shadow. Or one could create a shadow on the stage. This can be done with a darkened stage, a simple floodlight, and an object, perhaps on a stand that casts a shadow.

For fuller effect have the object hidden from the audience by a curtain or a stand of some type. When the room is dark, and the light is on, they will be able to see a shadow. The shadow is a real representation.

With the shadow in view, note three truths and then make observations.

- The presence of the shadow is the evidence of the reality.
  If there were no shadow, there could be no reality.
  We often think it is interesting that teachers and preachers and even biblical authors (!) can connect NT truths to OT events. The truth is, this is a backwards way to look at these events. The reality of Jesus is all through the OT because he was always there. He was always waiting to come, and the light of the Father was always there. Therefore, his shadow is on everything in the OT.
  We are cautioned not to project Jesus onto areas in the OT that were not envisioned by the biblical authors. In this way the metaphor works both ways. The light is not coming from us to the NT, to the Old. The light proceeded to us from before the OT and is explained to us by those who saw the shadows in the OT and the reality in the New.

- The shadow is an incomplete picture.
  While the shadow is evidence of a reality, it does not accurately represent the reality. The problem is time and space. The closer the object is to the light, the more accurate the representation of the original object. In the same way, a shadow, by its very definition, is not clear and precise. Thus, while the OT is a picture of Jesus, it is not a complete picture.

- The shadow is irrelevant when the reality is close.
  If I take the object and put it close to me, I no longer see the shadow. This is because the shadow is not relevant when the reality appears. In this way, the reality eclipses the shadow. It is of greater importance. In the same way, the majestic and meaningful shadows of the OT just seem flat and nostalgic when compared to the glory of Jesus.

The point you want to get across is simply this: "Living demands choosing our moments." An outline of this text might be:

- The work of Jesus is effective (vv. 1–10).
- The work of Jesus is singular (vv. 11–14).
- The work of Jesus is complete (vv. 15–18).

DISCUSSION QUESTIONS

1. Why was the original cultic system inadequate (Heb. 10:1–4)?

2. In what ways was the old system a shadow, assuming shadows point to reality (Heb. 10:1)?

3. Note the use of image (*eikon*) in verse 1. Is there a semantic relationship with its use in Colossians 1:15a?

4. How does our understanding of Psalm 40:6–8 change now that Barnabas has attributed it to Jesus (Heb. 10:5–10)?

5. What is the significance in the second use of Jeremiah 31:33 in Hebrews 10:15–18, and how does it differ from its use in Hebrews 9?

Hebrews 10:19–39

EXEGETICAL IDEA
Jesus as God's royal high priest, whose once-for-all self-sacrifice provided confidence to enter God's presence, warranted responsibilities, exhibited limitations for apostates, and expected the recollection of successes and perseverance in their faith in Jesus until he returns.

THEOLOGICAL FOCUS
Confidence in Jesus is limited to those who maintain their believing faith, because apostates will eventually face God's judgment.

PREACHING IDEA
Confidence demands evidence.

PREACHING POINTERS
The first-century world to which Barnabas was writing was hard. There were no social systems to take care of people in their time of need. It was easy to feel alone with no one to help. In their lowest moments, help was inaccessible. Faith in God might have seemed equally distant or as though God was inaccessible. The focus of the OT was not on his immanence but his transcendence. God was "wholly other." It was into this world that the word "confidence" (v. 19) comes streaking in like a meteor. What one did not have, ever, when approaching the throne of God, as represented in the Holy of Holies, was confidence. That confidence allowed them to draw near (v. 22). It motivated them to hold fast (v. 23) and stir each other up to good works (v. 24). Jesus brought them into the presence of hope.

Today people live without confidence for many reasons. Our confidence may be shaken with the crib death of our son, when our husband suffers a major heart attack and dies on Christmas day, when diagnosed with breast cancer, or when our daughter is being abused by her spouse. Where's God? Hurting people lean into their faith when they feel alone. Perhaps, not unlike in the first century, we live without confidence because we feel God is not accessible. To them God is aloof. God is real but apparently untouched by their suffering. Into this dark way of thinking bursts the Light of the World, who brings us near to the Father. For this reason, this passage may be more relevant now than ever. Confidence demands evidence.

ASSURANCES OF JESUS'S ROYAL-PRIESTHOOD (10:19–39)

LITERARY STRUCTURE AND THEMES (10:19–39)

In Hebrews 10:19–39, Barnabas recalled and essentially repeated Hebrews 4:14–16. Many commentators recognize this similar opening and closing to be a natural literary bracketing (or inclusio) whereby Barnabas indicated the opening and closing of 4:14–10:25 as though it were a single literary division of his homily/midrash/letter. Nevertheless, our twofold divisions are intended to stress Barnabas's perspective on who Jesus was (4:14–7:28) and then on what Jesus accomplished (9:1–10:39).

Hebrews 10:19–39 opened with a repeated confidence about the free access to God and Jesus as royal high priest that warranted the corporate worship of God, the corporate perseverance in confessions of faith, and the corporate considerations of how to improve life in the household community of faith (10:19–25). Barnabas then moved to underscore the limitations of Jesus's self-sacrifice and then warned of judgment for those who reject the Son; profane the new covenant; and insult the God who would avenge rebellion, judge people, and cause them to fear him (vv. 26–31). Barnabas closed with an expectation that the household family of faith would recall their past successes and encourage perseverance in their resolve about Jesus, God's exalted royal high priest, until he returns (vv. 32–39).

Barnabas's predominate themes addressed the efficacious nature of Jesus's self-sacrifice and God's judgment that awaits those who reject God's royal high priest.

- ***Confidence and Responsibilities (10:19–25)***
- ***Limitations of Jesus's Self-Sacrifice (10:26–31)***
- ***Remember Successes and Persevere until Jesus Returns (10:32–39)***

EXPOSITION (10:19–39)

Hardships experienced by the household family of faith were part of everyday life. Social support systems were essentially nonexistent. There were no Greco-Roman programs like welfare, Farm Aid, aid for military veterans and families, unemployment, Medicaid, Medicare, Social Security, etc. This lack of any social safety nets was accentuated by government-endorsed persecution whereby a person's property could be seized and people left destitute. In Hebrews 10:19–39, Barnabas compared the difficulties of the Jewish follower of Jesus living in Rome to that of a painful athletic contest whereby someone would often endure public humiliation or shaming. A Roman historian used similar language to describe Nero's persecution of Christians who were either tortured or employed as torches to light the circus by night in 63 B.C. (Tacitus, *Ann.* 15.44). Although the community fell short of suffering martyrdom, Barnabas pointed to the community's success in enduring suffering by their exposure to public humiliation. He offered assurances about Jesus as God's royal high priest, whose once-for-all self-sacrifice had provided a new way to enter God's presence that warranted responsibilities, exhibited limitations for apostates, and expected the recollection of successes and perseverance in their faith in Jesus until he returns.

Confidence and Responsibilities (10:19–25)

Free access to God and Jesus as royal high priest included two assurances that warranted the corporate worship of God, the corporate perseverance in confessions of faith, and the corporate considerations of how to improve life in the community.

10:19. Barnabas opened with yet another long Greek sentence (vv. 19–25) whereby he discussed two theological themes: assurance about Jesus (vv. 19–21) and reasoned responsibilities by members of the household family of faith (vv. 22–25). In essence, it concluded (οὖν, "therefore") what he had been arguing since 4:14. Barnabas began with a twofold assurance for members of the household family of faith (ἀδελφοί, "brothers *and sisters*"). First, they had "confidence" (παρρησίαν) to approach God in his heavenly place of rest (cf. 3:12–4:11). This ability for people to approach God differed from the limited ability to approach God in the tabernacle once a year by one person, the high priest (cf. 5:1–4; 7:27; 9:7–8).

10:20. The means by which the household family of faith had access to God was twofold. On the one hand, it was by means of Jesus's self-sacrifice (ἐν τῷ αἵματι Ἰησοῦ, "by the blood of Jesus") about which Barnabas spoke previously in 9:11–14 and 10:4–12. On the other hand, it was by means of "a new and living way" to God that did not exist while Judaism's cultic system was in place (9:8). Attridge (1989, 285 n. 26) and Koester (2001, 443) liken "way" to the literal creation of new roads in the Roman Empire. Barnabas, however, presented Jesus as "inaugurating" a new and living way to God, which recalled the "inauguration" of the new covenant (7:22; 8:6; 9:15). "Through the curtain" (διὰ τοῦ καταπετάσματος) drew specific attention to the literal veil that separated the inner chamber from the outer chamber of the tabernacle that prevented every priest except the high priest from approaching God (9:3; cf. Mark 15:38).[1] Yet here, Barnabas changed the literal to metaphorical: "the curtain, *that is*, his flesh" (τῆς σαρκός, gen. of ap.; cf. Attridge, 1989, 286). "His flesh" was a metaphor for Jesus's self-sacrifice, which recalled Barnabas's discussions about Jesus's sufferings (2:17–18; 5:7–8; 9:25–28; 10:10). Moffatt (1979, 143) suggests that the "flesh" had to be rent (Mark 15:38) before the "blood" could be presented before God in his "heavenly sanctuary" (cf. Bruce, 1990, 251). Yet, it's probably better to see Jesus's "blood" and "flesh" as parallel metaphors for his self-sacrifice whereby Jesus had entered into God's heavenly place of rest and thereby paved a new way for the household family of faith to approach God with confidence.

Some Recognizable Themes in Hebrews

The Believer's Confidence before God: 3:6; 4:16; 10:19, 35

The Believer's Access to God: 4:16; 10:22

Jesus's Suffering: 2:17–18; 5:7–8; 9:25–28; 10:10

Jesus's Exaltation as Royal High Priest: 5:5–10, 6:20, 7:17–21; 8:1

Jesus's Inauguration of the New Covenant: 8:7–13; 9:15–18; 10:14–17

10:21. The second assurance given to the household family of faith living in Rome was

1 D. Ulansey, "The Heavenly Veil Torn: Mark's Cosmic 'Inclusio,'" *Journal of Biblical Literature* 110.1 (Spring 1991): 123–25.

Jesus himself as "great high priest" (ἱερέα μέγαν; NLT). While the description "great high priest" may refer to the greatness of his priesthood as greater than all other Levitical priests (Ellingworth, 1989, 522; Lane, 1991b, 285), the emphasis served to remind the household family of faith about God's exaltation of Jesus as his royal high priest in 5:5–10, 6:20, 7:17–21, and 8:1 (cf. 1:3d, 13). At this point in Barnabas's argument, there was no "real" comparison to be made between Jesus and Levitical priests since his priesthood was that of the order of Melchizedek (7:14–17). Jesus was presented as God's exalted royal high priest who presided over the household family of faith (ἐπὶ τὸν οἶκον, "over the house"), a phrase Barnabas used previously in 3:6 where he described Jesus as "a son over God's house" (cf. 2:8–11). These two assurances, access to God and Jesus as royal high priest, served as reasons (ἔχοντες, "since we have") why the Jewish household family of faith in Rome had a threefold corporate responsibility (Lane, 1991b, 285).

10:22. Barnabas revealed the household family of faith's responsibility with three "let us" clauses (hortatory sbjv.) that may be summarized in this manner: let us draw near, let us hold fast, and let us consider (vv. 22–24). Each were reasoned expectations. First, "let us draw near" (προσερχώμεθα) was an expectation for the household family of faith to seize opportunities to corporately ("let us") worship God. While Barnabas's expectation to "draw near" (NET, ESV, NIV etc.) or "to go right into the presence of God" (NLT) echoed 4:14, there was a difference. Whereas 4:16 spoke of drawing near to God with confidence, here in verse 22 it spoke of drawing near to God with a "pure conscience" or "with a sincere heart" (ῥεραντισμένοι) reminiscent of a guilt-free conscience (9:14) revealing the inner disposition of an individual (Mitchell, 2001, 211). The reason (ἀπό, "because"; NET; BDAG, s.v. "ἀπό" 5c, p. 106) why people could approach God with a guilt-free conscience was because "hearts have been cleaned from an evil conscience" and "bodies have been washed in pure water" (Ellingworth, 1989, 523). On the one hand, the "clean conscience" and "washed heart" were considered parts of a person that represented the entire person (a synecdoche). So, the entire person was considered purified (BDAG, s.v. "ραντίζω" 2b, p. 903; s.v. "λούω" 2b, p. 603). On the other hand, the purification of the entire person was something accomplished on behalf of the members of the household family of faith (ῥεραντισμένοι, "have been clean"; and λελουσμένοι, "have been washed"; divine pass.). It was an act that God accomplished. These two metaphorical pictures stood in stark contrast to the inadequacies of Judaism's cultic system mentioned in 7:11 and 10:1–2 as well as the ritual baths (*Mikveh*) positioned at the entrance gates to Herod's temple and within the walls of Qumran where a portion of the Essene sect resided. So unlike people who were living under Judaism's cultic system, members of the household family of faith could approach God with a guilt-free conscence and bypass ritual bathings because of a divine act that had purified them from within and thereby made them worthy to draw near to God.

What Is a *Mikveh*?

Mikvehs first appeared during the first century B.C. in Judaea and eventually turned up throughout the Jewish Diaspora. They were bathing facilities whereby "living water" would be used for ritual purity. The water was expected to have contact with a natural source of water and thereby considered "living water." The *Mikveh*'s water, however, was to be able to cover the person's entire body. It was, in fact, a Jewish religous custom whereby a person would be totally immersed in water so that they might be declared "clean." For those living in Qumran, the daily practice of "baptism" was a prerequisite for entrance into the community (1Q28 2.25–3.12) and for partipating in the common meal (Josephus, *B.J.* 2.8.5 §129). Yet other situations existed for this Jewish cultic practice of baptism. A woman was considered unclean after giving birth and would go to a *Mikveh* for ritual purification (4Q265 2.15–17). A family who had contact with a dead family member was considered unclean and would go to a *Mikveh* for ritual purification (11Q19 49.5–21). Mikvehs were used for a variety of "unclean" people (cf. Lichtenberger, 2001, 85–89).

10:23. Second, "let us hold fast" (κατέχωμεν) recalled Hebrews 3:6 and 14. It remained an expectation that directed the household family about the hope they confessed. It was also a call to persevere corporately ("let us"). Thus, the object of Barnabas's expectation remained the same as in 3:6, a "confession of hope." Yet, here there was an emphasis to do so "without wavering" (ἀκλινῆ). While some translations offer "unwaveringly" (NET) or "tightly" (NLT) as though an adverb described the manner by which a person was to hold fast (Koester, 2001, 444), other English translations suggest "without wavering" (ESV). The latter is more descriptive of the firmness or conviction of confession held by someone and recalls "the image of hope as an anchor that keeps the believer steadfast" (Mitchell, 1989, 212; cf. 6:19–20). The reason (γάρ, "for") why members of the household family of faith were to persevere was because God who made promises kept them. "The one who [God] made the promise" (ὁ ἐπαγγειλάμενος) recalls Barnabas's discussions about Abraham in 6:13–15, who would eventually be declared faithful (11:11). Here God was considered "faithful" (πιστός) to keep his promise (cf. Deut. 7:9; 3 Macc 2:11; 1 John 1:9). So, the community was expected to persevere in their corporate confession of Jesus because God kept his promises (cf. Bateman, 2013, 89–125).

10:24. Barnabas continued (καί, "and") with the last of his three expectations, "let us consider" (κατανοῶμεν; ESV) or "let us think of ways" (NLT). And though this expectation was unparalleled in Hebrews, it was a rather important responsibility for the household family of faith to ponder for their corporate life ("let us") and was underscored with the assertion "one another" (ἀλλήλους). The goal was "to provoke" (εἰς παροξυσμόν; KJV, AV, NRSV) one another, not in a pejorative manner but in a positive one: "to love and good works" (ἀγάπης καὶ καλῶν ἔργων). It seems that many translations eliminate any pejorative misinterpretation with an assortment of translational options: "to spur" (NET, NIV), "to stir" (ESV, CNT), "to stimulate" (NASB), or "to motivate" (NLT) one another. Regardless of the translation, the point for the household family of faith was to contemplate how to actively care for one another, a point Barnabas would develop in chapter 13.

10:25. Naturally, extending care for one another was difficult to accomplish if people were absent from community gatherings. So, Barnabas offered an inappropriate means for accomplishing community care: "by abandoning" (ἐγκαταλείποντες, ptc. of means) or "by neglecting" (ESV, NRSV, NLT) or by separating one's self from community gatherings (BDAG, s.v. "ἐγκαταλείπω" 2, p. 273). Barnabas's concern focused attention on the "wrongful abandonment" of the family of faith's corporate gathering for worship (Attridge, 1989, 290). So, it was important to be part of the household family of faith's community gatherings. Barnabas then contrasted (ἀλλά, "but") the inappropriate with an appropriate means of caring for one another, "by encouraging" (παρακαλοῦντες, ptc. of means) or perhaps "by exhorting" (KJV, AV) each other. The call to exhort one another recalls Barnabas's previous exhortation to avoid hardened hearts (3:13–14). Whereas the emphasis in 3:13–14 was an exhortation "as long as it is called 'Today,'" the emphasis here is a bit more urgent: as "you see the day drawing near" (βλέπετε ἐγγίζουσαν τὴν ἡμέραν). Previously, "Today" was viewed more of the entire era during which Jesus was the primary spokes*man* (cf. 1:2). Here in 10:26, the emphasis was on the current era coming to an end, namely, Jesus was coming back soon (see 10:37–38). So, the community was expected to consider seriously the corporate care for one another because Jesus was about to draw this era to an end.

Limitations of Jesus's Self-Sacrifice (10:26–31)

The lack of a sacrifice and the prospect of judgment served as warnings of danger for those who rejected the Son, profaned the new covenant, and insulted the God who avenges sin, judges people, and was to be feared.

10:26. Barnabas provided the grounds (γάρ, "for") for the exhortation he gave at the end of verse 25. While representing an uncertain condition, "if we keep on sinning" (ἁμαρτανόντων, ptc. of cond.; Wallace, 1996, 632), Barnabas's concern was for any "deliberate" (NET, ESV, NIV, NLT, CNT) or "willful" (KJV, ASV, NASB) rebellion against God (= sin; cf. 2:2; 4:2; 10:29). "Deliberate" rebellion was considered any act based upon one's own volition (BDAG, s.v. "ἑκουσίως," p. 307). Although infrequently used, it reflected both a positive and negative sense. In a positive sense, people of their own volition voluntarily employed skills to build the tabernacle (Exod. 36:2), offered a sacrifice (Ps. 53:8), endured suffering (4 Macc 5:23), exercised church leadership (1 Peter 5:2; cf. the noun form in Philem. 14), and submitted to a ruler (Josephus, *A.J.* 12.3.3 §133). In a negative sense, a high priest of his own volition defiled himself (2 Macc 14:3); a couple had premarital sex (Josephus, *A.J.* 4.7.23 §251); people withheld service from God (Josephus, *B.J.* 2.16.4 §394); a person spoke falsehoods (noun: Josephus, *C. Ap.* 1.1 §3); and people committed murder (Josephus, *A.J.* 7.8.4 §185; Philo, *Det.* 26 §97; even suicide: Josephus, *B.J.* 4.7.5 §435). It was also used of Noah's generation to speak of a host of people who willfully and with premeditation competed for who could be the most rebellious (Philo, *Abr.* 40). Here in Hebrews 10:26, however, Barnabas's concern, which included himself, was the free volitional choice to continually rebel against God (cf. Rom. 6:12–14).

Naturally, this concern was addressed to Jewish members of the family of faith in Rome, namely, those "*after* receiving (μετὰ τὸ λαβεῖν) the knowledge of the truth." The content of this "truth" (τῆς ἀληθείας) was about God's spokes*man*, Jesus, through whom God had spoken (1:2b; 2:2:11–13; 10:5–9) and who was God's exalted royal high priest (1:5–13; 5:5–6; 6:20; 7:17, 21; 8:1). The time frame "*after* receiving" (temp. inf.; Wallace, 1996, 594) recalled Barnabas's previous warning about those who were enlightened, experienced the gift of salvation, and had been given a partnership (6:4–8). In Hebrews 6, the emphasis was on "no repentance" for the apostate. Here in Hebrews 10, the emphasis was on the fact that there "no longer remains a sacrifice" (οὐκέτι . . . ἀπολείπεται θυσία) for the apostate. The self-sacrifice of Jesus was once for all, never to be repeated (7:27; 9:12, 26, 28; 10:10). The effects of Jesus's self-sacrifice did not extend to the persistently willful rebellious or disobedient (see 10:18, 9:1–14). Apostates, according to Barnabas, had cut themselves off from Jesus, God's royal high priest (Bateman, 2012, 145).

The Dangers of Apostasy in Hebrews (Bateman, 2012, 145)		
Types of Dangers	**Danger**	**Reference in Hebrews**
Passive Dangers	Believers were encouraged not to drift away or lose sight of the message.	2:1
	Believers were encouraged not to neglect the message.	2:3
	Believers were encouraged not to fall short of the goal.	4:1
	Believers were encouraged not to lose hold of their confession.	4:14
	Believers were encouraged not to become dull in their understanding of the message.	5:11
	Believers were encouraged not to become sluggish in learning more about the message.	6:12 (cf. 5:12–14)
	Believers were encouraged not to lose their confidence.	10:19, 23
	Believers were encouraged not to lose heart.	12:3
	Believers were encouraged not to be carried away by strange teachings.	13:9
Active Dangers	Believers would develop a sinful, unbelieving heart that will turn away from the living God.	3:12
	Believers would exhibit disobedience that mirrors the Kadesh Barnea community.	4:11
	Believers would fall away from Jesus and hold him in contempt.	6:6
	Believers would neglect to meet together.	10:25
	Believers would persist, willfully, in sin and profane the blood of Jesus.	10:26
	Believers would reject God who speaks from heaven.	12:25
External Dangers	Believers would fall away due to the assaults that test their faith.	2:18; 4:16
	Believers would turn away due to their suffering through persecution.	10:32–34; 12:4
	Believers would reject the message due to the threat of torture and imprisonment.	10:33–34; 13:3
	Believers might forfeit future restoration or opportunity for a second repentance.	3:19; 6:4–8; 10:26–31; 12:16–17

10:27. In contrast (δέ, "but") to the members of the community who held fast their confession of faith in Jesus were those who rebelled against God's message about Jesus as his exalted royal high priest and who therefore faced the fearful prospect of judgment. Unlike Barnabas's previous mention of the emotive concept of fear as it related to entering God's heavenly place of rest in 4:1, here in 10:27 Barnabas spoke of God's judgment as something to be feared. This "fearful expectation" (φοβερὰ . . . ἐκδοχή) was, as Attridge (1989, 293) says, "an ominous note enhanced by the indefinite adjective" "only" (τις). Although this expression is more frequently translated as "fearful" (NET, KJV, RSV, NIV, NRSV, ESV), it is also translated "terrifying" (NASB; Lane, 1996b, 273; Koester, 2001, 452) or "terrible" (NLT; cf. BDAG, s.v. "φοβερός,"

p. 1060) with justifiable reasons. The term most frequently occurred in Josephus to speak of a person's attitude toward someone in power like Herod the Great (Josephus, *A.J.* 14.11.5 §286; *B.J.* 1.32.3 §631), but it also appeared in the Septuagint about the Persian king, Xerxes (Esther 15:6). Here in Hebrews 10:27, however, it was not a person to be feared but rather the prospect of judgment. Similar usage occurred in other Jewish literature. For instance, there was the fearful prospect of punishment for neglecting one's duty as a Roman soldier (Josephus, *B.J.* 3.4.7 §103; cf. Acts 12:1–4, 18–19) and of "fearful and woeful things to come" to one's soul for living in an unethical manner (Plato, *Phlb.* 32c; cf. Philo, *Det.* 140; *Gig.* 47). So, Barnabas used the adjective "fearful" quite candidly to issue a severe emotive warning about God's judgment. Whereas the appropriate response to Jesus's sacrifice was provided in 10:19–25, here in 10:26–31 Barnabas warned against an inappropriate response (i.e., deliberate rebellion against God's royal high priest). Thus, rebellion against God's anointed royal high priest would be one of fright or terror (cf. Ps. 2:4–7).

Barnabas continued (καί, "and") his emotive terror with imagery from Scripture (HB LXX) for divine judgment. Apostates were to expect "a fury of fire" (πυρὸς ζῆλος) in their future that "would consume" (ἐσθίειν) or "do away with them completely" (BDAG, s.v. "ἐσθίω" 2, p. 396). While Barnabas's description of God as a consuming fire echoed "For the Lord your God is a consuming fire; he is a jealous God" (Deut. 4:24; NET), Barnabas may have been citing Isaiah 26:11 and Zephaniah 1:18. Isaiah, in his anticipation of God's future judgment said, "O Lord, you are ready to act . . . yes, fire will consume your enemies." Likewise, Zephaniah spoke of the Lord's day of judgment in this manner: "In the day of the Lord's angry judgment, the whole earth will be consumed by his fiery wrath." Thus, Jesus's self-sacrifice had limitations in that it did not extend to willful rebellion against (or rejection of) God's exalted royal high priest; rather, apostates, according to Barnabas, would face the fearful prospect of God's judgment.

10:28. As he did in 2:1–4 and 4:1–11, Barnabas once again spoke of past violators of the legally binding law of Moses. People who "rejected," "declared invalid," or "ignored" (BDAG, s.v. "ἀθετέω" 1, p. 24) the law of Moses experienced a penalty: physical death. Idolatry was a chief example (Deut. 13:6–11). Idol worshippers "died" (ἀποθνῄσκει) "without compassion" (χωρὶς οἰκτιρμῶν; ASV), "without mercy" (KJV, NET, NASB, NRSV, NIV, NLT), or "without pity" (Lane, 1991b, 293). While all of these translations are possible, the latter is preferred because it conveys better the total lack of concern for their misfortune (BDAG, s.v. "οἰκτιρμός," p. 700). Naturally, there were to be at least two or three witnesses to validate a crime (Deut. 17:6). So, people under Judaism's cultic system were punished with physical death if they ignored the Mosaic law.

10:29. Barnabas then drew from this historical recollection about the Mosaic law a logical but heightened conclusion (*qal wahomer*)[2] applicable to one of Rome's household family of faith. Barnabas asked his readers, "how much worse" (πόσῳ . . . χείρονος) punishment will exist for those who disregard God's recent revelation from and about the messianic Son of promise? Following the logic of Barnabas's argument, for example, the verb "set aside" was used earlier in 7:18 and spoke of the entire Mosaic law being "set aside" (ἀθέτησις) due to its uselessness, and later in 8:13 the entire law was described as "obsolete" (παλαιούμενον). Finally in 10:9,

2 *Qal wahomer* is an argument of logic. Arguments begin with a less significant situation to something more significant. Thus, what applies in a less important case will certainly apply in a more important case. For other examples in Hebrews, see Bateman, 2012, 163–64.

the entire law was described as something God had "abolished" (ἀναιρεῖ τὸ πρῶτον). Its inadequacies warranted its replacement with God's new covenant inaugurated by the self-sacrifice of Jesus. Naturally, by the same lesser-to-greater logic, Barnabas was indicating that the divinely decreed consequences were going to be greater than physical death (cf. 2:1–4; BDAG, s.v. "τρισία," p. 1006).

Deliberate defiance defined the "sins" (ἁμαρτιῶν) of 10:26a. More specifically, "contempt" (καταπατήσας) for God's appointed messianic "Son" (cf. 1:1–14), "profaning" (κοινὸν ἡγησάμενος) the new covenant (cf. 9:15), and "insulting" (ἐνυβρίσας) God's spirit who testified about Jesus (cf. 2:4). They defined the meaning of "sin" in 10:26a. "Sin" then was rebellion against God's plan accomplished through Jesus, his appointed Son about whom God had declared his royal high priest. In essence, the words "contempt," "profane," and "insult" defined an apostate (Lane, 1991b, 294; Cockerill, 2012, 488–91).

10:30. Barnabas summarized (γάρ, "for") his candid warning with two verses from the Septuagint and a statement of fact in verse 31. Whereas the first passage was from Deuteronomy 32:35, "Vengeance is mine, I will repay," the second was from Deuteronomy 32:36, "The Lord will judge his people." Contextually, they came from a collection of verses that anticipated the nation of Israel's rebellion and the execution of divine judgment. Barnabas had already reminded the Jewish household family of faith in Rome about the Sinai event (Heb. 2:1–4) and the Kadesh Barnea event (3:7–4:11).

10:31. From these, Barnabas made a factual statement: "it is a terrifying thing to fall into the hands of the living God." "Terrifying" (φοβερόν) appears only in Hebrews (10:27, 31; 12:21). Unlike Hebrews 10:27, there was not the prospect of judgment that was to be feared, but rather the sense of being terrified of the power of the great King of all the earth (Ps. 47:2 [46:3 LXX]). (For examples of fear toward people in power, see discussion of "fearful" [φοβερός] in 10:27.) The phrase "falling into the hands" was a figure of speech for God (anthropomorphism) that Barnabas used to convey to the Jewish household family of faith the idea of coming under someone's power. Here it was God's power. As was the case elsewhere, the phrase had negative connotations (Deut. 32:39–41; cf. NET 430n19). Thus, Barnabas once again appealed to the members of the household family of faith to maintain a proper attitude about the terrifying and dreadful prospect of experiencing God's power. So, the lack of a sacrifice and the prospect of God's judgment for those who rejected the Son, profaned the new covenant, and insulted God's spirit would end with God's revenging their rebellion and thereby the Judge and his judgment should be feared.

Parallel Warnings (Adapted from Bateman, 2012, 146–47; Lane, 1991b, 296–97)		
The Apostate	**Descriptions in Hebrews 6:4–8**	**Descriptions in Hebrews 10:26–31**
Their sin	"they have committed apostasy" (6:6) "they display hostility to Jesus" (6:6) "they shame Jesus publicly" (6:6)	"they have committed apostasy" (10:26) "they have contempt for Jesus" (10:29) "they profane the new covenant" (10:29) "they insult God" (10:29)
Their salvation	"they experienced conversion" (6:4) "they experienced God's grace" (6:5) "they experienced a divine partnership" (6:5) "they experienced God's message (6:5)	"they experienced conversion" (10:26, 32)

Parallel Warnings (Adapted from Bateman, 2012, 146–47; Lane, 1991b, 296–97)		
The Apostate	**Descriptions in Hebrews 6:4–8**	**Descriptions in Hebrews 10:26–31**
Their difficulty	"it's impossible . . . to restore them to repentance" (6:4, 6)	"there's not another self-sacrifice to be offered by Jesus" (10:26)
Their future	"they are cursed" (6:8) "they are consumed in fire" (6:8)	"they are doomed for judgment" (10:27, 31) "they are consumed in fire" (10:27)

Remember Successes and Persevere until Jesus Returns (10:32–39)

Members of the household family of faith were expected to recall previous successes while suffering personal humiliation and loss and yet maintain their resolve about Jesus because Jesus would return, and God would judge all who apostate.

10:32. Barnabas contrasted (δέ, "but" or "instead") his warning about God's judgment of the apostate with an encouragement. He expected his recipients to "remember" (ἀναμιμνῄσκεσθε) an experience in the past. More specifically, they were to recall the time when they endured suffering. The phrase "in which" or "when" (NET, ESV, NIV, etc.; BDAG, s.v. "ἐν" 10b, p. 329) drew attention to a specific time and particularly "a great contest" (πολλὴν ἄθλησιν). Originally used for a warrior exerting himself in battle (Polybius, *Hist.* 5.64.6, 7.10.2–4, 27.9.1–13), here in Hebrews the "contest" was an athletic metaphor for a "severe struggle" (BDAG, s.v. "ἄθλησις," p. 25). In 4 Maccabees 17, there were those in a holy war who endured religious persecution like an athlete (ἄθλησις), competing in a contest for the Mosaic law. Here in Hebrews 10:32, it was a severe struggle that was accompanied "with suffering" (ESV), or the struggle might be described as "painful" (NET; παθημάτων, des. gen.).

This painful conflict occurred "*after* they had been enlightened" (φωτισθέντες; temp. ptc.). The term "enlightened" (NASB, NRSV) elicited Barnabas's similar use in Hebrews 6:4. Members of the Jewish household family of faith in Rome were to recall the hardships they experienced, not after baptism (Käseman, 1984, 187n10), but rather after their conversion (Lane, 1991b, 298; Johnson, 2006, 268).

10:33. Barnabas specified the nature of their sufferings mentioned in verse 33 (τοῦτο, "this" is anaphoric) with a parallel construction: "this on the one hand" (*τοῦτο μέν*) followed by "this on the other hand" (*τοῦτο δέ*). The opening phrases are generally translated as either "at times . . . and at other times" (NET) and "sometimes . . . other times" (NRSV, ESV, NLT; cf NIV). They are two separate but parallel thoughts (BDAG, s.v. "μέν" 1c, p. 630). Barnabas's use of these two anaphoric introductory phrases told how the household family of faith in Rome were struggling. Sometimes (or "on the one hand") their "painful struggle" was "by way of being" (γενηθέντες, ptc. of means) "exposed repeatedly to public humilation" (θεατριζόμενοι). It was the kind of public humiliation that involved some sort of "affliction" or "distress" (BDAG, s.v. "θλίψις" 1, p. 457) brought on by way of some sort of "public shaming" (BDAG, s.v. "θεατριζω," p. 446; deSilva, 2000, 359–60). It is possible that the household family of faith experienced both physical and verbal abuse (Johnson, 2006, 269).

Unfortunately, the word for "public shaming" (θεατριζόμενοι) was an extremely rare word that never occurs in the Septuagint, only once in the NT (Heb. 10:33), and only once in an inscription from the time of Trajan (ca. 102 to 114 B.C.; Jones, 1928; Cadbury, 1930). A Roman historian, however, used similar language to describe Nero's persecution of Christians who were either tortured or employed as torches to light the circus by night in 64 B.C. (Tacitus, *Ann.* 15.44; *TDNT* 3:42–43; Attridge, 1989, 298). In Hebrews 10:33, the verb was typically translated as either "you were made a gazing stock" (KJV), "by being made a public spectacle" (NASB), "by being publicly exposed" (RSV, NRSV), or "you were publicly exposed" (NIV, NET; similarly, NLT). Yet unlike the Jewish followers of Jesus in Jerusalem (Acts 7:54–60; 12:1–2) and those mentioned in Tacitus, the community in Rome fell short of suffering martyrdom (cf. 12:4; Lane, 1991b, 298). Nevertheless, Barnabas stressed the community's success in enduring their public humiliation.

Other times (or "on the other hand") it was "by way of becoming" (γενηθέντες, ptc. of means) co-sufferers with those who were publically shamed. "Co-sufferers" (κοινωνοί) or more often rendered as "partners" (ESV) or "sharers" (NASB), spoke of the household family of faith's taking part in something with someone (BDAG, s.v. "κοινωνός" 1aβ, p. 553). They made themselves partners with those who suffered. Perhaps it was by way of providing food and drink for those whose homes were confiscated and/or imprisioned as suggested in verse 34. There is a possible chiastic structure whereby Barnabas's recollections of verse 33 are expanded in verse 34:

A [33]sometimes by way of being exposed repeatedly to public humiliation,
  B and other times by being co-sufferers with those who were publically shamed.
  B' [34]for indeed, you had sympathy for the prisoners,
A' and you accepted the forcible confiscation of your possessions with joy,

TEXTUAL ANALYSIS: Conflicting Text Critical Reading: 10:34

There are two text critical issues for verse 34. The first is an exegetical issue. Manuscript support exists for both readings. Yet, it appears a scribe unintentionally omitted the first *iota* from the noun "prison" (δεσμίοις; 𝔓[46] 044 104 1739), which in turn led subsequent scribes to add "my" (μου, ℵ K P 88 614 1881). The text is the preferred reading (A 33 1739; cf. Lane, 1991b, 278; Metzger, 1994, 600).

txt. "for you also had compassion for those who were in **prison**" (καὶ γὰρ τοῖς **δεσμίοις** συνεπαθήσατε) (ASV, ESV, NASB, NET, NIV, NRSV)

var. "for you also had compassion for **my chains**" (καὶ γὰρ τοῖς **δεσμοῖς μου** συνεπαθήσατε) (KJV)

The second is a grammatical issue. Manuscript support exists for both readings. Yet, it appears the text was altered from "yourselves" (ἑαυτούς, acc.; 𝔓[13 46] ℵ A H 044 6 33 81 365 1505 1739) to "yourselves" (ἑαυτοῖς, dat.; D K 614 *Byz*), which led a subsequent scribe to add the preposition "among" (ἐν; 1 467 489 1881). The text is the preferred reading (Lane, 1991b, 278; Metzger, 1994, 601).

txt. "knowing that you **yourselves** possessed something better and more lasting" (γινώσκοντες ἔχειν **ἑαυτοὺς** κρείττονα ὕπαρξιν καὶ μένουσαν) (ESV, NASB, NET, NIV, NRSV)

var. "knowing that you possessed **among yourselves** something better and more lasting" (γινώσκοντες ἔχειν **ἐν ἑαυτοῖς** κρείττονα ὕπαρξιν καὶ μένουσαν) (ASV, KJV)

10:34. Barnabas introduced a twofold proof (καὶ γάρ, "for indeed") about members of Rome's household family of faith as co-sufferers. First, Barnabas pointed out that "you had sympathy" (συνεπαθήσατε) for "prisoners" (τοῖς δεσμίοις). Like the high priest in Hebrews 4:15, Barnabas described the household family of faith as exhibiting similar sympathy (BDAG, s.v. "συνεπαθέω," p. 958). Those for whom sympathy was expressed were followers of Jesus who had been shamed publicly and were imprisoned (B B'). It was not unusual for followers of Jesus to be imprisoned. And the Jewish household family of faith in Rome knew it. They knew the temple guard in Jerusalem imprisoned Peter and John (Acts 4:1–2). They knew Herod Agrippa I imprisoned Peter in Jerusalem (Acts 12:3–5). They knew magistrates in Philippi imprisoned Paul and Silas (Acts 16:22–24). They knew Roman governors imprisoned Paul in Caesarea (Acts 23:33–35). The believers in Rome knew Peter through Mark and knew of Paul through Romans and his arrival to Rome (Acts 28:16–18, 23–24). Yet, Paul's imprisonment in Rome was a house-arrest situation whereby he rented his own quarters, depended on others to supply his daily needs, and was guarded by a Roman centurion (Acts 28:16, 30–31; cf. Phil. 4:15–18; perhaps Col. 1:7; 4:12–13; Philem. 10–15). Perhaps the same sort of imprisonment was experienced by members of the Jewish household family of faith in Rome who were dependent on others to survive.

Barnabas continued (καί, "and") with a second proof. They accepted the "forcible confiscation" (NET, NIV; BDAG, s.v. "ἁρπαγή" 1, p. 133), "plundering" (NRSV, ESV), or "seizure" (NASB) of their property. "The loss of property that is most painful," says Johnson (2006, 271), "is that of one's house, and the image developed in chapter 11 of the patriarchs wandering in tents and of those persecuted wandering over desert and mountains and dens and caves of the earth (11:8–10, 38) supports the suggestion that the loss suffered was one of 'place.'" Within the ancient scrolls found at Qumran, there were examples of people who would willingly give their property to join the community (1Q28 6.14–16a) as well as examples of property being seized forcefully (1QpHab 12:1–10). Similarly, the Jewish community in Rome may have willingly given up their property as Jewish believers like Barnabas himself did for the needs of fellow followers of Jesus in Judaea (Acts 4:34–35). Yet here, Barnabas linked their sacrifices to a public humiliation (A A'). The NLT captures the historical event the best: "all you owned *was taken* from you." Yet rather than exhibiting grief and anger, Barnabas not only described the loss as something they "accepted" (προσεδέξασθε), but the manner in which they did so was "with joy" (μετὰ χαρᾶς).

10:35. Based (οὖν, "therefore") on the warning (vv. 31–32) and reminders of success (vv. 33–34), Barnabas issued a reasoned expectation from Rome's Jewish followers of Jesus. He first issued the expectation: "Do not throw away your confidence." "Do not throw away" (μὴ ἀποβάλητε) may have described a less vigorous act like that of a tree losing its leaves (Isa. 1:30 LXX; Tob 11:8) or it may have depicted the removal of a garment like that of blind Bartimaeus who "casts aside" his cloak and went to Jesus (Mark 10:50). Here in Hebrews, while it could be translated simply as "lose" (TEV, BDAG, s.v. "ἀποβάλλω" 3, p. 107), most commentators understand Barnabas's expectation to be a strong prohibition against a deliberate act of abandoning one's faith (Attridge, 1989, 300, Ellingworth, 1993, 550–51). It reinforced Barnabas's warning of verses 30–31 with a strong prohibition: "do not cast [fling] away" (KJV; Westcott, 1984, 335; Koester, 2001, 461) or "do not throw away" (NET, NASB, NIV, RSV, NRSV, ESV, NLT) your faith. Barnabas's concern was after all for the household family of faith's "confidence" (τὴν παρρησίαν). "Confidence" here may be viewed as both a feeling about and a belief in someone (BDAG, s.v. "παρρησία" 3b, p. 781). While Barnabas appealed frequently to "confidence" (3:6, 4:16, 10:19, 35), here the term's usage recalled Hebrews 3:6. Barnabas reiterated his initial concern, first evident in Hebrews 3:6, with a parallel warning: "do not to throw away your confidence" or "do not throw away your *resolve*." In essence, his readers were to maintain their resolve to listen to and obey the message from and about the Son.

Barnabas then provided his reason by way of a relative (ἥτις, "which") clause: "which has a great reward." The "great reward" (μεγάλην μισθαποδοσίαν) was perceived to be a reward received after death. It was a term unique to Hebrews used three times. Unlike in 2:2 where reward was used negatively as a "just penalty" (ἔνδικον μισθαποδοσίαν; NET) to motivate the community to heed his warning in 2:3, here and in 11:26 Barnabas used "reward" (μισθαποδοσίαν) positively about a future certainty (cf. Isa. 40:10, 62:11; Wis 5:15; Sir 2:8, 11:22). This future "reward" was "integrated into the plan of promise of God" and "a powerful motive in their moral struggle" (*TDNT*, 7.701).

TEXTUAL ANALYSIS: Conflicting Text Critical Reading: 10:38

Exegetical Issue: Perhaps the scribe of p13 omitted text so as to bring the Habakkuk 2:4 quote in line with Paul (Rom 1:17; Gal 3:11), which led subsequent scribes to follow (𝔓13 K P 044 81 614). Yet, older and reliable texts support the appearance of "my" (μου) after "righteous one" (δίκαιός; 𝔓46 ℵ A H* 104 257 383 1175 1739 1831 1875). The text is the prefered reading (Metzger, 1994, 601 contra Lane, 1991b, 278).

txt. "but **my** righteous one will live by faith" (ὁ δὲ δίκαιός **μου** ἐκ πίστεως ζήσεται) (ASV, ESV, NASB, NET, NIV, NRSV)

var. "but the righteous one will live by faith" (ὁ δὲ δίκαιός ἐκ πίστεως ζήσεται) (KJV)

10:36. Based (γάρ, "for") upon their "great reward," Barnabas said that they had a need to endure (cf. Lane, 1991b, 302). In other words, they needed to dig deep within themselves "to hold out or bear up" in the face of their difficulties (BDAG, s.v. "ὑπομονή" 1, p. 1039). Barnabas then provided an intended result ("so that"; BDAG, s.v. "ἵνα" 3, p. 477) for this need for mental and emotional resolution. "By doing" (ποιήσαντες; ptc. of means) God's will would result in receiving God's promise. Naturally, "God's will" was for members of the household family of faith to maintain their resolve about God's royal high priest (3:6). The intended result "can only be fulfilled for those who carry out its conditions" (Moffatt, 1979, 157; cf. Heb. 3:6, 12–14; 6:11–18). Thus, by continually doing God's will (= by maintaining your resolve about Jesus as God's exalted royal high priest), they would receive all that God had promised (= as heirs of God's promise: 6:12, 17).

10:37. The reason (γάρ, "for") why members of the household family of faith were to endure was because time was short. Barnabas recalled the concept of "the day is drawing near" (10:25) and further developed it here in verses 37–38. Barnabas's reasoning for enduring was based upon two passages from the Septuagint linked together due to a similar theological theme: divine judgment (*kayose bo bemaqom aher*;[3] cf. Gheorghita, 2003, 182). The first citation, Isaiah 26:20, was from a "Song of Isaiah" that dealt with taking shelter until the future coming of God's wrath had ended. Here in Hebrews, "in a very little while" also spoke of an expected future event. The Isaiah citation was then linked to a second passage from

3 *Kayose bo bemoaqom aher* means "as is found in another place." This rule involves the comparing of texts that have points of general, though not necessarily, verbal exactness (as expected with *gezerah shavah*). Thus, one verse of scripture is linked to another based upon conceptual similarities or parallels and thereby applicable to a new situation. For other examples in Hebrews, see Bateman, 2012, 165.

the Septuagint, Habakkuk 2:3–4.[4] Habakkuk was written in 609 B.C. (latter translated into Greek) about the coming of God's judgment to be executed by the Chaldeans. Yet, Habakkuk was to "wait" for it. It was a passage frequently found and reapplied in other Jewish texts. For instance, when the author of 1QpHabukkuk 6.12–8.3 quoted and then interpreted Habakkuk 2:1–4, the individual who was to "wait" was not limited to Habakkuk but broadened to include any member of the community who lived at Qumran. In fact, the interpretation was all-inclusive of the righteous—the faithful—based upon Habakkuk 2:4 (cf. Bateman, 1997, 89–116). Here in Hebrews those who were assumed to be waiting were the household family of faith. For whom they were to wait was Jesus, God's exalted royal high priest (= 1:3–14; 5:5–6; 7:17–21). "The one who is coming will come" (ὁ ἐρχόμενος ἥξει) spoke of Jesus's return.

10:38. Barnabas transitioned (δέ, "but") to another aspect of the OT citation from Habakkuk. The phrase "my righteous one shall live by faith" was not an appeal to be faithful and thereby a reference to lifestyle (Lewis, 1975–76, 91–94) but rather a life of perpetual trust in God and the one who accomplished his plan, namely, the exaltation of Jesus as royal high priest (BDAG, s.v. "πίστις" 2a, p. 819). The means by which a person was to live everyday life was "by faith" (πίστεως, gen. of means), which stood in contrast (καί, "and") to those who were "hesitant" with regard to trusting God and his exalted royal high priest (BDAG, s.v. "ὑποστέλλω" 2, p. 1041). Thus, they would "shrink away" (NET, ESV, NASB, NRSV, ASV), or "turn away" (NLT) or fail to do "God's will." According to Barnabas, God found "no pleasure" in "*anyone*" who would apostatize (NRSV, NLT). In fact, apostates "displeased" (οὐκ εὐδοκεῖ) God. Unlike verses 6 and 8 where the term "pleasure" (εὐδοκέω) was used positively in connection with Psalm 40 and God's delight in the sacrifice of Jesus, here in Hebrews 10:38 the term was used negatively to contrast the righteous of Habakkuk 2:4. In transposing the word order of Habakkuk 2:4, Barnabas stressed God's displeasure in anyone who would shrink back or fail to persevere till the very end of their physical life. In other words, God took no delight in quitters. Those who failed to please God were those who quit trusting him before their physical death, and according to Barnabas in Hebrews 10:39, they would perish.

10:39. With a rather strong contrast (δέ, "but"), Barnabas brought this unit to a close. In the first half of this verse he spoke "of the timid" (ὑποστολῆς, des. gen.). He quite emphatically (ἡμεῖς . . . *οὐκ ἐσμέν*) *did not* perceive himself and the members of the household family of faith as being "timid" (ὑποστολῆς) and thereby headed "toward destruction" (εἰς ἀπώλειαν). Although rarely used, the word for "timid" meant "reserve" with regard to troops being kept in reserve (Asclepiodotus Tactica 10.21) or "secrecy" with regards to Albinus, the Roman governor over Judaea, doing things in private (Josephus, *B.J.* 2.277). Here in Hebrews 10:39, "timidity" meant fainthearted (BDAG, s.v. "ὑποστολή," p. 1041; *TDNT,* 7:599) and could be rendered as "shrink back" (NET, ESV, NIV, CNT, NASB, NRSV) or "turn away" (KJV, NLT). The word "destruction," though frequent in the NT, appears only here in Hebrews. It tended to speak of people who attempted to thwart God's program like Judas (John 17:12) and the Antichrist (1 Thess. 2:3) or those who distorted God's message (2

4 For a detailed discussion about the textual differences of Habakkuk 2:3–4 in Hebrews 10:37–38, see Koester, 2001, 462–63 or for a more extensive discussion, Gheorghita, 2003, 148–224.

Peter 2:3, 3:16). It was used specifically of those who oppose the church at Philippi whom Paul said were doomed to destruction (1:28; 3:19; cf. Bateman, 1998, 39–62). Here in Hebrews 10:39, those who failed to persevere in their trust in God's deliverance would experience an everlasting state of torment and death like those people who opposed God and his program (2 Peter 3:7, cf. Matt. 7:13; *TDNT,* 1:394–96). For Barnabas, it recalled the exodus event in Hebrews 2, the Kadesh Barnea episode of chapter 4, and the future judgment of God in 10:27.

Barnabas then contrasted (ἀλλά, "but") those "of the timid" with those "of the faith" (πίστεως, des. gen.), namely, members who made it a practice to trust or have confidence in Jesus, God's exalted royal high priest (BDAG, s.v. "πίστις" 2dα, p. 819). It was this active continual resolute faith in Jesus that would "preserve their soul" (εἰς περιποίησιν ψυχῆς). "Preserve one's soul" was typically used of saving one's life from physical death. But here in Hebrews it meant to preserve one's life beyond death (Koester, 2001, 463). In other words, the Jewish followers of Jesus in Rome were among the many members of the household family of faith who "experienced security" as long as they maintained their faith in Jesus (BDAG, s.v. "περιποίησις" 1, p. 804; cf. Col. 1:21–23). The repetition of the word "faith" (πίστις) from Habakkuk 2:4 and the contrast between "those of timidity" and "those of faith" served as a bridge to Hebrews 11 (cf. Ellingworth, 1993, 557). Thus, Barnabas was of the rather strong opinion that he and those to whom he was writing would not be timid and perish but rather maintain their faith and be saved.

Statue of Habakkuk by Donatello (1386–1466). Public domain.

THEOLOGICAL FOCUS

The exegetical idea (Jesus as God's royal high priest, whose once-for-all self-sacrifice provided confidence to enter God's presence, warranted responsibilities, exhibited limitations for apostates, and expected the recollection of successes and perseverance in their faith in

Jesus until he returns) leads to this theological focus: Confidence in Jesus is limited to those who maintain their believing faith because apostates will eventually face God's judgment.

The predominate theological themes in this preaching unit are twofold. The first is about our confidence in Jesus's self-sacrifice. It was efficacious (vv. 5–10, 12–14; cf. 9:11–16, 24–26) except for those who turn away from God's high priest (vv. 26, 38–39). It was through Jesus, whose self-sacrifice provided forgiveness for all those who profess Jesus as God's royal high priest (vv. 16–17, 22), which in turn provided access to God (vv. 19, 22). The second is God's judgment. For anyone who turns from their faith in Jesus, there awaits God's judgment (vv. 27, 29–31, 39).

PREACHING AND TEACHING STRATEGIES

Exegetical and Theological Synthesis

This passage builds on the foundation of 9:23–24 which says, "Thus it was necessary for the copies of the heavenly things to be purified with these rites, but the heavenly things themselves with better sacrifices than these. For Christ has entered, not into holy places made with hands, which are copies of the true things, but into heaven itself, now to appear in the presence of God on our behalf."

Since we have the full assurance of the work of Jesus behind the veil, we enter with confidence (v. 19). As a result, we are lead to the three hortatory subjunctives ("let us") that function as commands: we are to draw near (v. 21), to hold fast (v. 23), and to think about how to lead others to good works (v. 24).

The flow of the passage then turns on the explanatory for (γάρ) of verse 26. The motivation to keep on is the very wrath of God! The logic was that those who turned aside the law of Moses were punished; therefore, whoever has "trampled underfoot the Son of God, and has profaned the blood of the covenant by which he was sanctified, and has outraged the Spirit of grace" (v. 29) would also face the vengeance of God.

The passage ended with the encouragement that their good works were the evidence that they could have confidence (v. 35), and therefore they should not quit but press on and preserve their souls (v. 39).

Preaching Idea

Confidence demands evidence.

Contemporary Connections

What does it mean?

What does it mean that confidence demands evidence? This simply means that if one is going to claim something, then there should be verifiable evidence. If there is not verifiable evidence, then the claim is not valid. If two children in the schoolyard are both claiming that their respective fathers are stronger than the other, these are claims that can be chalked up to boyish bravado. However, if one of the boys had a father that was an Olympic powerlifter, then he could reasonably say that his father is the stronger man.

Is it true?

Is it true that confidence demands evidence? It is one thing to be confident about something and another thing to have that confidence validated. Many times when people today exude confidence, it is unfounded. Imagine an athlete that guarantees his team will win the game. That pronouncement of winning does not cause him to win. No, he still has to play the game! The confidence in oneself means that they must produce evidence that backs up the claim.

In the same way, it is one thing to suggest that all our hope is in Jesus. And yet that assurance must be met with action. The action is the evidence that Jesus is in us. This is the tension that is expressed in Philippians

2:13–14, namely, that we must work out our salvation in cooperation with a God who is working in and through us (Moore et al., 2019, 147–50).

Now what?

Since confidence in Jesus demands the evidence of a changed life, the person who claims confidence in Jesus should evidence that confidence. Applications to this passage could be first to gain the confidence. This passage begs for an evangelistic appeal since all that is good hinges on receiving the confidence. Once we have the confidence, there are applications embedded in verses 19–25. First, draw near to God—this is the posture of seeking to live in God's presence. Second, we hold fast the confession by knowing what we believe and by not being swayed away from it. Third, we should agitate, in a good way, other people to obey God. This active application flows from the idea of confidence.

Finally, there is confidence in the encouragement to persevere in verses 32–39. We are not the kind of people who quit. Our confidence does not work that way. Rather, our confidence is validated in our endurance. In other words, as we endure through opposition and losses due to exercising our faith in Jesus, our confidence grows.

Creativity in Presentation

One creative way to present the idea that confidence demands evidence is to think about people who evoked confidence *without* assurance. One of the most obvious examples of this is fraud. Many times, investors are duped into believing that the money they are investing will have a huge return, when in reality the stock in which they are investing has no value. History is littered with stories of people who invested money, had no real evidence that they had financial security, and then later, toward the end of their life, had nothing. Reference could be made to some of the largest Ponzi schemes in American history.[5]

People in the audience could be asked with a show of hands how many would be willing to give you $5,000 to invest with no assurance of a return? No hands go up! Then, change the game. Since no one will invest $5,000 with no promise of return, then ask them simply to give their entire life savings. No hands go up at the laughable suggesting of investing more. Why? Because the thought of getting to the end of life and having nothing is terrible!

Now is a good time for a pause. After some silence the point is made that if we would not be willing to invest our financial resources without some evidence of a promised return, how would we be willing to entrust our eternity—something that once decided, can never be changed—to a faith that had no evidence? If we keep on deliberately sinning without any evidence that the Spirit is operative in our lives and causing us to endure, then we are banking eternity, including heaven and hell, on a life with no evidence! And a faith with no evidence is a faith with no confidence.

The point you want to get across is simply this: "Confidence demands evidence." An outline of Hebrews 10:19–39 may look like this:

- Remember your responsibilities (vv. 19–25).
- Remember Jesus's self-sacrifice (vv. 26–31).
- Remember successes and persevere until Jesus returns (vv. 32–39).

---

5 See "Top Ten Largest Ponzi Schemes of the Twentieth Century," Trending Stock, https://trendingstock.today/top-10-largest-ponzi-schemes-of-the-21st-century-2.

DISCUSSION QUESTIONS

1. What is the significance of the three commands in Hebrews 10:25? What do they each mean?

2. What exactly is the warning of this warning passage?

3. What does it mean to be apostate?

4. What is the "great reward" of Hebrews 10:35, and why is it a motivation to endure?

5. Why is it dangerous to say that we have faith if we have no confidence?

FURTHER READING

Bateman IV, Herbert W. (editor). 2007. *Four Views on the Warning Passages in Hebrews.* Grand Rapids: Kregel.

Bateman IV, Herbert W. and George H. Guthrie. 2017. "Understanding the New Covenant as Presented in Jeremiah, Understood at Qumran, and Fulfilled in Hebrews." Fifth Annual Let's Know the Bible Conference. Leesburg, IN: Cyber-Center of Biblical Studies.

Lowery, David K. 1992. "Christ, and the End of the Law," in *Dispensationalism, Israel and the Church: The Search for Definition,* 230–7. Edited by Craig A. Blaising and Darrell L. Bock. Grand Rapids: Zondervan.

Milgrom, Jacob. 2000. "Sacrifice." *Encyclopedia of the Dead Sea Scrolls,* Volume 2, 807–11. Edited by Lawrence H. Schiffman and James C. VanderKam. New York: Oxford University Press.

Omanson, Roger L. 1985. "A Superior Covenant: Hebrews 8:1–10:18," *Review and Expositor* 82: 361–73.

Peterson, David. 1979. "The Prophecy of the New Covenant in the Argument of Hebrews 8:1–10:18," *Reformed Theological Review* 38: 74–81.

APPLICATION (11:1—13:25)

As Barnabas moved to close out his exhortation (13:22) to the Jewish members of the household family of faith in Rome, he began with a lengthy list of figures from Scripture. Abel, Enoch, and Noah were commended as righteous, rewarded with life, and delivered from God's unforeseen and impending judgment (11:1–7). These patriarchs trusted God to provide a promised land (vv. 8–10, 13–16) and a promised offspring (vv. 11–12, 17–19) from Abraham and Sarah (vv. 8–19) to Issac (v. 20), to Jacob (v. 21), and finally to Joseph (v. 22). Similarly, Moses, his parents, people of the exodus generation, and Rahab (vv. 12–29) trusted God for future realities. Finally, there were those who experienced military success (v. 33), escaped from death (v. 34), suffered torture (v. 35), suffered physical punishment (v. 36), and suffered persecution and death (vv. 37–38). Each maintained their faith in God, even without the full realization of the promises and privileges that Jesus had provided (vv. 39–40). They all trusted God for future realities.

Based upon chapter 11 (cf. 12:1), several theological themes were woven throughout Barnabas's closing: belief in an unseen God (11:3, 6, 27), trust in promises made by this unseen God (11:9, 11, 13, 17, 33, 39; 12:2, 25), and commendations for looking forward to God's fulfilling of those promises (11:10, 14–16, 25, 35; 12:9, 22–24, 26, 28; 13:8) even if it meant suffering in the process (11:4–5, 7, 11–13, 17–31, 35–38; 12:2–3, 7; 13:3, 12–13, 23). There's also an emphasis on "peace" exhibited by Rahab (11:31) and expected by the household family of faith (12:11, 14), along with their entreating the God of peace.

This fifth division may be divided into four preaching units. The first draws attention to men and women of Israel who exhibited triumphs of faith throughout Israel's impressive story (11:1–40). The second underscores the importance of endurance and discipline by way of the endurance of an athlete and the instruction of a child (12:1–13). The third sermon is a warning about refusing God and the dangers and penalties involved (12:14–29). The fourth is a call to persist in loving one another in real-life situations (13:1–25). At the very end of this section is a list of books and articles for further reading that may be helpful in understanding these preaching units.

Hebrews 11:1–40

EXEGETICAL IDEA

Many well-known Jewish ancestors, who were recognized for their righteousness, believed in the certainty of an unseen creator God's existence and trusted him for their future realities.

THEOLOGICAL FOCUS

Righteous people believe in the certainty of an unseen creator God and trust him for future realities.

PREACHING IDEA

Faith is real confidence in unseen realities.

PREACHING POINTERS

Hebrews 11 is a literary monolith, yet one that has parallels in other Jewish literature (Sir, 3 Macc, CD). Barnabas's listing of Jewish heroes, however, draws attention to those who have triumphed in faith. It is as beautiful as it is daunting. While the beauty of this passage is appropriately well noted, what must not be missed it how breathtakingly intertextual this is. We have in this passage some explanations of the life of Noah and of Abraham that give us more information than in the original books of Genesis and Exodus, respectively! Beyond this, the OT characters are spoken of in terms of Jesus. For example, Moses is described as having considered the reproach of Christ. So, this beautiful passage helps us understand how the compositional nature of Scripture speaks to its oneness.

Throughout life we understand that people are successful because they believe. Like a golfer envisioning a ball going in the hole before he ever swings his putter, we know that successful people believe. They envision their success and therefore succeed. While that is true, what is going on here in Hebrews 11 is much deeper than that. This is not holy hoping. This faith is an absolute confidence in the kingdom of God. And as a result, this confidence is rewarded by God's commendation (v. 39). Faith is real confidence in unseen realities.

TRIUMPHS OF FAITH (11:1–40)

LITERARY STRUCTURE AND THEMES (11:1–40)

Moving from Scripture's declaration that the righteous live by faith and remain steadfast in that faith (Hab. 2:4), Barnabas drew specific attention to righteous people who triumphed in their belief in God during the antediluvian period, namely Abel, Enoch, and Noah (vv. 1–7). He then remembered the righteous who triumphed in their belief in God during the patriarchal period, namely, Abraham, Sarah, Isaac, Jacob, and Joseph (vv. 8–22). Barnabas then reminisced about the righteous who triumphed during the exodus period, namely Moses, the parents of Moses, the people who passed through the Red Sea as on dry land, the people who conquered Jericho, and Rahab (vv. 23–31). Barnabas closed out his list with the righteous who triumphed in their belief in God during the post-exodus period, namely Gideon, Barak, Samson, Jephthah, Samuel, David, and others (vv. 32–40). Thus many well-known Jewish ancestors, recognized for their righteousness, believed in the certainty of an unseen creator God's existence and trusted him for their future realities.

Barnabas's theme centered around people or groups of people who trusted in and remained faithful to God.

- ***Triumphs of Faith during the Antediluvian Period (11:1–7)***
- ***Triumphs of Faith during the Patriarchal Period (11:8–22)***
- ***Triumphs of Faith during the Exodus Period (11:23–31)***
- ***Triumphs of Faith during the Post-exodus Period (11:32–40)***

EXPOSITION (11:1–40)

Commendation and condemnation of people of the past were part of Jewish culture and evidenced in Jewish literature. Sometimes those memories of historical figures were to prevent the repeat of misconduct and divine judgment. This most certainly was the case for the exodus generation, fallen angels, and Sodom and Gomorrah. These three historical events were condemned, and their transgressions often repeated in canonical and noncanonical Jewish literary works as warnings.

Exodus, Fallen Angels, and Sodom and Gomorrah in Other Jewish Literature			
Type of Literature	**Exodus Generation**	**Fallen Angels**	**Sodom and Gomorrah**
OT Record	Numbers 13:1–14:45 (cf. Deut. 9:7–8)	Genesis 6:1–6	Genesis 19
Subsequent OT Record	Psalm 78 Psalm 95 Ezekiel 20:10–36		Deuteronomy 29:23 Isaiah 1:9; 3:9; 13:19 Jeremiah 49:18; 50:40 Amos 4:11 Ezekiel 16:46–56

Exodus, Fallen Angels, and Sodom and Gomorrah in Other Jewish Literature			
Type of Literature	**Exodus Generation**	**Fallen Angels**	**Sodom and Gomorrah**
Noncanonical Record	Sirach 16:6 3 Maccabees 2:6–7 CD 3.5–12	Sirach 16:5–7 3 Maccabees 2:4 CD 2:17–20 1 Enoch 6–7 (cf. 7–19; 21; 86–88; 106:13–17) Jubilees 5:1–2 (cf. 4:15, 22) 1QapGen 2:1; 6:20 T. Reub. 4:15, 22 T. Naph. 3:5 Josephus, *A.J.* 1.3.1 §72–73	Sirach 16:8 3 Maccabees 2:5 Testament of Naphtali 3:4
New Testament Reference	Acts 7:38–44 1 Corinthians 10:1–5 Hebrews 3:7–4:11 Jude 5–7	Jude 5–7 2 Peter 2:4	Matthew 10:15; 11:23–24 Luke 10:12, 17:29 Romans 9:29 Jude 5–7 2 Peter 2:6–10a

Similar lists were created to commend people for their good conduct. For instance, Ben Sira opened with "Let us now sing the praises of famous men, our ancestors in their generation" (Sir 44:1 NRSV) and then lists numerous Jewish figures along with a brief descriptive reason for praise (Sir 44:1–50:21). Appeals to endure hardship were sometimes based on historical figures such as Abraham and Daniel as in 4 Maccabees 16:18–23.

> Remember that it is for God's sake you were given a share in the world and the benefit of life, and accordingly you owe it to God to endure all hardship for his sake, for whom our father Abraham ventured boldly to sacrifice his son Isaac, the father of our nation; and Isaac, seeing his father's hand, with knife in it, fall down against him, did not flinch. Daniel also, the righteous one, was thrown to the lions, and Hananiah and Azariah and Mishael were cast into the fiery furnace, and all endured for the sake of God. Therefore, you who have the same faith in God must not be dismayed. For it would be unreasonable for you who know true religion not to withstand hardships. (trans. Anderson, 1985, 561)

Like his Jewish literary counterparts, Barnabas urged Jewish members of the household family of faith in Rome to recognize those who trusted God in the past. He too listed many well-known Jewish ancestors, recognized for their righteousness, who believed in the certainty of an unseen creator God's existence and trusted him for their future realities.

Triumphs of Faith during the Antediluvian Period (11:1–7)

Belief in the certain reality of the existence of God the creator of all things led to Abel's, Enoch's, and Noah's divine commendations of righteousness and divine approval as having pleased God.

11:1. Building upon Hebrews 10:39, Barnabas transitioned (δέ, "now") to a general but *not* exhaustive definition of faith (ἔστιν . . . πίστις;

"faith is").[1] While commentators often debate over Barnabas's limited definition, translations also wrestle with how to render Barnabas's opening statement. On the one hand, faith could be defined as the "assurance" (NASB, NRSV, ESV, CNT) of something: "faith *is* the assurance . . . ." The translation "assurance" underscores a person's confidence (subj.). "It is a personal state of certainty" (Koseter, 2001, 472) or "sure confidence" (NET, NIV; cf. BDAG, s.v. "ὑπόστασις" 3, p. 1040). "Assurance" was used earlier in this subjective sense concerning the believer's "confidence" (3:14; τῆς ὑποστάσεως).

On the other hand, it could be "the substance" (KJV, AV) or "the reality" (NLT) of something: "faith *is* the reality. . . ." The translation "reality" distinguishes faith from a mere "appearance." Faith is a guarantee or, as Moulton and Milligan say, "faith is the *title-deed* of things hoped for" (MM, 1930, 659; cf. BDAG, s.v. "ὑπόστασις" 4, p. 1040). In other words, "faith gives substance to our hope" (NEB) or "faith is the ground of things, which are hoped for" (Geneva). Cockerill (2012, 520) says it this way: "Faith is living as though the things hoped for are real" (cf. Attridge, 1989, 309–10; Lane, 1991b, 329). The objective meaning appeared earlier in Barnabas's description of the Son as being in the very image of God (1:3; τῆς ὑποστάσεως).

Both options have validity, but the latter has greater force because it more in keeping within Barnabas's immediate context of Hebrews 10. The fulfillment of God's plan about the exalted royal high priest who inaugurated a new covenant (10:23; cf. 3:6) that guaranteed the household family of faith's future promises was a present-day reality for which had anticipated (= hoped) ramifications (10:36; cf. 6:17–20). "Faith" gave substance to their "hope" (cf. NLT; BDAG, s.v. "ἐλπίζω" 1b, p. 319) and thereby served as the foundation upon which they had "hope" (cf. Geneva; BDAG, s.v. "ἔλεγχος" 1, p. 315). "Faith" was their "proof" (*TDNT*, 2:476) or as Käsemann (1984, 42) suggests, "certainty of the uncertain, a seeing of the invisible." Thus, faith was, for Barnabas, belief in realities and convinced of those realties that anticipated something not yet visible to the naked eye.

11:2. Barnabas confirmed ("for"; BDAG, s.v. "γάρ" 1d, p. 189) *his* definition of faith with specific examples. The phrase "by this" (ἐν ταύτῃ, anaphoric) was instrumental for introducing a select number of people in history past that exemplified what "faith" (= belief in unseen realties) looked like in everyday life (BDAG, s.v. "ἐν" 5b, p. 328). While some translations say, "people of old" (NET, ESV, NLT) or "the elders" (KJV, ASV), the more appropriate rendering is "our ancestors" (NRSV, cf. NIV; BDAG, s.v. "πρεσβύτερος" 1b, p. 862). Yet to limit the list to men (cf. NASB, CNT) would exclude the women in this catalog of people selected to exemplify faith (vv. 11, 23, 31, 35). Each person, man and woman, in Barnabas's record "received commendation" (NET), or more appropriately they were "well-spoken of" (BDAG, s.v. "μαρτυρέω" 2b, p. 618). This recognition should not be limited to God's commendations in Scripture (cf. NET, CNT; Lane, 1991b, 330) but should be more inclusive of many godly people. They had in fact "earned a good reputation" (NLT).

Similar lists appeared in other Jewish literature of the Second Temple period. The most notable list was found in the apocryphal writing entitled Sirach, chapters 44–50. Ben Sira opened with "Let us now sing the praises of famous men, our ancestors in their generation" (Sir 44:1 NRSV) and then listed Noah, Abraham, Aaron, Moses, Phinehas, Joshua, Caleb, Samuel, Nathan, David, Elijah, Hezekiah, Josiah, Ezekiel, Zerubbabel, and others. Each person was given a brief descriptive reason

1 The position of the verb (ἔστιν, "is") at the very front of the Greek sentence *equates* emphatically that "faith" and "ὑπόστασις" are equivalent (BDAG, s.v. "εἰμί" 2a, p. 283; cf. Attridge, 1989, 307; *TDNT*, 2:476 n. 4).

for praise. Of the Davidic kings, Ben Sira said, "Except for David and Hezekiah and Josiah all of them were great sinners, for they abandoned the laws of the Most High" (Sir 49:4 NRSV). So, there were a notable number of well-known Jewish ancestors who had received recognition from not only God but other godly people as examples about whom were worthy of attention.

Who Was Ben Sira?

Ben Sira, a scribe who lived and taught in Jerusalem before the Maccabean revolt of 167–164 B.C., wrote the apocryphal book entitled Sirach (also known as Ecclesiasticus or Wisdom of Jesus Ben Sira; cf. Sir 50:27). "Ben Sira," according to deSilva (2002, 153), "was no reactionary, but he was definitely a conservative voice of the first and second century B.C.E., calling his pupils to seek their fortune, their honor, and their good name through the diligent observance of the demands of the God of Israel first and foremost." The book was probably written sometime ca. 180 B.C. And though Sirach is a book of wisdom teachings about proper speech, riches and poverty, honesty, diligence, choice of friends, and sin and death, it is not totally proverbial. Sirach concludes with a hymn of praise about famous Jewish ancestors (41:1–49:16).

11:3. Before disclosing his list of examples, Barnabas interjected another element about faith. He began with "by faith *we understand*" (πίστει νοοῦμεν). Based on careful thought (BDAG, s.v. "νοέω" 1c, p. 674), the household family of faith was to grasp the creation account in Genesis wherein God established purposefully the temporal "universe" (ESV, NLT; or "world"; BDAG, s.v. "αἰών" 3, p. 33). In Hebrews 1:2, the "universe" was created through "a son," here it was created through God's direction, more pointedly "God's command" (ῥήματι θεοῦ). While "God's word" (ῥήματι θεοῦ) is another possible translation (ESV, KJV, NASB, NRSV, CNT), members of the household family of faith would probably recall God's "let there be . . ." commands in the opening chapters of Genesis (NET, NIV, NLT; cf. Bruce, 1990, 279). Thus, the translation "command" seems more appropriate. In either case, the result (εἰς . . . γεγονέναι; εἰς + infin.) of this creation process was this: from the invisible came the visible. For Barnabas, the emphasis was on the fact that God created the universe as evident in the following chiastic pattern (Ellingworth, 1989, 568; Koester, 2001, 474).

A were set in order (κατηρτίσθαι)
  B the universe (τοὺς αἰῶνας)
    C the command of God (ῥήματι θεοῦ)
    C' by the not visible (μὴ ἐκ φαινομένων)
  B' the visible (τὸ βλεπόμενον)
A' has its origins (γεγονέναι)

The origin (= set in order) of the physical universe (= visible) was by divine command (= invisible). Not that Barnabas argued for an *ex nihilo* doctrine of creation, but rather that he denied "the autonomy of the visible, created universe," and he affirmed the planetary and celestial "dependence on the power of God" (Attridge, 1989, 315; cf. Heb. 1:3).

Triumphs of Faith: The Antediluvian Period

Person	OT Reference	OT Event	Hebrews
Abel	Genesis 4:2–16	Abel offered an acceptable sacrifice to God.	11:4
Enoch	Genesis 5:22–24	Enoch pleased God and did not experience physical death.	11:5
Noah	Genesis 6:9–22	Noah heeded God's warning and built an ark, and he and his family lived.	11:7

TEXTUAL ANALYSIS: Conflicting Text Critical Reading: 11:4
Exegetical Issue: Manuscript evidence supports the text (𝔓[13* 46] 044 0285 1739 1881). Elsewhere in Hebrews "I offer" (προσφέρω) is not followed by "to God" (τῷ θεῷ; 5:1, 3, 7; 8:3, 4; 9:7, 9, 25, 28; 10:1, 2, 8, 11, 12; 11:27; 12:7). Thus, the early manuscript supporting the variant 𝔓[13] may represent an original reading, but the textual reading is preferred. There is strong evidence for questioning the decision and for favoring the variant reading, as with Hebrews 1:8 (see Textual Analysis on 1:8).

txt. "by faith Abel offered **to God** a more acceptable sacrifice than Cain" (πίστει πλείονα θυσίαν Ἄβελ παρὰ Κάϊν προσήνεγκεν **τῷ θεῷ**) (ASV, ESV, KJV, NASB, NET, NIV, NRSV)

var. "by faith Abel offered a more acceptable sacrifice than Cain" (πίστει πλείονα θυσίαν Ἄβελ παρὰ Κάϊν προσήνεγκεν)

11:4. With the phrase "By faith, Abel," Barnabas not only introduced the first well-known Jewish ancestor of the *antediluvian period*, but began a rather simple yet long anaphoric literary pattern[2] that eventually ended in verse 31 (BDF 260, §491). Moving beyond the fact that the story of Abel in Genesis said nothing about his faith, the biblical record about Abel was noticeably sparse (cf. Gen. 4:3–5) as were some of the retellings of the event in Jewish literature (e.g., Jub. 4:1–5). Nevertheless, the Genesis record recalled "at a designated time Cain brought some of the fruit of the ground for an offering" while "Abel brought some of the firstborn of his flock—even the fattest of them" (NET; cf. Ross, 1988, 157). As a result, God was pleased with Abel's sacrifice but displeased with Cain's. Unfortunately, the Genesis account offered no reason as to why Abel's sacrifice was accepted, and Cain's rejected. Jewish tradition about Abel suggested that it was because Cain honored himself before God (e.g., Philo, *Sacr.* 20; *QG* 1.60). In Jude 11 and Jewish tradition, Cain was an agent of wicked greed (cf. Bateman, 2015[17], 242–49). Contemporary commentators, however, link the reason to the Levitical code that described an acceptable offering (Ross, 1988,157; Wenham, 1987, 103), or they suggest that while Abel carried his "religious duty ideally," Cain merely "discharged his duty" and thereby revealed his indifference about his gift to God (Cassuto, 1978, 1:205). Nevertheless, Barnabas underscored Genesis's statement about God's pleasure in Abel's sacrifice wherein he concluded, interpretively, that Abel's sacrifice was "greater" (NET), "better" (NASB, NIV), or "more acceptable" (ESV, NRSV, NLT, CNT; BDAG, s.v. "πολύς" 1bα, p. 849) than Cain's. Yet, Barnabas's point was not about Abel's "*more acceptable* sacrifice." It was Abel's faith (Ellingworth, 1993, 571). It was *his faith* "through which" (δι' ἧς) Abel offered a sacrifice to God, and *that faith* pleased God.

Barnabas first recognized that Abel's faith was a divine commendation of righteousness (cf. vv. 1–2). Barnabas connected Abel with his previous reference to Habakkuk 2:4 in 10:38. And though Genesis was silent about Abel's being ascribed a "righteous" person, Jewish tradition was not. Josephus (*A.J.* 1.2.2 §53) described Abel as one who "had respect for *righteousness*, and, believing that God was with him at all his actions" (trans. Thackeray, 1978, 24–25; cf. T. Iss. 5:1–4). Thus, Barnabas echoed his Jewish contemporaries. Barnabas recognized that "though *he is dead*" (ἀποθανών; concessive ptc.), Abel's faith still spoke (ἔτι λαλεῖ, "still speaks"). While there was no evidence of Abel's heavenly existence (Koester, 1989, 476), the historical record of Abel's faith and divine commendation of

2 An anaphoric literary pattern is the repetition of a word or phrase at the beginning of successive clauses or sentences. In Hebrews 11:3–31, it's the repetitious use of "by faith" (Bateman, 2012, 191).

righteousness continued to speak of him and thereby was a well-founded starting point for Barnabas, as it was for Mathew when he discussed the coming of the kingdom and the divine judgment that would fall upon those who persecuted God's righteous people: "from the blood of righteous Abel to the blood of Zechariah, son of Barachiah" (Matt. 23:35; cf. 1 John 3:12).

"Cain leadeth Abel to Death" by James Tissot (between 1896 and 1902). Public domain.

11:5. "By faith, Enoch" introduced the second well-known Jewish ancestor of the *antediluvian period*. As it was the case with Abel, the Genesis account said nothing about Enoch's faith. Barnabas opened with Enoch's "being taken up" (μετετέθη). The verb means "to bring to another place," "to set in another place," or "transfer" (BDAG, s.v. "μετατίθημι" 1, p. 641; *TDNT,* 8.161). It was used in the Scripture (HB LXX) for resetting boundary markers (Deut. 27:17) and ancient landmarks (Prov. 23:10). In Acts 7:16, Stephen recalled how the bones of Jacob and others were "transferred" from Egypt to Shechem for burial. His body was transported from one geographical location and placed in another. Here in Hebrews 11:5, Enoch was "taken up" from this life on earth. He never experienced the sufferings associated with death (cf. Wis 4:10–11). His reward was escaping physical death (Johnson, 2006, 282). All three antediluvian figures, Abel, Enoch, and Noah, attracted special attention in Judaism. Yet, Ben Sira listed Enoch first in his praises of famous men of the Bible (Sir 44:1–50:24), and Enoch was well-known in Jewish literature (e.g., 1, 2, 3 En.; 4Q530–533; cf. Bateman, 2015[17], 300–15). Due to the years spent believing God's existence and living by faith (Heb. 11:6), Enoch was literally taken up into the heavens and, as suggested in Jubilees, "was with the angels" (4Q227 frag. 2.2; trans. Wise et al., 1996, 265). He was described as "the blessed and righteous man of the Lord" (1 En. 1:2).

The reason (γάρ, "for") for God's removal of Enoch from earth was not because he repented of sins as suggested in some Jewish literature: "Enoch pleased the Lord and was taken up, *an example of repentance to all generations*" (Sir 44:16 NRSV, emphasis added; cf. Philo, *Abr.* 17–18, 35; *QG* 1.82–85). Nor was it because "he walked with God" as was stated in the Hebrew Scriptures (MT: Gen. 5:22, 24). "Walk with [*hitpael* verb הָלַךְ, with אֶת] God" was a rare expression. In 1 Samuel, it was used of two groups of people who maintained a cordial and cooperative relationship as they worked and lived side by side in the fields (25:15). The expression "may imply that Enoch lived in close fellowship with God, leading a life of devotion and piety" (NET n. 11). So, Enoch's epitaph in Genesis 5:21–24 recorded his having had a "close fellowship with God" and then, after 365 years, "he was no more." "God took him." Barnabas, however, followed the Septuagint's interpretive translation of the expression "he walked with God" and wrote "he was well-pleasing" (εὐηρέστησεν; Gen. 5:22, 24; cf. Wis 4:10–15). "Before he was taken up" (πρὸ . . . τῆς μεταθέσεως) from earth to heaven, God had commended Enoch as one whose faith had pleased him. "It was, then, his disposition of faith during his life," according to Johnson, "that leads to God's gift of continuing life" (2006, 282). This rendering of Enoch's pleasing God served as Barnabas's transition to his further teaching about faith.

11:6. Barnabas paused to add (δέ, "and") yet another general truth about faith, namely, that "without faith it is impossible to please God." This was Barnabas's fourth and final "impossibility" (ἀδύνατον) cited in Hebrews. In 6:4, the adjective declared the absolute impossibility of an apostate to be renewed to faith. In 6:18, it asserted the absolute impossibility of God to make a false assertion. In 10:4, it asserted the absolute impossibility of animal sacrifices to take away sin. Here Barnabas declared the absolute impossibility to please God without faith. More would said about pleasing God in 12:28 and 13:16, 21.

Barnabas then provided for his original recipients two specifics (γάρ, "for") or requirements about his general statement about faith that pleased God. The first requirement was simply that people who approached (τὸν προσερχόμενον, "the one who approaches") God must believe God existed (ὅτι ἔστιν, "that he is"). While Barnabas admitted that God was an invisible realty (11:27) that no one had ever seen (John 1:18; cf. Exod. 33:20), God was still the object of faith (Heb. 4:16; 10:22). While Greco-Roman people tended to believe in many gods (polytheistic; cf. Acts 17:16–31; Philo, *Opif.* 1.170–72), Barnabas stressed the need to believe in the "one God" who created the universe (Heb. 11:3; cf. Acts 17:23–24). He emphasized that God was pleased when the household family of faith believed he existed. And yet, all of Judaism tended to confess God's existence as one God (Shema: Deut. 6:4; cf. 4 Macc 5:24).

Barnabas continued (καί [ὅτι], "and [that]") with a second requirement about faith that pleased God, namely, that this "one" God was the "rewarder" (μισθαποδότης; cf. Heb. 2:2; 10:35; 11:35). God had always been viewed as one who rewarded people. At Mount Gerizim, God promised to reward (= bless) all those who obeyed him with protection and physical prosperity (Deut. 28:1–14). Good actions were to lead to good outcomes (cf. Prov. 13:21). Yet, during the time of Barnabas, it had become clear that there was no *precise* relationship between good conduct and earthly rewards (cf. Job 8:6; Tob 1:3, 6–20; Josephus, *A.J.* 10. 6. 3 §98).

So, God's physical rewards were combined with something yet to come. For the household family of faith who were suffering persecution in Rome (10:32–35), the prospect of God's future reward would be encouraging. It pleased God when the household family of faith believed he would reward those who made it a practice to seek him. Thus, like Enoch, pleasing God *began* with believing that God not only existed but that God also rewarded those who sought out (τοῖς ἐκζητοῦσιν, "those who seek out") the God of creation and lived accordingly (cf. 11:26; 2 John 8).

11:7. "By faith, Noah" introduced the third and final well-known Jewish ancestor of the *antediluvian period*. As it was the case for Abel and Enoch, Genesis said nothing about Noah's faith. Yet, more so than Abel and Enoch, Noah's account was well attested in the NT (Matt. 24:37–39; Luke 17:26–27; 1 Peter 3:20; 2 Peter 2:5) as well as other Jewish literature (cf. Sir 44:17; Philo, *QG* 2.1–55; Jub. 5.19–6.16; 1Q19–20; 4Q422 2[frags. 2–6].1–13; Josephus, *A.J.* 1.3.2 §§75–79). Moving beyond the observation that Barnabas ignored the Septuagint's depiction of Noah as having "pleased" God (εὐηρέστησεν; Gen. 6:9)—which would have been a perfect verbal link to Enoch—Barnabas purposely steered his discussion in Hebrews 11:7 to "when he [Noah] was warned" (χρηματισθείς; temp. pass. ptc.). Noah received "a divine injunction" (BDAG, s.v. "χρηματίζω" 1α, p. 1089) about a forthcoming event "not yet seen" (τῶν μηδέπω βλεπομένων; cf. v. 3). God "warned him about things that had never happened before" (NLT). This warning fits naturally into Barnabas's overall context. He too had warned the household family of faith in Rome about unforeseen events that would occur to those who rejected Jesus, God's exalted royal high priest (cf. 2:1–3; 3:15–4:1; 6:1–6; 10:26–31).

In his recollection of Noah, Barnabas identified Noah as the first Jewish ancestor in this chapter who responded "by faith" to a divine message. On the one hand, his first "by faith" response was that he built an ark "out of reverence" (εὐλαβηθείς) for God (NET, NASB; Koester, 2001, 477). While "with fear" (KJV; cf. Sir 41:3; 2 Macc 8:16) and "with reverent fear" (ESV; cf. CNT) are other possible renderings, Barnabas's description of Noah paralleled that of Jesus's reverence for God (Heb. 5:7). However, unlike Jesus, Noah did so for "the physical preservation" (BDAG, s.v. "σωτηρία" 1, p. 985) "of his house" (τοῦ οἴκου αὐτοῦ = family household; cf. 3:1–6). On the other hand, his second "by faith" response (δι' ἧς, "through which"; fem. sg.) was that "he condemned the world." While it is possible that the very act of building an "ark" (fem. sg.) was "a visible evidence of his faith to his unbelieving and scoffing contemporaries" and thereby his life's actions of faith condemned the world (D. Guthrie, 1983, 230; Cockerill, 2012, 533; seemingly KJV, CNT), it seems more than likely that "by faith" (fem. sg.) Noah actually preached a message of condemnation (NLT; cf. Attridge, 1989, 319; Lane, 1991, 2:339). So, it was "by faith" that Noah (1) built an ark and (2) preached a message of an unforeseen divine judgment.

"Noah" Mosaic in Bailica di San Marco, Venice (12th–13th century). Public domain.

Barnabas continued (καί, "and") his proclamation about Noah with a historical testimonial about Noah. "Based upon his faith" (κατὰ πίστιν) or corresponding with his faith, Noah "became an heir of righteousness" (δικαιοσύνης ἐγένετο κληρονόμος). The term "righteousness" drew attention to Noah's correct response that resulted in a form of redemption for him and his family (BDAG, s.v. "δικαιοσύνη" 2, p. 247). While Josephus (*A.J.* 1.3.2 §75) contended that "God loved Noah for his righteousness," the author of Jubilees 10:17 commended Noah in this manner: "On account of his righteousness in which he was perfected, his life on earth was more excellent than (any of) the sons of men except Enoch" (trans. Wintermute, 1985, 76; cf. Jub. 5:19). Ben Sira praised Noah in this manner: "Noah was found perfect and righteous; in the time of wrath he kept the race alive" (Sir 44:17 NRSV). Thus, Noah's faith led him to construct an ark that delivered him and his family from God's unforeseen flood and to preach a message of divine judgment whereby he was deemed an heir of righteousness.

Despite the fact that the Genesis accounts about Abel, Enoch, and Noah said nothing of their faith, each figure of the *antediluvian period* was built from Barnabas's "interpretive key," which he established from Habakkuk 2:4 in Hebrews 10:38 (Koester, 2001, 481–83).

Triumphs of Faith: The Antediluvian Period			
Person	**OT Reference**	**OT Event**	**Hebrews**
Abel	Genesis 4:2–16	Abel offered an acceptable sacrifice to God.	11:4
Cain	Genesis 4:4	Cain offered an unacceptable sacrifice to God.	11:4
Enoch	Genesis 5:22–24	Enoch pleased God and did not experience physical death.	11:5
Noah	Genesis 6:9–22	Noah heeded God's warning and built an ark, and he and his family lived.	11:7

Barnabas echoed his contemporaries when he drew attention to the righteousness of Abel, Enoch, and Noah. What was unique to Barnabas's presentation, however, was his connection with Habakkuk 2:4 whereby these historically recognized people of righteousness lived by faith. Another Jewish author drew attention to righteous people in this manner: "Then the righteous will stand with great confidence in the presence of those who have oppressed them and those who make light of their labors" (Wis 5:1 NRSV). Thus, having believed in an unseen God as creator, having sacrificed to an unseen God, having pleased an unseen God, and having obeyed an unseen God; Abel, Enoch, and Noah were commended as righteous, rewarded with life, and delivered from God's unforeseen and impending judgment.

Triumphs of Faith during the Patriarchal Period (11:8–22)

Belief that God would keep his promise of land and offspring, the patriarchs obeyed and trusted God for their future realities.

Triumphs of Faith: The Patriarchal Period			
Person	**OT Reference**	**OT Event**	**Hebrews**
Abraham	Genesis 12:1–8; 23:4	Abraham migrated from Sumer for a new land.	11:8
Sarah	Genesis 17:15–21; 18:9–15; 23:4	Sarah, via an angel, was promised to conceive a son.	11:11
Abraham	Genesis 22:1–4	Abraham offered Isaac as a sacrifice.	11:17
Isaac	Genesis 27:27–29, 39–40	Isaac blessed Esau and Jacob.	11:20
Jacob	Genesis. 48:15–50	Jacob blessed his sons.	11:21
Joseph	Genesis 50:24–25	Joseph gave instructions about his burial in the Promised Land.	11:22

11:8. "By faith, Abraham" introduced the first well-known Jewish ancestor of the *patriarchal period*. Yet, this was the third mention of Abraham in Hebrews (cf. 6:13–15; 7:4–10). Naturally, Abraham's account was well attested in Jewish literature. He was described as "the great father of a multitude of nations, and no one has been found like him in glory" (Sir 44:19 NRSV; cf. Philo, *Spec. 1,2,3,4.* 3.228; *Abr.* 68–72, 77–83; 4Q252 1.ii.8.10; Josephus, *A.J.* 1.7.1 §§154–57). Barnabas, however, underscored two facts about Abraham's faith. The first "by faith" fact was his obedience: "he obeyed" (ὑπήκουσεν). Like Noah, Abraham received divine instructions. "When he was called" (καλούμενος; temp. ptc.) to move to another geographical location, "he followed instructions" (BDAG, s.v. "ὑπακούω" 1, p. 1028; cf. Gen. 12:1–2). And while the word "obey," did not appear in Genesis 12:1, Abraham's obedience to God's call was well known (cf. Gen. 22:18; 26:5; Philo, *Abr.* 60). Philo (*Migr.* 43), in his comments on Genesis 12:1, pointed out that Abraham's obedience testified to the trust that he had in God "not as called out by accomplished facts, but by expectation of what was to be" (trans. Whitaker, 1932, 32–33). Thus, Abraham obeyed God in anticipation of an inheritance. Barnabas then added (καί, "and") that Abraham "went without understanding" (ἐξῆλθεν μὴ ἐπιστάμενος) or "he was unacquainted" with the land to which God led him (BDAG, s.v. "ἐπίσταμαι" 1, p. 380). Attridge contends that "he was ignorant of his destination" (1989, 322). So, despite his uncertainty or ignorance, Abraham followed God's instruction. Barnabas's emphasis on Abraham's obedience recalled Jesus having learned obedience (Heb. 5:8) as well as his emphasis for "all those who obey" (5:9; Johnson, 2006, 289).

11:9. The second "by faith" fact (v. 9) about Abraham was that he moved from an affluent earthly society to a new geographical location. He migrated "to the land of promise" (εἰς γῆν τῆς ἐπαγγελίας). It was a land not his own where he lived as a foreigner or as a stranger (παρῴκησεν . . . ὡς ἀλλοτρίαν). He lived in the midst of other people groups. *He was an immigrant* (BDAG, s.v. "παρκοιέω" 2, p. 779) who lived in temporary dwellings as a nomad, namely, he lived "in tents" (BDAG, s.v. "σκηνή" 1a, p. 928). During the time of Abraham, it was not unusual to migrate from one country to another, especially when famines plagued a country (cf. Gen. 12:10; 41:56–57; Ruth 1:1). Abraham, as well as his immediate heirs, Isaac and Jacob, were nomadic people who pitched tents most of their lives (LXX: Gen. 13:3–5; 18:1–2; 31:25; but cf. 33:17). The "image of nomadic existence," says Attridge (1989, 323), "makes for a vivid contrast with the 'city,' an image of permanence and stability that is the ultimate goal." During the Greco-Roman period, immigrants or foreigners had no rights and were denied certain privileges associated with Roman citizenship (cf. Koseter, 2001, 485). In fact, a person could be stripped of such rights and privileges (Philo, *Flacc.* 53–54). For some, members of the Jewish household family of faith in Rome were disadvantaged (10:33–34). Perhaps some lost their Roman citizenship and lived *like* nomads in the city of Rome without any permanent dwelling (cf. Acts 18:1–3). Perhaps Barnabas was drawing a loose parallel with Abraham whereby some followers of Jesus lived in Rome as though they were *like* strangers and foreigners. So, unlike the Genesis account where Abraham's faith underscored a belief that God would give him an heir (Gen. 15:6), Barnabas emphasized Abraham's "by faith" response to follow God's instructions whereby Abraham moved to a place where he had no rights or privileges and thereby lived a nomadic life.

11:10. Barnabas's reason (γάρ, "for") why Abraham was willing to make such a move was because he looked forward to "a population center in contrast to a relatively uninhabited or rural area," namely, "a city" (BDAG, s.v. "πόλις" 1, p. 844). More specifically, Abraham looked forward to an unseen population center whereby the city's foundations were divinely designed and built by the ultimate craftsman, God (cf. 3:4; 12:22). Perhaps the household family of faith in Rome was hopeful for a successful Judaean war against Rome whereby God would, as in the past, "help" (עֶזְרָה; Ps. 46:4–5) Jerusalem, the city whose foundations he established (יְסוּדָתוֹ; Ps. 87:1; cf. Koseter, 2001, 486). Based upon Isaiah 54:11, there were those in Judaea who believed God built Jerusalem on the foundation of priests and not stones (4Q164 1–3). But eventually, Barnabas would clarify the city of which he spoke. It was not to be an earthly city, but rather a "heavenly Jerusalem" (12:12; 13:14). Naturally, the one who would govern the "heavenly city" was God's royal high priest, Jesus.

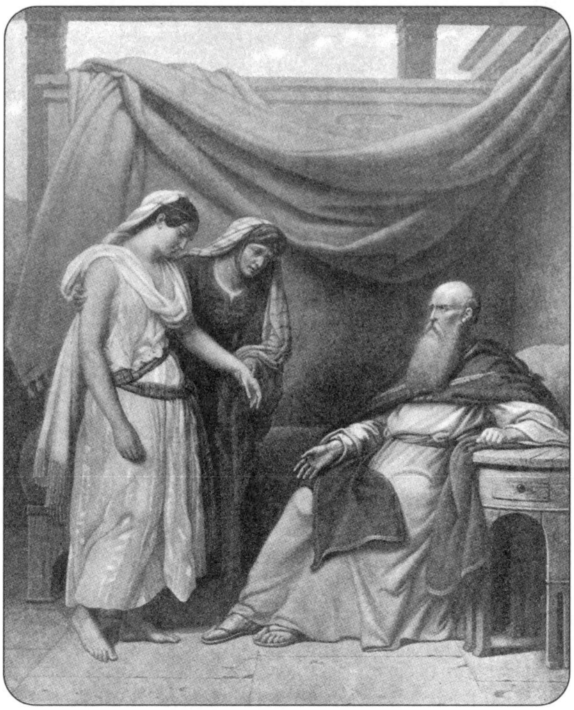

"Abraham, Sarah, and Hagar"
by Charles Foster (1897). Public domain.

TEXTUAL ANALYSIS: Conflicting Text Critical Readings: 11:11

Cultural/Exegetical Issue: Problems abound with this variant. First, "receive" (ἔλαβεν) could be translated as either "he received" or "she received." Thus, "he" (Abraham) became a "father" (σπέρματος; NIV, NRSV, NET). Or "she" (Sarah) became "pregnant" (σπέρματος; ASV, ESV, KJV, NASB). Second, "the barren one" (στεῖρα) was added (𝔓[46] P 044 81 88 1739). It seems more probable that "the barren one" (στεῖρα) dropped out of subsequent manuscripts (א A 33 614). Thus, the text is the preferred reading (Lane, 1991b, 344; Metzger, 1994, 602).

txt. "by faith—even though Sarah herself **the barren one**—he/she received power to conceive" (πίστει—καὶ αὐτὴ Σάρρα **στεῖρα**—δύναμιν εἰς καταβολὴν σπέρματος ἔλαβεν)

var. "by faith—even though Sarah herself—he/she received power to conceive (πίστει—καὶ αὐτὴ Σάρρα—δύναμιν εἰς καταβολὴν σπέρματος ἔλαβεν)

11:11. "By faith, even Sarah herself" introduced the second well-known Jewish ancestor of the *patriarchal period.* While some translations render Abraham as the grammatical subject (NET, NIV, NRSV; Attridge, 1989, 325–26; Koester, 2001, 487), Sarah appears to be the focus of this verse (KJV, RSV, NASB, ESV, NLT, CNT; Johnson, 2006, 291–92; Cockerill, 2012, 543–45). Barnabas provided an additional point (καί, "even") about Abraham's situation. "Even" (καί) his wife, Sarah, exhibited faith in God's promise. Abraham and Sarah were the first of two married couples in chapter 11 to be honored for their faith (cf. v. 23).

Despite the fact that Genesis presented Sarah as being somewhat skeptical concerning her ability to birth a child, Barnabas underscored her trust in God. First, Barnabas made it clear that Sarah was "beyond the normal age" (παρὰ καιρὸν ἡλικίας) for bearing children. "Beyond the normal age" was an idiomatic expression for "she was barren" (NLT, CNT; BDAG, "s.v. "ἡλικία" 2a, 436). Sarah's barrenness was clearly evident in Genesis (11:30; 15:11; 17:17; 18:11–12; cf. Philo, *QG* 4.15).

According to Genesis, she was also skeptical about her ability to give birth even after all the assurances God had given Abraham. At one point, she even took matters into her own hands and then blamed her husband for the outcome (16:1–5). She even laughed at the notion that she might give birth at ninety years of age (18:1–2, 3–8). Josephus (*A.J.* 1.11.2 §§197–198) described Sarah's response as a woman who "smiled [μειδιασάσης] and said that childbearing was *impossible* [ἀδύνατον], seeing that she was ninety years old and her husband an hundred" (trans. Thackeray). Yet, she was no more skeptical than Abraham when he questioned, "Can a son be born to a man who is a hundred years old" Can Sarah bear a child at the age of ninety?" (NET; Gen. 17:17). Nevertheless, Barnabas underscored how Sarah "received the ability to establish a posterity" (BDAG, s.v. "καταβολή" 1, p. 515). What Sarah saw as "*impossible*" (ἀδύνατος), God made "*possible*" (δύναμις). But in order for this divine intervention to occur, Sarah had to have sex with Abraham (cf. Rom. 4:17–22). "Abraham casts the seed," says Johnson (2006, 292), "but Sarah receives the power for it [the conception] to happen." Barnabas then moved to his interpretive conclusion about Sarah.

The reason (ἐπεί, "because") why she conceived and gave birth to a son, Isaac, was because she "considered" (ἡγήσατο) the "one who made the promise" (ἐπαγγειλάμενον; cf. 6:13–14) to be "faithful" (πιστὸν) to keep his promise and thereby behaved accordingly. "God did for Sarah what he had promised" (NET; Gen. 21:1–2).

11:12. Barnabas then explained (διὸ καί, "therefore" or "and so") the importance of Abraham's and Sarah's faith (vv. 8–11), namely, that their *joint* trust in God produced "children" (NET), "descendants" (ESV, NRSV, NIV, CNT) or a "nation" (NLT). Although the text reads "from one *they* were born" (ἀφ' ἑνὸς ἐγεννήθησαν; cf. KJV), English translations clarify "they" with a specific referent to "descendants." Clarifications of the Greek text continue for the phrase: "and *these* as good as dead" (καὶ *ταῦτα νενεκρωμένου*). Most translations render "these" (ταῦτα) as "him" (NET, ESV, NASB, KJV). Yet, the word "these" (ταῦτα; neut. pl.) in this parenthetical phrase referred to both Abraham and Sarah (vv. 8–11). Furthermore, the previous statement "from *one* [ἑνός; neut.] descendants were born" is also elusive. "From *one*" might be rendered "from *one* [*couple*] descendants were born" and not limited to "from *one* [*man*]" (NET, ESV, NIV, etc.). Like the word "man," "couple" would be considered an ellipsis (BDAG, s.v. "εἷς" 1, p. 291). So, "these" (ταῦτα) two people, Abraham and Sarah, who as a couple (ἑνός) were beyond childbearing years, trusted God, and acted on God's promise, which in turn contributed to God's fulfillment of his promise to them both. It was from this one married duo that God fulfilled his promise of numerous descendants: "like the number of stars in the sky and like the innumerable grains of sand on the seashore." Naturally, Barnabas may have been conflating God's initial promise to Abraham (and Sarah) here, but there were similarities in Genesis 22:17 and Daniel 3:36 (Lane, 1991b, 55; Attridge, 1989, 327). Nevertheless, the point remains: Abraham and Sarah trusted God for future unseen realities.

11:13. Barnabas placed, in the middle of this list of patriarchs who had triumphed in their faith, an interpretative observation: "these all died, in faith." Lane (1991b, 355) describes verses 13–16 as a "retrospective glance over the patriarchal period" (cf. Attridge, 1989, 329). Barnabas's retrospection, however, broke his anaphoric pattern of "by faith" in two ways. First, "these all died" was placed forward for emphasis. Consequently, the demonstrative pronoun "these" (πάντες) referred to all those mentioned in verses 9–12: Abraham, Sarah, Isaac, and Jacob. Second, Barnabas changed from "by faith" (πίστει) to "in faith" (κατὰ πίστιν). They died "in faith" "without receiving the promises." Although Barnabas just spoke of God's fulfilling his promise about children to Abraham and Sarah (v. 12) as he did in 6:15, here he spoke of "the promises" (τὰς ἐπαγγελίας) plural as unfulfilled. They were the land promises. The only land Abraham owned was the field of Machpelah, which he purchased from Ephron the Hittite in the presence of a group of Hittites so that he could bury Sarah (Gen. 23:4; cf. Jub. 19:1–9).

In contrast (ἀλλά, "but") to God's unfilled promise of land—the whole point for leaving Ur—Barnabas returned to the theme of living a nomadic way of life (v. 9). The patriarchs "confessed" (ὁμολογήσαντες; indep. ptc.) or "admitted" that they were "strangers and foreigners" (ξένοι καὶ παρεπίδημοί) in the land of Canaan even though Abraham had purchased the field of Machpelah (Gen. 23:4; cf. 49:29–32; Jub. 46:9–10). Jacob also described himself to Pharaoh a temporary resident of the land (Gen. 47:4, 9). The term "foreigner" or "aliens" conveyed the fact that the patriarchs were well aware of their inability to participate in civic matters (BDAG, s.v. "παρεπίδημος," p. 775; cf. Johnson, 2006, 292). The combination of "strangers and foreigners" (ξένοι καὶ παρεπίδημοί) expressed a single idea (hendiadys[3]), namely, that they were "sojourning strangers" (Lane, 1991b, 357). Perhaps some of the household family of faith in Rome felt alienated. Yet, there was an applicational distinction. Whereas the patriarchs felt like "sojourning strangers" in the specific land of Canaan, Barnabas expanded the description to be "on the earth" (ἐπὶ τῆς γῆς). Attridge (1989, 330) suggests that Barnabas's expanding of the patriarch's status to be "on the earth" was a contrast with his forthcoming discussion about a "heavenly homeland" (v. 14; cf. 13:14). And yet, it may recall Barnabas's previous dialogue about entering God's heavenly place of rest (4:1). Regardless, Barnabas used the word "confess" to link the patriarchs with his Jewish readers in Rome. Both conceded something or admitted something to be true (BDAG, s.v. "ὁμολογέω" 3a, p.708–9). Both made confessions (cf. 3:1; 4:14; 10:23).

11:14–15. Barnabas concluded (γάρ, "for") his interpretive retrospection of the patriarchs with an all-inclusive "the ones who speak in such a way" (οἱ τοιαῦτα λέγοντες) or "people who speak in such a way" (ESV). The patriarchs, or anyone, who said they were "strangers and foreigners on the earth" were, according to Barnabas, "seeking a homeland" (πατρίδα ἐπιζητοῦσιν). The idea of "seeking" tended to express a strong desire for something (BDAG, s.v. "ἐπιζητέω" 2a, p. 371).

Barnabas continued his conclusion (καί, "and") in verse 15 with a contrary-to-fact statement (εἰ μὲν . . . ἄν; second class cond.; BDF 182 §360): "if they had been thinking of from which they had gone out (which they weren't), they would have had the opportunity to return (which they didn't)." "From which they had gone out" (ἀφ᾽ ἧς ἐξέβησαν) was a typical idiomatic expression for "land" (NET, ESV, NRSV) or "country" (NLT, NIV, NASB). The phrase referred to the homelands of Abraham: Ur of the Chaldeans and Haran (Gen. 11:31). While Abraham's servant returned to Haran in search of a wife for Isaac (Gen. 24:4), and Jacob fled from Esau to Haran where his uncle

3 A hendiadys is a figure of speech whereby two words are used for one. In other words, two formally coordinate terms express a single concept in which one of the components defines the other (Bullinger, 1968; Trotter, 1997, 170–71; cf. Bateman, 2012, 194).

lived (Gen. 27:43), neither resided in Haran permanently (Koester, 2001, 490).

11:16a. In contrast (νῦν δέ, "but as it was") to returning to their original homelands, the patriarchs were said to "long for" or "desire" (BDAG, s.v. "ὀρέγω," p. 721) something "better." Their desire was an intense one (Attridge, 1989, 332). The term "better" (κρείττων) was a favorite term used throughout Hebrews (1:4; 6:9; 7:7, 19, 22; 8:6; 9:23; 10:34; 11:16, 35, 40; 12:24; cf. Bateman, 2012, 123). Here Barnabas spoke of a "better *homeland*," that is, "a heavenly *homeland*." Naturally, translations provide various insertions after the adjective "better": "better *land*" (NET), "better *place*" (NLT), and most often, "better *country*" (ESV, NIV, NASB, NASV, KJV). The same is true for "heavenly" (ἐπουράνιος): "heavenly *one*" (ESV, NIV, CNT, NASB, NASV; cf. KJV) because in both cases the noun was omitted (an ellipsis; BDF 125 §241). Yet, a "better *homeland*" and a "heavenly *homeland*" (NLT) renderings are in keeping with the context (πατρίδα, "homeland; v. 14). Finally, the appearance of "heavenly" corresponds with Barnabas's other "heavenly" emphasis: "heavenly call" (3:1), "heavenly gift" (6:4), and "heavenly Jerusalem" (12:22). Not that the patriarchs had the same theological understanding of heaven as Barnabas and his Jewish contemporaries, but that the patriarchs were trusting the God of heaven for their future unseen realities.

11:16b. Barnabas concluded (διό, "therefore") his retrospection about the patriarchs (vv. 8–16a) with a statement about God's feelings for them. There was to be no mistake about God's compassion for the patriarch's longing for something better. Barnabas wrote "God is not *ashamed* of them" (οὐκ *ἐπαισχύνεται* αὐτοὺς ὁ θεός) or "God is not too proud" to be called their God (BDAG, s.v. "ἐπαισχύνεται" c, p. 357). Jewish authors wrote of God as the God of Abraham, Isaac, and Jacob (1 Chron. 29:18; 2 Chron. 30:6b) and spoke of Abraham, Isaac, and Jacob with statements such as the "God of your fathers" (Exod. 3:15–16; Deut. 1:21; Josh. 18:3, etc.). Yet more importantly, God (הְוֹהָי, "Yahweh") explicitly declared himself to be the God of Abraham, Isaac, and Jacob: "[the LORD] said, 'I am the LORD, the God of your grandfather Abraham and the God of your father Isaac'" (Gen. 28:13; cf. Exod. 3:6, 15). Barnabas had already emphasized that Jesus was "not ashamed" (οὐκ ἐπαισχύνεται) to call his followers brothers and sisters (2:11), and God appeared to provide here a similar assurance. With the old covenant becoming obsolete (8:13) and the inauguration of the new covenant (9:15), Barnabas assured the household family of faith that just as the expression "I will be their God" was applicable to those under the Mosaic covenant (Gen. 17:8; Exod. 29:45; Jer. 24:7; 32:38; Ezek. 11:20; 14:11; 37:2, 27; Zech. 8:8), God would also be the God of the people under the new covenant (8:11; cf. Mitchell, 1989, 241; Koester, 2001, 490).

The reason (γάρ, "for") for God's undaunted feelings toward the patriarchs' longing for another city (cf. vv. 10, 14, 16) was because "he [God] had prepared a city for them" (ἡτοίμασεν . . . αὐτοῖς πόλιν; NET, NRSV, NIV, NLT). Lane (1991b, 359) contends that "the fervent longing of the exemplars [patriarchs] of faith was not misguided" because "a place of sanctuary is an important theme in apocalyptic literature (e.g., Rev. 12:6; 21:2; *2 Apoc. Bar.* 4:3; cf. John 14:2)" (cf. Ellingworth, 1993, 599).

11:17–18. The phrase "By faith, Abraham" served to reintroduce the first well-known Jewish ancestor that began this series of triumphs about the *patriarchs* as well as a return to Barnabas's anaphoric pattern of delivery. Here Barnabas recalled Abraham's offering of Isaac (Gen. 22:1–19). The recounting of the event was not unique to Barnabas. Numerous Jewish works recounted Abraham's story (Jub. 17:15–16; 18:1–19; Philo, *Abr.* 167–207; 4 Macc. 16:18–20; Josephus, *A.J.* 1.13.1–4 §§222–36). Like his contemporaries, Barnabas spoke of a time of Abraham's testing (πειραζόμενος, "when tested"; temp. ptc.). Yet, unlike Jubilees where an evil figure was responsible for the testing (like Job), Barnabas presented God as testing Abraham (Koester, 2001, 491). God's "testing," however, was done in a "favorable sense" in an endeavor to discover the nature or character of Abraham (BDAG, s.v. "πειράζω" 2b, p. 792). As a result, Abraham was not found wanting but "proved faithful" (Sir 44:20). He trusted God when "he offered up Issac." Abraham became a model for being successful in testing.

Barnabas expanded (καί, "and") Abraham's triumph with the addition of another specific (vv. 17b–18). Naturally, Abraham received the promise of an heir (Heb. 6:14–15; 11:11–12). Barnabas restated that Abraham "offered up Isaac," but now Barnabas underscored Isaac as his "only son" (τὸν μονογενῆ). Here Barnabas emphasized God's asking of Abraham to surrender the possibility of successors (cf. Lane, 1991b, 360). While it was true that Ishmael was his son (Gen. 16:15), God told Abraham that it was through Isaac's descendants whereby Abraham's name would flourish (Gen. 21:12).

11:19. Barnabas continued (καί, "and") with an interpretation. Abraham was presented as "having reasoned" (λογισάμενος). In essence, Abraham gave careful thought to God's request (BDAG, s.v. "λογίζομαι" 2, p. 597). The content (ὅτι, "that") of Abraham's careful thought was about restoring life to Isaac. The rare verb form "to raise" (ἐγείρειν) was used in Sirach to speak of Elijah's restoring life to a dead person: "You raised [ἔγειρον] a corpse from the dead" (48:5a NRSV; cf. Elijah: 1 Kings 17:17–24; Elisha: 2 Kings 4:32–37; cf. Mark 5:35–43; John 11:38–44). With the exception of Daniel 12:2, the OT concept of "resurrection" was that of restoring physical life to a person who had died. So, Abraham's concept of resurrection would have differed from the NT's eventual development of resurrection (consider the debates between the Pharisees and Sadducees; 2 Macc 7:9–14; 28–29; Josephus, *B.J.* 2.8.10 §153). Nevertheless, Abraham's willingness to obey God, even though Abraham was stopped just before killing Isaac on an altar, was symbolic of restoring Isaac's dead corpse from the dead (Mitchell, 1989, 245). With the knife to his throat, Johnson says, Isaac was "as good as dead" (Johnson, 2006, 295).

11:20. Barnabas ended this section about the patriarchs with three quick "by faith" statements about the three other patriarchal figures. The first was "by faith, Isaac also blessed. . . ." While this statement was an allusion to Genesis 27:27–40, Isaac's faith was never mentioned. Yet, Koester (2001, 492) suggests that Barnabas's description of Isaac as having pleased God (Gen. 48:15 LXX) was equivalent to faith based upon Hebrews 11:6—"without faith it is impossible to please him" (NET). So, if Isaac "pleased" God, ergo Isaac had faith.

Barnabas also limited his brief recall of Isaac to Isaac's paternal blessing of his two sons, Esau and Jacob. When Isaac "blessed" (εὐλόγησεν) his sons (Gen. 27:27; Jub. 26:19–33; 27:18), he was petitioning God to bestow upon his sons "special favor," especially as it concerned "God's gracious power" (BDAG, s.v. "εὐλογέω" 2a, p. 408). Barnabas made no mention of Esau's having sold his birthright or of Jacob's deception of his father (cf. Attridge, 1989, 335–36). And even though Barnabas indicated that both Jacob and Esau were given a blessing (cf. Gen. 27:38–40; Jub. 26:32–33; Philo, *QG* 4:231–33), that's not the case later in Hebrews 12:17. Furthermore, Barnabas showed no interest in the specifics of these blessings (Ellingworth, 1993, 604). His interest was simply in indicating Isaac's faith in petitioning God to bestow divine promises to his sons with no particular details given about certain "things to come" (Moffatt, 1979, 178).

Nevertheless, Barnabas defined these "things to come" (BDAG, s.v. "μέλλω" 3, p. 628) elsewhere throughout his work, namely, the inheriting of salvation (κληρονομεῖν σωτηρίαν; 1:14), "the world *to come*" (τὴν οἰκουμένην τὴν *μέλλουσαν*; 2:5), "the miracles of age *to come*" (δυνάμεις . . . *μέλλοντος* αἰῶνος; 6:5, NET), the law was "a shadow of the good *things to come*" (σκιὰν . . . τῶν *μελλόντων* ἀγαθῶν; 10:1), and the city "that is yet *to come*" (τὴν *μέλλουσαν*; 13:14). Thus, "he blessed concerning the *things to come*" (περὶ *μελλόντων* εὐλόγησεν) encompassed, for Barnabas, many *things to come* even though these eschatological specifics were unknown to Isaac at the time (Mitchell, 1989, 245; Koester, 2001, 492). These specifics were known, however, to Barnabas and the household family of faith only because of the coming of Jesus as God's royal high priest.

11:21. The phrase "By faith Jacob" was Barnabas's second example in his closing statement about the patriarchs. Like Isaac, Jacob's faith was never mention in Genesis. Although Jacob was not recognized as someone who was "faithful," he was recognized in Jewish tradition as a righteous man (Wis 10:10; Jub. 27:17), ergo a man of faith based upon Habakkuk 2:4 (Heb. 10:38; cf. Koester, 2001, 493). The period of Jacob's life upon which Barnabas dwelt was the blessing Jacob gave to his grandchildren born to Joseph, Manasseh and Ephraim. Isaac blessed his grandsons "as he was dying" (ἀποθνῄσκων, temp. ptc.; cf. Gen. 48:1, 21, 29). And just as it was the case with Jacob and Esau, so it was with Manasseh and Ephraim that Jacob "blessed" the younger, Ephraim, first then the older (Gen. 48:14–20).

After Jacob "blessed" (εὐλόγησεν) Joseph's sons, Barnabas alluded to a clause in Genesis: "then Israel bowed down at the head of his bed" (NET; Gen. 47:31). Chronologically, the clause initially appeared after Jacob blessed all of his sons and before blessing Manasseh and Ephraim. Yet, what Barnabas underscored was Jacob's worship during his final hours. Following the Septuagint's translation of Genesis 47:31, Jacob "worshipped as he leaned on his staff" (προσεκύνησεν ἐπὶ τὸ ἄκρον τῆς ῥάβδου αὐτοῦ). In other words, Jacob, as he was approaching death, expressed an attitude of complete dependence and submission to God (BDAG, s.v. "προσεκυνέω" 1bα, p. 183).

11:22. The phrase "By faith Joseph" was Barnabas's final example in his closing statement about the patriarchs. As it was with Isaac and Jacob, Jewish tradition identified Joseph as a righteous man (cf. Wis 10:13; Jub. 40:8; T. Benj. 5:4), ergo a man of faith based upon Habakkuk 2:4 (Heb. 10:38; cf. Koester, 2001, 493). By way of a euphemism, the period of Joseph's life upon which Barnabas dwelt was when he was about to die: "when his end *was near*" (τελευτῶν, temp. ptc.; BDAG, s.v. "τελευτάω" 2, p. 997; Gen. 50:24). So like Jacob, Barnabas underscored some of the final words of Joseph. Yet, unlike Jacob where Barnabas focused attention on Jacob's blessing descendants, Barnabas underscored two aspects about Joseph's faith.

First, Joseph expressed confidence about Israel's "exodus" (τῆς ἐξόδου) from Egypt (Gen. 50:24). While many translations say that Joseph "mentioned" (NET) or "made mention" (ESV, CNT, NRSV; cf. KJV) of the exodus as though they were to "remember" their departure from Egypt (BDAG, s.v. "μνημονεύω" 1c, p. 655), the exodus from Egyptian oppression had yet to occur (Koester, 2001, 493). One translation, however, captures the true sense of Joseph's faith: "he said *confidently* [ἐμνημόνευσεν] that the people of Israel *would leave* Egypt" (NLT), as it was also reflected in Jewish tradition (T. Jos. 20:1).

Second, Joseph gave instructions about the final burial "of his bones" (τῶν ὀστέων αὐτοῦ; cf. Gen. 50:25). Jewish tradition claimed that "no one has been born like Joseph; even his bones were cared for" (Sir 49:15; cf. Exod. 13:19; Acts 7:15–16). His confidence about returning to the land of promise and his final burial in the land was highlighted in subsequent Jewish literature (Jub. 46:5; T. Jos. 20:6; Josephus, *A.J.* 2.8.2 §200).

Triumphs of Faith: The Exodus Period			
Person	**OT Reference**	**OT Event**	**Hebrews**
Moses's parents	Exodus 2:1–2	After Moses was born, his parents hid him for three months.	11:23
Moses as a young man	Exodus 2:11–15	Moses identified himself with the Jewish people, killed an Egyptian, and fled from Pharaoh.	11:24–26
	Exodus 12:21–28	Moses kept (inaugurated) the Passover in Egypt.	11:28
Moses as a leader	Exodus 14:5–31	Moses led the exodus community across the Red Sea.	11:29
(Joshua)			
Rahab	Joshua 2:1–24; 6:17, 23–25	Rahab hid two Israelite spies and escaped the destruction of Jericho.	11:31

Triumphs of Faith during the Exodus Period (11:23–31)

Believing that God would provide and protect them, Moses, his parents, the people who passed through the Red Sea as on dry land, the people who conquered Jericho, and Rahab trusted God for future realities.

11:23. The phrase "By faith, Moses" introduced the first well-known Jewish ancestor of the *exodus period*. Although Barnabas had already spoken of Moses (3:1–6), here Barnabas provided a portrait of Moses during his younger years by way of three "by faith" statements. While this first "by faith" statement may grammatically refer to Moses as the subject, it was "his parents" (τῶν πατέρων αὐτοῦ) whose faith was given attention. They were the second married couple Barnabas honored for their faith (cf. v. 11). While Exodus singled out the mother's actions after the birth of Moses (2:2), Josephus underscored that both Moses's father Amram and his mother Jochabed conspired to hide him. Josephus (*A.J.* 2.9.4 §§218–23), reflecting Jewish tradition, contended that "their belief in the promises of God was confirmed by the manner of the woman's [Jochabed's] delivery" (trans. Thackeray, 1978, 258–59; cf. Philo, *Mos.* 1.9–11). Thus, Moses "was hidden for three months" (ἐκρύβη τρίμηνον; cf. Acts 7:20). The reason (διότι, "because") for concealing baby Moses was twofold. First, they concealed Moses because "the child was beautiful" (ἀστεῖον τὸ παιδίον; cf. Acts 7:20). Unlike others (Josephus, *A.J.* 2.9.4 §§228–31), Barnabas did not embellish the looks of baby Moses. He moved on to the second reason (διότι, ellipsis) for concealing Moses: "they were not afraid of the king's edict." Unlike Exodus 1:17 and 21 where the midwives disobeyed the king's edict because they feared God, here Barnabas maintained that the parents were not afraid of the king (cf. Josephus, *A.J.* 2.9.4 §§218–23). Thus, it was Moses's parents whom Barnabas praised for trusting God.

11:24. The second "by faith" fact Barnabas made about Moses appeared in a rather long Greek sentence (vv. 24–26) about Moses's transition to an adult. "When he was grown up" (μέγας γενόμενος; Exod. 2:11 LXX), Moses, an adopted son, left the home of "Pharaoh's daughter." While his age is difficult to determine, it may be that Moses was in his forties (cf. Acts 7:23). "At this stage," says Attridge (1989, 340), "Moses manifests his own faith by an act that parallels Abraham's rejection of the security of an earthly homeland." So, rather than focus attention to Moses's killing an Egyptian as a form of Jewish allegiance (Exod. 2:11–13), Barnabas limited his recollections of Moses to his abandoning his advantaged and privileged standing within Egyptian society. This example of having a privileged position in Egyptian society would have resonated with the Jewish Christians who had Roman citizenship because not everyone was privy to Romans civil rights.

11:25. How Moses identified with the persecuted Jewish people in Egypt, according to Barnabas, was "by choosing to be mistreated" along with the Israelites living a persecuted life as slaves in Egypt (v. 25). The phrase "by choosing" (ἑλόμενος, ptc. means) emphasized Moses's free chose (BDAG, s.v. "αἱρέω" 2, p. 28). While limited in use, the verb was used of Joseph who "chose" (εἵλετο) to suffer punishment "rather than" (μᾶλλον) indulge in the temporary physical pleasures offered him by Potiphar's wife (Josephus, *A.J.* 2.4.4 §50; cf. Jub. 39:1–10). It was also used of "choosing" death over life (Jer. 8:3 LXX). So, Moses "chose" to be mistreated "rather than" (μᾶλλον) enjoy the "fleeting pleasures of sin" (RSV, NLT) or "passing pleasures of sin" (NASB). The adjective "fleeting" (πρόσκαιρον) meant "lasting only for a time" or spoke of something that was merely "temporary," "momentary," or "transitory" (BDAG, s.v. "πρόσκαιρος," p. 881; *EDNT*, 3:171). In 4 Maccabees 15, the term was used of a mother choosing between "momentary safety" and "temporary maternal love" for her children (vv. 2, 8) or faith in God (v. 24). The mother chose devotion to God as she watched her children tortured and murdered before her eyes. In a similar vein, the choice between a temporal and an eternal good appeared in Hebrews 11:25 (D'Angelo, 29–30). Moses choose misery over momentary pleasure.

11:26. Barnabas's rationale for Moses's choosing misery over momentary pleasure was "because he considered" (ἡγησάμενος, ptc. cause) or because he realized intellectually (BDAG, s.v. "ἡγέομαι" 2, p. 434) that "the abuse" (τὸν ὀνειδισμόν) or acts of disparagement that resulted in his disgrace (BDAG, s.v. "ἡγέομαι" 2, p. 434) would be of greater value over all the wealth of Egypt. Koester (2001, 502) rightly connects "the abuse of Christ" (τὸν ὀνειδισμὸν τοῦ Χριστοῦ) with Psalm 89: "remember, O Lord, the abuse of your servant (τοῦ ὀνειδισμοῦ τῶν δούλων)" (Ps. 88:51 LXX [89:50 HB]). Barnabas applied "the abused" servant in Psalm 89:50 to be "the Messiah" (τοῦ Χριστοῦ).

11:27. The third "by faith" fact about Moses that Barnabas drew attention to was that "he left" (κατέλιπεν) Egypt. Like Abraham (v. 8), Moses "left" (κατέλιπεν) an affluent earthly society. Because the verb "left" meant to leave a place with a sense of finality (BDAG, s.v. "καταλείπεω" 2, p. 520), some debate whether Barnabas referred to Moses's leaving for Midian in Exodus 2:15 (Bruce, 1964, 312; Attridge, 1989, 342), leaving Egypt for Canaan in Exodus 13:17–22 (Wescott, 1984, 373), or if the statement was a conflated summary statement (Spicq, 1952, 359). The Midian view is somewhat weakened due to the use of verb "left," which appears only for Moses's leaving Egypt for Canaan in Josephus (*A.J.* 2.14.3 §302). Furthermore, Barnabas's claim that Moses fled Egypt without fear contradicted the account in Exodus (2:14–15). Just as Barnabas had earlier combined sacrificial practices (Heb. 7:27; 9:13) and dedication services (9:20–22; Koester, 2001, 504), so here he also combined the two departures into one as a summary statement (cf. D'Angelo, 1979, 59–62).

11:28. The fourth "by faith" fact about Moses that Barnabas highlighted was that he carried out a sacrifice. Like Abraham (v. 17), Moses performed a sacrifice, but one that would be performed annually, "the Passover" (τὸ πάσχα; Exod. 12:48; Num. 9:2; Josh. 5:104 Kgdms 23:31; Mark 14:16). The result (ἵνα, "so that") of the sacrifice was to protect the firstborn from "the one who caused destruction" (ὁ ὀλοθρεύων, subj. ptc.). On the one hand, the destroyer of the firstborn was God (Exod. 11:4–5; 12:27, 29). Elsewhere, the destroyer was a "destroying angel" (BDAG, s.v. "ὀλοθρεύω," p. 703; 2 Sam. 24:16; 1 Chron. 21:12, 15; Isa. 37:36). Similar diverse recollection occurred concerning God's giving of the Law to Moses on Mount Sinai (cf. Heb. 2:2). Regardless, God protected some children and allowed other firstborn children to be killed. God's judgments hurt.

11:29–30. "By faith they crossed the Red Sea" and "by faith the walls of Jericho fell" were two miraculous events whereby two different generations of the exodus community exercised faith in God. The first miraculous event Barnabas highlighted was about the exodus community, more specifically the first exodus generation, and their successful crossing the Red Sea *as though* on dry ground (Exod. 14:21–22; Wis 10:18–19). Under the leadership of Moses, God separated the waters of the Red Sea, and the first generation of the exodus community stepped out in faith and went through the parted waters. Their success was contrasted with the Egyptians who, when they attempted to cross through the parted waters, were swallowed up (NET), "drowned" (KJV, NRSV, NASB, ESV, NIV, NLT), or more accurately, completely destroyed (BDAG, s.v. "καταπίνω" 2b, p. 524).

The second miraculous event he underscored was also about the exodus community, but in verse 30 Barnabas drew attention to the second exodus generation and the defeat of Jericho under the leadership of another leader, Joshua (Josh. 6:6–25; Sir 46:1–8). In faith, an army of this second exodus generation stepped out and marched around Jericho for seven days, and trusted God for the walls to fall. They obeyed God's instructions, marched out in faith, and trusted God for the victory. Two exodus communities who obeyed God and God gave them victory over their enemies.

11:31. "By faith Rahab, the prostitute," introduced the final well-known Jewish ancestor of the *exodus period*. As was the case for many of those listed in chapter 11, Joshua said nothing about Rahab's faith, nor did Jewish literature (Josephus, *A.J.* 5.1–30 §§5–30). Yet Rahab, though at first a nonreputable Canaanite, was a "Jewish ancestor" in that she was eventually accepted into the Israelite community (Josh. 6:25; cf. Butler, 1983, 71) as a proselyte (*Mekilta* on Exodus), and perhaps even presented with her own land (Josephus, *A.J.* 5.1.8 §30). Woustra (1981, 116) observes that "purely racial components have never defined the people of God." Furthermore, Josephus (*A.J.* 5.1.2 §8) never referred to Rahab as a "prostitute," but she was described here and in James 2:25 as a person who "engaged in sexual relations for hire" (BDAG, s.v. "πόρνη" 1, p. 854). Unlike other prostitutes of her day, she was not a cultic prostitute. In Joshua, the spies she hid were referred to as "clients" (בּוֹא אֶל; NET),[4] and in Josephus she's presented as a person who owns an "inn" (καταγωγίῳ) whereby strangers visiting Jericho could take up lodging (*A.J.* 5.1.2 §8). Yet, Barnabas merely recalled the fact that Rahab was a prostitute who escaped Jericho's destruction.

The reason she was spared, according to Barnabas, was simply because "she welcomed" (τοὺς κατασκόπους; ptc. cause) the Jewish spies in peace. Rahab was aware of God's ability to destroy the enemies of the Israelite people. She knew God was on their side and placed her life and that of her family in the

4 The Hebrew idiom "come to" (בּוֹא אֶל) here in verse 3 and 4 probably has sexual connotations, as it does elsewhere when a man "comes to" a woman (Gen. 38:16; Judges 16:1). If so, the phrase could be translated "your clients." The instructions reflect Rahab's perspective as to the identity of the men (NET n. 14; cf. Woudstra, 1981, 69 n. 7, 70)

hands of God's people (Josh. 2:8–14). Koester (2001, 510) considers the inclusion of Rahab, the prostitute, in this catalog of faith beginning with Moses to be making a logical greater to lesser argument (*qal wahomer*): "if a prostitute can exhibit faith, how much more should faith be possible for the listeners."

Triumphs of Faith during the Post-exodus Period (11:32–40)

Believing in God during their successes and despite persecution and death, Gideon, Barak, Samson, Jephthah, Samuel, David and others maintained their faith in God and continued to trust God for their future realities.

Triumphs of Faith: The Post-exodus Period			
Person	**OT Reference**	**OT Event**	**Hebrews**
Gideon	Judges 6:11–12; 7:1–25	An angel of the Lord appeared to Gideon and addressed him as a mighty warrior. Gideon defeated the Midianites.	11:32
Barak	Judges 4:6–24	Barak defeated Sisera, army commander of King Jabin of Canaan, at Mount Tabor.	11:32
Jephthah	Judges 11:1–29; 12:1–7	Jephthah defended the Gadites against the Ammonites and later the Ephraimites.	11:32
Samson	Judges 13:24–16:31	Samson wreaked havoc with the Philistines and died destroying a Dagon temple.	11:32
Samuel	1 Sam. 7:2–16	Samuel subdued the Philistines at Mizpah and served as a judge in Israel.	11:32
David	1 Sam. 16–17; 2 Sam. 8:3–12	David served Saul, defeated Goliath and numerous enemies of Israel, and ruled as king over the nation of Israel.	11:32

11:32. In another very long Greek sentence, Barnabas shifted his literary pattern from the repetitious use of "by faith" to a "stirring summary" (BDF, 260, 262 §§491, 494). He opened his summary with a commonly used rhetorical question, "and [καί] what more shall I say?" followed by a common literary idiom, "for time will fail me" (NET, ESV, KJV). The rhetorical question that started verse 32 was the first of four rhetorical questions Barnabas would raise eventually (13:19, 22, 23). In the meantime, those about whom Barnabas could speak without end were six well-known Jewish ancestors of the *post-exodus period* (for the correct order in the HB, see the chart above). Ellingsworth (1993, 623) suggests that they be read as three pairs: Gideon and Barak, Samson and Jephthah, and David and Samuel. Regardless of how they may be read, four were judges: Gideon, Barak, Samson, and Jephthah; one was a king of Israel: David; and one was a prophetic prophet: Samuel (cf. 2 Chron. 35:18; Sir 46:13, 15).

While some commentators accept Barnabas's choices except one, Jephthah (Attridge, 1989, 348), others point out "they are not representative of the kind of faith Hebrews is generally interested in" (Mitchel, 2007, 257). On the one hand, Gideon doubted God and asked for a sign, Barak was reluctant, and Jephthah allegedly made an inappropriate vow. Yet for Bruce (1990, 320), when Judges points out that God's spirit ascended on Gideon (6:34), Jephthah (11:29), and Samson (13:25), it was "conclusive of their faith." On the other hand, David was known for his dedication (2 Sam. 23:3–5; Sir 46:1–22), Samson's self-sacrifice covered a multitude of inappropriate activities, and Samuel responded faithfully to God (Sir 46:13–15). Regardless, Barnabas listed these people, who by faith, trusted God.

Triumphs of Faith: Hebrews 11:33–34		
"military and political feats"	**"acts of deliverances"**	**"military valor"**
"they conquered kingdoms" • **Barak** overcame the Canaanite king, Jabin. • **Gideon** defeated Midianite kings. • **Jephthah** defeated the Ammonite king. • **Samson** overcame the Philistines. • **David** conquered surrounding kingdoms.	"they shut the mouths of lions" • **Samson**, through killing a lion, shut the mouth of a lion (Judg. 14:5–6). • **David**, through killing a lion, shut the mouth of a lion (1 Sam. 17:34–37; Sir 47:3). • **Daniel**, through prayer, shut the mouth of lions (Dan. 6:24, 25–27; cf. 1 Macc 2:60; 4 Macc 16:3, 21; Josephus, *A.J.* 10.11.6 §§257–58).	"they gained strength in weakness" ("weakness" is a metaphor for physical illness) • **Gideon's** band of brothers were given strength (Judges 6:15; 7:6). • **Samson**, in his blindness, was given strength to destroy a pagan temple (Judges 16:19–30).
"they administrated justice" • **Samuel** acted righteously (1 Sam. 12:3–4; 1 Kgdms 12:3–4 LXX). • **David** guaranteed justice for all people (2 Sam. [2 Kgdms LXX] 8:15; cf. 1 Chron. 18:14). • **Solomon** acted righteously (1 Kings [3 Kgdms LXX] 10:9; Pss. Sol. 17.23, 26).	"they quenched raging fire" • **Jewish captives**, Shadrach, Meshach, and Abednego, were cast into flames but not burned (Dan. 3:19–27; 1 Macc 2:59; 4 Macc 16:3, 21; Josephus, *A.J.* 10.10.5 §214).	"they became mighty in battle" • **Joshua** became mighty in battle against an Amorite coalition (Josh. 10:12–27, Sir 46:1–4). • **David** became mighty in battle against Goliath (1 Sam. 17:45–51; Sir 47:4–5; Josephus, *A.J.* 6.8.5 §189). • **Judah** Maccabee became mighty in power against the Greeks (1 Macc 3:17, 19; cf. 4:6–11, 30–33).
"they gained what was promised" • **Barak** experienced what was promised with his victory over the Canaanites (Judg. 6:16). • **Gideon** experienced what was promised with his victory over the Midianites (Judg. 5:7). • **David** experienced what was promised with his victory over the Philistines (2 Sam. 5:19–25).	"they escaped edge of the sword" (metaphor for death) • **David** escaped from Saul (2 Sam. 15:14) and Absalom (2 Sam. 15:14). • **Elijah** escaped from Jezebel (1 Kings 19:1–8). • **Esther** saved the Jewish people from a decree that would have destroyed them "by the sword" (Add Esth 13:6).	"they put foreign armies to flight" • **Gideon** put the Midianites to flight (Judg. 7:11, 14, 21; 8:11). • **Elisha** put the Syrians to flight (2 Kings 7). • **Hezekiah** put to flight, through prayer, the Assyrians (2 Kings 19:35; Isa. 37:14–36; Sir 48:19–21). • **Judas** put the Greeks to flight (1 Macc 2:7; 4:12, 26).

11:33–34. Having shifted from his anaphoric literary pattern with the repetitious use of "by faith," the opening "who through faith" (οἳ διὰ πίστεως) of verses 33–35 underscored the achievements of Gideon, Barak, Samson, Jephthah, David, Samuel, and many others. As it was with Jewish ancestors in this list, Scripture (HB LXX) did not draw attention to their faith. Nevertheless, they were considered righteous and therefore fit Barnabas's interpretive key (cf. v. 7). Attridge (1989, 348) suggests verses 33–34 may be divided into "three symmetrical groups." First, there are those "who through faith" achieved military and political feats, then there are those "who through faith" achieved acts of deliverances, and finally, there are those "who through faith" achieved military valor (cf. deSilva, 2000, 416–18). The following chart reflects and exemplifies the statements in Hebrews 11:33–34 as they appear in Attridge's three symmetrical groupings.

TEXTUAL ANALYSIS: Conflicting Text Critical Reading: 11:37

Exegetical Issue: Although minimally supported (𝔓[46] 1241 1984), the text reading is preferred. It appears "they were tempted" (ἐπειράσθησαν) was a scribal addition, primarily because "they were tempted" does not fit among the string of violent deaths enumerated in context (see Lane, 1991b, 381; Metzger, 1994, 604).

txt. "they were stoned to death, they were sawn in two" (ἐλιθάσθησαν, ἐπρίσθησαν) (ESV, NET, NIV, NRSV)

var. "they were stoned to death, they were sawn in two, **they were tempted**" (ἐλιθάσθησαν, ἐπρίσθησαν, **ἐπειράσθησαν**) (ASV, KJV, NASB)

11:35. Unfortunately, some translations insert an elliptical "and" (καί) suggesting that verse 35 belongs with verses 32–34 (NET; cf. Lane, 1991, 2:387). Yet, verse 35 actually began another one of Barnabas's long Greek sentences that ended in verse 38. He opened with "women received back their dead 'by resurrection' [ἐξ ἀναστάσεως]" (ESV, NASB, NRSV, KJV, etc.). Naturally, the statement recalled women such as the widow of Zarephath whose son Elijah raised (3 Kgdms 17:23), the Shunammite woman whose son Elisha raised (4 Kgdms 4:36), and we might add Mary and Martha whose brother Jesus raised (John 11:38–44; cf. BDAG, s.v. "ἀνάστασις" 2a, p. 71). All received "their loved ones back again from death" (NLT).

In contrast (δέ, "but") to women whose loved ones were raised to physical life again, there were those "who had been tortured" (ἐτυμπανίσθησαν) "not accepting release" (οὐ προσδεξάμενοι τὴν ἀπολύτρωσιν). "Tortured" actually meant to be severely beaten with an instrument (BDAG, s.v. "τυμπανίζω," p. 1019). According to Josephus (*C. Ap.* 1.148), an ill-tempered successor of Nebuchadnezzar was "bludgeoned" (ἀπετυμπανίσθη) to death. A notable Jewish scribe went to the "torture-rack" (τυμπανον) rather than succumb to eating pork (2 Macc 6:18–20; 27–30). Philo (*Flacc.* 85) described Jews being hung up, bound to a "torture wheel" (τροχιζόμενοι), and "brutally mauled" (καταικιζόμενοι) to death.

"Not accepting release" was understood in the common physical sense of "setting free" (NLT; cf. KJV: "deliverance") or as the noun is more typically translated, "release" (NASB, RSV, NRSV, NIV, ESV, NET). Employed in the negative, it spoke of martyrs and heroes of the faith *rejecting* "release" from torture. During the Maccabean revolt against Antiochus Epiphanes (167–164 B.C.), it was told that a man named Eleazar was offered "release" from torture and death if he, along with his seven brothers, would renounce practices dear to their Jewish faith (2 Macc 6:22, 30; 4 Macc 8:2; verb form ἀπολύω). They chose, however, not to accept the terms of "release." In return, they were tortured and died a painful death (2 Macc 6:18–31; 7:24–29; cf. 4 Macc 8:2–14). Rejecting the offer to exchange faith for freedom, they submitted to torture and death for a purpose (ἵνα, "in order that"): to obtain a resurrection to a better life. Barnabas recognized that for some, the triumphs of faith or rewards came only after death. Thus, in this roll call of faithful Jews, Barnabas intermixed people of faith from Scripture (HB, LXX) and other Jewish sources.

11:36–38. Barnabas continued (δέ, "and") this long sentence in verses 36–38 with a description of those who suffered persecution whether they were tormented, martyred, or marginalized (see chart for examples of each grouping).

Triumphs of Faith: Hebrews 11:36–38		
"tormented"	**"martyred"**	**"marginalized"**
"they were taunted" • **Jews in Egypt** were taunted (3 Macc 5:22). • **Seven brothers** were taunted (2 Macc 7:1, 24–29). "they were bound and even imprisoned" • **Micaiah**, the prophet, was placed in jail (3 Kgdms 22:27; [1 Kings 22:27]). • **Hanani**, the prophet, was placed in jail (2 Chron. 7, 10). • **Jeremiah**, the prophet, was placed in stocks (Jer. 20:2, 7; 29:26), flogged and imprisoned (Jer. 37:15), and cast into an empty cistern (Jer. 38:5–6).	"they were stoned" • **Zechariah**, the son of Jehoiada the priest, was stoned (2 Chron. 24:17, 20–22). • **Jeremiah**, the prophet, was stoned in Egypt according to tradition (Torrey, 1946, 31, 46). • **Prophets** in general were stoned (Matt. 21:35). "they were sawed apart" • Isaiah, the prophet, was sawed in two by Manasseh according to tradition (Torrey, 1946, 20, 34). "they were murdered with a sword" • **Uriah**, a contemporary prophet of Jeremiah, was murdered. Although he fled to Egypt to escape Jehoiakim, he was forcefully returned to Jerusalem and murdered (Jer. 26:20–23 [33:23 LXX]).	"they wandered in sheepskins and goatskins" • **Elijah**, the prophet, wore sheepskins and goatskins (3 Kgdms 18:46; 19:13 [1 Kings 18:46; 19:13]). • **Elisha**, the prophet, wore sheepskins and goatskins (4 Kgdms 2:8, 13, 14 [1 Kings 2:8, 13, 14]). "they were destitute, afflicted, and ill-treated" • **Elijah**, the prophet, was told by God to hide out in the Kerith Valley near the Jordan (3 Kgdms 17:2–16), and he hid in a cave (3 Kgdms 19:1–19 [1 Kings 19:1–19]). • **Elisha**, the prophet, wandered throughout Israel (e.g., Jericho, Bethel, Shunem) (4 Kgdms 2:23; 4:1–2, 8–12 [1 Kings 1:23; 4:1–2, 8–12]). • **Judah Maccabee** wandered throughout the mountain regions of Judah during his revolt against Antiochus IV (2 Macc 5:27).

11:39–40. Barnabas summed up (καὶ οὗτοι πάντες) his list of people who triumphed in faith by echoing his previous commendation of faith. In verse 2, Barnabas drew attention to the people of history who received God's commendation. Here in verse 39, Barnabas drew attention to those he himself had just commended "for their faith." Barnabas reinforced God's "approval" or "commendation" of a variety of exemplars whose faith were in keeping with Habakkuk 2:4. The chapter, according to Pfitzner (1997, 107), is "a celebration of faith with practical implications." Thus, divine commendation existed for those who exercised faith in truths such as the mystery of the invisible God and the mystery of creation that cannot be seen with the human eye (Heb. 11:3, 6, 27). Divine commendation existed for those who responded to God's word (11:8–12). Divine commendation existed for those who obeyed the call of God (11:8, 17) as opposed to rebelling against God (2:1–3; 3:12; 4:11; 6:6–8, 10:26–31). Divine commendation existed for those who trusted in the promises of God (11:9, 11, 13, 17, 33, 39). Divine commendation existed for those who remained faithful to God while facing suffering (11: 4–5, 7, 11–13, 17–31, 35–38). Divine commendation existed for those who looked to the future in which God had something better in store for believers (11:10, 14–16, 25, 35). The point was simply this: divine commendation existed for those who, like these various exemplars of history past, trusted God and kept the faith (cf. Pfitzner, 1997, 170–71).

THEOLOGICAL FOCUS

The exegetical idea (many well-known Jewish ancestors, who were recognized for their righteousness, believed in the certainty of an unseen creator God's existence and trusted him for their future realities) leads to this theological focus: Righteous people believe in the certainty of an unseen creator God and trust him for future realities.

The major theological theme that resonates throughout Hebrews 11 centers around people or groups of people who trusted in and were faithful to God. People of antediluvian, patriarchal, exodus, and post-exodus periods believed in an unseen God (11:3, 6, 27), trusted in promises made by this unseen God (11:9, 11, 13, 17, 33, 39), and were commended for looking forward to God's fulfilling of those promises (11:10, 14–16, 25, 35) even if it meant suffering in the process (11:4–5, 7, 11–13, 17–31, 35–38).

PREACHING AND TEACHING STRATEGIES

Exegetical and Theological Synthesis

This text illustrates the life of faith by listing OT saints, and perhaps intertestamental ones as well, that had completely given themselves for God's purposes. These are the stalwarts, the heavyweights of the faith.

The chapter began with a definition of faith as the substance of things hoped for and the evidence of things not seen, after which Barnabas cataloged the giants of the faith noting their profound faith. He began with those who lived before the flood (11:1–7), including Abel, Enoch, and Noah. Our understanding of Noah is framed by this passage as much as by the narrative in Genesis 6–9. Then Barnabas spent considerable time discussing the patriarchs, mentioning Abraham, Isaac, Jacob, Esau, and Sarah.

This was followed by a fascinating look at the life of Moses where, in a similar but more detailed way, we learn about what motivated Moses to live as a man of faith. The people of Israel and their journey of faith is noted as well.

Finally, the saints of the post-exodus period were mentioned, from Gideon, David, and Samuel, all the way to what presumably were saints in the intertestamental period.

Preaching Idea

Faith is real confidence in unseen realities.

Contemporary Connections

What does it mean?

What does it mean that faith is real confidence in unseen realities? A distinction needs to be made between faith as hopefulness versus faith as complete trust. This passage is calling for complete trust. A favorite topic of Jesus was the kingdom of God. He made it clear that the kingdom of God would have tangible expression. In Matthew 11:4–5, Jesus sent word to John that he should pay attention to what the people were seeing: "the blind receive their sight and the lame walk, lepers are cleansed and the deaf hear and he dead are raised up, and the poor have good news preached to them." This direct reference to the day of the Lord in Isaiah 61 communicated that the kingdom would have a visible reality. We would see things happening as a result of the kingdom moving. We know that the kingdom of God is invisible (Luke 17:20–21). But Jesus taught that the invisible world has a visible expression.

One of the best ways to explain intangible realities is with the emotion of love. When we are in school, we learn the difference between tangible and intangible realities. Love is intangible. Love is invisible. However, we are willing to make the most important decisions of our lives based on confidence that it is real. No one teaches us to do this; rather, it is intuitive. Many of us who are married spend their life savings, build lives, share bank accounts, and even raise children based on trust in the love of someone else. The love a husband and a wife share is very real even though it is unseen. A beautiful life with children and grandchildren, even many generations of them, can be built on this unseen love.

Is it true?

Is it true that faith is real confidence in unseen realities? The truth is that we express faith in the unseen in almost every area of our lives. We turn on lights when we cannot see the wiring. We turn keys that start car engines that we cannot see from the driver's seat. Something as simple as walking outside takes a tremendous amount of faith in the unseen! We believe in unseen gravity that will hold us to earth, and we trust that a meteor will not hit us or an errant solar flare melt us. We walk on the earth in the faith that the material universe is working, even though we cannot see it all.

Now what?

The people of Hebrews 11 illustrate that they walked with God like we walk on earth. Faith was the assumed posture. In the same way that we do not think twice about walking outside, they did not think twice about walking by faith. They simply chose to walk with God.

This text, applied to our lives, demands that we treat walking by faith in the spiritual realm as a default position in every arena in which we move. We give our money to kingdom causes because we believe in matters in ways we cannot see. We are obedient to God when no one sees because we believe he does see. We act in responsive obedience to the promptings of the Spirit because that matters. We are sensitive to the welfare of others, even when it costs us, because we believe their lives matter as much as if not more than ours. All of these are expressions of faith. They show that we are divesting in this world and investing in the world to come.

Creativity in Presentation

Since all of us walk by faith in the areas of our life, there are many ways to illustrate this. To illustrate this visually, one could place three items on the stage: a toy car, a small refrigerator, and a television. If the audience were asked if they could explain how these things worked, a show of hands for each one might reveal that very few actually know exactly how they work. And yet, we assume they will work, but we simply take this for granted. However, the use of these objects demands faith.

Once that point is made the deeper point could be made that all of life is like this. We take medicine even though we cannot explain how the medicine works. We sleep believing that this is not our last sleep but that we will in fact wake up. Existing as a human demands belief in things we cannot see. We were created to be people of trust.

The kingdom of God demands that we live this way, equally in the spiritual world as in the material world. Our default posture is to be one of trust. When seen this way, faith in God is not out of reach, but rather we can relate to the world we cannot see in the same way we relate to the world we can see, by faith. Faith is real confidence in unseen realities.

The point you want to get across is simply this: "Faith is real confidence in unseen realities." An outline for preaching Hebrews 11 as one sermon might be.

- Faith is identified (vv. 1–2).
- Faith is illustrated (vv. 3–38).
- Faith is incomplete (vv. 39–40).

DISCUSSION QUESTIONS

1. If you were writing Hebrews 11, what other OT saints could you include and why?
2. Why is the definition of faith in Hebrews 11:1 so memorable?
3. Why is it that we learn more about the faith of Moses from Hebrews 11 than from Exodus 2? What does this teach us about the nature of the Bible?
4. How should we respond to Hebrews 11:39 in terms of realizing that our faith today, in a sense, completes theirs from the first century? Thinking ahead, how does this discussion of faith anticipate Hebrews 12:1–4?

Hebrews 12:1–13

EXEGETICAL IDEA

Members of the household family of faith were expected to endure life's challenges, like an athlete, and to be encouraged that as members of God's family God was providing educational opportunities for them, like a father to his children.

THEOLOGICAL FOCUS

Enduring life's challenges and engaging in divine educational opportunities are commonplace for anyone who is a member of God's family.

PREACHING IDEA

Nothing of eternal value can be won without endurance and discipline.

PREACHING POINTERS

Greco-Roman life revolved around the household family and sporting events held at Rome's massive Coliseum located in the center of the city. Elite athletes ran great distances. But the reality was that even a runner of shorter distances, in a way, had to endure the race. They were expected to complete the race. The idea was always that running implied completing, whether the distance was 40 yards or 100 kilometers. Barnabas placed the context of the passage in the great hall of faith. So, the motivation for the running was the onlookers, the great cloud of witnesses. The cloud of witnesses was not just full of faith—they were also full of endurance. The Jewish household family of faith in Rome were running to join the cloud of witnesses.

Even today, we run to join the cloud of witnesses. And yet, this is not a pep talk to endure being given in a vacuum without context. Our motivation to endure comes from being under the discipline of the Lord. The Lord's discipline marks us believers. There is not an explicit sense that the discipline is necessarily *corrective*; it may equally be considered the *instructive* discipline of the Lord. This divine education comes with various opportunities to learn and involves a regimen of training that exercises our faith. So we are running, yes, but not just to run. We are running *into* the discipline of the Lord, toward something that is good for us. The goal is to finish the race set out for us. This is the explicit application of the faith we have as followers of Jesus, faith that endures as we embrace divine discipline. Nothing of eternal value can be won without endurance and discipline.

ENDURANCE AND DISCIPLINE (12:1–13)

LITERARY STRUCTURE AND THEMES (12:1–13)

Barnabas's emphasis in Hebrews 12:1–13 centered around sports and the family. He opened with enduring athletic Greco-Roman competitions such as running and participating in the pancration. The emphasis was not so much that of winning as it was finishing the events (vv. 1–4). Barnabas then shifted his emphasis to the family. By way of key verses from the book of Proverbs, Barnabas identified what it meant to be a legitimate child within God's household who received divine guidance for responsible living that was non-punitive yet educationally challenging (vv. 5–13). After quoting Proverbs 3:11–12 (vv. 5–6), he then interpreted these proverbs (vv. 7–11) and concluded with his application of the proverbs that was applicable for the household family of faith's current situation (vv. 12–13).

Barnabas's themes addressed the need to persevere through the challenges of life and God's paternal discipline.

- ***Endure Like an Athlete (12:1–4)***
- ***The Instruction of a Child (12:5–13)***

EXPOSITION (12:1–13)

Greco-Roman life revolved around the household family and sporting events held at Rome's massive Coliseum located in the center of the city. As noted earlier in Hebrews 2:10–18, the household was a family unit that consisted of *husband* and wife, *master* and slave, and *father* and children. The *husband*, *master*, and *father* are descriptive for the head of the household unit. It was believed that disorder in the household was a threat not only to the Greco-Roman family but also the Greco-Roman society.

The ruins of Rome's ancient Coliseum visible today, built after Nero's reign (begun in A.D. 72 and completed in A.D. 80), was symbolically located as the heart of Rome. Yet, the massive construction evidenced the prominence of sporting events to Roman society long before Vespasian and Titus built the Coliseum. Cities throughout the Greco-Roman world had amphitheaters where popular sporting events were held, such as running and wrestling. Another popular event was the pentathlon competition made up of five events: running, long jumping, discus throwing, javelin throwing, and wrestling.

Thus, Barnabas steered the Jewish members of the household family of faith in Rome to endure life's challenges, like an athlete, and to be encouraged that as members of God's family God was providing educational opportunities to them, like a father to his children.

Endure Like an Athlete (12:1–4)[1]

In view of the numerous people of faith who were watching, like spectators at a sporting event, the household family of faith was expected to endure life's challenges knowing that they had not yet endured any overly fierce competition.

---

1 While most commentaries break this unit at verse 3 (Attridge, 1989, 353; Bruce, 1990, 332; Lane, 1991b, 417; Mitchell, 2007, 264; Cockerill, 2012, 600), we follow Johnson (2006, 315) who views verses 1–4 as an entire section dominated by a single metaphor ending with Jesus as the means to success.

TEXTUAL ANALYSIS: Conflicting Text Critical Readings: 12:1

Theological/Exegetical Issue: With minimal support (𝔓[46] 1739), most translations appear to favor the variant reading. It has been suggested that the variant is evidence of a palaeographic error or a deliberate modification of "clings so closely" (ὑπερίστατον; cf. Lane, 1991b, 398–99 with Metzger, 1994, 604).

txt. "and the sin that **clings so closely**" (καὶ τὴν **εὐπερίστατον** ἁμαρτίαν) (ESV, NET, NRSV)

var. "and the sin that **so easily distracts**" (καὶ τὴν **εὐπερίσπαστον** ἁμαρτίαν) (ASV, KJV, NASB, NIV)

12:1. Barnabas transitioned (τοιγαροῦν καί, "therefore indeed") from his list of divinely commended righteous people (11:2, 39) who lived by faith to a twofold, all-inclusive inference. When Barnabas made his application, he included himself: "because *we* [ἡμεῖς] have a great cloud of witnesses surrounding *us* [ἡμῖν]." Barnabas drew specific attention to the numerous witnesses (= "cloud of witnesses") that surrounded and watched him and the entire household family of faith in Rome, *like* spectators attending an event at a Roman amphitheater. These "spectators" were witnesses who had already endured their own life's challenges. Barnabas then delivered a twofold expectation. To begin with, his readers were to consider themselves as athletes competing before a crowded amphitheater. He said to the household family of faith in Rome: "let us lay aside" (ἀποθέμενοι, ESV, NASB) or "let us rid ourselves" (BDAG, s.v. "ἀποτίθημι" 1b, p. 123) of anything that might hinder us. The more emphatic rendering might be "let us strip off" (NLT). Barnabas, along with his readers, were expected to rid themselves of any "behavior" (ἁμαρτίαν, "sin") that might

Panathenaic Runners (ca. 530–520 B.C.) Courtesy of the British Museum. Public domain.

impede their ability to complete the race God had prescribed for them. It was not unusual for Jewish authors to speak metaphorically of striping off clothing for ridding oneself of some sort of behavior. Philo (*Spec. 1,2,3,4.* 2.19 §102) spoke of businesspeople who "casting off all the sore burden of affairs which has lain heavy upon them from morn till eve, turn homewards and betake themselves to rest" (trans. Colson, 1937, 368–69). Josephus (*A.J.* 11.6.7 §223) used the term to speak Mordecai's refusal to "put off the habit" of mourning. Barnabas, however, spoke of stripping off sin (cf. Eph. 4:22; Col. 3:8). The sin was a specific sin (*τὴν* . . . ἁμαρτίαν, "*the* sin") for Barnabas, namely, *the* sin of apostasy (2:1–3a; 4:1–2; 6:4–6; 10:24–31; cf. Mitchell, 2007, 265).

The second expectation was to finish the race: "let us run" (τρέχωμεν) with endurance. "Race" was a metaphor for finishing life as a faithful follower of Jesus, God's royal high priest (cf. 2 Tim. 4:7). Barnabas, along with his readers, were expected to be loyal and dedicated to Jesus, an expectation inferred in previous passages (4:1, 11; 6:11–12; 10:23). The goal of faith was not to win but to be dependable as well as servants to others to build community (6:10; 13:1–17).

12:2. How Barnabas and his readers were expected to compete and complete their race was "by looking to Jesus" (ESV), "by keeping our eyes fixed on Jesus" (NET), or by directing attention, without any distraction, to Jesus (cf. BDAG, s.v. "ἀφοράω" 1, p. 158). Not only did Barnabas once again include himself in his expectation, but he used two significant titles for Jesus: "pioneer" (ἀρχηγὸν) and "perfecter" (τελειωτήν), exclusive for Jesus (Acts 3:15, 5:31; Heb. 2:10, 12:2). As it was in Hebrews 2:10, Jesus's title as "pioneer" (ἀρχηγὸν; RSV, NET) or "founder" (ESV) was more than merely the "author" (KJV, NRSB, NIV) of faith. As the pioneer, Jesus took faith to its ultimate goal, going where no one person had gone before (Heb. 11:4–38). He trailblazed (Heb. 6:20) and thereby led the way for the many sons and daughters (2:10) to experience all of God's promises, promises never before experienced by OT saints (11:39–40; cf. Koester, 2001, 523).

As "perfecter" (τελειωτήν) Barnabas affirmed that God's ultimate goal of faith was completed or accomplished in Jesus. Jesus was successful in fulfilling God's goal (2:10; BDAG, s.v. "τελειωτής," 997; *TDNT* 8:86). Jesus knew that God had something better for him. So, he endured the "shame" of dying a pitiful death on a Roman wooden cross (Deut. 21:22–23) but was raised to a place of honor, "at the right had of the throne of God," as royal high priest (cf. 1:3, 13; 8:1; 10:12–13).

> *TEXTUAL ANALYSIS:* Conflicting Text Critical Readings: 12:3
> Exegetical Issue: Manuscripts appear to favor the variant (𝔓[13 46] ℵ 044 33 1739) over the text (A P 104 326 1241). The text reading is prefered because there is difficulty in making sense out of the plural. *But* as with Hebrews 1:8 and 11:4, there is evidence for questioning the decision and for favoring the variant reading (cf. Lane, 1991b, 400 with Metzger, 1994, 604–05).
>
> *txt.* "against himself" (εἰς **ἑαυτόν**) (ASV, ESV, KJV, NASB, NET, NRSV)
>
> *var.* "against themselves" (εἰς **ἑαυτούς** [or] εἰς **αὐτούς**) "against themselves" (NIV)

12:3. Barnabas confirmed (γὰρ, "so then") his preceding exhortations with a candid expectation: "consider *him*" (NET, NRSV, ESV, NIV) or "reason, with careful deliberation, Jesus" (BDAG, s.v. "ἀναλογίζομαι," p. 67). Barnabas expected his readers to ponder the hostile opposition Jesus endured, namely, those who opposed him. Yet, despite the hostility, Jesus "endured" his sufferings and accomplished God's plan (cf. 1:3; 2:9; 10:10). Jesus was a model of trusting God who remained faithful to God despite his physical and emotional sufferings (cf. Mark 14:35–36; 14:45, 50, 56, 64; 15:12–13, 18–20, 24, 27–32, 34, 37). Barnabas had already commended his readers for having "endured a harsh conflict" (10:32; NET). Thus, Barnabas drew a parallel between their own sufferings and those of Jesus (Mitchell, 2007, 267).

The intended result (ἵνα, "so that") for reflecting on Jesus's resolution to trust and obey God in the face of persecution was so that the household family of faith might not give up. Barnabas expected that they not "grow weary" (NASB, NIV, CNT; cf. NLT), "fainthearted" (ESV; cf. KJV), or "exhausted in strength" (BDAG, s.v. "ἐκλύω," p. 306). Josephus (13.8.1 §233) used the same term to recall a soldier who saw his mother beaten and torn to pieces whereby he became "fainthearted" in spirit. On the other hand, Polybius (*Hist.* 29.17.4) used the term to tell of a person "weary" by toil, "like that of athletes in bad condition" (trans. Paton, 1937, 72–7)] and lacked endurance. Barnabas was concerned of both emotional and physical weariness (cf. 10:33–39; *TLNT* 1:455–56).

12:4. To help provide his readers with some perspective about their situation, Barnabas made an observation about their circumstances. They had yet to experience any overwhelming persecution: "You have not yet resisted to the point of bloodshed" (NET) or "you have not yet given your lives in your struggle" (NLT). On the one hand, "resist" or "oppose" (ἀντικατέστητε) was often used to rally military troops for resistance or to oppose someone in a bloody military encounter. On the other hand, it was used of those who opposed another in the political arena or court of law. For Barnabas, the resistance was neither military nor courtroom opposition, but rather an event in a sports arena (12:1b–3). In Hebrews 12:4, the verb "resist" may refer to two boxers "opposing" one another in the pancration—a brutal form of sport that combined wrestling and boxing with kicking, strangling, and the twisting of the limbs to defeat one's opponent. It was often a bloody competition (*TLNT*, 1:128–30; cf. Lane, 1991b, 417–18; Koester, 2001, 525). Thus, the imagery may be more metaphorical of a contestant who grappled with the everyday challenges that life tended to bring. Or more probably the referencing of a bloody resistance may be descriptive of the fierce opposition of a contestant, perhaps even brutal grappling with those within the household community of faith who opposed faith in Jesus as God's royal high priest (the sin of apostasy) that may indeed have led to personal suffering (6:4–6; cf. 2:3).

The Instruction of a Child (12:5–13)

An encouraging factor about being members of God's family was that God provided educational opportunities, just as human fathers did by way of paternal discipline.

12:5. As he continued (καί, "and") his argument, Barnabas somewhat abruptly took his readers in a different direction by way of a rhetorical question: "Have you forgotten the 'encouragement' [NIV, NLT] or 'exhortation' [KJV, NASB, RSV, NRSV, NET]?" In answering his own question, Barnabas appealed once again to Proverbs 3. Earlier in Hebrews 2:1, Barnabas appealed to Proverbs 3:21 as the reason for concentrating on what God had spoken through the Son (Heb. 1:2a), about the Son (vv. 2b–4), and to the Son (vv. 5–13). Here, Barnabas appealed to a portion of the twenty verses of instruction in Proverbs 3:1–20, more specifically 3:11–12. There is, however, a notable difference between the Hebrew Bible and the Septuagint. It is, however, the Septuagint from which Barnabas quoted.

HB	LXX
Son, do not despise the Lord's *discipline*	My son, do not despise the Lord's *discipline*
for [כִּי] the Lord *disciplines* [יוֹכִיחַ]	for [γάρ] the Lord *disciplines* [παιδεύει]
the one he loves	the one he loves
just as a father	and *chastens* [μαστιγοῖ]
the son in whom he *delights.*	every son whom he *receives.*

On the one hand, the identification of the community as "My son" was assuring (cf. 2:10), but the more salient admonition was for both sons and daughters. While the Septuagint translator added the pronoun "my," it was an implied subject in the Hebrew Bible (Attridge, 1989, 361; Pfitzner, 1997, 175). They, the sons and daughters, as members of the household family of faith, were not to treat lightly the Lord's "paternal discipline" (παιδείω, cf. Deut. 8:5). So, the addition of "my" (μου) was of no real significance. And yet, the Greek word for "discipline" was rather significant. While the Hebrew word for "discipline" (יָכַח) in Proverbs 3:11–12 contextually suggested some kind of corporeal discipline rather than mere verbal rebuke or cognitive correction, the Greek word for discipline (παιδεύει) did not. Thus, Barnabas defined suffering as paternal discipline (12:7).

12:6. On the other hand, the reason (γάρ, "for") for paternal disciple was educational (v. 6). In a very broad sense, "discipline" (παιδεύει) "denoted the upbringing and handling of the child who was growing up to maturity in need of direction, teaching, instruction and a certain measure of compulsion in the form of discipline or even chastisement" (*TDNT* 5:596). Proverbs 3:11 served as a nonpunitive informative or educational model of discipline (Koester, 2001, 527; cf. Cockerill, 2012, 617–18). Thus, members of God's household family of faith were to expect divine parental instruction because they were God's "children" (ὡς υἱοῖς, lit., "as sons"). The emphasis of Hebrews 12:7 was one of enduring God's informative discipline (cf. Heb. 10:32, 35; 12:1, 2, 3). This concept recalled another Jewish author's exhortation in the Psalms of Solomon: "The Lord is good to those who endure disciple" (10:2b) and "The Lord is faithful to those who love him in truth, to those who endure his discipline" (14:1; [trans. Wright, 1985, 661, 663]; cf. Jesus in 5:7–10). Thus, in Hebrews 12:5–12, "paternal discipline" spoke of divine guidance for responsible living that was nonpunitive, yet educationally challenging (BDAG, s.v. "παιδεία" 1, p. 748). Consequently, the basis for not being disappointed when God educated members of his family was because he loved his family and exerted paternal discipline on everyone who was in his family.

12:7. In his interpretation of Proverbs 3:11–12, Barnabas made a "direct and forceful application" (Attridge, 1989, 361). He exhorted the members of God's family in Rome to "endure" (ὑπομένετε, impv.) their difficult life situations as part of God's educational process: "endure *your suffering* as divine discipline" (cf. NET and NLT). The vivid and forceful application of Proverbs 3:11–12 was a reminder that "sonship" (sons and daughters) and suffering were linked together (12:7–13; cf. Jesus in 12:3; 5:7–9). In a similar manner, Mark also wrote to a group of followers of Jesus in Rome informing them that a call to discipleship was a call to suffering (8:35; cf. 10:28–31, 38–39, 43b–45).

What was self-evident (γάρ, "for") about Barnabas's application was simply that enduring God's educationally oriented life situations was experienced by every member of his family. By way of Proverbs 3:11–12, Barnabas made an everyday self-evident observation about human fathers. In his justifying the need to honor one's parents, Philo (*Leg.* 1.31 §99) said, "parents; they nourished us; they instructed us; they have been the causes of all good things to us" (trans. Colson et al., 1962, 212–13). Thus, Barnabas concluded that God "treats" (NET, ESV, NIV, NLT, CNT), "deals" (KJV, ASV, NASB) or "behaves toward" (BDAG, s.v. "προσφέρω" 3, p. 886) members of the household family of faith "as though they were his sons or daughters" (ὡς υἱοῖς, lit., "as sons"; cf. of Jesus in 2:11–13). They were the members of God's kingdom household family of faith.

12:8. Barnabas then contrasted (δέ, "but") the difference between legitimate and illegitimate family members. For the sake of his argument (εἰ "if", first class cond.), Barnabas assumed that an undisciplined (χωρίς . . . παιδείας, "without discipline") family member (υἱοί, "sons") was an "illegitimate" (νόθοι) child. The noun "illegitimate" (NASB, NIV, NRSV, ESV, NET) or "bastard" (KJV) spoke of a person "born out of wedlock or of servile origin and therefore without legal status or rights" (BDAG, s.v. "νόθος," p. 675). In Greco-Roman society, a bastard child had no legal rights. This custom was also evident in Jewish culture. The Mosaic law prohibited a "bastard" from inheriting from their father's estate (Jephthah, Judg. 10:6–11:39). Here in 12:8, a comparison was inadvertently made between legitimate and illegitimate "children" (cf. NLT). For Barnabas, evidence to support whether a child was a legitimate child (lit., "sons") was based upon whether or not that child "shared in" or "participated in" (μέτοχοι) God's discipline. Discipline was yet another item to add to their list of common partnership (μέτοχος; e.g., partners of a heavenly calling, 3:1; partners with Jesus, 3:14; and partners in God's spirit, 6:4; cf. Koester, 2001, 528). Members of the household family of faith who were "without" (χωρίς) discipline were assumed to be illegitimate children "without forgiveness" (9:22; Mitchell, 2007, 272) and with no kingdom rights (4:16; 10:19–22).

12:9. Barnabas reinforced (εἶτα, "furthermore") his application of Proverbs 3:11–12 with an example about human fathers (σαρκὸς ἡμῶν πατέρας; lit., "fathers of our flesh"). Due to their special status as fathers in Greco-Roman society who had absolute paternal authority, Barnabas underscored that they were still "respected" (BDAG, s.v. "ἐνετρέπω" 2, p. 341) when they exerted discipline within the family. In fact, children who respected their parents often respected their elders: "'One who pays respect' (αἰδούμενος) to an aged man or woman who is not of his kin may be regarded as having remembrance of his father and mother. He looks to them as prototypes and stands in awe of those who bear their image" (Philo, *Spec. 1,2,3,4.* 2.43 §237 [trans. Colson, 1937, 454–55]). Thus, Barnabas asked his readers a rhetorical question whereby he expected a positive answer in order to underscore not so much that they respected God but that they obeyed God who had even greater absolute paternal authority (BDAG, s.v. "ὑποτάσσω" 1b*β*, p. 1042). God was, after all, the God of "spirits," namely, celestial beings (cf. 1 En. 37–71; Jub. 10:7–9; 1QM).

12:10. Barnabas's reasoning (γάρ, "for") for expecting the household family of faith to submit to God's divine discipline, however, differed between human fathers and God (οἱ μέν, "*they* on the one hand" . . . ὁ δέ, "*he* on the other hand"). The duration of a parent's nonpunitive form of discipline was temporally limited (πρὸς ὀλίγας ἡμέρας, "for a few days"). Furthermore, all parental discipline was based upon what may seem good to the father. For instance, Philo (*Ebr.* 4 §14) recounted a pair of parents' resolve to present their case about their overly contentious and disobedient child to the leaders of the city, who in turn had him stoned to death. While Philo exemplified an extreme form of punitive discipline, the point to be made is that disciplinary practices differed from culture to culture, from generation to generation, or according to custom. Josephus (*A.J.* 16.6.1 §163) spoke of Jewish people who disciplined in the manner that seemed best to them at the time and according to custom. The same was true for nonpunitive forms of education. So, not all human forms of discipline were perfect.

In contrast (δέ, "but") to human fathers, however, God was the perfect and permanent educator (Spicq, 1952, 2:395). Barnabas recognized that God's instruction was for the "profit" (KJV, ASV), "benefit" (NET) or "good" (ESV, NLT, NIV, etc.) of the household family of faith. One Jewish author put it this way: "Having been disciplined a little, they will receive great good" (Wis 3:5a; NRSV). God's discipline was viewed as advantageous in that it provided his children educational opportunities with the intention (εἰς + inf.) "to participate" (τὸ μεταλαβεῖν) in God's "holiness" (τῆς ἁγιότητος αὐτοῦ, "his holiness"). Holiness, for Barnabas was moral transformation (cf. 2:11; 9:14; 10:10, 14, 29), a point to which he would return in verses 14–17.

12:11. Barnabas concluded (δέ, "now") his application of Proverbs' nonpunitive discipline by stating the obvious: education was not always a "pleasant" (χαρᾶς) activity. On the contrary (ἀλλά, "but"), Barnabas acknowledged that the pain of education was often formidable either mentally or emotionally (BDAG, s.v. "λύπη." p. 605). On the one hand, Bruce (1969, 344) highlights the "pedagogical value of suffering" evident in Elihu's interjective observations about the lengthy debate between Job and his friends (Job 32:2–37:24). Yet, Bruce's appeal appears more punitive (cf. Job 33:19–28). On the other hand, Barnabas appealed to mental or spiritual training (BDAG, s.v. "γυμνάζω," p. 208). People who yielded to their trainer, namely, discipline (γεγυμνασμένοις, "those who have been trained *by it*") reaped rewards. In contrast (δέ, "but') to whatever pain might occur, like a plant, it eventually "yields" (ἀποδίδωσιν, ESV) or "produces" fruit (NET; BDAG, s.v. "ἀποδίδωμι" 1, p. 109), namely, "acts of living rightly" (= "fruits of righteousness").

12:12–13. Barnabas concluded verses 1–13 with a self-evident (διό, "therefore") truth (Attridge, 1989, 364–65; Ellingworth, 1993, 657; Johnson, 2006, 323; etc.). Based upon several exhortations, God's family was to develop a renewed resolve to succeed under God's paternal discipline (12:12). First, his readers were expected to "straighten up" (ἀνορθώσατε). By way of metaphors from Isaiah 35:3, namely "listless hands and weak knees," Barnabas addressed the "dispositions of fidelity and endurance" of his readers (Johnson, 2006, 323). Cockerill (2012, 629), contends the metaphors were reflective of a boxer. They were to "put up their proverbial dukes and continue the fight." Yet, the metaphors appear to appeal to determination (Job 4:3–4; Koester, 2001, 530). Barnabas exhorted his readers to be determined in all situations and unwavering in their resolve about Jesus, their royal high priest.

In addition (καὶ, "and"; v. 13), members of household family of faith were to stay on target. Appealing once again to Proverbs, Barnabas echoed Proverbs 4:26, which was "a call to continued progress in their moral transformation" (Johnson, 2006, 323). The intended result (ἵνα, "so that") for members of God's family remaining true to their moral transformation was so that members of the household family of faith might advance (vv. 10–11; cf. 5:13–14). Thus, this *exhortation* from Proverbs 3:11–12, addressed to this Jewish community of believers (vv. 1–6), as well as Barnabas's subsequent *application* (vv. 7–13), served to remind his readers that sonship entailed nonpunitive discipline that might nevertheless involve pain (no pain, no gain) as evidence that they belonged to the Lord. As members of God's family, God's educational opportunities were to be taken seriously (deSilva, 2000, 447–50).

THEOLOGICAL FOCUS

The exegetical idea (members of the household family of faith were expected to endure life's challenges, like an athlete, and to be encouraged that as members of God's family God was providing educational opportunities to them, like a father to his children) leads to this theological focus: Enduring life's challenges and engaging in divine educational opportunities are commonplace for anyone who is a member of God's family.

The major theological themes in this preaching unit are twofold. First, there is the expectation that followers of Jesus persevere in facing the challenges of life. Believers are to "endure" life's challenges (vv. 1, 3, 4, 12) by following Jesus's example (v. 2). Second, there is the expectation to accept God's paternal discipline as legitimate members of God's family (vv. 6, 8). God's paternal designs are better than human parents (v. 10) and are to be obeyed and not just respected (v. 9), as it leads to living rightly (v. 13).

PREACHING AND TEACHING STRATEGIES

Exegetical and Theological Synthesis

Hebrews 12:1–13 begins with the challenge that we are to look to those who have run before us. In this way, the passage begins with a motivation. We are not running alone. This is a team event. We are to run with a pack, and the greats of all time are there. Our motivation for endurance is not based on our capacity to endure, but rather we are motivated by with whom we are running with. Based on this reality we are to run unencumbered.

Our model for endurance is Jesus himself. Jesus endured hostility from sinners, and in a sense, he endured the discipline of God. He too was a son, yet he learned obedience through enduring what he suffered (Heb. 5:8). He never needed to be corrected by divine paternal discipline, but rather the plan of God demanded that he submit to the will of his Father in order to accomplish the plan.

After discussing how Jesus the Son endured the cross, Barnabas explained that the discipline of the Lord has certain positive effects on us. For one, it reminds us that we are his children. This clarifies that the passage is not so much about endurance but enduring under the gracious discipline of the Lord. Submitting to the Lord's discipline, though not enjoyable but painful, is for our benefit in that it enables us to share in his holiness. This process eventually produces peace and acts of living rightly.

Preaching Idea

Nothing of eternal value can be won without endurance and discipline.

Contemporary Connections

What does it mean?

What does it mean that nothing of eternal value can be won without endurance and discipline? Everyone who succeeds must embrace the discipline necessary to endure. This is why the father of Proverbs 1:23 tells his son that he must turn *to* reproof. The idea is that the wise son knows to embrace discipline as something for his own good.

Ethiopian Haile Gebrselassie is one of the fastest distance runners in history. He ran a mile in under four minutes and a full marathon in just over two hours. What most of us would consider an all-out sprint he could sustain for more than twenty-six miles. Mind-boggling. After an interview with Gebrselassie, author Matt Fitzgerald concluded that the reason he kept winning races, and surprised people by getting faster with age, is that he enjoyed the *pain* of the workout. Imagine that. His favorite workouts were the hardest workouts.[2] But it makes sense: if training hard makes you faster, and you enjoy the pain of training, then you *will* get faster.

What brings Gebrselassie joy is the endurance required by running. If someone loves the training, as much as competing and winning, then naturally that person will run better and win more.

The discipline of the Lord does not seem enjoyable. No discipline ever does. But when we sense the gracious discipline of the Lord on us, we smile. We know that this is his favor; it is a reminder that we are his children, and it also is a reminder that we are still in the race. So, instead of running from discipline, we run to discipline.

2 M. Fitzgerald, *Run: The Mind-Body Method of Running by Feel* (Boulder, CO: Velo, 2010), 6.

Is it true?

Is it true that nothing of eternal value can be won without endurance and discipline? Can you imagine a child who wanted to be disciplined? Can you imagine a child who wanted a time-out, or a teen who wanted to be grounded? If so, it would be an anomaly! The reality is that children, even if they can tolerate the actual discipline, do not like the fact that they have disappointed their parents.

Yet, as parents, the discipline that we give is not always punitive. In fact, most of our discipline is both anticipatory and corrective. We anticipate that if we do not set a bedtime, our children will stay up too late. So we set, and enforce, a bedtime. We further anticipate that if our kids stay up too late, they will get a rough start to school the next day. A pattern of this can disrupt learning and lead to negative social behaviors. So, we shut off technology and we curtail caffeine intake. None of these actions are reactionary. We are not mad at our children. The discipline we impose is because we love them, we are proud of them, and we are rewarding their progress with more chances to progress. Of course, they do not see it this way! This is why Barnabas reminded us that God's instructive discipline is a reminder of his fatherly love. He is not trying to punish us. He is trying to parent us.

Now what?

If nothing of eternal value can be won without endurance and discipline, now what? This text is intensely practical. We first ask, in what ways God is trying to discipline us? Do we need to have more passion for our time with him? Do we need to control our food intake or our consumption of material things? Remember all of this is in the context of Hebrews chapter 11, which is about living for a world that we cannot see (cf. Phil. 3:20; Col 1:13). So, the discipline that the Lord may be pressing on us is a discipline to express our love for the kingdom that we cannot see more than the kingdoms that we can see. Once we establish where God is leading us, we press in. This is the sense of John 15:3, that like a productive vine, God prunes those he loves. So, we embrace the pruning and press into him.

Creativity in Presentation

In order to establish the thrust of this passage, we might use props or put slides up that represent what we associate with discipline. The slides should be shown one at a time. The title slide could simply say, "Discipline?" Explain that we are going to look at pictures and see which images we associate with discipline. The slides could be filled with examples that are obvious such as a drill sergeant working with new recruits, an adult going over an annual progress report with their boss, a college student or teenager getting tutored, or a child in time-out. However, without explaining why, mix in items that would qualify as instructive discipline: a toothbrush, a book, or running shoes.

After scrolling through the slides, ask which ones related to discipline. The point is that they all relate to discipline. Some discipline was corrective, and other discipline was instructive. Then, using the last three examples think what advantages a child would have if they loved to brush their teeth, if they loved to read, and if they loved to exercise. This is the idea. They are running *into* discipline, toward something that is good for them and offers certain benefits. And in the context of Hebrews 12, we not only receive the benefits of discipline, but the benefits of sonship as well.

The point you want to get across is simply this: "Nothing of eternal value can be won without endurance and discipline." An outline of Hebrews 12:1–13 could look like this:

- Run like an athlete (vv. 1–4).
- Endure discipline like a child (vv. 5–13).

DISCUSSION QUESTIONS

1. What was the cloud of witnesses in Hebrews 12:1?

2. How do witnesses motivate us to run?

3. What specifically are some practical examples of enduring under the discipline of the Lord?

4. How does God's discipline of us demonstrate his parentage of us?

5. Is God's discipline of us always in response to something we have done wrong?

Hebrews 12:14–29

EXEGETICAL IDEA

Barnabas encouraged living in harmony with all people despite their difficulties unlike the exodus generation, and he expected the Roman household of faith to pay attention to and not reject the message about Jesus and thereby join those in God's heavenly kingdom.

THEOLOGICAL FOCUS

All who live morally harmonious lives, who pay attention to and do not reject the message about Jesus, will join the righteous who currently inhabit the heavenly kingdom of God.

PREACHING IDEA

Living demands choosing our moments.

PREACHING POINTERS

Living harmoniously as a Roman household was paramount to people living during the Greco-Roman world. For the Roman Empire, maintaining the "peace of Rome" was essential. Yet, during the time Barnabas wrote Hebrews, a violent movement in Judaea was about to erupt. Yet, despite what was going on in Judaea, Barnabas insisted that the Jewish household family of faith in Rome live morally harmonious lives by refraining from decisions that would make it impossible for repentance, as was the case for the exodus generation. The events in Judaea were profound, disturbing, and tempting for Jewish people.

Even today, there are moments in life that are more profound than others. A first conversation with one's future spouse, or the moment we decide to put ourselves out there for a job or for a promotion, are examples. None of these things would be possible if we did not choose our moments. We call these instances "defining moments" because they cause the trajectory of our life to pivot or change course. And these changes forever become a part of who we are. Not only the choice to move forward, but also the choice to stand still, both have life-shaping consequences. There's no middle ground when followers of Jesus consider the dangers and penalties of refusing God. Living demands choosing our moments.

REFUSING GOD (12:14–29)

LITERARY STRUCTURE AND THEMES (12:14–29)

Barnabas began Hebrews 12:14–29 with an exhortation to live morally harmonious lives with all people (v. 14) and to refrain from making decisions that would make it impossible for repentance (vv. 15–17). He then redirected his attention once again to the Sinai desert where God's power was exhibited through nontangible things (vv. 18–21), but he contrasted the people of the exodus generation with the household family of faith and their anticipated entrance into God's heavenly kingdom (vv. 22–24). Barnabas concluded with an expectation to pay attention to God's message to prevent divine punishment (12:25). The intention for God's repeating an event from the past, with far greater force, was so that he might establish his kingdom (12:26–27). Based upon the fact that all members of the household family of faith were in the process of receiving an unshakable kingdom, they were to give thanks to and to serve God because he was to be feared (12:28–29).

Barnabas's themes centered around peace, moral conduct, God's kingdom, and a warning not to turn away from God.

- ***Living Morally Harmonious Lives (12:14–17)***
- ***Desert and Heavenly Contrasts (12:18–24)***
- ***Listening to God Prevents Punishment from God (12:25–29)***

EXPOSITION (12:14–29)

At the time Barnabas wrote to the Jewish household family of faith in Rome, a Jewish eschatological movement was at its apex in Judaea. It was a violent movement that was disturbing the *Pax Romana* ("peace of Rome"). There existed among the Jewish leaders in Judaea a radical theological principle that God alone was Lord and ruler to be obeyed, and an intense political belief about a forthcoming Messiah figure and freedom from Roman occupation. Jude described them as the "godless" (v. 4). They wanted to "free" Judaea from Roman occupation so that Judaea's kingdom under God might be ushered as a result of their movement. The momentum of their eschatological movement appeared in stages. The rebel rumblings began with local skirmishes with Rome (4 B.C.–A.D. 6). It was during these early local skirmishes that a group known as the Zealots took root under Judas the Galilean, founder of the group (Josephus, *A.J.* 18.1.6 §23–24). In both religion and in the recognition of political powers, God alone was their only Lord over Judaea (Bateman, 2015[17], 76–77; Hengel, 1997, 330–76; Aharoni et al., 1977, 157).

Yet despite what was going on in Judaea, Barnabas insisted that the Jewish household family of faith in Rome live morally harmonious lives by refraining from decisions that would make it impossible for repentance, as in the historical case of the exodus generation, and he expected them to pay attention to and not reject the message about Jesus and thereby join those in God's heavenly kingdom.

Living Morally Harmonious Lives (12:14–17)

The insistence that the household family of faith live morally harmonious lives with everyone was possible by coming alongside those who struggled with their confession of faith, by refraining from causing trouble, and by

JUDAEAN REVOLT AGAINST ROME

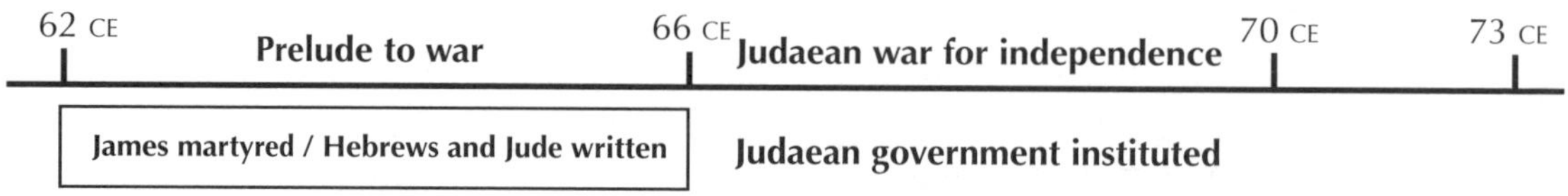

avoiding bold and rash decisions about Jesus that would make it impossible for repentance.

12:14. Barnabas opened with a very long Greek sentence (vv. 14–16) whereby he put forward an expectation and "how to" achieve it. First, translations render Barnabas's expectation as "pursue peace with everyone and holiness" (NET, NASB, NRSV), "strive for peace with everyone and holiness" (ESV, CNT), "make every effort to live in peace with all men and to be holy" (NIV), or "work at living in peace with everyone, and work at living a holy life" (NLT). When Barnabas spoke of "living at peace with everyone," he expected the household family of faith to live in "harmony" with all people, especially those with whom they had a "personal relationship" (BDAG, s.v. "εἰρήνη" 1a, p. 287). Closely related, this sort of harmonious living was tied to living a moral life (BDAG, s.v. "ἁγιασμός," p. 10). Similar concerns existed among the Essenes who lived at Qumran (1Q28 6.24–7.24). Like the desert-dwelling Essenes but unlike the war-driven Zealots, the Jewish household family of faith in Rome were to be holy in how they lived (vv. 15–16). The use of "holiness" should not be confused with Barnabas's earlier reference to the state of being made holy as a way to speak of their "sanctification" (2:11; 10:10, 14, 29) or as a way to speak of their being one of God's people (3:1) or one of "the saints" (τοῖς ἁγίοις; 6:10; cf. 13:24). Here, Barnabas spoke of living rightly or morally *before everyone* (12:11). The reason (elliptical γάρ, "for"; NET) for living a morally harmonious life with everyone, according to Barnabas, was because it contributed to their future entry into God's sanctuary (9:24; 10:19) as well as to their future celebration in God's sabbath rest (4:1, 9–11), and to actually see God (BDAG, s.v. "ὁράω" 1c, p. 719). For Barnabas, one's moral lifestyle mattered.

Who Were the Zealots?

The Zealots were a Judaean political/religious movement during the latter period of the Second Temple period (A.D. 6–73). Josephus referred to them as a "fourth sect." "The Zealots formed a relatively exclusive and unified movement with its own distinctive religious views," says Hengel (1989, 5), "and . . . they had a crucial influence on the history of Palestinian Judaism in the decisive period between A.D. 6 and 70." The movement began with Judas of Galilee in A.D. 6 and ended in A.D. 73 at Masada (cf. Hengel, 1989; Bateman, 2015[17], 51–80).

12:15. As this long Greek sentence continued, Barnabas provided the "how to" for living a morally harmonious life with everyone. The household family of faith was to be watchful (ἐπισκοποῦντες, impv. ptc. means), which translators have rendered in two different ways: "by seeing to it" (NET, ESV, NIV, CNT) or "by giving attention to it" (BDAG, s.v. "ἐπισκοπέω" 1, p. 379). Thus, the content about which Barnabas directed attention was threefold and easily identified by "that no one" (μή τις, "that no one"; vv. 15a, 15b, 16).

<u>Pursue</u> peace with everyone and holiness (v. 14)
by seeing to it "that no one" (μή τις) . . . (v. 15a)
by seeing to it "that no one" (μή τις) . . . (v. 15b)
by seeing to it "that no one" (μή τις) . . . (v. 16)

These three "how to" forms of living morally harmonious lives with everyone expanded Barnabas's previous expectation to "spur one another on to love and good works" (10:24). Yet here, Barnabas underscored the need to come alongside a brother or sister to avoid disharmony. They essentially served as a warning (Attridge, 1989, 367). The first "how to" was a general matter already addressed previously when Barnabas expressed his expectation to "let us hold fast" (3:6; 4:14; 10:23). The household family of faith was to see to it "that no one" *would fall short of* or *turn away from* God's grace (v. 15a; cf. 4:1; 3:12; 6:6). Naturally, the exodus generation at Kadesh Barnea would have come to mind for Barnabas's readers (cf. 3:7–19).

The second "how to" was a specific warning about troublemakers: by seeing to it "that no one caused trouble and defiled the community" (v. 15b). This "how to" response was based upon Scripture, specifically Deuteronomy 28:18 (LXX [29:17]). The "root of bitterness" in Deuteronomy initially spoke of idolatry and the abandoning the covenant community. Yet here, the "bitter root that springs up and causes trouble" (ῥίζα πικρίας ἄνω φύουσα ἐνοχλῇ) recalled the exodus generation as they stood at the geographical entrance of Canaan (Heb. 3:7–11). Ten spies rose up, caused trouble to the point of wanting to stone Moses, and turned away from God's desire for them (Num. 13:30–14:10). They were not living as a morally harmonious community. Similar concerns existed among the Essenes who lived at Qumran (1Q28 7.8b): "Whoever nurses a grudge against his companion—in blatant disregard of the *Yahad* statute about reproof on the same day—is to be punished by reduced rations of six months" (trans. Wise et al., 1996, 137). Barnabas realized that the household family of faith was struggling, just like the exodus generation. "Their [the household family of faith's] apostasy," says Johnson (2006, 324), "threatens the safety and integrity of all."

12:16. The third "how to" was another specific warning by way of a historical example: by seeing to it that no one repeated Esau's example and lost their inheritance (v. 16; cf. Gen. 25:29–34). Esau's example was one of "immorality" (πόρνος) or "godlessness" (βέβηλος). More specifically, the mention of Esau's selling of his birthright and his marriage to Gentile women (Gen. 26:34; 28:9; 36:2) were later construed in Jewish literature as an act of immorality because Esau yielded to satisfying his immediate physical desires (Jub 24:2–5; 25:1, 7–8; Philo, *Her*. 252–54; cf. Josephus, *A.J.* 1.18.1§257–58; 1.18.3–8 §263–77; cf. Attridge, 1989, 368–69; Koester, 2001, 533). He became the symbol of a corrupt age (4 Ezra 6:7–10). Philo (*QG* 4.197) described Esau as a person who did not think of "anything peaceful" and was "by nature rash and bold" (trans. Marcus, 1903, 486, 494). Furthermore, Philo (*QG* 4.201) described Esau as an "unrestrained, lecherous, impure, and unholy man" (trans. Marcus, 1903, 486, 494). These Jewish descriptions of Esau were not characteristic of a person who lived a morally harmonious life with everyone and was thereby to be avoided. Josephus described the Judaean Zealots as "tyrants" and "foolish" people who act "rashly" and exhibit "madness" as they promoted and pursued rebellion, pillaged and burned homes, and kidnapped and murdered Roman and countryman alike.[1]

12:17. The reasoned (γάρ, "for") support for Barnabas's perspective about Esau centered

1 In his descriptions of the Zealot, Josephus called them "tyrants" (τυράννος): Josephus, *B.J.* 1.1.4 §10; "foolish" (ἀφροσύνη), Josephus, *B.J.* 2.13.6 §651; manifest "rash" behavior (τόλμα): Josephus, *B.J.* 3.10.2 §479; 4.5.5 §347; exhibited "madness" (ἀπονοίας): Josephus, *B.J.* 2.13.6 §265; 3.9.8 §454; 3.10.2 §479; 4.6.1 §362; 5.1.5 §§34, 121, 424, 436, 436; 6.1.3 §20; 7.6.5 §213; 7.8.1 §267; 7.10.1 §412.

around Esau's "rejection" and his lack of an opportunity for "repentance." As "firstborn," Esau was entitled to the blessings typically granted to the firstborn son, but Esau gave his birthright to Jacob (Gen. 27:29). The event upon which Barnabas dwelt, however, occurred after he sold his birthright as triggered by the adverb "afterward" (μετέπειτα; ESV, NIV, NLT, NASB, KJV) or "later" (NET, NRSV). Although Esau wanted to inherit a blessing, "he was rejected" (ἀπεδοκιμάσθη). In other words, Esau was regarded as unworthy and unfit for inheriting a blessing (BDAG, s.v. "ἀποδοκιμάζω" b, p. 110). Granted, "inherit" does not appear in the Genesis account (27:30–40; cf. Josephus, *A.J.* 1.18.3–8 §263–77), but it was a theme Barnabas appealed to repeatedly (1:2, 14; 6:17; 9:15; 11:7). So, Barnabas's paraphrase of the Genesis account reflected his concern about the household family of faith forfeiting their spiritual inheritances (Attridge, 1989, 370).

Barnabas then explained (γάρ, "for") why Esau was considered unworthy of his inheritance: there was "no opportunity for repentance." The same word for "repentance" (μετάνοια) appeared in Hebrews 6:6 (cf. Wis 12:10b). Thus, Barnabas restated a previously developed theological truth: "Repentance after apostasy was impossible" (Attridge, 1989, 370; cf. Lane, 1991b, 459). Despite his tears, Esau was denied the opportunity to change his mind or to change what he had done (BDAG, s.v. "μετάνοια," p. 641; Koester, 2001, 533). Once again, this loss paralleled a similar loss at Kadesh Barnea, which was alluded to earlier in Hebrews 3:7–18. The exodus generation was denied entrance into Canaan, and despite their tears, they were condemned to die in the desert (Num. 14:1–4; 32–35; cf. Cockerill, 2012, 641). There was no opportunity to change what they had done for either the exodus generation or Esau. "Esau is brought to the attention of the assembled house church," says Lane, "as the person in whom the apostasy addressed in [Hebrews] 6:4–8 and 10:26–31 is realized" (Lane, 1991b, 458).

Esau sells his birthright to Jacob.
Courtesy of Circle of Matthias Stom. Public domain.

Desert and Heavenly Contrasts (12:18–24)

God's nontangible power that generated fear in the exodus generation in the Sinai desert was contrasted with the heavenly Zion where the righteous resided and the household family of faith anticipated participating in the life to come.

TEXTUAL ANALYSIS: Conflicting Text Critical Readings: 12:18

Exegetical Issue: Although many follow the variant (D K P 044 88 614 1739 1881 Byz), manuscript evidence supports strongly the text ($\mathfrak{P}^{46}$ ℵ A C 048 33 81 1175). Furthermore, there appears to be a scribal assimilation with Hebrews 12:22 where Mount Zion contrasts verse 18. The text is the preferred reading (Lane, 1991b, 441; Metzger, 1994, 605).

txt. "for you have not come to what may be touched" (οὐ γὰρ προσεληλύθατε ψηλαφωμένῳ) (ESV, NET, NRSV)

var. "for you have not come **to a mountain** that can be touched" (οὐ γὰρ προσεληλύθατε ψηλαφωμένῳ [**ὄρει**]) (ASV, KJV, NASB, NIV, NRSV)

12:18. Barnabas opened with yet another very long Greek sentence (vv. 18–21). The sentence served as Barnabas's conclusion (γάρ, "for") for the household family of faith based upon historical evidence and reasoning. Barnabas declared, by direct address, a converse statement: "you have not come to what may be touched" or "you have not come to manifestations that were tangible" (BDAG, s.v. "ψηλαφάω" 1, p. 1097). The nontangible items about which Barnabas spoke were items associated with God's power experienced by the exodus generation. God's power was first associated with a self-sustaining "burning fire" (κεκαυμένῳ πυρὶ) that may have recalled the burning bush (Exod. 3:2), the devouring fire at the top of Mount Sinai (Exod. 19:18; 24:17), or perhaps even the fire over the tabernacle (Exod. 40:38; Num. 9:15–16). God's power was also linked to "foreboding darkness" and "foreboding gloom" (BDAG, s.v. "ζόφος" 1, p. 429). "Darkness" most certainly conjured the remembrance of the three days of darkness over Egypt (Exod. 10:21–23) as well as God's voice being heard in the midst of darkness while stationed at the foot of Mount Sinai (Deut. 4:11; 5:22–23). God's power was also coupled with a "whirlwind" or more technically "atmospheric disturbance marked by violent gusts of wind" (BDAG, s.v. "θύελλα," p. 461). Perhaps this was a reference to God's atmospheric disturbance around Mount Sinai (Exod. 20:18; Josephus, *A.J.* 3.5.2 §79–80). Perhaps the whirlwind was associated with the cloud that hovered over the tabernacle (Exod. 19:16; 40:38; Num. 9:15; cf. Elijah, 2 Kings 2:1, 11) or God speaking out of a whirlwind (Job 38:1). Regardless, the fire, the foreboding darkness, and the whirlwind were demonstrations of God's nontangible power.

Mount Sinai (Gabal Musa). Public domain.

12:19. Barnabas continued (καί, "and") his list with two other nontangible items associated with God's power. On the one hand, there was the "sound of the trumpet" (σάλπιγγος ἤχῳ) that recalled the trumpet sound that would have signaled the exodus generation's ascent of Mount Sinai (Exod. 19:13; 20:18) or the exodus generation's having been set apart by God (Exod. 19:16). On the other hand, there was "the voice of words" (φωνῇ ῥημάτων). The concept of "the voice of words" was derived from Deuteronomy: "You heard the sound of words but saw no form; there was only a voice" (NRSV rendering of the LXX: Deut. 4:12; cf. Exod. 19:5, 19; Josephus, *A.J.* 3.4.4 §§89–90). There was a close relationship between the audio expressions, which Cockerill (2012, 648 n. 30) validates by way of a chiastic construction (cf. Attridge, 1989, 373 n. 373):

A "of a trumpet"
  B "a sound"
  B' "a voice"
A' "of words"

The "sound" (B) and "voice" (B') affected hearing. The "sound of the trumpet" and the "voice of word" served as a warning to the exodus generation not to approach Mount Sinai too closely lest they die (Johnson, 2006, 329–40). Yet, what Barnabas underscored was how God's voice affected the exodus generation: "those who heard God's voice begged [παρῃτήσαντο] to hear it no more" (cf. Exod. 20:19). Regardless of whether translated "entreated" (KJV, ASV) or more appropriately "begged" (NET, NIV, NLT, NASB; cf. ESV, NRSV), the net effect was a refusal to listen to and obey God (cf. Heb. 2:1; BDAG, s.v. "παραιτέομαι" 1b and 2, p. 764). The same verb appeared in verse 25 as a warning not to refuse the one who was speaking (Koester, 2001, 543). The exodus generation did not want God to speak to them directly. Barnabas's point was that God's power was evident to the exodus generation through at least five nontangible things: fire, darkness, whirlwind, the sounds of a trumpet, and God's voice.

12:20–21. Barnabas then presented the reason (γάρ, "for") why the exodus generation feared the threat they faced at the foot of Mount Sinai. They could not "bear" (NET, NIV, NASB) or "endure" (ESV, NRSV, CNT, ASV, KJV) the difficulty of the situation (BDAG, s.v. "φέρω" 9, p. 1052). The NLT captures this later sense best: "they staggered back under God's command." And though Barnabas paraphrased Exodus 19:12–13, God's command was still staggering: "if even an animal touches the mountain, it must be stoned." "If even" (κἂν; formed by crasis from καὶ ἐάν; cf. BDF, 11 §18) introduced an implied conditional statement (Moule, 1982, 138, 167) that insinuated a lesser to greater argument (*qal wahomer*).[2] So, if an animal was to be subjected to death for touching Mount Sinai, how much more would a person (Mitchell, 2007, 282)?

Barnabas followed his paraphrase of Exodus 19:12–13 with a "truth be told" (καί, "in fact") comment about the scene. It was "terrifying" (φοβερόν). The adjective "terrifying," or "fearful," appears only in Hebrews and reflected Barnabas's other recurring theme. There was the fear of death (Heb. 2:15; cf. 9:27), the fear of divine judgment (10:27), and the fear of experiencing the negative aspects of God's power (10:31). Unlike these previous references, Hebrews 12:21 was about standing in God's presence at the foot of Mount Sinai (Exod. 20:18–21). It was not unusual for Jewish writers to express attitudes of fear or terror concerning God's impartiality (LXX: Deut. 10:17), God's covenant-keeping attribute (LXX: Neh. 1:5; 9:32), God's deeds (LXX: Pss. 65[66]:3, 5; 145[146]:6), God's name (LXX: Pss. 98[98]:3; 110[111]:9), and the place of "the Existent Being" (Philo, *Somn.* 1.32 §184). Here in Hebrews 12:21, God's presence was "terrible" (KJV, NASB) or "terrifying" (NET, ESV, NIV, CNT, RSV, NRSV) to Moses. Moses, the national hero of the Jewish people (Heb. 3:2, 5), was quoted as saying, "I am terrified and trembling." There were two examples in Scripture (HB) about the fear of Moses. Moses was fearful of God's presence during the burning bush event (Exod. 3:6) and terrified to be in God's presence after exodus generation's sin of the golden calf at Mount Sinai (Deut. 5:5–11, 32–33 with 9:18–19). Barnabas, however, drew his quote from Deuteronomy 9:18–19. Thus, the term conveyed an attitude of fright at the prospect of standing face-to-face before the living God that perhaps revealed Barnabas's "stress on God's holiness" (Kistemaker, 1984, 390; cf. Exod. 34:34–35 with 2 Cor. 3:12–18).

12:22. Barnabas opened with yet another very long Greek sentence (vv. 22–24). The sentence served as Barnabas's contrast (ἀλλά, "but") between the earthly Sinai events (vv. 18–21) and Mount Zion (vv. 22–24). The Psalms often viewed "Zion," "the city of God," and "Jerusalem" as synonymous (51:18–19; 87:1–3; 102:21–22; Koester, 2001, 544). Historically, "Mount Zion" (Σιὼν ὄρει) was associated with the Davidic dynasty (2 Sam. 5:7; Pss. 2:6; 9:12; 48:2). David conquered the Jebusite stronghold in 1003 B.C. (2 Sam.

2 *Qal wahomer* is an argument of logic. Arguments begin with a less significant situation to something more significant. Thus, what applies in a less important case will certainly apply in a more important case. For other examples in Hebrews, see Bateman, 2012, 163–64.

5:6–10). Yet, prior to David and during the time of Abraham, it was Melchizedek's city known as Salem (Gen. 14:17–20; cf. Heb. 7:1–10). Similarly, "Jerusalem" was the city where Solomon eventually built the temple in 966 B.C. where God's presence was visible by way of a cloud (1 Kings 7:51–8:1, 10–11; Pss. 9:11; 48:1). Yet, Barnabas was not speaking of an earthly Zion or earthly Jerusalem as a place for a temporal rule of Messiah, a temporal kingdom for which the Zealots sought to achieve. God was frequently perceived as the "living God" (Deut. 5:16; Ps. 84:2) who had a "heavenly dwelling." Solomon, after building the temple in Jerusalem, recognized that no earthly temple could contain God, and he prayed, "hear from inside your heavenly dwelling place and respond favorably" (1 Kings 8:27–30 NET; Ps. 102:19).

In addition (καί, "and") to having approached the celestial city, there was the revelation that the household family of faith had communion with "myriads of angels" (μυριάσιν ἀγγέλων). Historically, it was believed that there were angels at Mount Sinai when Moses received the law (Deut. 33:2; cf. Josephus, *A.J.* 15.5.3 §136) and angels conversed with Moses (Acts 7:38). More contemporaneously to Barnabas's situation were the Essenes who lived at Qumran (cf. Bateman, 2012, 102–105). They believed that communion with the angels existed in worship (4Q400–407; cf. 1 Cor. 11:10) and during the final war between good and evil (1QM 1.15, 16.11–12; 12.1–9). "The Melchizedek scroll (11Q13) place(d) Melchizedek in opposition to Belial (the "evil one") and his angels, making Melchizedek a savior figure for the end time . . . Melchizedek clearly (was) depicted as a heavenly figure, a priestly savior" (trans. Mach, 2000, 26). Yet, unlike his contemporaries who often provided elaborations of the angelic world, Barnabas kept it simple. He made it clear that celestial beings resided in the heavenly city.

Statue of King David.
Courtesy of Jastrow. Public domain.

12:23. Barnabas continued (καί, "and") his lengthy sentence about those in heaven by moving beyond the myriad of angels in heaven to others present in heaven. First, he mentioned "the assembly of the firstborn" (ἐκκλησίᾳ πρωτοτόκων). The noun "assembly" was a typical reference for gatherings, whether a general assembly (Sir 26:5; Acts 19:39), an Israelite assembly (Deut. 31:30; Judg. 20:2; Pss. Sol. 10:6; Acts 7:38; Josephus, *A.J.* 12.4.2 §164; unlike the gatherings at Qumran where they called their groups "*Yahad*" 1Q28 1.1, 12, 22, etc.), or a gathering of the household family of faith (Rom. 16:5; 1 Cor. 11:18; Philem. 2). "Firstborn" also had various applications. Literally, "firstborn" spoke of the birth of a human father's first son (Exod. 22:29). Figuratively, "firstborn" spoke of the people who had a unique relationship with God: the nation of Israel was God's firstborn (Exod. 4:22–23; Num. 11:12; Jer. 31:9; Sir 17:17–18), and the Davidic king was recognized as having a unique relationship with God (2 Sam. 7:14; Pss. 2:7; 89:27). While some commentators limit "firstborn" to the household family of faith in Rome (Kistemaker, 1984, 393), most view "firstborn" as a figurative reference to those who follow Jesus (Westcott, 1984, 415; Guthrie, 1998, 420; cf. Lane, 1991b, 468–69). Yet, the relative clause "who are enrolled in heaven" referred to all people, not angels, listed in the heavenly registry whose future residence would be a heavenly one (Rev. 20:15; Attridge, 2989, 375; Mitchell, 2006, 283; cf. Bruce, 1990, 358). As was the case with Jesus's death for atonement of people not angels (2:16–18), the heavenly registry, according to Barnabas, consisted of human names and not those of angels (12:23).

Angelic Communion with People (adapted from Bateman, 2012, 102–05)

Old Testament	Extrabiblical Material
Genesis 18 did not seem to identify Abraham's three visitors as angelic beings.	The Ages of Creation (4Q180) identified the three men who visit Abraham as angels.
Angels were a benefit to people (Pss. 103:20; 78:25; cf. 2 Sam. 14:17, 20; 19:27; Zech. 14:5).	Angels were perceived at Qumran to have a dualistic division like that of humanity: those who were of the Sons of Light and those who were of the Sons of Darkness (1Q28 iii.13-iv.26).
Angels executed divine judgment or justice (Num. 22:23; Josh. 5:13; 2 Sam. 24:16; 1 Chron. 21:16; Ezek. 9:2; Zech. 1:8; 12:5). Often, they were represented as being armed with weapons (Josh. 5:13; cf. Num. 22:23; 1 Chron. 21:16, 30).	Angels were perceived at Qumran to execute judgment alongside human beings (1QM x.10–12; 1 En. 37–71).
Angels provided divine deliverance (Gen. 48:16; cf. Exod. 23:20–23; Judg. 2:1–5). It was the angel of the Lord who went out and put to death 85,000 of Sennacherib's army (Isa. 37:14–21; 33–37; cf. 2 Kings 19:32–34).	Josephus attributed the Sennacherib event as God delivering a sickness upon the army (Josephus, *A.J.* 10.1.4–5 §20–22).
The Hebrew Bible appeared to be silent about communion between human beings and angelic beings.	The members at Qumran communed with the Angels of Light only (Hodayot). This communion of people with angels formed one army in the eschatological battle against that of Belial and his angels (1QM i.10–11, ix.14–16).

Barnabas continued (καί, "and") with a second occupant of heaven: "God" (θεῷ). Barnabas referred to God as the "God who is judge over all things" (NLT) or "God, the judge of all" (NET, ESV, NASB, NRSV; Attridge, 1989, 376). Barnabas's allusion to God as judge who judges all appears in 1 Enoch. The book of 1 Enoch spoke directly of God's eschatological dealing with the godless (a *theophany*) that was on par with its Mosaic counterpart in Deuteronomy 33 and other texts from the Hebrew Bible (Bateman, 2015[17], 294).

Barnabas continued (καί, "and") with another group of occupants of heaven: "spirits of the righteous" (πνεύμασι δικαίων). These spirits were people who had died and whose souls had been separated from their bodies (1 Cor. 15:40, 42; 2 Cor. 5:8; unless of course there is soul sleep). More specifically, these were righteous saints like those mentioned but not limited to those in Hebrews 11. Righteous saints included all saints who followed Jesus (Westcott, 1984, 416; Kistemaker, 1984, 394; Lane, 1991b, 470). Barnabas described these Old and NT spirits of righteous people as those "who have been made perfect" (τετελειωμένων, perf. pass. ptc.). Thus, Barnabas described God's divine perfection of all upright people who had gone before (BDAG, s.v. "τελειόω" 2d, p. 996).

12:24. Barnabas continued (καί, "and") with one final occupant of heaven: "Jesus" (Ἰησοῦ). The use of the name of "Jesus" emphasized his humanity, which would be underscored with the forthcoming reference to "blood" (cf. 2:14–18; Ellingworth, 1993, 681; Lane, 1991b, 472). Naturally, Barnabas portrayed Jesus as "the mediator of the new covenant," a pronouncement declared earlier in Hebrews (8:6; 9:15). As mediator, Jesus was the one who mediated between two parties to resolve disagreements (BDAG, s.v. "μεσίτη," p. 634). He was the arbitrator between God and humanity that could be trusted and one who would negotiate peace.

Barnabas continued (καί, "and") with one further item in heaven: Jesus's human blood (αἵματι ῥαντισμοῦ; "sprinkled blood"). Some commentators consider Barnabas's reference to Jesus's blood as the blood of sprinkling that was sprinkled in heaven for accomplishing an eternal atonement and inauguration of the new covenant (10:22; BDAG, s.v. "ῥαντισμός," p. 903; cf. Attridge, 1989, 376; Bruce, 1990, 361; Lane, 1991b, 473). Barnabas, however, focused his final description about Jesus's blood as "a better word than the blood of Abel." While Abel's sacrifice was presented as a better sacrifice than Cain's (cf. Heb. 11:4), Jesus's sacrifice was even a "better word" (κρεῖττον λαλοῦντι) or more superior word than that of Abel's. While Abel's faith was personified as speaking from beyond the grave (11:4), here Jesus's "blood" was personified as speaking not from the grave but from heaven. The NLT renders the closing phrase about Jesus's blood in this manner: "and to the sprinkled blood, which speaks of forgiveness instead of crying out for vengeance like the blood of Abel."

Listening to God Prevents Punishment from God (12:25–29)[3]

Barnabas expected the household family of faith to pay attention to God's punishment of an older generation of disobedient Israelite people as well as to the future establishment of his kingdom, a kingdom about which household family members were in the process of entering and thereby expected to respond to God with thanksgiving by way of serving him.

3 For various perspectives on Hebrews 12:25–29, see H. W. Bateman IV (editor), *Four Views on the Warning Passages in Hebrews* (Grand Rapids: Kregel, 2007), 122–27; 197–205; 283–88.

12:25. Barnabas opened these final verses somewhat abruptly with a warning: "see to it [βλέπετε] that you do not refuse Jesus who is speaking." The absence of a connecting conjunction made verses 25–29 more forceful (Westcott, 1984, 418; Moffatt, 1979, 219). Barnabas was concerned that the household family of faith "did not reject" (μὴ παραιτήσησθε) or refuse to listen to the message about Jesus (BDAG, s.v. "παραιτέομαι" 2bα, p. 764). The statement was reminiscent of Barnabas's opening concern: "in these last days God has spoken to us through Jesus (1:2), and "therefore we must pay attention to what we have heard" (2:1). Thus, Barnabas offered a "cautionary prohibition" to listen to God who as the implied speaker spoke through Jesus's acts of obedience and self-sacrifice (Lane, 1991b, 475; cf. Westcott, 1984, 418).

Barnabas then presented the reason (γάρ, "for") for his expectation. Assuming a condition of fact for the sake of his argument (εἰ, "if"; first class cond.), Barnabas created another lesser to greater argument (*qal wahomer*). If during the former times (old dispensation) a previous generation were punished for disobeying God's message *spoken from Sinai*, "how much will we" (πολὺ μᾶλλον ἡμεῖς) who are living during this new era (new dispensation) be punished "*when* we turn away" (ἀποστρεφόμενοι, temp. ptc.) from God's message *spoken from heaven* (cf. Heb. 2:2–3). "Turning away" involved rejecting God's message about Jesus, the royal high priest (BDAG, s.v. "ἀποστρέφω" 23, p. 123). As he did earlier, Barnabas included himself in the warning: "how much will *we*" (πολὺ μᾶλλον ἡμεῖς; cf. 12:1–2). Similarly, Barnabas once again assumed that the household family of faith was in danger of turning away from the message about Jesus (3:12; 6:6; Koester, 2001, 547). Finally, Barnabas once again recalled God's speaking from heaven through either the prophets or the psalms (1:5–13; 3:7–11; 5:5–6; 8:8–12; 10:37–38; Koester, 2001, 547), as a way to curb any support of the revolutionary events happening in Judaea by the Zealots against Rome. So, the basis for the household family of faith to listen to God was based on God's severe punishment of people who did not trust in or disobeyed his expectations.

12:26. Barnabas appealed once again to God's voice (cf. 12:9, 25), but here, the emphasis recalled the time when God shook the earth at Sinai and then spoke. Although "once more" could convey the idea of "once again" as in a series of events (of sending a gift: Phil. 4:16; cf. 1 Macc 3:30; of visiting: 1 Thess. 2:18; cf. 2 Macc 3:37), here Barnabas had earthquakes in mind, which was clearly evident in Barnabas's quotation from the prophet Haggai. And though Barnabas typically quoted from the Septuagint, his additions to Haggai 2:6 "not only" (οὐ μόνον) and "but also" (ἀλλὰ καί) emphasized the thoroughness, "magnitude," and "finality" of God's future judgment (Koester, 2001, 547; Ellingworth, 1993, 687).

HB	LXX	Hebrews 12:26
Once again, in a little while I myself will shake ______ the heavens and the earth.	Once again, in a little while, I myself will shake ______ the heaven and the earth.	Once again, in a little while, I myself will shake *not only* the heaven *but also* the earth.

The mention of earth-shaking echoed Sinai events, when God's voice shook the earth in judgment (of Korah: Num. 16:20–35; cf. Judg. 5:4–5; Pss. 76[77]:18–20; 113[114]:1, 7; cf. 4 Ezra 3:17–19; 2 Bar 59.3–4). Through his restatement of Haggai 2:6, Barnabas redirected attention from merely earthquaking to a future shaking of both earth and heaven just as God originally promised in an oracle to those who returned from Babylonian captivity (ca. 539 B.C.) and who rebuilt the temple (ca. 515 B.C.). Haggai prophesied that God would "once again" "shake" the earth for a final judgment.

Haggai 2:6

Haggai 2:6 is the only verse from Haggai quoted in the NT.

OT Context: The book of Haggai consists of three oracles or sermons.

1. The first oracle, dated 1st Elui = August 29, 520 BCE, by the modern Julian calendar, exhorted the people to reorder priorities and to build the house of God (Hag. 1:1–11).
2. The second oracle, dated 7th Tishri = October 17, 520 BCE (2:1), by the modern Julian calendar, addressed the glory of the new house, namely, the temple (2:1–9).
3. The third oracle, dated 24th Kislev = December 18, 520 BCE, by the modern Julian calendar, offered a promise of a future blessing (2:10–19).

The Second Oracle: The second oracle, from which Barnabas quoted, may be divided into two major sections.

1. The first section was meant to be an encouragement to the governor Zerubbabel, the high priest Joshua, and the remnant of the Jewish community in Judaea (2:1–5).
2. The second section contained a promise of a glorious new house (2:6–9). There were at least two assurances mentioned in this section. One assurance consisted of "desired things" or "their treasures" (NET), which referred to the wealth of other nations, brought to Jerusalem (vv. 6–7; cf. Isa. 60:5; Ezra 6:8–12 [from Darius], 7:12–26 [from Artaxerxes], 2 Macc 3:3 [from Seleucus IV]). The other assurance emerged in the two promises made by God: (1) that the present house or temple would be greater than the glory of the former house (Josephus, *A.J.*) and (2) that God would grant peace to the place (Josephus *A.J.* [Salome Alexandria]; Hag. 2:9). The promises would have been understood with an earthly orientation and not a heavenly one, which is strictly a NT concept.

Haggai 2:6: Verse 6, the one quoted in Hebrews 12:26b, directed attention to God "shaking" the earth. The phrase "yet once more" indicated that there was a previous shaking of the earth, namely, at Mount Sinai (Exod. 19:16). In Haggai's time, the object shaken by God was "the heaven and earth." The totality of God's shaking things up was evident in the additional wording of "the sea and dry land." In all probability, the metaphor reflected the political instability of Darius's accession to power in 522 B.C. after the death of Cambyses. Here in Hebrews, Barnabas distinguished between a material and spiritual shaking of things and thereby escalated Haggai's prophetic word (cf. Smith et al., 2020, 105–09).

12:27. Here, Barnabas interpreted or explained (τὸ δέ, "now this") Haggai 2:6 (Kistemaker,1984, 399; Lane, 1991b, 481). The basis of Barnabas's argument (Ἔτι ἅπαξ, "yet once") implied a future event, namely, that *one final* temporal world-shaking event yet to come that would not only be a totally destructive quake but would reveal a heavenly kingdom that was unshakable and durable (11:10, 14–16; 12:22; cf. 4 Ezra

10:25–28; Matt. 24:29–30). Barnabas underscored for the household family of faith that God's voice would once again shake the earth as well as heaven so that he might establish his kingdom. It would not be a Zealot kingdom in Judaea but rather God's voice that would shake both heaven and earth. God would remove every created thing in both the material and immaterial world that could be shaken. In their comments on the phrase "unshakable kingdom" (Heb 12:28), one church father concluded "that we are not to be content with what God gives us in the present but are to give Him the greatest thanks for what is to come" (John Chrysostom, *Hom. Heb.* 33 cited in *TDNT* 7:70 n. 31).

Barnabas then provided God's intended result (ἵνα, "so that") for removing every created thing in both the material and immaterial world. It was so that only that which was unshakable would "remain" (μείνῃ). Those things that continue to exist (BDAG, s.v. "μένω" 2b, p. 631) would be those things that were not shaken. Thus, God's repeating an event from the past, with far greater force, would occur again so that God might establish or reveal his unshakeable kingdom.

12:28. Barnabas concluded (διό, "therefore") his comments about God's thorough and future shaking of his created order (Moffatt, 1979, 222). On the one hand, the Jewish household family of faith in Rome were in the process of receiving the Son's unshakable kingdom. Thus, Barnabas provided the reason for the final shake-up: "since we are in the process of receiving" (παραλαμβάνοντες, ptc. of reason; NET, NLT, NIV, NASB, NRSV, CNT). "Receiving a kingdom," according to Attridge (1989, 382), is "apocalyptic imagery" typically found in Daniel: "The holy ones of the Most High will receive the kingdom and will take possession of the kingdom forever and ever" (Dan. 7:18 NET). Yet, the fact that members of the household family of faith were receiving the kingdom not only modified Haggai 2:6, it implied that they were already becoming members of God's kingdom (Pfitzner, 1997, 189). Thus, this "unshakeable kingdom" (βασιλείαν ἀσάλευτον) was not to be confused with the Judaean Zealots who wanted to reestablish a Judaean earthly kingdom (Bateman, 2015[17], 51–80; cf. Morris, 1981, 181). Barnabas emphasized an eternal heavenly kingdom ruled by God's exalted royal high priest, Jesus (Lane, 1991b, 484; Koester, 2001, 557).

Barnabas then delivered a twofold expectation whereby he urged the household family of faith to unite with him (Wallace, 1996, 464). First, he exhorted the Jewish household family of faith in Rome to give thanks to God: "Let *us* give thanks" (ἔχωμεν χάριν). A response of gratitude to God's generosity was reasonable, hence Barnabas's appeal. Gratitude was the response "through which" (δι' ἧς) the household family of faith were to unite yet another appeal for action. Second, Barnabas thus exhorted them to serve God: "Let *us* serve (λατρεύωμεν; KJV, ASV, NASB) God acceptably with reverence and awe" (BDAG, s.v. "λατρεύω," p. 587). Some translations render "serve" as "worship" (NET, ESV, NIV, CNT, NRSV), which would have included approaching God in boldness (4:14–16; 10:19–22) as well as living a morally harmonious life with everyone, which included acts of good works (cf. 10:24–26; 12:14–15; 13:16, 21). So, based upon the fact that members of the Jewish household family of faith in Rome were in the process of receiving the Son's unshakable kingdom, they were to give thanks to God, and they were to serve God "with reverence and awe" (μετὰ εὐλαβείας καὶ δέους). Whereas "reverence" (εὐλαβείας) revealed a caution to avoid giving an offense to God (BDAG, s.v. "εὐλάβεια," p. 407), as in the case of Jesus (5:7) and Noah (11:7), "awe" (δέους) was an emotion of profound respect and reverence for deity" (BDAG, s.v. "δέος," p. 218). It was "a more uneasy fear" (Koester, 2001, 557).

12:29. Barnabas then presented the reason (γάρ, "for") why God was to be served with reverence and awe. It was because he was a "consuming fire" (πῦρ καταναλίσκον). Barnabas's emblematic description of God presented God as though he were "fire." The metaphor came from Scripture, specifically Deuteronomy 4:24. Deuteronomy's context emphasized a warning to the nation of Israel. If they were to abandon the Mosaic covenant, they would forfeit God's promise of protection (Deut. 29:9–29). Here, members of the new covenant were given the same warning: turning away from God's new covenantal promises completed through Jesus would result in divine punishment.

THEOLOGICAL FOCUS

The exegetical idea (Barnabas encouraged living in harmony with all people despite their difficulties unlike the exodus generation, and he expected the Roman household of faith to pay attention to and not reject the message about Jesus and thereby join those in God's heavenly kingdom) leads to this theological focus: All who live morally harmonious lives, who pay attention to and do not reject the message about Jesus, will join the righteous who currently inhabit the heavenly kingdom of God.

While common words link these verses together—the participle "speaking" (vv. 24 and 25), the mention of "fire" (vv. 29 and 18), the mention of "voice" (vv. 26 and 19), and the mention of "heaven" (vv. 22–23 and 25–26)—the predominate theological themes in this preaching unit are fourfold. First, there was the theme of living at peace with all people (v. 14). Second, there was an emphasis on moral conduct, particularly as it concerned maintaining their faith (vv. 15–17, 25). Third, there was the theme God's heavenly kingdom as it was first described, namely, as a heavenly Zion (vv. 22, 28). Warnings were weaved through 12:14–29 where Barnabas offered a final "word of warning." Whereas verses 14–24 served to introduce the warning, verses 25–29 clearly served as Barnabas's direct warning that closely resembled Hebrews 2:1–5.

PREACHING AND TEACHING STRATEGIES

Exegetical and Theological Synthesis

This passage comes off the heels of a call to follow the discipline of the Lord in Hebrews 12:1–13. That call to honor the paternal love of the Father in action is complemented by an equally clear call to respond. Now, we are not just to be responsive to the Father's discipline, but to the general call to follow God in life.

The call begins with a call to live a life of moral fortitude as described in 12:14–17. The idea, however, is not just on living the life but on *deciding* to live the life. Barnabas made the fine point here by using the illustration of Esau who, in a moment, made a decision from which he never recovered. He later found that this moment could not be reversed.

The motivation to respond to the call of God comes in 12:18–24, namely, that we are not coming to Mount Sinai with its fire and smoke, but we are coming to Mount Zion. We are coming to the city of God in the celebration of the new covenant.

This heavenly city is also an unshakable kingdom (12:25–29). When Jesus brings the unshakable kingdom, he will make all things new! What a glorious promise that God's immutable character will be represented in an unchanging kingdom.

Preaching Idea

Living demands choosing our moments.

Contemporary Connections

What does it mean?

What does it mean that living demands choosing our moments? At every juncture of life we make choices that define us. Scripture is filled with examples of people such as the midwives of Exodus 2, Joseph, Ruth, Esther, and even Jesus's disciples, who when faced with a choice, made—often in just a moment—a life-altering decision. They chose and they did not look back. In the context of life today, the same is true. Those who are effective in their pursuits as athletes, students, or in business make decisions and press on. As someone said, defining moments are defiant moments.

Is it true?

Is it true that living demands choosing our moments? Yes, it is true. We don't need to look to the Bible or even to history to illustrate this. We know this from our lives. Everyone who lives has experienced a moment that defined them. Graduating from high school or college are defining moments. Securing your first job or accepting a promotion are choses that are defining moments. That first kiss or first date could be a choice that ends as a defining moment. Everyday life demands choices, many of which are defining moments. It is a truism that with all the planning we do, much of life turns on a few key moments, a few key decisions.

Now what?

If living demands choosing moments, then the application to this passage, like the warning passages of Hebrews, is profound. We must respond to the discipline of the Father, and we must, in the moment that we have, choose not to refuse the one who is speaking to us. It could be God is encouraging us to make a choice through our Scripture readings, our favorite radio pastor, our spouse, our boss, our parents, or our teachers at school. Refusing God would be a disastrous decision. The call of this passage is to compare our lives to people like Esau and to the exodus generation of Israelites, who, in their moments of decision, decided against following God and paid with extreme consequences.

Creativity in Presentation

If a rocket ship is taking off to the moon, the engineers set it on a trajectory. Many things have to be considered. Factors in the launch include the place where the rocket is taking off from, the weight of the ship, the amount of fuel, the amount of cargo, the weather, and the rotation of the earth. The reason all these things are to be taken into consideration is obvious. The moon is so far away that if the rocket is off by a few inches when it leaves the earth, it may miss the moon by miles. The trajectory is very important.

To illustrate this, one could show a graph of a rocket ship on its way to the moon. Throughout that long journey, you will see that there is a little arch at the beginning of the journey. The little arch, though a very small part of the journey, determines everything else! It's a small moment in time that determines the destination. If this was on a massive graph, then the small part where the rocket took off and set this trajectory would be the most influential part of the entire journey.

Another way to illustrate this is with money. If someone saves a small amount of money early in their life and invests it with compound interest, the growth in value over enough time yields a massive return. The key is that the money must be invested early in one's life. Such a person sets an early trajectory for wealth building. That small decision can have a significant payoff.

We see this in our lives as well. Decisions we make early in our lives often have far-reaching consequences. This is the appeal of the text: to own the moment, to choose well, and to not find out when it's too late that we missed our intended destination.

The point you want to get across is simply this: "Living demands choosing our moments." An outline of Hebrews 12:14–24 could look like this:

- Choose to live in morality and peace; we are under the new covenant (vv. 14–24).
- Choose to listen; our God is a consuming fire (vv. 25–29).

DISCUSSION QUESTIONS

1. How did the use of Esau as an illustration in Hebrews 12:17 clarify the importance of making the right decision?
2. What was meant by the phrase "the assembly of the firstborn" in Hebrews 12:23?
3. What was significant about the comparison of the two mountains in Hebrews 12:18–25?
4. What did Barnabas mean in Hebrews 12:28 by "a kingdom that cannot be shaken"?
5. What is the motivation for offering God acceptable worship in Hebrews 12:28?

Hebrews 13:1–25

EXEGETICAL IDEA
Barnabas's admonition to persist in loving one another involved expectations for ethical living regarding hospitality and concern for others, the private life relating to social nuptials and confidence in God as helper, and community life concerning its leaders and the continuity of God's message about the sacrificial death of Jesus, which served as the basis for rejecting Judaism's cultic system.

THEOLOGICAL FOCUS
Persistent love for one another manifests itself in caring for others, honoring marriage vows, revering church leaders past and present, and maintaining God's message about Jesus as exalted royal high priest.

PREACHING IDEA
How do we recognize the real family of God?

PREACHING POINTERS
For Rome's Jewish household family of faith, there was an expectation in the culture to exhibit unselfish dispositions and practices that involved mutual sharing of possessions and participating in community activities. These were forms of "brotherly love." Barnabas admonished the household family of faith to persist in loving one another, which comprised expectations for ethical living regarding hospitality and the concern for others. For private life, this included honoring marriage in society and trusting God to provide despite societal threats; and for community life, this included remembering and obeying leaders and ensuring the continuity of God's message about the sacrificial death of Jesus, whom God had not only raised but also exalted as royal high priest.

Even today families have expectations. This final chapter of Hebrews carries much of the language of family (brothers, and brotherly love) and the idea of community. There is a community identity to a group of people who alone exclusively have the right to eat around a certain table, a table that by its very existence includes some and excludes others. In fact, this idea of family as community here in this final chapter is a fitting ending to the sermon series on the book of Hebrews. The high view of Jesus allows us to see practically what Jesus won for his household family of faith by giving us, his family, access to the throne of God. As well, the warning passages are warnings to those who think they are in the family but do not have the character traits (such as endurance) of family members. The mood of the text flows forth from the expectation of a confident, enduring believer. We do not endure on our own, but in the family of faith, and as such, we live out all aspects of our life together with family expectations in view.

A CALL TO PERSIST IN LOVING ONE ANOTHER (13:1–25)

LITERARY STRUCTURE AND THEMES (13:1–25)

In this final preaching unit (13:1–25), Barnabas presented numerous expectations of the household family of faith who followed Jesus, God's royal high priest. The opening admonition to persist in loving one another (v. 1) governed three groupings of activities that revealed devotion to one another. First, persistent love for one another was to be evident in ethical living that included extending hospitality and helping those under house arrest or in prison (vv. 2–3). Second, persistent love for one another was to be marked by honoring social nuptials of marriage and being content with what God provided (vv. 4–6). Third, Barnabas concluded his opening admonition of persistent love for one another with one last appeal about remembering and obeying their leaders, maintaining the continuity of God's message about the sacrificial death of Jesus, their rejection of the current affairs of Judaism, and prayer for others (vv. 7–19). Barnabas closed with a benediction for the God of peace to enable the household family of faith to experience the internalized new covenant, and then he offered a salutation (vv. 20–25).

Barnabas's theme in this final chapter focused on the call to persistent love for one another that affect relationships with other people.

- ***Expectations for Ethical Living (13:1–3)***
- ***Expectations of the Private Life (13:4–6)***
- ***Expectations for Community Life (13:7–19)***
- ***Benediction and Salutation (13:20–25)***

EXPOSITION (13:1–25)

During the time of Barnabas's writing to the members of Rome's household family of faith, there was an expectation to exhibit unselfish dispositions and practices that involved mutual sharing of possessions and participating in community activities. These were forms of "brotherly love" (ἡ φιλαδελφία μενέτω; Acts 4:34–37). As a result, society emphasized the importance of maintaining household codes, hospitality, respecting governing officials, and maintaining the peace of Rome (*Pax Romana*), just to name a few. Naturally, these societal norms were ideals practiced in various ways throughout the Roman Empire. And yet, elements of these ideals were often carried over into the church: love one another (Rom. 13:10; Eph. 5:1–2; James 2:8; 1 John; etc.), honor household codes (Eph. 5:22–6:6; Col.3:18–22; cf. 1 Tim. 6:1–2; 1 Peter 2:18–3:7; etc.), practice hospitality (3 John 8; cf. 1 John 3:17), honor governing officials (Rom. 12:9; 13:1–2; 1 Peter 2:17; cf. church leaders: 1 Tim. 5:17), and live at peace with all people (Rom. 12:16, 18; 1 Peter 3:11).

Barnabas, like his co-laborers of the faith, made similar emphases. In Hebrews 13:1–25, Barnabas admonished the Jewish household family of faith in Rome to persist in loving one another, which comprised expectations for ethical living regarding hospitality and the concern for others. It encompassed the private life relating to social nuptials and confidence in God as helper. It involved community life concerning leaders of the faith and the continuity of God's message about the sacrificial death of Jesus, which served as the basis for rejecting Judaism's cultic system. Barnabas closed with an appeal to

God for the community to enable the household family of faith experience the internalized new covenant.

Expectations for Ethical Living (13:1–3)

The admonition to persist in loving one another involved extending hospitality and helping those who were under house arrest or imprisoned.

13:1. Barnabas opened with an expectation: "persist in loving one another" (ἡ φιλαδελφία μενέτω) or "*continue* [μενέτω] in your love for one another" (cf. BDAG, s.v. "μένω" 2b, p. 631). He did not use a connecter to connect this verse with 12:29, and yet the admonition echoed the expectation to live morally harmonious lives in 12:14 and the call for serving God in 12:28. His appeal to exercise brotherly love, however, was not uncommon. It was also evident in Plutarch's work *On Brotherly Love* (*Mor.* 4.9–21 §482–92). Johnson (2006, 339) summarizes Plutarch in this manner: "Brotherly love is not merely a matter of sentiment, but it involves a complex set of dispositions and practices . . . it involves mutual sharing of possessions and activities." Similar examples appeared in Judaism as well. Eleazar, a Levitical high priest who stood before the Greek king Antiochus IV, was willing to offer himself as a sacrifice for the sake of the people of Judaea with whom he shared religious dispositions and practices (4 Macc 5:16–6:26; cf. Paul in Rom. 9:3). Similarly, after a tremendous amount of torture, brothers were portrayed as sharing the same values, companionship, moral character, pain, and torture (4 Macc 13:23–26).

13:2. Exhibiting persistent love or "brotherly love" (ἡ φιλαδελφία μενέτω) involved hospitality. Barnabas exhorted the household family of faith, "do not neglect hospitality." "Do not neglect" (*μὴ* ἐπιλανθάνεσθε; imper. ptc.; NET, ESV), however, was perhaps an indication that the household family of faith was "overlooking" (NLT) or they showed an "inattentive" pattern of behavior concerning hospitality (BDAG, s.v. "ἐπιλανθάνομαι" 2, p. 374). "Hospitality" (τῆς φιλοξενίας) was not merely a social expectation but often linked with being a godly person, as was evident and even expected among the Johannine churches (3 John 8; Bateman, 2018, 392–93).[1]

The reason (γάρ, "for) Barnabas gave for maintaining hospitality was because "through *hospitality*" (διὰ *ταύτης*, "though *it*") people in the past had actually entertained angels "without realizing it" (ἔλαθόν; NLT), "without knowing it" (NET, NASB; BDAG, s.v. "ἔλανθάνω," p. 586) or "unawares" (KJV, ASV, ESV). Several examples may include Abraham and Sarah (Gen. 18:2–15), Lot (Gen. 19:1–14), Gideon (Judg. 6:11–18), Manoah (Judg. 13:3–22), and Tobit (Tob. 12:1–20).

Hospitality

What did hospitality mean during the first-century culture? According to Delling, the idea of supporting someone was not limited to hospitality but extended to even protecting those who were persecuted (*TDNT*, 4:15; cf. BDAG, s.v. "ὑπολαμβάνω" 1, p. 1038).

This understanding was a clear expectation in Hebrews 13:3. Similarly, John in his letter to Gaius expanded a directive issued not only to Gaius but to all those who claimed to follow Jesus (3 John 8).

All followers of Jesus were obligated or *expected* to offer various kinds of support to those whose vocation it was to proclaim Jesus, the Messiah. No pastor or missionary was be living in a state

1 D. W. Riddle, "Early Christian Hospitality: A Factor in Gospel Transmission," *Journal for Biblical Literature* 57.2 (1938): 141–54.

of poverty. They were to be provided for in a manner worthy of God.

13:3. Exhibiting persistent love or "brotherly love" (ἡ φιλαδελφία μενέτω) involved an expectation that the Jewish household family of faith would "remember prisoners" (μιμνῄσκεσθε τῶν δεσμίων). Historically, early church leaders were at one time or another "prisoners" (τῶν δεσμίων). For example, Paul, who was well known to the household family of faith in Rome, was placed under house arrest (Acts 23:18; 25:14, 27; 28:16; cf. Philem. 1, 9; Eph. 3:1) and imprisoned (Acts 16:25, 27; cf. 2 Tim. 1:8). Barnabas, having already praised his readers for their efforts in this area (Heb. 10:34), wanted to ensure that they continued that practice. The manner by which prisoners were to be remembered was "as though *they were* imprisoned *together*" (ὡς συνδεδεμένοι; NET, ESV; Lane, 1991b, 513). While Barnabas left out the connector (καί, "and"), the expectation to remember included "*those who are* ill-treated" (τῶν κακουχουμένων; subj. ptc.). To motivate members of the household family of faith, Barnabas expected them "to imagine how they would feel if their bodies were being maltreated" (Koester, 2001, 558).

Expectations of the Private Life (13:4–6)

The admonition to persist in loving one another continued concerning matters of honoring social nuptials of marriage and being content with what God provided despite any societal threats.

13:4. Exhibiting persistent love or "brotherly love" (ἡ φιλαδελφία μενέτω) involved distinguishing proper and improper sex within a marriage. On the one hand, the social nuptials of "marriage" (ὁ γάμος) were to be "held in honor" or "respected" (BDAG, s.v. "τίμιος" 1c, p. 1005) "among all" (*ἐν πᾶσιν*) the members of the household family of faith (cf. Moffatt, 1979, 227; Lane, 1991b, 516). On the other hand, Barnabas continued (καί, "and") to develop his theme of marriage with an emphasis on improper bedtime activities: "the bed undefiled" (ἡ κοίτη ἀμίαντος). While "the bed" may reference a literal structure for lying down, here Barnabas mentioned "the bed" (ἡ κοίτη) as a place where sexual activity occurred, namely, "adultery" (BDAG, s.v. "κοίτη" 12a, p. 554). Thus, the use of "undefiled" spoke of the activities of "immoral people" (BDAG, s.v. "ἀμίαντος" a, p. 54).

Barnabas's reason (γάρ, "for") was clear: "God will judge" (κρινεῖ ὁ θεός). This prediction about God echoed Barnabas's previous statement about God's judgment: "the Lord will judge his people" (10:30, from Deut. 32:36). Equally clear were those he would judge: the "immoral" (πόρνους) and the "adulterer" (μοιχοὺς). Whereas the "immoral" person was one who practiced sexual immorality, namely, a fornicator (BDAG, s.v. "πόρνος" 1, p. 855), the "adulterer" acted unfaithfully to his or her spouse (BDAG, s.v. "μοιχός" 1, p. 657). It was not unusual for men and women in power to defile their nuptial vows. Claudius's (A.D. 37–41) fourth wife, Valeria Messalina, was so unfaithful that Tacitus (*Ann.* 11.12) said she would compete with prostitutes to see who could have the most sexual partners in a night. In Judaea, Herod Antipas (4 B.C.–A.D. 39) divorced his first wife in order to marry his brother's wife, Salome (Mark 6:16–20).

13:5. Exhibiting persistent love or "brotherly love" (ἡ φιλαδελφία μενέτω) also involved money. "The life" (ὁ τρόπος) of any member of the household family of faith was to exclude "loving money" (ἀφιλάργυρος). Yet, English translations offer various renderings: "Your conduct must be free from the love of money" (NET), "Keep your life free from the love of money" (ESV; cf. NIV, NRSV), or "Make sure that your character is free from the love of money" (NASB). Regardless of how the expectation is nuanced, Barnabas's point was simply this: "Don't love money" (NLT). To be a lover of money would conflict with Barnabas's admonition to love and care for others. Yet, more importantly was Barnabas's continuation of his concern: "be content with what you have" (NET, ESV, CNT, NRSV; cf. NASB, KJV) or "be satisfied with what you have" (NLT). Barnabas's expectation to "be content" (ἀρκούμενοι) was a common admonition (BDAG, s.v. "ἀρκέω" 1, p. 131). Barnabas connected contentment with persistent love "for the sake of serving others in the confidence that God would give them a future reward (Heb 10:35; 11:26)" (Koester, 2001, 559).

Barnabas underscored his twofold expectation with a promise repeated in two verses in Deuteronomy 31: "I will never leave you and I will never abandon you" (vv. 6, 8). Contextually, God's promise in Deuteronomy was to assure the Israelites that they need not worship idols. This promise from God, however, may have echoed God's promise to Jacob in a dream before he fled from Esau and went to Haran (Gen. 28:15). God made a similar promise to Joshua just before crossing over the Jordan to confront the inhabitants of Canaan (Josh. 1:5). David reapplied God's promise to his son Solomon concerning the building of the temple (1 Chron. 28:20). Here in Hebrews, Barnabas assured the household family of faith that God would be with them, and he would not abandon them as it concerned their physical needs for everyday living, which in turn enabled them with a capacity to share with others (cf. Attridge, 1989, 388).

Barnabas's linking of sexual immorality and money reflected a common theme during the time of his writing. In the Testament of Judah (18:2), it was said, "Keep yourselves, therefore, my children from sexual impurity and the love of money" [trans. Lane, 1991b, 517]. Cain was frequently presented as a person who exemplified greed for wealth, which was well documented in Jewish literature (Jude 11; Bateman, 2015[17], 241–49).

TEXTUAL ANALYSIs: Conflicting Text Critical Readings: 13:6

Grammatical/Exegetical Issue: Manuscript support exists for both readings: text (𝔓[46] A D 044 0121b 0243 1881) and variant (א* C* P 33 1175 1739). A scribe wishing to bring the quote into conformity with the LXX may have added "so" (καί). Its absence may be the author's deliberate alteration of the LXX for emphasis. The text reading is preferred (cf. Lane, 1991b, 509).

txt. "The Lord is my Helper, [**so**] I will not be afraid" (Κύριος ἐμοὶ βοηθός, [**καὶ**] οὐ φοβηθήσομαι) (KJV, NET)

var. "The Lord is my Helper; I will not be afraid" (Κύριος ἐμοὶ βοηθός; οὐ φοβηθήσομαι) (ASV, ESV, NASB, NIV, NRSV)

13:6. The result (ὥστε, "so that") of Barnabas's expectation to be content was of particular importance. It provided the ability "to speak confidently" (θαρροῦντας . . . λέγειν; NET, ESV, NLT, NRSV; Lane, 1991b, 520; Attridge, 1989, 389). Once again, Barnabas included himself "*we* [ἡμᾶς] can speak with confidence" (BDAG, s.v. "θαρρέω," p. 444). By way of another truth from Scripture, namely, Psalm 118 (117 LXX), Barnabas continued to underscore his twofold expectation about money and contentment. In three clauses, Barnabas revealed three truths from Psalm 118:6 (117:6 LXX). First, Barnabas spoke about trusting God: "*The Lord* [Κύριος] is to me a helper" (Bruce, 1990, 374). The household family of faith was to "live with confidence in God's promises and power" (Cockerill, 2012, 688; Heb. 11:1–6). Barnabas purposely placed "to me" (ἐμοί) in an emphatic position, revealing the personal element of his confidence.

Historical Events of the Second Testament (Bateman et al., 2012, 312 revised)		
First Emperors of the Roman Empire	**Jewish Rulers and Major Conflicts with Rome**	**Transition in Redemption History: The Age of Fulfillment**
Julio-Claudian Dynasty	***Herodian Dynasty***	***Davidic Dynasty Restored (already / not yet)***
Augustus (31 B.C.–A.D. 4)	Herod the Great (40–4 B.C.)	Jesus's birth (late 5 / early 4 B.C.)
	Archelaus: Judaea (4 B.C.–A.D. 6)	
Tiberius (14–37)	Philip: Northeast Galilee (4 B.C.–A.D. 37)	Jesus's death and resurrection (A.D. 33)
Caligula (37–41)	Antipas: Galilee and Perea (4 B.C.–A.D. 39)	***New Testament Testimonies***
Claudius (41–54)	Agrippa I (37–44)	James and Galatians (mid- to late 40s)
		1–2 Thessalonians (early 50s)
Nero (54–68)	Agrippa II (50–92?)	1–2 Corinthians, Romans (mid- to late 50s)
		Colossians, Philemon, Ephesians, Philippians, Titus, 1 Timothy (early 60s)
		Mark, Hebrews, 1 Peter, Jude (early to mid-60s)
Roman civil war (68–69)	Jewish wars against Rome (66–73)	Matthew, Luke–Acts, 2 Timothy, 2 Peter (mid- to late 60s)
Flavian Dynasty		
Vespasian (69–79)		
Titus (79–81)		
Domitian (81–96)		John, Johannine Letters, Revelation (mid-80s to mid-90s)

Second, this personal element about God as "helper" generated a result: "so, I will not fear" (NLT). While most translations do not translate the connector (καί "so"), it appears to be linked with an expression (e.g., "the Lord is to me a helper") that introduced a result (BDAG, s.v. "καί" 2d, p. 496). For Barnabas, the community was not to live in a state of apprehension; they need not be frightened or live in fear (BDAG, s.v. "φοβέω" 1, p. 1060). For Barnabas, "fear" was reserved for entrance into God's heavenly rest (4:1), not for everyday needs (cf. Rom. 8:31–39).

Third, Barnabas asked a rhetorical question that expected a negative response (D. Guthrie, 1983, 270). Can any onslaught by any man or woman hurt the household family of faith? The assumed answer was no! At the time Barnabas and the household family of faith in Rome lived, they did so under an unstable dictator, Nero. He could and would confiscate all of a person's physical possessions, imprison, and even send a person into exile (see the introduction). Looking to God as one's personal helper was to be the basis for setting aside fear, particularly of people (ἄνθρωπος) like Nero: "What can mere people do to me?" (NLT; cf. NRSV). Absolutely nothing (Rom. 8:31–38)! So, while Barnabas warned the household family of faith about fearing God's judgment (Heb. 2:2–3; 4:1, 12–13; 10:26–27, 30–31; 12:29; 13:1), they were not to fear people.

Expectations for Community Life (13:7–19)
The admonition to persist in loving one another concluded with further expectations about remembering and obeying leaders and maintaining the continuity of God's message about the sacrificial death of Jesus, which served as the basis for rejecting Judaism's cultic system; a further expectation was that of prayer for others.

13:7. Exhibiting persistent love or "brotherly love" (ἡ φιλαδελφία μενέτω) involved the household family of faith's leaders. Barnabas expected them to remember their leaders. "Those who lead you" (τῶν ἡγουμένων ὑμῶν) referred to the original leaders of the household family of faith in Rome (Moffatt, 1924, 231; Attridge, 1989, 391; Lane 1991b, 526; Koester, 2001, 559). Barnabas evoked a historical remembrance, namely, of their original leaders "who spoke" (ἐλάλησαν; const. aor.) God's message (= God's word). "God's word" (τὸν λόγον τοῦ θεοῦ) conjured God's message about Jesus that Barnabas repeatedly reinforced for the Jewish household family of faith (1:5–13; 2:4; 5:5–6; 7:14–17). Barnabas had already underscored a portion of that message with his mention of the new covenant in Jeremiah, namely, that God would no longer remember their evil or lawless deeds (8:12; 10:17).

13:8. Barnabas made it clear that the message, like Jesus himself (Heb. 1:12), would not change. First, Barnabas made it perfectly clear that Jesus was the Christ (Messiah): "Jesus, the Messiah."[2] Whereas "Jesus" (Ἰησοῦς) was a personal name, "Christ" (Χριστός) was a title in apposition to "Jesus" (like "God, the Father"). Despite the false messiahs that often rose and drove the Judaean revolt against Rome (Bateman, 2015[17], 59–66), Barnabas reinforced the fact that Jesus was the one and only true Messiah through whom God accomplished his work as well as underscored the message regarding Jesus about whom God gave credence (1:5–13; 2:4; 5:5–6; 7:14–17). Neither the message about Jesus nor the exalted work of Jesus would change. They would stay "the same" (ὁ αὐτός). "Yesterday" (ἐχθές) stood for the past in general concerning Jesus's pioneer work about which the leaders had spoken (Moffatt, 1924, 232 cf. Lane, 1991b, 529–30). "Today" (σήμερον) stood for the present time in general and yet alluded to Jesus's specific intercession on behalf of the household family of faith (4:14–16; 10:19–24; cf. Westcott, 1984, 435; Lane, 1991b, 530 with Bruce, 1990, 375; Kistemaker, 1984, 415). Attridge (1989, 392) contends that the formula "yesterday and today" (ἐχθὲς καὶ σήμερον) was a common theological expression among Jewish writers for continuity (Exod. 5:14; 2 Sam. 15:20; Sir 38:22; 1 Macc 9:44; Heb. 6:16–18). Here, Barnabas emphasized the continuity in both the work of Jesus and the divinely confirmed message about him.

13:9a. Exhibiting persistent love or "brotherly love" (ἡ φιλαδελφία μενέτω) involved the Jewish household family of faith's avoidance of "diverse and strange teachings" (διδαχαῖς ποικίλαις καὶ ξέναις). For Barnabas, this expectation was rather important because he defended it in seven verses (vv. 9–15). Although the NLT inserts the idea that these teachings were "new ideas," such teachings more frequently involved Jewish teachings (BDAG, s.v. "διδαχή" 2, p. 241). Teachings could be considered teachings of Judaism in general (Bloomfield, 1836, 510), or more specifically they could be teachings of the Essenes (Bruce, 1990, 377). Yet, the major historical event during the time of Barnabas's writing was the Judaean revolt where "diverse" (ποικίλαις) ideas of various leaders and false messiahs were vying for leadership in their

2 For the argument against Christ being merely a "name" for Jesus without titular force, see C. Blomberg, "Messiah in the NT," in *Israel's Messiah in the Bible and the Dead Sea Scrolls,* eds. R S. Hess and M. D. Carroll R. (Grand Rapids: Baker Academic, 2003), 111–50.

rebellion against Rome (Bateman, 2015[17], 51–80). Support for Jewish events happening in Judaea informed the description of the teachings as "strange" (ξέναις). "Strange" was something that was emerging "outside the community" (BDAG, s.v. "ξένος" 1aα, p. 684). The "strange teachings" appeared to be the Judaean leaders' rhetorical calls to support an eschatological movement that led numerous Jewish people astray in Judaea. While Barnabas wrote as a Jew viewing the Judaean situation from a distance, Jesus's brother Jude and the Jewish historian Josephus wrote as Judaean eyewitnesses of the emerging of the Jewish revolt against Rome. As Bruce (1990, 376) notes, "the language here suggests something *more* than a relapsing into orthodox Judaism" (emphasis added). Nevertheless, many commentators and translations suggest that the two words, "teaching" and "strange," were a single idea (= hendiadys; Lane, 1991b, 531–32; Ellingworth, 1993, 707; cf. NET, ESV, NLT, NASB, NRSV).

13:9b–10. The reason (γάρ, "for") Barnabas gave for ignoring the eschatological teachings of the Zealots in Judaea was that it was "good for the heart to be strengthened by grace." The means by which the heart was to be strengthened was "by grace" (χάριτι) not war. For Barnabas, "grace" was the gracious deed of Jesus, who had died once for the salvation of many (BDAG, s.v. "χάρις" 3b, p. 1080). Naturally, Jesus's death replaced "ritual foods" (οὐ βρώμασιν) associated with ceremonial sacrifices offered repeatedly in the tabernacle (9:9–10; 10:1, 4, 11). Barnabas made a further statement about these ceremonial foods of sacrifice. They were both inadequate and of no benefit (cf. 9:1–10; 10:1–4).

In a contrastive-like statement, Barnabas shifted to a new place of worship: "We have an altar." Later, Barnabas employed "altar" as a symbol for the Mosaic law's Levitical cultic system of sacrifice. That system of sacrifice (cf. 13:15–16), performed first in the tabernacle and then Jerusalem's temple, was replaced (made obsolete) with a different altar. Here, "altar" recalled the death of Jesus (Bruce, 1990, 378; Lane, 1991b, 537–38; 1993; Ellingworth, 1993, 711). Furthermore, the Jewish household family of faith need not participate in the Levitical system of sacrifice any longer, but rather they were a community of faith who shared in the benefits of Jesus's sacrifice (4:14; 6:19; 8:2; 10:19). Barnabas underscored the ineffectiveness of the Levitical system when he drew attention to the Jewish priesthood, namely, "those who serve in the tent" (οἱ τῇ σκηνῇ λατρεύοντες; 9:1–10; cf. Westcott, 1984, 439; Lane, 1991b, 539).

13:11. In a somewhat loose connection (γάρ, "for"), Barnabas moved from his general principle about the Levitical system (old covenant) of sacrifice to a specific and developed example about sacrificed animals: "Under the old system, the high priest brought the blood of animals into the holy place as a sacrifice for sin, and the bodies of the animals were burned outside the camp" (NLT; cf. Attridge, 1989, 397). In Judaism's cultic system, the consuming of the entire animal (Exod. 29:14; Ezek. 43:21) was performed to prevent anyone from eating animal remains. The blood taken into the holy place was Barnabas's way of referring once again to the "Day

THE TABERNACLE

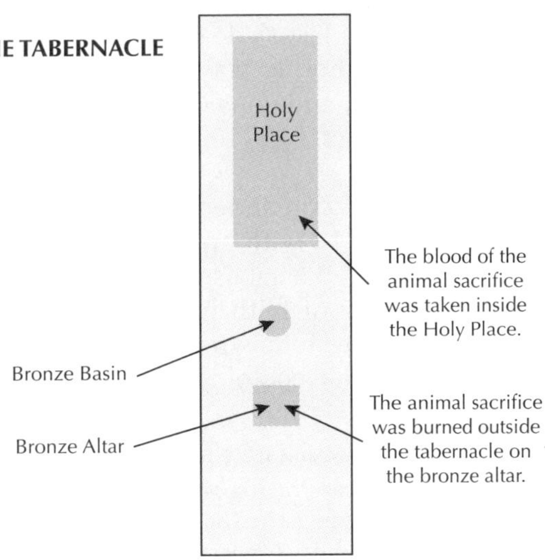

of Atonement" (Lev. 16:11–19; Heb. 9:7, 12–14, 18–22, 25; cf. Lane, 1991b, 540).

13:12. Barnabas continued (διὸ καί, "so also") his specific example with an application about Jesus's sacrifice. The specific use of the personal name "Jesus" pointed once again to his humanity and physical sufferings: "he suffered outside the gate" (ἔξω τῆς πύλης ἔπαθεν; Westcott, 1984, 440; Lane, 1991b, 541–42; Koester, 2001, 570). Barnabas then shifted the images of past sacrifices to the most recent image of Jesus, who was crucified. Rather than referencing the altar of sacrifice outside the Holy Place, Jesus was presented as a self-sacrifice offered up to God outside the city gates of Jerusalem (cf. Mark 15:16–22).

The purpose (ἵνα, "in order that") for Jesus's sacrifice was to "sanctify people through his blood." As the atoning sacrifice "through his own blood" (διὰ τοῦ ἰδίου αἵματος), Jesus entered the heavenly tabernacle (= tent) and offered his blood as the means by which he cleansed the consciences of people (Heb. 9:14). "People" here were people of the new covenant. Unlike 12:14 where "holiness" addressed moral living, here "holiness" (ἁγιάσῃ) spoke to the state of being made holy as a way to speak of their "sanctification" (2:11; 10:10, 14, 29). Yet, Barnabas recalled Jesus's death outside the city of Jerusalem as another way to picture his rejection, mocking, and conviction as a criminal (re-crucify Jesus; cf. Heb. 10:26–27).

13:13. Barnabas concluded (τοίνυν, "therefore") verses 11–12 with an expectation: "Let *us* go out to him." Barnabas wanted the Jewish household family of faith in Rome to go out to Jesus and leave Judaism behind, renounce Judaea's Zealot eschatological revolt, and put away the old covenant (cf. D. Guthrie, 1983, 274; Lane, 1991b, 545–46; Ellingworth, 1993, 717). Barnabas's threefold appearance of the phrase "outside the camp" (ἔξω τῆς παρεμβολῆς; vv. 11, 13) was an emphatic metaphor about Judaism: leave it (Westcott, 1984, 442; Bruce, 1990, 382; cf. Lane, 1991b, 543). "Camp" (παρεμβολῆς) typically referred to a literal "army in battle array" (BDAG, s.v. "παρεμβολή" 3, p. 775) that reinforced Barnabas's admonishment to reject Judaism's cultic system and ignore the military events happening in Judaea against the Romans whereby Zealot leaders believed they needed to assist God in reestablishing Judaea as God's kingdom on earth. But God's kingdom was at hand during Jesus's ministry (Mark 1:15), already present with Jesus's exaltation (Heb. 1:8) and an anticipated kingdom yet to come (Heb. 12:26–28).[3]

The way by which the household family of faith was to leave Judaism was "by bearing" (φέροντες; ptc. of means) the same abuse Jesus experienced: rejection, mocking, physical suffering, and if necessary physical death (cf. Mark 15:14–37; Heb. 10:32–34). These were all "acts of disparagement that result[ed] in disgrace" (BDAG, s.v. "ὀνειδισμός," p. 710).

13:14. Barnabas's reason (γάρ, "for) for leaving Judaism that led to disgrace was his contrast between two cities. On the one hand, there was the earthly city that would not last, namely, the city of Jerusalem where Judaism's ceremonial practices were taking place and where the activities of certain Judaeans were leading to a war to expel the Romans from Judaea and disrupt the peace of Rome. On the other hand (ἀλλά, "but"), Barnabas and the Jewish household family of faith in Rome would continue to

3 J. L. Burns, "Israel and the Church" in *Three Central Issues in Contemporary Dispensationalism: A Comparison of Traditional and Progressive Views*, ed. H. W. Bateman IV (Grand Rapids, Kregel, 1999), 263–291; idem, "The Future of Ethnic Israel in Romans 11" in *Dispensationalism, Israel and the Church*, eds. C. A. Blaising and D. L. Bock (Grand Rapids: Zondervan, 1992), 188–229.

"seek" (ἐπιζητοῦμεν) a heavenly Jerusalem city yet to come (12:22; Bloomfield, 1836, 511; Lane, 1991b, 546; Koester, 2001, 571). Naturally, this heavenly city was a metaphor for God's heavenly kingdom (Heb. 12:25–28).

> *TEXTUAL ANALYSIS:* Conflicting Text Critical Readings: 13:15
> Style/Syntax Issue: Manuscript support exists for both readings: text (A C K 056 0121b 0142 0243 0285 81 88 614 1739) and variant (𝔓[46] ℵ* D* P 044). It seems easier to explain a scribe's desire to add οὖν because it's a natural place for a conclusion, though one might argue that it was inadvertently omitted. Yet, "therefore" (οὖν) in Hebrews is infrequent (2:14; 4:1, 6, 11, 16; 7:11; 8:4; 9:1, 23; 10:19, 35). The variant is the preferred reading (cf. Lane, 1991b, 524).
>
> *txt.* "through him, **therefore**, let us offer the sacrifice of praise" (δι' αὐτοῦ **οὖν** ἀναφέρωμεν θυσίαν αἰνέσεως) (ASV, ESV, KJV, NASB, NET, NIV, NRSV)
>
> *var.* "through him let us offer the sacrifice of praise" (δι' αὐτοῦ ἀναφέρωμεν θυσίαν αἰνέσεως)

13:15. Barnabas concluded (οὖν, "therefore") his expectation for his readers to leave Judaism's cultic system with yet another appeal to "Jesus" (δι' αὐτοῦ, "through him"). He exhorted members of the household family of faith to "offer up a sacrifice of praise" (ἀναφέρωμεν θυσίαν αἰνέσεως). Barnabas expected a habit-forming "continuous praise" (ἀναφέρωμεν; sbjv. cust. pres.). To whom this praise was to be made was "to God" (τῷ θεῷ; cf. 12:28) just as Jesus did with the household family of faith (2:12). Barnabas then explained (τοῦτ' ἔστιν, "that is") what he meant with a figure of speech: "the fruit of lips" (καρπὸν χειλέων). "The fruit of lips" was figurative language that spoke frequently of expressing thanks (Prov. 18:20; Hos. 14:3; Pss. Sol. 15:3; 1Q28 9.4–5). The fruit of Jesus's sacrifice was expected to produce verbal praise to God (Lane, 1991b, 550; Koester, 2001, 572).

13:16. Barnabas continued (δέ, "and") his expectation of persistent love for one another (Heb. 13:1) with a household community's belief, which he previously emphasized: "do not neglect to do good and to share what you have." While some translations say, "do not forget" (NIV, NLT, CNT; BDAG, s.v. "ἐπιλανθάνομαι" 1, p. 374), others read "do not neglect" (NET, ESV, NASB, NRSV). Regardless of which translation is preferred, Barnabas wanted the household family of faith to be intentional (BDAG, s.v. "ἐπιλανθάνομαι" 2, p. 374). Previously, Barnabas wanted the household family of faith in Rome not to neglect meeting together (10:25), not to neglect hospitality (13:2), and now not to neglect doing good and sharing (13:16). Barnabas's reason (γάρ, "for) given to the household family of faith was that such a sacrificial lifestyle pleased God: "God is pleased with such sacrifices." God took delight in intentional acts of kindness extended to others.

13:17. Barnabas heightened his expectations of persistent love or "brotherly love" (ἡ φιλαδελφία μενέτω) by writing once again about the church leaders in Rome's household family of faith. He moved from merely "remember your leaders" (μνημονεύετε τῶν ἡγουμένων ὑμῶν) of the past to expectations about current church leaders: "obey your leaders" (πείθεσθε τοῖς ἡγουμένοις ὑμῶν) as well as "submit" (ὑπείκετε). While obeying refers to specific injunctions (Westcott, 1984, 444), submitting has mixed renderings. Some translations insert "to them" (NET, ESV, CNT; Attridge, 1989, 402; Bruce, 1990, 385), yet others insert "to their authority" (NIV; Hagner, 1981, 247; Lane, 1991b, 555). In either case, Barnabas's reason (γάρ, "for) for urging the household family of faith to obey and submit to their leaders was because they were concerned for their "souls" (τῶν ψυχῶν ὑμῶν;

"your souls"). The soul was considered the center of both the earthly and the transcendent life (BDAG, s.v. "ψυχή" 2e, p. 1099) and therefore a metaphor for the spiritual well-being of the members of the household family of faith (Morris, 1981, 140; Ellingworth, 1993, 723). Similarly, Attridge (1989, 402) attaches Barnabas's mention of the "soul" to what he rightly considers the main focus of Hebrews's salvation message anchored in heaven (6:19), renewed by faith (10:39) and exemplified by the example of Jesus (12:3).

Barnabas justified his expectation with yet another expectation (ἵνα . . . τοῦτο ποιῶσιν): "Let them do this" (NET, ESV, NASB, NASV) or "that they may do this" (KJV). "This" (τοῦτο) referred back (anaphoric) to their leader's obligation to care for the household family of faith's spiritial well-being (Westcott, 1984, 445; Moffatt, 1924, 239). Barnabas emphasized that leaders were to exercise their responsibility "with joy." "Joy" (χαρᾶς) involved the experience of gladness (BDAG, s.v. "χαρά" 1a, p. 1077). Barnabas continued (καί, "and") with a contrasting emotion: "without groaning" (μὴ στενάζοντες) due to "undesirable circumstance(s)" (BDAG, s.v. "στενάζω" 1, p. 942). Refusing to submit to church leaders, whose role it was to care for the spiritual well-being of the household family of faith, would be self-destructive.

13:18. Persistent love or "brotherly love" also involved prayer for others. While Barnabas did not use a connector to attach his expectation to what went before, he nevertheless expected members of the household family of faith to "pray for us" (προσεύχεσθε περὶ ἡμῶν). The request to pray was not a one-time event, but rather Barnabas insisted on the household family of faith to "make it a practice to pray" (προσεύχεσθε, cust. pres. imper.). The "us" for whom they were to pray referred to Barnabas and his companions (Westcott, 1984, 435; Lane, 1991b, 556; Ellingworth, 1993, 724–25).

Barnabas's basis (γάρ, "for) for his request for prayer was that his conscience and those of his companions were clear. Barnabas's "clear conscience" had a twofold reference. On the one hand, Barnabas's conscience concerned his teaching against the Levitical ceremonial system of sacrifice (9:13, 25–26; 10:1–4, 11–12; cf. Kistemaker, 1984, 428). On the other hand, Barnabas's conscience concerned his conduct as honorable: "act honorably" (καλῶς θέλοντες ἀναστρέφεσθαι) or "to conduct oneself in terms of certain principles" (BDAG, s.v. "ἀναστρέφω" 3, p. 72). Barnabas did not ask something of others that he himself did not believe or practice.

13:19. Barnabas continued (δέ, "and") his initial expectation for prayer in verse 19 with a sense of urgency: "I urge you all the more to do this." "This" (τοῦτο) referred back (anaphoric) to Barnabas's request for prayer in verse 18. The content of their prayer (ἵνα, "that") was to focus attention on his return to Rome: "I may be restored to you" (BDAG, s.v. "ἀποκαθίστημι" 2, p. 111). Barnabas wanted to return and was anticipating his returning to Rome.

Benediction and Salutation (13:20–25)

In closing, Barnabas made an appeal to the God of peace on behalf of the household family of faith to enable the fulfillment of the new covenant inaugurated through Jesus, the shepherd King, before closing with encouraging salutations.

13:20. Barnabas introduced a transition (δέ, "and" or "now") that shifted his request for prayer to an appeal to the "God of peace" (ὁ δὲ θεὸς τῆς εἰρήνης) on behalf of the Jewish household family of faith in Rome. "Peace" (εἰρήνη) was something God conferred (Westcott, 1984, 447; Lane, 1991b, 560) and something to be kept: "Pursue peace with everyone" (12:14). Barnabas described God (ὁ, "who") as "having brought up from the [realm of the] dead" (BDAG, s.v. "ἀνάγω" 1, p. 61; cf. NLT) "our Lord Jesus." While Barnabas's specific use of the personal name "Jesus" pointed once again to his humanity and physical sufferings, he described Jesus as "the shepherd of the sheep, the great one." The phrase emphasized that Jesus related to "the sheep" (= household family of faith; cf. Heb. 2:14–17) as a "shepherd." This description was also applicable to Davidic kings (1 Chron, 11:2; Ezek. 34:5; 37:23–28; cf. Johnston, 2012, 177–79). Jesus was God's promised royal shepherd.

Descriptions of Jesus in Hebrews	
Christ (= Messiah)	3:6; 5:5, 7; 9:11, 14, 24, 28
Pioneer	2:10, 12:2
Great High Priest	4:14
Mediator	8:6; 9:15; 12:24
Great Shepherd	13:20

How Jesus was related to the household family of faith as a royal shepherd was "by (ἐν) the blood of the eternal covenant." "Blood" (αἷμα) once again pointed to Jesus's life as the means to ratify the "eternal covenant" (διαθήκης αἰωνίου: Lane, 1991b, 563). The NLT captures this understanding the best: Jesus "ratified an eternal covenant with his blood" (cf. Heb. 9:15–18).

TEXTUAL ANALYSIS: Conflicting Text Critical Readings: 13:21

There are three issues in this verse, the first theological and the second and third exegetical.

Theological Issue: Though manscripts support the variant (C K M P 0243 0285 33 1739 1881 Byz), the text (𝔓[46] ℵ D* 044) is the preferred reading. Perhaps there was an intentional addition made to align Hebrews 13:21 with 2 Thessalonians 2:17 (Lane, 1991b, 559; Metzger, 1994, 605).

txt. "with every good thing" (ἐν παντὶ ἀγαθῷ) (cf. NASB, NET with ESV, NIV, NRSV)

var. "in every good **work**" (ἐν παντὶ **ἔργῳ** ἀγαθῷ) (ASV, KJV)

Exegetical Issue: Manuscript support exists for both readings: text (𝔓[46] ℵ A K M 0243 0285 33 81 104 326 1175 1241 1739 1881) and variant (C P 044 6 88 629* 630 1505). Perhaps a scribe altered the text due to the preceding "you" (ὑμῖν). The text is the preferred reading (Lane, 1991b, 559; Metzger, 1994, 606).

txt. "working in **us** that which is pleasing in his sight" (ποιῶν ἐν **ἡμῖν** τὸ εὐάρεστον ἐνώπιον αὐτοῦ) (ASV, ESV, NASB, NIV, NRSV)

var. "working in **you** that which is pleasing in his sight" (ποιῶν ἐν **ὑμῖν** τὸ εὐάρεστον ἐνώπιον αὐτοῦ) (KJV, NET)

Exegetical Issue: Manuscript support exists for both readings: text (𝔓[46] C D 1241) and the variant (ℵ A C* K P 0243 0285 33 1739 1881). Perhaps a scribe lengthened the text to agree with similar doxologies in 1 Timothy 1:17 and 2 Timothy 4:18. In Hebrews 5:6; 6:2; 7:17, 21, however, the shorter form occurs: "forever" (εἰς τὸν αἰῶνα). The variant is the preferred reading (Lane, 1991b, 559; cf. NET note and Metzger, 1994, 606).

txt. "to whom be glory forever [**and ever**]. Amen" (ᾧ ἡ δόξα εἰς τοὺς αἰῶνας [**τῶν αἰώνων**]. ἀμήν) (ASV, ESV, KJV, NASB, NIV, NRSV)

var. "to whom be glory forever. Amen." (ᾧ ἡ δόξα εἰς τοὺς αἰῶνας. ἀμήν) (NET)

13:21. Barnabas then petitioned God "to equip" or "to make perfect" (καταρτίσαι) the household family of faith (Westcott, 1984, 449;

Lane, 1991b, 564). Barnabas presented God as the agent of equipping (BDAG, s.v. "ἐν" 6, p. 329). He looked to God who would cause things to function harmoniously (BDAG, s.v. "καταρτίζω" 1b, p. 526), namely, "every good thing to do his will" (NET). Barnabas described God's will when he spoke of the new covenant and Jesus's fulfillment of it: "I will put my laws in their minds and I will inscribe them on their hearts. And I will be their God and they will be my people" (Heb. 8:10, quoting Jer. 31:33), namely, trust God and care about the welfare of other people. Thus, the "good" (ἀγαθῷ) referred to an inner endowment from God to do God's will (Lane, 1991b, 564–65). How this "good thing" was made possible was "through [διά] Jesus, who is the Christ [= Messiah]." This "good thing" was for all (ἡμῖν, "us") followers of Jesus, which was established in the inauguration of the new covenant and intended to be lived out daily.

13:22. Barnabas introduced another transition (δέ, "and" or "now") that shifted from his appeal to God to what he had just written to the household family of faith. First, the appearance of "brothers *and sisters*" (τὸν ἀδελφόν) conveyed tenderness for and an association with his readers. It underscored that they were partners in the faith (3:1, 14; 6:4), supported one another to do good works (10:24), lived morally harmonious lives (12:14), and pursued love for one another (13:1). Second, Barnabas then appealed to his work as a whole (Bruce, 1990, 389; Lane, 1991b, 568; Ellingworth, 1993, 731). He had exhorted the community to "bear with" (NET, ESV, NIV, NRSV, NASB, KJV), "pay attention" (NLT), or "listen patiently" (BDAG, s.v. "ἀνέχω" 1bα, p. 78) to the reading of his encouraging words. Barnabas's appeal may indicate that his readers thought it too long, and thus the household family of faith may have found it a bit wearisome (Lane, 1991b, 568–69). Letters of antiquity were on average 295 to 995 words, but Hebrews has 4,954 words (Bateman, 2012, 26–27). This idea may be further supported with his next clause. Barnabas's reason (γάρ, "for"), which he gave with a degree of emphasis (καί, "indeed"), was that the household family of faith was to "listen patiently" to his message because, from his perspective, he merely wrote "briefly" or "in a few words" (BDAG, s.v. "βραχύς" 3, p. 183). The expectation to "listen patiently" or to "pay attention" echoed Barnabas's expectation in Hebrews 2: "Therefore we must pay closer attention to what we have heard, so that we do not slip away" (v. 1).

13:23. With no connector, Barnabas shifted abruptly to some good news for the Jewish household family of faith in Rome: "you should know" (γινώσκετε; impv.). What Barnabas wanted them to know was that Timothy had been "freed" or "released" (ἀπολελυμένον). Timothy had been permitted to leave his house arrest or imprisonment (BDAG, s.v. "ἀπολύω" 1 and 3, p. 117; cf. Westcott, 1984, 4; Lane, 1991b, 569): "Timothy has been released from jail" (NLT). Obviously, the household family of faith knew of Timothy because of the expression "our brother" (τὸν ἀδελφὸν ἡμῶν). Some even identify Timothy with Paul's close coworker (Moffat, 1924, 244; Koester, 2001, 580).

Who Was Timothy?

Son of a Gentile father and a Jewish mother, Timothy lived in Lystra (Acts 16:1). Whether Timothy was a convert of the apostle Paul is unknown. Timothy was already converted when he was first mentioned with Paul (Acts 16:1). Perhaps his mother (Eunice) and grandmother (Lois), who had a significant impact on his faith (2 Tim. 1:5, 3:14–15), led him to Jesus.

Since Timothy had one Jewish parent, he was regarded as a Jew. Paul felt it expedient to have Timothy circumcised so that he might be able to associate with Jews with the result that his ministry among the Jews might be more effective (cf. 1 Cor. 9:20); Paul did not object to adherence to the Mosaic law and to circumcision on the part of Jewish believers (Acts 21:18, 20, 24), but he strenuously insisted that the law and circumcision could not be imposed on Gentiles.

13:24. Barnabas closed his work, which was typical for a letter: "Greetings to" (BDAG, s.v. "ἀσπάζομαι" 1a, p. 144; Bateman, 2012, 20–25), namely, the ones leading the household family of faith as well all the household family of faith. The repeated "all" (πάντας) was Barnabas's way to be emphatic that no one was to be excluded in his closing salutation (Moffatt, 1979, 246).

To this personal greeting, Barnabas added greetings from "those from Italy" (οἱ ἀπὸ τῆς 'Ιταλίας). While two English translations appear to pinpoint Italy as the origin of Hebrews, William Tyndale's 1526 translated edition of the NT and the 1611 edition of the King James Version end this work "To the Hebrews" with "Written to the Hebrewes, from Italy, by Timothie" (cf. 'Εγράφη ἀπὸ 'Ιταλίας *διὰ* Τιμόθέου; Nestle, 1936). Yet, current NT Greek texts (e.g., Nestle-Aland[28]) and English translations exclude the subscription (NASB, NRSV, ESV, NIV, NET). Nevertheless, Vanhoye (2015, 14) still argues that Barnabas wrote from Italy.

Yet, these were people "from" (*ἀπό*) somewhere that indicated that they were in geographical locations other than where they lived (Acts 2:5; 10:23, 38; 17:13; 21:27). As a result, some commentators suggest that the Italian Christians and Barnabas himself were somewhere other than the Italian peninsula (Moffatt, 1924, 247; Strathmann, 1937, 70–71; Hiebert, 1977, 85). Still others are a bit more specific: Riggenbach (1922) suggests Cyprus. Regardless, of where these Italian brothers and sisters lived, they offered their greetings to the members of the household family of faith in Rome.

TEXTUAL ANALYSIS: Conflicting Text Critical Readings: 13:25

Exegetical Issue: Manuscript support exists for both readings: text (𝔓[46*] ℵ*) and variant (A C D H K P 044 0121b 0243 81 1739 1881). It seems almost impossible for a scribe to have resisted placing "amen" (ἀμήν) at the conclusion of this sermonic letter. The text is the prefered reading (Lane, 1991b, 567; Metzger, 1994, 607).

txt. "Grace be with you all" (ἡ χάρις μετὰ πάντων ὑμῶν) (ESV, NASB, NET, NIV, NRSV)

var. "Grace be with you all. **Amen**!" (ἡ χάρις μετὰ πάντων ὑμῶν. **ἀμήν**) ASV, KJV)

13:25. Barnabas's final word was that God's grace be with the entire household family of faith. "Grace" (ἡ χάρις) was Barnabas's closing desire for his readers, namely, that they might experience "divine favor" (BDAG, s.v. "χάρις" 2c, p. 1079). The use of "grace" at the beginning of a letter (Rom. 1:7; 1 Cor. 1:3; 2 Cor. 1:2; Eph. 1:2; Phil. 1:2; etc.) and at the end of a letter (Rom. 16:20; 1 Cor. 16:23; 2 Cor. 13:13; Eph. 6:24; Phil. 4:23; etc.) became a fixed formula among NT letters. Yet, it was not merely a formula without significance. It was a practical application concerning God's goodwill being extended to everyone within the household family of faith (μετὰ πάντων ὑμῶν, "with all of you").

THEOLOGICAL FOCUS

The exegetical idea (Barnabas's admonition to persist in loving one another involved expectations for ethical living regarding hospitality and concern for others, the private life relating to social nuptials and confidence in God as helper, and community life concerning its leaders and the continuity of God's message about the sacrificial death of Jesus, which served as the basis for rejecting Judaism's cultic system) leads to this theological focus: Persistent love for one another manifests itself in caring for others, honoring marriage vows, revering church leaders past and present, and maintaining God's message about Jesus as exalted royal high priest.

The primary theological theme and thrust of this preaching unit is the call to persistent love for one another within community. It was to be evident in ethical living that included extending hospitality and helping those under house arrest or imprisoned (vv. 2–3). It was to be marked by honoring social nuptials of marriage and being content with what God provided (vv. 4–6). It was about remembering and obeying their leaders, the continuity of God's message about the sacrificial death of Jesus, their rejection of the current affairs of Judaism, and prayer for others (vv. 7–19).

PREACHING AND TEACHING STRATEGIES

Exegetical and Theological Synthesis

The flow of this passage was familial, as there were references to brotherly love (v. 1), marriage (v. 4), and brothers and sisters (vv. 22, 23). The feel of the passage was also communal. The household family of faith were commanded to remember, obey, and submit to their leaders (vv. 7, 17, 20); they had an altar, a symbol of Jesus's death, from which only they could eat because of their faith in Jesus (v. 10); and they were expected to share what they had with others (v. 16). The passage therefore develops a feeling of life in the community.

In the community life, there was an expectation to maintain a certain ethical standard personally (vv. 1–3). This standard included showing hospitality to strangers; keeping an eye for those on the margins; holding a high standard of sexual morality and honoring marriage; and living a life of contentment and trust in God, free from the love of money.

There was also an expectation that they would protect the community of believers. This was to be done by looking to the leaders of the past (v. 7) and by not being diverted by "strange" eschatological teachings involving the then current affairs of Judaea or errant theological ideas of various leaders and false messiahs (v. 9). As well, the community was privileged since they, through Jesus's self-sacrifice, had an altar from which others could not eat, giving them access to God (vv. 10–16). This unit ended with an exhortation for the household family of faith to obey their leaders and to pray for Barnabas, for he had a clear conscience about his teaching against Judaism's now obsolete system of sacrifice as well as his honorable conduct. He asked them to pray that he would return to them in Rome soon.

A final appeal was given to the brothers that they heed the words of the exhortation, be encouraged that Timothy was released, and both give and receive greetings and grace (vv. 22–25).

Preaching Idea

How do you recognize the real family of God?

Contemporary Connections

What does it mean?

What does it mean that the real family of God is recognizable? Naturally, every family has expectations for living. If two or more people share a home, this forms a community, and the rules of living in the community are either explicit or implicit. If anyone comes into the house, it is to their benefit to have the expectations of the household made clear to them. For instance, culturally we have rules of everyday etiquette that transcends time, gender, and age for all households. There are websites for "Teaching Kids Good Table Manners"[4] and books like *Everyday Etiquette: How to*

4 K. Lee, "Teaching Kids Good Table Manners," Verywell Family, updated May 03, 2020, https://www.verywellfamily.com/teaching-kids-good-table-manners-620306.

Navigate 101 Common and Uncommon Social Situations,[5] where Patricia Rossi deals with social media, home, business and other forms of etiquette. While not all households or businesses may follow to the "letter" these codes of everyday etiquette, they are twenty-first-century guidelines for people to follow and are extremely helpful to know, especially for households. Thus the harmony inside a home is directly related to the sense that there is a common set of expectations for the behavior of the members of the household, and a shared desire to meet those expectations.

Conversely there is tension in a home when such expectations are unclear, ill-defined, or perceived as unreasonable and thus rejected or merely set aside. There is also tension when there is so much passivity in a home that no one says anything when expectations are not met! The people in such a home may feign unity by not acknowledging that things are not right, but eventually this leads to disharmony and breakdowns in the family's relationships.

Is it true?

Is it true that the real family of God is recognizable? Where there is a family, there are expectations that need to be met. Every family has in some way been touched by a tragedy. This often involves at least one or more people who do not want to live according to the family's expectations. This is the son or daughter that rebels and will not follow the leadership of the parents. Or there may be indirect family members who decide to exclude themselves from the family. These are examples of people who did not feel they could, or wanted to, meet family expectations, so they, either passively or aggressively, withdrew.

In extreme cases this does not take the form of passive withdrawal but of active abuse. This is the extreme example where someone who not only does not live up to the family's expectations let alone society's expectations, but abuses those in the family. All these realities remind us that being in a family comes with certain expectations.

Now what?

What is the real family of God to do? This passage has direct applications for the family of God. While the applications can be applied to the universal invisible church, they are more directly for the local body of believers. The applications are clear: we are to look to leaders of the past and emulate their faith; to show love in marriage, and to those in prison; and to revere and obey our leaders.

However, there is an application that seems less direct but is very compelling. The motivation not to follow the Judaic dietary rules was that the family of faith had their own table. In this beautiful rhetorical move, the Lord's table is underscored as itself restrictive to believers. Therefore, the exclusive nature of our relationship to Jesus, makes us steadfast. As a result, we are not tempted to theological fads or by other faiths. We have our own identity! Our identity is with the family at the table. A place where others have no right to eat. Therefore, we are motivated to obey. In this way we are recognized as the real family of God.

Creativity in Presentation

The reality that every family has family expectations could be communicated with an idea that would take a little work in advance. Ask people beforehand to take an online survey. This can be accomplished easily through email with one of many free online survey tools.

On the survey include questions asking the person's age, gender, and role in the family (son, wife, etc.). Then ask questions in the survey that might trigger different responses

5 P. Rossi, *Everyday Etiquette: How to Navigate 101 Common and Uncommon Social Situations* (New York: St Martin's Press, 2011).

from different positions in the family. For example, a mom might expect a bedroom to be cleaned nightly, and a teen might think it should be done monthly. A father expects his teen daughter to be home at ten o'clock, whereas she thinks midnight is reasonable. The brave among us could ask questions about marriage: How often should we date our spouses, expect meaningful conversations, or expect time away from one's spouse to pursue hobbies and interests? The differences would be telling. Plus, they would have more meaning if they were a sampling from the group that was present.

When the answers are revealed the mood could go from very funny to very sobering. What makes this funny or sobering is the distance between the expectations, thus making the point that the joy of the family community is tied to knowing the expectations.

The point you want to get across is simply this: "How do you recognize the real family of God?" An outline of Hebrews 12:14–24 could look like this:

- We are expected to show hospitality (vv. 1–3).
- We are expected to live in purity (vv. 4–6).
- We are expected to live in community (vv. 7–19).
- Benediction and salutation (vv. 20–25)

DISCUSSION QUESTIONS

1. What did it mean to "entertain angels" (Heb. 13:2)?
2. Who were the "leaders" mentioned in Hebrews 13:7?
3. What was the motivation not to return to Judaic dietary practices (Heb. 13:9–16)?
4. What are the contemporary implications of obedience for church and its pastor(s) and leader(s) (Heb. 13:17)?
5. What did it mean that Jesus was the "great shepherd of the sheep" (Heb. 13:20)?

FURTHER READING

Bateman IV, Herbert W. (editor). 2007. *Four Views on the Warning Passages in Hebrews*. Grand Rapids: Kregel.

Evans, C. A. 2000. "Abraham." In *Encyclopedia of the Dead Sea Scrolls*, volume 1:2–4. Eds. Lawrence H. Schiffman and James C. VanderKam. New York: Oxford University Press.

Nickelsburg, George W. E. 2000. "Enoch, Books of." In *Encyclopedia of the Dead Sea Scrolls*, volume 1:249–53. Eds. Lawrence H. Schiffman and James C. VanderKam. New York: Oxford University Press.

Reeves, John C. 2000. "Enoch." In *Encyclopedia of the Dead Sea Scrolls*, volume 1:249. Eds. Lawrence H. Schiffman and James C. VanderKam. New York: Oxford University Press.

REFERENCES

Aharoni, Y. and M. Avi-Yonah. 1968. *The Macmillan Bible Atlas*. New York: Macmillan.

Aharoni, Y., M. Avi-Yonah, A. F. Rainey, and Z. Safrai. 2002. *The Carta Bible Atlas*, 4th ed. Jerusalem: Carta..

Aland, B., K. Aland, J. Karavidopoulos, C. M. Martini, and B. M. Metzger, eds. 1993. *The Greek New Testament*. 4th ed. Stuttgart: United Bible Societies.

Allegro J. M. 1968. 4Q161 or "Commentary on Isaiah (A)." In *Qumran Cave 4.I*. Discoveries in the Judaean Desert 5, 11–15. Oxford: Clarendon.

Allen, D. A. 2010a. *Lukan Authorship of Hebrews*. NAC Studies in Bible and Theology 8. Nashville: B&H Academic.

______. 2010b. *Hebrews: An Exegetical and Theological Exposition of Holy Scripture*. New American Commentary 35. Nashville: B&H.

Anderson, C. P. 1966. "The Epistle to the Hebrews and the Pauline Letter Collection." *Harvard Theological Review* 59 (4):429–38.

______. 1966. "Who Wrote 'the Epistle from Laodicea'?" *Journal of Biblical Literature* 85 (4):436–40.

______. 1975–76. "Hebrews among the Letters of Paul." *Studies in Religion* 5 (3):258–66.

Anderson, G. A. 2000. "Worship, Qumran Sect." In *Encyclopedia of the Dead Sea Scrolls*, edited by L. H. Schiffman and J. C. VanderKam, 2:991–96. New York: Oxford University Press.

Anderson, H. 1985. "4 Maccabees: A New Translation and Introduction." In *The Old Testament Pseudepigrapha*, edited by J. H. Charlesworth, 2:531–64. Garden City: NY: Doubleday.

Andrews, J. N. 1873. *The Complete Testimony of the Fathers of the First Three Centuries Concerning the Sabbath and First Day*. Battle Creek, MI: Steam Press, Seventh-day Adventist Publishing Association.

The Apostolic Fathers. 1912–13, 1914–17. Translated by K. Lake et al. 2 vols. Loeb Classical Library. Cambridge, MA: Harvard University Press.

Aquinas, T. *Commentary on the Epistle to the Hebrews*. Translated by C. Baer. South Bend, IN: St. Augustine's Press, 2006.

Archer, G. L. 1964. *A Survey of Old Testament Introduction*. Chicago: Moody Press.

Argall, R. A. 1995. *1 Enoch and Sirach: a Comparative Literary and Conceptual Analysis of the Themes of Revelation, Creation and Judgment*. SBL Early Judaism and Its Literature, edited by W. Adler. Atlanta: Scholars Press.

Attridge, H. W. 1989. *Hebrews*. Hermeneia. Philadelphia: Fortress.

______. 1990. "Paraenesis in a Homily (*logos paraklēseōs*): The Possible Location of, and Socialization in the 'Epistle of the Hebrews." *Semeia* 50:211–26.

______. 2002. "God in Hebrews: Urging Children to Heavenly Glory." In *The Forgotten God: Perspectives in Biblical Theology*, edited by A. A. Das and F. J. Matera, 197–209. Louisville: Westminster John Knox.

______. 2012. *Essays on John and Hebrews*. Grand Rapids: Baker Academic. Originally published 2010 by Mohr Siebeck (Tübingen; Wissenschaftliche Untersuchungen zum Neuen Testament 264).

Aune, D. E. 1987. *The New Testament in Its Literary Environment*. Edited by W. A. Meeks. Philadelphia: Westminster.

Averbeck, R. E. 2010. "Psalms 103 and 104: Hymns of Redemption and Creation." In *Interpreting the Psalms for Teaching* and Preaching, edited by H. W. Bateman IV and D. B. Sandy, 132–48. St. Louis: Chalice.

Badcock, F. J. 1935. *The Pauline Epistles and the Epistle to the Hebrews in Their Historical Setting*. New York: Macmillian.

Barclay, J. M. 1996. *Jews in the Mediterranean Diaspora: From Alexander to Trajan*. Edinburgh: T&T Clark.

Bartlet, J. V. 1902. "Barnabas and His Genuine Epistle." *Expositor* Sixth Series 5:409–27.

Bateman IV, H. W. 1992. "The Use of Psalm 110:1 in the New Testament." *Bibliotheca Sacra* 149:438–53.

______. 1995. "Two First-Century Messianic Uses of the Old Testament: Hebrews 1:5–13 and 4QFlorilegium." *Journal of the Evangelical Theological Society* 38 (1):11–27.

______. 1997. *Early Jewish Hermeneutics and Hebrews 1:5–13: The Impact of Early Jewish Exegesis on the Interpretation of a Significant New Testament Passage*. American University Studies, Series 7. New York: Lang.

______. 1998. "Were the Opponents at Philippi Necessarily Jewish." *Bibliotheca Sacra* 155:39–62.

______, ed. 1999. *Three Central Issues in Contemporary Dispensationalism: A Comparison of Traditional and Progressive Views*. Grand Rapids: Kregel.

______. 2001. "Psalm 45:6–7 and Its Christological Contributions to Hebrews." *Trinity Journal* 22NS (1):3–21.

______. 2007. "Defining the Titles 'Christ' and 'Son of God' in Mark's Narrative Presentation of Jesus." *Journal of the Evangelical Theological Society* 50 (3):537–59.

______, ed. 2007. *Four Views on the Warning Passages in Hebrews*. Grand Rapids: Kregel.

______. 2008. *The Letter to the Hebrews*. Dallas: u.p, 1988; revised edition, Winona Lake, IN: u.p.

______. 2010. [Bateman[1]] "Psalm 110: A Psalm of Assurance in the Midst of Change." In *Interpreting the Psalms for Preaching and Teaching*, edited by H. W. Bateman IV and D. B. Sandy, 150–61. St. Louis: Chalice.

______. 2010. [Bateman[2]] "Second Temple Exegetical Practices: Extra-biblical Examples of Exegesis Compared with Those in the Book of Hebrews." The Dead Sea Scrolls issue of *Southwestern Journal of Theology* 53 (1):26–54.

______. 2012. *Charts on the Book of Hebrews*. Kregel Charts of the Bible. Grand Rapids, Kregel.

______. 2013. *Interpreting the General Letters: An Exegetical Handbook*. Handbooks for New Testament Exegesis, edited by J. D. Harvey. Grand Rapids: Kregel.

______. 2015[17]. *Jude*. Evangelical Exegetical Commentary, edited by H. Harris. Bellingham, WA: Lexham Press. First published in digital in 2015. Citations refer to the 2017 edition.

Bateman IV, H W., and D. B. Sandy, eds. 2010. *Interpreting the Psalms for Preaching and Teaching*. St. Louis, Chalice.

Bateman IV, H. W., D. L. Bock, and G. H. Johnston. 2012. *Jesus the Messiah: Tracing the Promises, Expectations, and Coming of Israel's King*. Grand Rapids: Kregel.

Bateman IV, H. W., and A. C. Peer. 2018. *John's Letters: An Exegetical Guide for Preaching and Teaching*. The Big Greek Idea Series. Grand Rapids: Kregel.

Bauer, W. F., W. F. Arndt, F. W. Gingrich, and W. Danker. 1958. *A Greek-English Lexicon of the New Testament and Other Early Christian Literature*. 2nd ed. Chicago: University of Chicago Press.

Baumgarten, A. I. 1997. *The Flourishing of Jewish Sects in the Maccabean Era: An Interpretation*. Supplements to the Journal for the Study of Judaism 55. New York: Brill.

Baumgarten, J. M. and D. R. Schwartz. 1995. "Damascus Document." In *The Dead Sea*

Scrolls: Volume 2. Damascus Document, War Scroll, and Related Documents, edited by J. H. Charlesworth. Tübingen: Mohr Siebeck.

Baur, F. C. (1838) 1963. "Uber der Ursprung des Episcopats in der Christlichen Kirch." *Tübinger Zeitschrift für TheologieI* 11:1–185.

Beale, G. K. 2012. *Handbook on the New Testament Use of the Old Testament: Exegesis and Interpretation*. Grand Rapids: Baker Academic.

Begrich, J. 1998. *Introduction to Psalms: The Genres of the Religious Lyric of Israel*. Translated by J. D. Nogalski. Macon, GA: Mercer University Press.

Black, D. A. 2001. "Who Wrote Hebrews? Internal and External Evidence Reexamined." *Faith and Mission* 18 (2):3–26.

Black II, C. C. 1988. "The Rhetorical Form of the Hellenistic Jewish and Early Christian Sermon: A Response to Lawrence Wills." *Harvard Theological Review* 81 (1):1–18.

Blass, F. 1903. *Der Brief an die Hebräer: Text mit Angabe der Rhythmen*. Halle: Niemyer.

Bleek, F. 1828–1840. *Der Brief an die Hebrër, erläultert durch Einleitung, Übersetzung und fortlaufenden Kommentar*. 3 Vols. Berlin: D¨mmler.

Bloch, R. 1978. "Midrash." In *Studies in Judaism and Its Greco-Roman Context*. Vol. 5 of *Approaches to Ancient Judaism: Theory and Practice*, translated by M. H. Callaway; edited by W. S. Green, 29–50. Brown Judaic Studies 32. Missoula, MT: Scholars Press.

Bloch, R., with W. J. Sullivan. 1978. "Methodological Note for the Study of Rabbinic Literature." In *Studies in Judaism and Its Greco-Roman Context*. Vol. 5 of *Approaches to Ancient Judaism: Theory and Practice*, translated and edited by W. S. Green, 51–75. Brown Judaic Studies 32. Missoula, MT: Scholars Press.

Bloomfield, S. T. The Greek New Testament. Volume 2. Second ed. London: Longman, Orme, Brown, Green, & Longmans, 1836

Boccaccini, G. 1991. *Middle Judaism: Jewish Thought, 300 B.C.E. to 200 C.E.* Minneapolis: Fortress.

Bock, D. L. 1996. *Luke 9:51–24:53*. Baker Exegetical Commentary on the New Testament 3B. Grand Rapids: Baker Books.

______. 1999. "The Structure of the Biblical Covenants." In *Three Central Issues of Contemporary Dispensationalism: A Comparison of Traditional and Progressive Views*, edited by H. W. Bateman IV, 140–51. Grand Rapids: Kregel.

______. 2008. "Single Meaning, Multiple Contexts and Referents." In *Three Views on the New Testament Use of the Old Testament*, 105–68. S. N. Gundry, series editor. Grand Rapids: Zondervan.

Boehme, C. F. 1825. *Epistola ad Hebreaeos*. Lipsige: Barth.

Borgen, P. 1992. "Philo's Writings." In *Anchor Bible Dictionary*. Vol. 5, O–Sh, edited by D. N. Freedman, 334–36. New York: Doubleday.

Bornhaüser, K. B. 1932. *Empfänger und Verfasser des Briefes an die Hebräer*. Beiträge zur Förderung christlicher Theologie 35.3. Gütersloh: Bertelsmann.

Bowker J. W. 1967–68. "Speeches in Acts: A Study in Proem and Yelammedenu Form." *New Testament Studies* 14:96–111.

Bowman. J. W. 1962. *Hebrews, James, I & II Peter*. Layman's Bible Commentary. London: SCM.

Braun, F. M. 1955. "L'arrièr-fond judaïque du quatrième évangile et la Communauté de l'Aliance." *Revue biblique* 62:5–44.

Briant, P. 2002. *From Cyrus to Alexander: A History of the Persian Empire*. Translated by P T. Daniels. Winona Lake, IN: Eisenbrauns.

Brooks, A. E. 1896. *Origen: Commentary on the St. John's Gospel*. 2 vols. Cambridge: Cambridge University Press.

Brown, R. 1997. *An Introduction to the New Testament*. New York: Doubleday.

Bruce, F. F. 1962–63. "'To the Hebrew' or 'To the Essenes'?" *New Testament Studies* 9 (3):217–32.

______. 1964. *The Epistle to the Hebrews*. New International Commentary on the New Testament. Grand Rapids: Eerdmans.

Buchanan, G. W. 1983. *To the Hebrews*. Anchor Bible. New York: Doubleday.

Buck, D. E. 2002. "The Rhetorical Arrangement and Function of OT Citations in the Book of Hebrews: Uncovering Their Role in the Paraenetic Discourse of Access." PhD diss., Dallas Theological Seminary.

Bullinger, E. W. 1968. *Figures of Speech Used in the Bible*. Grand Rapids: Baker. Originally published 1898 by Eyre and Spotiswoode (London). Citations refer to the Baker edition.

Burns, J. L. 1992. "The Future of Ethnic Israel in Romans 11." In *Dispensationalism, Israel and the Church*, edited by C. A. Blaising and D. L. Bock, 188–229. Grand Rapids: Zondervan.

______. 1997. "Israel and the Church of a Progressive Dispensationalist." In *Three Central Issues in Contemporary Dispensationalism: A Comparison of Traditional and Progressive Views*, edited by H. W. Bateman IV, 263–317. Grand Rapids: Kregel.

Cadoux, C. J. 1922. "The Early Christian Church in Egypt." *Expository Times* 33 (12):536–39.

Caird, G. B. 1959. "The Exegetical Method of the Epistle to the Hebrews." *Canadian Journal of Theology* 5 (1):44–51.

Carpzov, J. B. 1750. *Sacrae exercitationes in S. Pauli epistolam ad Heraeos ex Philone alexandrine*. Amsterdam: n.p.

Carson, D. A., and D. J. Moo, eds. 2005. *An Introduction to the New Testament*. 2nd ed. Grand Rapids: Zondervan.

Champlin, E. 2003. *Nero*. Cambridge, MA: Harvard University Press.

Chapman, J. 1905. "Aristion, Author of the Epistle to the Hebrews." *Revue bénédictine* 22 (1–4):50–64.

Charlesworth J. H., ed. 1985. *The Old Testament Pseudepigrapha*. 2 vols. New York: Doubleday.

Charlesworth, J. H., with J. M Baumgarten et al., eds. 1995. *Damascus Document, War Scroll, and Related Documents*. Vol. 2 of *The Dead Sea Scrolls: Hebrew, Aramaic, and Greek Texts with English Translations*. Princeton Theological Seminary Dead Sea Scrolls Project. Tübingen: Mohr Siebeck.

Chiappetta, Michael. 1953. "Historiography and Roman Education." *History of Education Journal* 4 (4):149–56.

Childs, B. 1985. *The New Testament as Canon: An Introduction*. Philadelphia: Fortress.

Chisholm R. and H. W. Bateman IV. 2016. *How to Read, Understand, and Interpret the Book*. In Let's Know the Bible. Leesburg, IN: Cyber–Center for Biblical Studies.

Cockerill, G. L. 2007. "'If We Neglect Such Great Salvation': A Wesleyan Perspective." In *Four Views of the Warning Passages*, edited by H. W. Bateman IV, 257–92. Grand Rapids: Kregel.

______. 2012. *The Epistle to the Hebrews*. New International Commentary on the New Testament. Grand Rapids: Eerdmans.

Collart, P. 1937. *Philippes, ville de Macédoine depuis ses origines jusqu' a la fin de l'époque romaine*. Paris: E. de Boccord.

Collins, J. J. 2010. *The Scepter and the Star: The Messianism in Light of the Dead Sea Scrolls*. 2nd ed. Grand Rapids: Eerdmans.

Comfort, P. W., and D. P. Barrett. 1999. *The Complete Text of the Earliest New Testament Manuscripts*. Grand Rapids: Baker.

Crawford, M. 1992. *The Roman Republic*. 2nd ed. Cambridge, MA: Harvard University Press.

Dando-Collins, S. 2010. *The Great Fire of Rome: The Fall of the Emperor Nero and the City of Rome*. Cambridge, MA: De Capo.

D'Angelo, M. R. 1979. *Moses in the Letter to the Hebrews*. Society of Biblical Literature Dissertation Series 42. Missoula, MT: Scholars Press.

Daniélou, P. J. 1958. *The Dead Sea Scrolls and Primitive Christianity*. Translated by S. Attanasio. Baltimore: Helicon.

Danker, F. W., W. Bauer, W. F. Arndt, and F. W. Gingrich. 2000. *A Greek-English Lexicon of the New Testament and Other Early Christian Literature*. 3rd ed. Chicago: University of Chicago Press.

Davidson, M. J. 1992. *Angels at Qumran: A Comparative Study of 1 Enoch 1–36, 71–108 and Sectarian Writings from Qumran*. Supplement Series. Sheffield, England: Sheffield Academic Press.

deSilva, D. A. 2000. [deSilva1] *Honor, Patronage, Kingship and Purity: Unlocking New Testament Culture*. Downers Grove, IL: InterVarsity Press.

______. 2000. [deSilva2] *Perseverance in Gratitude: A Socio-Rhetorical Commentary on the Epistle "to the Hebrews."* Grand Rapids: Eerdmans.

Dibelius, F. 1910. *Der Verfasser des Hebräerbriefes: Eine Untersuchung zur Geschichte des Urchristentums*. Strassburg: J. H. Ed. Heitz [Heitz & Mündel].

Dickie, J. 1913. "The Literary Riddle of the "Epistle to the Hebrews." *Exp* 8 (2):371–78.

Dio Casius. 1914–24. *Dio's Roman History*. Translated by E. Cary et al. 9 vols. Loeb Classical Library. New York: G. P. Putman's Sons.

Dixon, J. W. 1911. "Anchor." In *Encyclopaedia Britannica*, 947–49. Cambridge: Cambridge University Press.

Dowley, T. 2003. *The Kregel Bible Atlas*. Grand Rapids: Kregel.

Dubarle, A. M. 1939. "Rédacteur et Destinaires de l'Epitre aux Hébreux." *Revue Biblique* 48:506–29.

Dunn, J. D. G. 1980. *Christology in the Making: A New Testament Inquiry into the Origins of the Doctrine of the Incarnation*. Philadelphia: Westminster.

Edmundson, G. 1913. *The Church in Rome in the First Century*. London: Longmans, Green.

Ellingworth, P. 1993. *Commentary on Hebrews*. New International Greek Testament Commentary. Grand Rapids: Eerdmans.

Ellingworth, P., and E. A. Nida. 1983. *A Translator's Handbook on the Letter to the Hebrews*. New York: United Bible Society.

Eskola, T. 2001. *Messiah and the Throne*. Wissenschaftliche Untersuchungen zum Neuen Testament. Tübingen: Mohr Siebeck.

Eusebius. *Ecclesiastical History*. 1926. Vol. 1. Translated by K. Lake. Loeb Classical Library 153. New York: Putnam.

______. *Ecclesiastical History*. 1932. Vol. 2. Translated by J. E. L. Oulton, taken from the edition published in conjunction with H. J. Lawlor. Loeb Classical Library 265. New York: Putnam.

Evans, L. H. 1985. *Hebrews*. Communicators Commentary. Waco, TX: Word Books.

Falk, D. K. 2000a. "Moses." In *Encyclopedia of the Dead Sea Scrolls*, edited by L. H. Schiffman and J. C. VanderKam, 1:576–77. New York: Oxford University Press.

______. 2000b. "Moses, Texts of." In *Encyclopedia of the Dead Sea Scrolls*, edited by L. H. Schiffman and J. C. VanderKam, 1:577–81. New York: Oxford University Press.

Fanning, B. M. 2007. "Apostasy and Security in Hebrews: A Reformed Perspective." In *Four Views of the Warning Passages*, edited by H. W. Bateman IV, 172–219. Grand Rapids: Kregel.

______. 1994. "A Theology of Hebrews." In *A Biblical Theology of the New Testament*, edited by R. B. Zuck and D. L. Bock, 369–416. Chicago, IL: Moody Press.

Feine, P., J. Behm, and W. G. Kümmel. 1963. *Einleitung in das Neue Testaments*. Heidelberg: Quelle & Meyer.

Feld, H. 1985. *Der Hebräerbrief.* Darmstadt: Wissenschaftliche Buchgesellschaft.

Fensham, F. C. 1971. "Hebrews and Qumran." *Neotestamentica* 5:9–21.

Fiensy, D. A. 1994. *New Testament Introduction*. College Press NIV Commentary. Joplin, MO: College Press.

Filson, F. V. 1967. *"Yesterday": A Study of Hebrews in the Light of Chapter 13*. Studies in Biblical Theology 4. London: SCM.

Fitzgerald, M. 2010. *Run: The Mind-Body Method of Running by Feel*. Boulder, CO: Velo.

Fitzmyer, J. A. 1967. "Further Light on Melchizedek from Qumran Cave 11." *Journal of Biblical Literature* 86:25–41.

Ford, J. M. 1966. "The First Epistle to the Corinthians or the First Epistle to the Hebrews?" *Catholic Biblical Quarterly* 28:402–16.

Foulkes, F. 1958. *The Acts of God: A Study of the Basis of Typology in the Old Testament*. London: Tyndale.

Freeman, R. E. 1992. "Tabernacle." In *Anchor Bible Dictionary*, 242–300. New York: Doubleday.

Futato, M. D. 2007. *Interpreting the Psalms: An Exegetical Handbook*, edited by D. M. Howard. Handbooks for Old Testament Exegesis. Grand Rapids: Kregel.

Gärtner, B. 1965. *The Temple and the Community in Qumran and the New Testament*. Society for New Testament Studies Monograph Series 1. Cambridge: University Press.

Gheorghita, R. 2003. *The Role of the Septuagint in Hebrews: An Investigation of Its Influence with Specific Consideration to the Use of Hab 2:3–3 in Heb 10:37–38*. Wissenschaftliche Untersuchungen zum Neuen Testament 160. Tübingen: Mohr Siebeck.

Gibson, J. C. L. 1977. *Canaanite Myths and Legends*. Edinburgh: T&T Clark.

Girdwood, J., and P. Verkruyse. 1997. *Hebrews*. College Press NIV Commentary. Joplin, MO: College Press.

Glassner, J.-J. 2004. *Mesopotamian Chronicles*. Writings from the Ancient World, edited by Benjamin R. Foster. Atlanta: Society of Biblical Literature.

Gleason, R. 2007. "The Warnings in Hebrews as Covenantal Discipline: A Moderate Reformed Perspective." In *Four Views of the Warning Passages*, edited by H. W. Bateman IV, 336–77. Grand Rapids: Kregel.

Glen, D. R. 1982. "Psalm 8 and Hebrews 2: A Case Study in Biblical Hermeneutics and Biblical Theology." In *Walvoord: A Tribute*, edited by D. K. Campbell, 39–51. Chicago: Moody Press.

Goppelt, L. 1982. *Typos: The Typological Interpretation of the Old Testament in the New*. Translated by D. H. Madvig. Grand Rapids: Eerdmans. Originally presented as the author's thesis (doctoral—Erlangen, 1939).

Gordon, C. H. 1965. *Ugaritic Textbook: Grammar, Texts in Transliteration, Cuneiform Selections, Glossary, Indices*. Rome: Pontifical Biblical Institute.

Gordon, R. P. 2008. *Hebrews*. 2nd ed. Readings: A New Biblical Commentary, edited by J. Jarick. Sheffield: Sheffield Phoenix Press.

Goulder, M. 2003. "Hebrews and the Ebionites." *New Testament Studies* 49:393–406.

Gramacki, R. G. 1974. *New Testament Survey*. Grand Rapids: Baker.

Green, G. L. 2008. *Jude and 2 Peter*. Barker Exegetical Commentary of the New Testament. Grand Rapids: Baker.

Greenlee, J. H. 1989. *Introduction to New Testament Textual Criticism*. Grand Rapids: Eerdmans.

_______. 1998. *An Exegetical Summary of Hebrews*. Dallas, TX: Summer Institute of Linguistics.

Gregory, C. R. 1907. *Canon and Text of the New Testament*. Edinburgh: T&T Clark.

Gregory of Elvira. 1900. *Tractatus Origenis*, edited by P. Batiffol and A. Wilmart. Parisilis: A. Picard.

Grenfell, B. P., and A. S. Hunt et al., eds. and trans. 1898–1987. *Oxyrhynchus Papyri*. 54 vols. London: Egypt Exploration Society.

Grotius, H. 1645. *Christ's Passion: A Tragedy with Annotations*. Translated by G. Sandys. London: I. L.

______. 1646. *Annotationes in Acta Apostolorum et in epistolas catholicas*. Paris: n.p.

Guthrie, D. 1983. *The Letter to the Hebrews: An Introduction and Commentary*. Tyndale New Testament Commentaries. Grand Rapids: Eerdmans.

______. 1990. *New Testament Introduction*. 4th ed. Downers Grove, IL: InterVarsity Press.

Guthrie, G. H. 1994. *The Structure of Hebrews: A Text-Linguistic Analysis*. Supplements to Novum Testamentum. New York: Brill.

______. 1998. *Hebrews*. NIV Application Commentary. Grand Rapids: Zondervan.

______. 2001. "The Case for Apollos as the Author of Hebrews." *Faith and Mission* 18 (2):41–56.

Hagner, D. A. 1973. *The Use of the Old and New Testaments in Clement of Rome*. Supplements to Novum Testamentum 34. Leiden: Brill.

______. 1983. *Hebrews*. Good News Commentary. San Francisco: Harper & Row.

______. 2002. *Encountering the Book of Hebrews*. Encounter Biblical Studies. Grand Rapids: Baker.

Hamerton-Kelly, R. G. 1973. *Pre-Existence, Wisdom and the Son of Man*. Society for New Testament Studies Monograph Series 21. Cambridge: University Press.

Hanson, A. T. 1965. *Jesus Christ in the Old Testament*. London, UK: Society for Promoting Christian Knowledge.

Harnack, A. J. 1900. "Probabilia über die Addeesse und den Verasser des Hebräerbriefes." *Zeitschrift für die Neutestamentliche Wissenschaft und die Kunde der älteren Kirche* 1:16–41.

Harrington, H. K. 2000. "Purity." In *Encyclopedia of the Dead Sea Scrolls*, edited by L. H. Schiffman and J. C. VanderKam, 2:724–28. New York: Oxford University Press.

Harris, M. J. 1984. "The Translation of *Elohim* in Psalm 45:7–8." *Tyndale Bulletin* 35:65–89.

Harris, W. V. 1989. *Ancient Literacy*. Cambridge, MA: Harvard University Press.

Hatch, W. H. P. 1951. *Facsimiles and Descriptions of Minuscule Manuscripts of the New Testament*. Cambridge, MA: Harvard University Press.

Heen, E. M., and P. D. W. Krey, eds. 2005. *Hebrews*. Ancient Christian Commentary on Scripture: New Testament 10. Downers Grove, IL: InterVarsity Press.

Hegermann, H. 1988. *Der Brief an die Hebräer*. Theologischer Handkommentar zum Neuen Testament. 16. Berlin: Evangelische Verlagsanstalt.

Hengel, M. 1985. *Studies in the Gospel of Mark*. Translated by J. Bowden. Philadelphia: Fortress.

______. 1997. *The Zealots: Investigations into the Jewish Freedom Movement in the Period from Herod I until 70 A.D.* Edinburgh: T&T Clark, 1989.

Herodotus. 1921–28. *The History of Herodotus*. Translated by A. D. Godley et al. 4 vols. Loeb Classical Library, 117–20. Cambridge, MA: Harvard University Press.

Hewitt, T. 1960. *The Epistle to the Hebrews*. Tyndale New Testament Commentaries. Grand Rapids, Eerdmans.

Hiebert, D. E. 1977. *An Introduction to the New Testament*. Vol. 3, *The Non-Pauline Epistles and Revelation*. Rev. and enlarged ed. Chicago: Moody Press.

Hodges, Z. 1983. "Hebrews." In *Bible Knowledge Commentary*, edited by R. Zuck and J. Walvoord, 779–80. Wheaton, IL: Victor Books.

Hohner, H. W. 1977. *Chronological Aspects of the Life of Christ*. Grand Rapids: Zondervan.

______. 1980. *Herod Antipas: A Contemporary of Jesus Christ*. Grand Rapids: Zondervan.

Holladay, C. R. 2017. *Introduction to the New Testament: Reference Edition*. Waco, TX: Baylor University Press.

Holmén, T. 2001. *Jesus and Jewish Covenant Thinking*, edited by R. A. Culpepper and R. Remdtorff. Biblical Interpretation Series 55. Leiden: Brill.

Holsteen, N. D. 2011. "The Trinity in the Book of Hebrews." *Bibliotheca Sacra* 168: 334–46.

Hoppin, R. 1997. *Priscilla's Letter: Finding the Author of the Epistle to the Hebrews*. Fort Bragg, CA: Lost Coast Press.

Horgan, M. P. 2002. "Isaiah Pesher 4 (4Q161 = 4QpIsaa)." In *Pesharim, Other Commentaries, and Related Documents*. Vol. 6B of *The Dead Sea Scrolls: Hebrew, Aramaic, and Greek Texts with English Translations*, edited by J. H. Charlesworth and H. W. Rietz et al., 70–73. Princeton Theological Seminary Dead Sea Scrolls Project. Tübingen: Mohr Siebeck.

Hornung, E. 1982. *Conceptions of God in Ancient Egypt: The One and the Many*. Translated by J. Baines. Ithaca, NY: Cornell University Press.

Hughes, P. E. 1977. *A Commentary on the Epistle to the Hebrews*. Grand Rapids: Eerdmans.

Isaac B. G. 1997. "Hillel." In *The Oxford Dictionary of the Jewish Religion*, edited by R. J. Z. Werblowsky and Geoffrey Wigoder, 323. New York: Oxford University Press.

Isaac, E. 1985. "1 (Ethiopic Apocalypse of) Enoch." *The Old Testament Pseudepigrapha*, edited by J. H. Charlesworth, 1:5–89. New York: Doubleday.

Jeremias, J. 1969. *Jerusalem in the Time of Jesus: An Investigation into Economic and Social Conditions during the New Testament Period*. Translated by F. H. Cave and C. H. Cave. Philadelphia: Fortress.

Jeremias, J., and Strathmann, H. 1963. *Die Briefe an des Timotheus und Titus; Der Brief an die Hebräer*. Translated and explained by J. Jeremias and H. Strathmann. Das Neue Testament Deutsch 9. Güteringen: Vandenhoeck & Ruprecht.

Jerome. 1829. *De viris illustribus*, edited by G. Herdingii. Lipsiae: Aedibus B. G. Teubneri. Originally published A.D. 392–93.

Johnson, T. L. 2006. *Hebrews A Commentary*. New Testament Library. Louisville: Westminster John Knox.

Johnston, G. H. 2012. "Messianic Trajectories in Genesis and Numbers." *Jesus the Messiah: Tracing the Promises, Expectations, and Coming of Israel's King*, by H. W. Bateman IV, D. L. Bock, and G. H. Johnston, 37–58. Grand Rapids: Kregel.

Jones, E. D. 1934–35. "The Authorship of Hebrews xiii." *Expository Times* 46 (12): 562–67.

Josephus. 1976. The Life, Against Apion. Vol. 1. Translated by H. St. J. Thackeray. Loeb Classical Library. Cambridge, MA: Harvard University Press, 1926.

______. 1978. *Jewish Antiquities*, Books I-IV. Vol. 4. Translated by H. St. J. Thackeray. Loeb Classical Library. Cambridge, MA: Harvard University Press.

______. 1989. *The Jewish Wars*, Books I-III. Vol. 2. Translated by H. St. J. Thackeray. Loeb Classical Library. Cambridge, MA: Harvard University Press.

______. 1990. *The Jewish Wars*, Books IV-VII. Vol. 3. Translated by H. St. J. Thackeray. Loeb Classical Library. Cambridge, MA: Harvard University Press.

______. 1978. *The Jewish Wars*, Books IX-XI. Vol. 6. Translated by R. Marcus. Loeb Classical Library. Cambridge, MA: Harvard University Press.

______. 1958. *The Jewish Wars*, Books XII-XIV. Vol. 7. Translated by R. Marcus. Loeb Classical Library. Cambridge, MA: Harvard University Press.

______. 1963. *The Jewish Wars*, Books XV-XVII. Vol. 8. Translated by R. Marcus. Loeb Classical Library. Cambridge, MA: Harvard University Press.

______. 1965. *The Jewish Wars*, Books XVIII-XX. Vol. 9. Translated by L. H. Feldman. Loeb Classical Library. Cambridge, MA: Harvard University Press.

Jurgens, W. A., trans. 1970. *Pre-Nicene and Nicene Eras*. Vol. 1, The Faith of the Early Fathers. Collegeville, MN: Liturgical Press.

________, trans. 1979a. *Post-Nicene and Constantinopolitan Eras through St. Jerome*. Vol. 2, The Faith of the Early Fathers. Collegeville, MN: Liturgical Press.

________, trans. 1979b. *St. Augustine to the End of the Patristic Age*. Vol. 3, The Faith of the Early Fathers. Collegeville, MN: Liturgical Press.

Käsemann, E. 1984. *The Wandering People of God: An Investigation of the Letter to the Hebrews*. Translated by R. A. Harrisville and I. L. Sandberg. Minneapolis: Augsburg.

Kee, H. C. 1985. "Testaments of the Twelve Patriarchs (Second Century B.C.)." In *The Old Testament Pseudepigrapha*. 2 vols., edited by J. H. Charlesworth, 775–828. New York: Doubleday.

Keel, O. 1978. *The Symbolism of the Biblical World: Ancient Near Eastern Iconography and the Book of Psalms*. Translated by T. J. Hallett. New York: Seabury.

Keil, C. F. 1885. *Kommentar über den Brief an die Hebrëer*. Leipzig: Dorffling and Franke.

Kenneth, H. 1981. *Hebrews Commentary from Erasmus to Beza 1516–1598*. Tübingen: Mohr Siebeck.

Kistemaker, S. 1961. *The Psalm Citations in the Epistle to the Hebrews*. Amsterdam: G. Van Soest.

Kittel, G., and G. Friedrich, eds. 1964–76. *Theological Dictionary of the New Testament*. 10 vols. Translated by G. W. Bromiley. Grand Rapids: Eerdmans.

Kling, H., et al. 1978. *Mitteilungen aus der Papyrussammlung der Giessener Universitätsbibliothek*. Vol. 6, *Griechische Verwaltungsurkunden von Tebtynis aus dem Anfang des dritten Jahrhunderts n. Chr.* (P. bibl. univ. Giss. 47–53), edited by G. Rosenberger. Papyrology on Microfiche, ser. 2, vol. 25. Missoula, MO: Scholars Press. First published 1939 by Töpelmann (Giessen). Citations refer to the 1978 edition.

Koester, C. R. 2001. *Hebrews: A New Translation with Introduction and Commentary*. Anchor Bible. New York: Doubleday.

Kosmala, H. 1959. *Hebräer-Essener-Christen*. Leiden: Brill.

Kümmel, W. G. 1966. *Introduction to the New Testament*. Translated by A. J. Mattill. Nashville/New York: Abingdon.

______. 1972. *The New Testament: The History of the Investigation of its Problems*. Translated by S. M. Gilmour and H. C. Kee. Nashville: Abingdon.

Kurianal, J. 2000. *Jesus Our High Priest: Ps 110,4 as the Substructure of Heb 5,1–7, 28*. Europäische Hochschulschriften 23. New York: Lang.

Laansma, J. 1997. *"I Will Give You Rest": The Rest Motif in the New Testament with Special Reference to Mt 11 and Heb 3–4*. Wissenschatliche Untersuchunge zum Neuen Testament 2.98. Tübingen: Mohr Siebeck.

Lake, H., and K. Lake. 1982. *Codex Sinaiticvs*. Detroit: Brown & Thomas. Originally published by Oxford at the Clarendon Press in 1911. Graecus Codex Vaticanus originally published in 1868.

Lane, W. L. 1985. *Call to Commitment: Responding to the Message of Hebrews*. Nashville: Nelson.

______. 1991a. *Hebrews 1–8*. Word Biblical Commentary. Dallas: Word Books.

______. 1991b. *Hebrews 9–13*. Word Biblical Commentary. Dallas: Word Books.

Le Déaut, R. 1969. "Apropos d'une definition du Midrash." *Biblica* 50:395–413.

______. 1971. "Apropos a Definition of Midrash." Translated by M. C. Howard. *Interpretation* 25:259–82.

Legg, J. D. 1968. "Our Brother Timothy: A Suggested Solution to the Problem of the Authorship of the Epistle to the Hebrews." *Evangelical Quarterly* 40:22–23.

Leonard, W. 1939. *The Authorship of the Epistle to the Hebrews*. London: Oates and Washbourne.

Lewis, T. W. 1975. "'. . . And if he shrinks back' (Heb. X.38 b)." *New Testament Studies* 22 (1):88–94.

Lichtenberger, H. 2000. "Baths and Bapitism." In *Encyclopedia of the Dead Sea Scrolls*, edited by L. H. Schiffman and J. C. VanderKam, 1:85–89. New York: Oxford University Press.

Lindars, B. 1989. "The Rhetorical Structure of Hebrews." *New Testament Studies* 35 (3):382–406.

Linnemann, E. 2002. "A Call for a Retrial in the Case of the Epistle to the Hebrews." Translated by D. E. Lanier. *Faith and Mission* 19 (2):19–59.

Lipschits, O., and M. Oeming, eds. 2006. *Judah and the Judaeans in the Persian Period*. Winona Lake, IN: Eisenbrauns.

Lipschits, O., G. N. Knoppers, and R. Albertz, eds. 2007. *Judah and the Judaeans in the Fourth Century B.C.E.* Winona Lake, IN: Eisenbrauns.

Loisy, A. 1935. *Remarques sur la littérature épistolaire du Nouveau Testament*. Paris: É. Nourry.

Longenecker, R. N. 1999. *Biblical Exegesis in the Apostolic Period*. 2nd ed. Grand Rapids: Eerdmans.

Lowery, D. K. 1992. "Christ, and the End of the Law." In *Dispensationalism, Israel and the Church: The Search for Definition*, edited by Craig A. Blaising and Darrell L. Bock, 230–47. Grand Rapids: Zondervan.

Luther, M. 1958. *Commentary on Genesis: Chapters 1–21*. Translated by J. T. Mueller. Grand Rapids: Zondervan. Originally published Minneapolis: Luther Press, 1910.

______. 1960. "Preface to the Epistle of Hebrews." In *Lectures on Titus, Philemon, and Hebrews. Vol. 29 of Luther's Works*. Translated by C. M. Jacobs, revised by E. Theodore Bachmann, and edited by E. T. Bachmann, 394–95. Philadelphia: Muhlenberg. Originally published St. Louis, MO: Concordia Publishing House, 1955.

Mach, M. 2000. "Angels." In *Encyclopedia of the Dead Sea Scrolls*, edited by L. H. Schiffman and J. C. VanderKam, 1:24–27. New York: Oxford University Press.

MacLeod, D. J. 1987. "The Theology of the Epistle to the Hebrews: Introduction, Prolegomena and Doctrinal Center." ThD diss., Dallas Theological Seminary.

Maier, P. L., trans. and ed. 1988. *Josephus: The Essential Writings*. Grand Rapids: Kregel.

Maier P. L., and R. C. Linnenbugel, eds. 2016. *Foxe's Book of Martyrs*. Abridged and rev. ed. Grand Rapids: Kregel.

Malherbe, A. J. 1988. *Ancient Epistolary Theorists*. SBL Sources for Biblical Study 19. Atlanta: Scholars Press.

Martinez, F. G. 1992. "The Eschatological Figure of 4Q246." *Qumran and Apocalyptic: Studies on the Aramaic Texts from Qumran*, 162–79. Studies on the Texts of the Desert of Judah 9. Leiden: Brill.

Martinez, F. G., and E. J. C. Tigchelaar, eds. 2000a. *The Dead Sea Scrolls Study Edition*. Vol. 1, *1Q1–4Q273*. Leiden: Brill; Grand Rapids: Eerdmans. First published 1997 by Brill (Leiden).

______, eds. 2000b. *The Dead Sea Scrolls Study Edition*. Vol. 2, *4Q274–11Q13*. Leiden: Brill; Grand Rapids: Eerdmans. First published 1998 by Brill (Leiden).

McKnight, S. 1992. "The Warning Passages of Hebrews: A Formal Analysis and Theological Conclusions." *Trinity Journal* 13 (1):21–29.

Meier, J. P. 1985a. "Structure and Theology in Heb 1:1–14." *Biblica* 66 (2):168–89.

______. 1985b. "Symmetry and Theology in the Old Testament Citations of Hebrews 1:5–14." *Biblica* 66 (4):504–33.

Ménégoz, E. 1894. *La Théologie de l'épître aux Hébreux*. Paris: Fischbacher.

Merrill, E. H. 1987. *Kingdom of Priests: A History of Old Testament Israel*. Grand Rapids: Baker.

______. 1993. "Royal Priesthood: An Old Testament Messianic Motif." *Bibliotheca Sacra* 150:50–61.

Metzger, B. M. 1992. *The Text of the New Testament: Its Transmission, Corruption, and Restoration*. 3rd enlarged ed. New York: Oxford University Press.

______. 1994. *A Textual Commentary on the Greek New Testament*. 2nd ed. New York: United Bible Society.

Metzger, B. M. and Roland Murphy, eds. 1991. *The New Oxford Annotated Apocrypha: The Apocryphal/Deuterocanonical Books of the Old Testament*. New York: Oxford University Press (1965, 1977).

Michalak, A. R. 2012. "Angels as Warriors in Late Second Temple Literature." *Wissenschaftliche Untersuchungen zum Neuen Testament*. Tübingen, Germany: Mohr Siebeck.

Milgrom, J. 2000. "Sacrifice." In *Encyclopedia of the Dead Sea Scrolls*, edited by L. H. Schiffman and J. C. VanderKam, 2:807–11. New York: Oxford University Press.

Mitchell, A. C. 2007. *Hebrews*. Sacra Pagina 13. Collegeville, MN: Liturgical Press.

Moffatt, M. 1979. *A Critical and Exegetical Commentary on the Epistle to the Hebrews*. International Critical Commentary 40. Edinburgh: T&T Clark. First published 1924. Citations refer to the 1979 edition.

Mohler Jr., R. A. 2017. *Exalting Jesus in Hebrews*. Christ-Centered Exposition. Nashville: Holman Reference.

Moore, T. and T. Sprankle. 2019. *Philippians*. Kerux Commentaries: A Commentary for Preaching and Teaching. Grand Rapids, Kregel.

Morris, L. 1981. "Hebrews." In *Expositor's Bible Commentary*, edited by F. E. Gaebelein, 12:123–158. Grand Rapids: Zondervan.

Moule, C. F. D. 1950. "Sanctuary and Sacrifice in the Church of the New Testament." *Journal of Theological Studies* 1:29–41.

______. 1984. *An Idiom Book of New Testament Greek*, 2nd ed. Cambridge: Cambridge University Press. First published 1959.

Moulton, J. H., and G. Milligan. 1930. *The Vocabulary of the Greek Testament: Illustrated from the Papyri and Other Non-literary Sources*. Grand Rapids: Eerdmans.

Mowinkel, S. 2014. *Psalms Studies, Volume 1*. Translated by M. E. Biddle. History of Biblical Studies 2. Atlanta: SBL Press.

Neill, S. and T. Wright, 1988. *Interpretation of the New Testament* 1861–1986. New Edition. Oxford: Oxford University Press. First published 1964 by Oxford University Press.

Nestle, Eb., and Er. Nestle. 1936. *Greek New Testament: Edited with Critical Apparatus*. 16th ed. New York: American Bible Society.

Nestle, Eb., Er. Nestle, K. Aland, and B. Aland, eds. 1993. *Novum Testamentum Graece*. 27th ed. Stuttgart: Deutsche Bibelgesellschaft.

Newsome, C. S. 2000. "Songs of the Sabbath Sacrifice." In *Encyclopedia of the Dead Sea Scrolls*, edited by L. H. Schiffman and J. C. VanderKam, 2:887–89. New York: Oxford University Press.

Nickelsburg, G. W. E. 2000. "Enoch, Books of." In *Encyclopedia of the Dead Sea Scrolls*, edited by L. H. Schiffman and J. C Vander-Kam, 1:249–53. New York: Oxford University Press.

Norris, F. W. 1992. "Antioch of Syria." In *The Anchor Bible Dictionary*. Vol. 1, A–D, edited by D. N. Freedman, 265–69. New York: Doubleday.

Olivier, J. P. J. "The Sceptre of Justice and Psalm 45:7b." *Journal of Northwest Semitic Languages* 7:45–54.

Osborne, G. 2007. "The Warning Passages of Hebrews: An Arminian Perspective." In *Four Views of the Warning Passages,* edited by H. W. Bateman IV, 86–128. Grand Rapids: Kregel.

Pfitzner, V. C. 1997. *Hebrews.* Abingdon New Testament Commentaries. Nashville: Abingdon.

Phillips, J. 1988. *Exploring Hebrews: An Expository Commentary.* Rev. ed. John Phillips Commentary Series. Grand Rapids: Kregel.

Philo. 1929–62. *Philo.* Translated by F. H. Colson and G. H. Whitaker. 9 vols. Loeb Classical Library. Cambridge, MA: Harvard University Press.

______. 1953. *Questions and Answers on Genesis.* Translated by R. Marcus. Supplementary vol. 1. Loeb Classical Library. Cambridge, MA: Harvard University Press.

Pixner, B. 1992. "The Jerusalem Essenes, Barnabas and the Letter to the Hebrews." In *Intertestamental Essays in Honour of Józef Tadeusz Milik,* edited by Z. J. Kapera, 167–78. Qumranica Mogilanensia 6 (pt. 1). Kraków: Enigma Press.

Plato. 1925. *Poiticus and Philebus.* Translated by H. N. Fowler. Loeb Classical Library. New York, NY: G.P. Putnam's Sons.

______. 1930–35. *Respublica.* Translated by P. Shorey. 2 vols. Loeb Classical Library. Cambridge: Harvard University Press.

Plutarch. 1914–21. *Lives.* Translated by B. Perrin. 11 vols. Loeb Classical Library. Cambridge: Harvard University Press.

Polybius. 1922–27. *The Histories.* Translated by W. R. Paton. 6 vols. Loeb Classical Library. Cambridge, MA: Harvard University Press.

Poster, C., and L. C. Mitchell, eds. 2007. *Letter-Writing Manuals and Instruction from Antiquity to the Present.* Columbia: University of South Carolina Press.

Pritchard, J. B. 1958. *The Ancient Near East.* Vol. 1, *An Anthology of Texts and Pictures,* translated and annotated by W. F. Albright et al. Princeton, NJ: Princeton University Press.

Puech, É. 1996. *Qumran Cave 4 XVII.* Discoveries in the Judaean Desert 22. Oxford: Clarendon.

Qimron, E., and J. Strugnell. 1984. "An Unpublished Halakhic Letter from Qumran." In *Biblical Archaeology Today: Proceedings of the International Congress on Biblical Archaeology, Jerusalem, April 1984,* edited by J. Amitai, 400–407. Jerusalem: Israel Exploration Society.

Ramsay, W. M. 1899. "The Date and Authorship of the Epistle to the Hebrews." *The Expositor* 9:401–22. (There is a problem with the library copy—p. 401 is actually labeled as p. 26.—Ed.)

Rhee, V. (S.-Y.). 2001a. "Chiasm and the Concept of Faith in Hebrews 12:1–29." *Westminster Theological Journal* 63 (2):269–84.

______. 2001b. *Faith in Hebrews: Analysis within the Context of Christology, Eschatology, and Ethics.* Studies in Biblical Literature 19. New York: Lang.

Rice, G. E. 1981. "The Chiastic Structure of the Central Section of the Epistle to the Hebrews." *Andrews University Seminary Studies* 19 (3):243–46.

Richardson, P. 1996. *Herod: King of the Jews and Friend of the Romans.* Columbia: University of South Carolina Press.

Riggenbach, E. 1922. *Der Brief an die Hebräer.* 2nd ed. Kommentar zum Neuwn Testament 14. Leipzig: Deichert.

Rissi, M. 1987. *Die Theologie des Hebräerbriefs: Ihre Verankerung in der Situation des Verfassers und seiner Leser.* Tübingen: Mohr Siebeck.

Ritschl, A. 1866. "Über die Leser des Hebrâebriefes." *Theologische Studien und Kritien* 39:89–102

Robertson, A. T. 1934. *Grammar of the Greek New Testament in Light of Historical Research*. Nashville: Broadman Press.

Robinson, J. A. T. 1976. *Redating the New Testament*. Philadelphia: Westminster.

Roeth, E. M. 1836. *Epistolam vulgo "ad Hebraeos" non ad Hebraeos, id est Christianos genere Judaeos, sed ad Christianos genere Gentiles et quidem ad Ephesios datem esse demonstrare conatur*. Frankfurt: Schmerber.

Ross, A. P. 2011. *A Commentary on the Psalms: Volume 1 (1–41)*. Kregel Exegetical Library. Grand Rapids: Kregel Academic & Professional.

______. 2013. *A Commentary on the Psalms: Volume 2 (42–89)*. Kregel Exegetical Library. Grand Rapids: Kregel Academic & Professional.

______. 2016. *A Commentary on the Psalms: Volume 3 (89–150)*. Kregel Exegetical Library. Grand Rapids: Kregel Academic & Professional.

Rossi, P. 2011. *Everyday Etiquette: How to Navigate 101 Common and Uncommon Social Situations*. First edition. New York: St. Martin's Press.

Rutgers, L. V. 1994. "Roman Policy towards the Jews: Expulsions from the City of Rome during the First Century C.E." *Classic Antiquity* 13 (1):56–74.

Salmon, G. 1888. *Introduction to the New Testament*. 3rd ed. London: Murray.

Sandegren, C. 1955. "The Addressees of the Epistle to the Hebrews." *Evangelical Quarterly* 27 (4):221–24.

Sanders, J. A. 1959. "Habakkuk in Qumran, Paul and the Old Testament." *Journal of Religion* 39 (4):232–44.

Sandmel, S. 1974. *A Jewish Understanding of the New Testament*. New York: Ktav. Originally published 1956 by Hebrew Union College (Cincinnati).

Sandy, D. B. 2002. *Plowshares and Pruning Hooks: Rethinking the Language of Biblical Prophecy and Apocalyptic*. Downers Grove, IL: InterVarsity Press.

Sappington, T. J. 1991. *Revelation and Redemption at Colossae*. Journal for the Study of the New Testament Supplement Series 53. Sheffield: JSOT Press.

Scarre, C. 1995. *Chronicle of the Roman Emperors: The Reign-by-Reign Record of the Rulers of Imperial Rome*. London: Thames & Hudson.

Schaff, P., and H. Wace, eds. 1979. *A Select Library of Nicene and Post-Nicene Fathers of the Christian Church*, Second Series. Vol. 3, *Theodoret, Jerome, Gennadius, Rufinus: Historical Writings*, etc. Grand Rapids: Eerdmans. Originally published 1892 by The Christian Literature Company (New York).

Schiffman L. H., and J. C. VanderKam, eds. 2000. *Encyclopedia of the Dead Sea Scrolls*. 2 vols. Oxford: Oxford University Press.

Schürer, E. 1973. *History of the Jewish People in the Age of Jesus Christ (175 B.C.–A.D. 135)*, vol. 1. New English ed. Revised and edited by G. Vermes and F. Millar. Edinburgh: T&T Clark. First published 1885.

Schwartz, D. R. 2009. "Philo, His Family, and His Times." In *The Cambridge Companion to Philo*, edited by A. Kamesar, 9–31. New York: Cambridge University Press.

Seager, R. 2002. *Pompey the Great: A Political Biography*. 2nd ed. Oxford: Blackwell.

Skehan, P. W., trans. 1987. *The Wisdom of Ben Sira: A New Translation with Notes*. Introduction and commentary by A. A. Di Lella. Anchor Bible 39. New York: Doubleday.

Smith, G. and T. Sprankle. 2020. *Zephaniah—Malachi*. Kerux Commentaries: A Commentary for Preaching and Teaching. Grand Rapids, Kregel.

Snell, A. 1959. *New and Living Way: An Exposition of the Epistle to the Hebrews*. London: Faith.

Sowers, S. G. 1965. *The Hermeneutics of Philo and Hebrews: A Comparison of the*

Interpretation of the Old Testament in Philo Judaeus and the Epistle to the Hebrews. Basel Studies of Theology 1. Zurich: EVZ-Verlag.

Spicq, C. 1947. "L'Authenticité du chapitre XIII de l'Épître aux Hébreux." *Coniectanea Neotestamentica* 11:226–36.

______. 1949–50. "Le philonisme de l'Épître aux Hébreux." *Revue biblique* 56(1949):542–72; 57(1950):212–42.

______. 1951. "Alexandrismes dans l'Épître aux Hébreux." *Revue biblique* 58:481–502.

______. 1952. *L'Épître aux Hébreux*. 2 vols. Paris: Gabalda.

______. 1959. "L'Epître aux Hebreux: Apollos, Jean-Baptiste, les Helléniste, et Qumran." *Revue de Qumran* 1:365–90.

______. 1996. *Theological Lexicon of the New Testament*. Translated by J. Ernest. 3 vols. Peabody, MA: Hendrickson.

Stedman, R. C. 1992. *Hebrews*. IVP New Testament Commentary Series. Downers Grove, IL: InterVarsity Press.

Stegner, W. R. 1988. "The Ancient Jewish Synagogue Homily." In *Greco-Roman Literature and the New Testament*, edited by D. E. Aune, 51–69. SBL Sources for Biblical Studies 21. Atlanta: Scholars Press.

Stowers, S. K. 1986. *Letter Writing in Greco-Roman Antiquity*. Library of Early Christianity 5, edited by W. A. Meeks. Philadelphia: Westminster.

Strabo. 1917–32. *The Geography of Strabo*. Translated by H. L. Jones. 8 vols. Loeb Classical Library. Cambridge, MA: Harvard University Press.

Strathmann, H. 1963. *Der Brief an die Hebräer*. Translated and explained by H. Strathmann. Das Neue Testament Deutsch 9. Güteringen: Vandenhoeck & Ruprecht.

Straus, M. 1998. *The Challenge of Bible Translation & Gender Accuracy*. Downers Grove, IL: InterVarsity Press.

Stuckenbruck, L. T. 2006. "Formation and Re-Formation of Daniel." In *Scripture and the Scrolls*. Vol. 1 of *The Bible and the Dead Sea Scrolls*, edited by J. H. Charlesworth, 117–20. Waco, TX: Baylor University Press, 2006.

Suetonius. 1914. *The Twelve Caesars*. Vols. 1–2 of *Suetonius*, translated by J. C. Rolfe. Loeb Classical Library. Cambridge, MA: Harvard University Press.

______. 2007. *The Twelve Caesars*. Translated by R. Graves Revised with an introduction and notes by J. B. Rives. Penguin Classics. New York: Penguin Books.

Swetnam, J. 1969. "On the Literary Genre of the 'Epistle' to the Hebrews." *Novum Testamentum* 11 (4):261–69.

Tacitus. 1969a. *The Annals*, translated by J. Jackson. Vols. 3–5 of *Tacitus*. 3 vols. Loeb Classical Library. Cambridge, MA: Harvard University Press.

______. 1969b. *The Histories*, translated by C. H. Moore. Vols. 2–3 of *Tacitus*. Loeb Classical Library. Cambridge, MA: Harvard University Press.

Tasker, R. V. G. 1935–36. "The Integrity of the Epistle to the Hebrews." *Expository Times* 47:136–38.

Tertullian. 1959. *Treatises on Penance: On Penitence [De Paenitentia]; On Purity [De Pudicitia]*. Ancient Christian Writers 28. Translated and annotated by W. P. Le Saint. New York: Newman.

Thompson, J. W. 2008. *Hebrews*. Paideia Commentaries on the New Testament. Grand Rapids: Baker.

Thucydides. 1919–23. *History of the Peloponnesian War*. Translated by C. F. Smith. 4 vols. Loeb Classical Library. Cambridge, MA: Harvard University Press.

Thyen, H. 1955. *Der Stil der jüdisch-hellenistischen Homilie*. Forschungen zur Religion und Literatur des Alten und Neuen Testaments 47. Göttingen: Vandenhoeck & Ruprecht.

Todd, M. N. 1918–19. "Notes on Two Published Inscriptions." *Annual of the British School at Athens* 23: 94–97.

Torrey, C. C. 1911. "The Authorship and Character of the So-Called Epistle to the Hebrews." *Journal of Biblical Literature* 30 (2):137–56.

______. 1946. *The Lives of the Prophets: Greek Text and Translation*. Society of Biblical Literature Monograph Series. Philadelphia: Society of Biblical Literature and Exegesis.

Toussaint, S. D. 1997. "Israel and the Church of a Traditional Dispensationalist." In *Three Central Issues in Contemporary Dispensationalism: A Comparison of Traditional and Progressive Views*, edited by H W. Bateman IV, 227–62. Grand Rapids: Kregel.

Trotter Jr., A. H. 1997. *Interpreting the Epistle to the Hebrews*. Guides to New Testament Exegesis 6. Grand Rapids: Baker.

Trudinger, L. P. 1972. "*ΚΑΙ ΓΑΡ ΔΙΑ ΒΡΑΧΕΩΝ ΕΠΕΣΤΕΙΛΑ ΥΜΙΝ* [*Kai gar dia bracheōn epesteila ymin*]: A Note on Hebrews XIII. 22." *Journal of Theological Studies* 23 (1):128–30.

Tyndale, W., trans. 2008. *The New Testament: A Facsimile of the 1526 Edition*. Peabody, MA: Hendrickson.

Ulansey, D. 1991. "The Heavenly Veil Torn: Mark's Cosmic 'Inclusio.'" *Journal of Biblical Literature* 110.1: 123–25.

VanderKam, J. C. 2004. *From Joshua to Caiaphas: High Priests after the Exile*. Minneapolis: Fortress.

______. 1973. "The Theophany of Enoch I 3b–7, 9." *Vetus Testamentum* 23 (1973): 129–150.

Vanhoye, A. 1964. *A Structured Translation of the Epistle to the Hebrews*. Translated by J. Swetnam. Rome: Pontifical Biblical Institute.

______. 1967. *Épître aux Hébreux: texte Grec structure*. Rome: Pontifical Biblical Institute.

______. 1969. *Situation du Christ: Épître aux Hébreux 1–2*. Lectio Divina 58. Paris: Cerf.

______. 2015. *The Letter to the Hebrews: A New Commentary*. Translated by L. Arnold. New York: Paulist.

Vanhoye, A. P. 1976–77. "La question littéraire de Hébreux xiii. 1–6." *New Testament Studies* 23 (2):121–39.

Vermes, G., and M. D. Goodman. 1989. *The Essenes: According to the Classical Sources*. Oxford Centre Textbooks 1. Sheffield: JSOT Press.

Von Harnack, A. 1900. "Probabilia uber die Adresse und den Verfasser des Hebraerbriefs." *Zeitschrift für die Neutestamentliche Wissenschaft und die Kunde der Älteren Kirche* 1 (1):16–41.

Wallace, D. B. 2004. "Hebrews: Introduction, Argument, Outline." New Testament: Introductions and Outlines. Published June 28, 2004. https://bible.org/seriespage/hebrews-introduction-argument-and-outline.

Walton, F. A. 1955. "The Messenger of God in Hecataeus of Abdera." *Harvard Theological Review* 48 (4):255–57.

Walton, J. H., and D. B. Sandy. 2013. *The Lost World of Scripture: Ancient Literary Culture and Biblical Authority*. Downers Grove, IL: IVP Academic.

Weinfeld, M. 1970. "The Covenant of Grant in the Old Testament and in the Ancient Near East." *Journal of the American Oriental Society* 90 (2):368–81.

Weiss, B. 1888. *Der Brief an die Hebräer*. Kritisch-exegetischer Kommentar über das Neue Testament 13. Göttingen: Vandenoeck & Ruprecht.

______. 1889. *Manual of Introduction to the New Testament*. 2 vols. Translated by A. J. K. Davidson. Foreign Biblical Library. New York: Funk & Wagnalls.

Welch, A. 1898 *The Authorship of the Epistle to the Hebrews: And Other Papers*. Edinburgh: Oliphant, Anderson & Ferrier.

Westcott, B. F. 1984. *The Epistle to the Hebrews: The Greek Text with Notes and Essay*.

Grand Rapids: Eerdmans. Reprint of the 1892 edition by MacMillan (London).

White, J. L. 1988. "Ancient Greek Letters." In *Greco-Roman Literature and the New Testament,* edited by D. E. Aune, 85–105. SBL Sources for Biblical Studies 21. Atlanta: Scholars Press.

Wickham, E. C. 1910. *The Epistle to the Hebrews.* London: Methuen.

Wieseler, K. G. 1884. *Chronologie des apostolische Zeialters bis zum Tobe der Apostel Paulas und Petrus: En Versuch.* Göttingen: Banbenhoeck & Ruprecht.

Wikenhauser, A. 1958. *New Testament Introduction.* Translated by J. Cunningham. Freiburg: Herder & Herder.

Williams, C. R. 1911. "A Word-Study of Hebrews 13." *Journal of Biblical Literature* 30 (2):129–32.

Williamson, R. 1970. *Philo and the Epistle to the Hebrews.* Arbeiten zur Literatur und Geschichte des hellenistischen Judentums 4. Leiden: Brill.

Wills, L. 1984. "The Form of the Sermon in Hellenistic Judaism and Early Christianity." *Harvard Theological Review* 77 (3–4):277–99.

Wilson, R. M. 1987. *Hebrews.* New Century Bible Commentary. Grand Rapids: Eerdmans.

Windisch, H. 1931. *Der Herbräerbrief.* Handbuch zum Neuen Testament 14. Tübingen: Mohr Siebeck. First published in 1913.

Wintermute, O.S. 1985. "Jubilees: A New Translation and Introduction." In *The Old Testament Pseudepigrapha,* edited by J. H. Charlesworth, 2:35–142. Garden City: NY: Doubleday.

Wise, M., M. Abegg Jr., and E. Cook. 1996. *The Dead Sea Scrolls: A New Translation.* San Francisco: HarperSanFrancisco.

Witherington III, B. 1998. *The Acts of the Apostles: A Socio-Rhetorical Commentary.* Grand Rapids: Eerdmans.

Wood, A. 2008. *Of Wings and Wheels: A Synthetic Study of the Biblical Cherubim.* Beihefte zur Zeitschrift für die alttestamentliche Wissenschaft 385. New York: de Gruyter.

Wray, J. H. 1998. *Rest as a Theological Metaphor in the Epistle to the Hebrews and the Gospel of Truth Early Christian Homiletics of Rest.* SBL Dissertation Series 166. Atlanta: Scholars Press.

Wrede, W. 1906. *Das literarische Rätsel des Hebräerbriefes: Mit einem Anhang über den literarischen Charakter des Barnabasbriefes.* Göttingen: Vandenhoeck & Ruprecht.

Wright, A. G. 1966a. "The Literary Genre Midrash: Part One." *Catholic Biblical Quarterly* 28 (2):105–38.

______. 1966b. "The Literary Genre Midrash: Part Two." *Catholic Biblical Quarterly* 28 (4):417–57.

Wright, N. T. 1996. *Jesus and the Victory of God.* Minneapolis: Fortress.

______. 1992. *The New Testament and the People of God.* Minneapolis: Fortress.

Wright, R. B., trans. 1985. "Psalms of Solomon." In *Expansions of the "Old Testament" and Legends, Wisdom and Philosophical Literature, Prayers, Psalms, and Odes, Fragments of Lost Judeo-Hellenistic Works.* Vol. 2 of The Old Testament Pseudepigrapha, edited by J. H. Charlesworth, 639–70. New York: Doubleday.

Yadin, Y. 1978. *Bar-Kokhba: The Rediscovery of the Legendary Hero of the Last Jewish Revolt against Imperial Rome.* London: Weidenfeld and Nicolson.

Zahn, T. 1977. *Introduction to the New Testament.* 3 vols. Translated by J. M. Trout, W. A. Mather, L. Hodous, E. S. Worcester, W. H. Worrell, and R. B. Dodge. Minneapolis: Klock & Klock. Reprinted previously 1953 by Kregel (Grand Rapids). First published 1909 by T&T Clark (Edinburgh). Citations refer to the 1977 edition.

Zerwick, M. 1963. *Biblical Greek: Illustrated by Examples.* Translated and adapted by J. Smith. Scripta Pontificii Instituti Biblici 114. Rome: Biblical Institute Press.

Zimmermann, J. 1998. "Observations on 4Q246—The 'Son of God.'" In *Qumran-Messianism,* edited by J. H. Charlesworth, H. Lichtenberger, and G. S. Oegema, 175–90. Tübingen: Mohr Siebeck.